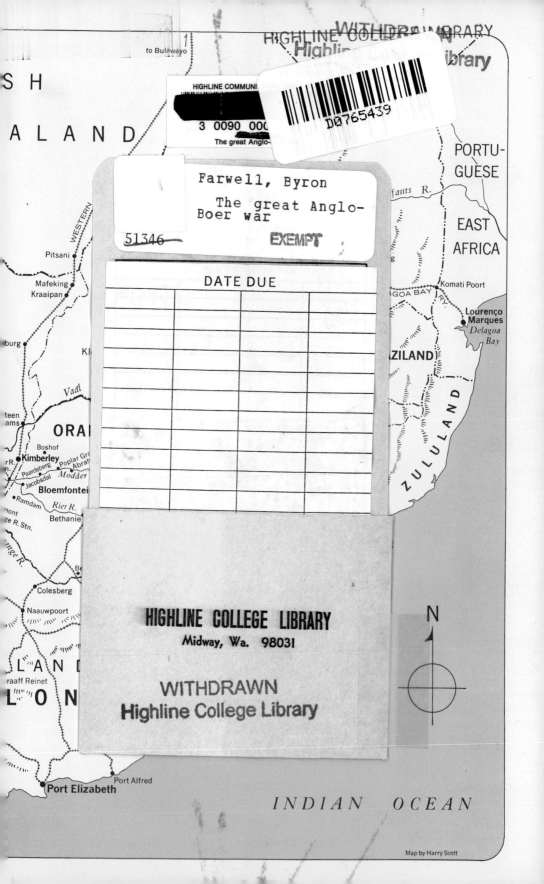

Map by Harry Scott

THE GREAT ANGLO-BOER WAR

THE GREAT
ANGLO-BOER WAR

Byron Farwell

HARPER & ROW, PUBLISHERS
New York, Hagerstown, San Francisco, London

TO MY SISTERS

Mary Chenoweth
Helen Peter

FIRST EDITION

Designed by C. Linda Dingler
Endpaper map by Harry Scott
Text maps by E. M. Scheel
Reproductions of contemporary drawings by Jim Kalett

Library of Congress Cataloging in Publication Data

Farwell, Byron.
  The great Anglo-Boer war.
  Bibliography: p.
  Includes index.
  1. South African War, 1899–1902. I. Title.
DT930.F37 1976   968.04   74–15822
ISBN 0–06–011204–2

76 77 78 79 10 9 8 7 6 5 4 3 2 1

CONTENTS

ACT II

ACT III

ILLUSTRATIONS

A section of photographs follows page 306.

MAPS

CONTEMPORARY DRAWINGS

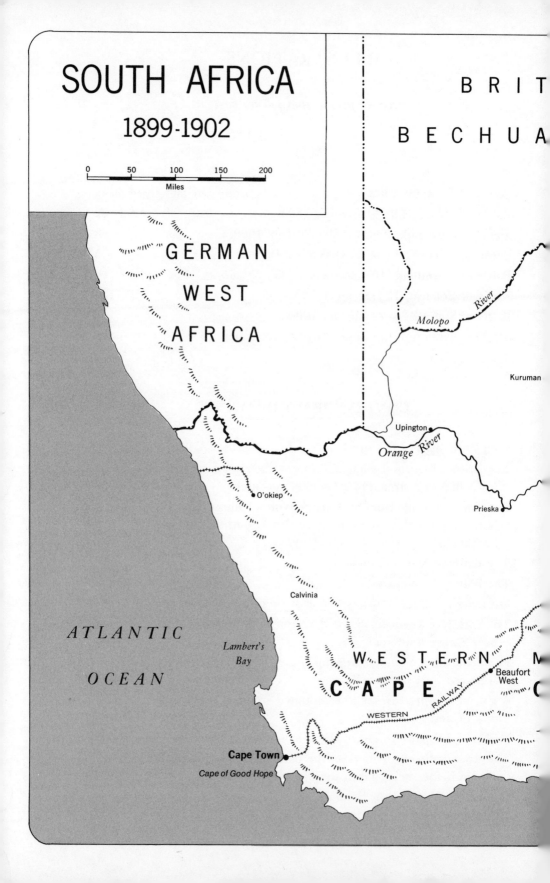

SOUTH AFRICA
1899-1902

0   50   100   150   200
Miles

B R I T

B E C H U A

GERMAN

WEST

AFRICA

Molopo

River

Kuruman

Upington

Orange River

O'okiep

Prieska

Calvinia

ATLANTIC

*Lambert's
Bay*

W E S T E R N   M

Beaufort
West

OCEAN

C A P E   C

RAILWAY

WESTERN

Cape Town

Cape of Good Hope

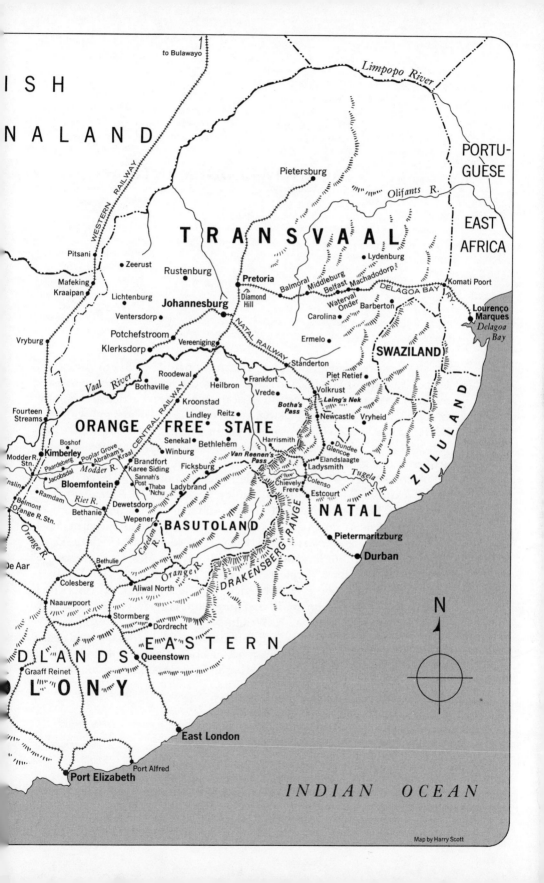

ACKNOWLEDGEMENTS

I wish to express my gratitude to the many people in South Africa, the United Kingdom, Switzerland, and the United States who have assisted me in my research. Three South Africans have been particularly helpful, devoting much time and taking great pains to provide me with new material: George Aschman, former editor of the *Cape Times;* Maria Bosman, daughter of Captain J. W. "Koos" Bosman of the Transvaal Staats-artillerie; and G. E. Steyn, daughter of President M. T. Steyn.

Among others who have provided me with valuable material, I would like to express my gratitude to Stanley Beadle, G. M. Botha, Frank R. Bradlow, J. H. Breytenbach, Mrs. J. Canning, W. H. Carter, Anthony de Crespigny, Lillian du Preez, Austin M. Fraser, Etrechia Fichardt, H. J. Graham-Wolfaard, Jock Hasswell, Doris Heberden, Carl Hegardt, David Hillhouse, Albert Hollingsworth, Adelaide Jacobs, Mrs. G. V. Kearns, V. Leibbrandt, Petrovna Metelerkamp, C. E. More, Woody Nel, L. Oxenham, William la Roux, J. H. Schoeman, J. J. J. Scholtz, C. E. Sherwood, George and Lillian Tatham, E. S. Thompson, Casper Venter, Rolf Wiklund, Buller Willis, and W. E. Wright.

I owe a special debt of gratitude to my wife, Ruth, who devoted nearly a thousand hours to making this a better book. I am deeply indebted to her for her sound advice, penetrating insights, keen criticism, and sustained enthusiasm.

PREFACE

The war is the biggest thing since the Mutiny. It is great in itself; It is great in its incidents; It is great in its issues.

—Lord Lorning in a letter to Lady Edward Cecil, 11 December 1899

Although this book deals with politicians and warriors, with politics and battles, it is neither a military nor a political history in the conventional sense, but a description of a great human drama that encompassed, as Jan Smuts said, "a vast tragedy in the life of a people, whose human interest far surpassed its military interest."

In popular interest the Anglo-Boer War was eclipsed by the Great War which followed it only a dozen years later, the deaths of millions overshadowing the deaths of mere tens of thousands, but it was an important war—important at the time and important for its effect on the affairs of the world since.

There is little similarity between the Anglo-Boer War and the two world wars; in its early stages the Second War of Independence (as the Afrikaners now prefer to call the Anglo-Boer War) was reminiscent of the wars of a century earlier, with formal, almost stately set-piece battles; in its later stages it more nearly resembled the wars of the last quarter-century, those in Southeast Asia or the wars of the Portuguese in their African colonies.

In the two world wars of this century the actions of individuals or their units could determine the outcome of a battle only when massed with tens or hundreds of thousands of others; whether the actions of any one man or any one regiment were brave or cowardly, wise or foolish, scarcely mattered except in their aggregate. Battalions and regiments, even divisions, often seemed to lose their identity, to be lost in the swirling mists of battle, disappearing or returning decimated with no noticeable effect on the course of the war. The Anglo-Boer War was different. Although a major war, it was small enough for the actions of individuals and small units to be significant.

In September 1899 Britain stood at a point in history and occupied a place in world affairs analogous to that of the United States sixty years later. She was, or conceived herself to be, the greatest power in the world: a belief as yet uncontested and thus untested. Rulers and statesmen thought, as they are ever prone to do, in terms of conventional national power and of the conventional way in which that power historically had always been tested: through war. Not in eighty-four years, since Waterloo, had any major world power seriously contested Britain's position in the world—the Crimean War posed no real threat to the Empire, and the Indian Mutiny, which did, was, after all, a mutiny and not even a rebellion —but when the Boers invaded Britain's South African colonies in 1899 it marked what is sometimes seen as the beginning of the end of the British Empire, though it certainly did not seem so at the time.

The Anglo-Boer War, like the American entanglement in Southeast Asia, involved a highly industrialized nation's attempt to subdue a smaller agricultural country; in both instances the smaller nations resorted to that form of combat in which the intelligence, imagination, and character of the people count most and the quantity and quality of the weapons least: guerrilla warfare. In both cases the basic limitations and weaknesses of the great powers were revealed to an envious world and to its jealous and ambitious rulers and statesmen.

Britain won the great Anglo-Boer War, but at the cost of its reputation. The number of men, the amount of matériel, and the length of time required by mighty Britain to subdue a relative handful of South African farmers jolted Britain and amazed the world. Among the many interested spectators to this revelation of Britain's limitations, none perhaps was more interested than the Kaiser and the Great General Staff of the German army, which produced a detailed two-volume study of the conflict. The exact extent to which the Kaiser and his generals were influenced by the spectacle of the British army's performance in South Africa cannot be determined, but certainly they saw little to discourage their aggressive ambitions.

Whether history has lessons to teach is a debatable and much debated issue, but always men have sought to learn from what others did in the past. As often as not men have learned the wrong lessons, for, like the pronouncements of the oracle at Delphi, the past is capable of many interpretations and is often misunderstood. Men seek solutions to specific problems, and, as history never really repeats itself, these kinds of solutions history rarely provides. What it does offer is a vast array of examples which illustrate general principles. A lesson the British thought they had learned from the Anglo-Boer War was the importance of mounted men in modern warfare—and so they sent thousands of horsemen to France in 1914. The real lessons, of course, concerned the more general principles of the importance of mobility to an army. Young W. E. Davies of the Rifle Brigade discovered the kind of lessons history teaches when he found that the Anglo-Boer War was "exactly like every other war in that it was unlike any other war."

We might, however, learn something from the erroneous conclusions men have drawn from history, particularly the history of wars. After some earlier and all subsequent major wars there have been those who concluded, as did John Atkins after the Anglo-Boer War, that "weapons . . . are too terrible for wars to continue." History has repeatedly illustrated that there is no weapon so terrible that some nation will not sometime use it.

The great principles concerning men's conduct are, of course, continually being demonstrated, and the recitation of history's examples— including a roll call of the sins which men and nations are prone to commit—serves as a reminder of the vast range of deeds, good and evil, which men and women are capable of performing. History reminds us too that rulers and statesmen are, after all, men and women.

For most Britons the Anglo-Boer War has come to seem quaint; few remember why it was fought, the way it was fought, or its consequences. The Americans, who had citizens fighting on both sides, who (most of them) expressed strong pro-Boer sentiments, and who profited mightily from the sale of horses, mules, and tinned beef to the British, remember the war but none of its details, and they have completely forgotten their own interest and involvement in it. For the Afrikaners, however, the war is still a vital, living issue, though the facts have dissolved into myths, leaving in the hearts of many a distilled bitterness. Although nearly all those who took part in the war are now dead, the fears, hopes, attitudes, and prejudices it generated remain, and they influence the actions of the Afrikaner people and the South African government. South Africa is a land in whose history bizarre, improbable events have occurred with astonishing frequency, but no event has left a more lasting imprint on the minds and hearts of her people than the Second Anglo-Boer War, and no one can hope to understand the country or those who today rule it without an understanding of this conflict.

The best detailed, blow-by-blow account of the war is to be found in *The Times History of the War in South Africa 1899–1902*, a seven-volume work written by a variety of hands over several years under the general direction of L. S. Amery. I have made frequent reference to this as simply *The Times History*. The *Official History* had too many tendentious editors. From the array of conflicting numbers available—casualty figures and sizes of forces engaged, for example—I have tried to select those which seemed to me the most reliable or at least the most plausible.

The best of the modern accounts is Rayne Kruger's *Good-bye Dolly*

Gray, first published in 1959. This is a military history with scant attention paid to the concentration camps and none to the prisoners of war, who by war's end outnumbered the fighting burghers in the field. Since Kruger's book appeared, a number of studies of men and events connected with the war have been published in South Africa—the works of Johannes Meintjes, for example—and much new material is now available to the historian which throws light on many aspects of the war. And I have received an astonishing amount of unpublished material from helpful and interested South Africans and Englishmen.

To mitigate as far as possible the annoyance of footnotes, all citations of sources are numbered and tucked away in the back of the book for those interested; in the few instances where it seemed desirable to add notes of substance, asterisks have been used and notes placed at the foot of the page.

Finally, it should perhaps be explained that when shrapnel is mentioned the reference is to the type of shell (or its missiles) invented by Henry Shrapnel, a projectile timed to explode in the air and to disperse a number of metal pellets, and not, as the word is commonly used by journalists, to describe high-explosive shells or their fragments.

PROLOGUE

1

THE BIRTH OF A PEOPLE

South Africa is a land bathed in sunshine, with air so bright and clear that one can see great distances across its unforested hinterland, that vast plateau called the high veld. Nature seems to have done its best to protect this fair land from desecration by man: its few high-banked rivers are unnavigable, and the red soil resists the growth of most alien crops. Behind the high veld (for the land seems to face southeast) is the great Kalahari Desert; in front of it lies a series of mountain ranges curving along the escarpment for 1,400 miles, and, on the southeastern edge of the plateau, the Karoo—a strip of high, arid tableland. These separate the high veld from the low veld and the littoral which begins in the hot, tropical northeast at Mozambique and sweeps down south to the temperate Cape of Good Hope. South of the Cape there are only the wastes of Antarctica and the invisible dividing line between the Indian Ocean and the Atlantic. Along South Africa's nearly 2,000 miles of gale-swept coastline there are few natural harbours, few points at which strangers from the sea can penetrate. Yet men have been here, though never in great numbers, for a very long time. And always they have fought each other.

There has been a conflict of cultures here, a "race problem," for as long as men can remember—longer even, for archaeologists and anthropologists have exhumed the problem from the prehistoric past, a past so distant it is not certain the protagonists were actually human. In that dimly seen period of history, hundreds of thousands of years ago, two types of humanoid creatures lived on this land. Then, several thousands of years later, there was but one: *Homo sapiens*. South Africa's first cultural conflict ended in the complete and utter extermination of one humanoid creature by another.

The survivors were perhaps the ancestors of the Bushmen and the Hottentots. These first known inhabitants of the Cape were yellow-skinned people, short in stature, who spoke languages characterized by a number of clicking sounds which served for some of their consonants. The men had protuberant bellies; the women had pendulous breasts and enormous buttocks. The taller Hottentots developed a more advanced culture and eventually subdued or drove away the Bushmen.

In 1498, when Vasco da Gama rounded the Cape and landed at Mossel Bay, he found only Hottentots (at least these are the only people mentioned), for the black men were still far to the north. Other Europeans followed Da Gama, but none stayed until on 6 April 1652 Johan (Jan) van Riebeck of the Dutch East India Company, landed at Table Bay with about one hundred men and four women to form a settlement which, it was hoped, would be able to provide meat and fresh vegetables for the Company's ships going to and from the East Indies. Van Riebeck built a fort, planted crops, and soon was demanding that more women be sent out—not soft, town-bred girls, but "lusty farm wenches."

Conflict with the Hottentots was perhaps inevitable. In the unequal struggle the Europeans soon displayed their superior strength, and the last serious organized resistance of the Hottentots was crushed in 1677. With their easy adaptability, the Hottentots turned from warring against the white man to working for him. Those who survived the white man's diseases began the process of interbreeding with other races that was to result in their extermination as a separate race.

In 1688, thirty-six years after Van Riebeck landed, there arrived at the Cape a group of about 175 Huguenots—men, women, and children—who had been driven from France by the revocation of the Edict of Nantes. Within two generations the French language was forgotten and the descendants of these refugees merged with the Dutch community, adopting their language, religion, and mode of life but adding an astonishing number of French surnames which survive to this day through generations of prolific families.

After the Huguenots came a number of German peasants, lured by the offer of free land, and these three nationalities—Dutch, French, and German—alloyed to become a new and distinct people called Boers (the word means "farmers") or Afrikaners, speaking a variation of seventeenth-century Dutch known at first as Taal and then as Afrikaans. Later the mixture was enriched by the addition of Britons, mostly Irish and Scots.

For a century after the last war with the Hottentots the colonists experienced a relatively peaceful time, raising cattle and crops, quarrelling with the Dutch officials, moving ever further from government control, seeking ever more land, and breeding themselves into what Conan Doyle called "the most rugged, virile, unconquerable race ever seen upon earth." Almost from the beginning they were discontented with the rule of the Dutch East India Company. In spite of the Company's efforts to contain the colony within controllable limits and to curb the wanderlust of its people, the boundaries of the colony expanded, mostly to the northeast, as people moved further and further inland. About the middle of the eighteenth century they collided with the blacks in the neighborhood of the Fish River.

The blacks—called Kaffirs until the twentieth century and now Bantu, after the type of languages they speak—crossed the northern edge of what is now the Republic of South Africa, perhaps driven south by more warlike tribes in the interior. They remained at first in the rich agricultural lands north of the Kei and Orange rivers; later they began to move south between the Drakensberg range and the Indian Ocean until eventually but inevitably they encountered the advancing whites. Blacks and whites competed for grazing lands and began a sporadic conflict which was to last for more than a century until the blacks were beaten into submission and settled down to living and working by the white man's rules.

In 1795, when a French-inspired republic replaced the royal government in Holland, the Prince of Orange fled to England and asked the British to take charge of Dutch colonial possessions until he could return to his throne, thus ending the 143-year reign of the Dutch East Africa Company in South Africa. The Afrikaners liked the British government no better than they had the Dutch; they had, in fact, already developed an almost inbred detestation of any form of government. They continually complained, protested, revolted, and made themselves generally troublesome.

In 1802, as one result of the Peace of Amiens, Cape Colony was restored to Holland, but less than four years later, in January 1806, a British expeditionary force captured it to keep it out of the hands of the French and in 1814 it was formally ceded to Britain. This time the British came to stay. But British concepts of justice and humanity conflicted with those of Britain's truculent white South African subjects. From the beginning, her policies were designed to protect what she regarded as the interests of the natives and to prevent the abuse of slaves and Hottentot servants, who often lived in a state close to slavery. To the Boers it seemed that their British rulers were unduly interested in the welfare of these people, for the Boers believed in the right of every white man to "beat his own nigger" and that the relationship between a master and his servants and slaves was a private, domestic affair of no legitimate concern to the government.

In 1813 the British instituted a series of circuit courts to hear the complaints of servants against their masters. This was promptly damned as the "Black Court"; the Boers were incensed that the word of a slave or servant should carry any weight in a court of law.

In 1815 a Boer named Frederick Cornelius Bezuidenhout, who owned a farm on Baviaan's River in eastern Cape Colony, ignored the summonses of three circuit courts to appear and answer charges of cruelty to a Hottentot servant. A lieutenant and twelve Hottentot policemen sent to arrest him were fired on as they approached his farm. They returned the fire and Bezuidenhout was killed. This incident was to have repercussions that lasted for well over a century.

Eastern Cape Colony was inhabited by tough-minded Boer frontiersmen, accustomed to fighting for what they had and to getting what they wanted. To them it appeared monstrous that the government would send Hottentots to arrest a white man. And even more monstrous that the government would sanction Hottentots killing a white man—and this over a mere matter of a man's treatment of his servant. Bezuidenhout's brother led his neighbours in a hopeless revolt: sixty men against the British Empire.

The revolution was soon crushed. Forty-seven men were captured and tried. Thirty were sentenced to be banished and six to be executed. One of the six was pardoned; the other five were publicly hanged at Slachter's (or Slagter's) Nek.

The executions were, from the British point of view, a simple act of justice; they underestimated or failed to understand their significance for the Boers. Politically they were a serious blunder: they created martyrs. The Bezuidenhouts and the five hanged rebels were enshrined in Boer martyrology, and the hanging at Slachter's Nek is remembered to this day as an example of British repression, brutality, and injustice.

The problems of the British rulers multiplied. On the frontiers there was constant dissatisfaction and unrest, and a series of wars with the Bantu. The rise of the Zulu nation to the north and its expansion into the lands of its neighbours drove tens of thousands of Bantu south, overpopulating the land on the northeastern frontier and increasing the friction between blacks and whites. The British added to the problem by settling some 6,000 Germans there. The Boers complained of too much government and the British settlers of too little. Both grumbled about their insecurity. The garrisons of Imperial troops were indeed too small, for the mother country was unwilling to bear the expense of providing soldiers and the colony could not afford to hire them. Then too the British continued their attempts to protect the rights of Hottentots, Bantu, Asians, and Coloureds (those of mixed races). British policy regarding these people raised for the Boers the frightening spectre of equality.

In 1828 laws were passed which permitted the Hottentots to move about freely without a pass in the land which had once been theirs, and attempts were made to limit what had been the near-absolute authority of their white masters. Then, by act of Parliament in distant London, the British abolished slavery. Every one of the 39,021 slaves in the colony was to be emancipated by 1 December 1834—just at the time of the wheat harvest, noted the Boers bitterly. Compensation was promised, but instead of the more than £ 3 million expected, only £ 1,247,401 was provided—payable in London. In South Africa, where the economy was based on slave labour, this spelled ruin for many farmers. The Boers were enraged at this government philanthropy at their expense. Meetings were held, and many determined to flee whatever the cost. "All England's power on land and water will not prevent the emigration of her subjects from her territories,"[1] said the Reverend Daniel Lindley.* Deneys Reitz, himself a Boer, speaking more than a century later, said: "Knowing my countrymen as I do, I think the cause of their leaving was not so much hatred of British rule as dislike of any rule."[2]

In the autumn of 1836 advance parties were sent north to scout the land beyond the Karoo, beyond the Orange River, beyond the frontiers of Cape Colony and the reach of the British. There on the high veld the scouts found a vast land largely depopulated by the tribal wars of the Bantu. In February 1837 the first large body of voortrekkers, as the pioneers were called, moved out of Cape Colony under their leader, Pieter Retief (1780–1838).

By September some two hundred Boers had crossed the Orange River. By the end of the year there were more than a thousand ox wagons on the high veld between the Orange and the Vaal rivers. It was the beginning of that mass migration the Boers call the Great Trek.

2

VOORTREKKERS AND THEIR REPUBLICS

The voortrekkers moved in two directions: north onto the high veld and northeast into Natal. They travelled at the pace of the ox wagon and their grazing herds, taking with them their families and servants, their guns and their Bibles, their faith in God and in themselves. They quickly became a nomadic, pastoral, self-sufficient people, leading remote and isolated lives, yet united in their common language, religious beliefs, occupations, race, cultural attitudes, and, above all else, in their fierce desire for independence, for which they willingly faced savage beasts, lived among primitive men, and suffered all the hardships of a life almost completely divorced from civilized comforts.

The voortrekker vrow gave birth to her young while lying in the wagon's bed or on the bare red sands of the veld. To survive, a child had to be hardy and strong; it grew up among horses and oxen and wild beasts, the boys learning early to ride, shoot, and manage oxen. The

*Daniel Lindley (1801–1888) was an American, son of the president of Philadelphia College, who came to South Africa in 1833, learned Dutch, and in 1843 was ordained in the Dutch Reformed Church.

child's world was the great open veld and the narrow confines of his own family, ruled by its patriarch, who presided over children, grandchildren, daughters-in-law, servants, and slaves. His home was the sturdy ox wagon, and there were no schools. From itinerant predikants (ministers of the Dutch Reformed Church) and from relatives the child tried to learn to read the Bible in Dutch. There was no other literature available, wanted, or even tolerated, so that children grew up suspicious of all beyond their own narrow culture. Early in life they developed into strong men and tough-fibred women.

Wherever they went the Boers established republics. A quarrelsome, contumacious people, they argued endlessly among themselves about where to settle, about religion (there were degrees of Calvinistic strictness), and about who their leaders should be. When feelings ran too high, the dissidents took to their horses and ox wagons and moved on to found other republics elsewhere. The little republic founded at Winburg, the first important settlement north of the Orange, split four ways. The trekker states often took their names from the districts or towns (usually mere villages) which they made their capitals—Potchefstroom, Lydenburg, Zoutpansberg, and Winburg—but some had more colourful names such as Stellaland, Goshen, and New Republic. All of these either were annexed by the British or were absorbed into the two large republics which eventually emerged.

The trekker republics had certain features in common: the use of Roman Dutch law, a state church, a white male franchise, the obligation of every man and boy over fifteen to turn out with his horse, wagon, and provisions to fight a common enemy, and, most important of all, an all-powerful legislative body called a volksraad. The chief officials were the president and the commandant-general; each district had a landdrost (magistrate), a commandant who led the district's commando in time of war, and a veld kornet (field cornet) who served as an administrator for both the landdrost and the commandant. All were elected. Even in war, most of the major decisions were made not by the commandant alone but by a krygsraad (council of war) which was usually attended by everybody in the commando. It was almost true, as was said, that every Boer was a general.

When Piet Retief led his people out of Cape Colony, he took them to Natal, where in February 1838 he concluded an agreement with Dingaan, King of the Zulus, giving him and his voortrekkers a large tract of land between the Umzimvubu and Tugela rivers. No sooner was the agreement signed, however, than Dingaan called out his warriors, killed Retief and those with him, and sent his impis to attack Boer laagers scattered throughout Natal. Of the 3,500 voortrekkers there, at least 350 men, women, and children fell under the slashing, stabbing assegais of the Zulus.

Retief's place as trek leader was taken by Andries Pretorius (1798–1853), who at once assembled a 500-man commando to fight the Zulus.

It was a handful against a horde, but it was ever characteristic of the Boers to be disdainful of numerically superior enemies and to put their faith in their own fighting capabilities and in God—and when the Boers put their trust in God they expected His active cooperation and support. No Christian people in modern times have so firmly and wholeheartedly believed in the righteousness of their causes and so confidently relied on God's support.

To move into the vicinity of the enemy, take up a good defensive position, and wait to be attacked was a characteristic Boer tactic. In a vast land where occupation of ground was strategically unimportant and where the enemy invariably possessed superiority in numbers, this was sound military doctrine, for attackers generally suffer greater losses than defenders. This was the tactic used by Pretorius; he led his commando into Zululand and beside the Blood River formed a strong laager—ox wagons in a circle, prepared for defence—and there, on 16 December 1838, the Zulus found them and launched a savage unsuccessful attack. Unable to close with their enemy, a tactic imposed on them by the short assegai, they fell before the flintlocks of the Boers. It is said that 3,000 Zulus were killed at a cost to the Boers of 3 wounded. The number of Zulus killed is doubtless an exaggeration, but certainly the Boers attained a remarkable victory. It is still remembered, for 16 December became Dingaan's Day (now called Day of the Covenant in keeping with the oath of perpetual remembrance taken by Pretorius and his men), and each year it is celebrated by Afrikaners as a proud day of solemn thanksgiving.

A year after Pretorius's victory the voortrekkers raised their own flag at Durban, but their fragile republic, Natalia, was not allowed to grow. In 1842 a British force under that redoubtable old warrior Sir Harry Smith (1787–1860), hero of the First Sikh War, occupied Durban, dismantled the republic, raised the Union Jack, and three years later formally annexed Natal to the British Empire. It was to become the most British of all the South African colonies, for the Boers left, carrying with them an abiding sense of injury and injustice, a bitter hatred of the British who had robbed them of the land for which they had fought and bled.

The Boers from Natal joined those from the Cape in climbing onto the high veld, and ten years after the start of the Great Trek there were perhaps 15,000 Boers there. Most stayed in the land lying between the Orange and Vaal rivers, but some trekked on, ever northward, beyond the Vaal and up into the wild Zoutpansberg; soon the whole area between the Orange and the Limpopo (160,000 square miles) was sprinkled with trekker republics.

The British could not quite decide what, if anything, they should do about these people. They did not like the idea of Boer republics on the flanks of Natal and Cape Colony; missionaries continually protested against the enslavement of the natives by the Boers and demanded that Britain exercise its power to bring British justice onto the high veld; on the other hand, most politicians in London quailed at the expense and difficulty of attempting to administer these vast, sparsely populated lands inhabited by such troublesome people. Wavering British attitudes were reflected in wavering British policies over a long period.

In 1847 Sir Harry Smith became governor of Cape Colony and claimed authority over the land between the Orange and Vaal rivers. The Boers there, led by Pretorius, took up arms to defend their independence, but Sir Harry crossed the Orange with a mixed force of regulars, colonials, and Griquas* and defeated them at Boomplaats. Three years later the land was formally annexed as the Orange River Territory.

The Boers could set up all the republics they chose, but they could never really consider themselves free until and unless the British ceased to consider them British subjects and agreed not to interfere with them. Actually, as they eventually learned, they would not be safe even then. However, the voortrekkers in the three republics beyond the Vaal—Potchefstroom, Zoutpansberg, and Lydenburg—having at last trekked far enough away from all British authority, did manage to achieve formal recognition of their independence. In January 1852 Boers and Britons met at the Zand (Sand) River and signed a document which became known as the Zand River Convention. The meeting appears to have been somewhat haphazard—not all the Boers were represented; the authority of the British commissioners was vague—and the document itself was informal, being entitled: "Minutes of a Meeting between . . . H.M. Assistant Commissioners . . . and a Deputation of Emigrant Farmers Residing North of the Vaal River." There were a number of clauses about facilitating trade, extradition of criminals, and free movement across the frontier, but the meat of the document was the agreement on the part of the Boers to prohibit slavery and the promise of the British not to interfere with their internal affairs. The British thus gave up all claim to the area between the Vaal and the Limpopo rivers.

In February 1854 another Anglo-Boer agreement was signed: the Bloemfontein Convention gave independence to the inhabitants of the land between the Orange and the Vaal. The Zand River Convention had promised not to impose British rule; the Bloemfontein Convention promised to withdraw the existing British authority, to abandon all responsibility not only for the Boers but for the 40,000 Bantu (mostly Basutos) and Coloureds who lived there. The actual withdrawal took place without celebration or ceremony when the 300 men of the garrison at Bloemfontein marched south and crossed the Orange into Cape Colony. It would be nearly half a century before British troops recrossed that boundary.

The new Orange Free State, as the Orange River Territory became, went through three presidents in the first ten years of its existence. Then, in 1864, Johannes Hendricus Brand (1823–1888) was elected president,

*The Griquas are a people of mixed origins: Hottentot, European, and Bantu. They proudly called themselves Bastards until missionaries told them the word was pejorative.

and for twenty-four years he wisely guided the infant republic's destiny. Although he often nettled the British, he was careful never to give them cause to meddle. This was not easy. The aggressive and powerful British resented the very presence of the two republics, and the Free Staters had to tread warily, even in the face of such wrath-provoking British arrogance as the annexation of the diamond fields in 1872, an action which left a bitter taste in the mouths of the Free Staters and confirmed their traditional distrust of Great Britain. It is not surprising then that not long after they were quick to see in the high-handed actions of the British in the Transvaal a threat to their cherished independence.

The Transvaal had not been as fortunate in its leadership and had fallen into a chaotic state: burghers refused to pay taxes, government debts mounted, there was no money for schools, roads or public buildings; the volksraad argued and quarrelled and accomplished nothing. By 1877 the Bapedi, a hostile tribe, were causing trouble on the southeastern frontier and Zulu impis were poised for an invasion. Although slavery was forbidden, a law designed to provide for orphans permitted a system of "apprenticeship" that was very close to it. Every successful commando returned with orphans, and questions were seldom asked about the parents when a Boer registered apprentices. Once indentured the children could be sold, and there was a considerable trade in them. At least once a wagonload of black "orphans" was openly sold in the streets of Potchefstroom. The British thought it was perhaps time to take under its imperial wing this immoral, bankrupt country drifting towards anarchy and war. They sent Theophilus Shepstone (1817–1893) to investigate and, if necessary, to act.

He arrived in Pretoria, capital of the Transvaal, on 22 January 1877 with a small staff which included the twenty-one-year-old future novelist H. Rider Haggard and an escort of twenty-five mounted policemen. Many of the people with whom he spoke favoured annexation, and he thought the conditions of the country seemed to justify this action. Haggard said:

> Anything more hopeless than the position of the country on 1st January 1877 it is impossible to conceive. Enemies surrounded it. . . . In the exchequer there was nothing but over-due bills. The president was helpless, and mistrustful of his officers. . . . all the ordinary functions of Government had ceased, and trade was paralysed. . . . the majority of the inhabitants, who would neither fight nor pay taxes, sat still and awaited the catastrophe, utterly careless of all consequences.[1]

In the Victorian era a curious belief was prevalent that sovereign states ought to have governments that were reasonably efficient and solvent.

It was true that some of the burghers were apathetic, others saw annexation as the only solution to the government's woes, and probably a few even believed Shepstone's assurances that annexation would be a blessing and that Britain's motives were entirely philanthropic, but there was a sizable number—a majority as it turned out later—who, although disliking their own government, liked the idea of British rule even less.

This view was forcefully expressed by the volksraad, which stated its strong objections. Britain ignored these, as it ignored also the provisions of the Zand River Convention, although a case could be made that the Transvaal had violated the Convention by permitting conditions very near slavery to exist.

In April 1877 the Transvaal was annexed and Shepstone became the first British governor. Although he promised at the outset "the fullest legislative privileges compatible with the circumstances of the country and the intelligence of the people," no elected legislative body was ever assembled and the Boers were left with no effective voice in their government.

There was some talk of armed rebellion and much grumbling. Former Vice-President Paul Kruger even made two trips to London, once with a petition signed by a majority of the male population, protesting the annexation and begging for independence; nothing came of it.

Less than two years after the annexation of the Transvaal the British went to war with the Zulus, crossing the Buffalo River and invading Zululand at three points. The results were disastrous. Near a hill called Isandhlwana the Zulus fell upon a large part of the main column and almost completely exterminated it. Nearly 900 men were left dead amidst a welter of broken wagons and scattered supplies. Only a few days after the start of the invasion, what was left of the British army came limping back across the Buffalo.

Britain was appalled. That black savages armed with assegais could defeat a large force of British regulars armed with modern rifles and artillery seemed incredible. The Boers in the Transvaal raised their eyebrows: they remembered how Pretorius, with a handful of men armed with muskets, had beat off Dingaan's impis; the famed British army was not, after all, invincible, even against savages. Although the British rushed reinforcements to Natal and the Zulus were eventually crushed, the defeat at Isandhlwana made a lasting impression on the Transvaalers.

When the news of this British disaster reached London, the government sent out Sir Garnet Wolseley, the most brilliant general of the Victorian era. He was appointed high commissioner for South Africa, and although the Zulu War was finished before he arrived, he undertook a campaign that crushed the troublesome Bapedi. Wolseley was soon made aware of Boer discontent, but he was contemptuous of it: "Ignorant men, led by a few designing fellows, are talking nonesense on the High Veld," he said. He advised the Boers to forget about independence, for "so long as the sun shines, the Transvaal will remain British territory." But in a dispatch home on 29 October 1879 he warned that "the main body of the Dutch population are disaffected to our rule."

The Transvaalers continued to hope, and with some reason, that the British would change their minds. No one had been louder in his denunciations of the annexation than William Ewart Gladstone, who had called it a hideous and treacherous crime. His speeches, together with those of political leaders who agreed with him, were given much space in Transvaal newspapers, and some of the speeches were published as pamphlets. When, in the spring of 1880, Gladstone became prime minister they waited expectantly for their independence to be restored, a hope finally dashed by Gladstone himself when he informed them: "Looking at all the circumstances . . . our judgement is that the Queen cannot be advised to relinquish the Transvaal."

The Boers digested this information for six months and then rose in revolt.

3

THE FIRST ANGLO-BOER WAR

No one dreamed that the Boers in the Transvaal would fight. The British officials there did not think so, the colonials in Natal and Cape Colony did not think so, and certainly no one in London thought they would be so rash. There were, indeed, sound reasons for holding such a belief.

The Boers had, after all, quietly accepted the annexation only three years earlier; they were widely scattered and armed only with hunting weapons; and they were uneducated, many illiterate. And consider the audacity of the thing: for some 50,000 people—less than half the population of Kensington or of Peoria, Illinois—spread over more than 110,000 square miles, to challenge the might of the British Empire with its hundreds of millions of people, its army alone more than three times larger than the entire white population of the Transvaal, its navy twice the size of any other and undisputed master of all the oceans and seas—no, it was unthinkable.

But the British underestimated the depth and extent of Boer discontent. Only a spark was needed to ignite the flame of revolt, and Piet Bezuidenhout (believed to be a descendant of the Bezuidenhouts who started the revolt at Slachter's Nek in 1815) provided the spark. It began simply enough when he refused to pay his taxes—a common enough thing among the Boers. The government sued him for £27 5s, but Bezuidenhout pointed out that this was £14 more than he owed. The court agreed, reduced the tax due, and assessed him £13 5s court costs. When he balked at this, his ox wagon was seized.

The stoutly built, half-tented ox wagon was to the Boer more than just a farm wagon. Often it was a family's most valuable and valued possession, and frequently their home as well. In native wars it was a movable fort from which a man could defend himself. Efficient and economical, it made the trekboer's life style possible, and he usually had an attachment to it in excess of its material value. With it and six to eight span of oxen the vast spaces of the open veld were his, for he had no need of roads. To lose an ox wagon was a serious matter; that the government would seize one for a mere £13 5s debt was, felt most Boers, rank injustice.

Piet Bezuidenhout's ox wagon was scheduled to be sold in the public square of Potchefstroom at 11 A.M. on 11 November 1880. Early that morning some one hundred Boers assembled in front of the landdrost's office to protest. Indignant speeches were made, and, having stirred themselves up, they moved on to the public square. When an official mounted the wagon to read the conditions of sale, Piet Cronjé dragged him off and kicked him. Oxen were brought up, and the wagon was triumphantly hauled back to the Bezuidenhout farm.

One hundred and forty Scots Fusiliers and two guns were sent to restore order and to enforce the government's authority. Marching out to meet Cronjé, they found him on his farm surrounded by thoroughly aroused, armed Boers. The Fusiliers prudently withdrew to Potchefstroom and settled themselves to wait for tempers to cool, throwing up some earthworks and making a little fort just outside the town. But the British underestimated the fighting fever of Cronjé and his men; in the early afternoon of 15 December some 500 of them, led by Cronjé, rode into Potchefstroom and occupied its principal buildings and streets. The troops and some of the townspeople retreated to the fort.

The following day a small party of Boers trotted defiantly out towards the fort. One called out, "Why don't you fight, you damned cowards?"

When a lieutenant and thirteen men sent out to drive them away rode purposefully towards them, they wheeled their ponies and dashed for town, the troopers on their heels. At the edge of town four or five Boers raised their rifles and fired. The troops returned the fire and Commandant Frans Robertse was hit in the arm.

The war had begun.

In December 1880 nearly 5,000 men, women, and children gathered at Paardekraal, a farm near present-day Krugersdorp, and proclaimed themselves to be free in a long manifesto which said in part:

We therefore make it known to everybody, that on the 13th of December 1880 the Government has been re-established. Mr. S. J. P. Kruger has been appointed Vice President, and shall form with Mr. M. W. Pretorius and Mr. P. Joubert, a Triumvirate that shall execute the Government of the country. The Volksraad has recommenced its sitting. . . .[1]

Before the day was over, every person there found a stone and placed it on a symbolic heap, pledging themselves to the task of regaining their independence. They declared Heidelberg to be their temporary capital, and there on 16 December, Dingaan's Day—the Boers always attached importance to historic dates—the long declaration of independence was read and the four-coloured flag, the Transvaal Vierkleur, was hoisted in defiance. In Pretoria rifles were handed out from the back of a wagon to everyone who looked as if he could shoot one.

The Transvaalers' hopes and dreams were set forth in a "Petition of Rights" that they sent to the government of the Orange Free State in the hope of enlisting their support. It listed their grievances in great detail, ending with: "With confidence we lay our case before the whole world, be it that we conquer or that we die; liberty shall arise in Africa as the sun from the morning clouds, as liberty rose in the United States of North America. Then will it be from the Zambezi to Simon's Bay, Africa for the Afrikaner!"

The British were unperturbed. At Lydenburg young Elsa Dietrich warned Lieutenant Colonel Philip Robert Anstruther of the 94th Foot that the Boers were plotting rebellion and that the British were not safe. Anstruther laughed. "Do you think, Miss Dietrich, that the British army is asleep?" She might have answered in all truth, "Yes." The British army was completely unprepared. The forces in the Transvaal at the begining of the revolution were certainly inadequate, and they were split into tiny garrisons sprinkled about the country.

A few days later Anstruther knew beyond any doubt that Miss Dietrich had spoken the truth. Marching with a column of 250 men and three women, he reached Bronkhorstspruit, about 38 miles east of Pretoria, his destination, on 20 December. The band was playing and he was marching across Mr. Grobler's farm when a horseman carrying a white flag dashed up and handed him a message, a demand for immediate surrender. Anstruther refused and the Boers opened fire, shooting from concealed positions. Before the soldiers could shake out of their marching formation into skirmishing order, the battle was over. Fifty-six soldiers and one of the women were killed; 101 were wounded, of whom 20 died later. Only one officer survived, and he was badly wounded.

As soon as the firing ceased, the Boers came forward to help; tents were set up and the battlefield became a hospital. Farmer Grobler supplied what he could, bread, butter, and fruit. From Pretoria came doctors and a stream of townspeople bringing food and books and other comforts. One of the doctors was amazed at the number of multiple wounds the soldiers had suffered, stating that there were "on an average, five wounds per man," an exaggeration perhaps, but the Boers were among the finest marksmen in the world.

The dead soldiers were buried on Mr. Grobler's farm, and it is said that from the seeds of peaches in their knapsacks sprang flourishing peach trees.

It was more than a month before another pitched battle was fought, although throughout the Transvaal the British were besieged in all their little garrisons by Boer commandos that simply sat down around them to starve them out. In Natal the British were hurriedly throwing together an army to rescue the besieged garrisons and to restore the authority of the crown. In command was Major General Sir George Colley, forty-five years old and considered by many to be the brightest intellect in the British army, but he was apprehensive about his performance, for this was his first independent command. In a letter home he wrote: "Whether I . . . shall find that South Africa is to me, as it is said to be in general, 'the grave of all good reputations', remains to be seen."[2]

His opponent was Petrus ("Piet") Jacobus Joubert, the forty-six-year-old commandant-general of the Transvaal Boers. He had fought in native wars, but he lacked the temperament, training, and inclination to be a soldier; he was a farmer-politician, a man who disliked war.

The Boers seized the initiative, not waiting for the British to invade. Some 2,000 crossed the frontier into Natal and took up favourable positions at Laing's Nek (Langenek). There on 23 January 1881 Colley found them and ordered them to disperse. The Boers showed a disposition to bargain but not to be cowed. They replied:

. . . we declare that we would be satisfied with a rescinding of the annexation and the restoration of the South African Republic under a protectorate of Her Majesty the Queen, so that once a year the British flag shall be hoisted. . . . If your Excellency resolves to reject this, we have only to submit to our fate; but the Lord will provide.

The Lord provided. In a short, simple battle the British soldiers charged and the Boers shot them down. There were 195 British casualties.

In this battle the 58th Regiment carried its colours into battle; it was the last British regiment ever to do so.

Joubert failed to follow up his victory, and ten days later Colley had recovered sufficiently to make an effort to clear his line of communication and "meet and escort some waggons expected from Newcastle." He set out on 8 February, a fine and bright morning, with 273 infantry, 38 mounted men, and four guns. Thomas Fortescue Carter, a newspaper correspondent who accompanied the expedition, noted that "everyone was in good spirits at the prospect of an outing." Colley did not expect to be attacked. He thought his guns would deter the enemy, who had no artillery of their own.

But about noon, at Schuin's Hoogte near the Ingogo River, the Boers opened fire on the column. The battle lasted all afternoon. About five o'clock rain began to fall and the British huddled on a piece of rising ground while the Boers lay back and picked them off. At dusk some British reinforcements arrived, but they were too late. Seven officers and 69 men were killed and 3 officers and 64 men wounded. Under cover of darkness Colley retreated, leaving most of his wounded lying in the rain.

The British suffered defeat in three successive engagements, but they were small affairs; no decisive battle had yet been fought. As the two armies sat facing each other on the Natal-Transvaal border, Colley made a careful study of the Boer position. It was located below a steep, high hill, an extinct volcano actually, called Majuba, or Amajuba, which did not appear to be held. It was the key topographical feature, and Colley saw that if he occupied it he could prise the Boers out of their positions.

On the night of 26 February orders were quietly passed for 494 soldiers and 64 sailors to assemble with arms, ammunition, greatcoats, entrenching tools, and three days' rations. Including the medical staff, some Bantu porters, and three newspaper correspondents, there were about 600 men.

At ten o'clock on this moonless night Colley led his force towards Majuba. As they passed near the farm of R. C. O'Neill a dog barked, but the silent men marched on and the dog roused no one. On a ridge at the base of the hill two companies were detached and ordered to entrench. The horses of the officers were also left, and the troops began the long, hard climb to the summit. In old age Ian Hamilton, then a lieutenant in the Gordon Highlanders, wrote: "I remember, as if it were yesterday, the tense excitement of that climb up with a half-dozen shadowy forms close by, which were swallowed up and disappeared if they got further away from me than half a dozen paces." It was three o'clock in the morning before they reached the top, exhausted but exultant. Many men, weighed down by their 58 pounds of equipment and provisions, had lagged be-hind and in the dark had lost contact with their own units; straggling in, they were sent to positions that seemed short of men. Thus the units were not well organized under their own officers, and no attempt was made to sort them out. They could now rest for a few hours, but most were too excited to sleep, and besides it was cold in the early morning hours.

The top of Majuba was about 400 yards long and 300 yards wide, and in the centre was a basinlike depression. No effort was made to entrench or to throw up any effective defences. Neither was the position properly reconnoitred, for some men were posted to defend a side that was quite adequately protected by a sheer precipice.

Dawn revealed the Boer laager below them. "Looking down from our position right into the enemy's lines, we seemed to hold them in the palm of our hands," said Thomas Carter, one of the correspondents. Colley looked around and remarked, "We could stay here forever." Highlanders stood up and gleefully shook their fists. One called out, "Come up here, you beggars!"

Down in the Boer laager it was Hendrina Joubert, wife of the Com-mandant-General, who first saw the British on Majuba. Hendrina always accompanied her husband on commando, and it was said that she was the soldier in the family. She had slept badly and at first light had got up, dressed, and gone out of the tent to put a kettle on the fire. Looking up at Majuba, she saw Colley's men on the rim and ran to rouse her husband: "Piet, come here. There are people on the kop."

Joubert sounded the alarm, and the laager sprang to life. Nicolaas

Smit, one of the bravest and best of the Boer generals, called for volunteers to climb Majuba.

Lieutenant Ian Hamilton, in charge of an advanced piquet outside the basin, saw the first of the volunteers beginning to climb, and he hastened to report to Colley. The general thanked him politely for his information and sent him back. Three times more that morning Hamilton reported the progress of the advancing Boers. The last time he found Colley asleep.

There was a small detached knoll on the east side where Hamilton was stationed, and some of the first Boers to come within rifle range occupied this, pouring a heavy fire into his position. Hamilton was forced to retreat; the Boers gained the rim of the basin. Once more Hamilton dashed back to Colley, now awake, and petitioned him: "I do hope, General, that you will let us have a charge, and that you will not think it presumption on my part to have come up and asked you."

"No presumption, Mr. Hamilton, but we will wait until the Boers advance on us, then give them a volley and charge."

Minutes later Colley fell dead, a bullet through his head. The Boers were overrunning the British position. Back with his men, Hamilton seized a rifle, but before he could raise it a bullet shattered his left wrist.

Everywhere the soldiers fled from the Boers. The commands and threats of their officers did nothing to arrest the headlong flight. "I'll shoot you if you don't come back," one officer shouted, but the men ran blindly on. The newspapermen ran too. Thomas Carter found himself racing shoulder to shoulder with a stalwart Highlander. Directly in front of them was the hospital area with the wounded men stretched out on the ground. They swerved around the wounded, and Carter, aware that the Highlander had the inside track, begrudged him the advantage. All around them running men pitched forward as the Boers poured a murderous fire into their backs. Carter heard one cry, "Oh, my God!" as he fell. He leaped over him and pounded on.

At the edge of the rim Carter and the others were forced to pull up. A 40-foot cliff fell away before them. A bullet from the rear toppled one of the men near him, and Carter, fearing a broken neck less than a bullet in the back, dropped to his stomach and launched himself over the side. Clutching at the tufts of heather, he managed to break his fall and land unhurt at the bottom.

He and those who followed his example found themselves in a ravine. They tried to run down it, but the Boers were soon above them sending down a shower of bullets that impinged off the rocks around them. All were forced to surrender. Carter, like the other correspondents, carried a pistol, but he thought it would "look better" if he was found unarmed, and he managed to bury his revolver in the sand before he gave himself up. Among the Boers' prisoners was Lieutenant Alan Hill of the 58th Foot who only a month earlier had won the Victoria Cross for rescuing two wounded men under heavy fire at Laing's Nek. Now he was holding a bloody arm, ripped open from the elbow to the wrist.

In the general rout Ian Hamilton also fled, clutching his shattered wrist. Then a spent bullet or chip of rock struck him on the head and he fell unconscious. When he recovered, two boys of about fourteen were turning him over and removing his sword and equipment. They were chased off by an old Boer with a black beard, and when he was on his feet Hamilton was led to identify Colley's body.

J. H. J. Wessels, one of his captors, attended to Hamilton's wound, binding his wrist with an improvised splint made from the top of a bully-beef tin and tying it with his own red bandana. Thirty years later Lieutenant General Sir Ian Hamilton again met Mr. Wessels and presented him with a new handkerchief in a silver box.

Hamilton was allowed to wander about, and for a while he carried water to the wounded. He heard one Boer, looking at the shambles around him, piously declare that such was the fate of those who chose to fight on the Sabbath. About dusk he slipped away, tried to climb down the hill and make his way back to camp, but darkness fell, there was a heavy rain, and he lost his way. Exhausted and in pain, he sank down and lost consciousness. A dog's tongue licking his face roused him; Patch, his fox terrier, had come out with a search party and had found his master. Hamilton's arm was forever crippled, but at the age of ninety-one he could still say: "Majuba was worth an arm any day."

Majuba was the last battle of the war. General Evelyn Wood, who now took command of the British forces in South Africa, was ordered to arrange an armistice. The British wanted peace. The Transvaal did not seem important enough to shed blood over it.

Majuba, although a small affair, was particularly mortifying for Britain; never before in its long history had British arms suffered such a humiliating defeat: a group of unsoldierly farm boys had completely routed a British force containing elements of the Royal Navy and regulars from some of the most famous regiments in the British army, and a force, moreover, that was six times larger than that of the Boers and in what ought to have been an impregnable position.

A Royal Commission was appointed to go to Pretoria to treat with the Boers, and on 3 August 1881 the Pretoria Convention, as the peace terms were called, was signed and published. It gave the Transvaalers "complete self-government, subject to suzerainty of Her Majesty." Britain retained control over external relations, the right to move troops through the country, and a veto over laws affecting the Bantu; the Transvaalers agreed to permit foreigners to enter, live, and work in the country without interference and to exempt from military service British subjects registered with the British Resident.

What the Transvaal Boers had been unable to accomplish with argument they had achieved with bullets—and their bravery, determination, and sheer audacity.

In England reaction to the Pretoria Convention was mixed. Some regarded it as a generous gesture on the part of Gladstone's government, but most saw it as a shameful capitulation. Conan Doyle said, "It was the height of idealism, and the result has not been such as to encourage its repetition. . . . the Boers saw neither generosity nor humanity in our conduct, but only fear."[3] Queen Victoria warned her ministers that there would be disastrous results from such a humiliating peace made on the heels of military defeat. The army was thoroughly outraged. Lieutenant Colonel Hugh McCalmont of the 7th Hussars expressed a common feeling when he wrote in a letter home: "Why have Colley and all his men been sacrificed if there was a foregone conclusion of the Government that there was nothing worth fighting about?"

The British inhabitants of South Africa were dismayed. In the market square of Newcastle, Natal, there was "raving, weeping and blaspheming." In Pretoria loyalists folded a Union Jack in a coffin and held a bitter funeral. C. K. White, president of the Committee of Loyal Inhabitants of the Transvaal, spoke of men crying like children. He sent letters protesting the peace to Gladstone, Lord Kimberley, and the House of Commons together with a petition signed by thirty-four loyalists: "Unless the supremacy of England be vindicated," it declared, "inhabitants of British descent living in South Africa will be subjected to continual insult and injury, not only from the Boers, but also from native tribes who have witnessed our defeat and humiliation."[4] In reply Gladstone blandly stated that it had been thought that the Transvaalers wanted British rule, but now it was clear they did not and "Her Majesty's Government have thought it their duty to avail themselves of the earliest indications on the part of the Boers of a disposition to a reasonable adjustment, in order to terminate a war which threatened the most disastrous consequences, not only to the Transvaal but to the whole of South Africa."[5]

The First Anglo-Boer War created only a brief sensation in the world outside South Africa. There were too many other dramatic events following close on the heels of the armistice in 1881: on 12 March the French occupied Tunis; the next day Alexander II, Czar of Russia, was assassinated; Disraeli died on 12 April; and on 2 July James Garfield, newly inaugurated President of the United States, was shot.

Three years after the war, under the terms of the London Convention, the British gave up the right to march troops through the Transvaal and the right to any control over the treatment of the Bantu. Paul Kruger was now president of the new republic, which officially called itself the Republic of South Africa, and at his insistence there was no mention of British suzerainty in the London Convention. Majuba Day was already enshrined as a memorable date among the Boers, but it was evidently a much less significant date for the British, for the London Convention was signed on 27 February 1881, the third anniversary of Britain's humiliating defeat.

The Boers were now relatively content. The British had removed the menace of the Zulus and the Bapedi, introduced some order into the government, and returned the government to them. A president and volksraad had been elected, and all the trappings of a trekker republic were restored. So things might have remained, and perhaps Boer and Briton would have learned to live side by side had not a disaster struck the Transvaal: gold was discovered on the Witwatersrand.

4

THE JAMESON RAID

The Rand (short for the Witwatersrand—meaning "Ridge of White Water") is a 60-mile-long ridge running roughly east and west, its centre about 30 miles south of Pretoria. It was, and is, the largest gold field in the world. The uncovering of its buried riches solved the financial difficulties of the South African Republic, but it created tragic problems of its own, and no one foresaw this more clearly than President Paul Kruger, who told his countrymen in a prophetic statement: "Instead of rejoicing you would do better to weep, for this gold will cause our country to be soaked in blood."

When the gold of the Rand was discovered in 1887 a flood of foreigners—uitlanders, the Boers called them—poured into the country. These gold seekers, many of them footloose adventurers, were a different breed of men from the farmers and small tradesmen who had previously been drawn to the Transvaal, and the government was ill-prepared to cope with them. Less than 15 percent were married men who had brought their families with them and intended to settle. The rest were either single or men who had left their families in their home countries and intended to go back as soon as they had made their fortunes. They congregated in and around Johannesburg, where John Merriman, a Cape politician, described them as "a loafing, drinking, scheming lot" who would, he said, "corrupt an archangel, or at any rate knock a good deal of bloom off its wings."

The Transvaal government tried to be helpful, but the size of the uitlander population increased so rapidly that it was frightening: they were fast outnumbering the Boers themselves, and they made little or no effort to settle into Boer ways; they were, in fact, strident in their demands for concessions, changes in the laws, even, as they were the most heavily taxed, the right to vote. Most of all, they wanted things done the right way. Their way.

Although most of the uitlanders were of British origin, there were representatives from the United States, Australia, and every country in Europe. Miners, prospectors, and speculators poured in, and behind them came gamblers, businessmen, thieves, financiers, prostitutes, and engineers. There were adventurers of all classes, all eager to make a fortune, all greedy. Some were poor, and some were rich already but wanted more; some were stupid, and a few were very clever indeed. Among the rich and clever was Cecil Rhodes (1853–1902), who had already made a fortune from diamonds at Kimberley and who, in a remarkably short period of time, had become the richest man in the Western world. In 1890, at the age of thirty-seven, he became prime minister of Cape Colony as well.

Rhodes was a man of big dreams, one of which was a united South Africa—united under the Union Jack—and of a British Africa extending from the Cape to Cairo. In 1895 he thought he saw in the complaints of the uitlanders an opportunity for Britain to reannex the Transvaal.

The Boers, too, had a vision of a united South Africa, but of an Afrikaner state under a republican flag. In the course of events the dreams of both were realized, but for neither Boer nor Briton was 1895 the right time.

Within the Transvaal government there were undoubtedly inefficiencies and some corruption, but the causes of the uitlanders' discontent were annoyances, not oppressions; Conan Doyle's contention that "their whole lives were darkened by injustice" was a gross exaggeration; their grievances were certainly not adequate excuses for rebellion. Yet there was violent talk, and in Johannesburg a sixty-six-man "Reform Committee" made seditious noises. Rhodes encouraged them. When they determined to revolt, he supplied them with arms, smuggling rifles and ammunition into the country in coal wagons and oil drums of the De Beers Company, which he controlled.

Just over the Transvaal frontier nearest Johannesburg Rhodes stationed a force of some 500 armed and mounted men with instructions to wait until the revolt on the Rand began and then ride in and assure its success. In charge of this operation was Dr. Leander Starr Jameson (1853–1917), Rhodes's friend, employee, confidant, and sharer of his dreams of empire and glory.

The conspiracy was not very secret. Everyone in Johannesburg knew about it, and naturally Kruger knew too. Sir Hercules Robinson, the British high commissioner in Cape Town, and Joseph Chamberlain, the colonial secretary in London, also knew about it, although they tried to avoid knowing and persisted in pretending that they did not know. When Sir Hercules's imperial secretary tried to tell him more, he snapped, "The less you and I have to do with these damned conspiracies of Rhodes and Chamberlain the better." What no one knew, not even the conspirators themselves, was the date. Several dates were fixed, but each time the event was postponed. The plotters were not professional revolutionaries, or even politicians; for the most part they were prospering businessmen and well-paid workmen. Rhodes's brother, Colonel Frank Rhodes, a British army officer then in the Transvaal, wrote on 25 October 1895 that "so long as people are making money individually in Johannesburg they will endure a great many political wrongs."

Many of the uitlanders would have preferred to see a reformed Transvaal government rather than British annexation. They disliked Britain's native policy and the meddling of Parliament and the philanthropic societies, for the uitlanders' view of the position of nonwhites in society was little different from that of the Boers.* The Americans, of whom there were a goodly number, including eight on the Reform Committee, were almost unanimous in rejecting the idea of British rule, and many refused to participate when they learned that it was intended to hoist the Union Jack. There was much bickering and vacillation. Rhodes was growing impatient, and Jameson, in whom patience was never a plentiful commodity, was growing more so. But old Paul Kruger—Oom (Uncle) Paul, his people called him—was patient, and he counselled patience to his burghers: "Take a tortoise," he told them. "If you want to kill it you must wait until it puts out its head, and then you cut it off."

Jameson with his troopers sat on the border in the dusty little village of Pitsani and fretted. He was the same age as Rhodes, but somehow seemed younger. Like Rhodes, he was a bachelor who had no interest in women. He was by nature an adventurer and a gambler who, apparently without qualms, gave up a successful medical practice in Kimberley and succumbed to the dreams of Rhodes. Everyone liked him, for he was a man with charm, and in Rhodes's cause he charmed nearly everyone. But he did not charm Oom Paul Kruger.

Jameson was sure that if he rode in he could prod the reluctant Reform Committee into action, and, all patience gone, he warned Rhodes: "Unless I hear definitely to the contrary, shall leave tomorrow morning." Rhodes's answer—"On no account must you move. I strongly object to such a course"—never arrived, so Jameson mounted and rode over the border with 494 men, eight Maxim machine guns, and three light field pieces.

The Jameson Raid was a fiasco from the beginning. The detail of troopers assigned to cut the telegraph line to the Transvaal got drunk and cut the line to Cape Town instead. Thus, Rhodes did not know what was happening, but Kruger did. A Boer commando surrounded Jameson and his men about 10 miles outside Johannesburg, and on the morning of 2 January 1896 they were forced to surrender.

---

*Not even missionaries and liberals in England suggested equal political rights. A schoolbook explained it: "To the natives . . . the British flag means protection and security. It does not mean complete equality before the law, still less does it mean political equality. In a land where the natives are so many more in number than the whites, and where the natives are not by nature either intelligent or law-abiding, they must be restrained in matters where white men are left free."[1]

The uitlanders in Johannesburg had gone so far as to pass out a few of Rhodes's rifles, nothing more. They had no stomach for fighting. At the invitation of the Transvaal government, they sent a deputation to Pretoria, the capital. There these shrewd Johannesburg businessmen proved themselves the most inept of revolutionaries, for when the Boer officials questioned their credentials and demanded to know whom they represented, they proudly handed over a complete list of the members of the Reform Committee and the other plotters. The Boers, list in hand, arrested them all.

When Rhodes learned of the capture of Jameson he told his friend W. P. Schreiner, attorney general of Cape Colony, "Old Jameson has upset my applecart. . . . Twenty years we have been friends, and now he goes in and ruins me." Rhodes was indeed ruined, but he kept his head and acted like a man—which is more than can be said for Joseph Chamberlain, the colonial secretary. Rhodes accepted the blame for his part in the affair, and in spite of heavy pressure to denounce Jameson he refused to turn his back on him.

As soon as the news of the Jameson Raid reached Europe, the Germans began to rattle their sabres. The Kaiser sent a cruiser to Delagoa Bay, and when Jameson was captured he telegraphed congratulations to Kruger on repelling the "armed bands which invaded your country." This raised a storm of anti-German sentiment in England, and there was a music hall glorification of Jameson as a champion of England against what was regarded as German-Boer intrigue. Still, as far as the British government was concerned, the raid was the cause of acute political embarrassment. "If filibustering fails," Lord Salisbury told Chamberlain, "it is always disreputable."

As a result of the raid and the abortive revolt some of Johannesburg's most substantial inhabitants were in gaol, where they became one of the sights of the town and were duly called on by distinguished visitors, including Mark Twain. Five of the conspirators were sentenced to death, including Colonel Frank Rhodes and John Hays Hammond, a wealthy American mining engineer. Part of the beam of the gallows used by the British to hang the five rebels at Slachter's Nek was brought out, and it was suggested that it would be appropriate to hang the conspirators from it. However, the British and American governments moved to save their people: Jameson was eventually turned over to the British government for punishment while the others were given heavy fines only. Both Jameson and Rhodes were ordered to testify before a Select Committee of the House of Commons.

When Jameson gave his evidence he said, "I know perfectly well that as I have not succeeded the natural thing has happened; but I also know that if I had succeeded I should have been forgiven." He was right and everyone knew it. All Britain would have cheered, considering his action only a neat bit of needful skulduggery. There was much criticism of the Select Committee. Still, it resulted in Jameson being sent to prison for

SCOUTS: THE EYES OF THE ARMY.

a few months and Rhodes being strongly condemned. Its report stated: "Whatever justification there might have been for the action on the part of the people of Johannesburg, there was none for the conduct of a person in Mr. Rhodes' position."

What was Rhodes's position? The difficulty was that he held too many positions. If Rhodes as simply a wealthy man had helped the uitlanders, this would have been understandable and excusable; if, as a director of the British South Africa Company, he had mobilized an armed force on the border in case of emergency, he might have been praised for his foresight; if, as prime minister of Cape Colony, he had, like Robinson and Chamberlain, simply closed his eyes to the planned revolt and failed to warn either his neighbour or his own government, this would have been overlooked; and if, as head of De Beers, he had permitted the company's resources to be used to further the aims of the revolutionists, it is doubtful if the shareholders would have protested. But doing all these things in all his capacities at the same time was too much. It was this which *The Times* called the "unjustifiable character of Mr. Rhodes's action."

Rhodes refused, in spite of his lawyer's entreaties, to implicate Chamberlain and the British government, as he could easily have done. In December 1896 his career was at its nadir. He had been forced to resign from all his public offices and to give up most of his directorships; his brother, through trying to help him, had lost his commission in the British army and was in a Transvaal gaol; his friend Jameson was a convicted criminal. In addition, there was trouble in Rhodesia—the Mashona were in revolt—and his house at the Cape, Groote Schuur, which he loved, burned to the ground. He also suffered from ill health: malaria, influenza, and heart trouble. He had suffered a fall so great that he would never completely recover from it. Yet, he woke up his friend Albert Grey one night and asked him if he had ever considered how fortunate he was to be an Englishman.

The Jameson Raid had a profound effect upon the Boers. They were alarmed to discover that the uitlanders presented not only an internal threat but an external danger; war seemed again a possibility. Some of their gold, they decided, had best be spent for arms. Forts were constructed at Johannesburg (which the uitlanders believed were designed to control them), and expenditures for arms and equipment were increased fivefold; most important of all was the purchase of modern Mauser rifles, to replace their old Martini-Henrys, and some of the finest artillery made in Europe.

Kruger's handling of the Jameson Raid raised his prestige enormously. John Merriman said, "President Kruger . . . now occupies without dispute the leading position in South Africa. His faults are forgotten in admiration of his success and the conviction that both in diplomacy and in war he is more than a match for the English."[2]

The raid also brought the two Boer republics closer together. As M. T. Steyn, soon to be president of the Orange Free State, said: "After the Jameson Raid it was clear to me that the fate of the Free State, whether we wished it or not, was tied up with that of the Transvaal for better or for worse."[3]

And so the explosive powder of mutual distrust and enmity was prepared. So too was the portfire of uitlander discontent left smouldering. The man who put the fire to the powder and blew up South Africa was Alfred Milner, ably assisted by his superior, Joseph Chamberlain, and his opponent, Paul Kruger.

5

MOVING TOWARDS WAR

"It is the British race which built the Empire, and it is the undivided British race which can alone uphold it. . . . Deeper, stronger, more primordial than material ties is the bond of common blood, a common language, common history and traditions." Such was the firm-seated belief of forty-three-year-old Sir Alfred Milner in 1897 on the eve of his departure from England to take up the posts of governor of Cape Colony and high commissioner for South Africa.

He was an extraordinary man, Alfred Milner. Few felt indifferent towards him; he aroused intense hatred in some and the warmest admiration in others. Jan Smuts, after meeting him for the first time, told his wife that "there is something in his very intelligent eyes that tells me he is a very dangerous man." He referred to himself as "a civilian soldier of the Empire." And this he was. Yet many remarked on his un-British personality—he seemed more German than English—and his contempt for democratic processes. Sir Henry Campbell-Bannerman, soon to be head of the Liberal party, regarded him as an opinionated and dangerous man of doubtful judgement.

As a boy he had attended school in Germany, and at King's College, London, he proved to be a brilliant student, taking prizes in classics, history, and literature and at eighteen winning the first scholarship at Balliol College, Oxford. There he won four successive scholarships, took a first class in *literae humaniores,* and was elected to a fellowship at New College. He has been described at this period as "tall, dignified, and grave beyond his years . . . eager to organize rather than to influence, and fearful to give generous impulses full rein." He had already decided that marriage would interfere with a career and that he would postpone it until he retired, a resolution which, like all his other resolutions, he kept.

He refused a tutorship at New College and went instead to London to study law, being called to the bar in 1881. Finding no success at the law, he turned to journalism and worked for the *Pall Mall Gazette,* floundering as do many promising young men looking for the right career. He ran for Parliament and was defeated. Then he accepted a position as secretary to George Goschen, who in 1886 became chancellor of the exchequer in Salisbury's ministry, and in this capacity he displayed such an extraordinary grasp of finance that in 1889 Goschen obtained for him the post of director-general of accounts in Egypt. Here, for the first time, he prospered. Three years later Goschen brought him back to England to become chairman of the Board of Inland Revenue, and in another three years he was knighted (KCB).

When Joseph Chamberlain offered Milner the posts of governor of Cape Colony and high commissioner for South Africa, Milner was delighted and told his friend R. B. Brett (later Viscount Esher) that "though I know perfectly well that I may break my neck over it, I am wild to go." On 5 May 1897 this financial expert arrived in South Africa and went to work applying his genius to its very human problems. South Africa never recovered from the experience.

His first nine months in office were spent learning Dutch and Afrikaans, studying the local problems, and struggling, he said, "against the temptation to say anything of substantial importance." Then in a private letter to Chamberlain dated 23 February 1898 he gave as his considered opinion that "there is no way out of the political troubles in South Africa except reform in the Transvaal or war. And at present the chances of reform are worse than ever."

To conclude that a country neighbouring a British colony must change its ways or Britain would have to go to war was a violent reaction to the situation existing in South Africa. To understand how Milner arrived at such an extraordinary conclusion it is necessary to look beyond the facts and fantasies concerning the position of the uitlanders in the Transvaal to the set of attitudes which Milner brought with him to South Africa. To believe, as Milner did, that the British were natural rulers and that British rule was the best rule was a common enough belief among the British; throughout the world self-assured Englishmen ruled over people of other races and other cultures. To believe, as Milner did, that other races or people of other cultures ought not to rule over Englishmen, that it was not right that they should do so, that it was somehow morally wrong—this was a new conception of the imperial doctrine, a conception which, as such a situation had never before occurred (at least in modern history), had never before been examined. Milner now demanded that it be examined, and his own conclusion was already fixed: Englishmen must not be ruled by others.

Although in an excellent position to promote his viewpoint, or rather to embody his attitude in policy and thus provoke war, Milner needed the

support of his chief. Joseph Chamberlain (1836–1914) had been appointed colonial secretary only six months before the Jameson Raid. In
the ten years he held the post he was to give it an importance it had never
before assumed and never would again. With his monocle ever screwed
in his eye and an ever-present orchid on his lapel he looked every inch
an aristocrat, but in fact he came from a prosperous middle-class family
of business people and he himself had been a successful screw manufacturer before entering politics at the age of thirty-eight. He was thrice
married; by one wife he had a son who became prime minister and by
another a son who became chancellor of the exchequer. He was called
"Pushful Joe" and "Imperial Joe" and, of course, a good many other less
complimentary names. Sir Hercules Robinson considered him "dangerous as an enemy, untrustworthy as a friend but fatal as a colleague."[1]
Queen Victoria, however, thought him "sensible," and he was immensely
popular with jingos, for he came to personify the imperial ideal. When
he took office as colonial secretary he claimed to have two important
qualifications for the post: "These qualifications are that, in the first
place, I believe in the British race. I believe that the British race is the
greatest of governing races that the world has ever seen . . . and I believe
that there are no limits to its future."[2]

He was, then, a man after Milner's heart; but Chamberlain was, as
Milner was not, a shrewd politician aware of the political sensibilities of
his countrymen; he also knew that it was he who would have to answer
to his colleagues and to Parliament for Milner's actions. Chamberlain
asked Milner to come home and explain his views.

During Milner's absence from South Africa his place was taken by
Major General William Butler (1838–1910), commander-in-chief of the
British forces in South Africa. Butler was a curious specimen of Victorian
soldiery. He had seen much active service in West Africa, Egypt, the
Sudan, and Canada (where he had recommended the formation of the
Northwest Mounted Police), and he had also served in Burma, India, and
with Wolseley in South Africa. Like many Victorian officers, he loved war
and thought "a battle by far the most exciting and enthralling of all life's
possibilities to its mortals." Yet the only campaign in which he had taken
part that he thought morally defensible was the Gordon Relief Expedition—and that was a failure. Although he had little formal education, he
possessed a brilliant mind, and he was one of the most literate of the
Victorian generals, the author of more than a half-dozen books and a
friend of Victor Hugo. Butler was a man of strong opinions, and he was
not hesitant in expressing them, even when they were unpopular. Of his
lack of tact, General Evelyn Wood once said, "That he was generally right
in his conclusions does not indicate that he always went the right way of
obtaining them."

Butler arrived in South Africa shortly after Milner left, and the two
men did not have an opportunity to confer. Butler wrote later: "I went
out blindfolded to South Africa in 1898; the bandages soon fell off." Like

Milner, he carefully studied the problems he found, but he arrived at diametric conclusions: he believed that South Africa needed "a rest cure and not an operation." He was undoubtedly right, but he also saw that, in spite of anything he might do, the surgeons would have their way. Never modest, he later wrote: "I was able to judge of a possible war between us and the Boers with a power of forecast of a quite exceptional character."

What was there about the problems in South Africa that led men to consider such a drastic solution as war?

Both sides wanted a united South Africa, though, of course, they differed in their ideas of who should dominate it. For the Boers, an Afrikaner South Africa seemed a distant aspiration; for the British a united but British South Africa seemed not only desirable but a possible and even necessary goal. There was much talk of the need to maintain British paramountcy, though no one was quite sure exactly what this meant or why it was necessary. It was with this idea in mind that the British had included the vague phrase about suzerainty in the preamble to the Pretoria Convention. It had been omitted from the London Convention, but with curious logic the British now maintained that the preamble to the earlier document was assumed to be part of the later one. There was much official correspondence about this, and Milner noted that the word "suzerainty" had "a curiously maddening effect" on the Boers.

The concept of an imperial mission, of the desirability—the nobility even—of one nation assuming suzerainty over another, or of one nation arrogating to itself a position of paramountcy in a part of the world containing other nations, is today an unpopular one. Yet it was commonly held prior to World War I. Englishmen believed in the "white man's burden," in what was regarded as the heavy, thankless duty of civilised men to rule and teach all lesser, more inferior races. L. S. Amery espoused these ideals but noted that not quite everyone felt this way and that there existed "a notion . . . that nationalism is in itself a desirable thing and that, apart from all question of political principle, it is in some unexplained way identical with political liberty. . . . Little sympathy is bestowed on the great peoples rightly struggling for mastery, for the supremacy of higher civilization and higher principle."

Lofty principles are often not formulated until after war has been declared, and so it was with the Anglo-Boer War. It was a week after hostilities had actually begun that Chamberlain told the House of Commons why Britain was fighting:

We are going to war in defence of principles—the principles on which this Empire has been founded, and upon which alone it can exist. . . . The first principle is this—if we are to maintain our existence as a great power in South Africa, we are bound to show that we are both willing and able to protect British subjects everywhere when they are made to suffer from oppression and injustice.

. . . The second principle is that in the interests of the British Empire, Great Britain must remain the paramount Power in South Africa.

So much for lofty principles. Some of the specific principles sound somewhat curious in relation to the grander ones. Chamberlain declared that Britain must "protect British subjects everywhere," but to demand that British subjects be permitted to become citizens of a republic was a curious extension of the protection.

The uitlander mine owners—known as Randlords—complained of corruption, and certainly this existed (although often it was the Randlords themselves who did the corrupting), and they particularly objected to a dynamite monopoly granted by the Transvaal government which made it necessary for them to pay dearly for this needed article. Uitlanders also complained of high taxes, and a bill to impose a modest 5 percent tax on mining profits was cited as "an indication of how far the rights of arbitrary taxation might be carried." (Today the tax is computed on a complicated formula but is close to 60 percent.) They complained, too, that there were not enough English schools and that the language of the laws and of the courts was the language of the country. All of these ills could be cured, they felt, if only they were given the franchise—the right to vote—and they were convinced of their right to demand it.

The reluctance of the Boers to give the uitlanders the franchise was understandable—"For the little sheep my door is always open," said Oom Paul Kruger, "but the wolf I mean to keep out"—but they were unsophisticated in their methods. Before 1882 only one year's residence had been required before an immigrant could become a citizen; then the requirement was raised to five years. In 1890 fear of the uitlander vote caused the volksraad to raise the residency requirement to fourteen years, and the clamour grew. Uitlanders ground out a continuous stream of complaints and did their best to turn minor incidents into models of oppression.

Among the uitlanders it was much resented that all public officials were Afrikaners, and it was particularly galling that the Boer policemen, called Zarps (after the initials of the Zuid-Afrikaansche Republiek Politie), whom they considered corrupt and inefficient, should be permitted to arrest Englishmen. Of the provocative incidents which helped lead the way to war, none was more celebrated than the Edgar case, though it is difficult to see why. On the night of 18 December 1898 a powerfully built Englishman, Tom Edgar, fighting with another Englishman, beat him severely. The Zarps arrived and Edgar fled. The police pursued him to his home; there he resisted arrest, and in the scuffle he was shot and killed. As General Butler said, "Had this drunken brawl occurred in any other city in the world out of the Transvaal it would have occasioned no excitement outside of the people immediately concerned in it." But the uitlanders at once seized the incident as an example of police brutality. Indignation meetings were called, a petition to the Queen was prepared, and dozens of letters and telegrams were dispatched to British politicians and officials. It somewhat detracted from the case as a propaganda vehicle that the policeman's name was Jones, but when his trial resulted in acquittal it was hailed as an example of the lack of justice to be found in the Transvaal courts of law.

Reporting the incident to London, Butler said, "I have no doubt that cases of rough usage by police have occurred in Johannesburg; but we must bear in mind that the town is probably the most corrupt, immoral, and untruthful assemblage of beings at present in the world." He was not the only one with such an unflattering opinion. J. A. Hobson, a keen observer of the scene there, wrote: "As for general liberty and even license of conduct, it existed nowhere if not in Johannesburg. Every luxury of life, every extravagance of behaviour, every form of private vice flourished unchecked; every man and woman (except Kaffirs, who do the work and don't count) said and did what seemed good in his or her own eyes." Even Chamberlain characterized Johannesburgers as "a lot of cowardly, selfish blatant speculators who would sell their souls to have the power of rigging the market."

The Jews of Johannesburg were flourishing and in general did not join with other uitlanders in complaining to the government, but Butler suspected them of being at the root of the troublemaking, and in a dispatch to the War Office he wrote: "If the Jews were out of the question, it would be easy enough to come to an agreement; but they are apparently intent upon plunging the country into civil strife." This was also the view of Hilaire Belloc, who said that the war was "openly and undeniably provoked and promoted by Jewish interests in South Africa."

Jews had indeed flocked to the Transvaal from all parts of Europe— about half came from Germany or Central Europe—and Johannesburg boasted three synagogues. Many were poor but managed to establish themselves in businesses and trades, performing valuable functions outside the competence of the Boers in the urban life that sprang up in the boom town that was Johannesburg. Few, however, took any part in the agitation or signed their names to the many complaints sent to the British high commissioner. Those from Central Europe (it was thought amusing by the uitlanders to call these "Peruvians") had never enjoyed any political rights in their home countries, and they found the Boers' almost complete lack of anti-Semitism refreshing. Some even sent declarations of support to Kruger, disassociating themselves from the clamouring of the other uitlanders.

Milner was not completely successful in England; in spite of his best efforts he had not entirely convinced Chamberlain and his colleagues that war was inevitable. On 8 May 1896 Chamberlain had told the House of Commons:

A war in South Africa would be one of the most serious wars that could possibly be waged. It would be in the nature of a civil war. It would be a long war, and a costly war, and, as I have pointed out already, it would leave behind it the embers of a strife which I believe generations would be hardly long enough to extinguish.[3]

He was, of course, absolutely right, and it was unfortunate that three years later Milner was able to persuade him to change his views.

Chamberlain, sympathetic to Milner's views but afraid that the British public was not yet prepared for war, asked him to sum up the situation and his views in a dispatch which might be made public. Milner did so in a long telegram which L. S. Amery called "one of the most masterly State documents ever penned." It became famous as the "Helots Dispatch":

> It seems a paradox but it is true that the only effective way of protecting our subjects is, to help them to cease to be our subjects. . . . It is idle to talk of peace and unity. . . . The case for intervention is overwhelming. . . . The spectacle of thousands of British subjects kept permanently in the position of helots, constantly chafing under undoubted grievances, and calling vainly to Her Majesty's Government for redress, does steadily undermine the influence and reputation of Great Britain and the respect for the British Government within its own dominions.

The Helots Dispatch reached Chamberlain on 5 May 1899, but it was not immediately released. M. T. Steyn, president of the Orange Free State, and William P. Schreiner, prime minister of Cape Colony, proposed that Milner and Kruger meet face to face at Bloemfontein, the Free State capital; Chamberlain thought this an excellent idea; Milner was less enthusiastic but could hardly refuse. He had no skill in diplomacy, or at least no taste for it. Just before leaving Cape Town for Bloemfontein he wrote: "My view has been and still is . . . that if we are perfectly determined we shall win without a fight or with a mere apology for one."

The conference lasted only from 31 May until 5 June. Facing Milner across the table was Paul Kruger, described by Henry M. Stanley, who had met him a few months before, as "a Boer Machiavelli, astute and bigoted, obstinate as a mule, remarkably opinionated, vain and puffed up with the power conferred on him, vindictive, covetous and always a Boer, which means a narrow-minded and obtuse provincial of the illiterate type," and by Kipling as "sloven, sullen, savage, secret, uncontrolled" and "cruel in the shadow, crafty in the sun." But these were British opinions. To his own people he was a strong, resourceful leader: cunning, obstinate, and uneducated—yes, but wise in the ways of his own *volk* and sensitive to their needs and aspirations.

Stephanus Johannes Paulus Krüger (1825–1904), to give him his full and correct name, exhibited most of the strengths and weaknesses of his race in bold relief. Born on a farm near Venterstad in Cape Colony, he had been taken by his parents on the Great Trek and by the time he was twenty-one had seen action against the Bantu, had twice married (his first wife died young), and had settled on his own farm near Rustenburg in the Transvaal.

He was a deeply religious man, a member of the Dopper sect of the

Dutch Reformed Church. The strictest of Calvinists, Doppers interpreted the Bible so literally that Kruger once assured Captain Joshua Slocum, the American circumnavigator, that the world was flat. He read nothing but the Bible, not even a newspaper; the words of the Old Testament were constantly on his lips, and all of his life he served as a lay preacher. He had had only three months of schooling and he wrote with difficulty, even forming his signature labouriously, but his mind was quick; he was shrewd and he had a remarkable memory. In the wars against the Bantu he had earned a reputation for bravery; in the internal squabbles of the early trekker republics he became renowned for his astuteness.

When in 1883, at the age of fifty-eight, he was first elected president of the Transvaal, he continued to live as he always had: he rose each morning at dawn, read his Bible, and then held a religious service for his family—he had seven daughters and nine sons. After that he sat on the front stoep of his unpretentious house in Pretoria, drinking innumerable cups of coffee, his pipe ever in his mouth, and conducted the business of the state. His people also came to him here with their agricultural and domestic problems, for he was considered wise in these matters. Gezina, his wife, kept cows and chickens, thriftily sold milk and eggs to her neighbours, and freely dispensed her great supply of home remedies for all diseases.

Kruger was a huge man with an enormous head that carried one of the world's ugliest faces. His left thumb was gone—torn off when as a young man his gun exploded as he was shooting a rhinoceros. Stanley said that he spoke "in a voice that was like a loud gurgle" as "the great jaws and cheeks heaved and opened. His speeches sounded like sermons." He often had a surly manner, and to some he seemed uncouth, but he had a kind of gnarled grandeur and he impressed men with his rhetoric and by his resourcefulness and strength of will.

When the conference began Kruger tried to bargain, but Milner was obdurate. He had been instructed by Chamberlain to "lay all stress on the question of the franchise," and this he did by simply stating his terms —five years' residency—and refusing to budge. Kruger told him: "I understand from His Excellency's arguments that if I do not give the whole management of my land and government to strangers there is nothing to be done. . . . I am not ready to hand over my country to strangers." Milner simply sat cold, impassive, insistent.

President Steyn did everything in his power to keep the conference going and to prevent a deadlock. Kruger offered to ask the volksraad to reduce the residency requirement from fourteen years to seven. To Steyn this seemed a major concession, and he had a private talk with Milner in an attempt to persuade him to accept this and take up other issues—the teaching of English in the schools, and customs, postal, and railway unions—but Milner was so uncompromising that Steyn despaired. When he left the meeting he went directly to his office, where he sat down and ordered 2,000 Mauser rifles and a million rounds of ammunition. He was too late: war began before the arms arrived.

Chamberlain, too, was anxious for the talks to continue, and he cabled Milner that it was "of the utmost importance to put the President of the South African Republic clearly in the wrong." But the impatient Milner had already slammed the door and closed the conference. Kruger summed it up simply: "It is my country you want." As he drove away there were tears streaming down his rutted, homely face.

Although undoubtedly disheartened, Kruger did not cease his efforts to keep his country from plunging into war. As he told Milner he would, he went home and persuaded his volksraad to reduce the residency requirement to seven years. Seven years was not as good as five, but it was not worth going to war for the extra two years. In Britain there were sighs of relief. *The Times* announced that the crisis was over. No, no, no, cried Milner. There were other aspects of the case; the conditions were not as good as they appeared; the real issue was not the franchise after all but British paramountcy in South Africa. Speaking of the new franchise law in a dispatch, Milner said that "if it is enforced rigidly, there will be practically unlimited opportunities of excluding persons whom the Government considers undesirable." Why a country should not be allowed to exclude undesirable foreigners was not explained. He now proposed a joint inquiry into Transvaal reforms. Chamberlain, following Milner's lead, decided to ignore the Transvaal's conciliatory gestures and released Milner's Helots Dispatch.

The British public, even the Cabinet, had shown little interest in South Africa, but the dramatic dispatch created a sensation, and not just in Britain. The British in South Africa reacted as well. Throughout the winter months in South Africa—June, July, and August—there were anti-Boer demonstrations, public meetings, petitions, and incidents of all kinds, not only in the Transvaal, but in Natal and Cape Colony as well.

On 26 June Chamberlain gave a bellicose speech in Birmingham in which he said:

We have tried waiting, patience, and trusting to promises which were never kept. We can wait no more. It is our duty, not only to the Uitlander, but to the English throughout South Africa, to the native races, and to our own prestige in that part of the world, and to the world at large, to insist that the Transvaal falls into line with the other states in South Africa, and no longer menaces the peace and prosperity of the world.

Difficult as it may have been to see how the Transvaal was menacing the peace of the world, Chamberlain had now thrown down the gauntlet, not only to the Boers but politically to his party and particularly to his colleagues in the Cabinet. They had either to go along with him or to disown him. Since he was too powerful a political figure to be dismissed, the Cabinet reluctantly supported him. Balfour grumbled to Salisbury about Chamberlain's "favourite method of dealing with the S. African sore . . . by the free application of irritants," but when Chamberlain asked for troops he reluctantly agreed that they should be sent: "I cannot think it wise to allow him to goad on the Boers by his speeches, and to refuse him the means of repelling Boer attack." Lord Salisbury, the prime minister, in a letter to Lord Lansdowne, the secretary for war, spoke of the uitlanders as "a people we despise" who were living in "territory which will bring no profit and no power to England." The Cabinet, he complained, was committed to "act upon a moral field prepared for us by Milner and his jingo supporters."

While Chamberlain and his supporters were preparing Britain for war, frantic efforts were being made in Pretoria to prevent it. In mid-August Jan Smuts, the twenty-nine-year-old state attorney of the Transvaal, met secretly with W. Conyngham-Greene, British agent in Pretoria, to work out new proposals. The result was an agreement on the part of the Transvaal to a five-year residency for the franchise if only Britain would agree not to interfere in future with the domestic problems of the country and to submit points in dispute to arbitration by third parties. On 28 August Chamberlain gave what he called "a qualified acceptance" to the agreement, but which was, in fact, a complete rejection; he had gone too far now to turn back. At a garden party he made a speech in which he referred to the Transvaal dribbling out reforms like a "squeezed sponge." Milner, worried that the Transvaal might agree to all his terms, suggested to Chamberlain that Britain should now demand that the Transvaal disarm, a condition they certainly would not accept. This, at the moment, seemed too crude for Chamberlain, although he told Milner: "I dread above all the whittling away of differences until we have no *casus belli* left."

Chamberlain had no cause to worry. On 8 September he sent a telegram to South Africa stating that it was the unanimous decision of the Cabinet to repudiate the claims of the Transvaal to be a sovereign international state and that Britain would not consider any proposal which appeared to acknowledge such claims. That did it. On the same date the Cabinet ordered an increase in the number of troops in South Africa to 22,000. Incredibly, although Milner and Chamberlain had been relentlessly pursuing a policy which they and all the leaders of government saw would probably lead to war, almost no provision whatever had been made to fight a war in South Africa. It was not until June that the Cape Command was even ordered to collect regimental transport.

Milner constantly urged Butler to prepare for war, but Butler had received no orders from the War Office and so had done nothing. He was later much criticised for this. A British South African named Aubrey Woolls-Sampson, who had been one of the staunchest members of the Reform Committee, devised a scheme for raising a volunteer force, but Butler objected, saying that raising such a force would only alarm the Boers still more and increase the tension. He refused to sanction it, and Milner said to him bitterly, "It can never be said, Sir William, that *you* precipitated a conflict with the Dutch."

Indeed it could not. During his brief period as acting high commissioner while Milner was in England, Butler had done everything he could to dampen the rising flames of uitlander discontent, and all that he had done had met with Milner's disapproval. When Milner returned and Butler reverted to his position as commander-in-chief, the old general tried to hold his tongue as he watched Milner pursue his provocative diplomacy, but tongue holding was not easy for him.

In his dispatches home Milner complained constantly of Butler and his "policy of obstructive pacifism." On 14 June he wrote Chamberlain:

> The General. He is too awful. He has, I believe, made his military preparations all right, but I cannot get him to make the least move or take the slightest interest. . . . He will wait for his W.O. orders, but till he has commands to mobilize, he will not budge an inch. . . . His sympathy is wholly with the other side. *At the same time there is nothing to lay hold of.* He never interferes with my business and is perfectly polite. But he is absolutely no use. . . .

It was a curious situation: a diplomatist doing his best to start a war and a general doing his best to prevent it. Milner cast about desperately for an excuse to get rid of this pacifist general.

When the War Office sent Butler an order to purchase mules, asked some questions concerning supplies, and concluded by asking if he had any "observations," Butler seized this as an excuse to air his opinion on the political situation: "I believe war between the white races . . . would be the greatest calamity that ever occurred in South Africa." The War Office rebuked him, saying that political observations had not been requested. Milner wrote to Chamberlain: "I am sorry to say that in my opinion the strength of the General's political opinion impairs his efficiency, whatever his military capacity." He asked for Butler's recall. Butler was forced to resign, and his resignation was accepted on 9 August 1899, scarcely more than a month before the beginning of the war.

As Viscount Esher later told King Edward VII: "Sir W^m met the fate of those who give unpalatable advice. That much of the advice he gave has since proved correct, is not possibly of advantage to him in certain quarters."

6

EVE OF WAR

The stage was now set for war. Boers and Britons were psychologically prepared for it: all had been driven to the proper state of exasperation by the futile meetings, the legal technicalities, the endless correspondence. Most men were now impatient for the talk to end and the action

to begin. The Boers were maddened by Milner's intransigence and outraged by the threat to their cherished independence; the British were
swept by a tremendous surge of imperial sentiment such as they had
never before experienced. Practical considerations on both sides delayed
the start of hostilities for a few weeks: Britain waited for reinforcements
to arrive in South Africa; the Boers waited for the spring grass to cover
the veld, grass to sustain the horses and ponies of their commandos.

Both sides expected the war to be short. The Boers thought that
Britain would be unwilling to accept the cost in lives and treasure necessary to subdue them, and that she would, as in 1881, back off; they
underestimated the determination of the British to see the thing through
this time, to conquer them once and for all. The Boers had a misplaced
confidence in the intervention of European powers on their behalf if the
war should last longer than a few months; the British had an ill-founded
confidence in the efficacy of their army, and they underestimated both the
military capacities of the Boers and their determination to resist.

There were still some futile diplomatic gestures in the final weeks
before the hostilities began. Just as on the British side it had been the
commander-in-chief in South Africa, General Butler, who had striven for
peace, so among the Boers it was the commandant-general, Piet Joubert,
hero of Majuba, who tried at the last minute to stave off the war. He wrote
a long missive to Queen Victoria entitled "An Ernest Representation and
Historical Reminder to Her Majesty . . . in View of the Prevailing Crisis."
He sent copies to the Kaiser and the Czar. The Queen of the Netherlands
also wrote to Queen Victoria, pleading with her to use her influence to
prevent war in South Africa, but Queen Victoria replied, "If President
Kruger is reasonable, there will be no war, but the issue is in his hands."

No one had worked harder to preserve the peace than Marthinus
Theunis Steyn (1857–1916), who knew that when Britain went to war with
the Transvaal his own country would inevitably become involved, not
only because of the mutual defence pact between the two republics but
also because of the sentiments of his own people and the certainty that
if the Transvaal fell the Orange Free State could not long survive as a
republican island surrounded by British colonies. He wrote an urgent
plea for peace and asked Milner to send it to London. Milner reluctantly
agreed to relay it; then, without Steyn's knowledge, he cut out portions
of the message—because of its "enormous length." Steyn also sent off a
message to President William McKinley pleading for American intervention. But the United States had just concluded an imperialistic war of its
own in which it had acquired the Philippines, and since the Filipinos liked
the Yankees no better than they had liked the Spaniards and wanted their
freedom, the Americans were occupied in suppressing them. Besides,
Britain had sided with the United States in the war with Spain and had
in many little ways been helpful. The South African republics were not
likely to find help in this quarter.

On 17 June 1899 Sir Henry Campbell-Bannerman, ingenuously looking only at the facts, declared that there was nothing in the South African situation to justify preparing for war. But as John Adams had said more than a century before, "A Torrent is not to be impeded by Reasoning." The lust for war is not to be controlled by logic nor its gratification deterred by facts.

The War Office apparently agreed with Campbell-Bannerman and, despite repeated warnings from Lord Wolseley, the commander-in-chief, continued to turn a blind eye and a deaf ear to what was going on in the nation and declined to bestir itself sufficiently to prepare for a major conflict. No plan for a campaign in South Africa existed.

In June the British had only about 10,000 regulars and 24 field guns in all South Africa. On 8 June Lord Wolseley recommended the mobilization in England of an army corps and a cavalry division under the command of a general who would take it to South Africa if needed. However, as a Royal Commission discovered after the war, "This was never seriously entertained by the Government." Two weeks later two officers were sent to South Africa to buy 1,340 animals (less than 1 percent of the number which would actually be required), but the secretary of state for war refused to authorize remount buyers to be sent to Italy and Spain.

While Milner was stirring the pot and keeping it boiling in South Africa, the generals were growing uneasy, and General Sir Redvers Buller, who had been selected to take an army to South Africa should it be required, wrote direct to the prime minister, telling Salisbury that "before the diplomatist proceeds to an ultimatum the military should be in a position to enforce it. . . . So far as I am aware, the War Office has no idea of how matters are proceeding, and has not been consulted." On the same day, 5 September, Wolseley wrote in a minute: "The Government are acting without complete knowledge of what the military can do, while the military authorities are equally without full knowledge of what the Government expects them to do, nor are they given authority to make such antecedent preparations as will enable them to act with the least possible delay."[1]

On 16 September, with war less than a month away, Milner sent a request for "speedy reinforcements of troops and men of war." Only then did the government agree to send out reinforcements from India and to order Lieutenant General Sir George White, V.C., out from England to take command in Natal. By the time hostilities actually began, the British had mustered only about 22,000 men and 60 guns in South Africa; more than a quarter of the men had been locally recruited and were largely untrained. Just over half of these were stationed in Natal.

The British army, as was soon to be revealed, was not adequate to the strain which was about to be put upon it. The Empire had grown enormous and at a rapid rate; while the army, too, had expanded, it had, through no fault of its own, not grown large enough to handle all of the wide-flung commitments expected of it and to fight a major war at the same time. On paper, at least, there were 249,466 regulars and about

90,000 reservists, but only 70,000 were available for service in South Africa, even including those intended for home defence. In spite of this shortage of soldiers, the government made a decision which deliberately deprived the army of one of its greatest sources of trained manpower.

It was decided that the war in South Africa was to be a "white man's war," the experienced Indian army would not be used, and the Bantu and other Coloured races in South Africa would not be formed into combat units or employed as local levies. As L. S. Amery put it in *The Times History*, "it was held inadvisable to make use of any but white soldiers in a war fought between white men in a country where the black man presents so difficult a problem."[2] The Boers had similar views, so the white men on both sides warned the Basutos, Zulus, Swazis, and other Bantu to stay out of their war.

However, if the war was to be fought exclusively by white men, Britain would have to find more. There was no lack of volunteers. Even before the war began, in July and August, the Australian colonies and New Zealand offered to send men, and the day after war was declared Canada offered 1,000 volunteers. Offers of men to fight the war came from all corners of the globe. Indian princes offered men, horses, and material; the Malay States wanted to send 300 Malay States Guards, the governor of Lagos 300 Hausas, and small groups of Englishmen everywhere proposed to rush to the Empire's aid.

The military authorities were cool to these offers: colonials, they felt, would be difficult to manage and probably troublesome. Nevertheless, it was thought to be a generous gesture, and it seemed politically wise to allow the "white colonies," as a favour, to participate in the war. Pressure was put on the War Office, and on 3 October the colonies were told by telegraph that they could contribute some volunteers, but "in view of the numbers already available, infantry most, cavalry least serviceable." This telegram was much cited—usually misquoted in the form of "dismounted men preferred"—as evidence of how little the generals knew about the nature of the war they were to fight.

Before the war was over, some 25,000 Australians, New Zealanders, and Canadians were gratefully accepted—"All independent, queer an' odd, but most amazin' new," Kipling wrote. And so they must have seemed to the British regular, for the army he lived in was a closed little world of its own. British officers formed almost a separate caste; most were the sons of officers, civil servants, Anglican clergymen, squires, or professional men; few were the sons of businessmen, and fewer still were the sons of artisans or labourers. The common soldiers were drawn from the lowest classes; more than two-thirds were poor Scots and Irish; many were illiterate. From Irish bogs and Glasgow slums they turned to the army as the only escape from starvation and dulling poverty. Officers did not expect much of them. Lieutenant Colonel Forbes Macbean, who became commanding officer of the Gordon Highlanders, described his recruits:

It is natural not to expect much in the way of individual intelligence either from the recruit who comes from the part of the population which is poorest, worst fed from infancy, least educated, and brought up largely in crowded towns, or from the recruit who, though a country lad, is not naturally a man gifted with intelligence.[3]

Unlike the Boers, who enrolled boys and old men, the British infantrymen and calvarymen initially sent to South Africa were all at least twenty years old with one year's service; artillerymen had to be nineteen years old with nine months' service. Officers excepted, there were few soldiers in South Africa over thirty-five; most were between twenty and thirty.

It was easier for the British to find the men than the necessary supplies. Economy had ever been in the minds of the members of Parliament when examining the military estimates; the nation was now to pay dearly for it. After the failure of the Bloemfontein conference Wolseley had recommended that stores, ordinance, and transport be accumulated in South Africa, but the Cabinet had rejected the idea. Now, three months later, with war almost upon them, the army found itself woefully unprepared: in the army depots there were only scarlet and blue uniforms, none of the new khaki adopted for field service in the Sudan campaign of 1898; there were no reserves of horses, saddles, or horseshoes: the rifles in the reserve all had defective sights; and there were only eighty cavalry swords to spare. Worst of all, the supplies of ammunition were inadequate: there were only 200 rounds per gun for the horse, field, and mountain batteries; of 151 million rounds of rifle ammunition in stock, 66 million were Mark IV, commonly called dumdums (bullets with a slightly cylindrical cavity at their head covered by a hard envelope which expanded on contact and created dreadful wounds). The First Peace Conference, held at The Hague, had just ended 12 July, and twenty-six nations, including Britain, had agreed that dumdums were too barbarous to use. How many were actually fired during the war in South Africa is unknown, but both sides indignantly accused the other of using them, and there is ample and reliable evidence that both sides did.

Not only was there a shortage of everything that would be needed to wage war, but no one at the War Office thought to alert armaments manufacturers until sometime in October that they might expect increased demands on their facilities; in other words, not until a few days before, or perhaps after, the war began. Either the makers of arms, ammunition, and other war supplies did not think there would be a war or, if they did, it appears not to have occurred to them that war would create an increased need for their products. They were, in any case, as unprepared for war as was the army.

Even more serious than the shortage of men and supplies was the fact that the army was neither organized nor trained to fight a major war against an enemy armed with modern weapons. There was no general staff; the mobilization plan was crude; none of the units later thrown together into brigades and divisions had ever worked as a unit; the regu-

lar army, militia, yeomanry, volunteers, and colonial forces had no or-
ganic connection with each other. Ammunition and money had been
saved by trimming musketry training, and the result was that British
soldiers could march better than they could shoot; mounted troops were
given no musketry training at all, although they were issued carbines.

Money had been saved as well by skimping on the Intelligence Department. Considered not a very important unit, it worked out of an old
house in Queen Anne's Gate on a budget of £18,000. This at a time when
the German army's intelligence unit operated with a budget of £270,000
and a staff that included 300 officers. At Queen Anne's Gate the entire
Foreign Intelligence Section, including clerks, numbered fourteen. The
mapping section numbered only 30 persons—versus 230 in the French
army's equivalent—and the lack of maps of South Africa was to prove a
costly economy. In spite of these handicaps the Intelligence Department
did collect some valuable information, but almost none was passed on to
those who were to command in South Africa.

General F. W. Forstier-Walker, Butler's replacement, who arrived in
South Africa just five weeks before the shooting started, later complained
that he had received no instructions from the War Office other than to
take command: "As to the actual state of affairs and the imminence of war,
practically nothing was known beyond the reports which appeared in the
daily press." Sir George White left England to take command of the
forces in Natal on 16 September—less than thirty days before war was
declared—yet neither the military authorities nor any of the politicians
explained the situation to him, outlined British policy, or discussed possible strategies. He did not think of talking with Military Intelligence, nor
did anyone suggest it.

The Boers were almost as ignorant of the British army as the British
were of theirs, and they had given as little thought to their war plan.
However, they began the war with a number of distinct advantages: they
were familiar with the country; they had interior lines of supply and
communication; their forces in the theatre of operations outnumbered
the British; they possessed superior weapons; their organizational structure was simpler and better suited to the type of war they would have to
fight; and their fighting men knew how to ride and shoot.

The Boer armies of the Transvaal and the Orange Free State, numbering between fifty and sixty thousand (although it is doubtful if more
than forty thousand were ever in the field at one time), consisted simply
of every able-bodied male between the ages of sixteen and sixty, and
there were many above and below those ages who also served. Except for
the small numbers in the police force (some units of which fought in the
army) and the artillery, it was an army without uniforms, medals, bands,
insignia of rank, or pay: there were none of the trappings usually considered necessary to encourage men to become soldiers, and there were
none of the rules and regulations usually considered necessary to turn
men into fighting machines. There was no marching, drilling, or saluting,
and no formal training. In each electoral district (eighteen in the Orange

Free State and twenty-two in the Transvaal) there were from two to six "wyks," or wards, under an elected field cornet. The men of each district formed a commando of indeterminate size under a commandant, also elected. Some of the larger field cornetcies were broken down into corporalships or "seksies" (sections). Each republic had an elected head of its army— a commandant-general in the Transvaal and a commander-in-chief in the Free State—and later there were lesser ranks of generals: assistant commandant-generals and vecht (fighting) generals. Mobilization was a simple matter: the field cornet in each wyk called up the local burghers and they assembled in a nearby town or on a convenient farm, each man with his horse, bridle, saddle, rifle, thirty or more cartridges, and eight days' provisions. They were then ready to move and to fight.

An exception to the undisciplined, slouching horsemen in the commandos was the staatsartillerie (state's artillery). This was in both republics well organized, disciplined, and trained by officers who had served in the German army. They wore German-style uniforms, and on parade they marched with the goose step. These few uniformed artillerymen (about 400 in the Orange Free State and 800 in the Transvaal) were in striking contrast to the rest of the Boer army, who went to war clothed in whatever each man deemed appropriate; many from the towns wore business suits and neckties; some of the older men, particularly officers, wore high-crowned hats and frock coats with clawhammer tails; but the most characteristic attire was marked by a broad-brimmed hat, corduroy pants, and a bandolier of ammunition slung over the shoulder.

The only item of equipment which the Boer governments provided was the Mauser rifle. Like the British Lee-Metford and Lee-Enfield, the Mauser had a five-cartridge magazine, but there was an important difference: the magazine of the British rifles had to be loaded one cartridge at a time and the soldiers carried their bullets loose in ammunition pouches; the Boers carried their cartridges in clips, and a five-round clip could be inserted quickly by a push of the thumb. Thus, while a British soldier could fire five rounds as fast as a Boer, the latter could fire fifty rounds faster than the soldier could fire twenty because of the speed at which he could reload. The Mauser also had fine and exact sights, and it could kill at 2,200 yards. It was, then, altogether a better weapon than the British rifle. In this rifleman's war the superiority of the quick-firing Mausers made an immense difference on the battlefield, and the British were soon made aware of it, but in the course of the war no improvements were made in their rifles; no one suggested buying better ones or even using captured Mausers.*

*British regulars began the war with old Lee-Metfords. Although a few years earlier the army had decided to adopt the improved Lee-Enfield, which differed from the older rifle in the number, depth, and width of the grooves, it had been determined, with typical military economy, to allow the regulars to wear out the old rifles and, except for 25,000 issued to reservists, the Lee-Enfields (some 200,000) were put in the reserve of rifles. Three months after the war started, when the army began to issue the new Lee-Enfields to the Imperial Yeomanry, it was discovered by the yeomanry that all these new rifles were badly sighted, firing 18 inches to the right at 500 yards!

The laws provided penalties for failure to heed the summons to join a commando when called and for desertion, but in actual fact these penalties were rarely imposed. If a man did not like his field cornet or commandant, he simply left his unit and joined another. A burgher was supposed to obtain permission from his officers to go on leave, but frequently, when a man's wife or his cow took sick, or he himself became homesick, he simply left the war and went home. This unauthorized leave-taking was the bane of every Boer general's existence.

There were military advantages to this independence. Accustomed to thinking for himself, the Boer was capable of acting in emergencies without waiting for orders. The officers knew that the men with them were highly motivated and trusted them. Battle plans were agreed upon at krygsraads, and each man knew the plan and could act independently to carry it out. Captain Alfred Thayer Mahan, the American naval officer and historian, noted: "Every Boer organization seems susceptible of immediate dissolution into its component units, each of independent vitality, and of subsequent reunion in some assigned place."[4] The British found this disconcerting; Sir Redvers Buller was to complain that Boer units were like those living organisms which can be cut apart without destroying the individual life of the fragments.

Every Boer rode a horse, and with the exception of the staatsartillerie, the entire Boer force consisted of what was essentially mounted infantry. From early childhood most of the men had been raised with horses and oxen: they understood their management. Unlike the British soldiers, they knew how to take care of themselves on the veld and how to take advantage of its terrain. Many of the British soldiers, officers and men, found it difficult to estimate distances in the clear air of the high veld, and this affected their sighting; this was the natural element of the Boer, and he was very good at judging distances; he was familiar with the veld's bushes, anthills, and kopjes; from his experiences in hunting and in fighting Bantu he knew how to take advantage of cover, both for offence and for defence. To his opponents, coming from the cities and towns of Britain, and even to British farm lads, the veld was strange, its kopjes different from the hills with which they were familiar, its flora and fauna alien and exotic.

The Orange Free State still had some outmoded cannon, but the staatsartillerie of the Transvaal was equipped with sixty or seventy modern guns of the latest design: from France the Transvaal government had bought 75mm and 155mm Creusot guns equipped with recoil mechanisms (the latter came to be known as "Long Toms"); from Germany they purchased 120mm Krupp howitzers; and from England—yes, England—twenty-two or twenty-three 37mm Vickers-Maxim automatic quick-firing guns (called pompoms from the sound they made) which fired a belt of ten 1-pound shells at a rate of one every two seconds and had a range of about 4,000 yards. The pompom had been designed for naval use, but the Boers thought it would be a handy weapon on the veld, as indeed it was. All of these guns used smokeless powder, which made them difficult to locate. Seeing how valuable a weapon the pompom was in the hands of their enemy, the Royal Artillery finally ordered some for themselves.

Both sides used machine guns, mostly .303-inch Maxims, although their proper employment was not understood. They were mounted on carts, and men could not seem to make up their minds whether they were infantry weapons or artillery pieces. It is curious that neither side used mortars. This uncomplicated weapon was known to earlier generations of soldiers, and a lightweight mortar would have been most useful and practical, but apparently no one ever thought of it. Hand grenades were not used either, except for some homemade varieties.

Both the telephone and the telegraph existed in 1899—Johannesburg had a telephone exchange in 1895—but their use on the battlefield was limited, commanders not understanding their full potentiality. Before the war was over, a wireless message had crossed the Atlantic, but none crossed the veld.

Observation balloons, made of goldbeater's skin, were employed by the British, but there is no evidence that a commanding officer ever went up in one, and often they were not sent up when they would have been most useful. It does not appear that anyone ever thought of equipping the observer with a telephone; he reported his observations by signals.

The British had a small photographic unit, but their generals preferred to rely upon the more familiar sketches made by officers. It is curious that the provincial and pastoral Boers used every modern device they could lay their hands on and were not afraid of innovation while the British officers, representing one of the most technologically advanced nation in the world, scorned the fruits of technology and were hidebound traditionalists.

The Boers were no longer quite as homogeneous as they had been in the early voortrekker days; there were now greater economic and cultural differences. There were town Boers, many of whom had been educated in Europe; trekboers who continued the roving life of the voortrekkers; a few primitive "wild Boers"—often called *takhaaren* from their custom of trimming their hair around a bowl—mostly nomadic big-game hunters from the Zoutpansberg area; but most were still simply farmers. Indeed, the farm was always the Boer's status symbol: even the town Boers, and certainly politicians, including intellectuals such as Jan Smuts, possessed a farm.

Most visitors to South Africa who met the Boers for the first time found themselves admiring them. Richard Harding Davis, the American war correspondent and novelist, wrote his mother from the Transvaal that "personally I know no class of men I admire so much or who to-day preserve the best and oldest ideas of charity, fairness and good-will to men."[5] Even the British correspondents were impressed, or many of them. G. W. Steevens wrote:

They are big, bearded men, loose of limb, shabbily dressed in broad brimmed hats, corduroy trousers, and brown shoes; they sit their ponies at a rocking-chair canter easy and erect; unkempt, rough, half-savage, their tanned faces and blue eyes express lazy good-nature, sluggish stubbornness, dormant fierceness. . . . their bearing stamps them as free men. A people hard to rouse, you say—and as hard, when roused, to subdue.[6]

By September 1899 the Boers had girded up their loins for war. They knew what they would be fighting for: their independence. The British were not only unprepared, they were still not quite certain why they were going to fight, at least not officially. Chamberlain told Milner that although "the casus belli is a very weak one" the Cabinet had agreed to send the Transvaal an ultimatum. This decision was reached on 29 September; on the same day the volksraad passed a resolution giving immediate and full rights to all foreigners who were willing to fight for the country's independence. Chamberlain thought that the British public had now been sufficiently propagandized to accept the war, and he told Milner that "the majority of the people have recognized that there is a greater issue than the franchise or the grievances of the Uitlanders at stake and that our supremacy in South Africa and our existence as a great Power in the world are involved. . . . Three months ago we could not— that is, we should not have been allowed to—go to war on this issue. Now we shall be sufficiently supported."[7]

The first week of October, with Boer and Briton poised on the brink of war, both sides were silent. No words, written or spoken, were exchanged between the tense men in London and Pretoria. It was, as Anthony Nutting said, "As in a motion picture when the reel is stopped, the characters in the drama were frozen into immobility."[8] A New York newspaper cabled Kruger to ask if the Boers would really fight. Smuts replied for him: "Yes. It will be a fight that will stagger humanity."

The British ultimatum as approved by the Cabinet demanded "a complete surrender on the part of the Boers either by agreement or by war." Among its demands were that the Transvaal repeal all legislation passed since 1881 which affected the rights of the uitlanders, that it grant home rule to the inhabitants of the Rand, that there be arbitration without third parties in disputes, that the Transvaal "surrender" its rights to import arms through Mozambique, and, just to make sure that their ultimatum would be rejected, the British demanded that the Transvaalers disarm.

In the end it mattered very little what the British ultimatum said. For incomprehensible reasons it was not telegraphed but sent by mail steamer to South Africa, and in the meantime the Boers had been busy drafting their own ultimatum and they delivered theirs first: on 10 October 1899, Kruger's seventy-fourth birthday, the Transvaal ultimatum, largely drafted by Jan Smuts but signed by F. W. Reitz as state secretary, after reminding the British of the terms of the London Convention respecting uitlanders, demanded that Britain withdraw her troops from the border, remove from South Africa all troops that had arrived since 1 June, and send back the troops now on the high seas bound for South Africa. Unless "an immediate and affirmative answer" to these demands was received by five o'clock on the afternoon of Wednesday, 11 October 1899, the Transvaal would consider the British to have declared war. A British government Blue Book was to call this "the most egregious document ever addressed to a great Power by a petty state."

De Tocqueville said that "in a political democracy the most peaceful of all people are the generals." So it was in the Transvaal. When the ultimatum was approved by the volksraad in secret session, four of the seven dissenting votes were cast by Piet Joubert, Koos de la Rey, Lucas Meyer, and Louis Botha—all future leaders in the Transvaal army and destined to play principal roles in the fighting. De la Rey, addressing the members, declared that it was foolish even to talk of war with Great Britain, but added, "I shall do my duty as the Raad decides."

President Steyn of the Orange Free State was still making frantic efforts to prevent the inevitable. He wrote pleading but futile letters to both Kruger and Milner. Kruger replied: "Peace is entirely out of the question." Milner ignored him. When all about him have gone mad, the man of reason is helplessly ineffectual.

"They have done it!" exclaimed Chamberlain with delight when he received news of the Transvaal's ultimatum. "Accept my felicitations," Landsdowne wrote him. "I don't think Kruger could have played our cards better than he has. . . . My soldiers are in ecstasies."

The Free Staters quickly cast their lot with the Transvaalers. President Steyn, bowing to the inevitable, told the Free State volksraad, "I believe that nothing happens without the will of the Almighty and that He, who helped our forefathers in such a marvelous way, will take pity on us. In any case, His will be done."

ACT I

7

WAR BEGINS

At five o'clock on 11 October 1899—just at tea time, noted *The Times*—
the war officially began. The time of trying to make sense of the muddled
issues was over. Slogans would do now: "Independence!" for the Boers;
"Avenge Majuba!" for the British. A declaration of war is an abandonment of reason; the time for negotiations which end only in exasperation
is past; there is an end to argument and the kind of suspense which debate
generates. The hopes and fears of compromise are in an instant wiped
from the mind. Suspense is ended in the relief of action, the comfort of
a decision taken.

The declaration of war told every man, woman, and child capable of
understanding in the Transvaal and the Orange Free State that they had
all been launched upon an momentous enterprise. None knew just how
momentous. Dangerous it surely would be, but none knew how dangerous, nor did any suspect the tragic effect the war would have upon the
women and children. The beginning of a war is like the setting out on a
perilous journey to an unknown land: reactions vary from fear to delight;
between these emotional poles, varying degrees of anxiety and excitement surge through the populace.

As a people the Boers faced the war with confidence and determination; their morale was high, their cause was just, and surely God would
help them, provide miracles, and give them ultimate victory. Still, a declaration of war becomes a personal matter, and each considers what he or
she might lose and in what ways life will be altered: the strange becomes
familiar; the familiar strange.

In the eastern Free State three of the Pohl boys were on their way
home from a swim when they met their sister Sophia running breathlessly
towards them calling out that the war had begun. Almost immediately a
young neighbour came riding up with orders for Stephen and Frederick

Pohl to join the Ladybrand Commando which was assembling at Van Rooyen's farm. All the older Pohl boys had, like the other burghers, been issued Mauser rifles; one had even been given to thirteen-year-old Victor.

The two oldest boys left at first light the next morning. They tried to appear calm as they left, forcing their impatient ponies to a seemly walk until they were out of sight of home and those waving good-bye. Then they dashed off to Van Rooyen's farm. When the commando assembled, there were speeches, a prayer, and then they all sang a hymn: "Slechts vertrouwen dat is al" (Simply trusting, that is all).

It was a scene repeated in every town and throughout the countryside in every district of the two republics. The field cornets sent out the assembly orders; the women hurried to bake bread, pack biltong, prepare clothing for their menfolk; the men looked to their horses, harnesses, and rifles; then there were the farewells and the men rode off. Once assembled, the commandos set off for the frontiers, the jumping-off points for the invasion of Cape Colony and Natal.

It was all simple and very informal. Another Pohl boy, Willie, was visiting in the Transvaal when war was declared; he did not bother to return to the Free State, but simply joined a Transvaal commando with his brother-in-law. Both were soon fighting on the Natal front. Hjalmar Reitz, eldest son of the Transvaal's state secretary, was even further away, studying law in the Netherlands, but he at once left his studies to hurry back for the war.

Alida Badenhorst rose early the morning of the day her husband was to leave to join his commando. She had his packing to do and much to occupy her, but she stood for a moment looking down at the great bearded man still asleep in the bed. A revelation came to her such as comes to many women in wartime, and through the long years of the war she never forgot the moment: "Have I then," she thought, "always had this great treasure in the house and not before fully known it?"

For the young, excitement usually crowded out other emotions. Freda Schlosberg, the fourteen-year-old daughter of a Russian immigrant in the boarding school of the Loreto Convent in Pretoria, wrote in her diary on 25 September 1899:

> There is not much study going on. Everybody is excited, expecting war to break out, and almost every class is divided into pro-Boers and pro-Britishers. We discuss, argue and quarrel, and sometimes almost fight. Our Lady Superior called us together and told us that in future the discussion of politics was forbidden. But who can stop us talking politics?[1]

Just before the declaration of war Freda was taken from the convent to her parents' farm at Bronkhorstspruit, where she saw trains being loaded with horses and men for the journey to the front and watched the resolute farewells of the mothers, wives, and sweethearts gathered to see their men off. "Few, very few tears were shed by the women at the station. Why should they weep? The war will not last long and their men would return triumphant, having driven the English into the sea and taken over their farms and homes."[2] When a commando bivouacked at the farm one day, the convent-raised young girl delightedly discovered another aspect of war: "These young commandos are very audacious and seem always to be looking at me."

Friends and relatives, even members of the same family, sometimes found themselves on opposite sides of the conflict. Shortly after the war started, T. N. Leslie visited the home of a family he knew in Heidelberg and found a mother with her two daughters: the husband of one daughter was fighting with the British; the husband of the other daughter and the father of the family were with Boer commandos. There were many such divided families in Cape Colony.

Loyalist Cape Colony families living near the border were fearful of a Boer invasion, but few had any definite plans in case it really occurred; most were unable to make up their minds to any course of action. Dr. G. A. "Jack" Heberden, a thirty-nine-year-old district surgeon at Barclay West, knew exactly what he wanted to do. "Every Englishman strong enough ought to offer his services for the Queen," he told his young wife Winifred, and they rode off to Kimberley, their three-year-old son tied to the doctor's back by a blanket.

The British, if not ready, were eager; in England there was wild enthusiasm for the war. The disgrace of Majuba Hill, the humiliating peace terms of the first war, the fiasco of the Jameson Raid, could all be put behind them; there would be no more shilly-hallying. Britain was, after all, the greatest Power (always capitalized) in the world, and the world would be made to know it. These last years of Queen Victoria's reign have been called the "braggart years," and indeed the British had never before so preened themselves: never before, nor since, had Britons swelled with such an intensity of imperial pride.

Their Empire was growing by leaps and bounds: in the preceding thirty years alone nearly 5 million square miles of land and some 88 million people had been added to it. There was a firm, unshakable belief that Britain had not only the capability but the *right* to rule over such vast dominions. That in sixty years it would all disappear would have been thought an impossibility. Even the Queen seemed indestructible: she had sat on the throne for sixty-two years and most people could not remember living under any other sovereign. For the Queen and Empire then; for the enfranchisement of the uitlander and for British paramountcy, to avenge Majuba and protect the natives, and from sheer national pride, the British people went joyfully into war.

Scarcely anyone believed that the war would seriously strain Britain's resources or that it would last more than six months. Most would have agreed with the member of Parliament who told the House of Commons: "I believe the war will be brief and that we will be victorious and that such a result will be to the advantage of the Boers, the blacks, and the British alike."[3] There were, however, a few unbelievers. Wilfred Scawen Blunt, that singular Englishman, vociferous in his hatred of the British Empire, wrote in his diary on the first day of the war: "I look upon the war as perhaps the first nail driven into the coffin of the British Empire. I believe that if the Boers can hold out for six months Europe will intervene."[4]

More typical was the reaction of Rudyard Kipling, who embraced the war with fervour. He formed a volunteer company in the village of Rottingdean, near Brighton, and then turned to raising money for the Soldiers' Families' Fund. Of the more than two dozen poems the war inspired him to write, "The Absent Minded Beggar," his plea for the Fund, was the most celebrated at the time. It began:

> When you've shouted "Rule Britannia," when you've sung "God Save
>   the Queen,"
> When you've finished killing Kruger with your mouth,
> Will you kindly drop a shilling in my little tambourine
>   For a gentleman in *kharki* ordered south?
> He's an absent minded beggar, and his weaknesses are great—
>   But we and Paul must take him as we find him—
> He is out on active service, wiping something off a slate—
>   And he's left a lot of little things behind him!
> Duke's son—cook's son—son of a hundred kings—
> (Fifty thousand horse and foot going to Table Bay!)
> Each of 'em doing his country's work
>   (and who's to look after their things?)
> Pass the hat for your credit's sake, and pay—pay—pay!

First published in the *Daily Mail* on 31 October 1899, it was an instant success; Mark Twain said that the "clarion-peal" of its lines "thrilled the world." The celebrated actress Mrs. Beerbohm Tree recited the poem daily for fourteen weeks from the stage of the Palace Theatre; each time she reached the lines "pay—pay—pay!" the stage was showered with coins, and she raised £70,000 for the Fund. Lines from the poem were reproduced on cigarette packages, ashtrays, tobacco jars, plates, and even pillowcases; Sir Arthur Sullivan set the words to music, and the song swept the country.

Badly prepared and poorly equipped as the British army was, its officers and men were eager to fight; everyone was wild to go. Sergeants even gave up their stripes to be included in units scheduled to leave for the front. Orders for South Africa were a cause for celebration, and some regiments celebrated almost to the moment of departure: when the 1st Battalion of the Gordon Highlanders left Edinburgh for South Africa one officer commented on the fact that "the battalion was sober with the exception of the grooms, who were nearly all drunk, my man being the most so."[5] The Oxfordshire Light Infantry was showered with letters and telegrams of congratulations when its orders came. Retired officers sent gifts; one former private sent the magnificent sum of twenty guineas, and a telegram signed "Rothschild" was received: "Hope you will kindly inform me when regiment starts for seat of war, as I shall like to send men pipes and tobacco. . . ."

When in the early morning hours the Guards marched from their barracks to the railway station on their way to war there was such a crowd of cheering men and women that they could hardly make their way through it. Lieutenant George Cornwallis-West, Lady Randolph Churchill's young lover, wrote: "Over Westminster Bridge, our ranks almost degenerated into a rabble, so great was the crush of civilians."[6] And the *Daily Mail* (23 October 1899) reported that "even total strangers, carried away by the enthusiasm, broke into the ranks and insisted on carrying rifles, kit bags . . . and at Waterloo all semblance of military order had disappeared. The police were swept aside and the men were borne, in many cases, shoulder high to the entraining platform, while others struggled through in single file."

Three months later when the first contingent of the CIV (City of London Imperial Volunteers—the most famous of the volunteer units) marched to the station, Colonel W. H. Mackinnon, their commanding officer, recorded their difficulties in his diary: "January 13—The detachment marched out of Bunhill Row at 7 A.M., but, owing to the enormous crowds lining the streets, it took three hours and twenty minutes to get to Nine Elms. Several men were exhausted, and many articles of equipment were lost."[7]

Departing officers were loaded with gifts from friends and relations: bars of chocolate, bottles of meat tabloids, field glasses, compasses, Mappin and Webb's wrist watches, Kodak cameras, stomach bands, sparklet squeezers, and copies of Colonel R. S. S. Baden-Powell's *Aids to Scouting*. Fortnum and Mason offered a "South African War Service" to provide officers with luxuries. Included in the piles of officers' baggage were cases of wines and spirits, tinned foods, sporting guns, expensive saddles, and dressing cases with silver fittings.

Khaki was all the rage, the day's most popular colour, and officers were even given khaki pajamas. There was a song called "Khaki." Bonds floated to finance the war were called khakis, and the general election of 1900 was known as the khaki election. The Royal Marines dyed their white belts with tea, and the Scots Greys even coloured their horses khaki. "Kakies" was the name the Boers were soon to give to all British soldiers.

On 2 October 1899 *The Times* reported on the scene in Johannesburg as the Boers prepared for war:

Since yesterday afternoon the officials have been busy commandeering men, horses, and supplies. Several hundred men have been despatched from here to the Natal border, and a considerable number of special trains, heavily laden with men and munitions, have passed through bound for the same destination. . . . All the horses belonging to individuals, including many British Uitlanders, have been indiscriminately commandeered.

Margret Broadfoot, an English actress and singer with a theatrical troupe, was in Johannesburg in early October and wrote home to a friend: "I was driving home from the theatre on Friday when two soldiers on horseback rode up and stopped the carriage; of course I got rather a start, and most certainly looked for a bullet through me. However, it was the horses they wanted. We were allowed to drive to the hotel, but they took the cabman's horses after that."[8]

British intelligence had estimated that 5,000 Boers would be needed to control the uitlanders when war broke out, but in fact none was required, for the uitlanders who had clamoured loudest for war were now in a panic at the thought of it; their one desire was to flee to the safety of Durban or Cape Town. An ex-Londoner described the crowds at the railway station in Johannesburg as being "as bad as the Underground at six o'clock," and another witness to the scene wrote:

> The departure platform . . . is crowded every night with eager, excited masses. All are rushing hither and thither jostling and pushing. Faces already pale from excitement are rendered ghastly by the glare of the lamps and the rays of the electric light. Standing upright in open cattle-trucks, penned like sheep, exposed to the glaring sun, the biting winds, the soaking rains, they leave Johannesburg. Fortunate are they who have secured the shelter of covered carriages for their womenfolk and little ones.

The plight of the women and children standing in the open cattle and coal trucks on the long journey to Cape Town was sad indeed. At least once, at the Vereeniging station Boer railway officials, with the help of other passengers and some bystanders, ejected all the men from the first-class carriages and gave their places to women and children.

In Johannesburg, houses were abandoned with all their furniture in place, whole streets were deserted, and all major buildings were barricaded with corrugated iron and wooden slats. It was estimated that 45,000 uitlanders and British sympathisers fled from the Transvaal and the Orange Free State. Cape Town was flooded with refugees, and accommodation for them became a problem. Some of the wealthy uitlanders who had left early holed up in the Mount Nelson, Cape Town's most luxurious hotel, which became known as Helots Rest.

The refugees were happy to provide the Natal and Cape newspapers with a steady supply of atrocity stories. There were tales of English women being clubbed with rifle butts and whipped with sjamboks (a rawhide whip or riding crop), of babies torn from their mothers' arms, of men and women "robbed and reviled with brutal oaths and jeers." One Englishman was said to have been kicked to death. A young correspondent for the *Morning Post*, Winston Churchill, wrote on 5 November 1899 from East London:

> I . . . heard the first confirmation of the horrible barbarities perpetrated by the Boers on the trainloads of refugees. A British officer on special service was also explicit. . . . The Boers plundered the flying folk mercilessly, and had insulted or assaulted men and women. . . . "One woman," said the officer, "had been flogged across the breasts, and was much lacerated."[9]

There were a number of accounts of passengers who had been dragged from railway carriages and forced to shout "Long live Kruger!" There was not much truth in any of this, although there was indeed a fracas at one railway station when a group of miners from the Rand stood on the platform and insisted on singing "Rule Britannia." Cape Town newspapers carried for days a running story of abuses suffered by one well-known uitlander in Boer hands and finally a sensational story of his death. It was embarrassing when soon after he turned up alive and well.

The Boers also had their anxieties. In 1899 a successful lighter-than-air airship had not yet been built, but the internal combustion engine had been invented and airships were technically possible; Alberto Santos-Dumont in France and Count Ferdinand von Zeppelin in Germany were working furiously to create one. There was much talk of this fantastic marvel, and in South Africa the most widespread rumour among the Boers was that the British planned to attack them from the air. Even the Transvaal government accepted the notion, and orders were sent out to all telegraph offices to report any airships that might be sighted. Plenty were. There was hardly a locality that did not report seeing at least one, often with "a powerful light," and a considerable amount of ammunition was expended on inoffensive stars. Pretoria was bombarded with telegrams; typical was this from Vryheid: "Airship with powerful light plainly visible from here in far off distance towards Dundee. Telegraphist at Paulpietersburg also spied one, and at Amsterdam three in the direction of Zambaansland to the south-east."[10]

By 12 October some 38,000 burghers (23,000 Transvaalers and 15,000 Free Staters) were in the field and ready to fight. The general plan of the campaign was to attack on two fronts: to invade northwestern Natal, defeat the only field army the British possessed in South Africa at Dundee or Ladysmith, and then to sweep through Natal to Durban; on the western front to move across the Orange Free State frontiers into Cape Colony and Bechuanaland, capturing Kimberley, Vryburg, and Mafeking, and then to march south, where it was expected that thousands of Cape Afrikaners would rise in revolt and join the republican forces. With Natal and most of Cape Colony in Boer hands, it was believed that the British would sue for peace or that European powers would intervene.

The first action of the war took place on the western front when a small force led by Koos de la Rey, a part of the larger force under Piet Cronjé, moved across the Transvaal border and, halfway between Vryburg and Mafeking, stumbled upon an armoured train carrying artillery destined for the defence of Mafeking. Without the loss of a single man, De la Rey captured the train and took thirty prisoners.

Although Cronjé's main force soon crossed the frontier and laid siege to Kimberley and Mafeking, the main theatre of action at the beginning of the war was not on the western front but on the Natal-Transvaal frontier where Commandant-General Piet Joubert had 14,000 Transvaalers under his command; in addition, 6,000 Free Staters under Marthinus Prinsloo were moving up along the Drakensberg range. Only 12,000 South African volunteers and British regulars under Sir George White were ahead to oppose them.

THE DRIVERS MANAGED SOMEHOW TO GET THEIR GUNS OVER THE ROCKY
BED OF A STREAM TO A FAVORABLE POSITION.

The Transvaal army on the Natal front was divided into four parts: Lucas Meyer was on the far left, then S. P. Erasmus, then Joubert with the main force, and J. H. M. Kock on his right. Joubert's main laager was jammed with armed men and the wives of many of them, including, of course, the commandant-general's wife, Hendrina. (One determined young woman was there dressed as a boy and carrying a Mauser; discovered, she was sent back to Johannesburg.) Men and women shared the space with cattle, oxen, horses, ponies, and a mad array of vehicles: ox carts, spiders, laundry wagons, trollies, and butchers' carts, many of which had been commandeered and bore the names of the companies or individuals who had owned them. The burghers themselves were amused by the incongruity of a cart painted "P. Amm & Sons Tea Merchants" beside one of the Krupp guns. There was nothing formal about this army of farmers. Joubert's tent was open to all, and one burgher came in to ask the commandant-general for the loan of a shoe lace.

Joubert's invasion was slow off the mark, and he moved cautiously. He need not have done so, for the British did not defend a single pass; they did not blow up a single bridge or tunnel, nor did they destroy the railway. This was not negligence on the part of the British, but economy. Bridges and tunnels were expensive, and the British had the curious notion that if they left these valuable structures for the Boers that the Boers would do the same for them.

Seventeen-year-old Deneys Reitz, a son of the Transvaal's state secretary, was with the forces under S. P. Erasmus, and he was stirred as he moved forward with the invading host: "As far as the eye could see the plain was alive with horsemen, guns and cattle, all steadily going forward to the frontier."[11] At the Buffalo River near Newcastle the lines of horsemen reined in and looked across at the land they were about to invade. Erasmus, tall and dark, dressed in the top hat and frock coat in which he went to war, rode up and spoke to them: Natal was a land taken from their forefathers by the British, he said; now they would win it back. Then, "amid enthusiastic cries we began to ford the stream. . . . the cheering and the singing of the 'Volkslied' [national anthem] were continuous, and we rode into the smiling land of Natal full of hope and courage."[12]

Roland Schikkerling, nineteen years old, was with the Johannesburg Commando, a part of the force that entered Natal over Botha's Pass and bivouacked on the upper Ingogo River. At the frontier the border police had fled so hastily that he found a spread table of still-warm food. His first sight of British soldiers was a group of prisoners:

How I was disillusioned by the appearance of these men! They were small, and some had the naked bully beef slapped in their pockets, so that the grease oozed through. They had neither, it seemed, the accent nor the gait of Christians. I saw none of the sullen haughtiness I had pictured. . . . They had, it appeared, lost their way in the vicinity of Dundee.[13]

"We have lost time, a misfortune in war, and in preparing for war, which is deplorable," Wolseley told Lansdowne. "We have committed one of the very greatest blunders in war, namely, we have given our enemy the initiative." However, some of the 5,700 British troops from India had already landed and others were on the water only a few days out of Durban; a battalion each had been ordered to South Africa from Malta, Crete, Egypt, and Gibraltar. In England, mobilization of the reserves was ordered, and Britain was hurriedly assembling an army corps of 47,000 men under General Sir Redvers Buller, V.C. The most famous regiments in the British army were alerted for active service: fusiliers, Highlanders, and Guards; hussars, dragoons, and lancers. Once this giant force reached South Africa these arrogant farmers would be easily and quickly crushed. Or so it was believed.

8

TALANA: THE FIRST BATTLE

When Lieutenant General George White arrived to take command of the army in Natal just six days before war was declared, it seemed to him that when the Boers invaded, as they were expected to, the best place to make a stand would be Ladysmith: it was a British cantonment, strategically located, and the most important town in northern Natal. But Sir Walter Hely-Hutchinson, governor of Natal, protested. Ladysmith, he maintained, was too far back from the border, too far south on the railway line leading to the Transvaal; the British must hold Dundee, a small mining town 40 miles further north, otherwise its valuable coal fields would be lost and the colonists in Natal and the Cape would lose all confidence in the British army; to allow the Boers to penetrate as far as Ladysmith would be an exhibition of weakness and would lead to a native uprising. Sir Walter was warmly supported by Major General Sir William Penn Symons, whom White superseded as commanding general in Natal but who was to remain under White's command. He was certain that Dundee could easily be held against what he saw as an attack by simple farmers armed with rifles who would certainly crumble before British regulars. Four months earlier he had discussed the possibility of war with the Bishop of Natal: "It would be indeed a grievous thing," he told the bishop. "We none of us want to be sent to kill the ignorant Boer farmers." His sentiments were less pious when told later that the Boers were gathering at Laing's Nek: "I wish every commando in the Transvaal was collected there so that I could make one sweep of the lot of them."

Doubtless Penn Symons's reputation and experience, if not his reasoning, counted much with White, for Penn Symons had seen a great deal of active service in Burma and on India's Northwest Frontier; besides, many years before he had fought in two campaigns in South Africa: the war against the Gaika in 1877–1878 and the Zulu War of 1879. It was a fault in White's character that he lacked the faith in his own ideas and convictions which they often deserved. He allowed himself to be persuaded to maintain the dispositions already made by Penn Symons: about 8,000 troops remained in Ladysmith under White's immediate control, and a brigade of 4,000 men stayed in Dundee under Penn Symons. But White remained uneasy about this isolated brigade and at the last minute changed his mind and instructed Penn Symons to fall back on Ladysmith, an order Penn Symons chose to ignore; he told his officers: "I feel perfectly safe, and I am dead against retreating."

On 13 October Joubert occupied Laing's Nek and was pleased to find the railway tunnel there intact; the force under Erasmus roamed ahead and on the afternoon of the 18th skirmished with a British patrol out of Dundee. Penn Symons found it impossible to believe that a Boer force, whatever its size, would be so rash as to attack a British brigade; certain that he was in no danger, he neglected the most elementary precautions.

Dundee was surrounded by hills, the most dominant being Impati, 1,500 feet high, rising north of the town, and Talana and Lennox, a pair of kopjes about 2 miles east, 800 feet high and, like most South African hills, relatively flat on top. There was not even a picket posted on any of these heights, although Impati held the town's water supply. The British camp was about three-quarters of a mile west of the town, almost in the centre of a topographical saucer, in the bottom of what a former French officer, Georges Villebois de Mareuil, described as a chamber pot.

At six o'clock on the evening of 19 October some 4,000 of the Boers east of the Buffalo River assembled in a pelting rain. Predikants of the Dutch Reformed Church led them in prayer and urged them to fight like men and to trust in God. Their devotions over, the commandos rode off through the mud towards Dundee, dragging with them four field pieces and two pompoms. At two thirty the next morning some of their scouts stumbled upon a picket of the Royal Dublin Fusiliers, and young Lieutenant Cecil Thomas Wrigley Grimshaw, in charge of the picket, heard bullets fired in anger for the first time. He wisely fell back to a better defensive position and sent a sergeant hurrying back to camp with the news. But it was not until he had sent a second message, reporting that he was in danger of being surrounded, that Penn Symons sent out two companies of infantry to support him.

At five o'clock, in a dull drizzling rain, the brigade paraded as usual. Penn Symons, unconcerned about the attack on his picket by what he imagined to be a Boer raiding party, did not even inform his senior

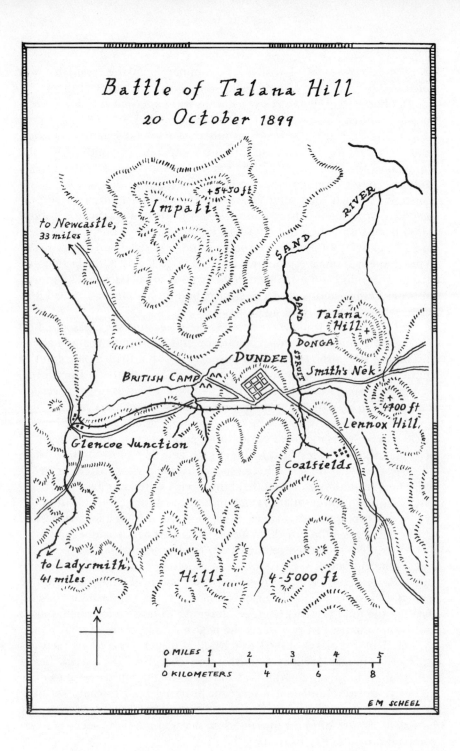

Battle of Talana Hill
20 October 1899

Impati
+5450 ft

to Newcastle,
33 miles

SAND RIVER

SAND SPRUIT

Talana
Hill +

DONGA

DUNDEE

BRITISH CAMP

Smith's Nek

+ 4700 ft
Lennox Hill

Glencoe Junction

Coalfields

to Ladysmith,
41 miles

Hills 4-5000 ft

N

0 MILES 1   2   3   4   5
0 KILOMETERS   4   6   8

E M SCHEEL

officers, nor did it occur to him to give his men an early breakfast in anticipation of a battle. The brigade was dismissed without any special orders or any indication that they were in danger. The guns and limbers of the artillery were unhitched, and the horses were led towards their watering place about a mile away. One battalion moved out to drill on the plain; others were dismissed and the men removed their accoutrements to prepare for the routine fatigues of camp life.

During the night the Utrect and Wakkerstroom commandos with some artillery under Major J. F. Wolmarans of the staatsartillerie—in all about 1,500 men—had climbed to the top of Talana, while Lucas Meyer led the Middleburg, Vryheid, and Pietretief commandos to occupy Lennox and other hills to the southeast, and Erasmus with the vanguard of Joubert's forces climbed Impati. The Boers now occupied the heights to the north and east of the valley where Dundee and Penn Symons's brigade rested in unsuspecting confidence. Their plan of action was typical of Boer tactics: their guns would stir up the British beehive and then they would wait for the British to attack their entrenched positions.

Wolmarans positioned his guns in the centre of Talana and began constructing protective emplacements while the impatient burghers (most of whom had never heard a cannon fired) crowded around, urging the gunners to open fire: "Why don't you say good morning to the English?" Lucas Meyer was also impatient and sent word for Wolmarans to stop wasting time and to get his guns into action.

In the valley a British soldier looked up from his work towards Talana, standing black and well defined against the pale eastern sky, and saw the hill covered with men. He cried out and others looked where he pointed. Excitement swept through the camp. Thousands of heads turned towards Talana. Officers took out their field glasses for a first look at their enemy. Then a shell, the first of the thousands that were to fall on Natal, arced through the air and exploded on the outskirts of Dundee. A second buried itself in the mud a few feet from General Penn Symons's tent but failed to explode. The British camp jumped to life; officers and noncommissioned officers barked orders, and men ran for their rifles, buckling on their equipment as they ran.

The British artillerymen were particularly quick in swinging into action. Horses were recalled, teams speedily hitched, and two batteries at a gallop went thundering through little Dundee; just beyond the town they whirled smartly around and took up positions on a small knoll. Knots of the town's citizens, excited and curious, gathered to watch. Whips cracking, teams were hustled to the rear; at a range of 3,650 yards the British guns, loaded with shrapnel, opened fire on the Boers.

After a few trial rounds white puffs of smoke could be seen directly over the Boers' position on the crest and their artillery was silenced as Wolmarans was forced to withdraw his exposed guns. The effect of the British shelling on the Boers was profound. As the shells burst overhead and the shrapnel rattled on the rocks around them, the brave took cover behind boulders; those less brave retreated to the foot of the hill; some went further, running to their ponies and ignominiously fleeing the field.

Although negligent of the precautions he should have taken against attack and slow to recognize danger, William Penn Symons knew how to conduct a battle. Leaving a battery and one battalion to defend his camp, he launched the rest of his brigade at the enemy on Talana. As the troops surged down the road through Dundee, men, women, and children stood by the wayside and cheered; an inspired town guard seized their rifles and joined the infantry.

The Dublin Fusiliers and the Irish Fusiliers were ordered to advance on Talana in extended order while a battalion of the King's Royal Rifle Corps gave them support. The troops advanced in waves, the Dublin Fusiliers leading. They were delayed by a stream bed, into which they tumbled, one line on top of the other, the units becoming hopelessly jumbled. Finally the officers sorted them out and at about seven thirty they scrambled out and raced for a wood of blue gum trees.

In the open space before the wood they came under an intense fire from the Boer rifles above them, but with the haven of the trees before their eyes they pressed on without faltering, the artillery moving closer to support them. Once in the shelter of the wood the infantry showed some reluctance to move out, and Penn Symons dispatched two staff officers to his second-in-command, Brigadier General James Yule, with an order: "Assault!" Yule replied that he would as soon as he was able. Fiery Penn Symons, dissatisfied with this answer, decided to go to the wood himself.

Spurring his horse, he jumped a fence and at a gallop crossed the open ground. Inside the wood he dismounted and gave orders for everyone, even the reserve, to move on through the wood. On the far side the forward troops came up against a low stone wall, and Penn Symons rashly stepped through a gap to look at the position. He was barely through when he turned to a staff officer and said quietly, "I am severely—mortally—wounded in the stomach."

Soldiers carried him down through the wood and then, at his order, put him on his horse. Supported by officers, he made the agonizing ride back as far as the guns; here he was eased from his horse and carried back to camp, there to die a slow, painful death.

Yule, now in command, carried on. With difficulty he collected his men and led them in a charge out of the wood and up the slope to another stone wall on the hillside through the fierce and accurate fire of the Boers' rifles. It was the first time that British troops had ever faced modern musketry, and it was a sobering experience. One officer described it:

I don't suppose I am ever likely to go through a more awful fire than broke out from the Boer line as we dashed forward. The ground in front of me was literally rising in dust from the bullets. . . . Half way over the terrace I looked round over my shoulder. . . . At that moment I was hit for the first time, just as

I reached the foot of the hill beyond the terrace. I was hit through the knee. The actual shock was as if someone had hit me with their whole strength with a club. I spun round and fell, my pistol flying one way and helmet another. . . . I felt numbed at first but no actual pain. I gathered up my property and hopped to the foot of the rise from the terrace to the top. There I began to pull myself up by holding on to the rocks and bushes and long grass with which the hillside was covered. . . . About 15 to 20 yards up the hill I was hit a second time by a shot from above; the bullet hit me in the back above my right hip and came out in front of my thigh. After a short rest I got up and began to crawl to the top. I had reached the crest line and was leaning against a rock when a Boer stood up twenty yards in front of me and faced me. We both looked at one another for a moment and then almost simultaneously he threw up his rifle and covered me and I took a step forward and covered him with my Mauser pistol. My first wound saved me, for in stepping forward I forgot my wounded leg, and as I pulled the trigger the leg gave way and I fell flat on my face. Whether the Boer fired or not I cannot say, there was too much din to distinguish one rifle from another even at that short range. After falling, I drew back under cover of the rock and raised myself carefully, ready to shoot if I spotted my man again. He was gone, however, and, as I was looking, I was hit a third time, this time in the back, the bullet coming out just by my spine. . . . The fire was gradually dying down, only to bring to our ears what was infinitely more painful to hear, the moaning of wounded men from the terrace below and the hillside round us. . . . I had just taken off my accoutrements and was beginning to bandage my leg when a shrapnel shell burst overhead. . . . We could see our artillery on the plain below us. . . . It seemed impossible that they should not have seen our advance from the wall, especially as they had ceased firing for over half an hour previously. I sat anxiously watching, and presently I saw another flash from a gun, and then, with a scream and a crash, a shrapnel shell burst just behind us. There was no room for error this time; the artillery was shelling us. . . . I felt rather beat then. I didn't feel as if I could do anything to help myself, and a feeling of despair came over me for a while. It seemed so hard, after escaping the Boers so far, to be killed by our own people. . . . below me on the terrace I watched the wretched fellows who were wounded trying to drag themselves to the wall for shelter. Presently a shrapnel burst right over our heads, and the bullets struck the ground all round us. Our men were now flying off the top of the hill for shelter below, and the Boers from both flanks, seeing their chance, began firing again as hard as they could load.[1]

A signaller of the Royal Irish Fusiliers leaped onto a boulder and tried to signal to the guns below, only 1,500 yards away. The firing stopped, then began again, and effectively cleared the crest of friend and foe alike.

Satisfied at last that its work was done, the artillery stopped. The British infantry then painfully regrouped itself and occupied Talana. The Boers were now streaming eastward in flight.

The British had been fortunate that Lucas Meyer's men on neighboring Lennox Hill had not reinforced their comrades on Talana but had contented themselves with providing only a long-range flanking fire, and that Erasmus, with his force of 4,000 on Impati, had made no move to attack the British camp and threaten their rear.

As soon as Talana was captured and it was evident that the Boers were fleeing, Lieutenant Colonel Edwin Pickwoad, who was in charge of the two batteries which had shelled their own men, was ordered to take his guns to Smith's Nek, the saddle between Talana and Lennox hills. It was now two o'clock in the afternoon and raining steadily, but from Smith's Nek Pickwoad could see almost the entire Boer force in full flight across the plain only a thousand yards from the muzzles of his guns. Here was an opportunity to turn the Boers' leisurely retreat into a rout, for as *The Times History* said, "Rarely has such a mark fallen to the portion of artillery in war." Pickwoad's twelve guns could have created havoc among the long lines of horsemen, wagons, and artillery. His guns were unlimbered and he was in an excellent position. He had only to open fire. Instead, he sent a messenger back to Yule asking what he ought to do.

It is not clear, either from his own report or from other accounts, why Pickwoad failed to seize this opportunity. He had already blundered badly this day; undoubtedly he was shaken by what he had done and was perhaps fearful of repeating his mistake, for British cavalry and mounted infantry had worked their way around to the Boer rear. Perhaps he feared he would hit Boer ambulances; some of the retreating Boers may have raised a white flag. We will never know for sure. There is also a possibility that Pickwoad thought a truce had been declared.

An hour and a half earlier he had talked with an officer who was looking for General Yule. A Boer messenger had given him a note (addressed to Penn Symons) from Lucas Meyer who, according to L. S. Amery, "was suddenly seized with the strange inspiration to ask for a temporary suspension of hostilities to enable the wounded to be safely removed to the field hospitals."[2] Pickwoad had urged the officer to advise Yule against granting the request, but he had no way of knowing the outcome of the affair. It is difficult to know exactly what did happen. The officer with the message was unable to find the Boer messenger who had given him Meyer's note. Lucas Meyer later claimed that Penn Symons had granted the truce, but this seems unlikely. In any case, the Boers suffered no further harm that day from the British artillery.

The British infantry also failed to follow the retreating Boers. Having struggled all day and at such cost to reach the top of Talana, they marched back down again and returned to their camp, reaching it at about five thirty in the afternoon. There was some excuse for this. The men had not eaten since the previous day and they had been marching and fighting in the mud and rain since early morning; besides, Yule was fearful of the Boers on Impati, who might yet attack his camp.

The action of the cavalry this day forms a separate story. The 18th Hussars and some mounted infantry, all under the command of Lieutenant Colonel Bernhard Drysdale Möller, had been ordered by Penn Symons to sweep around the north end of Talana and harass the Boer rear. The 18th Hussars had not been in action since Waterloo, more than eighty years before, and their commanding officer had never seen an enemy in all his twenty-six years of service. On that morning of 20 October he rode off at the head of his regiment to fight his first and last battle. He first took up an excellent position north of Talana and then sent Major Eustace Knox with two squadrons of hussars to roam behind the enemy's positions. Knox's squadrons trotted about in the drizzling rain and came upon several isolated groups of Boers. These were charged, boot to boot with flashing sabres, in the approved cavalry style. But the sabres of British cavalry (except in India) were, in accordance with regulations, kept sheathed in steel scabbards; as a result, they were so dull that the hussars could not even cut through their enemies' homespun clothing. Nevertheless, some uncut but battered and bruised Boers were taken prisoner and tied together in a file behind a Scotch cart.

As Möller with the rest of the mounted men came up to join Knox, the Boers could be seen streaming down the slopes of Talana and Lennox. Möller now sent Knox off to the south while he took up a position directly across the path of the retreating Boers, his mounted infantry and the Maxim detachment of the 18th Hussars in front and he himself with his two remaining squadrons positioned behind them. It is difficult to conceive how Möller could have imagined that 120 rifles and one machine gun would stop the entire Boer army, which, although discouraged, was not demoralized. Pressed by overwhelming numbers, he was, of course, unable to maintain his position and slowly retreated northward in a series of retirements. The Maxim machine gun, mounted on a cart, bogged down in the thick mud and its crew were all killed or wounded valiantly trying to save it. Möller, instead of leading his force back to Dundee by the way it had come, appears to have lost his way in the mist and blindly galloped on until he came up behind Impati. There two or three hundred of Erasmus's men under Commandant Piet Trichardt found him. Möller threw his force into a group of farm buildings and prepared to defend himself, but Trichardt brought up a couple of guns and after firing only half a dozen rounds forced him to surrender. Knox managed to return safely.

The British counted Talana a victory, but many more such victories would destroy them. Conan Doyle called it "a tactical victory but a strategic defeat." They lost 41 killed, of whom 10 were officers, and 185 wounded; 9 officers and 211 other ranks were prisoners or missing. Boer losses were considerably less: 23 killed, 66 wounded, and 20 missing. Nevertheless, the *Natal Witness* put out a special edition to announce this victory to British arms in the first real battle of the war. Back in England they were soon singing:

> Bravo the Dublin Fusiliers! Bravo the Dublin Fusiliers!
> Crossed the ocean for the Boers to fight,
> Put ten thousand of the Boers to flight,
> Bravo the Dublin Fusiliers!

9

ELANDSLAAGTE

On 18 October 1899, two days before the battle of Talana Hill, a Boer patrol rode into Elanslaagte, a village of tin houses surrounded by a few trees on the railway line about 14 miles north by east of Ladysmith and about the same distance south of Dundee. The town was undefended, but they caught an army supply train in the station and made prisoners of the few soldiers they found there. At ten thirty the following morning General Johannes Kock arrived, after a 20-mile march, with 1,200 men and two guns. His force consisted of town Boers from Johannesburg, a Free State contingent, and a number of foreign volunteers. They slept and rested most of the day, and that evening some of them organized a "smoking concert" at the Elandslaagte inn; the British prisoners were invited to join them, and they lustily sang songs in English and Afrikaans, including both the "Volkslied" and "God Save the Queen." The war was young and exciting and so far bloodless; they had not yet experienced its grimmer meaning. Within forty-eight hours some of the singers would be dead, some would be suffering untended wounds, and all would have a greater understanding of the nature of the enterprise upon which they had embarked.

Johannes Hermanus Kock was a sixty-three-year-old white-bearded patriarch who, like many other burghers, brought his wife along to the war to look after him. As an infant he had been taken on the Great Trek, and as a twelve-year-old boy he had taken part in the battle of Boomplaats. He had served as landdrost of Potchefstroom, was a member of the Transvaal volksraad, and since 1891 had been a member of the Executive Council.

On the day Kock arrived at Elandslaagte, Major General John French (1852–1925), the man who in fifteen years' time would lead the British Expeditionary Force to France, arrived in Ladysmith to take temporary command of the British cavalry in Natal. Short, chunky, and sitting hunched in his saddle, he looked not at all like a dashing cavalry commander—yet this was the reputation he was to acquire in South Africa. He had a hot temper and he was moody; he was a man eager for responsibility and—a rare quality in a British general in this era—he was willing to take risks.

The son of a captain in the Royal Navy, French was entered as a cadet in HMS *Britannia* when he was fourteen, but his career in high-masted ships was short: he suffered from vertigo. After serving briefly in the militia, he obtained a commission in the 8th Hussars at the age of twenty-two. Until he arrived in South Africa his only active service had been in Egypt during the Nile expedition of 1884–1885, where he had taken part in two engagements. French had no personal fortune of any size—an embarrassing situation for a British cavalry officer, whose mess bill alone usually exceeded his salary—and he had expensive tastes. He loved beautiful women and was said to be as gallant in the bedroom as on the battlefield; it was whispered that he had once seduced his colonel's wife. Financial problems plagued him. He had engaged in some unwise speculations—including some highly speculative Transvaal gold shares—and he was heavily in debt.

On the day after his arrival at Ladysmith, French led a small force of cavalry on a reconnaisance up the railway line towards Dundee. Two small Boer patrols were captured, and from the prisoners it was learned that the enemy was at Elandslaagte. The following day General White in Ladysmith, having heard of the battle of Talana and being anxious to keep his communications with Yule open, ordered French to clear the Boers out of Elandslaagte and to repair the railway and telegraph lines. French advanced to within sight of the town and was surprised to discover the Boer force there so large. Nevertheless, he ordered up the Natal Volunteer Field Battery, which began to shell the town, their second round inadvertently hitting the Boer field hospital. The Boers returned the fire with two Krupps. In the short artillery duel that followed, the Boers gave the British a sharp lesson in modern gunnery: with their second shot they found the range and pounded the wretched little battery of the Natal Volunteers, whose miserable muzzle-loading 7-pounder screw guns were no match for the efficient Krupps. French wisely decided to withdraw his men and guns out of range and call for help.

White at once sent up sizable reinforcements under Colonel Ian Hamilton, the same Ian Hamilton whose wrist had been shattered by a Boer bullet at Majuba eighteen years earlier. The sensitive, soft-voiced, and literate Hamilton and the moody, reckless French now began together to lay the foundations for their future great reputations and to become the victors of the last battle the British would win for many weeks.

Elandslaagte sits on the level veld, but just south of it is an irregular horseshoe-shaped piece of high ground, its toe, broad and low, facing south. On the eastern side of this horseshoe the ground is higher and a hogsback ridge runs along it, ending in a kopje that rises 300 feet above the veld. It was on this eastern ridge and kopje that the Boers took up their positions to wait for the British attack. Within sight of the ridge, now backed by a dark storm cloud, Hamilton called his men together and explained to them what they were to do. He was an advocate of a new school of military thought which believed that attacks should be made in extended order in short rushes. This was the way he wanted them to storm the Boer positions. It was already the middle of the afternoon, but he assured them that their work would be done before sunset, and he ended with the rousing words that the next morning newsboys in the streets of London would be calling out the news of their victory. The men waved their helmets and cheered.

Hamilton threw his men at the Boers: the Devonshire Regiment in a frontal attack while the Manchesters and Gordon Highlanders went round the south side of the ridge to roll back the flank. The Imperial Light Horse dismounted and joined the flankers, taking a position to the right of the Manchesters. The ILH was a locally formed unit. Two of its majors were W. D. "Karri" Davies and Aubrey Woolls-Sampson, who had helped to organize it. Most of its troopers were Johannesburg uitlanders. On the hill above, lying in wait for them, was the Johannesburg Commando, and it, too, had a number of uitlanders from the town: it was to be neighbour against neighbour.

In the wings, hawklike, watching the infantry and waiting for them to flush their prey, sat a squadron each of the 5th Lancers and the 5th Dragoon Guards under the command of Major St. John Corbet Gore.

In the open formation Hamilton had ordered, the infantry moved to the attack. It was not the comforting shoulder-to-shoulder formation the men had been taught, but they were cheered by the pipes of the Highlanders playing "Cock o' the North," the familiar tune sounding bravely above the crack of Boer musketry, the shriek of the shells, and the thunder that now rolled through the hills. The men cheered as they advanced; there were cries of "Remember Majuba!" A heavy rain fell briefly and drenched them, but their enthusiasm remained undampened as they climbed the rock-strewn slope.

A contingent of German volunteers dashed out from behind a farm house at the ILH and were mowed down. Colonel John Scott-Chisholme, in command of the ILH, led his men forward holding a red silk scarf tied on a stick. "To see that little red rag going on and on and on without a falter was the bravest sight I have ever seen in my life," said Ian Hamilton. Here and there the advance was slowed down by farmers' wire fences. The intensity of the Boers' fire increased; so, too, did their accuracy. Men fell singly and, where they bunched up at gaps in the wire, in batches. Of the Highlanders' officers, half were dead or seriously wounded by the time the Gordons were halfway to the top. In the face of the increasingly intense fire the troops wavered for a critical moment. Hamilton scrambled towards the front of the line, he and his staff sweeping up all those who had dropped back or were hesitating, the cautious and the frightened; these he pushed forward, providing needed reinforcement to the line. He ordered a bugler to sound "Charge." Other buglers took up the call, and the British infantry, shouting and cheering, bayonets bared, charged and cleared the crest, killing or capturing all of the Boers who had not fled.

CARRYING A MESSAGE FROM SIR GEORGE WHITE, A MESSENGER WAS
BLINDFOLDED BEFORE ENTERING THE BOER OUTPOST OUTSIDE
LADYSMITH.

Hamilton ordered the "Cease Fire" when a small group of Boers holding up a white flag was pointed out to him. Minutes later there was a furious burst of musketry as some 50 Boers who had lain hidden just below the crest of the ridge leaped to their feet and fired into the cheering soldiers. Led by old Kock himself in his black frock coat and his tall hat, they ran forward, firing as they came. The confused soldiers reeled and fell back; for a moment it seemed that the ridge, won with such gallantry, was now to be lost. Colonel Scott-Chisholme was one of the first to fall, still holding his little red flag, a bullet in his leg and one in his chest. "My fellows are doing well," he was heard to gasp, and then a third bullet crashed into his skull. A soldier in the Gordons fell mortally wounded, crying, "And me a time-expired man!" Some men panicked.

An officer of the ILH called out, "For God's sake, men, don't retire!" But some heard only the word "retire" and began to fall back. Lieutenant Mathew Meiklejohn of the Gordons sprang forward to rally the disorganized mass but fell with half a dozen bullets in his body. Other officers, and Hamilton too, rushed to stem the rout; the troops were steadied and, aided by the timely arrival of several companies of Devons, the crest was cleared for a second time, Kock falling mortally wounded and his remaining men fleeing in disorder. The Devons, Manchesters, Gordons, and ILH dashed for the Boer laager below shouting "Majuba!"

A few of the Boers in the laager surrendered, but most mounted their ponies and galloped off. The lancers and dragoons on the flank still watched and waited as single men, then small groups of burghers left the field of battle and made off across the veld. Now there was a steady stream of fugitives. Daylight was fast fading. It was time to strike. Major Gore sang out the orders: sabres were drawn and lances lowered as in extended order they walked their horses over the rise which had concealed them. Three hundred yards in their front was a straggling group of mounted Boers in retreat. With a yell the troopers thundered down the slope and crashed into them.

A few of the victims tried to defend themselves by shooting from the saddle; others threw up their hands; some, unhorsed, fell on the ground and begged for mercy. Charging cavalry has no mercy. The lancers and dragoons on their long-striding heavy cavalry horses bowled them over. After riding through the fugitives, Major Gore rallied his men, re-formed them, and turned them around. Then they rode at the Boers again. A lancer who took part wrote: "We charged them and they went on their knees, begging us to shoot them rather than stab them with our lances, but in vain. The time had come for us to do our work and we did it." The Boers were horrified; one Boer prisoner said, "Men on horses carrying sticks with spikes on top, came galloping at us as we were running to our horses. They pushed us up on the spikes like bundles of hay. They came through us once, then again, altogether five times. And you English call yourselves civilised people!" Even when the Boers fell, the lancers continued to stick them; one lancer wrote home: "We gave them a good dig as they lay. Next day most of the lances were bloody." One young Boer, still alive, was found to have sixteen lance wounds.

The charge had accomplished its purpose: the orderly retreat was turned into a rout of panic-stricken men. The cavalry now began to take prisoners, rounding them up with sabres and dripping lances into frightened groups.

To pursue fleeing foes and demoralise them was one of the purposes of cavalry, and the dragoons and lancers had done their duty with éclat. But the Boers never forgave them for their bloody work at Elandslaagte. Their hatred was particularly directed at the 5th Lancers, for they regarded the lance as a barbarous weapon—a long-handled assegai—not to be used by civilised men. Some vowed they would kill any lancer who fell into their hands. There was also a feeling shared by many Boers, including Commandant-General Joubert, that it was un-Christian to attack a fleeing foe. But waging war in such a fashion was beyond the understanding of the British—or, for that matter, any other nationality.

Not all of the British soldiers were as bloody-minded as the cavalrymen. One said: "They were dressed in black frock coats and looked like a lot of rather seedy businessmen. It seemed like murder to kill them." Ian Hamilton saw a dozen Boers continue to fire on the Gordons until the Highlanders with their bayonets were on top of them; then they threw up their arms to surrender. According to the rules by which the British fought, these men had no right to mercy, but, as Hamilton later told it:

Several of the Highlanders, being new to the bloody game, drew back their rifles for the lunge but could not drive the bayonet home. I have a perfect picture still in the eye of memory which shows me a fair-haired young Boer with the down on his cheek, wearing a grey felt hat from which dangled a bunch of coloured ribands. Two Gordons could not, between them, find the heart to kill him.[1]

Night fell on a battlefield littered with the remains of bleeding, broken men lying on the cold, stony ground in the rain. Some were still alive. A noncommissioned officer of the 5th Dragoon Guards volunteered to help look for the wounded:

The lamps of search parties—Briton and Boer—flickered out in many places, and the calls to attract the attention of the wounded could be heard in every direction. We had a whistle and blew it occasionally, then listened; we were some time before we found anyone, and then near a wire fence we came across a few who had fallen quite close together. All the wounded had been attended to so that we could do no more than to give them a drink, and, if possible, cover them over. There were no complaints; one fellow asked me for a cigarette, and an officer in the Manchesters, though shot in the groin and in terrible pain, only said what a grand fight it had been. The wounded seemed to suffer from the cold more than their wounds, and one poor fellow of the Gordons asked me to take the cloak off a dead man, he was so cold. We did all we could—which was, I'm afraid, very little —and made our way back to the bivouac. . . . We sat over the fires most of the night, but though our faces were scorched by the fire our backs were cold, and I thought of those on the field.[2]

One of those left on the field was a young officer who had been hit in the shoulder by a dumdum fired from an elephant gun. (Some Boers preferred their more familiar hunting rifles to the new Mausers, and most of the illegal bullets fired by them came from these weapons.)

I shall never forget the horrors of that night as long as I live. In addition to the agony which my wound gave me, I had two sharp stones running into my back, I was soaked to the skin and bitterly cold, but had an awful thirst; the torrents of rain never stopped. On one side of me was a Gordon Highlander in raving delirium, and on the other a Boer who had had his leg shattered by a shell, and who gave vent to the most heart-rending cries and groans. War is a funny game, mother. . . . I lay out in the rain the whole of the night.[3]

Captain Donald Paton of the Manchester Regiment also lay on the rain-swept hill that night, but one of his men, Private Rogers, watched over him, trying to shield him from the rain and to keep him warm by lying through the night with his arm around him.

Woolls-Sampson of the ILH, wounded in the leg, was carried back on a litter sometime during the night. The soldiers carrying him stumbled frequently over the rough ground in the dark, and once even fell and dropped him. His leg had been roughly spliced on the battlefield with a rifle used as a splint; the next day it was found that the rifle was still loaded, the muzzle pointing towards his armpit.

Among the severely wounded was the aged father of General Johannes Kock, shot in the shoulder and groin. When found by the British high up on the hill the old man said in a strong voice and with simple dignity, "Take me down the hill and lay me in a tent. I am wounded by three bullets." The dying have a right to command. General Kock's wife, meanwhile, was searching for news of her husband among the defeated and dispirited burghers returning from the battle. Deneys Reitz saw her the next morning when she was trying to find a way to reach the British lines, "the memory of her tear-stained face giving me my first hint of what women suffer in time of war."[4] Four members of the Kock family fell this day at Elandslaagte.

G. W. Steevens of the *Daily Mail* described the scene at a makeshift hospital:

The tent was carpeted now with limp bodies. . . . In the rain-blurred light of the lanterns—could it not cease, that piercing drizzle, to-night of all nights at least? The doctor, the one doctor, toiled buoyantly on. Cutting up their clothes with scissors, feeling with light firm fingers over torn chest or thigh, cunningly slipping round the bandage, tenderly covering up the crimson ruin of strong men —hour by hour, man by man, he toiled on.[5]

British losses were 55 killed and 205 wounded; Boer losses were 46 killed, 105 wounded, and 181 missing or taken prisoner. It should be noted that all figures for Boer losses are approximate, for this battle and all others; accurate records were not kept.

Elandslaagte marked the beginning of what was to become a bitter running controversy in the conduct of the war: Kock's attack after the white flag had been shown was the first of many infractions of the rules concerning its use by both Boer and Briton, each side accusing the other of misuse and abuse of the flag in battle after battle. In principle, only the commanding officer of a unit could order a white flag to be raised, and then the entire unit was assumed to have surrendered. In earlier wars, when units were kept in tight formations, there had been few problems, but the magazine-fed rifle and quick-firing guns had now ended that type of fighting. Isolated groups that chose to surrender created problems on both sides, the victors not knowing the size of the group surrendering and perhaps exposing themselves to the fire of other members of the unit who either did not see the white flag or did not choose to surrender themselves; commanding officers, faced by an unauthorized white flag raised by their own men, were often unsure whether they should honour it.

In the Bantu wars the white flag had never been used, and many Boers were unfamiliar with the conventions attached to it. Lucas Meyer telegraphed Joubert about an incident in which the British had "twice hoisted the white flag, but our burghers continued to fire, not understanding that one must cease fire as soon as a white flag is raised."[6] However, even when its meaning became known, the individualism and lack of discipline among the Boers led to its abuse; a burgher frequently saw no reason why he should not use it to indicate that he and the group with him were willing to surrender even if the rest of his commando wanted to continue fighting.

J. A. Hobson said: "A conscientious reader of the *Cape Times* and the *Argus* during the opening days of hostilities would have come to the conclusion that Boers divided their time pretty equally between firing upon the white flag and upon the red cross."[7] H. H. S. Pearse of the *Daily News* (London) wrote:

It is . . . impossible to find excuses, or to give the Boers credit for good intentions always in their use of the white flag. They seem to regard it as an emblem to be hoisted for their own convenience or safety, and to be put aside when its purpose has been served, without any consideration for the other party.[8]

Similar accusations were brought against the British in a telegram Louis Botha sent to General Schalk Burger on 5 November 1899:

The messenger was shot at from the dense bush while he was still carrying the white flag. . . . The enemy twice used the white flag in order to take up better positions. . . . the enemy put out the white flag, and while negotiating, they re-commenced firing, resulting in two of our men being killed; Dum-dum bullets were removed from their wounds by the doctor.

Both sides charged that the red cross was fired on, and the truth is that both sides did inadvertantly fire on hospitals and ambulances, particularly artillerymen, who could not distinguish from a distance the red cross from the Union Jack or the Vierkleur. From photographs it would appear that the red crosses painted on the sides of ambulances were too small and the flags in front of hospital tents were certainly inadequate as markers. Both bullets and shells could go beyond the range of normal eyesight, and there were mishaps, but there is no proof that either side deliberately fired on the wounded.

10

THE BATTLE OF LADYSMITH

The British, having won the battles of Talana and Elandslaagte, now behaved as if they had lost them. White sent urgent messages to Yule and French to retire on Ladysmith. Death had removed Penn Symons, the most vocal opponent to his plan for consolidating his forces, and he was now more anxious than ever to do what he had wanted to do in the first place: bring his men together at Ladysmith. The Boers had appeared in greater strength than had been predicted, and they had proved themselves such formidable foes that in spite of his victory Yule was in real danger of being cut off and it was obvious that he must extricate himself as quickly as possible; to fall back on Ladysmith made sense. White's reasons for withdrawing French from Elandslaagte at the same time are less clear, since by remaining where he was French was in an excellent position to cover Yule's withdrawal.

With French, reckless and even brilliant exploits were frequently followed by depression and despair; resolute and confident under fire, he seemed to grow fearful in the calm that followed. He had just won, with Hamilton's help, a complete, crushing victory; now he obeyed the order to withdraw with undue alacrity, tumbling back on Ladysmith so hastily that, as Hamilton later described it, "the withdrawal became a skedaddle: the victorious forces looking over their shoulders at the blank horizon, and the last train especially seeming to be rather filled with fugitives than conquerors."[1] Large quantities of captured stores, arms, and ammunition were simply abandoned. Strangest of all was the abandonment of 30 or 40 Boer prisoners who, to their surprise, were simply left to wander back to their commandos.

Yule slipped away from Dundee at night, leaving his camp standing with three months' supply of provisions, large quantities of ammunition, and even the kits of the officers and men. The Town Guard was not told of the move and was left to its fate. And so, too, were the wounded, including General Penn Symons, who died the next day a few hours after the Boers rode in to claim the town and the camp.

The Boers had been astonished to learn of the British departure from Dundee, but they were quick to occupy the town, and they enjoyed the looting. Deneys Reitz described it:

> Soon 1,500 men were whooping through the streets, and behaving in a very undisciplined manner. Officers tried to stem the rush, but we were not to be denied, and we plundered shops and dwelling houses, and did considerable damage before the Commandants and Field-Cornets were able to restore some semblance of order. It was not for what we got out of it, for we knew that we could carry little or nothing away with us, but the joy of ransacking other people's property is hard to resist, and we gave way to the impulse. My brother and I . . . brought away enough food for a royal feast, and after living on half-cured biltong for all these days, we made up for lost time.
>
> There was not only the town to be looted, but there was a large military camp standing abandoned on the outskirts, and here were entire streets of tents, and great stacks of tinned and other foodstuffs, and, knowing the meagre way in which our men were fed and equipped, I was astonished at the numberless things an English army carried with it in the field.[2]

One burgher was seen riding out of Dundee with a bicycle strapped to his horse. News of the looting put the commandant-general into a rage, for he had a horror of such thievery. Joubert stormed at his men, accusing them of being more interested in looting than in fighting. He berated the Johannesburg Commando for allowing Yule and his men to escape from Dundee. He found reasons to quarrel with Lucas Meyer and Prinsloo. There seemed hardly enough wrath to go around, but he found time and sufficiently cooled his temper to write a letter of condolence to the widow of General Penn Symons.

Sixty-seven-year-old Piet Joubert, the "Hero of Majuba," was a man who had had military fame thrust upon him. He was basically a pacifist —"Blood is precious. I hate to waste it," he once said—and he was not really a good general. He never claimed to be. He gave credit for his victories to God—where perhaps the credit belonged. Once when he was introduced as a great general, he brushed this claim aside, saying, "Heaven won my battles." He was short (5 feet 7 inches tall), broad, and rather stout, and his voice was high, almost a falsetto. A chronic complainer, continually drawing up lists of grievances, he took criticism badly and was sometimes vindictive. It is difficult to reconcile vanity and ambition with humility in the character of one man, yet such were to be found in this energetic, quarrelsome, intelligent, soft-hearted, self-educated man.

By Boer standards Joubert was rich. He was an able farmer who owned all or part of some thirty farms; he was also an astute businessman and a successful speculator in gold shares. At the age of thirty-four he had been elected to the volksraad, at one time serving as its chairman, and for one period of fourteen months he had served as acting president of the republic. Next to Kruger he was the most popular politician in the Transvaal; even the uitlanders thought well of him, for he understood the Johannesburg financiers and speculators and had been their champion in the volksraad debates.

In 1884 he briefly resigned his position as commandant-general. On leaving office he turned in his revolver, sabre, and field glasses, which were the property of the government. The government made him a present of the field glasses and the sabre; the revolver was given to his wife, Hendrina, sometimes called the "real" commandant-general. Gaunt, small-boned, tight-lipped, about the same age as her husband, she wore steel-rimmed glasses and held herself stiffly erect. Fort Hendrina in the Zoutpansberg district was named after her. Piet Joubert had been twenty-one years old when he was called on commando for a war with the Bakwena tribe; he was already married and Hendrina was pregnant, but it was then that she established the pattern of accompanying her husband to war. She gave birth to their child, the first of eight, in a laager during the campaign. Although Joubert was appalled by the number of women who were with the commandos in Natal and issued strict orders for all to be sent home, it did not occur to him—and probably not to anyone else —that this should include Hendrina.

Joubert had won most of his wars with the Bantu by surrounding his enemies and then waiting for them to surrender. This took time, but it saved lives and was effective. He now proposed to do the same with the British, and General White was accommodating him by drawing into sleepy, dusty little Ladysmith all the British forces in Natal—about 13,000 men.

Ladysmith was named after the wife of Sir Harry Smith, an exotic Spanish girl whom he had met when she sought his protection after the battle of Badajoz in 1812. As *The Times History* described it, there was nothing exotic about the town:

It is a quaint little place, Ladysmith, just a little tin-roofed township nestling in one of the dips of the vast rolling hills; hugging a kopje and a deep-delved stream, and shaded by a few green trees standing out pleasantly amid the bare veld—a town of two parallel streets and a few detached villas, that is all.

It was an ideal place for a peacetime cantonment area and supply depot, situated on the main line from Durban to Johannesburg beside the Klip River in the centre of northern Natal. It was not, however, an easy place to defend, sitting as it did on a small plain surrounded by hills which were too far away to be included in a defensive perimeter but close enough for an enemy to mount guns on them.

All the world was soon to know of this small town, now filled to overflowing with troops, stores, and ordnance. There was a cantonment 2 miles out, and in the town itself every public building had been requisitioned by the army; schoolhouses and churches bulged with boxes, bales, and sacks, and hourly trains arrived from Durban with more supplies.

They would be needed, for Joubert was closing in. French's cavalry patrols had had several skirmishes, and the enemy could be seen constructing gun emplacements on Pepworth Hill about 5 miles north-northeast
of the town.

By 29 October White had collected all his forces at Ladysmith. The
Boers were taking up positions in the surrounding hills but had not yet
completed their investment of the town: the Transvaalers were in the hills
on the north and east, but the Free Staters were not yet in their places.
White decided to launch an elaborate, large-scale attack on both forces
and break up their line before they could complete their arrangements.
The orders he issued for this event were so vague that it is difficult to
understand in detail exactly what he intended to do. Called the battle of
Ladysmith, it was actually three distinct engagements, often designated
as separate battles. For the British, the entire operation was an unmiti-
gated disaster.

Early on the morning of 30 October a brigade under Colonel Geoffrey Grimwood Grimwood was flung at Long Hill, about 5 miles northeast
of the town. Although this was thought to be held by the enemy, no Boers
were there; the British had attacked a deserted kopje. Once on Long Hill,
the brigade came under a heavy flanking fire from Pepworth Hill just west
of it. Grimwood, although he had seen considerable action in India,
appears to have become hopelessly confused and unnerved; he was unable to remember where his men were positioned, and he issued no
orders at all. French, who was supposed to have his cavalry to the right
of this brigade, ended up in the wrong position and got into difficulties.

Also from Pepworth Hill a "Long Tom" opened fire on Ladysmith,
causing near-panic among the civilians. White had no heavy artillery with
which to reply, but, dramatically, in the midst of the battle a train from
Durban carrying 280 sailors from HMS *Powerful* with four 12-pounders
and two 4.6-inch guns pulled into the Ladysmith station. Although these
were immediately put into action, they were not enough to turn the tide
of battle. Everywhere the British troops were pinned down by the Boers'
firepower and unable to come to grips with or even to see their enemies.
By the end of the morning the attack had so hopelessly bogged down that
White decided to withdraw.

The infantry, which had had quite enough of the Boer musketry, was
more than willing; the retreat, far from orderly, was almost a rout, and
the Boers' rifle and artillery fire increased as the soldiers stood up and
turned their backs on them. French's cavalry also beat a fast and disor-
derly retreat, riding back in a mass as fast as their horses would carry
them. Throughout it all the British artillerymen behaved with great gallantry, the gunners standing by their guns while the infantry flowed past
and behind them. Now was the moment for the Boers to charge, and
Joubert's officers begged him to mount his men and pursue the enemy,
but he refused, telling them that when God offers a finger it is not right
to claim the whole hand.

Depressed as White was by the check he had received, he still did not

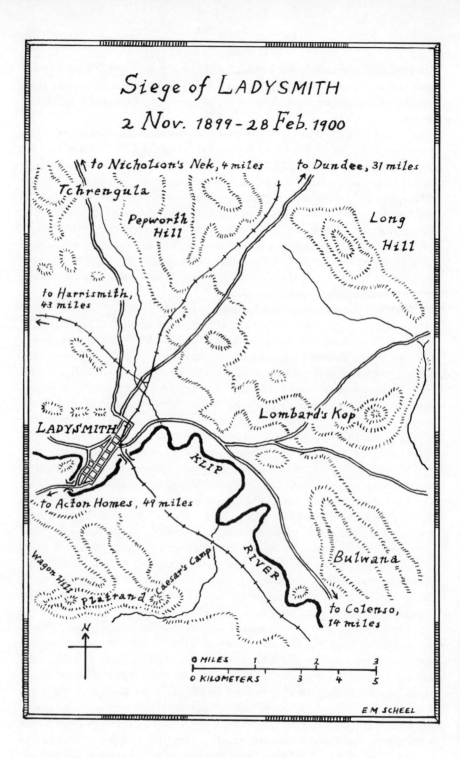

Siege of LADYSMITH
2 Nov. 1899 - 28 Feb. 1900

↑ to Nicholson's Nek, 4 miles

to Dundee, 31 miles

Tchrengula

Pepworth
Hill

Long
Hill

to Harrismith,
43 miles

LADYSMITH

KLIP

Lombard's Kop

to Acton Homes, 49 miles

Wagon Hill

Caesar's Camp

Platrand

RIVER

Bulwana

to Colenso,
14 miles

N

0 MILES   1   2   3
0 KILOMETERS   3   4   5

E M SCHEEL

know the worst. The night before the attack he had sent a force under Lieutenant Colonel Frank Carleton north on the Newcastle road with orders "to occupy the kopjes on each side of the pass at the north end of Nicholson's Nek to keep the enemy from the left flank of the main force." Although Carleton had been in the army for twenty-six years, he had never seen a battle. His force consisted of six companies (520 men) of his own Royal Irish Fusiliers, five and a half companies (450 men) of the Gloucestershire Regiment and No. 10 Mountain Battery (140 men). In addition to the mules of the mountain battery there were another 100 pack mules carrying extra ammunition, a Maxim machine gun, two heliographs, and several kegs of water. The men leading the mules were simple soldiers and not experienced muleteers.

This force was late in leaving Ladysmith and slow in moving. By 2:00 A.M. Carleton, having decided that they would be unable to reach Nicholson's Nek before first light, even though it was only 2 miles away, turned off the road to the left to take up a position on Tchrengula Hill, the Irish Fusiliers leading the way and the Gloucesters bringing up the rear, the mules and the mountain battery between them. Three or four hundred yards from the road the hillside turned steep, and in the dark the soldiers tripped and stumbled over the loose rock as they climbed. The leading Fusiliers had reached the crest, the Gloucesters were still on the road below, when disaster struck the column: the mules stampeded.

The exact cause of the stampede is unknown, but it started with the leading mules just behind the Fusiliers. Terror-stricken, they came kicking and squealing down the rocky slope in their headlong flight, throwing small boulders before them onto the mules and soldiers below. They crashed into the mountain battery and spread their mindless panic. Within minutes almost every mule in the column was thundering down the hill towards the Gloucesters. The terror of the mules was communicated to the men, some of whom came running down shouting, "Boer cavalry!"

The perplexed Gloucesters fixed bayonets and stood in the road, not knowing the nature of the danger or what to expect. Some nervous men in the rear fired off a few wild rounds, adding to the confusion. Then the frenzied mules crashed into them. Soldiers were knocked down, thrown into the ditch, trampled on, and then the mules were gone in a clatter of hooves, the splintering of ammunition boxes sounding behind them as they disappeared down the road.

After strenuous efforts on the part of the officers, the men were calmed and brought under control, although some 40 Gloucesters and 70 gunners appear to have run with the mules; they drifted into Ladysmith the next morning. The remainder were at last got to the top of Tchrengula, but the water kegs and heliographs were gone; a few mules had been saved, but there were only twenty rounds per man of reserve ammunition, and although the Gloucesters managed to save their Maxim, there were not enough parts left in the mountain battery to assemble even one gun. Carleton ought now to have retreated, but he was understandably reluctant to go back and tell White that he had been defeated by his own mules.

Like many South African kopjes, Tchrengula was fairly flat on top and of irregular shape. Carleton's force occupied the southern end of the hill, but not the higher northern end, which was not even reconnoitred. The men had no entrenching tools, so they began to construct stone sangers (breastworks) in front of their positions. Carleton's march had been undetected by the Boers until the uproar caused by the stampeding mules alerted them. Then they at once began to close in. At dawn, about 4:45 A.M., the first shots were fired.

One of the axioms of British musketry training held that soldiers ought not to be allowed to fire their weapons independently but only in volleys on orders of an officer when the enemy appeared in masses. A few soldiers did shoot at dodging, ducking, creeping Boers, but they were ordered to stop. Lieutenant William Temple saw the Johannesburg Police galloping across the valley below him in small groups; it was an irresistible target, and he opened fire with the Maxim, but he was at once ordered to stop.

Relentlessly the Boers closed in on Carleton's force and, mounting the high northern end of the hill, poured a hot fire into the Gloucesters on that side. All morning the soldiers huddled behind their sangers while the Boer musketry, according to one of the officers present, played on them "like a garden hose on a flower bed." Under the cover of their fire the Boers stalked closer and closer.

Carleton tried to get word of his predicament to White: an unsuccessful attempt was made to fashion a heliograph from a biscuit tin; signal flags were wagged at the observation balloon which floated "serene and unresponsive" over Ladysmith. At noon he received a heliographed order: "Retire on Ladysmith as opportunity offers." But this was no longer possible. There would be no opportunity.

By 12:30 P.M. Company B of the Gloucesters had taken so many casualties that Lieutenant Charles Knox ran back to get reinforcements. On the way he saw a group of Boers drawing in on the flank of an unsuspecting unit commanded by Captain Stephen Willcock. Knox shouted and waved his arms to alert them, but he was too far away for his words to be heard, and Willcock interpreted his signals as an order to retire; he passed the message to Company C. As the men in Company C left the safety of their sangers to fall back across the open grass slope behind them, the Boers closed in and poured a merciless fire into their backs. Out of 83 men in the company, 13 were killed and 23 wounded; nearly all were losses suffered during the retirement.

At one isolated outpost on the hill Captain Stuart Duncan, finding himself amid a shambles of dead and wounded men, tied a white towel to his sword and held it up in surrender. Carleton, informed of it, hesitated. He had considered trying to cut his way out with the bayonet, but he had seen in the distance some of White's defeated men streaming back into Ladysmith and he knew that within an hour his own ammunition supply would be exhausted. He ordered a bugler to sound the "Cease Fire." The bugler was so nervous that he had to try several times before he could produce a note, and when he finally succeeded the call was so quavering and unclear that later it gave rise to a rumour that a Boer had sounded the call. The Irish Fusiliers had been only lightly engaged and could hardly be made to believe that the entire force had been surrendered. Some of them went on firing for several minutes. Some of their officers broke their swords in angry indignation. But it was all over.

The soldiers were disarmed; it was time to count the dead and tend the wounded. Estimates of the size of the Boer force vary wildly from 200 to 2,000, though the evidence seems to indicate that the true figure was nearer the former than the latter. Boer losses were said to be only 4 killed and 5 wounded. British casualties were 38 killed and 105 wounded; nearly 1,000 soldiers were made prisoner. Not in a century had so many British soldiers laid down their arms and surrendered to a foe.

Both Christiaan de Wet (at this stage in the war a commandant) and his brother Piet were present at this battle, which the Boers called "Little Majuba." Christiaan de Wet remembered the cries of those who had fallen: "The condition of the wounded touched my heart deeply. It was pitiable to hear them cry 'Water! Water!' "[3] It was the middle of a summer afternoon; Boers and Britons had been fighting since dawn, and all were parched, for neither side had water. The Boers did what they could for the wounded, then they sang a hymn of praise and marched their prisoners down the hill on the first stage of their journey to prison in Pretoria. Captain Gerard Rice, adjutant of the 1st Irish Fusiliers, had been wounded and was carried down from the hill on the back of a giant Boer; he was astonished when the man refused the gold piece offered him for this piece of humanity. The British still had much to learn about their foes.

No greater boost to Boer morale could have been given than the sight of a thousand British prisoners being marched through the streets of the Transvaal capital. The doubters, the waverers, all those who had found a pretext for not going to the war, now seized their rifles and rode off to join their commandos.

It was a sad night in Ladysmith when news of the disaster came. The next morning G. W. Steevens went to the camp of the Royal Irish Fusiliers, and in the tent that served as the officers' mess he found only the doctor, the quartermaster, and a young second lieutenant fresh from Sandhurst who had just arrived. Another officer, pale and haggard, came in. They were all that was left of the regimental mess. "They had been busy half the night packing up the lost officers' kits to send down to Durban. . . . Tied up in a waterproof sheet were the officers' letters—the letters of their wives and mothers that had arrived that morning. . . .[4]

It was a grey, raw day in London when the news of the battle of

Ladysmith was announced. Horse-omnibuses stopped to allow passengers to buy newspapers, which were silently read and solemnly folded. It was "Mournful Monday."

G. W. Steevens ended his dispatch to the *Daily Mail* with bitter words: "At the end, when the tardy truth could be withheld no more—what shame! What bitter shame for all the camp! All ashamed for England! Not of her—never that!—but for her. Once more she was a laughter to her enemies."[5]

11

BULLER

The full significance of the battle of Ladysmith was not at first apparent —perhaps it was simply too shocking to be believed: for nearly a century the British army had repeatedly engaged enemy forces of vastly superior numerical strength and defeated them; now an almost equal number of Boers and Britons had fought a major battle on nearly equal terms and the British had been soundly beaten. No one in Britain dared say it, or even think it: the Boer had shown himself to be, man for man, a better fighter than the Briton.

At the end of the first fortnight of war the situation looked very grave indeed for the British: on the western front the Boers had won small victories, Kimberley was besieged and Mafeking was about to be, and there seemed nothing to prevent the Boers from sweeping down off the high veld into the heartland of Cape Colony; on the Natal front the British had lost about 1,200 men and the Natal Field Force was almost bottled up in Ladysmith; there was no serious force between Joubert's army and the sea, nothing to prevent the Boers from overrunning Natal. But help was on the way. A full army corps, 40,000 strong, the largest expeditionary force in British history, had been put together in England, and daily at Southampton troops, horses, guns, ordnance, and stores were being loaded on transports for the more than 6,000-mile voyage to South Africa. A long line of ships already dotted the sea, and on one of them was the commander of this mighty host, the man on whom all Britain's hopes were pinned: General Sir Redvers Buller, V.C. Everyone —the government, the army, and the people—had complete confidence in him—everyone, that is, except Buller himself.

"My confidence in the British soldier is only equalled by my confidence in Sir Redvers Buller," said Lord Salisbury, the prime minister. Sir Evelyn Wood, who had soldiered with Buller, said he was "careful of his men's lives, reckless of his own, untiring and unflinching in the performance of his duty." Walter Jerrold summed up the general feeling of Britons when he wrote: "His fitness for the job now entrusted to him cannot be questioned. He is the best soldier of his standing available for the present crisis."[1] Churchill more moderately described him as "a characteristic British personality. He looked stolid. He said little and what he said was obscure. He was not the kind of man who could explain things, and he never tried to. . . . he was regarded as a very sensible soldier."[2] Conan Doyle called him "a heavy, obdurate, inexplicable man."

Redvers Henry Buller was born on his father's estate in Devon on 7 December 1839 of a family that could trace its history in the west of England back three centuries. His mother was a granddaughter of the twelfth Duke of Norfolk; his father was a wealthy country squire. Young Redvers was sent first to Harrow and then to Eton, but in neither school did he distinguish himself. He was eighteen—tall, big-boned, and strong —when he was given a commission in the 60th Regiment (King's Royal Rifle Corps), and six months later he was in India. He first saw action in the China War of 1860. There his front teeth were kicked out by a horse so that ever after he spoke indistinctly and with a lisp. In 1862 he was promoted lieutenant and joined the 4th Battalion of his regiment in Canada.

Like most young officers in this era, he knew almost nothing about his profession and took little interest in it: with nothing required of him except that he act bravely should he find himself in combat, he filled his time contentedly enough with horses, billiards, and cards. Then one day his colonel asked him to be battalion adjutant. He accepted reluctantly, but, to his own surprise, he began to take an interest in the army and proved to have a talent for military administration.

In 1869–1870 he took part in the bloodless Red River Expedition in Canada led by Garnet Wolseley (1833–1913) against a half-breed rebel in Manitoba. His career was made, for he impressed Wolseley and became one of his protégés. In 1871 he entered the Staff College, but when given the opportunity to join Wolseley in fighting the Ashanti, he quickly dropped his books and sailed for West Africa. His next two campaigns were in South Africa, where he fought in the Sixth Kaffir War and played an active part in the Zulu War of 1879, winning the Victoria Cross.

He was forty-two when he married the daughter of a marquis, and he was on his honeymoon when Wolseley invited him to go to Egypt as his chief of intelligence in the expedition against Arabi. From Egypt Buller wrote to his bride to explain his feelings about war: "I do believe that it is wicked and very brutal, but I can't help it; there is nothing in this world that so stirs me up as a fight."

For his part in this campaign he was knighted. After a brief spell in

London, he returned to northeast Africa in 1884 to fight the Dervishes in the eastern Sudan and was promoted major general for distinguished services. When it was decided to send a force under Wolseley to attempt the rescue of Charles "Chinese" Gordon besieged at Khartoum, Buller was again on the staff.

The Gordon Relief Expedition was Buller's last campaign until his appointment to the South African command. Sixty years old and a full general, he was in command of the troops at Aldershot when the Anglo-Boer War broke out. He appeared to have all the qualifications for high command: he was a brave and experienced battlefield officer; he was a good administrator; and he was solicitous for the welfare of his men, by whom he was liked and trusted. Yet, something curious was observed during the manoeuvres held in Britain in the summer of 1898 when Buller commanded one side and the Duke of Connaught commanded the other. The Duke handled his forces with greater skill than the more experienced Buller, who was at times overly cautious and indecisive.

Throughout his fighting career Buller had served under Wolseley, and it had been this brilliant general who had planned every campaign and battle; Buller was the able executer of his chief's strategy. While on the Gordon Relief Expedition he wrote his wife, telling her how pleased he was to have the position of chief of staff; it was a position, he said, "involving all the responsibilities of execution without those of invention and preliminary organization. I have never credited myself with much ability on the inventive side; all mine, if I have any, is on the executive side, and possibly if I have a strong point it is resource, which is a great help in execution."

Given clear orders, Buller carried them out with vigour and resolution, but he had never in his life been in charge of planning and directing a campaign. He had no head for it, and, not being a fool, he knew it. When offered command of the army corps to be sent to South Africa, he hesitated. Honest with others as well as himself, he plainly told Lord Lansdowne, secretary for war: "I have always considered that I was better as second in a complex military affair than as an officer in chief command. . . . I had never been in a position where the whole load of responsibility fell on me."[3] Finally he went to consult with his mentor, Wolseley, telling him frankly that he did not want the command and that he would relinquish it at the first opportunity. Such words must have sounded strange to Wolseley, his memory often failing him now but eager as ever for battle. When Buller did at last accept, Wolseley wrote: "Buller will I am sure end the war with complete success for England. . . . But how I envy him!"

It had been fifteen years since Buller had taken part in a battle. During his desk assignments in Britain he had changed: good food and soft living had made him stout and given him a double chin. In that time there had been changes, too, in the art of war, for improved weapons now called for changes in tactics.

On the dozens of battlefields where British soldiers fought during Queen Victoria's long reign there had not been, except in Wolseley's campaigns, much military genius displayed; there had not been much need of it. The greatest asset of the British army was its infantry, and British generals tended to rely rather too heavily upon it. The strength of British infantry lay in the stolid discipline exhibited by the men in the ranks, in the bravery, often reckless, of its officers, and in the regimental esprit which animated them all. Generals usually knew how to inspire their men in battle, and they seldom missed an opportunity to seize their swords and lead a charge, but in planning a battle, in the deployment of troops, in the coordination of the available arms and services, in overall strategy, in the organization of proper staffs and their best employment, in the use of the increasing technology which was available to them—in all these matters the knowledge and skill of most generals was deficient.

The British army, like most armies, was a conservative institution that resisted change, and always had. It had long delayed the switch from muskets to rifles, from muzzle-loading cannon (which, incredibly, they were still using) to breech-loading guns, and most officers chose to adopt a supercilious attitude towards machine guns, which tended to be forgotten or left behind when going into battle. Lord Rawlinson once saw a battalion commander deploying troops over ground on which his machine gun stood. It interfered with the movements of his infantrymen, and he shouted at the subaltern in charge of it: "Take that damned cart out of the way!"

When civilian volunteers entered the army for the war in South Africa many asked questions which regular officers had never thought of asking: Mortimer Memper, an artist and a marksman, asked why telescopic sights were not used when in the clear South African air the conditions were perfect for them; no one could give him an answer. In the cavalry the sword and lance were favoured and the carbine despised; in the infantry the bayonet was preferred, and it was the object of every general to close with the enemy as quickly as possible so that this knife on the end of a rifle, this inferior descendant of the pike, could be made formidable or at least effective. Had some commander-in-chief, wise enough and respected enough to overcome the objections of every other officer in the army, ordered that all bayonets be thrown on the scrap heap the army might then have been forced to learn tactics based on firepower rather than knives and lances. No such general existed—not then and not later. Most Victorian generals never realized that the magazine-fed rifle made obsolete the tactics and the training which had enabled the British to win their earlier wars.

There were a few officers—Ian Hamilton was one of them—who realized the importance of musketry training and understood that against modern rifles and quick-firing guns troops had to be deployed in open order and be allowed to take advantage of available cover. Buller still clung to conventional views on such matters, views which were reflected in a memorandum he issued to officers at Aldershot asserting that battles were won not by "jacks-in-boxes" but by resolute, enthusiastic men who kept on their feet. "Jacks-in-boxes," he explained, were men who "bob up, fire, and bob down again." Officers under fire did not "bob" and such antics should not be encouraged in their men. This memorandum was issued only a few weeks before he embarked for South Africa to lead resolute, enthusiastic British soldiers against an entire army of jacks-in-boxes.

One final quality unfitted Buller for the command of an army in the field. Behind this brave man's gruff manners, his stern immobile face, and stout, four-square indomitable figure there lurked too tender a heart. Few knew this, and no one realized the disadvantage of such a possession to a man whose business was to send others to be killed.

Such was the man whom Britain was about to send to South Africa to salvage its imperial fortunes.

On 5 October Buller met with the Queen and assured her that he did not think there would be much hard fighting. On 14 October he left London amid a pandemonium of enthusiasm: men, women, and children shook with emotion as they watched this stolid-looking warrior of proved valour, appearing to typify the British leader of men in battle, depart to take command at the seat of war. No general going to war ever enjoyed such complete and unbounded confidence. Who could doubt that once this man arrived on the scene all would be put right in South Africa? For Buller himself, already loaded with honours as he was, it was anticipated that the future would bring even more, and a peerage certainly.

On board the *Dunottar Castle* which carried him to South Africa was a "mutograph" or "cinematograph," a motion picture camera in the shape of a huge square box on an iron tripod, its innards full of "burring electrical works," for this was to be the first war recorded on film for the biograph, as the cinema was called—and is still called in South Africa. It was a cumbersome affair, and John Atkins, one of the many newspaper correspondents on board, said, "It looks as though it would require a team of artillery horses to bring it into action on the field."[4] When it was set up on the hurricane deck where Buller and his staff strolled before dinner, Buller gruffly told the camera crew: "You can catch me if you can, but I won't pose for you." Among the newspaper correspondents on board was Winston Churchill, who had himself considered a scheme to take motion pictures of the war but had abandoned the idea when he learned that the American Biograph Company had already made arrangements to do it.

The three-day passage to Madeira was rough, and Churchill was "grievously sick." All on board had hoped that there would be some late news of the war waiting at Madeira, but there was none. It was a two-week sail from here to the Cape, and until almost the end of the voyage the commander-in-chief, his staff, and the newspaper correspondents were incommunicado. On 29 October they sighted the *Australasian,* a home-ward-bound troopship. One might think that it would have been of some importance for the two ships to have paused long enough for the com-mander-in-chief to obtain the latest intelligence, but no one thought of it, and they silently passed each other. However, from the deck of the *Australasian* a large blackboard with white lettering was held up:

> BOERS DEFEATED
>
> THREE BATTLES
>
> PENN SYMONS KILLED

This was discouraging news; it seemed as if the war would be won by the time they arrived. A staff officer said to Buller: "It looks as if it will be over, sir."

But Buller was sanguine: "I dare say there will be enough left to give us a fight outside Pretoria."

On 31 October, the day after White's defeat at Ladysmith, the *Dunot-tar Castle* arrived at Cape Town. Buller's reception there was no less enthusiastic than it had been in London and Southampton. When, at 9:00 A.M. precisely, he stepped on the gangway, the guard of honour presented arms, the harbour batteries banged out a salute, the deck hands and stokers of the *Dunottar Castle* gave three cheers, crowds on shore roared a welcome, and the cinematograph buzzed noisily, recording it all. As he was driven from the ship to Government House in a carriage with a mounted escort along streets gay with flags, jubilant masses lined the way, shouting "Bravo General!" and "Avenge Majuba!" He had brought no troops with him, and not even an adequate staff, but his appearance alone was inspiring: imperturbable, impassive, he had the bearing of a man who could not fail.

Behind that calm mask which so impressed the crowds there was many a self-doubt; in fact, he seems to have had a premonition that the future held little glory for him. Shortly after his arrival in Cape Town he wrote to his younger brother, Tremayne: "I am in the tightest place I have ever been in. . . . I don't know if I shall ever get out of it, and I think if I fail that it is fair my family should know afterwards what at any rate I had to say in my own defence." It was a long letter, a detailed apologia for defeats he had not yet suffered, placing the blame for them squarely on the politicians, especially Lansdowne, of whom he wrote bitterly and petulantly. It was an astonishing letter for Buller, or any man in his position, to write.

Some difficult and crucial decisions had to be made immediately. The campaign Buller had intended and for which all his plans had been made was simply a straightforward march of his entire army corps from the Cape to Bloemfontein and Pretoria, in the course of which he would defeat the Boer armies, seize their capitals, and end the war. The troop-ships loaded with men and supplies were all headed for Cape Colony ports; elaborate arrangements and intricate timetables had been designed to carry out the first phase of the original campaign plan, the march north from Cape Colony into the Free State. But in the two weeks that Buller had been en route too much had changed: three towns, containing more than half of the entire British force in South Africa, were besieged or about to become so.

On the western front little Mafeking, where a cavalry colonel named Baden-Powell with a handful of locally raised volunteers was holding out, did not seem important yet, but Kimberley contained not only the largest diamond mines in the world and a force of British regulars, but also the world-famous Cecil Rhodes. And Rhodes was screaming for help: he was not pleading, he was *demanding* that the British army relieve Kimberley —NOW. On the Natal front White at this stage still thought it possible to break out of Ladysmith and take up a position behind the Tugela River, but the effect on public opinion of a retreat from Ladysmith was incalculable, and all things considered, he thought it would be better to hold on and allow himself to be invested; he telegraphed this proposal to Buller, who agreed. Thus the Natal Field Force, including its splendid but now almost useless cavalry, ceased to be a field force and became merely the garrison of a beleaguered town and sat waiting to be relieved. After the disaster of 30 October White never again sought a general engagement.

The problem of the besieged towns was not the only difficulty confronting Buller. On the day of his arrival he had a far from encouraging talk with Milner, who told him, as he also told young Winston Churchill in an interview, that Cape Colony was "trembling on the verge of rebellion." He wanted Buller to divert some of his troops to northern Cape Colony to prevent the Afrikaners from rising. Buller grumbled that it seemed he was expected to conquer not just the two Boer republics but all of South Africa. The army corps, large as it was, could not provide enough troops to relieve the besieged towns, defend Cape Colony, prevent rebellion, and invade the Orange Free State.

On the day after Buller's arrival it appeared that Milner's worst fears were about to be realized: a Free State commando seized the railway bridge over the Orange at Norval's Pont; the Bethulie and Smithfield commandos crossed the river at Bethulie. North central Cape Colony had been invaded; eager young Cape Afrikaners were joining the enemy. Buller feared that the British garrisons at Naauwpoort and Stormberg, which lay in the path of the invading commandos, might be overwhelmed or besieged, and although he knew nothing of the strength of the British positions there, he ordered the troops immediately to fall back south along the railway. Major Frederick Heath of the Royal Engineers was at Cape Town, and he knew all about the situation at Stormberg, for he had just returned from inspecting the fortifications there, but he was having his hair cut when the withdrawal decision was being discussed and by the time he returned from the barber the orders had been sent.

Buller now decided that in view of the deteriorating situations in Natal and Cape Colony his triumphal march through the Boer republics must be postponed and the army corps on its way to Cape ports would have to be broken up to meet the variety of crises which had developed. Lieutenant General Paul Sanford, Lord Methuen, was directed to lead a full division to the relief of Kimberley; Lieutenant General Sir William Gatacre, who was to have commanded a division in the army corps, was left with a bare brigade and told to hold down rebellion and prevent further Boer incursions in north central Cape Colony. The situation in Natal was, Buller decided, the most critical. Louis Botha, Joubert's protégé, had made some forays south of Ladysmith and Boers were now ranging south of the Tugela, where the British forces were "strung out like beads on a chain, no direction, only a general terror and paralysis."[5] When the first contingent of the army corps reached the Cape on 9–15 November the troops did not disembark; instead the transports were ordered to carry them on up the coast to Natal, where two brigades, together with a force of local volunteers, all under the command of Major General C. F. Clery, were ordered to assemble at Estcourt on the main railway line 30 miles south of Ladysmith.

The first advance of the British forces, however, was not in Natal but on the western front. Neither Buller nor Methuen expected the relief of Kimberley to be a difficult operation. It lay only 75 miles north of the Orange River, and there were few natural obstacles to bar the way. Methuen had 8,000 men, and it was believed that the Boers, with large forces tied up in the sieges of Kimberley and Mafeking, would not be able to put more than 5,000 men across his path. Buller reported to the Queen that "Sir Redvers does not anticipate that the force will meet with very serious difficulties."[6] Methuen only hoped he would see some action on the way.

12

METHUEN

Paul Sanford (third Baron) Methuen (1845–1932), the youngest lieutenant general in the army, was educated at Eton and commissioned in the Scots Fusilier Guards in 1864 at the age of nineteen. He served as a staff officer with Wolseley in the Ashanti War of 1873–1874 and again in the Egyptian Campaign of 1882. His first and only experience as a commander in the field was as the leader of a regiment of local volunteers in the bloodless Bechuanaland Expedition under Sir Charles Warren in 1884–1885. During the Tirah Campaign on India's Northwest Frontier he served as press censor at headquarters.

He was a tall, bony man with a determined chin and a drooping, reddish moustache under a short nose. Always courteous, he was well liked by his fellow officers; he took his profession seriously, and he was conscientious, hard-working, persistent, and brave. He had, perhaps, only one defect: he was not very clever.

On the banks of the Orange River in the southwestern corner of Griqualand West Methuen assembled his division for the advance on Kimberley. It was a convenient and strategically valuable location: men and supplies could be lifted there by rail from Cape Town, and the very presence of his force gave some security to this portion of Cape Colony. Between Methuen and his objective there was only open veld with, here and there, kopjes standing out like islands on the flat plain. There were only three places on his proposed line of march where kopjes linked by ridges were clustered in such a way as to offer tempting defensive positions that might encourage the Boers to contest his progress, and none was so extensive that it could not be outflanked. The Modder River, which also lay across his path, did not appear to be a formidable obstacle. Methuen sent word to the besieged in Kimberley that they could expect to be relieved in about a week.

He was pleased with the infantry assigned to him, as well he might be, for it included battalions from some of the most famous regiments in the British army: a 1st or Guards Brigade (Grenadiers, Coldstreams, and Scots) and a 9th Brigade (Northumberlands, Northhamptons, Yorkshires, and Lancashires), with a Highland Brigade (Black Watch, Argylls, Highland Light Infantry, and Seaforths) still on the line of communication when he began his march but soon to join him. He had, too, an armoured train, and a naval brigade of 400 bluejackets and marines with four 12-pounder guns came up after the march had begun. The greatest weakness of the division was its lack of sufficient mounted troops, for there were only the 9th Lancers, three companies of mounted infantry, and two small colonial units, the New South Wales Lancers and Rimington's Guides.

It took about a week to assemble the troops, stores, and ordnance and to make all the preparations for the march. Much khaki paint was employed to dull the glitter of the regiments, for the army had already learned one lesson: shiny objects attracted the attention of Boer marksmen. All buttons and gleaming bits of accoutrements were painted; officers were advised to abandon their Sam Browne belts, swords, and brass insignia. A sergeant wrote home: "I believe they will be making us dye our whiskers khaki colour next." Methuen described himself as looking "like a second-class conductor in a khaki coat with no mark of rank on it and a Boer hat and in Norwegian slippers."

Early on the morning of 21 November 1899 Methuen's khaki-coloured army turned its back on the muddy Orange River and began its march towards Kimberley. Most of the soldiers had been too excited by the prospect of early battle to sleep; they had sat up late around fires of mimosa thorn, talking and singing. Now dawn found the two brigades marching briskly across the level veld; the air was pure and bracing, and the men stepped out with a will, their progress halted only briefly from time to time by wire fences. Methuen did not have a map—not an adequate one—but he could not get lost, for he had only to follow the railway line that led straight to Kimberley. By noon the division had marched 10 miles; then it halted for the day at an ostrich farm where there was a reservoir of water and a patch of green trees.

Another 10 miles was covered the next day. The Boers, well aware of all Methuen's movements, saw that he followed the railway track, assumed that he would continue to do so, and prepared themselves accordingly. That evening British cavalry patrols drew fire from Boers positioned on kopjes near Belmont railway station. British and Boer guns exchanged a few rounds, then everyone went to sleep, knowing that the next morning they would be in battle.

The Boer force in the kopjes across Methuen's line of march consisted of less than 2,000 Free Staters under Jacobus Prinsloo, but due to the inadequacies of British reconnaissance techniques, Methuen had no way of knowing their strength. It was suggested by several staff officers that the Boer positions be outflanked, but Methuen rejected the idea. To Colonel Willoughby Verner he said, "My good fellow, I intend to put the fear of God into these people," and he told Colonel Henry Streatfield that he intended to "attack the position in front, trusting to the courage and stubbornness of our troops to gain the day."

The troops left their camp at two o'clock in the morning in order to be close up on the enemy at first light. Their intended positions were indicated on a rough map made the evening before by Colonel Verner, but dawn revealed that Verner had made a mistake: the enemy-held kopjes were still 1,000 yards away. In spite of this, it did not occur to Methuen to recall his troops and fight another day. They marched on. The Scots Guards were within 350 yards of the enemy, their band playing, when the first shots were fired. As Julian Ralph, an American who was serving as the correspondent for the London *Daily Mail*, described it, "there ran along the crest of the kopje quick, vivid jets of fire like jewels flashing in a coronet . . . the rim of fire beads flashed along the crest and died away, and raced along the crest again as tiny gas-jets blow out and re-ignite in a heavy wind." The infantry, unshaken, pushed on, pausing at the foot of the kopjes only long enough to catch their breath and fix bayonets before throwing themselves on the slopes. The kopjes before them were surprisingly high and steep, rising 100 to 200 feet above the veld, but the troops clawed their way up, sometimes on their hands and knees, while the Boer marksmen leaned over their sangers and fired on the helmeted heads below them. The fire slackened as they neared the crest, and by the time they had heaved themselves to the top the enemy had fled down the hill, mounted their ponies, and ridden off. The troops were well pleased with themselves; it was the first battle for most. When the Grenadier Guards reached the crest of the kopje they had assaulted they proudly raised a chorus of "Soldiers of the Queen," but in the distance a retreating young burgher was seen to turn in his saddle, raise a hand with extended fingers, and put his thumb to his nose.

The British had lost 75 officers and men killed. There were also 220 wounded, not counting Mr. E. F. Knight of the *Morning Post,* who was struck by a dumdum and lost his arm: the first casualty among the war correspondents. In spite of these losses the British considered themselves victors. Methuen was elated and told the Guards, who had borne the brunt of the fighting, "With troops like you, no general can fear the result of his plans." He was indeed fortunate to have such soldiers, considering that he had made very few plans and such as he had made proved faulty. Belmont has been called a "soldiers' battle," and so it was, for as General Sir Henry Colvile, commanding the Guards Brigade, said, "The men did for themselves what no general would have dared ask of them."

Prinsloo, who was considerably shaken by the vigour of the British charge, considered himself defeated and reported to Bloemfontein: "Nov. 23rd. This morning there was a terrible fight to our disadvantage, as we had to leave the field. According to Dr. Voortman, who went over the field of battle, we lost about twelve killed and forty wounded."[1] Boer losses were actually higher than this, for the British found some thirty Boer dead, but, whatever the true figures, Boer casualties were certainly less than half those of the British. They would have been higher if Methuen had had a brigade of cavalry and more horse artillery, and if Prinsloo's retreat had not been covered by a Transvaal force of some 800 men under De la Rey who arrived just in time and successfully ambushed the pursuing lancers and mounted infantry.

The Boers did not retreat far, and two days later Methuen again found them across his path at a place called Rooilaagte between Enslin and Graspan. Here the combined forces of Prinsloo and De la Rey, just over 2,000 men with five guns, had taken up positions on a series of steep-sloped kopjes. Captain L. March Phillips with Rimington's Guides described the country as it appeared to him: "A wide plain in front of me, four miles across, flat as the sea, and all along the further side a line of kopjes and hills rising like reefs and detached islands out of it."[2]

On the night before the battle the naval brigade was told that it would have the honour of leading the assault. "By Jove, what sport!" exclaimed a midshipman. "Is it really true, sir?" an excited marine sergeant asked. "The news seemed almost too good to be true," wrote one officer later, "and it was some short time before we could believe it and realize our luck."[3] Early in the morning the still-elated naval brigade formed into neat lines and stepped out towards the waiting Boers. Colonel Verner watched them and noted how "each hard, clean-cut face was from time to time anxiously turned toward the directing flank, so as to satisfy each individual that the interval and dressing were properly kept. . . . No better kept line ever went forward to death or glory." It was impossible for them to stay extended, however, and in places they were soon almost shoulder to shoulder. The Boers waited patiently until they were only 650 yards away and then opened "a fierce hurricane of fire" that swept across their front and, more deadly still, enfiladed them from their left.

Verner watched as they "were picked off like deer, but they never flinched and fell with their faces to the hill and their officers walked ahead with their swords drawn." The officers, who had insisted on walking in front, on carrying their swords, and on wearing polished belts, were nearly all hit. Major John Plumbe of the Marines fell dead beside his fox terrier, which had been trotting beside him. Broad, bearded Captain Prothero, commander of the naval brigade, was one of the first to drop, calling as he fell: "Take that hill and be hanged to it!" Midshipman C. Huddart of HMS *Doris* was twice hit but staggered on until a third bullet killed him. Nearly half the brigade was down before they reached the foot of the kopje; yet, without swerving or changing their pace, the survivors pressed on. Supported by the Yorkshires and North Lancashires, they carried the kopje, but by the time they reached the crest the Boers had once again mounted their ponies and ridden off.

"Did you watch the naval brigade?" asked Lieutenant Colonel Charles Baxter of a staff officer. "By Heaven, I never saw anything so magnificent in my life!" *The Times History* said that the charge, now almost forgotten, "will live to all time as one of the most splendid instances of disciplined courage." It was disciplined, of course, and courageous certainly; it was also tragically anachronistic. The days of stand-up, shoulder-to-shoulder attacks were past. Casualties were almost 50 percent. Nearly all the petty officers and marine noncommissioned officers were killed or wounded.

The correspondent for *The Times* reported that the vacated Boer positions were "almost dripping in blood; not a boulder escaped its splash of crimson." In actual fact, only 21 dead burghers were found on the hills. The men who had done the fighting and who were still alive were tired, hot, and, above all, thirsty. They now retraced their steps, some stopping to help the wounded who had been left in the wake of their charge and who cried out for water. There was none to be had. One man, his arm shattered and unable to pull out the stopper of his water bottle, had in his frenzy bitten off the metal neck. No one seemed to know where the water carts were. On the plain men crowded around the locomotives begging for water from the boilers, but the engine drivers had their orders and refused to part with any. One frantic man crawled under an engine and lay on his back trying to catch drops from a steam pipe.

Methuen sent such cavalry as he possessed in pursuit of the Boers, but the British horses were thirsty too, and tired, and the Boers fought a skilful rear-guard action.

The Boers saw no disgrace in being forced to retreat, but they were dispirited by their failure to halt the British advance and they had lost confidence in Prinsloo, who had proved himself an unimaginative and irresolute leader. Determined to stop Methuen at all costs, they pushed Prinsloo into the background and Piet Cronjé and some Transvaalers under Koos de la Rey, drawn from the forces besieging Mafeking and Kimberley, came down to take over the task of blocking Methuen.

Pieter Arnoldus Cronjé (1835–1911), stubborn and hot-headed, was one of the two Boer leaders (the other was Piet Joubert) with an established military record, and as a result of his part in the First Anglo-Boer War he was called the Lion of Potchefstroom. Attached to him as an "adviser" was Jacobus Herculaas de la Rey (1847–1914), called "Koos," who was to emerge as one of the outstanding generals of the war. He possessed the most engaging and enigmatic personality to be found on either side. He was a handsome man of fifty-two, standing 6 feet 1 inch tall with a large head, hawk nose, shaggy eyebrows, a long square beard beginning to turn grey, and expressive eyes. He did not look like a fighter. Harold Spender said: "Benevolence shone from every feature . . . the kindly grandfatherly eyes . . . like a warm-hearted Norfolk farmer." John Buchan said that he had "a face which I have never seen equalled for antique patriarchal dignity." This kindly, gentle, pipe-smoking man who in the volksraad had voted against the war could be fiercely passionate in battle, lashing his burghers with his sjambok and shouting, "Fight!" and "Fire!" and "God is on our side!" He was speaking the simple truth when he said, "I fear God—and nothing else on earth." A man with a vast store of sound common sense, he nevertheless believed in visions and prophecies. With him throughout the war was a bizarre character, Niklaas van Rensburg (1862–1926), called the *Siener* (seer), who, although himself frequently confounded by his visions, was credited by De la Rey and others with the ability to foresee the future.

Like most of the Boer generals, De la Rey had little formal education —"a handful of wisdom is worth more than a head full of learning," he said—but he was intelligent and had, said Deneys Reitz, "a fine gift of simple speech."

The Boer forces, consisting now of about 3,500 men with six Krupp guns and three or four pompoms—about half the size of Methuen's division—decided to make their next stand where the Modder and Riet rivers meet, about 25 miles south of Kimberley. Here the rivers had cut into the soft soil of the veld and flowed in deep troughs some 30 feet below the surface of the plain, their steep banks lined with bushes and willows. It was De la Rey's idea not to contest the crossing of the Modder in the usual fashion by posting men and guns to cover the riverbanks but to utilise the banks themselves as natural defences, posting men in their shelter as if in a giant trench.

On Sunday, 26 November, they started work on their new positions, converting farm buildings and kraals in the area into improvised forts, making hidden gun emplacements and riflemen's pits, and marking out ranges by positioning white stones and biscuit tins at measured distances in front of them. De la Rey supervised the work. Cronjé was supposed to be in charge, but by the time he arrived De la Rey's plans were already being put into operation. Cronjé disliked De la Rey and had resented having him assigned as his "adviser," but he made no change in the dispositions of the men or the plan of battle and gave no orders, choosing instead to stay aloof from all the preparations by withdrawing to the Island Hotel, a small inn located on the tongue of land that the configuration of the two rivers made almost an island.

On Monday the British left Enslin and made a 14-mile march to within 6 miles of the Modder. Cavalry patrols ranging ahead were fired upon, and they reported to Methuen that the Boers were concentrating their forces near the now destroyed railway bridge across the river. Late in the day Methuen himself rode out to look. His glasses swept the landscape, but he could see nothing of note, only the dark green foliage that marked the course of the river, the rolling open veld beyond, and, in the distance, the blue hills of Magersfontein and Spytfontein, where he believed the Boers would make a final attempt to stop him and where he expected to fight his last battle before entering Kimberley, now only 25 miles away.

Methuen's map of the area was a hastily drawn affair made a few weeks earlier by Captain Walter O'Meara, R.E., who had not used any instruments because he did not want to be seen "spying about." Almost every detail in it was wrong. Most important of all, the peculiar wanderings of the Modder and Riet rivers were incorrectly shown. This would not have mattered if Methuen had stuck to his original plan, which was to provide his men with five days' rations, cut himself off from the railway, and, swinging through Jacobsdal, 10 miles east of the railway, attack what he believed to be the enemy's flank at Spytfontein. Such a manoeuvre, however mistaken in its objective, would certainly have taken the Boers by surprise, for he would probably have struck a long line of Cronjé's supply wagons, which were leisurely moving across his flank not 10 miles away, and in that case the Boers would have quickly fallen back. However, Methuen made a last-minute change in plans and decided to do exactly what the Boers expected him to do: make another frontal attack.

Methuen's decision simply to butt his way through the Boers he encountered in his path requires some explanation. It was based in part upon his desire to defeat his enemies in open battle, to demoralise them by winning a decisive victory. Frontal attacks had succeeded at Talana and Elandslaagte, he knew, and he himself had been successful with the same tactic at Belmont and Rooilaagte; it would do equally well here without the risk of elaborate and possibly more dangerous manoeuvres. Perhaps the most decisive factor in Methuen's thinking, however, was his fear of leaving the railway. Not only was it the source of all necessities and all comforts, but his orders included specific instructions to repair the line as he went along, and it was envisaged that it would probably be necessary to evacuate the noncombatants from Kimberley once it had been relieved. Deliberately to abandon, even temporarily, the single railway (there were no proper roads) stretching back to all bases and hospitals seemed a dangerous proceeding, for the Boers might then sweep down and destroy it, leaving him stranded on the vast, unknown veld. It appeared best to hug the railway, to try again the same simple tactic, to rely again upon the brave hearts and bright bayonets of his infantrymen.

At four o'clock in the morning on Tuesday, 28 November, the infantry were turned out, including the Argyll and Sutherland Highlanders, who had arrived by train only a few hours earlier. The men were not fed; they could breakfast after crossing the Modder. Cavalry patrols rode out ahead and again reported that they had drawn fire near the broken railway bridge, but Methuen thought the Boers were not there in any great force. The sun was well above the horizon by the time the infantry topped the last fold of ground south of the rivers. It was a crisp, clear summer morning, and not a Boer was in sight; before them stretched the picture of a peaceful South African countryside: the wide plain broken only by the lines of green bushes along the rivers, a few clusters of poplar trees, some white-walled farm buildings and kraals. Beyond the river was the Modder River railway station and a few houses surrounded by eucalyptus trees. Methuen scanned the scene with his glasses: there was not a sign of the more than 3,000 riflemen hidden along the riverbanks. Turning to General R. Pole-Carew, commanding the 9th Brigade, he remarked that there were "probably no Boers at all"; if there were, he thought there were not more than 400. He pointed out one of the houses near the railway station which he thought would be a good place to make his headquarters, and two of his staff officers trotted off towards it to make preparations for his arrival.

From the Island Hotel Cronjé, who had just finished his breakfast, watched the advancing British infantry. He had just given his only order of the day: to De la Rey's horror, he ordered two guns to be moved from their prepared positions in the centre to the left flank. This movement, at about seven o'clock in the morning, gave the British their first sight of the enemy. A battery of the Royal Horse Artillery detached itself and smartly galloped into position, the gunners swinging their guns into action and accurately shelling the Boer guns at a range of 4,000 yards. The Boer artillerymen withdrew their guns out of range and out of sight.

Not even the appearance of the enemy guns ruffled Methuen and his staff. Several officers expressed the opinion that "they'll never stand against us here." Not here, not on open, level ground against regular British infantry.

But snuggly hidden by the river's banks the Boer marksmen silently watched the massed ranks of infantry march across that level, open ground, well aware that it offered the best shooting conditions they could ask for.

"They are not there," said Methuen to Sir Henry Colvile.

"They are sitting uncommonly tight if they are, sir," Colvile replied.

At that moment the Boer line, nearly 4 miles long, opened fire. The range was 1,200 yards. The British had walked into what one man called "a three-mile jaw full of sunken teeth." The soldiers threw themselves on the ground, trying their best to find cover behind the low, leafless bushes of the plain and the scattered anthills. Then the Boer artillery opened fire. One of the first shells killed Lieutenant Colonel Horace Stopford, commander of the 2nd Coldstream Guards, as he was trying to move his men forward. A string of pompom shells killed the entire crew of the Scots Guards' Maxim, leaving the gun on its cart standing upright, unmanned and alone, for the rest of the day, the only object standing on a plain of prone men.

On the right of the British line the Scots Guards attempted a flanking movement and to their surprise encountered the Riet River, wide, muddy, and at this point unfordable. The Boers had not tried to defend the banks here. Colvile ordered men to search for a place to cross, but they failed to find Besman's Drift, an easy crossing for men and guns only a couple of miles downstream. A well-used path led to the drift; mounted patrols had skirmished near it; yet neither Colvile nor Methuen knew of its existence.

The day grew hotter and then hotter. All along the centre of the line the soldiers lay flat on their stomachs in the scorching sun. The temperature climbed to 110 degrees, and the men were hungry and, above all, thirsty, but any movement provoked the fire of the deadly, unseen riflemen. This fighting against unseen foes was maddening. "It's fighting against rocks. You have nobody to shoot at, damn it!" one soldier complained. Lieutenant Colonel Alfred Codrington wrote Lady Florence Poore that although he had been in three battles he had seen only three Boers. There was a feeling among the soldiers that Boer tactics were not quite cricket: "Why doesn't the Boer come out in the open and fight us fair in the teeth?" asked one.

Shortly after noon a herd of black and white goats wandered across the fire zone. The Boers used them to correct their range; their accuracy, already good, was improved. It became even more dangerous to move an arm or a leg. The men stretched motionless on the ground listened to what has been described as "the silky breath of the Mauser."

Boer bullets striking anthills disturbed the ants, who streamed out to take their revenge on the helpless men. Lying still on the sandy ground, the hot sun beating on their backs, ants and flies crawling over them, a deadly foe in front of them, some of the soldiers simply fell asleep. One who did wrote in a letter home: "I dropped off to sleep. I don't know how long I slept, but I was rudely awakened by the scream of a shell from a Boer 'Buck-up gun,' which exploded about thirty yards from me, and took the right leg off one of our chaps. I didn't go to sleep again."[4] The Highlanders suffered most from the sun, for the backs of their knees reddened and blistered.

Methuen wandered about the battlefield and gave no orders of any importance; his commanders seldom knew where to find him. At one point he took over a subaltern's command, leading a party of Argyll and Sutherland Highlanders down a small gully. Later in the afternoon, when he was again where he ought not to have been, he was shot in the thigh. Methuen found it easier to be gallant than to be wise.

Almost the only damage done to the Boers was inflicted by the British artillery, even though the gunners, too, suffered from the Boers' musketry. An officer from the 62nd Battery wrote:

We took up our position 800 yards from the Boer trenches, and, by Jove! the Boers let us have a fearful reception. Before I got my horses out they shot one of my drivers and two horses . . . and brought down my own horse. We then got my gun around on the enemy, when one of my gunners was shot through the brain and fell at my feet. Another of my gunners was shot whilst bringing up a shell, and I began to feel queer.[5]

In spite of their casualties the artillerymen continued to work their guns, and they had such a demoralising effect upon the Free Staters on the Boer right that late in the afternoon they fell back. The British infantry exploited the advantage and some troops actually managed to cross the Modder and capture a small village.

When it grew too dark to see, the shooting stopped, both sides remaining where they were while their leaders debated their next move. Methuen made up his mind to sit tight and renew the attack in the morning; the Boers, ever sensitive about their flanks, were alarmed by the one British success on their right and the withdrawal of the Free Staters there, some of whom had fled the field for good. In spite of the bitter objections of De la Rey, the krygsraad decided to retreat during the night.

That afternoon De la Rey had seen his nineteen-year-old son Adriaan (called "Adaan") severely wounded in the abdomen by shrapnel. Now, even with the battle over, it was not possible to get back to him. Once the retreat was decided on, his men streamed away from the field in such haste that for a while it appeared that the guns would be abandoned and he had personally to see that they were got safely away. By the time he got back, at the end of the long day, the boy was dying.

"Are your cannon safe?" Adaan asked as his father bent over him.

There were no ambulances. De la Rey and some of his aides carried the boy on a blanket down the hill and set off down the road to Jacobsdal. Sick at the thought of retreating, sick at the thought of his dying son, De la Rey, himself slightly wounded in the right shoulder, trudged down the road in the dark. Cronjé and his staff came riding up behind.

"Well, Vechtgeneraal, how did the battle go?" Cronjé called out.

De la Rey swelled with rage. In a fury he accused Cronjé of shirking his duty and of leaving the burghers in the lurch. The dying boy was set down on the road while the generals wrangled.

Cronjé put an end to it by riding off. De la Rey and his men took up the boy and resumed their sad and bitter march. Then from behind came a small wagon hitched to a mule. It was driven by Field Cornet Coetzee, and in the back was his son, Hansie, barely alive with a gaping wound where his throat should have been. Hansie Coetzee and Adaan de la Rey had been classmates at the Staatsmodel School in Pretoria. Adaan was lifted into the wagon beside his friend. It was nearly dawn before they reached Jacobsdal and found the hospital. All of the beds were occupied; the boys were laid on the floor. Someone brought De la Rey a cup of coffee as he sat on the floor beside his son; he offered some to Adaan, but the boy could only shake his head. Minutes later he died. De la Rey telegraphed his wife: "Today there slipped to death so softly in my arms our loved son Adaan. . . . Tomorrow the body will be committed to earth here in Jacobsdal. How hard it still is for us all. But God has so decided. . . ."[6]

Men on both sides were beginning to understand some of war's grim realities. A private in the Loyal North Lancashire Regiment wrote to his mother: "I wrote you a letter the night before the battle of Modder River, stating what fine sport war was in my idea, but tore it up as soon as I saw my poor old friend lying dead on the battlefield."[7] Another soldier wrote: "Most terrible of all was a tall red-bearded Boer who had been wounded fearfully by a shell, and walked to and fro, his whole face one mass of blood, his eyes torn out, calling frantically for his comrades."[8] Lieutenant Cornwallis-West wrote: "I am sick of this war, three big battles in six days is enough for any man, and I think most of us think the same." The war had just begun.

When the next morning the first light of dawn touched the silent battlefield on the Modder, the naval guns threw a few shells at what had been the Boer positions. There was no response. In the continuing silence the British realised that their enemy had left. Methuen sent off a dispatch to London announcing another victory. It was, he said, "one of the hardest and most trying fights in the annals of the British army." It was not that. The British army in its long history had certainly fought fiercer battles, and in this one most of his men had simply lain out in the sun trying not to be seen by the enemy. Still, he had lost 70 officers and men killed and 413 wounded.

13

MAGERSFONTEIN

For twelve days Methuen sat inactive by the Modder River, accumulating supplies and receiving reinforcements. Two more Highland battalions arrived, the Black Watch and the Seaforths, completing the complement of the Highland Brigade, and there were now almost as many kilts as trousers in his army, for in addition to the Highland Brigade there were the Gordons and (although trousered) a battalion of the Scots Guards.

In command of the Highland Brigade was Major General Andrew Wauchope (1846–1899), called by his men "Andy" or "Red Mick"; he had a "strangely ascetic face" and was the only clean-shaven general officer in the British army. Like French, he began his service in the Royal Navy. He was fourteen at the time. After three years he left, spent two years in retirement, and, at the age of nineteen, obtained a commission in the Black Watch. He served in the Ashanti War of 1873 and was twice wounded, once severely. During the Egyptian Campaign of 1882 he was again severely wounded. Andy Wauchope was not lucky in battle. He took part in the Nile expedition of 1884–1885 and was wounded still again at the battle of Kirkeban. He then retired on half-pay for a time to devote himself to his family estates and business affairs, for on the death of his elder brother he had become one of the wealthiest men in Scotland. In 1892 he stood for Parliament, contesting without success the seat held by Gladstone. Then he returned to active duty with the army, taking part in the 1898 campaign in the Sudan, where for the first and only time he fought a war without being wounded.

In addition to the two new Highland battalions, Methuen also received as reinforcements the 12th Lancers, 100 mounted infantry, a battery of horse artillery, a howitzer battery, a 4.7-inch naval gun that was nicknamed "Joe Chamberlain," and a "war balloon." Other units, including contingents of newly arrived Canadian and Australian infantry, were brought up to hold his line of communication.

Methuen was in communication with the forces inside Kimberley through searchlights, heliographs, and occasional messengers; he knew the besieged town was not in any immediate danger and he felt under no great pressure to hurry. Except to repair the railway bridge over the Modder, he did nothing to prepare for his advance, to interfere with the enemy's preparations to meet him, or even to discover the nature of the Boer defences. In spite of his observation balloon and his light cavalry —in neither of which he reposed much confidence—he knew nothing of the enemy's numbers or dispositions. He estimated their strength to be about equal to his own 15,000, although the Boer forces actually numbered only about 8,000, even with the reinforcements that had recently come up, and he assumed, this time correctly, that they would be waiting for him at a farm known as Magersfontein where a series of kopjes offered them good defensive positions. Ten miles away on his right flank was Jacobsdal, where the Boers kept their almost undefended laagers crammed with wagons, supplies, women, and children, but it seems not to have occurred to him that a raid in that direction might shake them and disrupt their preparations. Apparently it did not occur to the Boers either. They assumed that Methuen would continue his march straight up the railway line and would again launch another frontal attack. They were right.

The Boers were busily digging trenches and making breastworks on the crests of the Magersfontein kopjes when De la Rey conceived what *The Times History* called "one of the boldest and most original conceptions in the history of war." So original did it seem that one officer claimed that "if it had been displayed by a young British officer in an examination for promotion, it would probably have injured that officer's prospects." De la Rey's scheme was to dig the main line of trenches on ground level in front of the hill instead of on the crests. It would deceive the British and would give the Boer riflemen a sweeping fire range. Piet Cronjé disagreed. At this point President Steyn arrived and settled the quarrel; he agreed with De la Rey's plan and forced Cronjé to accept it. The trenches, deep, narrow, and well camouflaged, were dug at the bottom of the hills.

After the battle much was made of what seemed to be another novelty in warfare: barbed wire. An American, Joseph Glidden, had invented this twenty-five years earlier, but it had never been used in a defensive manner by soldiers. At Magersfontein it appears that by chance some barbed wire that had been strung by farmers stood in front of parts of the Boer position, but at this time it was not used deliberately.

Methuen also had a plan for the battle, and he called together his senior officers to explain it. There was nothing remarkable about it: he intended to bombard the Boers, then move the Highland Brigade up close to the Boer positions during the night and attack at dawn. Although night marches in the face of the enemy, even for short distances, were regarded as complicated maneuvers involving some risk, it was the same plan Wolseley had used to win his victory over Arabi in Egypt seventeen years earlier, and in spite of miscalculations, it had worked successfully for Methuen himself at Belmont. He was confident it would work again. He left all the details to his brigade commanders, and later he was to say of the Highland Brigade, "No detailed orders as to the formation to be adopted were given by me." Wauchope listened glumly while Methuen explained his battle plan. As he left Methuen's tent he said to Colonel Charles Douglas, the chief staff officer, "I don't like the idea of this night march."

At three o'clock on Sunday afternoon, 10 December, in a pouring rain the Black Watch, screened by the 9th Lancers, moved out of camp and advanced in extended order "like a well-oiled piece of machinery" towards the hills of Magersfontein. They stopped while still out of range of the enemy's rifles and, on order, lay down in the mud. The purpose of this manoeuvre is obscure, but probably Methuen thought it a safeguard in case the Boers should attack his guns, which, as soon as the Highlanders were in position, began a two-hour bombardment of the crests, using a powerful new explosive called lyddite. "Shells tore through the air with precisely the noise of an express train rushing at full speed," reported one correspondent. They exploded with a force that tossed huge rocks into the air and covered the crest with great clouds of greenish yellow smoke. Everyone was impressed. The Black Watch lay on the veld and watched. A sharp-eyed sergeant noticed that when shells fell short of the hill, near the base, the earth thrown up was of a different colour. "There must be trenches there," he said. But no one paid any attention.

Methuen was delighted by the artillery display, confident that he was inflicting severe losses and shaking the enemy's morale considerably. In fact, the total result of the bombardment was three burghers wounded. If anything, it reinforced, even raised, the morale of the Boers, who, as they lay snugly in their trenches, safe from all but direct hits, had time to realise the full beauty of De la Rey's plan.

The war balloon was to have made its ascent this day, but the pelting rain prevented it, and it did not occur to Methuen to delay his attack until he could see where the enemy was and the real effect of his bombardment.

The Black Watch, having lain in the mud throughout the bombardment, now rose and moved back. As Captain Charles Stewart, commanding Company B, said, "Thus having given the Boers warning that we were likely to attack first thing in the morning, we retired and bivouacked together, one Highland regiment behind the other."

After the bombardment Methuen met again with his staff and brigade commanders. As the meeting broke up, Colvile remarked to Wauchope that since his Guards Brigade were to be in the reserve he would not see much action. "Things don't always go as they are expected. You may not be in reserve long," Wauchope said glumly. It was, however, to be a Scottish battle; even the farm on which the battle took place was owned by John Bisset, a Scot.

Shortly after midnight the Highland Brigade was roused from its sleep on the damp, rocky ground and put into close formation of quarter columns, a dense rectangle of 4,000 men in ninety-six successive lines, the Black Watch in front followed by the Seaforths, the Argylls, and the Highland Light Infantry. Then they marched off in the rain and dark towards the Magersfontein kopjes. Wauchope carried his sword, his old claymore. Thunder rolled across the veld, and lightning flashed from time to time above them as they marched. In the distance ahead of them the blinking violet-white light of the Kimberley searchlight could be seen; it was at about this time that messages were being sent by some of the town's wealthier citizens to their bankers in Cape Town.

To keep the Highlanders in their close formation and marching in the right direction, officers holding ropes were on both ends of the marching column. An artillery officer, Major George Elliot Benson, led the way. They had marched about far enough; the rain had stopped; dawn was near; the outline of the kopjes could be dimly seen. Major Benson twice suggested that it was time to deploy, but Wauchope wanted to be close

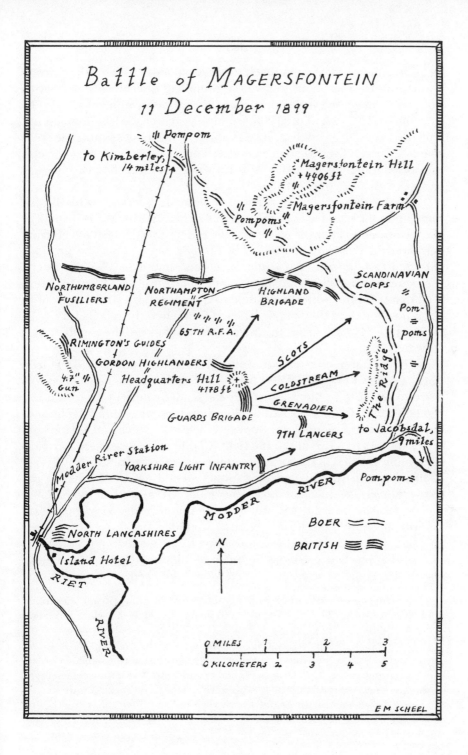

Battle of MAGERSFONTEIN
11 December 1899

to Kimberley, 14 miles

Pompom

Magersfontein Hill +4406 ft

Pompoms

Magersfontein Farm

NORTHUMBERLAND FUSILIERS

NORTHAMPTON REGIMENT

HIGHLAND BRIGADE

SCANDINAVIAN CORPS

Pom-poms

65TH R.F.A.

RIMINGTON'S GUIDES

GORDON HIGHLANDERS

Scots

4.7" Gun

Headquarters Hill 4178 ft

Coldstream

The Ridge

GUARDS BRIGADE

Grenadier

9TH LANCERS

to Jacobsdal, 9 miles

Pompoms

Modder River Station

YORKSHIRE LIGHT INFANTRY

MODDER   RIVER   Pompoms

BOER

BRITISH

NORTH LANCASHIRES

Island Hotel

N

RIET

RIVER

0 MILES 1 2 3
0 KILOMETERS 2 3 4 5

E M SCHEEL

in by first light, and he knew that his men could move faster in their closed formation. He was about to give the command to change from quarter column to extended order (five-pace interval between men) when they encountered a patch of prickly thorn bushes and he decided to wait until they had passed through it. The leading elements of his brigade were about 700 yards from the kopjes, and although neither he nor anyone else suspected it, he was only 400 yards from the Boer trenches when he was at last ready to deploy. At that moment disaster struck.

There exist a variety of versions of how the Boers knew the British were upon them and who gave the signal to fire. Among the British there were stories told after the battle of spies and traitors, lantern signals from farmhouses, that sort of thing, but nothing better than the previous afternoon's bombardment could have been found to alert the Boers. They were obviously waiting expectantly. One burgher, O. van Oostrun, said that trip wires with tin cans tied to them had been strung in front of their positions and they simply listened for them to be touched. Perhaps he was right. He was there. In any case, the massacre of the Highland lads now began.

The Boer musketry was rapid and, at such close range, deadly indeed for the massed brigade. When the firing began Wauchope stepped forward to see how far the Boer trenches extended and sent his cousin and aide-de-camp, Lieutenant Arthur Wauchope, running along the lines to find Lieutenant Colonel John Coode of the Black Watch and tell him and other officers to move out to the right. Coode valiantly tried to move his men but was killed in the attempt. So too was Lieutenant Colonel Gerald Goff of the Argylls. Lieutenant Colonel Gerald Hughes-Hallett of the Seaforths was the only battalion commander left untouched. When Lieutenant Wauchope made his way back, he found Andy Wauchope dead. Shortly after, he himself was seriously wounded.

Caught in a dense formation so close to the enemy's lines the Scots did not have a chance. Colour Sergeant McInnes of the Argyll and Sutherland Highlanders tried to describe what happened:

> The brigade seemed to stagger under the awful fire, but yet held their ground and did not break. The order was given to lie down, but in that close formation we were getting shot like sheep.
>
> I remember distinctly the 91st [Argylls] getting the order to move to the right, and we started moving in that direction when several contradictory orders rang out, some calling to "fix bayonets and charge" etc. Then, this seemed to me what happened—the Black Watch, who were in front, could stand it no longer, and were driven back on the Seaforths, who likewise started to shout "retire" and the next minute the brigade had lost all shape and were converted into a dismayed mob, running to seek cover anywhere and getting shot by the score as they did so.[1]

Another Highlander said, "When we started to extend they opened fire on us, and such a hailstorm of bullets I don't want to experience

again. It was seen that someone had blundered." A soldier in the Highland Light Infantry said, "What could we do? It was dark. The men did
not know where they were. Somebody shouted 'Retire!' and we did—
well, not a retire, but a stampede; 4,000 men like a flock of sheep running
for dear life." His commanding officer, Lieutenant Colonel Henry Kelham, who was only slightly wounded, was knocked down and trampled
on by his own men.

Not everyone panicked; there were brave men and brave actions.
Jimmy McKay, corporal piper of the Argylls, stood up and began to play
"The Campbells Are Coming." Several other pipers followed his example. Corporal John Shaul won a Victoria Cross by turning a group of men
around and leading them in an advance. William MacFarlan, adjutant of
the 2nd Black Watch, led a small group of men straight up the southeastern point of the hill, but the British artillery came into action and shells
from their own guns drove them down again. Lieutenant Ernest Cox of
the Seaforths also broke through with three or four men. All were killed.
Lieutenant H. E. M. Douglas and Lieutenant E. T. Inkson of the Royal
Army Medical Corps crawled about the battlefield administering aid to
the wounded, their valour earning them Victoria Crosses. Major William
Lambton, wounded, refused to allow himself to be carried from the field
for fear of attracting fire and endangering the bearers; he lay on the
ground for thirty-seven hours without food or water.

In addition to the frightened and the brave, there were the foolish.
A soldier of the Highland Light Infantry blundered about among his
prone and cursing comrades pursued by a blizzard of bullets bawling,
"Anyone seen my mess tin?"

Had he not in a crucial moment hesitated, Lieutenant Robert Wilson
of the Seaforths might have changed the outcome of the battle and
indeed the entire course of the war. He had found a hole in the Boer lines
and led some hundred Highlanders through it and around to the reverse
slope of the hill. He was headed for the crest, and if he had gained it, the
plunging fire he could have poured into the Boers' rear would almost
certainly have turned the tide of battle. But he and his soldiers were not
the only men on the slope.

The Boers had had a wet and uncomfortable night. Cronjé had tried
to sleep in the damp without success; in the dark of the early morning,
shortly after the Highlanders had begun their march, he had given up the
attempt and set off with six of his staff on a tour of inspection. Stumbling
around in the dark, they had lost their way so thoroughly that they were
still wandering about in the early dawn when they saw Lieutenant Wilson's Highlanders. Cronjé did not hesitate. "Schiet, kerels! Schiet!"
(Shoot, boys! Shoot!), he shouted. Throwing themselves behind rocks,
the seven opened a hot fire. Glory and victory sometimes hang by a
slender thread indeed. Had Wilson charged he would have gained the
crest (there were no other Boers on this side of the hill) and killed or
captured Piet Cronjé, a prize indeed. There were only seven Mausers

against a hundred Lee-Metfords, but so furiously did Cronjé and his aides fire that the Highlanders, when a charge would have gained them everything, stopped and sought cover. They returned the fire, but they had lost their chance. Several hundred yards back other troops, Seaforths and Black Watch, were hurriedly trying to join Wilson, but the Boers rushed to close the gap in their lines and give support to Cronjé and his band. Then British artillery opened up on the area. Assaulted on all sides, Wilson and his men fought gallantly until their ranks were reduced to thirty or forty survivors and they were forced to surrender.

Day broke bright, clear, and fresh after the night's storm, revealing the broken remains of the Highland Brigade strewn over the veld in front of the Boer positions. From time to time parties of men led by officers attempted to charge the trenches. One group of Black Watch managed to get within 150 yards before they were halted.

Over their kilts the Highlanders wore khaki aprons, but parts of their dark tartans showed up on the brown veld, often revealing their position. Again, as at the Modder River, the backs of their legs blistered as they lay in the sun. Not, however, the legs of Lieutenant Bertram Lang. Now twenty-one years old, he was destined not only to live through this battle but others as well and to be one of the very last surviving veterans of the war. Lang showed an early talent for survival: before the battle he pulled on a pair of long black woman's stockings with the feet cut off.

All attempts to rally the demoralised Highlanders, to get them off their stomachs, to get them moving forward, failed. As one Argyll said: "The men's hearts were broken at the start, and they were like children all day." Throughout the morning men who could not see the point of lying in the sun to be shot at all day crept back. Wauchope's cousin lay seriously wounded behind an anthill which only partially concealed him; he was wearing a bright new pair of gaiters which attracted the attention of the Boer marksmen, and he was several times hit in both legs, suffering injuries from which he never recovered.

At eleven o'clock in the morning the Gordons were thrown into the battle and charged through the prone Highland Brigade. They got as close to the Boer trenches as any, but in the end they joined the Black Watch on the ground, their gallantry wasted.

The Boers did not escape unscathed. One group of 50 Scandinavian volunteers, occupying an advanced outpost, was relentlessly pounded by Battery G, Royal Horse Artillery (which in this battle fired 1,250 rounds —the greatest expenditure of ammunition by one battery in the war). Then a charge by a group of Seaforths overwhelmed them. Forty-three were killed or seriously wounded in this action; only seven escaped.

On both sides the gunners took casualties, both from the enemy's guns and from musketry. Willie du Plessis of the staatsartillerie, visiting the battlefield sixty-four years later, still remembered: "If my gun position could talk it would tell you what I had to endure here." British gunners, too, had much to endure; at Magersfontein, as in other battles in the war, British artillerymen, fighting with inferior weapons but with splendid discipline and great gallantry, added to the laurels of their arm. Captain Henry Farrell, a gunner who had been shot through the left leg at Belmont and in the right leg at the Modder River, was still fighting his guns at Magersfontein.

It had not occurred to Methuen that the attack of the Highland Brigade would fail. Although he had the Guards in reserve, they were 3 miles back and he had no alternative plan. He simply left the Highlanders stretched out on the veld in front of the Boer lines and sent word that they were to hang on where they were for the rest of the day, hoping that the Boers would quietly go away when night fell as they had done on the Modder River. The balloon was sent aloft, now that it was too late, and the Boer positions, already discovered the hard way, were revealed.

By midday the battle appeared to be a stalemate all along the length of the battlefield. About 1:30 P.M. on the right of the line the commando from Fricksburg made a gallant effort to secure a position from which they could enfilade the Highlanders. Lieutenant Colonel Hughes-Hallett ordered two companies to pull back and swing around to meet the attack. Officers, seeing the retrograde movement and unaware of Methuen's order to hang on until dark, assumed that a general retirement had been ordered. The movement communicated itself from one end of the line to the other, and soon the whole front of the brigade rose up and made for the rear. Lieutenant Colonel Henry Kelham said later: "I saw the whole extended line rise up and slowly retire, so deliberately that I felt sure it was the result of an order."

The retreat began in an orderly fashion. Lieutenant Colonel Forbes Macbean, now in command of the 1st Gordons, walked leisurely back, turning now and then to look at the enemy while adjusting his monocle. At least one of the soldiers with him was impressed by his imperturbability: "A shell burst just behind us and the base went hurtling along the ground between him and me, and I tried to look as if I didn't mind."[2] But the coolness of their officers could not hold the troops steady in the ferocious fire poured into them by the Boers, who stood up in their trenches the better to shoot as the Highlanders rose and turned their backs. What began as an orderly retreat soon turned into a rout.

On a hill in the rear the correspondent from the *Morning Post* watched: "Back they came in a wave that no officer could stop. . . . One could see them swarming like bees over the veldt till they were almost out of range, and the guns left out in the open with no one to support them. It was, perhaps, the most unpleasant sight that a British soldier of today has ever beheld."[3]

More Highlanders were killed and wounded in this retreat than had been shot down in the attack.

As soon as the officers discovered that no retirement had been ordered, they tried desperately to rally their men. Just out of rifle range rallying points were established; water carts were ordered up and the parched men clustered around them. It was then that the Boer field guns, three Krupps which had been strangely silent all day, opened fire, their targets the men swarming about the water carts. The Highlanders fled in a second retreat still further to the rear. Scotland's pride, the flower of British infantry, was a demoralized mob.

Of the 4,000 men who had been on the field, only a portion remained, and most of these were stretched flat on the ground; some, as at the Modder River, had fallen asleep, and there were isolated groups of men who had rightly reasoned that it was more dangerous to leave than to stay. One small group of the Black Watch in an advanced position, with only

THE BATTLE AT MAGERSFONTEIN.

three men unwounded, fought on until the Boers, impressed with their fortitude, called out to them that if they would cease firing they would not be fired on and, finally, at sunset, called out again that if they left behind their arms and ammunition they could walk back to their lines in safety.

In another part of the line, young Frederick Pohl noticed among the dead and wounded left behind one man who still clutched his rifle with both hands. Pohl had been fighting long enough to be cautious. He worked his way around to the right of the corpse and called "Hands up!" The "dead man" released his rifle, sat up, and to Pohl's surprise turned to a lifeless comrade beside him and said, "Get up, Tom, the game's up."

Behind the British lines Dr. Nathan Rutherford came upon a young Highlander sans helmet, rifle, and accoutrements sitting motionless on an anthill. He looked up at the doctor in a daze and said dully, "All the battalion is wiped out, and all the officers killed."

James Barnes, a newspaper correspondent well in the rear, heard the firing die down and thought that the battle was over and that it would be safe for him to go forward; he assumed the British had won. He was soon disillusioned:

> The first man I met was a wounded Highlander. . . . his face wore a set, puzzled expression, and now and then he glanced back over his shoulder. I spoke to him, but he did not reply, and kept on. And now I could see them swarming back, some limping, some running, others dodging from bush to ant-hill, and almost all occasionally looking back over their shoulders. . . . Something had gone wrong! . . . I stopped a bare headed Seaforth and asked him.
>
> "We're a' that's left," he said, including perhaps twenty men near him with a sweep of his hand. . . .[4]

The British howitzers and naval guns dropped shells on the Boers in a desultory fashion; from time to time a rifle cracked; the Highlanders were re-formed well to the rear, but no further attacks were ordered.

At dawn the next morning Colvile repaired to Methuen's headquarters and found the general discouraged and inclined to retreat. Colvile did his best to dissuade him and Methuen seemed to waver, but an hour later, at a council of war, most of his staff came out in favour of retirement: both ammunition and water were in short supply, and the Highlanders were in a state of shock. In these terms retirement seemed the wisest course; they had no way of knowing that the Boers were thirsty too and that their supply of rifle ammunition was so low that they could not have sustained another day of hard fighting.

While Methuen and his officers debated, the Guards were brought up and exchanged shots with the Boers, but about the middle of the morning, before any orders were given, the firing died down of itself and then ceased. A rumour spread along the front that an armistice had been arranged to allow the dead and wounded to be collected. Nothing of the sort had happened, but from both sides ambulances, doctors, and bearers, Boers and Britons, started moving out onto the silent battlefield.

As sometimes happens, orders followed rumours; the fight was over, the British drew back, and began their retreat to the Modder. Their casualties amounted to approximately 7 percent of Methuen's force: 23 officers and 182 men killed; 45 officers and 645 men wounded; 76 men were missing or prisoners. Total British casualties: 971. The Highlanders suffered the worst, of course; the Highland Brigade lost more than a quarter of its officers. For the Black Watch in particular the battle was a catastrophe: 17 out of 22 officers and 338 out of 943 men had fallen. Not since the regiment had fought the French at Ticonderoga in 1757 had it taken such casualties. Total Boer losses were about 250 killed and wounded.

The Highlanders' feelings were best expressed by one Black Watch soldier who declared that his regiment had been "led into a butcher's shop and bloody well left there." An anonymous Black Watch private wrote:

> Tell you the tale of the battle, well, there's not much to tell;
> Nine hundred men went to the slaughter, and nigh four hundred fell.
> Wire and Mauser fire, thirst, and a burning sun
> Knocked us down by hundreds ere the day was done.

Although it was clearly Wauchope's fault that the brigade had not extended when it should have, the Highlanders refused to blame their dead commander. It was Methuen who had been responsible, they said: it was he who had ordered them to attack in quarter columns in spite of Wauchope's protests; the rumour spread that Wauchope himself had fastened the blame on Methuen with his dying words. Lieutenant Lang wrote home: "Everyone here is furious with Methuen for his bad generalship."

When the news of the disaster reached Scotland there was general mourning, and in Edinburgh all dances were cancelled. Conan Doyle said that "it may be doubted if any single battle has ever put so many families of high and low into mourning from the Tweed to the Caithness shore."[5] Wauchope was buried in a small private burial ground at nearby Majestfontein; a piper played "Lochaber No More" over his grave.

For long afterwards the controversy raged over who had been responsible for the fiasco. Although Methuen in his official dispatch had stated, "I attach no blame to this splendid brigade," he clearly felt that the Highlanders had let him down.

While no Highlander was willing to admit that the conduct of his own regiment had been in any way blameworthy, most were willing to concede that other Highland regiments had crumpled. Lieutenant Colonel Kelham of the Highland Light Infantry said, "The troops in front of us [that is, the Black Watch, Seaforths, and Argylls] were thrown into complete disorder." An Argyll and Sutherland officer, referring to those in front of his regiment (the Black Watch and the Seaforths), said, "They turned and bolted." A Seaforth sergeant said, "The Black Watch, who were in front, could stand it no longer and were driven back on the Seaforths, throwing them into confusion." The Black Watch, however, refused to take any blame. One officer said in the face of all the contrary evidence: "The Black Watch never retired. . . . What other regiments did I only know from hearsay." And Captain Charles Stewart of the same regiment wrote: "The Black Watch behaved as they should, I think, but I have heard some queer stories of other regiments." The newspapers, for the most part, were kind: the *Daily News* said, "All that mortal man could do the Scots did. They tried, they failed, they fell, and there is nothing left now but to mourn for them and avenge them."

The Scotsmen in their kilts were curiosities to the Boers. F. S. ("Frikkie") Badenhorst wrote to his wife Allie: "We had a great battle. . . . A lot of men have been brought in as prisoners: they are called 'Highlanders' or mountain Scotch. They wear a very strange dress. A yellow jacket with a short skirt above the knee, and long stockings. The skirt is made of Scotch stuff, with some bears' tails sewn on their front."[6]

The Boers clearly owed their victory to the inspired plan of Koos de la Rey, but on the day of the battle he had disappeared. Perhaps it was still too soon after the death of his son for him to face another fight; more probably, he could not stand the thought of serving in another battle under Cronjé. It is not clear exactly where he was on 11 December, but it appears that he spent the day in the vicinity of Kimberley.

For the British, Magersfontein was not only a major defeat but the retreat of Methuen to the Modder meant that Kimberley and Mafeking could not be relieved, at least not in the immediate future. Britons at home found news from the front sad reading indeed, for in addition to Methuen's defeat there was also the extraordinary event which had taken place in another part of Cape Colony only twenty-four hours earlier when General Gatacre attacked the Boers at Stormberg.

14

STORMBERG JUNCTION

The Boers had begun the war by invading the territory of their neighbours in three places: over the Drakensberg range into Natal; across their western frontiers into Bechuanaland and Griqualand West; and south into north central Cape Colony, striking at the heartland of Britain's oldest and most populous South African colony. It was this third thrust which, although the weakest, put fear into the heart of Alfred Milner, who anticipated a large-scale rebellion on the part of the Afrikaner colonists there who, when they spoke of "our victories," usually meant Boer victories.

The invaders moved south following the two railway lines which crossed the Orange River at Bethulie and at Norval's Pont. To cope with these threats the British divided this theatre of war into two parts: the western commanded by French (who had left Ladysmith on the last train) and the eastern by Lieutenant General Sir William Gatacre. In Buller's original plan Gatacre was to have commanded a division, but units had been withdrawn to fight in Natal, and by 1 December 1899 his command consisted of two infantry battalions, 300 mounted infantry, and 1,000 men in local corps such as the Cape Mounted Rifles, Brabant's Horse, and the Cape Police—in all, about 3,000 men. Although Buller had with unnecessary haste ordered the withdrawal of Gatacre's troops from Stormberg in early November, the Boers had not occupied it until three weeks later. It was an important railway junction, and with its occupation by the enemy Gatacre's lateral railway communications with French were severed. When on 5 December Gatacre was reinforced by a battalion of the Royal Scots and two batteries of field artillery, he decided to attack Stormberg Junction.

Sir William Gatacre (1843–1905) was a small, spare man with a bristling moustache on what Conan Doyle described as "a gaunt Don-Quixote face." Now aged fifty-six, he weighed 142 pounds, exactly his weight as a twenty-year-old subaltern in India. He was inordinately proud of this, for he made a fetish of physical fitness, never drank or smoked, and delighted in performing feats of physical endurance. G. W. Steevens said of him that "his body was all steel wire" and Major (later Lieutenant General) Edward Ellis called him "the hardest man I ever met." Winston Churchill described him as "the exhausted victim of his own vitality." Gatacre was not only hard on himself, but hard on his men as well, and he had no patience with those whose energy and endurance did not approach his own. His men called him "General Back-acher." He was a martinet who did all things in strict accordance with army regulations, insisting that those under him do likewise, and as his second wife charmingly phrased it, "He never shrank from the disagreeable duty of rebuke."[1]

He had been commissioned at eighteen, but had had as a young man no opportunity to distinguish himself in action; as yet, his only claim to fame was that he, who took so little interest in food, was the inventor of a mess tin. Of another distinction he was less proud: he was divorced. After fifteen years of marriage his wife had gone off with another man. He was then with the Bombay army at Poona, and it was at about this time that he was bitten by a jackal. Whether as a result of his experiences with his wife or the jackal, Gatacre's mind became unhinged; he complained that howling jackals kept him awake and in his terror had all the windows of his bungalow fitted out with bars to keep them from leaping in. But that had been eight or nine years ago. Since then he had remarried (at age fifty-two); commanded a brigade in the relief of Chitral, where he distinguished himself by riding standing in his stirrups because of a boil on his buttocks; and commanded another brigade in Kitchener's army in the Sudan, where his efforts earned him a knighthood (KCB).

Stormberg is the name given to the great Drakensberg range in this part of Cape Colony. Bleak and inhospitable, it long resisted the advances of civilisation. Bushmen retreated here, and their splendid artistry can still be seen on the walls of the many caves and on the rock faces of the cliffs. There had been lions in the area less than fifty years before; it was now the haunt of hyenas, lynxes, baboons, and, superstition said, of unknown monsters and legendary creatures. The only town actually located in the Stormberg range was Molteno, a small village that contained more loyalists than did most of the towns in this area. Stormberg, less than 10 miles away, was described by Steevens as a "little junction station. A platform with dining-room and telegraph office, a few corrugated iron sheds."[2]

Gatacre planned to launch a surprise attack on the Boers ensconced in the hills around Stormberg by bringing his troops up as far as Molteno by train in the afternoon and then making a night march to the Boer positions. That his troops after all this movement and lack of sleep might not be very fresh for an attack on stoutly defended hills the following morning did not seem to have occurred to him. The scheme required good timing, and of course it was essential that the troops not get lost in the dark. There seemed little chance that they would, for he planned to follow a road that ran beside the railway tracks; there would be moonlight in the early hours of the night; and he would take local guides.

The troops available were in scattered locations, but he managed to assemble at Molteno the Northumberland Fusiliers, the Irish Rifles, two batteries of field artillery, and a hotchpotch of mounted infantry, engineers, Cape Police, and a field hospital—about 2,700 men, not many for the size of the task. He was to have had 400 additional troops, four more guns, and a Maxim, which were stationed at Pen Hoek, but the telegraph clerk to whom the order was given forgot to transmit the message.

Gatacre and his staff arrived in Molteno on the afternoon of 9 December, and there he received a report that the Boers had erected wire entanglements in front of the positions he planned to attack. The report was false, but it worried him and he changed his plans. Three roads led north from Molteno. Instead of the centre one beside the railway track which he had intended to use, he decided to take the west road and make a flank attack. The night march would be a few miles longer, but this hardly worried Gatacre. There was also some danger of losing the way, for they would have to turn off the road near their objective, but Sergeant W. S. Morgan and four other Cape Police who had been selected as

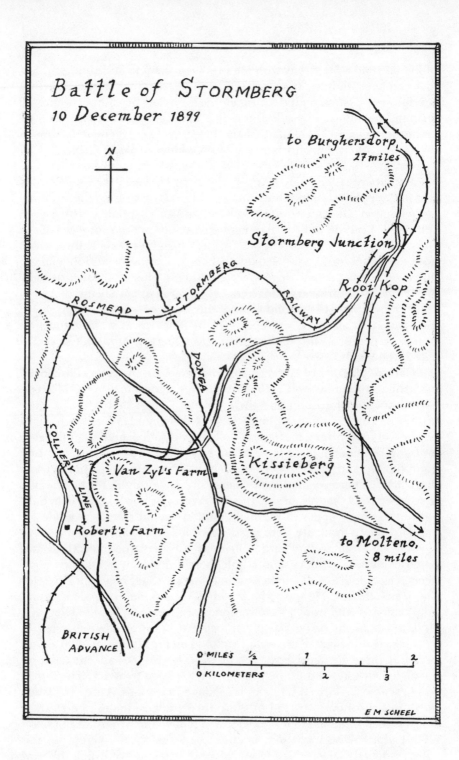

Battle of STORMBERG
10 December 1899

N

to Burghersdorp,
27 miles

Stormberg Junction

Rooi Kop

ROSMEAD — STORMBERG RAILWAY

DONGA

COLLIERY LINE

Van Zyl's Farm

Kissieberg

Robert's Farm

to Molteno,
8 miles

BRITISH
ADVANCE

0 MILES ½ 1 2
0 KILOMETERS 2 3

E M SCHEEL

guides assured him that they knew every inch of the ground.

As the trains arrived packed with sweating, dusty soldiers, Molteno schoolboys raided their mothers' kitchens for tidbits to exchange for bully beef and army biscuits—and the soldiers were eager to trade. No one in town had ever seen so many men before, and everyone watched with interest as the troops formed up in the dusty streets and marched past the Central Hotel and Mrs. Annie Rörich's boarding house. Gatacre had planned to leave at 7:15 P.M., but the troops from Pen Hoek, who had not received their orders, naturally failed to arrive, and the last troop-carrying train was late, not pulling in until 8:30 P.M. because the line had been blocked by a trainload of mules. The troops, who had been up since 4:00 A.M. and had spent most of the day standing around on railway platforms or sitting in open trucks under the African sun, were tired before they started out on their long night march at 9:15 that evening. The Irish Rifles, who led the way, were ordered to march with fixed bayonets, a wicked, unnecessary order which forced a man to carry his rifle at an awkward and tiring angle and forbade the easing of the strain by frequent shifts of position.

When after a long march the head of the column struck a railway track, a branch line that was known to be 2 miles beyond the planned turnoff for their objective, it was obvious that the guides had missed the turn. It was by this time past midnight and the moon had set. Gatacre called a halt at a nearby farm and gave his men an hour's rest while he conferred with his guides, who, reluctant to admit their mistake, insisted that they had simply avoided some wire and a bad piece of track and were only a mile and a half from the enemy's positions. In actual fact, they were at this moment sitting midway between two Boer forces.

Gatacre's column was not the only British force that was lost. There was also a collection of odds and ends, including the field hospital, the bearer company, and the Maxim of the Irish Rifles, all led by Colonel John Edge, RAMC, who had been late in starting and had not been informed of the change of route. Marching along the centre road, they encountered three journalists on their way back from an unsuccessful attempt to find Gatacre. Assured that Gatacre was nowhere along the road he was following, the perplexed Edge decided to wait where he was while the journalists rode on to Molteno to find out what he ought to do. But not even Colonel Wallscourt Waters, Gatacre's chief intelligence officer, left in charge in Molteno, had been informed of the changed plan. Wakened from a sound sleep, he assured them that all was well; Edge was certainly on the right road. Galloping back with all speed, they met Edge, who, tired of waiting, had turned back. Wearily he turned his column around and started once more down the road. The column was still plodding along at 2:30 A.M. when noises of men and wagons in the darkness to their left proved to be five policemen and two mule wagons, one of which carried the reserve ammunition of the Northumberland Fusiliers. They, too, were lost. Edge now wisely decided to wait where he was until dawn. Shortly, two of Gatacre's staff officers, who had also lost their way, joined them. At this point a considerable portion of Gatacre's force was scattered and all—including Gatacre—were lost. So thoroughly confused was he that a month after the battle a sketch map he drew to accompany his dispatch showed that even then he had no idea of where he had been.

About 2 A.M. he led his men out of the barnyard. They recrossed the railway tracks of the branch line and moved eastward along a miserable track into a dark mass of hills. Gatacre was under the impression that he was approaching Stormberg from the northwest; many of his regimental officers thought they were approaching from the southeast. All were wrong. Approaching from the southwest, the column arrived—it was 3:45 A.M.—at the exact point Gatacre had wanted to reach and just at the time, shortly before dawn, he wanted to be there. Above him on his right were the heights he had wanted to seize in order to dominate the Boer position. The trouble was that he not only did not know where he was, but, worse, he thought he knew—and he thought he was several miles away from where he wanted to be. They marched on.

Dawn found the weary infantry stumbling along in column of fours, the artillery and mounted troops behind, following a rough track across Louis Jacobus van Zyl's farm. Not a single scout had been sent out. The unsuspecting Boers were only a few hundred yards away, and the unsuspecting British were marching straight for the laager of Commandant Jan Hendrik Olivier.

In the column's wake were a number of exhausted soldiers who had dropped behind, and some of these were tempted by the sight of Mr. Van Zyl's sheep. The prospect of roast mutton seemed infinitely more appealing than trying to keep up with General Back-acher, who hardly seemed to know where he was going anyway. Van Zyl, astonished to see soldiers tramping across his fields so early in the morning, strolled out to see what they were doing and found, to his horror, that they were killing his pregnant ewes. He went to get his gun.

On the other side of the kopje on Gatacre's right lay a Boer outpost, 60 men and a Krupp gun under Hans Swanepoel. At about 4:30 A.M. one of the burghers, yielding to his bowels' commands, stumbled sleepily away from camp to the other side of the hill. His trousers were lowered and he was about to squat when he saw below him in the early morning light the glint of Gatacre's bayonets. Grabbing up his trousers, he ran for camp yelling, "Die kakies! Die kakies!" Each man seized his rifle and ran to the top of the hill. The young were fastest, and Hendrik Coetzee, a teen-aged boy who had left his school at Wellington in Cape Colony to join a commando, fired the first shot. He was quickly joined by the others and, 60 against 2,000, they poured a hot fire into Gatacre's column. The sound of their musketry gave the alarm to all the other Boers in the area.

At the first shot Gatacre ordered the Irish Rifles to deploy and seize a detached kopje on the left. Three companies got the order right; the rest, together with the Northumberland Fusiliers, went storming up the steepest and most rugged side of a mountain on the left. Gatacre was left sitting on his horse with no more infantry to command, the battle already almost out of his hands. There was still the artillery, of course, and he directed that the guns come up and into action. By the time Lieutenant Colonel Henry Eagar and a handful of the Irish Rifles had arduously scrambled up almost to the crest of the mountain, Gatacre's gunners, the rising sun in their eyes, shelled them. Several rounds of shrapnel burst directly over their heads: Eagar and six others were wounded and the rest were effectively driven back down the slopes.

Meanwhile, in the rear, an angry farmer Van Zyl started his own battle: he opened fire on the soldiers slaughtering his ewes.

Gatacre's men, subjected to a galling fire from several points, bewildered by an almost invisible enemy sheltering behind rocks, nevertheless returned the fire, and some of their bullets took effect. Field Cornet Harm Olivier, father of twenty children and a prosperous farmer from the Burgersdorp district, was there in the fight with three of his sons. A British bullet pierced his eye.

The entire battle lasted scarcely an hour and a half. Gatacre, having clumsily stuck his hand into a hornets' nest and been badly stung, then tried to withdraw it and flee. He ordered his remaining men recalled and began his retreat. No longer in formations, the infantry, exhausted and demoralised, staggered away. One of the guns became inextricably stuck in the mud on Van Zyl's farm and was abandoned. Its breech block was first removed, a piece of foresight which should have rendered the gun useless to its captors, but it was tossed into an ammunition wagon which in turn bogged down and the Boers were able to assemble a fine British gun.

Now was certainly the time for a Boer counterattack on Gatacre's exhausted and disheartened men. Probably 300 stout burghers could have swept up the lot. In fact, their leaders had a quarrel about this, but it was, after all, Sunday, and besides, the burghers were impatient to collect the loot on the battlefield; Gatacre was allowed to limp back unmolested to Molteno.

The British gone, the Boers came down onto the battlefield to collect prisoners and loot, to bury the dead and tend the wounded. When Jacobus Petrus Bosman, a young schoolteacher, found one soldier, both legs shattered, sitting with his back to an anthill smoking a cigarette, he was struck with the feeling of comradeship that so often takes over after a battle: "Suddenly we were enemies no more, but friends, human beings in the fullest sense. Would I have been so calm and collected in such a maimed condition?"[3]

In one part of the field men were startled to hear a single shot ring out. A soldier had ended the agony of a friend shot through the kidney by putting a bullet through his head.

About eleven o'clock in the morning the wreck of Gatacre's little army began to stumble, footsore, hot, thirsty, hungry, and dispirited into Molteno; it was not until late in the day that the last stragglers arrived.

Gatacre was disheartened. But he had yet to learn the worst: the casualty report was a stunning blow. He was seen sobbing in the waiting room of the Molteno railway station after it was delivered to him: more than 700 casualties, about one-third of his entire force. What had become of all these men? Had it really been such a ferocious battle? Hardly. Only later did he learn the embarrassing, shameful, the near-incredible truth: only 29 of his men had been killed and 57 wounded; the rest—633 officers and men—had been left behind.[4] Forgotten. Receiving no order to retreat, they had stayed and had been abandoned on the sides of the kopjes —and Gatacre had not missed them.

Sometime that morning, when the abandoned men discovered that they were alone, that their general had marched off and left them, they raised white flags and quietly surrendered; Commandant Floris du Plooy and his Bethulie burghers rounded them up.

The Boer force that routed Gatacre numbered no more than 800 men. Their losses were 6 killed and 27 wounded. After spending the morning burying, bandaging, looting, and rounding up prisoners, they held a thanksgiving service. Then, to commemorate their victory, each man took a stone and put it on a pile, topping it with a sign reading MET GOD VOOR VRYHEID (With God for Freedom). It had been the first battle for most; some resolved it would be their last. As battles go, it had not been particularly bloody, but there were those who, seeing the dead and wounded, found that war was not to their taste and decided to go back to their farms and families.

Three days after the battle Gatacre brought himself to tell his wife about it. It was, he said,

a most lamentable failure, and yet within an ace of being the success I anticipated. . . . The fault was mine, and I was responsible of course. I went rather against my better judgement in not resting the night at Molteno, but I was tempted by the shortness of the distance and the certainty of success. It was so near being a brilliant success.[5]

He had to tell Buller, of course, and he telegraphed a report. Buller replied: "I think you were quite right to try the night attack and hope better luck next time."

It was three months before the British occupied Stormberg, and by that time the Boers had simply abandoned it.

One of Louis van Zyl's Coloured workers informed on him, and he was arrested, tried, and acquitted. In a farming community no one was willing to condemn a man for defending his sheep. Van Zyl's reputation among his Afrikaner neighbours as the man who had defied the might of the British Empire to save his pregnant ewes grew with the years, the story losing nothing in the telling and the number of soldiers he was said to have shot rising to seven.

15

BEFORE COLENSO

Buller did not remain long in Cape Town. He diverted more and more troops to Natal, then decided that this sector required his personal attention. Leaving most of his staff behind, and without bothering to tell Milner, he set off with only his military secretary and a few aides-de-camp, arriving at Pietermaritzburg, the capital of the colony, on 25 November.

Buller had no intention of assuming personal command of the forces in Natal. He merely wanted to inspect the situation, give some advice, and straighten out a few matters; he intended to return to Cape Town in two or three weeks. At this time Methuen appeared to be progressing well: he had won the battle of Belmont and that very day he had won another victory at Enslin; he was expected to relieve Kimberley within a few days. General French in north central Cape Colony was pushing out cavalry patrols from Naauwpoort; Gatacre too was moving troops north from Queenstown and was planning his attack on Stormberg. Buller could feel confident that he had done the right thing in coming, for it was important, he thought, that Ladysmith be relieved before he could revert to his original plan of a triumphal march north from Cape Colony through the Orange Free State into the Transvaal. He anticipated some hard fighting in Natal, but with the large force now at hand success seemed certain.

The army for the relief of Ladysmith was assembling at Frere and Estcourt, and John Atkins watched as "along all the road north towards Frere moved one long, slow line of cavalry, troops, guns, waggons, teams of sixteen oxen, teams of mules ten-in-hand (often enough ten-out-of-hand), equipment, the pantries and the kitchens of an army, bakers, cooks, farriers, followers of all sorts, doctors, bearers, ambulance waggons—the wonderful dusty spectacle of an army moving."[1] It was an army which was said to be, and probably was, the finest force Britain had put in the field since the Crimean War nearly fifty years before.

General Cornelius Francis Clery (1838–1926) was in command in Natal. The son of an Irish wine merchant, Clery was a graduate of Sandhurst and the Staff College, and although he had seen action in the Zulu War and in Egypt and the Sudan, he had always been on the staff and had never before held a command. More of a student of war than a warrior, he had been a professor of tactics at Sandhurst and had served as commandant of the Staff College. For thirty years his book *Minor Tactics* had been a text in the British army. He was a bachelor and a dandy, dressing with fastidious care, his clothes well cut, his figure elegant. In the Sudan campaign, when the other officers adopted the new-fashioned, drab khaki, he habitually wore scarlet jackets and soft boots with gold spurs, although he forwent the traditional tight cavalry breeches; they galled his varicose veins. His whiskers were elaborate and he dyed them. Bennett Burleigh once heard a soldier describe him: "Oh, you can't mistake him at all—thin, queer-looking bloke with a puzzle beard and blue whiskers."

While Clery took charge of the troops assembling at Frere, Buller busied himself for the next ten days with the supply, transport, and medical arrangements at Pietermaritzburg. He was very good at this work. No Victorian general was more solicitous for the welfare of his troops than Buller. Unlike most, he personally assured himself that the facilities for the care of the sick and wounded were the best that could be had, and he took a special interest in the medical arrangements for hospital trains (then an innovation) and hospital ships. Dr. Frederick Treves, a consulting surgeon, later testified to his solicitude: "No engagement was commenced without the medical staff getting a message from Headquarters to prepare for the number of cases expected, and General Buller was full of anxiety as to how the sick were to be accommodated."[2]

He tried to give every soldier at least one hot meal a day, and he made an effort to see that they had fresh meat and vegetables. He established Field Force Canteens, the first attempt to make available to soldiers in the field small necessities and luxuries. Some felt that Buller coddled his men and that too much emphasis was placed on supplies. Major W. R. Birdwood said: "It is the exact opposite of the Crimea where they starved. Here troops are if anything overfed and the generals are bound hand and foot by their supply columns."[3]

Buller was, however, the best-liked general in South Africa. John Atkins noted the magical effect of his presence on the morale of the troops when on 5 December he moved up to Frere:

> The notion of advancing is no doubt something, but the arrival of Sir Redvers Buller is almost everything. I have never seen troops re-tempered like this by one man since I saw the extraordinary change which came over the American army on the sudden arrival of General Miles before Santiago.[4]

Three days after Buller's arrival at Frere the railway bridge there, which had been damaged, was repaired and all was ready for the advance to Ladysmith. There were now 18,000 men assembled—four brigades of infantry, a brigade of mounted troops, five batteries of field artillery, and some large naval guns—besides about 2,500 men on the line of communications. Buller, unable to confine himself to the role of adviser, now took direct personal charge, although Clery was not superseded and the curious fiction was maintained that Buller was merely visiting the front; all orders were issued over Clery's signature even though all knew that Buller was actually in command.

Between Buller's army and White's beleaguered men were the Boers led by Louis Botha, entrenched in unknown strength along 7 miles of kopjes north of the Tugela River 12 miles south of Ladysmith. The small settlement of Colenso—a dozen tin-roofed houses, a railway station, and a goods shed—was on the south side of the Tugela (the name means "the terrible one"), where lay open plain with only slight folds in the terrain. It was over this flat, open grassland that Buller now began to manoeuvre his army, watched by the hidden Boers on their kopjes across the river. It was not clear what Buller intended to do, and probably he himself was not entirely certain. Originally he had planned to make a wide flanking movement around the Colenso kopjes. On 12 December he telegraphed Lansdowne that "a direct assault upon the enemy's position at Colenso and north of it would be too costly," but on the same day he ordered a brigade of infantry under Major General Geoffrey Barton with six 12-pounders and two 4.7-inch naval guns to move up to within 7,000 yards of Colenso. The next day two infantry brigades moved up and the naval guns opened fire on the Boer positions, first from 10,000 yards and then from 7,000 yards. The Boers, under strict orders to conceal their positions until the British infantry advanced to the river, did not reply.

By heliograph Buller informed White that he would attack on the 17th, and White accordingly began preparations for a sally in some force to assist him. On the morning of 14 December Buller's guns moved to within 4,000 yards of Colenso and began a day-long bombardment of the kopjes across the river and of Hlangwane (pronounced shlang-wahn-ee), a dominant height south and east of the river. Clouds of green-yellow lyddite smoke hung over the hills, spurts of red dust rising where shells struck, but of the enemy there was not a sign. Watching intently through their glasses, Buller and his officers were unable to see what effect, if any, the bombardment was producing. They seemed to be shelling an empty landscape. Some began to wonder if there were any Boers there at all. Buller, too, may have had some doubts, but that evening he called together his brigade commanders to announce that they would attack the Boer positions at Colenso in the morning.

Why Buller told the secretary for war that an attack on Colenso would be too costly to be considered, then reversed himself and helioed White that he would attack on the 17th, and finally and abruptly, without informing either Lansdowne or White of his change in plans, decided to attack on the 15th is an enigma—one among several connected with Buller's strategy. He had received no new intelligence of the enemy that could have accounted for such drastic changes. The news of the defeats of Gatacre and then Methuen had come to him, stunning blows which may have made a quick, decisive victory seem more desirable than a time-consuming flanking movement, and perhaps the studied silence of the Boers under his bombardment changed his estimate of their strength. The plan of battle which he set before his brigade commanders was essentially a three-pronged frontal attack. Major General Arthur Fitzroy Hart was to lead his brigade in an attack on the left, where there was believed to be a drift; Major General Henry Hildyard's brigade was to attack the centre of the line, straight down the railway tracks through Colenso; the brigades of Generals N. G. Lyttelton and Geoffrey Barton were to be held in reserve. Hlangwane was to be attacked by Lord Dundonald's mounted brigade.

The orders for the attack, signed by Clery, were not issued until 10 P.M. and could not have been digested by the brigade commanders and their staffs before midnight. The orders were far from clear, and the objectives of the attacking brigades were vague. As to where the Boers were located, the brigade commanders were told only that "the enemy is entrenched in the kopjes north of Colenso bridge." Hart was ordered to cross the "bridle drift immediately to the west of the junction of the Doornkop spruit and the Tugela," but there were two spruits (streams) here, and both were incorrectly marked on the map. Hildyard was ordered to march on "the iron bridge," but there were two iron bridges, one for the road to the west of the village and another for the railway north of Colenso.

General Lyttelton, one of the brigade commanders, later complained that there had been "no proper reconnoitering of the ground, no certain information as to any ford by which to cross the river, no proper artillery preparation, no satisfactory targets for the artillery, no realization of the importance of Hlangwane."

Of all Lyttelton's list, the last, the failure of Buller and his staff to grasp the importance of Hlangwane, is by far the most baffling. Standing 3,616 feet high, the most prominent feature in the landscape, it so clearly controlled the surrounding terrain that the youngest lieutenant from Sandhurst ought to have easily seen that wherever in the vicinity the Boers were entrenched it was vital to seize Hlangwane if they were to be dislodged. And it was south of the Tugela, so that it was not even necessary to cross the river to reach it. Buller seems to have known what ought to have been done once the hill was captured, for he told Dundonald to try to take a position on it from which he could "enfilade the kopjes north of the iron bridge," yet he had told Lansdowne that "its possession did not in any way assist the crossing." It would appear that in Buller's mind Dundonald's part in the battle was simply to create a diversion from the main attacks of Hart and Hildyard, although why mounted troops were used to attack a precipitous hill when two spare infantry brigades were available is unfathomable.

That Buller did not see the importance of Hlangwane is inexplicable; that his brigade commanders and Clery, the expert on minor tactics, all failed to grasp the tactical significance of this commanding height can be attributed only to their awe of Buller's reputation. Although Hlangwane's importance became obvious to all later—nine weeks and 3,205 casualties later—it would seem that none of these generals offered any objections when Buller explained his battle plans at the 14 December meeting: no one pointed out the absolute necessity of securing Hlangwane, and no one questioned the wisdom of sending a thousand horsemen and a battery to attack it. There may have been some less senior officers with doubts, however, for at the conclusion of the meeting one staff officer was heard to murmur, "And may the Lord have mercy on our souls."

Louis Botha (his name pronounced as in French) was born near Greytown in Natal in 1862, the seventh of thirteen children, and was taken by his parents to the Orange Free State when he was five. He had little formal education, perhaps no more than three years, plus what could be acquired from itinerant Dutch tutors who travelled the veld in this era. He was twenty-one when, after the death of his father, he and a younger brother set off with an ox wagon for northern Natal. There he attached himself to Lucas Meyer, who in the tradition of the voortrekkers, established De Nieuw Republiek (The New Republic).

In 1886, at the age of twenty-four, he married Annie Emmet, a schoolteacher of Irish descent who spoke little Afrikaans; Botha spoke little English. Perhaps they communicated through music, for she was said to be a fine musician and he played the accordian. Botha was a good farmer and he prospered, eventually owning 16,000 acres spread over several farms. The New Republic soon became part of the Transvaal, and in 1898 he was elected to its volksraad, representing Vryheid. In the vote on going to war, he abstained.

Louis Botha was a natural politician, happiest with people around him. Although he possessed a brilliant mind, the Bible and a biography of Abraham Lincoln were the only books he is known to have read. People, not books, interested him, and with consummate tact, patience, courtesy, and charm he managed them, for his personal magnetism was hard to resist. Jan Smuts said that he had "an intuitive power of understanding and appreciating men which was very rare."[5] He had feelings that were easily wounded, he could not stand criticism, and he felt deeply; tears came easily to his eyes.

Tielman Johannes de Villiers Roos (1875–1935), who was acting as a correspondent for Reuters (which maintained correspondents on both sides of the lines), was at Colenso and described Botha's headquarters and the conditions in which he (and most Boer generals) worked:

General Botha's tent at Colenso was an ordinary bell affair captured at Dundee. In this there was a convertible stretcher and chair, generally occupied by the general. In front of this was a packing case serving as a table. . . . Botha being a young man with a becoming reverence for age, always rises when a white haired burgher enters and gives him the stretcher chair, while he literally sits at his feet on the ground. . . . Burghers drop into the tent all day long to hear the news or bring reports. The general has no private life. He eats, drinks and sleeps before a coming and going procession. Reports are received and dispatches dictated in the presence of a dozen chance visitors.[6]

Botha was to prove himself a master strategist and a fine tactician, but at Colenso he was preparing to fight his first battle as a general, and he discovered that he needed all of his political and social skills to carry the day. It was fortunate for the Boer cause that he possessed these skills to such a high degree.

Inexperienced as he was, Botha had quickly understood that Hlangwane was the hinge to the Boer positions and must be held at all costs, but the burghers were reluctant to occupy it. A commando had been on the hill for a time, but the men were uneasy, having no safe line of retreat; after the bombardment by the naval guns they had climbed down and recrossed the river, leaving this vital height undefended.

On 14 December, at about the same time that Buller was meeting with his senior officers, Botha called a krygsraad to settle the problem. The commandants attended, but they were stubborn, almost all were older than Botha, and he probably would not have been able to budge them if he had not had the foresight to appeal to President Kruger. Oom Paul, after consulting with Joubert and Lucas Meyer, sent a telegram adjuring them to hold Hlangwane at all cost. Armed with this, Botha pleaded and cajoled, finally bringing the commandants around. Still, no one wanted to go there himself. In the end lots were drawn and the task fell to the brave and able Jozua Joubert of the Wakkerstroom Commando, who accepted his fate calmly: "The choice of the lot is the choice of God," he said.

Jozua Joubert and his 600-man commando occupied Hlangwane only a few hours before Buller launched his attack. Had Buller directed a major assault on the hill it would surely have fallen, held as it was by such a slender force, but Botha was content to have a single commando there, for he was confident that Buller's main force would march straight down the railway tracks. *The Times History* noted: "Nothing indeed, at this stage of the war, is more astonishing than the contempt the Boer generals showed for their opponents, except the fact that that contempt was almost invariably justified by the event."

Many of Botha's burghers did not share his confidence in Buller's ineptitude; the older ones remembered the reputation he had earned in the Zulu War twenty years earlier and they were apprehensive. Botha moved about, breathing confidence, giving encouragement and stressing over and over again the importance of holding their fire until the British were very close; he hoped that some of the troops would have crossed the river before he would be forced to disclose his positions.

Buller made no effort at all to conceal his dispositions or his intentions; feints and deceptions such as Garnet Wolseley had planned in his campaigns were beyond him. On the night before the battle the British camp was spread out on the plain only 4 miles from the kopjes where the silent Boers waited and watched.

16

COLENSO

Dawn at Colenso on 15 December 1899 found Buller's brigades in motion across the open rolling veld under a clear blue, cloudless sky. There was not a breath of wind; it was the beginning of a fiery hot summer's day. Across the plain they marched towards the Tugela, their feet churning up dust which in the still air lay in a low cloud below their waists so that the marching columns appeared to be wading through it. Ahead they could see the waves of hills that stretched beyond the river in the direction of Ladysmith. At 5:30 A.M. the silence of the morning was broken by the naval guns which began to shell the Colenso kopjes at 5,000 yards.

In their trenches and shelters the Boers waited. Willie Pohl was nervous as he peered out at the columns of British infantry moving so purposefully towards them. Beside him in the trench an old burgher from time to time calmly bit off a chunk of tobacco, stroked his long beard, and worked the bolt of his Mauser. "Trust in God," he said, "lie low, and don't waste ammunition."

The battle began with an unforeseen action on the part of Buller's artillery commanded by Colonel Charles Long, a fire-eater who had arrived on the scene only the day before. Long had served much of his career in India, where he became famous as a pig sticker, having once killed fifty boars in one day. He had served in the Afghan War of 1879–1880 and had recently distinguished himself by his handling of the artillery at the battle of Omdurman in the Sudan.

Under the protection of Barton's infantry Long moved forward on the right of the railway with the 14th and 66th batteries (twelve guns) and six naval guns. His orders were to support the attack on the centre by Hildyard's brigade, which was to launch itself straight down the railway to Colenso. Buller had told Long that he would probably have to rely solely on his naval guns in the beginning of the battle, for it would be too dangerous to push forward his field pieces, adding that he would be quite content to have the fire of the naval guns alone. Long, however, had his own ideas as to how field guns should be employed: his theory was that they should be shoved well forward and worked rapidly at close range— or, as he put it, "The only way to smash those beggars is to rush in at 'em."

Long and his guns started out marching as ordered with Barton's brigade, but about six o'clock in the morning, while still 3 miles from the river, he ordered his guns to move smartly forward. Guns, caissons, and limbers went jingling and clattering past the infantry. Barton, taken unawares by this manoeuvre, sent the first of several messages to Long asking him to wait for his infantry, but Long and his guns galloped recklessly on. They were only 700 yards from the river and more than a mile ahead of the infantry when he swung his guns into position. He later admitted that "the light was deceptive, and I got a bit closer than I intended."[1] No sooner had the gunners prepared for action than a single gun from the Colenso kopjes banged out a signal and the Boer riflemen opened fire.

Long said later: "In spite of the sudden and rather unexpected fire that was opened, the field batteries came up perfectly steady and were brought into action in an excellent line." The value of guns brought into a perfect line on a battlefield was nonexistent, and doing so under fire was preposterous, but Long's guns were smartly unlimbered and drawn up as though on parade; all was neat and even, a beautiful line of twelve guns, none equipped with shields, on the open, unprotected plain. Until the infantry came up, they were the Boers' only target, and more than a thousand Mausers were aimed at them. Two artillery officers were killed and four wounded in the first few minutes. The Boer artillery also opened fire, and soon Long himself was down with a shrapnel ball through his liver. He liked later to say that his liver had always been rather sluggish until the Boers tickled it up a bit.

The disciplined British gunners fought their guns bravely and well, and even managed to beat down the enemy's fire somewhat, but they took severe losses. Twelve gunners had been killed and 29 were wounded when, after less than an hour's firing, their ammunition was exhausted and the order was given to retire to the shelter of a donga. Even then they fell back in good order, carrying their wounded with them. Long refused all medical attention until his men had been given aid. When someone suggested that perhaps the guns would have to be abandoned, he protested: "Abandon be damned! We never abandon guns!" Captain Percy Herbert rode back to hurry forward the ammunition wagons, still some 3 miles in the rear.

The naval guns were also hurrying forward, but, being pulled by oxen, were further behind; their Coloured and Bantu drivers fled at the first shot—it was, as the white men said, their war. Two of the big guns stuck in a small donga and the rest were scattered, but the naval officers managed to get them all into action, even if they were not in a neat line.

Buller intended to leave the actual conduct of the battle to Clery while he stationed himself on a low kopje in the rear to watch. His attention was first directed to the action taking place on his left where Hart's brigade, led by the 2nd Dublin Fusiliers, was moving to the attack —or at least towards the river. Hart, who was called "General No Bobs" because he had never been known to duck when under fire, had been in

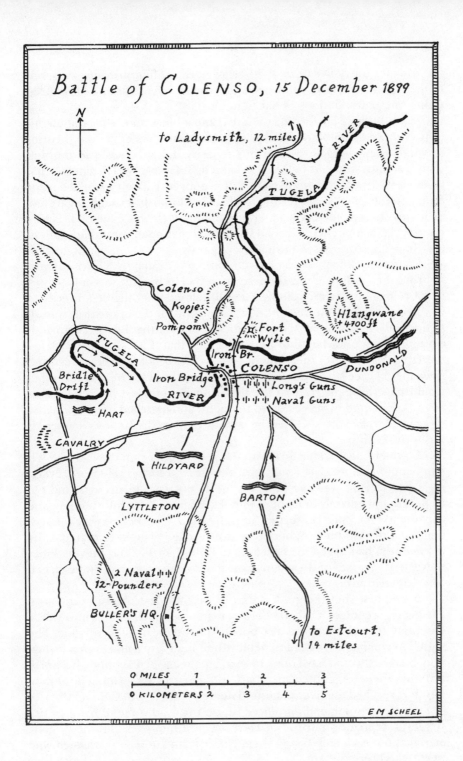

Battle of COLENSO, *15 December 1899*

N

to Ladysmith, 12 miles

TUGELA RIVER

Colenso
Kopjes

Pompom

Hlangwane
4700 ft

Fort
Wylie

DUNDONALD

TUGELA

Iron Br. COLENSO

Iron Bridge

Bridle
Drift

RIVER

Long's Guns

Naval Guns

HART

CAVALRY

HILDYARD

LYTTLETON

BARTON

2 Naval
12-Pounders

BULLER'S H.Q.

to Estcourt,
14 miles

0 MILES   1   2   3
0 KILOMETERS 2   3   4   5

E M SCHEEL

the army for thirty-five years and was a veteran of four previous wars, but in this age of smokeless powder and magazine-fed rifles he harboured some antiquated notions about fighting.

It was Buller's misfortune to have commanders who, while not plentifully endowed with brains, had possessed themselves of tactical theories to which they clung with ferocious tenacity. Long believed in pushing guns well forward; Hart believed in keeping infantry "well in hand." That is, in close formation. None of this new nonsense about open order for him; resolute men shoulder to shoulder could push through regardless of losses. Except for his leading battalion, which was extended, Hart's entire brigade marched in broad daylight across open country in sight of the Boer lines in masses of quarter columns.

"A general who is courageous and stupid is a calamity"; Hart was now to prove the wisdom of this Chinese proverb. His brigade was only a short distance from the river, following a well-defined track that led directly to it, when the guides for inexplicable reasons insisted that the drift was off to the right. It was one of the curiosities of the war that British commanders more than once failed to grasp the idea that if a well-used track led directly toward a river there might conceivably be a ford where track and river met. Three hundred yards more along the track he was following would have brought Hart to the drift, but he followed the implausible advice of his guides, veered off to the right, and marched his brigade into a peninsularlike space created by a great loop in the sinuous Tugela. It was a death trap.

Colonel Charles Murdock with the 1st Dragoons on the extreme left flank could see, as Hart could not, the Boer trenches. He sent several messages to Hart warning him that the Boers were in strength and entrenched immediately in front of him. Hart ignored the information, and the brigade marched on further into the loop. The Boers, watching patiently, adjusting their sights, were now arched around him across the river. Botha had urged his burghers to hold their fire and they had, but these dense masses of the enemy now so close were an irresistible target. They opened fire.

At the first shot the guides disappeared, never to be seen again. In a rising crescendo of musketry the Boers pumped their bullets into Hart's Irishmen; several Boer guns also opened fire on the helpless brigade. The battalion commanders tried to deploy their men into a more open formation, but Hart would have none of that, and he dashed about on his horse ordering them to get their men back into close order again. The Dublin Fusiliers reached the river but found no ford. Lieutenant Colonel Charles Cooper, their commanding officer, started to lead some of his men upstream in search of a drift, but Hart ordered him back and the brigade marched on, each step taking them closer to the unseen marksmen who were slaughtering them. The leading ranks had no idea of where they were going; Hart had none either. The guides, before they bolted, had vaguely indicated the end of the loop; Hart had not sent scouts ahead to discover whether or not a drift actually existed there (none did), but marched his entire brigade, less one battalion left to line the riverbank, towards an unfordable spot on the river. It ended in disaster.

The ranks crumpled and men began to throw themselves on the ground and to seek such scanty cover as there was. Several isolated groups in front made valiant efforts to go forward: a colour sergeant was heard to cry, "Fix bayonets, men, and let's make a name for ourselves!" before he fell. One small party reached a kraal near the end of the loop; others found some low scrub near the river and looked in vain for a drift. Among these was John Dunn, a handsome fourteen-year-old bugler of the Dublin Fusiliers. He had been ordered to the rear but had remained with his company instead. Now, without orders, he lifted his bugle to his lips and sounded the advance. A number of men fixed bayonets and charged into the Tugela, which at this point was about 10 feet deep. Some drowned, some managed to swim across but were shot down by the Boers, and some, having crossed, saw they were too few to go further and swam back. Bugler Dunn himself was wounded in the arm and chest and lost his bugle.*

Buller, who had watched Hart's disaster, was unable to remain any longer a passive spectator and came riding down to the salient, having told Lyttelton: "Hart has got into a devil of a mess down there. Get him out of it as best you can." Lyttelton moved up two battalions and threw them across the open end of the loop, and Hart was ordered to withdraw his men through them. The entire affair—it can hardly be called an attack—was begun and finished in an hour and a half. Hart's brigade suffered 532 casualties; 216 of them were Dublin Fusiliers.

The retirement of Hart's brigade began just as Long's guns fell silent, while on the right flank Dundonald was trying to storm Hlangwane with the 13th Hussars, one battery, and about 600 mounted infantry, mostly colonials who had never before seen action—and he nearly succeeded.

Handsome and gay, Douglas Mackinnon Baillie Hamilton Cochrane, twelfth Earl of Dundonald (1852–1935), was a remarkable man with an inventive mind. He was a type of Briton whom the Victorians usually admired, frequently had need of, produced in profusion, and generally neglected. He had invented a light machine gun, a light and comfortable ambulance, a gun carriage of hickory and steel that could be pulled by a single horse, and a waterproof bag capable of supporting a man crossing a river. All of these devices might have been useful in South Africa,

*Instead of the hiding he deserved, young Dunn became a hero. Invalided home, he was given a tumultuous welcome. At Portsmouth the crowd carried him on their shoulders. There was some execrable poetry written about him, and he was taken to Osborne to meet the Queen, who presented him with a new silver bugle with a suitable inscription. Queen Victoria, writing of him in her journal, described him as "a nice-looking, modest boy." Richard Harding Davis, the American newspaper correspondent and novelist, declared that the only people who emerged from the war with any distinction were Sir George White, Baden-Powell, John French, Winston Churchill, and Bugler Dunn.

but the army had refused to adopt any of them. He also had some novel ideas about using smoke to screen the movement of troops or ships.

Dundonald was commissioned and gazetted to the 2nd Life Guards at the age of eighteen and rose to be the commanding officer of that elegant regiment twenty-five years later. He remained active all his life, and thirty-five years after the battle of Colenso, at the age of seventy-seven, he sailed a 14-ton boat across the Atlantic to South America. An intelligent and imaginative man, he was not much admired in the army, which placed little value on these qualities; some of his men called him "Dundoodle," and one of his officers, Captain Hubert Gough, described him as being "another of Buller's weaker subordinates. . . . hesitating, vacillating and vain."[2] Gough also charged that Dundonald took credit that properly belonged to his subordinates.

At 7:15 A.M. Dundonald dismounted his men in the bed of a spruit about a mile from Hlangwane and threw his colonials across bare mealie fields in a loose attack formation. They encountered heavy fire but reached the scrub and loose rocks at the foot of the hill, and the South African Light Horse, led by Julian (later Lord) Byng, a future field marshal, made some progress up the slope while the mounted infantry were sent down the valley to the east in an attempt to outflank the Boer positions. Dundonald used all the force available to him—the only commander to do so this day—but the Boers tenaciously resisted. On the crest of Hlangwane Jozua Joubert walked about calmly, making jokes and encouraging his men, until he was hit by a shell fragment just below the knee.

When the attack slowed down Dundonald called on Barton for reinforcements: one battalion of infantry was all he needed, he believed. According to the orders of the day, Barton's brigade was to supply support for Dundonald and Hildyard, but Barton had just received orders from Buller not to commit his troops. Some initiative on Barton's part, a willingness to go beyond the letter of his orders, would probably have enabled Dundonald to take Hlangwane, but Barton refused to give his support. Perhaps he had rightly interpreted his chief's thinking, for Buller, in an extraordinary piece of logic, had explained to Lansdowne earlier that "if I took it [Hlangwane] and then failed at Colenso I should eventually have to evacuate it." Dundonald's men were thus left clinging to the slopes of the hill, pinned down by the plunging fire of the Boers.

Dundonald might have made a personal appeal to Buller if he had been able to find him, but Buller, commander-in-chief of all the British forces in South Africa, was now busy acting as a battery commander. After seeing that Hart's brigade was being extricated from the loop, he gave no thought to renewing the attack in that quarter and decided that all his efforts must be thrown behind Hildyard's attack on the centre, just now getting under way.

Henry Hildyard had seen very little active service during his thirty-two years in the army, but he had had the opportunity while at Aldershot to train the brigade he was now leading, and he had trained it well. Unlike Hart, Hildyard ordered his men—Devons, Queen's, East Surreys, and West Yorks—to advance swiftly in extended order and in lines. But they walked erect, and Bennett Burleigh of the *Daily Telegraph* was lost in admiration as he watched them: "With death filling the air and tearing the ground, onward they went, the most superb spectacle of invincible manhood."[3]

Hildyard's brigade advanced under heavy fire but with light losses on the left of the railway and pushed on into Colenso itself. Some of the Queen's even managed to get on the iron road bridge across the Tugela. From houses, sheds, and over walls in the village they poured such an effective fire into the Boer positions that the burghers left their trenches on the opposite bank for others higher up behind them. The naval guns had been ably supporting this attack, but they lost sight of the Queen's and Devons when they entered the village. As the swarm of Boers left their trenches and scampered up the sides of the kopjes the muzzle of every gun was leveled at them; then someone shouted, "They're our men!" The gunners held their fire and missed the best target presented to them all day.

Hildyard's leading battalions were nearing Colenso when Buller with Clery and some staff officers rode across to oversee the operation. On the way they encountered Captain Herbert, who had been sent to hurry up the ammunition for Long's guns, and from him Buller learned that the two field batteries were out of action. This was bad news indeed; first the failure of Hart's attack, now this misfortune. The news was particularly distressing because Herbert gave the impression that the naval guns were also out of action. Buller and his party at once cantered towards the guns, drawing considerable fire from the Boers as they rode.

It was just half past nine in the morning when Buller reached the donga where the artillerymen had taken refuge and stared out at the twelve field guns sitting unattended in their parade ground formation. Around him in the donga were the wounded and the remains of the gun crews. Long was delirious and raving about his poor brave gunners. The fear of losing his guns now seemed to dominate Buller's thoughts to the exclusion of all else—the fate of Dundonald's brigade on his right or the success or failure of Hildyard's attack on his immediate left or anything else.

Buller had eight battalions at hand that had seen little or no action; he had dozens of other guns; ammunition was available; the situation was not hopeless. Hildyard and Dundonald, if supported, had every chance of success, and the best way for Buller to save those wretched guns was to defeat the Boers, but he was no longer capable of seeing the unfolding of the entire battle.

Whatever the private soldier may think, and however inspiring it may be to have the general commanding in a battle in the front lines, there are advantages to having him cool and comfortable in the rear, away from

THE BATTLE OF COLENSO.

the hurly-burly of the front-line action, for it is on his judgement that his men's lives as well as victory or defeat depend, and that judgement ought to be exercised in surroundings conducive to clear thinking. Buller had been pounding about the battlefield all morning and hearing only bad news; the sun was hot and he was portly and no longer young; he was fighting the first battle which he himself had arranged and for which he alone was responsible. Being a brave man who loved action but feared responsibility for the lives of others, it was tempting for him to lose himself in the details of the action, but in succumbing to this temptation he lost control of the battle itself.

Standing now amid the wounded in the donga, bullets flying about him, shells bursting near him, Long's guns standing reproachfully in front of him, he was in no condition to be objective and far-seeing. His mental and emotional state was not improved when his staff surgeon was killed beside him and he himself was struck in the side and badly bruised by a spent shell fragment. Through it all he appeared to others to be as stolid, upright, and impassive as ever, unaffected by the tragedies around him, in control of his destiny and theirs.

With Long out of action, Major A. C. Bailward was left in charge of the guns, but Buller turned to one of his aides-de-camp, Captain Harry Schofield of the Royal Horse Artillery, and told him to try to get the guns away. Schofield called for volunteers, and two limber teams of the 66th Battery came forward; so too did two other staff officers: Captain Walter Congreve and Lieutenant the Honourable Frederick S. Roberts, only son of Field Marshal Lord Roberts of Kandahar, who was serving as one of Clery's aides-de-camp.

Schofield organized teams of horses, and with them and his volunteers he dashed out to rescue the guns. Lieutenant George Salt of the Royal Welsh Fusiliers witnessed the attempt and tried to describe it in a letter home:

I was on a rise of a hill to the right, and could see every inch of the ground from start to finish. One could see the bullets striking all around them, and it seemed a marvel that they were not hit. When they were about half way across, one team came to grief, and had to lie where they were under a hot fire. Another was struck, and became a struggling mass before they reached the guns. Three got to the guns, hooked on their teams, and started to gallop back. A shell, as far as I could see, struck one of the guns, and it turned right over, but the other two got safely back. It was an awful sight, but fearfully exciting.[4]

Young Lieutenant Roberts, exhilarated, had dashed out laughing and twirling his stick like a jockey. He had not gone 30 yards before he was shot from his saddle. Captain Congreve lived to describe his experience:

I have never seen, even at field firing, bullets fly thicker. All one could see was little tufts of dust all over the ground, and one heard a whistling noise and a phut where they hit and an unceasing rattle of musketry somewhere in front. My first bullet went through my left sleeve and just made the point of my elbow bleed; next a clod of earth caught me no end of a smack on the other arm; then my horse got one; then my right leg one; my horse another and that settled us, for he plunged and I fell off about a hundred yards short of the gun we were going to.[5]

Although horseless and wounded, Congreve crawled to the aid of Roberts. Major William Babtie of the Royal Army Medical Corps also crawled out to Roberts, wounded now in three places, and the two officers managed to drag him into a sheltered spot.

Schofield himself came through untouched, although he had six bullet holes in his uniform. "I can't believe it even now," he said later to John Atkins of the *Manchester Guardian*, "that we got through so well." He paid tribute to the coolness of the soldiers with him and indirectly to the result that years of strict, repetitive gun drill can achieve: "I'll show you how cool those drivers were. While I was hooking on one of the guns, one of the drivers said, 'Elevate the muzzle, sir'—that's a precaution for galloping in rough country. But I shouldn't have thought of it—not just then."[6]

The next attempt to save the guns was made by Captain Hamilton Reed of the 7th Battery, who with a group of volunteers dashed out with three wagon teams. He never reached them. Thirteen out of twenty-two horses and seven out of thirteen men were shot down; Reed was wounded in the leg. In the kopjes across the river Louis Botha watched through his glasses the executions by his riflemen and later told a friend: "I was sick with horror that such bravery should have been so useless."[7] Seven Victoria Crosses were won in these mad attempts; Roberts, who died the following day, became the first to receive the medal posthumously.

For Buller it was a terrible thing to stand and watch these men die trying to save his guns. He had not the fortitude to endure the sufferings of others, to stand sweating in the sun and watch these young men shot from their saddles and lie writhing in agony in the dust. He must have wished that he was again a junior officer, thirty or forty years younger and thirty or forty pounds lighter, and without the weight of a general's insignia on his shoulders. When he saw Reed and his men go down in a bloody tangle of horses, harnesses, and limbers he called a halt. He could stand no more. Without considering other alternatives, he abandoned the guns.

Months later, testifying before a royal commission, Long said indignantly, "The idea of abandoning the guns never entered my head, nor did it occur to any of the battery officers. . . . I consider the guns were deserted of support."[8] But Buller said categorically: "I do not believe any living man could have got those guns away." Perhaps not, but he might have considered a plan for removing the guns under cover of darkness; he might have ordered men to crawl out and remove the breech blocks; he might even—had he been capable of forgetting the wounded around them—have ordered his heavy naval guns to destroy them with shell fire. But he did none of these things. His abandonment of these ten guns was complete. More than that, he gave up the battle as well.

To the commander of the naval guns he said, "Out of this, please," and with some difficulty the big guns were moved further to the rear: the Bantu drivers could not be found, and thirty-two of the oxen had been shot.

It was only eleven o'clock in the morning, but Buller was later to tell a royal commission that by this time his men were already exhausted and that if he had continued the fight they would have been "utterly prostrated" by the end of the day. If then, as he feared, the Boers had crossed the river and attacked "we should have had a rough and tumble on the bank in which I fully believe we would have been worsted." Buller was describing his own condition rather than that of his men. He was finished. He wanted to be done with this battle. Ignorant of Hildyard's success and Dundonald's situation, he sent orders for Hildyard to withdraw his men at once and then mounted and rode out of the donga to recall Dundonald.

The Times History said: "Bad in its conception, worse in its execution, Colenso was worst of all in its abandonment." The dismounted Mounted Brigade was extricated from its scattered positions on the sides of Hlangwane with the greatest difficulty. It would certainly have been easier and less costly to have thrown in more men and taken the hill than to have attempted to bring back the men on the hillsides in broad daylight, but Buller wanted them back. The process took three hours, and Dundonald lost more men in the retirement than he had in the attack.

Withdrawing Hildyard's brigade was not easy either. The Boers had telegraph lines connecting their main positions, but Buller's communications were no better than Wellington's had been at Waterloo. It was well past noon before the order to retreat reached the Devons; still, most of Hildyard's brigade managed to retire in good order, and by the middle of the afternoon they were back in camp pitching the tents they had struck early that morning.

On the south side of the river where the slaughter had taken place the area was dotted with dead and wounded British soldiers lying in the still hot sun of the late afternoon. Ambulance men began to move among them. The Boers crossed over at several points, among them Field Cornet Cheere Emmet, Botha's English-speaking brother-in-law, who came with oxen and some volunteers to carry off the guns. There were others too who wandered about the shambles.

Mr. W. K.-L. Dickson, the motion picture man from the American Biograph Company, went out to see the battlefield. Although apparently too horrified to take any pictures, he described what he saw in a letter:

> It was the most harrowing thing I ever witnessed. Khaki uniformed men lying about everywhere, deluged in blood, faces horribly distorted and swollen and black. A piece of shell had caught one in the head and opened up his brain. I was inexpressibly affected by the sight, and after covering up as many faces as we could, turned away.[9]

There were on the battlefield still a number of stray soldiers who had not yet received the order to retire and did not quite realize that the battle was over or who forgot that the battlefield belongs to the victor. Major Nathanial Barton of the Connaught Rangers, part of Hart's brigade, found himself alone with the wounded when he was surprised by a troop of mounted Boers. The leading burgher raised his rifle, but Barton called out, "Don't be a damned fool! I can make no resistance." The rifle was lowered and the two men talked. In a letter to his wife, Ellen, Barton wrote: "After a lot of questioning, etc., he was very civil and let me go —on giving my parole. To explain how I came to be there you must know that the brigade *retired* at eleven, and we were never let know."[10]

Among those who never received the order to retire was Lieutenant Colonel George Bullock, commanding the 2nd Battalion of the Devonshire Regiment, who with three other officers and 33 men was ensconced in a small donga not far from Long's guns. When Emmet and his burghers appeared, Bullock and his Devons opened fire. Instead of answering fire with fire, Emmet commandeered a British ambulance orderly and under the protection of the red cross walked up to Bullock's position and told him the battle was over and that he should surrender. Bullock refused. He demanded that Emmet and his men go back and fight it out. Burghers and soldiers stood about watching and listening while their officers argued. It ended when one exasperated burgher, shouting, "Surrender, you brave idiot!" clubbed Bullock on the head with his rifle.

In still another place fighting switched from bullets to words on this extraordinary battlefield. Over on the British left, stranded in the bushes by the river in the retreat of Hart's brigade, was Lieutenant Colonel

Thomas Thackery, commanding officer of the 1st Battalion of the Innis-killing Fusiliers, and a small group of his men. Late in the afternoon, about the same time that Emmet was crossing over to get the guns, another commando crossed the Tugela and demanded that the Inniskill-ings surrender. Thackery refused, and he and the Boer commandant, each with armed and uncertain men at their backs, stood on the battlefield arguing it out. Thackery won and triumphantly marched his men back to their camp. Lieutenant George Warren with a half company of the Border Regiment had a similar experience. Other scattered groups, faced with less generous or more stubborn captors, were rounded up and made prisoner.

It had been a strange day. Although all accounts spoke of the din of guns and musketry, there were from time to time unaccountable lulls in the firing; Bennett Burleigh noticed that in these curiously silent mo-ments he could hear birds singing and crickets chirruping.

It was said, although it was not true, that Buller was "the first British general for nearly a century to incur the stigma of losing guns."[11] To lose one gun was a disgrace. To lose ten of them—and without a single one of the enemy ever actually touching them until they hauled them away— was unthinkable. Yet it had happened. Nearly two years later Buller gave a speech in which he spoke of the battle: "I attacked Colenso on Decem-ber 15. I was unsuccessful; it was a very trying day; I was thirty-six hours at work; I was fourteen hours in the saddle. It was the hottest day we had the whole of the time I was out there, and I had rank bad luck. . . ." [12]

Yes, Buller had had bad luck, but it would have taken extraordinary good luck to have made up for such bad generalship. John Atkins watched Buller and his staff return to camp: "The General climbed down limply and wearily from his horse like an old, old man."

Lyttelton was later to say that Colenso was "one of the most unfortu-nate battles in which a British army has ever been engaged and in none has there been a more deplorable tactical display."[13] It was more than unfortunate and deplorable: it was sheer madness, all of it. Buller was to tell a royal commission: "I never attacked on the 15th at all. . . . I made no attack. I stopped at the very earliest moment in the morning every general from moving."[14] A Dublin Fusilier agreed: "Fight? Och, it was no fight at all, at all." In a sense Buller and the Fusilier were right. There was no real attack, only men led up to the Boer lines to be shot down as though they were tin soldiers at a shooting gallery. Total British casual-ties were 1,139 officers and men, of whom 143 were killed: heavy casual-ties for a battle in which neither side attacked.

Military men everywhere heard the story with bewildered wonder-ment: a brigade led in a dense mass into a loop made by an unfordable river surrounded on three sides by a concealed and sheltered enemy; guns and their crews thrown miles ahead of the infantry and put in parade ground order in a completely exposed position and then abandoned; an inadequate force of mounted men sent to take a precipitous hill; armed men, foes, facing each other and quarrelling like children over the rules of the game. It did not make sense, not any of it.

There came towards the end of that hot afternoon a kind of neutral time. The guns were silent. The British had nearly completed their withdrawal; the Boers had not yet left their trenches. Overhead the vultures swung in great arcs waiting for their banquet hall to be cleared of the butchers. It was then that there occurred one of this day's last bizarre, inexplicable events. An old man, unarmed, in civilian clothes, mounted on an artillery horse, appeared alone on the battlefield. There was something strange, evasive, and wild about him as he wandered about. Was he a Boer? Some soldiers brought him in. His saddlebags were found to be stuffed with curious loot he had picked up on the field: bits of broken harness and worthless scraps of militaria. Then someone recognized him: he had once been a British officer. John Atkins saw him and asked for an explanation. Where had he come from? Why had this crazy old war horse, this remnant of a man, returned to this field of battle? "Oh, sunstroke in India or something of that sort, you know," he was told.

The day of madness ended with a lone madman being led from the battlefield.

17

BLACK WEEK

"The God of our fathers has today granted us a brilliant victory." So Louis Botha began his dispatch to President Kruger describing the battle and the capture of Long's guns, those "big, beautiful cannons," and of "about 170 of their best men." He estimated his own casualties at "about 30 killed and wounded"; as for the British, "the enemy's losses must have been terrible"—he thought about 2,000—but he had not ordered a body count; this, he felt, would be too callous. (The real figure appears to have been 38 for the Boers, of whom 8 were killed.) Botha asked the government "to proclaim a general day of prayer to thank Him who gave us this victory." This was done, for the following day was Dingaan's Day when, exactly sixty-one years earlier, this same breed of men had driven off Dingaan's Zulu hordes; now they had repelled the British host. The God of their fathers and grandfathers did indeed seem to be watching over them. In the Transvaal and the Orange Free State there was rejoicing, but there was neither the wild jubilation that such stunning victories would have provoked in other countries nor was there surprise, for they believed their cause just and it seemed only natural that the stern, just God they worshipped should guide the bullets of their Mausers to the breasts of the kakies.

At Colenso the British asked for an armistice to bring in their dead and wounded, and this was agreed to until midnight on the 16th. All day long on that day the ambulances and bearers were busy, and on into the night, in spite of a full eclipse of the moon which hampered their work.

Although Joubert, who visited the battlefield three days after the fight, saw some of the British dead still on the field and exposed to the vultures, most of the bodies had by then been collected and buried. It was a heavy, loathsome task; burial services were brief and one service did for many, for there is no more sickening sight than raw corpses that have been left exposed to an African sun, and no smell more nauseous. As soon as a row of graves had been dug, field ambulances brought up the dead. Great clouds of blue flies swarmed out when the canvas curtains were thrown back, and the ceremonial burial parties shrank back, sickened by the stench of yesterday's cheerful, brave companions.

The wounded were carried to four field hospitals where the busy surgeons worked long and hard. Sir William MacCormac described them:

> Each of the three operating tents contained two operating tables, and as fast as a patient was taken off a table another took his place. Awaiting their turn, the wounded were lying outside in rows, which were continually being augmented by the civilian bearers coming in from the field. As each man reached the hospital he was served with a hot cup of Bovril, large cans of which were boiling outside the tents. . . . The Royal Army Medical Corps officers of these hospitals had started their surgical work about 3 A.M., and when I visited them in the evening they were still hard at it, having had no food meanwhile and no time for rest, and the work went on for hours afterwards. Altogether some 800 patients passed through the field hospitals during the day. The men showed the utmost pluck and endurance.[1]

A drummer boy of about fourteen, his left arm shattered, sat on the back of an ambulance eating a biscuit while waiting his turn on the surgeon's table. An officer, pitying him and admiring his fortitude, walked up and, in what seems today a curious expression of sympathy, offered him half-a-crown. The money—a day and a half's pay for a private soldier—was appreciated: "Thank you," said the boy, "but would you mind putting it in my pocket? I mustn't let go of the biscuit."

A hospital train shuttled between the field hospitals at Colenso and a general hospital at Chievely. Lieutenant Roberts was brought into 4th Brigade Field Hospital in the evening and the next day was sent on to Chievely, where he died that night. The death of Field Marshal Lord Roberts's only son had a profound effect upon Englishmen everywhere. In Ladysmith Lord Rawlinson wrote in his journal:

> Today I had news which affected me more than any since the beginning of the war. Little Freddy Roberts was killed at Colenso. The helio message says "He

was shot in the groin whilst gallantly trying to save the guns." He was such a charming and fine lad, and I fear to think of the effect his death will have on his family.[2]

Joubert wrote a letter of condolence to his parents. So too did Queen Victoria, and to her they replied: "Our loss is grievous, but our boy died the death he would have chosen."

The Queen learned of the disaster at Colenso when she went to breakfast on 16 December and was handed "a very unsatisfactory telegram" which the War Office had received from Buller. It had been sent at eleven fifteen the night before and it began: "I regret to report serious reverse. . . ." He calculated that the Boers must have 145,000 men in the field of whom 85,000 were Transvaalers, but Lansdowne noted that the entire population of the Transvaal—men, women, and children—was only 90,000.

Buller could hardly face the enormity of his failure; he blamed Hart and particularly Long. But the fault lay not with others, but with himself. He was a Victorian Hamlet, wanting action, provoking it, yet afraid of the consequences of acting on his own judgement. He did not, like Hamlet, contemplate suicide, but he did that which for a general is worse: he expressed his conviction that he could not win. He advised the War Office that he considered himself incapable of relieving Ladysmith, and he sent off two extraordinary messages by helio to White in the besieged town saying, "The enemy is too strong for my force . . . I cannot break in," and suggesting that he fire off as much ammunition as he could, destroy his cypher books, and make the best terms possible with the Boers. White could not believe the message was genuine. He thought the Boers had sent it. When it was confirmed he signalled back: "The loss of 12,000 men here would be a heavy blow to England. We must not think of it."

It was mid-winter and a thick cold fog hung over England; London in particular was submerged in a dense, dark mist. To those living in this dim and dismal land there came daily news from the southern hemisphere where their soldiers were fighting and sweating under a hot sun. The news they received that second week in December was all bad, and it arrived in profusion: Stormberg on 10 December, Magersfontein on the 11th, and Colenso on the 15th. "What a national fiasco so far!" exclaimed Lord Esher. "The gloomiest week in our history for close upon a hundred years," said Prevost Battersby. Conan Doyle wrote: "The week which extended from 10 December to 17th December, 1899, was the blackest one known during our generation, and the most disastrous for British arms during the century."[3] *The Times History* noted: "There were no outward signs of panic. . . . All the same, the nation was more deeply stirred, more profoundly alarmed, than perhaps at any period since the eve of Trafalgar."[4]

"Our generals," said Herbert Asquith, "seem neither able to win victories nor to give convincing reasons for their defeats." Throughout the world Britain's enemies rejoiced. Her famed military might had, not once, but three times in less than a week, gone down to defeat before the rifles of a collection of rustics from a pair of tenth-rate republics. Prince Bernhard von Bülow, Germany's secretary of state for foreign affairs, wrote: "The vast majority of German military experts believe that the S.A. war will end with a complete defeat of the English." Englishmen living amidst strangers felt this gleeful hostility most. Cecil Spring Rice in Persia wrote (20 December 1899):

Life is a prolonged nightmare now. The daily telegrams are a horror and working in the morning or late at night is a terrible thing; one lies alone with a living and growing fear staring one in the face. But after all, I have some faith left in the strength and determination and courage of the people and the colonies. And the fellow feeling of America is a real and constant delight. . . . But, oh, the present horror of it—and out here with vindictive and sneering faces—and the utter helplessness.[5]

The New York *Journal* tried to explain the feelings of the British to its American readers:

The bewildering thing to the British mind has been the mauling received at the hands of bewhiskered farmers by many regiments which were favorites, whose records so blazed with glory that they were popularly accounted invincible. For instance, "The Black Watch" . . . has traditions which are superior to that of any regiment in the world perhaps. Very well—an unimposing body of men who don't wash very often batter this regiment out of shape.[6]

The British were indeed humiliated, but no people on earth bear up under military disaster more stoutly. Their resolve stiffened. When Arthur Balfour mentioned the disasters of Black Week to the Queen she cut him short: "Please understand that there is no one depressed in *this* house; we are not interested in the possibilities of defeat; they do not exist." From the Queen to the poorest commoner there developed a determination that this time there would be no giving in as after Majuba. In fact, in the popular mind the uitlanders and their problems were already forgotten and the reason for the fighting was reduced to the slogan: "Avenge Majuba!"

F. I. Maxse once noted that "Britons do not give personal service to the State until a war is half lost." Now men from every station in life clamoured to enlist. At the outbreak of the war many prominent men had offered to raise, some even at their own expense, volunteer units for active service, but the authorities at the War Office, contemptuous of military amateurs, repeatedly declined these offers, declaring they would not be needed; besides, there was no War Office staff to handle this function. However, on 18 December, three days after Colenso, the government, purely as a political measure to provide an escape valve for the pent-up enthusiasm of the nation, reluctantly announced that it would permit twelve battalions of militia and some 20,000 selected volunteers from the yeomanry to go to South Africa.

Tens of thousands of men besieged the recruiting depots, and it was now that the most famous of the English volunteer units was formed: the City of London Imperial Volunteers, universally known as the CIV. It was raised by Sir Alfred Newton, Lord Mayor of London, under Royal Warrant dated 24 December 1899. Although rifles were drawn from the Tower, all of the equipment and clothing, including the smasher slouch hats turned up on one side, as well as a Maxim machine gun and six 12½-pounder quick-firing guns of the latest pattern bought from Vickers, were paid for out of a special Mansion House Fund to which the public subscribed £100,000.

The CIV was in many respects remarkable. In addition to the battery of artillery, it contained a battalion of infantry and two companies of mounted infantry, 1,550 men in all—almost a miniature army in itself. Its commanding officer, Colonel W. H. Mackinnon, was a regular army officer, as were most of his staff; there were a few regular army noncommissioned officers, but most of the unit, officers and men, had had no previous military experience. Even Colonel Mackinnon, a half-pay guardsman, had seen no active service during his thirty years in the army.

For the first time in British history social classes other than the highest and the lowest were part of the fighting force: the CIV included an officer of the crown, nine barristers, seven architects, two bankers, thirty civil servants, four schoolmasters, and a ship owner. Tom Cockrane was elected to Parliament while serving in its ranks. Colonel Mackinnon was astonished and amused by the quality of his men. Inquiring of a sentry what his profession was, he was told: "I have none, sir, but my amusement in life is archaeology." On shipboard, he inquired about a sergeant who in rough weather was exceptionally steady on his feet, and was told that he owned a yacht. Their manners, while impeccable, were incongruously civilian, and Mackinnon had cause to complain of his sergeants: "The conversational style in which some of them give commands to strong squads is not conducive to efficiency."

The CIV was hastily raised. The first men were sworn in on 1 January 1900, and less than two months later the first detachment, about 500 strong, embarked for South Africa. Within a month all had sailed. Friends gave the unit 2,000 bottles of whiskey and enough beer to issue five gallons to every man.

A popular magazine reported: "The sole fear of the soldiers who are going out late is that the war will be over before they arrive and have a chance to win a medal."[7] It was said that "many young men about town justified their existence for the first time." There were other volunteer units besides the CIV. Twenty-two peers of the realm and twenty-seven members of Parliament volunteered, most of them in the yeomanry. Among the regulars there was some dissatisfaction because the volunteers were paid more, but the men in a unit known as the Duke of Cambridge's Own were all men of substance who paid their own way, equipped and provisioned themselves in style, and donated their pay to the Widows and Orphans Fund. By the end of February some 4,900 of these ill-trained volunteers had sailed for South Africa, some being shipped out free of charge by the steamship lines.

This surge of jingoism was not confined to Britain. Australians, New Zealanders, and Canadians sank their complaints about the mother country in a fierce pride in the Empire. The prime minister of New Zealand expressed the sentiments of most colonials when he said:

> The war is only nominally with the Boers; actually it is with all who are jealous of the growing power of the British Empire, and who, rejoicing in our reverses, are aiding and abetting the Boers. The reverses suffered are only temporary; they will be followed by the invariable, inevitable success of British arms.

An innocent victim of the fervid patriotism stirred up by Black Week was Sir William Butler. He who had done so much to try to prevent the war was now viciously attacked in the press. He pleaded with the War Office either to defend his character or to allow him to defend it himself, but he received a cold reply from Lansdowne: "I am to state that it is not desirable that officers should take note of criticisms in the Press as to the manner in which they have discharged their duties."

Many thoughtful Britons deplored the war but were convinced that it had to be fought—and won. Lord Grey was one such, and in a letter to Katherine Lyttelton, Sir Neville's wife, written shortly after the war started, he said:

> I am depressed about this war: I admit the necessity of it and that it must be carried through, but it has no business to be popular, and the cry of "Revenge Majuba" dishonours us and destroys our reputation for good faith. I should like to break the heads of all the Music Halls first and then go out and teach the Boers gravely and sternly the things which they do not know.[8]

A small but literate and vocal minority opposed the war from the beginning to the end. It included W. T. Stead, one of the most famous journalists and publishers of the period, who began a weekly paper called *War Against War in South Africa;* Beatrice Webb, mother of modern socialism; Leonard Courtney, a member of Parliament who headed a "Stop the War Committee"; and two future prime ministers: Sir Henry Campbell-Bannerman and David Lloyd George. Few went as far as Wilfrid Scawen Blunt, who was actually pro-Boer and openly jubilant in the midst of Black Week. In his diary for 17 December he wrote: "The Boers are making a splendid fight for their freedom, and are winning all along the line. Every honest man, English or not, ought to rejoice."[9]

Beatrice Webb had ambiguous feelings, for, as she said, "Any criticism of the war at present is hopelessly unpopular. . . . And who can fail to be depressed at the hatred of England on the Continent: it is comforting to put it down to envy and malice, but not convincing."[10] Indeed, the flood of hatred for the British which swept Europe was deeply felt, but it helped to increase British solidarity. The Boers were encouraged by all this pro-Boer, anti-British sentiment to hope that one or more of the European powers would intervene, but this was an *ignis fatuus,* for as Winston Churchill later said in his maiden speech in the House of Commons: "No people in the world received so much verbal sympathy and so little support."[11]

Many Americans and many Boers made a comparison between the war in South Africa and the revolution of the colonists in North America 120 years earlier. The bulk of popular sentiment in the United States favoured the Boers, but President William McKinley and the American government were well aware of the embarrassing moral position of the United States at that moment. The country had just finished an imperialistic war of its own with Spain, a war in which Britain had taken a position actively friendly to the United States. Furthermore, the Americans had taken the Philippines as part of their booty, and the American army was actively engaged in suppressing those Filipinos who wanted their freedom. It would obviously be contradictory, not to say hypocritical, of the American government to express sympathy for the Boers struggling for their independence while shooting Filipinos who were struggling for theirs. The pro-Boer American consul in Pretoria was replaced by Adalbert Hay, son of the secretary of state, whose sympathies were with the British; the Americans undertook to look after British interests in the Transvaal, and young Hay was particularly solicitous for the welfare of British prisoners of war. Before it ended, the war was to see many Americans fighting on both sides.

When news of Black Week reached the United States, Theodore Roosevelt, himself of Dutch ancestry, soon to be president and now governor of New York, wrote to his friend Cecil Spring Rice in Persia:

I have been absorbed in interest in the Boer War. The Boers are belated Cromwellians, with many fine traits. They deeply and earnestly believe in their cause, and they attract the sympathy which always goes to the small nation. . . . But it would be for the advantage of mankind to have English spoken south of the Zambesi just as in New York; and as I told one of my fellow knickerbockers the other day, as we let the Uitlanders of old in here, I do not see why the same rule is not good enough in the Transvaal. . . . the fighting will be hard and bloody beyond doubt. But the end is inevitable.[12]

Difficult as it was for the British government to absorb the shock of the three military defeats, the prospect of worse to come set off alarm bells throughout the higher reaches of Whitehall. Buller's message to White suggesting surrender sent shivers down ministerial spines. The public was not told, but the Queen through her secretary expressed her sentiments to Lansdowne: "I thought it quite impossible to abandon Ladysmith." Salisbury, Lansdowne, and his colleagues agreed, and Buller was told, "Her Majesty's Government regard abandonment and consequent surrender of White's force as a national disaster of the greatest magnitude."

In Ladysmith itself, not only White but all of his officers were incensed at the supposition that they might surrender, for such an idea had not occurred to them. Some were bitter. Ian Hamilton wrote in his diary: "After all, a nation which possesses a Roberts and a Buller and selects the latter for a vital undertaking deserves almost any misfortune which it is possible to imagine."[13] Roberts's name came to the minds of politicians in London as well. He had taken pains to see that it would. On 8 December, just before Black Week, he had written to Lansdowne from Dublin:

I am much concerned to hear of the very gloomy view which Sir Redvers Buller takes of the situation in South Africa. . . .

As I have, I think, often remarked to you, it is impossible to gauge a general's qualities until he has been tried, and it is a regretable fact that not a single commander in South Africa has ever had an independent command in the field. It is the feeling of responsibility which weighs down most men, and it seems clear . . . that this feeling is having its too frequent effect on Buller. He seems to me overwhelmed by the magnitude of the task imposed upon him, and I confess that the tone of some of his telegrams causes me considerable alarm. From the day he landed in Cape Town he seemed to take a pessimistic view of our position, and when a Commander allows himself to entertain evil forebodings, the effect is inevitably felt throughout the army.

I feel the greatest possible hesitation and dislike to expressing my opinion thus plainly, and nothing but the gravity of the situation and the strongest sense of duty would induce me to do so, or to offer—as I now do—to place my services at the disposal of the Government.

The difficulty of making this offer is greatly increased by the fact that, if it is accepted, I must necessarily be placed in supreme command, and to those who do not know me I may lay myself open to misconception. But the country cannot afford to run any avoidable risk of failure. A serious reverse in South Africa would endanger the Empire.[14]

This was a remarkably candid letter, and timely. Lansdowne showed it to Salisbury, but the sixty-nine-year-old prime minister thought that sixty-seven-year-old Roberts was too old. Lansdowne therefore politely thanked Roberts, said he would keep his offer in mind, and pointed out that Buller had not yet had an opportunity to show what he could do and that he might "achieve a brilliant success on the Tugela within the next two or three days." Lansdowne's letter was dated 10 December. Just six days later—when the news of Stormberg, Magersfontein, and Colenso had reached London—Roberts looked like a prophet.

When Buller's report of his message to White arrived, the government lost no time deciding what must be done. Salisbury hurriedly met with Lansdowne and a few other cabinet members and, without consulting Wolseley, the army's commander-in-chief, or the Queen, decided to send Lord Roberts to supersede Buller as head of the army in South Africa. To back him and to overcome Salisbury's objection to his age it was decided that Lord Kitchener, forty-nine, should go out with him as his chief of staff. Lansdowne telegraphed Roberts in Dublin to come at once to London and to be prepared to leave immediately for South Africa.

Roberts received Lansdowne's message on the same day that a telegram from Buller was handed him telling that his son had been seriously wounded at Colenso. Torn between anxiety for his son and elation at the prospect of a high command, Roberts left for London. He arrived on Sunday, 17 December, and that same day met with Salisbury, Lansdowne, and other ministers at No. 10 Downing Street; he was offered and accepted the appointment as commander-in-chief of the largest army England in its history had ever sent from its shores.

The telegram announcing that Freddy had died of his wounds reached Dublin that afternoon and was forwarded to Lansdowne, who located Roberts late in the afternoon at Mackeller's Hotel and broke the news to him: "The blow was almost more than he could bear, and for a moment I thought he would break down, but he pulled himself together. I shall never forget the courage he showed, or the way in which he refused to allow this disaster to turn him aside from his duty."[15]

The following week was a busy one for Roberts; fortunately so, work being a blessing in time of grief. One of his final duties was to see the Queen at Windsor, and on 22 December she wrote in her journal: "Saw Lord Roberts after tea. He knelt down and kissed my hand. I said how much I felt for him. He could only answer, 'I cannot speak of *that*, but I can of anything else.' "

The following day he went with his wife and daughter to Southampton, there to board the *Dunottar Castle,* the same ship which had carried Buller to South Africa. On hand to see him off was a crowd of the great and famous as well as the unknown and the curious: "A dense and unmanageable crowd, with danger of being squashed," the Prince of Wales grumpily reported to his mother. It was a grey, overcast winter's day, and Roberts, standing on deck, was dressed in a black coat and a top hat, which he raised to the cheering crowd. *The Times* described him as a "little, vigorous, resolute, sorrowful man in deep mourning." His farewells said, the well-wishes of the crowd acknowledged, he turned to pace the deck, doubtless to think of South Africa, where his son now lay in his grave and where his country expected him to turn defeat into victory, the greatest challenge he had ever faced.

ACT II

18

LORD ROBERTS AND LORD KITCHENER

Britain's two greatest generals in the late Victorian era, rivals for military glory and honours, were Garnet Wolseley, "our only general," and Frederick Roberts, "our other general." Each had but one eye—Wolseley had lost his in the Crimea and Roberts his as a result of "brain fever"—and each had a peculiar aversion—Wolseley could not stand the sight of raw meat and Roberts was afraid of cats—but here all similarities ended. What Roberts thought of Wolseley is unknown; Wolseley thought Roberts a "cute, little, jobbing showman," "a snob," "a scheming little Indian," and "a man of whose abilities I have a poor opinion. . . . a very inferior fellow." But Wolseley met Roberts only once, his opinions were biased, and certainly his was a minority view.

Lord Rawlinson thought Roberts was "the greatest and most loveable man I have ever known." Young Churchill was impressed with him, and L. S. Amery called him "the greatest British soldier of the century between Waterloo and the world wars." Bron Herbert in *The Times History* wrote:

> His unaffected geniality and kindliness won the hearts of all officers who served with him, while his personal gallantry, his success, and his genuine and untiring interest in the welfare of the common soldier endeared "Bobs" to the army as a whole. . . . Of the qualities essential to generalship he was gifted with the imaginative intuition necessary to divine the movements and the intentions of the enemy, with the courage of his own judgement, and with the true thirst for victory. . . .[1]

Field Marshal Frederick Sleigh Roberts, first Baron Roberts of Kandahar (1832–1914), known as "Bobs" and frequently as "little Bobs"

151

because he stood only 5 feet 3 inches tall,* was a son of General Sir Abraham Roberts born in Cawnpore. British children born in India were usually shipped off to Britain to grow up, and Frederick Roberts was carried there when he was two years old. After Eton, Sandhurst, and Adiscombe (the military college of the Honourable East India Company), he was gazetted at the age of nineteen to the Bengal artillery and returned to India. He served first under his father on the Northwest Frontier, and then, when the great Indian mutiny shook the Empire, he saw much active service and won the Victoria Cross in a cavalry charge.

Later he took part in the Umbeyla Campaign on the Northwest Frontier, was sent to Abyssinia for the war against the Emperor Theodore, and to the Northeast Frontier for the arduous Lushai Campaign. During the Second Afghan War he was given command of one of the three invading columns, and for his victory at Peiwar Kotal he was promoted major general, knighted (KCB), and given the thanks of Parliament.

After a lull the hostilities resumed and Roberts again led an army into Afghanistan, defeating the Afghans at Charasia and occupying Kabul. He then captured the imagination of the British public and became a popular hero by marching 300 miles south with an army of 10,000 men for the relief of besieged Kandahar. A special Kabul-to-Kandahar medal was struck: Roberts was awarded a GCB, created a baronet, and made commander-in-chief of the Madras army. He fought no more battles but was made a baron in 1892 and three years later became a field marshal. He was commander-in-chief in Ireland, an honourable post in which to conclude a fine military career, when he was called to take the field in South Africa.

Roberts was, all things considered, the best choice the British government could have made from among the eight field marshals and nineteen full generals on the active list. Some had never been in battle or had seen little active service; others had, in their day, been fine battlefield commanders—Wolseley, Evelyn Wood, William Lockhart—but all were over sixty and most had not survived their years of campaigning with their faculties unimpaired. Of those senior to Buller, only the Duke of Connaught might have been as good as Roberts, but there was great reluctance on the part of the politicians to expose members of the royal family to the dangers of the battlefield, and the Duke's royal blood had always been a hindrance to his career. Even had the government been willing ignominiously to jettison Buller—which they were not—there were no military geniuses among the more junior generals. Aging but agile and tough Little Bobs was not only the logical choice but practically the only choice for the command in South Africa.

*Had he not been born into one of the classes of society from which British officers were drawn, Roberts could never have been a professional soldier, for the minimum height required by the regular army for other ranks was 5 feet 5½ inches, reduced during the war in South Africa to 5 feet 2 inches for the Royal Artillery and 5 feet 3 inches for other regiments of the line.

By accepting the appointment, Roberts put his own reputation on the line. Certainly he had more to lose than to gain. By his intellect, gallantry, character, and a reasonable amount of luck he had won for himself the Victoria Cross, a peerage, and a field marshal's baton; he was also one of the most popular of Britain's soldiers. There was little then in the form of honours or acclaim which success could bring him, while there existed the possibility that his military reputation might be shattered. Although he had not heard a shot fired in anger for twenty years, Roberts, unlike Buller, had no doubts about his own abilities and he was absolutely confident that he would succeed.

Wolseley was furious when told of Roberts's appointment, and he predicted that Buller, his protégé, would resign as soon as he heard that he was to be superseded. Lansdowne apparently thought so too and intimated as much in breaking the news to Buller. But instead of being disgruntled, Buller seemed actually relieved that the responsibilities of commander-in-chief were to be lifted from his shoulders. From Camp Frere he telegraphed a confidential message to Lansdowne:

I have for some time been convinced that it is impossible for one man to direct active military operations in two places distant 1,500 miles from each other. . . . Lord Lansdowne is kind enough to suggest that the decision may be distasteful to me, but I trust that any decision intended for the interests of the Empire will always be acceptable to me.[2]

Before leaving Southampton Roberts telegraphed to Buller asking him to stay on the defensive until he arrived. From Gibraltar and Madeira he sent similar messages. The voyage itself was not pleasant; Roberts was a poor sailor. He occupied his time reading books on South Africa and the American Civil War. At Gibraltar he was joined by Kitchener, who had come up from the Sudan.

Roberts had met Kitchener once before, only eight months earlier in Ireland at the suggestion of Henry Rawlinson. The short, kindly Roberts and the tall, cold Kitchener seemed to take a liking to each other, though it is hard to see how or why. George Younghusband pointed out their dissimilarities:

Lord Roberts was the modern Bayard, *chevalier sans peur et sans reproche* [sic]. Lord Kitchener was fashioned more on the lines of Bismarck. Both were born British, but one developed into the highest type of English gentleman, the other acquired more Teutonic characteristics. It would therefore be somewhat difficult for an honest admirer of Lord Roberts to be an equally honest admirer of Lord Kitchener.[3]

Horatio Herbert Kitchener, first Baron Kitchener of Khartoum (1850–1916), had only recently become a hero by conquering the Sudan. He was in many respects a peculiar hero for the British to embrace, for he lacked compassion and his eccentricities were not endearing. Cold, calculating, ruthless, and arrogant, he had great energy and was driven by a fierce ambition. He never loved a woman, and the only people in the world for whom he ever exhibited any affection were two of his young aides, one of whom disappointed him by marrying. He formed few friendships and made no acquaintances except with those whom he felt might be helpful, and these he did not hesitate to turn against when they were no longer useful and when it suited his purpose to do so. He had risen in the army by virtue of his intelligence and his energetic devotion to the tasks assigned to him—and in spite of the fact that few of his colleagues liked him. He did not cultivate the friendship of those beneath him in social or military rank, and he never spoke to a common soldier except to give an order. He was never known to allow love or hate or even his likes and dislikes to interfere with his decisions; personal feelings never kept him from doing what was best for his own interests. He could, and frequently did, lose his temper, raging and screaming, revealing that behind his great thick moustache and stern, impassive face there lurked a highly emotional nature. He preferred things to people or ideas, and as soon as he had the means he began to collect *objets d'art,* not hesitating to add to his collections by looting when opportunity offered.

Like many Victorian soldiers, Kitchener was the son of a soldier. As a boy he attended school for five years in Switzerland, where he became fluent in French, then went on to the Royal Military Academy, Woolwich, obtaining his commission in the Royal Engineers in January, 1871. Military duties occupied very little of his career, for he spent most of his time in engineering work, mostly surveying, in Cyprus and Palestine. His first real experience with troops was late in 1882 when he took an appointment as second-in-command of the cavalry in the new Egyptian army Britain created after destroying the old one and occupying the country. He learned Arabic and served as an intelligence officer during the unsuccessful attempt to rescue Gordon from Khartoum. After more survey work in East Africa he was appointed governor general of the Eastern Sudan.

On 17 January 1888 Kitchener fought his first battle when he marched against Osman Digna, one of the best of the Dervish generals. It was not a well-conducted operation. His force was soundly trounced, and he himself was severely wounded in the jaw. After a number of other appointments in Egypt, Kitchener, although only a colonel in the British army, was appointed sirdar, or commander-in-chief, of the Egyptian army in 1892. Sir Evelyn Baring (later Lord Cromer), who had recommended him, was impressed not with his military abilities but with his sense of economy; he described him as "a sound man of business." There is no doubt that he was a good organizer, and although he kept his army in rags to save money, he put together a sizable force of well-trained Egyptians and southern Sudanese. When in 1898 Britain decided to invade the Sudan in Egypt's name, he at last had the chance to achieve the glory he craved.

Exhibiting great logistical skill, he moved an Anglo-Egyptian army into the heart of the Sudan and at the battle of Omdurman mowed the Dervishes down with his rifles, cannons, and machine guns. For this he was raised to the peerage, received the thanks of Parliament, was feted, and was sent back as governor general of the Sudan. He was serving in this post when he was asked to go to South Africa with Roberts. Although his title was chief of staff and he was not a very senior general (he ranked 41st among major generals on the 1899 Army List), he really served as second-in-command and Roberts was to use him as his alter ego.

On 10 January 1900 Roberts and Kitchener arrived in Cape Town. The problems of the British in South Africa had not diminished while they were on the high seas: Gatacre was struggling to maintain his position; rebellion in the Cape midlands was still a threat; French had tried and failed to wrench Colesburg from the forces of Christiaan de Wet; Methuen was still sitting on the Modder River unable to advance; Ladysmith, Kimberley, and Mafeking were still besieged. The only encouraging factor, but an important one, was that men, guns, and supplies were pouring into South Africa at a prodigious rate and the fighting strength of the forces had risen to 86,730 men and 270 guns. The men came not just from Great Britain itself, but from all her "white colonies"; from India, Ceylon, and smaller possessions came groups of white colonials. Several thousand Indians also came to South Africa to serve in noncombatant roles.

While bringing in men and supplies herself, Britain took steps to cut the Boers' supply line. The only route to the outside world available to the republics, the only route which did not lead through British colonies, was the railway line that ran from Pretoria to the port of Lourenço Marques on Delagoa Bay in Mozambique (Portuguese East Africa). In December 1899 and January 1900 the British adopted some high-handed methods, stationing men-of-war to blockade the bay and even boarding several foreign vessels and hauling them off to Durban to have their cargoes examined. As these tactics produced some unpleasant diplomatic reactions, the British switched to the simple expedient of stationing agents at Lourenço Marques to buy up the cargoes as they landed.

One of the ever present fears of the British—Milner was haunted by it—and one of the great hopes of the republican Boers was that the Afrikaners in Cape Colony, who in rural areas outnumbered colonists of British descent, would rise en masse in rebellion against their British masters. Had there been a rebellion in the Cape of major proportions the complexion of the war would certainly have changed; that it did not happen was due to the peculiar attitudes of the "Cape Dutch" and to the wisdom of Britain's policy of self-government for all colonies capable of it.

There was certainly a considerable amount of sympathy on the part of the Afrikaners in the Cape for the republicans and their cause. They were united to the Boers in the north by language, religion, and culture. Until martial law was finally proclaimed in April 1901 seditious sentiments were openly expressed: republican flags and emblems were frequently displayed and young Afrikaner girls delighted in flaunting ribbons in the colours of the republics—red, white, and blue, plus orange for the Orange Free State and green for the Transvaal. Boer commandos invading from the Free State were invariably greeted with cheers and smothered in flowers. When J. H. Olivier rode into Aliwal North with a Free State commando there was a local celebration and a daughter of a former member of the Cape Parliament led the inhabitants in the singing of the Free State "Volkslied." Many Cape Afrikaners, particularly the young men, were eager to join commandos, and it has been estimated that before the end of the war as many as 10,000 Cape rebels fought for the republics.

Still, strong as were the Cape Afrikaners' sympathies for their republican neighbours and however content they might have been to live in an Afrikaner republic, they had no great grievance against the Imperial government, and the feelings of most did not extend to risking life and property in the republics' cause; there was no spontaneous uprising such as the Boer leaders had hoped for.

Most of the Cape politicians were Afrikaners, and some had relatives fighting with the Boers. A crisis of conscience afflicted many, perhaps most. W. P. Schreiner, the prime minister of Cape Colony, was the brother of Olive Schreiner, one of the most fervent pro-Boer writers in the Empire, and his wife was the sister of Francis Reitz, state secretary of the Transvaal. Schreiner's position was a difficult one—in fact, impossible. He had strongly opposed the policies of Milner and Chamberlain which had led to the war, and he was sympathetic to the cause of the republics; at the same time he felt a strong loyalty to the government he served and he could not countenance rebellion. He tried to prevent the imposition of martial law and he opposed drastic penalties for rebels while at the same time doing all in his power to prevent revolution. In the end he was damned by the British for doing too little to help them win the war and by the Afrikaners for doing too much.

Fear of the local inhabitants dominated Milner's thoughts. He even feared rebellion in Cape Town itself and persuaded Admiral Sir Robert Harris to keep 500 bluejackets in readiness to land should this happen. On New Year's Eve 1899 there was a rumour that Milner was to be kidnapped and that this would be the signal for a general rising. Guards were doubled and special precautions taken. Nothing happened.

During Roberts's stay in Cape Town he was fully exposed to Milner's anxiety complex, but he refused to be influenced by his apprehensions, and he all but drained the colony of troops for the development of his own strategy. However, only two weeks after he landed and before he could carry out his own scheme, Buller again took the offensive on the Tugela.

19

TABANYAMA: PRELUDE TO SPION KOP

On 15 November, in a minor action of the war, Winston Churchill had been captured during an attack on an armoured train near Estcourt. Only five days before he had written to General Evelyn Wood: "I think we ought to punish people who surrender troops under their command—and let us say at once—No exchange of Prisoners."[1] Less than two weeks later, a prisoner in Pretoria, his thinking had changed radically, and he was badgering his captors for permission to send home a press release urging prisoner exchange. Churchill did not wait to be exchanged, however; using an escape plan devised by Aylmer Haldane, he fled from Pretoria—although regrettably leaving Haldane behind—and he was now one of the few British heroes of the war. In a London music hall T. E. Dunville, a Lancashire comedian, warbled:

> You've heard of Winston Churchill
> This is all I have to say—
> He's the latest and the greatest
> Correspondent of the day.

Churchill was not on hand to enjoy his celebrity, for he had rejoined Buller's army, and in a dispatch to the *Morning Post* the "greatest correspondent of the day" alerted his readers that the next dramatic action of the war was about to take place: "The long interval between the acts has come to an end. The warning bell has rung. Take your seats, ladies and gentlemen. . . . The curtain is about to rise."

It was about to rise on Buller's second attempt to break though to Ladysmith. In spite of Roberts's advice to remain on the defensive, Buller made plans for a new attack at a new location, and by the time Roberts landed in Cape Town he was ready to shift his army 20 miles west of Estcourt and establish a new base at Springfield. Buller reported his plan to Roberts, who, not being intimately acquainted with the situation in Natal and reluctant to order Buller to give up a scheme already begun, gave his consent. Although apprehensive about the operation, the only advice he offered was that Buller move quickly: "Rapidity of movement is everything against an enemy so skillful in strengthening defensive positions."[2] This sound counsel was ignored.

It would first appear that Buller's plan was to make a flank attack—Roberts apparently thought this was what he had in mind—and had he moved with speed and vigour that is what it would have been. Moreover, it would surely have been successful, for the Boers would have been unable to throw up any effective opposition. But in fact he moved so slowly, in such a cumbersome fashion, that the Boers had ample opportunity to shift men and guns and to prepare new positions. Buller's scheme, then, turned out to be only another frontal attack at a new location.

Buller had been receiving a steady flow of reinforcements and he now had 30,000 men in his field army; the Boer force, on the other hand, was somewhat diminished, for a number of burghers, bored or homesick, had left the front. There were now only about 16,000 fighting burghers in Natal, half of whom were sitting around Ladysmith keeping White and his 12,000 men bottled up, while Botha stretched the remainder along the Tugela to prevent Buller from relieving them.

Leaving Barton's brigade to guard his base at Estcourt, Buller on 10 January 1900 moved out with 19,000 infantry, 3,000 cavalry, and 60 guns, including six large howitzers capable of throwing 50-pound lyddite shells and ten long-range naval guns (two 4.7-inch guns and eight 12-pounders). It was a ponderous operation. Thousands of men, guns, horses, oxen, wagons, carts, and ambulances plodded and ploughed through a pouring rain towards the village of Springfield. John Atkins described the march for the *Manchester Guardian:*

> The hills seemed to melt down like tallow under heat; the rain beat the earth into liquid, and the thick, earthy liquid ran down in terraced cascades. . . . From Estcourt to Frere the division waded, sliding, sucking, pumping, gurgling through the mud: the horses floundered or tobogganed with all four feet together.[3]

Dundonald's mounted troops splashed ahead to make sure the town was secure, and then Dundonald, exceeding his orders, advanced towards the Tugela and seized a prominent height called Spearman's Hill which overlooked the river and commanded a ford, Potgieter's Drift, by which Buller's army could cross. When the sun came out heliographic communication was established with Ladysmith; Lyttelton's brigade and later one of the new brigades, Talbot Coke's, occupied the hill and began to entrench. On the morning of 12 January Buller rode up and inexplicably ordered the entrenching to cease; it was "folly," he said.

From the summit of Spearman's Hill Buller had a magnificent view of the landscape, the twisting Tugela and the hills beyond: highest of all was whale-backed Spion Kop (in Afrikaans: Spiocnkop, "spy" or "lookout" hill); then, stretching westward, the 7-mile-long Tabanyama ridge with Bastion Hill, Sugar Loaf Hill, Three Tree Hill, and Green Hill at the ends of fingerlike projections pointing south towards the Tugela. In the distance was the beckoning twinkle of the Ladysmith heliograph, and in the hills between were the Boers. They had been slow to react to Buller's shift of front, and although they were now entrenching madly, the number opposed to Buller was insignificant. He could have walked through to Ladysmith with very little opposition had he made the attempt. But, ignorant of the chance he had, he occupied himself with his long supply columns.

Lieutenant General Charles Warren had arrived on the scene at the end of December, and Buller had reorganized his army, dividing it into two parts between Clery and Warren. Then he had reorganized again and put nearly the whole of his army under Warren and assigned him the task of forcing the heights beyond the Tugela. How Warren came to command such a force and to receive a mission of such importance is an enigma. Among the many incompetent British generals in South Africa, Warren was perhaps the worst; certainly he was the most preposterous. Yet Buller, who personally disliked him, turned over to him almost his entire army.

The son of a major general, Sir Charles Warren (1840–1927) was educated at Woolwich and commissioned in the Royal Engineers at the age of seventeen. He had already acquired a monocle. He spent his first twenty years in the army surveying, teaching surveying, and doing archaeological excavations in Palestine. It was not until the Gaika War of 1877, when he commanded a locally raised unit, that he saw action for the first time. He was severely wounded in the battle of Perie Bush.

In 1886 he was appointed chief commissioner of the London Metropolitan Police. During the two years he spent in this post he quarrelled with the home secretary, was accused of "military high-handedness," and was much criticised for his failure to track down Jack the Ripper. When he resigned he was named commander of troops in Singapore and spent five years quarrelling with the governor and bombarding the War Office with complaints. Buller, then adjutant general, finally wrote him: "All I want to say is for heaven's sake leave us alone."

Warren was fifty-nine years old and had been on the retired list for a year when he was unexpectedly and inexplicably given command of a division in South Africa and promoted lieutenant general. He was also given what was called a Dormant Commission, a secret document which entitled him to assume command of all the forces in South Africa should anything happen to Buller. When he arrived in Cape Town during Black Week he found waiting for him a telegram from the War Office ordering him to supersede Methuen. Wolseley thought that both Gatacre and Methuen should be removed from active commands at the front and given assignments on the lines of communication. Buller violently objected:

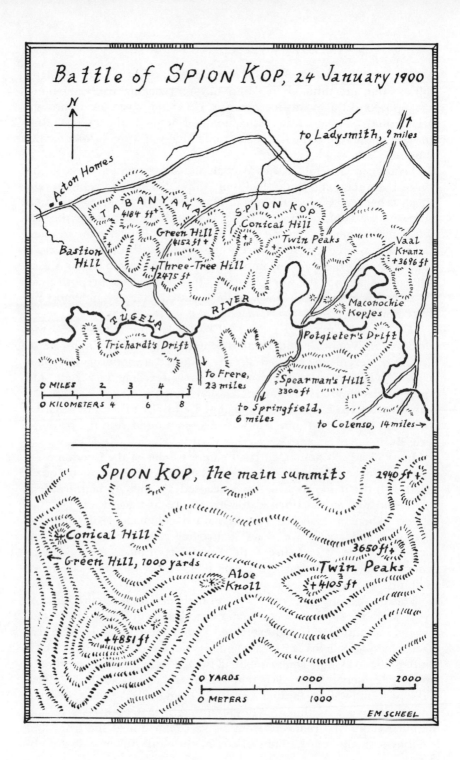

Battle of SPION KOP, 24 January 1900

N

to Ladysmith, 9 miles

Acton Homes

TABANYAMA
4184 ft +

SPION KOP
Conical Hill

Green Hill
4152 ft +

Twin Peaks

Vaal
Kranz
+3696 ft

Bastion
Hill

+ Three-Tree Hill
2475 ft

RIVER

TUGELA

Trichardt's Drift

Maconochie
Kopjes

Potgieter's Drift

to Frere,
23 miles

Spearman's Hill
3300 ft

to Springfield,
6 miles

to Colenso, 14 miles →

0 MILES   2   3   4   5
0 KILOMETERS 4   6   8

SPION KOP, the main summits   2940 ft +

+ Conical Hill

← Green Hill, 1000 yards

3650 ft +

Twin Peaks

Aloe
Knoll

+ 4105 ft

+ 4851 ft

0 YARDS   1000   2000
0 METERS   1000

EM SCHEEL

I cannot agree with the Commander-in-Chief and allow Methuen, who has done very well, to be superseded by Warren. Commander-in-Chief, comfortable at home, has no idea of the difficulties here. It would, I think, be a fatal policy to supersede every general who failed to succeed in every fight, but I offer no objection in my own case, if thought desirable.[4]

Buller was allowed to have his way, and Warren, by this time 500 miles north of Cape Town on his way to the Modder River, was stopped and ordered back; he was to follow his original instructions and assume command of a division in Natal.

When Warren joined Buller, he found his chief "rather reserved" and noted with surprise that he appeared to have "taken to heart his reverse at Colenso." His suggestion that Buller should take a month's rest was not kindly received. Neither was his expressed opinion that Hlangwane was the key to the problem of forcing the Boer positions on the Tugela. On the *Norham Castle* en route to South Africa he had occupied his time playing war games with his staff. At the mention of Hlangwane Buller turned on him and asked bluntly, "What do you know about it?" Warren's answer was necessarily lame: "General knowledge and war games." Buller ignored him.

Like Buller's other generals, Warren came equipped with his own military theories. He had told Wolseley that he thought the Boers could be defeated "either by sweeping over them with very long lines of infantry attacking simultaneously" or "by pounding away at them with artillery till they quailed."[5] His most eccentric notion was that troops should be "introduced" to the enemy before allowing them to fight, that there should be what he called a "dress rehearsal." He told his staff that he would no more take his men into battle without this rehearsal and introduction than "take a team of cricketers who had no experience of football to compete in a football match."

On the difficult march in the rain to Springfield Warren was in his element. "I knew all about the details of putting on extra spans of oxen and hauling on ropes," he said. "I was the only general intimately acquainted with these matters." Warren was now in command of more troops than he had ever seen in one place before, but instead of supervising them he "turned out in my old capacity as leader or ganger and helped manually." A preoccupation with oxen was to be revealed as one of Warren's defects as a general.

Other ranks always enjoy watching officers pitching in, shovelling dirt and hauling on ropes instead of tending to their business, so the sight of their monocled lieutenant general messing about with ox teams no doubt pleased them. Warren's bathing arrangements were a diversion too. One blistering hot day he was scrubbing himself in his mackintosh bath filled with steaming water and set up outside his tent, his men crowding round to watch, when Buller and his staff rode up. Warren draped a towel around his waist to greet his chief and then dressed. "I felt that I had done what I could for the day to amuse the troops," he said. Whatever his impressions on the men, Warren failed to impress most of his officers, one of whom was heard to refer to him as "this dug-out policeman."

Buller, after some indecision as to where to cross the river, ordered Warren to take 36 field guns, three brigades, and 1,500 mounted men, cross the river at Trichardt's Drift, and attack the Boer positions on the long Tabanyama ridge. Intelligence reported that the Boers had two long-range guns there, and Warren asked for the use of the naval guns, but Buller did not believe the intelligence reports and he refused. Warren persisted and tempers rose. If he could not have the naval guns he would have to capture Spion Kop, Warren argued; Buller said that would not be necessary.

On the evening of 16 January Warren's troops moved out of their camp near Springfield towards the Tugela. Although it was called a flying column, Warren's force, with its thousands of oxen and its laden wagons, was about as dashing as a centipede. Nevertheless it was an impressively martial sight. Lieutenant G. Burne of the Naval Brigade wrote that "the men in their greatcoats marching along with the horses and guns mixed up with them reminded me strongly of scenes in pictures of Napoleon's wars."[6]

Shortly after midnight the head of Warren's column reached Trichardt's Drift. In the hills opposite them there were at this moment not more than 500 Boers. Instead of crossing at once—infantry and cavalry could have crossed without a bridge—Warren contented himself with assembling his force on the south bank of the river, and not until morning did he order his engineers to construct a pontoon bridge. He then began a leisurely crossing of his men and guns and supplies. Buller rode over in the morning and sat all day with him watching the oxen and wagons, men, horses, and guns crossing the river. On the following day, 19 January, Warren occupied himself in moving his cattle and wagons 3 miles west of the drift to Venter's Spruit. There was no opposition, but by now the Boers could clearly see where they would be attacked and they were rushing up reinforcements and strengthening their defensive works under the eyes of Louis Botha, who had arrived only the day before. Still, Warren was in no hurry. He wanted to have his dress rehearsal and "to introduce Mr. Thomas Atkins to Mr. Boer and bid them come together."

Meanwhile, the dashing Dundonald, whose orders were to guard Warren's left flank, had already began to probe the Boers' far right. With only 700 troopers (to his intense indignation he had been compelled to give up 500 mounted men to guard oxen) he made a wide flanking movement west and then north towards Acton Homes, where, on a road that led from Ladysmith into the Orange Free State, he ambushed a 300-man commando. The Boers lost 20 men killed or wounded, and Dundonald took two dozen prisoners. He then threw himself into some kopjes along the road and sent word to Warren that he needed some artillery and the return of his cavalry. Never imagining that Warren would spend three days watching his oxen cross a river, he innocently assumed that infantry would follow in his wake and exploit his success.

There is little doubt that had Warren moved rapidly with his infantry and artillery he could have turned the Boer flank and moved behind the enemy's positions, demoralising them and relieving Ladysmith. But this was not Warren's way. He was mentally and temperamentally incapable of realizing the importance of Dundonald's actions and of exploiting the opportunity now open to him. He sent Dundonald a squadron and a half of cavalry but no artillery. The next day, over Dundonald's furious protests, he ordered the mounted brigade to return.

Buller later told a royal commission:

On the 19th* Lord Dundonald . . . had taken the right flank of the Boer position, whereas General Warren had advanced to the westward and was crossing Venter's Spruit. I was dissatisfied with Warren's operations, which seemed to me aimless and irresolute. Dundonald's movement was a decided success, and should have been supported by artillery, while Warren's infantry should have attacked the salient, which Dundonald's success had left exposed.[7]

At the time, however, Buller made no attempt to countermand Warren's orders or to interfere with him in any way.

Warren, even at this date, had no concrete plan of action. He considered several schemes, built another bridge, and shifted about his men, wagons, and guns in a purposeless manner. John Atkins overheard two soldiers talking:

"What are we waiting 'ere for? Why don't we go on?"

"Don't yer know?"

"No."

"To give the Boers time to build up their trenches and fetch up their guns. Fair—ain't it?"

What was obvious to the men in the ranks was not, apparently, capable of being grasped by their general. When Warren announced that he was not going to do anything for another two or three days in order "to adopt some special arrangements," even Buller grew impatient with his languid advance to battle. He later confessed:

On the 19th I ought to have assumed command myself. I saw that things were not going well—indeed everyone saw that. . . . I blame myself now for not having done so. I did not, because I thought that if I did I should discredit General Warren in the estimation of his troops; and that if I were shot, and he had to withdraw across the Tugela, and they had lost confidence in him, the consequences might be very serious.[8]

At long last, on 20 January, Warren decided on an attack—a frontal attack directed towards Three Tree Hill at the end of one of the fingers projecting south from the Tabanyama range. Warren designated Clery, that expert on minor tactics, to conduct the battle, and at 3:00 A.M. the

*Actually the 18th.

troops moved out, led by E. R. P. Woodgate's brigade with Hart in reserve. Three hours later the leading elements of Woodgate's brigade reached the summit of Three Tree Hill and discovered what a couple of scouts might have learned had they been sent out, or what might have been observed from the balloon that was available: the hill was unoccupied.

The sight of the great army advancing on them had badly shaken the Boers, but with the arrival of Botha and the reinforcements he had summoned they had taken heart and, under Botha's energetic direction, had quickly constructed an excellent line of trenches and sangars well back on the high end of the slanting table that constituted the top of Tabanyama ridge. These were so placed that everywhere they commanded from 600 to 2,000 yards of sloping, grassy glacis with a clear field of fire. Field Cornet Jan Kemp said later: "Though I have to say it myself, our officers certainly knew what they were doing when they selected those positions."[9] Botha's right was in the air and weak—he had only 2,000 men on the ridge—but by now he was convinced that British generals would always make frontal attacks. His belief was confirmed by the result.

Clery sent Hart's Irish Brigade climbing up the fingers of Tabanyama to the west of Three Tree Hill and ordered up batteries to support the advance. The guns were soon in action, bombarding the Boer positions. As Hart's infantry neared the top the Boers fell back to their well-prepared positions at the opposite end of the glacis.

By 3:30 P.M. the British line had reached a point where only the open glacis separated them from the Boer trenches, and here they paused. Hart —brave and hot-headed—was about to draw his sword and lead his men in a charge up the glacis when Clery, tormented by misgivings about the whole enterprise, fearful of the casualties he would suffer if his men tried to rush up that exposed slope, called a halt. Clery communicated his doubts and fears to Warren, who agreed that a further advance ought not to be attempted at this time. Twenty-eight officers and men had been killed and 280 wounded in the aborted attack.

There was no thought, apparently, of making a night attack on Tabanyama, and Hart's brigade was pulled back somewhat from the edge of the glacis, although it remained on the ridge. Colonel Frederick Walter Kitchener, Lord Kitchener's younger brother, led an attack on the Boer right flank, an attack which might well have succeeded had not Clery abruptly ordered it stopped. Churchill, who was observing the action on Tabanyama, began to wonder if "perhaps the task before Sir Redvers Buller and Sir Charles Warren is an actual impossibility.[10]

Warren moved his headquarters up to Three Tree Hill near Clery; Buller came around and, although he gave no orders, criticised almost everything. He found, he testified later, that Warren had "divided his fighting line into three independent commands, independent of each other and apparently independent of him, as he told me he could not move any batteries without General Clery's consent."[11] In other words,

Warren was delegating his responsibilities just as Buller himself had done.

It was unfortunate for the British that two generals such as Buller and Warren should have been placed in command of the forces on the Tugela. Both were, though for different reasons, indecisive; together their incompetence was compounded. Neither was particularly clever. Buller knew he was not; Warren was convinced that he was, and even when it was dramatically proven he was not, he ever kept a high opinion of himself. Buller's mistakes were those of a simple, honest soldier, determined to do his duty but thrust into a position where he was expected to assume more responsibility than he wanted or could handle. Failure resulted from his lack of skill in planning battles involving large bodies of men, his own awareness of his deficiencies (though he tried to hide them from others), and his deep compassion for those he led, which he concealed behind a gruff, uncommunicative manner. Warren's mistakes were those of an arrogant man caught in the net of his own absurd theories and deceived by his own conceit. He hid his lack of experience, his uncertainty, and his lack of ability behind a mask of bouncing self-confidence. Buller was a blunderer, but Warren was a fool.

Buller distrusted Warren's theories; he was aware of his lack of experience, and Warren's personality grated on him. But perhaps he envied him his self-confidence and believed, or wanted to believe, that Warren was capable of extricating him from his difficulties on the Tugela. In any case, he placed in Warren's incapable hands his own reputation, the lives of most of his soldiers, the fate of Ladysmith, and the credit of the British army in the eyes of the world. Then he compounded his mistake by meddling. Warren left to himself was a menace; under the carping criticism and interfering "suggestions" of Buller he became a disaster.

None of the generals produced any comprehensive battle plan, and they wandered over the front wondering what they should do. Warren briefly considered renewing the attack on the Boer right, but after worrying the idea a bit he decided against it and hit upon the uninspiring plan of a frontal assault on the Boer trenches opposite Three Tree Hill. But first he wanted a four-day artillery bombardment. He asked for more troops, more guns, and once again the large naval guns. Buller gave him another brigade of infantry and four howitzers, ignoring the request for the naval guns, and the following day rode over to have another talk. It was a fateful conversation.

Buller scoffed at the notion of demoralising the enemy with a long bombardment, regarding it as a time-wasting activity which Warren was using as an excuse to delay making the painful decisions as to where and when and how he should attack. He told Warren that either he must attack at once or he would order his forces withdrawn behind the Tugela. He himself favoured an attack on the Boer right, but he gave no positive orders. Warren was against this; he feared it would leave his base camp inadequately protected—and what might not the Boers do to his oxen?

He insisted that he could not attack in the centre without the long bombardment which Buller had vetoed. If he attacked on his right, he said, he would first have to seize Spion Kop. All right, then take it, said an exasperated Buller. And thus in a heated exchange between two irritated generals was the fateful decision made to attack Spion Kop.

Indecisive generals hold councils of war. As soon as Buller left, Warren summoned every available general to come and debate what should be done and to consider the off-hand decision, if decision it can be called, to attack Spion Kop. At the meeting someone again suggested an attack on the Boer right, but Clery the tactician argued vehemently against this, advancing an extraordinary argument: If successful they would then be committed to a series of attacks on all the enemy positions on the ridge. This is what is usually considered the highly desirable objective of rolling up the enemy's flank. No one pointed this out. In the end there was a kind of agreement to attack the hill called Spion Kop. Later Buller said that Warren "had evidently not thought the matter out." Neither had he. No one had.

20

SPION KOP

While Warren and Clery were fighting their inconclusive battle on Tabanyama, Lyttelton had been conducting a series of demonstrations with his brigade on the right of the British line. He wanted to do something more, to be helpful if he could. He was independent of Warren and reported directly to Buller, but every day he inquired of Warren how he could best cooperate with him; he made suggestions, such as a night attack; he was willing to consider any plan. Warren could think of nothing for him to do. Barton, left at Colenso, also made some demonstrations, carrying out a vigorous reconnaissance in force in the direction of Hlangwane and other Boer positions. The Boers were alarmed, but had no need to be, for Buller, incapable of effectively orchestrating the movements of his subordinates, was not the man to exploit such opportunities, and nothing was accomplished.

Although Buller had already agreed to the attack on Spion Kop, he still felt that an attack on the Boer right was better, and he sent Warren a letter in which he outlined a promising plan for such an operation. It was not an order, not a plan Warren was directed to follow, merely a suggestion. Warren ignored it.

Buller's behaviour was becoming increasingly vacillatory. *The Times History* summed it up: "He was determined not to let Warren work out his own plan in his own way; he could not bring himself to insist that Warren carry out the plan he himself was convinced was the right one; he would not take over the command himself."[1]

Warren had given Buller to understand that Spion Kop would be seized that night, 22 January. The man selected to lead the attack was Major General John Talbot Coke, a veteran of forty years in the army who was still lame from a recently broken leg. It was late in the afternoon when he was summoned to Warren's tent and given his orders. Coke protested that some of the troops selected were still at Venter's Spruit; he also sensibly suggested that he ought first to have a look at the position he was to attack. Warren readily agreed and the operation was postponed, although Warren neglected to inform Buller. When Coke left Warren's tent it was dark, and although his own camp was not far away, he became so hopelessly lost that he was forced to spend the night in the open. That a lame general who could not find his way home in the dark was a poor choice to lead a night attack on a strange height did not occur to Warren.

Early the next morning Warren and Coke with Major General E. R. P. Woodgate and some other officers rode out to look at Spion Kop, looming 1,470 feet above them. Tabanyama ridge ends on the east with a height called Green Hill; from here the ground drops sharply into a gully on the other side of which is Conical Hill, the northeastern end of Spion Kop, which extends 3 miles to the east. A spur, or arête, extends to the southwest, and on the eastern edge of the triangular-shaped summit of Spion Kop proper is a prominent rise called Aloe Knoll. Beyond, further east, are two commanding heights known as Twin Peaks.

The inspection of Spion Kop by Warren and his officers was cursory, and they appear to have viewed it from only one angle, most of their attention being directed to the arête running to the southwest by which the troops would ascend. From where they stood they were unable to see Twin Peaks or Aloe Knoll. Their failure to discover the existence of the latter was to prove tragic. Had one of the generals ascended in the balloon or had Warren ordered an engineer to make a sketch this oversight would not have occurred. But the balloon was not sent up and no sketch of any description was made; those responsible for the attack had only the vaguest notion of the configuration of the hill.

Warren returned to his tent to find Buller there waiting to hear his report on the occupation of Spion Kop. When Buller heard that no attack had yet been made, that it had been delayed without his knowledge, he exploded. Warren did his best to calm him with assurances that there would be no more delay, that the attack would be launched that night without fail. Buller had to be satisfied with that, but when told that Coke was to lead the attack he balked. He did not like the man anyway, and he pointed out that a lame man was not the best choice as a commander for so energetic an enterprise. Warren had to agree. He gave the command to Woodgate, a fifty-five-year-old general in poor health.

The force selected included the Lancashire Fusiliers, six companies of the Royal Lancasters, and two companies of the South Lancashires. In addition to these regulars, 200 troopers from Lieutenant Colonel A. W. Thorneycroft's Mounted Infantry (composed mostly of Johannesburg uitlanders) and a half company of Royal Engineers were selected—a total force of 1,700 men. Although a field telegraph unit was available, the communications were put in charge of an artillery officer with a small staff of signallers. The mountain battery would have been useful—in the event, decisive—but it had been left behind at Frere and no one thought of it until it was too late. No one thought of taking machine guns either. There was, in fact, very little thought of any sort.

No one had any clear conception of the reasons for attacking Spion Kop. Buller, when asked by a staff officer what the force on Spion Kop was to do after it had secured the summit, thought about this for a few moments and then said, "It has got to stay there." No consideration had been given either as to what the rest of the army would be or should be doing. Lieutenant Colonel Charles à Court (afterwards Repington), a member of Buller's staff assigned to Warren as liaison officer, later wrote: "Some 1,700 men were to assault a hill . . . in the centre of the Boer position, and the rest of Buller's 20,000 men were to look on and do nothing."[2]

Selected to lead the way up Spion Kop was Lieutenant Colonel Alexander Thorneycroft, a heavily built man, 6 feet 2 inches tall, in command of a mounted infantry unit. He was supposed to have two Bantu guides, but one bolted and the other proved useless. Nevertheless, Thorneycroft had spent much of the day looking at the arête along which they were to climb and memorizing a series of landmarks; he felt confident that he could lead Woodgate and his men to the top.

At seven thirty in the evening on 23 January Woodgate's force assembled below Three Tree Hill. The men were told that their work was to be with the bayonet, and to make sure no one fired his rifle, all magazines were carried empty. An hour later they began their march, down a gully and past a large pile of empty sandbags which some intelligent officer had supplied with the intention that each man should carry one with him for use on the summit. However, as no one remembered to give the order to pick them up, they were left behind.

About eleven o'clock in the evening they reached the foot of Spion Kop and the actual climb began. It was a dark night and there was a slight drizzle. The climb was slow and arduous, and it took four hours to reach the last of Thorneycroft's landmarks; here the slope grew less steep, but they were enveloped in a heavy mist. Quietly the word was passed to fix bayonets and extend in long lines. The advance continued cautiously. Suddenly there was a challenge from a Boer sentry: "Werda?" The soldiers threw themselves in the damp weeds on the hard and rocky ground, as they had been instructed to do, while the Boer picket—about seventy men of the Vryheid Commando and some German volunteers—emptied their magazines into the misty night. Then Thorneycroft jumped to his feet and yelled, "Charge!" His own men and the Lancashire Fusiliers leaped forward shouting "Majuba!" One burgher was killed: he died on a bayonet wielded by Lieutenant Vere Awdry, an athletic young man who swung him into the air like a bale of hay. The rest of them fled, some in their stocking feet. It was 3:30 A.M. Woodgate formed up his men and ordered them to give three cheers to let the army below know that the position was won, and he sent Lieutenant Colonel à Court down to give Warren a firsthand account of their victory. Then, instead of sending out officers to discover the configuration of the hill, he ordered his engineers to lay out a line of trenches where they were and the men began to throw up stone sangars and to scratch out the trenches which were to become for many of them their graves. The ground was hard and stony; the entrenching tools were few and flimsy. Woodgate did not know that he was on a false crest, still more than 100 yards from the true crest line. And of course he was ignorant of the existence of Aloe Knoll, the dominant height on the summit.

As soon as Botha learned what had happened he sent messengers galloping to all the laagers with an urgent call for volunteers: "Spion Kop must be taken this day." But many burghers, assuming that this was the beginning of a general British offensive, panicked. Wagons and saddlebags were hastily packed and men streamed down the road north. To stem the headlong flight Botha himself galloped out to the road where he pleaded and argued with the fugitives, tried shaming them by pointing out a group of foreign volunteers steadfastly making for Spion Kop, and even lashed out with his sjambok. Many turned back, but few went to Spion Kop.

Not all the burghers took fright or had to be driven to battle. Commandant Hendrik Prinsloo, the thirty-eight-year-old leader of the Carolina Commando, was a veteran of the First Anglo-Boer War and of several Kaffir wars; leading 88 men from his commando, he was the first to move to the attack. It was seven o'clock in the morning before they reached the foot of the hill. They left their horses and like stalking hunters advanced from rock to rock up the northern side of Spion Kop. They encountered no resistance, for although it was daylight the top of the hill was still covered with a thick mist. Meanwhile, Botha was hastening forward more men and ordering his guns to shell the British as soon as their exact position could be determined.

At eight thirty in the morning the dissolving mist, a parting curtain on this hilltop stage, revealed to the actors the setting for the tragedy to be enacted. Only now could the British see that their too shallow trenches were located in the wrong place. They were in a death trap. Prinsloo's men had already occupied Aloe Knoll, and as soon as the mist cleared enough for them to sight their rifles they poured an enfilading fire into the Lancashire Fusiliers on the right flank of the British position. Many soldiers never knew where the fire was coming from. Some 70 of the dead were found to have been shot through the right side of the head.

Prinsloo had carried up a heliograph and it flashed away, relaying fire control data to the Boer gunners, who soon began to lay down an accurate and deadly fire. Woodgate tried to signal for artillery support, but his one heliograph was knocked out of action and his flag signallers had a hard time making their signals understood. Besides, the Boers were familiar with the peculiar configuration of Spion Kop and the British were not. Although the British had nearly ten times as many guns as the Boers, the soldiers on Spion Kop received practically no help from their own artillery.

At eight forty-five Woodgate with his brigade major, Captain Naunton Vertue, was standing to the left of the main trench talking with Lieutenant Colonel Charles Bloomfield of the Lancashire Fusiliers, who was pointing out the Boer reinforcements which could be seen coming up below Aloe Knoll. These were mainly men from the Pretoria Commando under "Red Daniel" Opperman. Suddenly and silently Woodgate crumpled with a Mauser bullet lodged in his head. Bloomfield and Vertue knelt over him; he was still alive but quite obviously no longer able to function. Lieutenant Colonel Malby Crofton of the Royal Lancasters, the next senior officer, now assumed command.

The Boers, too, were taking losses. Berend Badenhorst, field cornet from Vryheid, was standing behind a large rock shooting. Suddenly he swung on his heel and with a groan sank to a sitting position, his back against the rock. Although hit between the eyes, he was still alive. Two Americans fighting with the Boers, Alan Hiley and John Hassell, wrote a description of his death:

> Hour after hour he sat with wide open eyes. His death certain, no one moved him. . . . Men with spare ammunition hurrying past would give this well known man a glance of pity. . . . The noise of the battle and the passing men had no apparent effect on the deadened brain or staring gaze, but sitting erect until noon, suddenly, with a gutteral she-e-e-t (shoot) a stream of blood poured from the hole in his forehead and the bravest man we ever knew sank dead and limp to the earth.[3]

Young Deneys Reitz had followed behind the Pretoria men when red-bearded Daniel Opperman led them up Spion Kop:

> Dead and dying men lay all along the way, and there was proof that the Pretoria men had gone by for I soon came upon the body of John Malherbe, our Corporal's brother, with a bullet between his eyes; a few paces further lay two more dead men of our commando. Further on I found my tent-mate, poor Robert Reinecke, shot through the head, and not far off L. de Villiers of our corporalship lay dead. Higher up was Krige, another of Isaac's men, with a bullet through both lungs, still alive, and beyond him Walter de Vos of my tent shot through the chest, but smiling cheerfully as we passed. Apart from the Pretoria men there were many dead and wounded, mostly Carolina burghers from the eastern Transvaal. . . .

Half-way across lay the huddled body of a dead man and now that I had time to look more carefully at him I recognized Charles Jeppe, the last of my tent-mates. His death affected me keenly for we had been particularly good friends. . . . The English troops lay so near that one could have tossed a biscuit tin among them, and whilst the losses which they were causing us were only too evident, we on our side did not know that we were inflicting even greater damage upon them. Our own casualties lay hideously among us, but theirs were screened from view behind the breastwork, so that the comfort of knowing that we were giving worse than we received was denied us.[4]

Cramped on the top of Spion Kop, excited and fearful but without rancour, Britons and Boers slaughtered each other. Without the comfort of bitterness or hatred, weapons were aimed and fired into the faces beneath slouch hats and pith helmets. *The Times History* noted that "rarely has a war been carried on with less personal hatred on both sides," and of Spion Kop it is remarkable that in not a single one of the many accounts of this desperate fight between soldiers and burghers is there one expression of hatred for the enemy.

Each man had an arduous role to play. The Transvaal farmers and their sons, the Lancashire plough boys, and the sweeps of city slums— all were to face on this hot summer's day an ordeal beyond any of their imagining, for the concentrated hell that Spion Kop became was beyond any man's experience. Compressed on the hill in the heat and smoke and din was all the courage and endurance that some 2,500 men could muster. Some found courage but could not sustain it; some found they could endure but not endure enough; and some found that they were without either courage or endurance. To retreat, to flee down the hill, was not difficult. It was not fear of punishment that held those who stayed and endured. A sense of duty, a fear of shame greater than physical fear, a sentiment that a man must not desert his comrades—these held most through the long hours of the morning.

Neither Boer nor Briton had considered Spion Kop of great importance, yet now it had become the whole battle; indeed, on this day it became the entire war. Hundreds of miles away Methuen sat listlessly on the Modder and Cronjé in his trenches at Magersfontein; Gatacre, De Wet, Roberts, and De la Rey were all inactive. Boers and Britons in and around Ladysmith, Mafeking, and Kimberley, besiegers and besieged, were quiet while on this triangular piece of ground, roughly 400 yards on a side, war raged with an insane fury. Even the remainder of the two armies facing each other for miles along the Tugela, burghers and sol-diers, were spectators, watching and waiting and wondering. For miles around, on all sides of Spion Kop, the sounds of the battle could be heard. Soldiers and civilians in Ladysmith could see "little white balls of smoke breaking over the summit" and hear the distant roar of cannon and musketry. The Boers in their laagers and trenches on Tabanyama watched and listened too, and the Bantu wagon drivers on both sides and the locals in their scattered kraals watched in fear and wonder the fury of the white men. It was as though each side had sent its champions to this high hilltop to decide the fate of them all. But no one had selected them as the bravest and best; only destiny had chosen them; on each side the men were representative of their respective armies; it was a fair sample that each sent.

The Boer guns took a heavy toll of the Lancashire boys, but for the most part it was a primitive fight with rifles and bayonets. There was no cavalry; there were no machine guns, no grenades, no elaborate fortifications. Men came to battle on this treeless, boulder-strewn hilltop almost barehanded, without water or food or medical comforts—at least not nearly enough.

At Warren's headquarters on Three Tree Hill the first definite news from Spion Kop had been received when à Court arrived with his description of the easy conquest of the hilltop. When shortly after the naval officers, seeing through their telescopes Boers moving among the rocks on Aloe Knoll, opened fire with their 4.7-inch naval guns, Warren sent them an urgent message: "We occupy the whole summit and I fear you are shelling us seriously. Cannot you turn your guns on the enemy's guns?" The naval guns shifted their fire. The Boers were spared a bombardment of heavy shells and the British on Spion Kop were deprived of artillery support.

The next news to reach Warren was a frantic message sent by signal flags: "Colonel Crofton to G.O.C. Force. Reinforce at once or all lost. General dead." Warren was not too disturbed. He had just sent off two more battalions—the Middlesex and the Scottish Rifles (Cameronians)—and so he signalled Crofton that reinforcements were on the way, concluding his message with: "Hold on to the last. No surrender." He then relayed Crofton's message to Lyttelton, asking him what he could do on the right, and he sent Coke up to replace Woodgate, giving him as parting words: "Mind, no surrender." It was shortly after eleven o'clock in the morning when Coke with his bad leg began to climb. Coke thought a machine gun might be useful, so he ordered one to be brought along with him, but as he explained later, "unfortunately it overturned."

Buller was following the action, and he could see more from his headquarters on Spearman's Hill than could Warren on Three Tree Hill, but instead of taking command he simply continued to criticise and to make suggestions. At eleven forty-five he sent Warren the following message: "Now Woodgate is dead I think you must put a strong commander on top; I recommend you put Thorneycroft in command."

Warren at once signalled to Crofton that Thorneycroft was in charge with the rank of brigadier general. Crofton felt aggrieved; as he said later, he was "hurt most deeply being superseded during an engagement by an officer so much my junior." Warren did not tell Buller that he had already appointed Coke, who, still climbing up the arête, was not informed that he had been superseded before he had even arrived.

On the summit a signals officer went off to inform Thorneycroft of his appointment, but he stopped to lead forward a rush of men to a section where reinforcements were urgently needed, then he became caught up in the fighting, lost the message (it was later picked up by the Boers), and it was hours before he found Thorneycroft. Another messenger found Thorneycroft but was shot dead at his feet, his message undelivered. Eventually a lieutenant tracked him down and shouted to him above the noise of the musketry and the crashing shells: "Sir C. Warren has heliographed that you are in command. You are a general."

When Coke arrived on the summit early in the afternoon he found what he described with some understatement as a "scene of considerable confusion." Throughout the morning there had been a bitter struggle for the crest. The British had pushed out from their main trenches and established themselves in positions on the true crest, but the Boers had at once begun to drive them back. Beginning on the right of the line they attacked a section of Thorneycroft's Mounted Infantry and wiped them out. Then, creeping around to the right rear, they wiped out another section. The British mounted two attacks to regain their lost ground, one led by Thorneycroft himself, but the men were swept away by the fury of the Boer musketry. The main trenches became their front line, and these were clogged with dead and wounded. The two forces were so close at some points that the Boers could hear the shouts of the British officers and the British could hear the encouraging calls in Afrikaans of the Boer leaders—and all could hear the piteous cries of the wounded.

Accounts of the battle written by participants, Boer and British, fail to give a clear picture of what actually happened on Spion Kop this day. Although the length of the battlefield was not much more than 400 yards, the actors in the drama, including the leaders on both sides, appear to have been completely absorbed in what was taking place in their immediate neighbourhood.

The sun was a ball of fire overhead, and there was no water for anyone on the firing line on either side; heat and thirst added their torments to the confusion, fear, and pain of the struggling men. What the survivors seem to remember most clearly was the intermingling of the living and the dead, the wounded and the fit, and the individual acts of courage. Captain Charles Muriel of the Middlesex Regiment was shot through the cheek, but he continued to lead his company until a bullet lodged in his brain. Major William Scott-Moncrieff of the same regiment was wounded three times but kept to his post until a fourth bullet felled him. Captain Fergus Murray, adjutant of the Cameronians, with five dripping wounds, continued to stagger about among his men and even led a charge before he was killed. An officer of the Middlesex later described how he was wounded:

I fired at one Boer, and then another passed. We were fighting hand to hand. I shot the Boer and he dropped, clinging, however, to his rifle as he fell, and covering me most carefully. He fired, and I fell like a rabbit, the bullet going in just over and grazing the left lung. I lay where I fell until midnight.[5]

Two soldiers were seen burning, shells having set fire to their clothes. One soldier, his arm blown off close to the shoulder by a shell, picked up his shorn arm and screamed, "My arm! My arm! Oh, God, where's my arm?" Churchill's description was perhaps not overpainted: "The dead and injured, smashed and broken by the shells, littered the summit till it was a bloody, reeking shambles."[6]

It was too much for some men. A few days after the battle Benjamin Walker, a trooper in Thorneycroft's Mounted Infantry, wrote to his father:

Now that I am writing a private letter which will never go out of our circle I must tell you how we were deserted by the regulars. Their conduct was disgraceful. Twice they bolted and were rallied by our Colonel. Three of us were alone in the midst of a crowd of Lancashires who lay with their heads rolled up in their arms, laying flat on the ground not daring to lift their guns to shoot, shaking and trembling with fear. It was horrible.[7]

About one o'clock in the afternoon some Lancashire Fusiliers on the far right of the British position, hard pressed by Opperman's burghers, discovered that all their officers had been shot away. "Where are the bosses?" one Fusilier cried. Leaderless and demoralised, men began to wave white handkerchiefs over their heads. The Boers ceased firing, and some, thinking the battle over, stood up. They were immediately shot down by those on the British side who either did not see the white flags or refused to recognize them. Someone shouted for those who wanted to surrender to come out. No one moved. Then Jan Celliers of the Pretoria Commando boldly ran forward, leaped over the parapet, and called out, "Who is your officer?" There were no officers, only a group of frightened soldiers who stood up and raised their hands. Other Boers, waving handkerchiefs, then ran over to join Celliers.

At this critical moment a sergeant from Thorneycroft's Mounted Infantry came up. A private tore the rifle from his hands and told him, "You're a prisoner."

"No, no," the sergeant protested. "They're surrendering to us. The reinforcements have come." Then, seeing all around him soldiers with their hands over their heads, he bolted and ran to find his colonel.

Thorneycroft had badly twisted his knee, but when told of this disaster he called to the men around him to follow as he limpingly ran to the right of the line. The Boers were rounding up their prisoners when this huge, angry-faced man came hopping and limping up to them shouting, "I'm in command here! Take your men back to hell, sir! I allow no surrender!"

Then there occurred another of those battlefield arguments. It was short and furious, but Thorneycroft lost. The thoroughly demoralised Lancashire men, 167 of them, tamely went off with their Boer captors and

Thorneycroft retreated to the shelter of some rocks. At that moment a company of the Middlesex Regiment which had just arrived on Spion Kop appeared on the scene. Thorneycroft took these men and his own and led them in a charge that drove the Boers off that section of the crest.

The Boers lost eleven men killed during the capture of the Lancashires. One of the dead was elderly Marthinus Wessels of Kroonstad, father of nine children and a cousin of President Steyn. Because of his age Steyn had tried to persuade him to go home, but the old man had replied that he wanted to take part in just one battle.

A half hour after the surrender incident the morale of the soldiers in the centre of the line crumbled and they deserted their trenches in batches and made for the rear. Crofton rushed forward, had his bugler sound the "Advance," and rallied some of them. Again, just in time, another company of the Middlesex arrived and swept forward through the panic-stricken Lancashires to reoccupy the trenches. Croften, Thorneycroft, and the Middlesex had narrowly averted another Majuba.

The morale of the Boers was weakening as well. Deneys Reitz described the situation on the Boer side:

> The sun became hotter and we had neither food nor water. Around us lay scores of dead and wounded men, a depressing sight, and by mid-day a feeling of discouragement had gained ground that was only kept in check by Commandant Opperman's forceful personality and vigorous language to any man who seemed wavering. Had it not been for him the majority would have gone far sooner than they did, for the belief spread that we were being left in the lurch. . . .
>
> As the hours dragged on a trickle of men slipped down the hill, and in spite of his watchful eye this gradual wastage so depleted our strength that long before nightfall we were holding the blood-spattered ledge with a mere handful of rifles. I wanted to go too, but the thought of Isaac and my other friends saved me from deserting. . . .
>
> The hours went by; we kept watch, peering over and firing whenever a helmet showed itself, and in reply the soldiers volleyed unremittingly. We were hungry, thirsty and tired; around us were the dead men covered with swarms of flies attracted by the smell of blood. We did not know the cruel losses that the English were suffering, and we believed that they were easily holding their own, so discouragement spread as the shadows lengthened.
>
> Batches of men left the line, openly defying Red Daniel who was impotent in the face of this wholesale defection, and when at last the sun set I do not think there were sixty men left on the ledge.[8]

At Warren's headquarters there was increasing anxiety. Winston Churchill, still a war correspondent but now also holding a commission as a second lieutenant in the South African Light Horse, went up to Captain Cecil Levita, an artillery officer on Warren's staff, and said, "For God's sake, Levita, don't let this be a second Majuba Hill!"

Levita shrugged and suggested that Churchill talk with Warren, who was pacing up and down nearby. Second Lieutenant Churchill ap-

proached Lieutenant General Warren and offered his advice. Levita overheard snatches. Churchill was in full flow: "Majuba Hill . . . the great
British public. . . ." Warren stopped his pacing and glared through his
monocle; then he turned to Levita and bellowed, "Who is this man? Take
him away! Put him under arrest!"

Thorneycroft, who throughout the day remained too far forward to
give general direction to the fight, sent a message to Warren at 2:30 P.M.
begging for more reinforcements. Meanwhile Coke, still unaware of
Thorneycroft's appointment, formed the impression that the summit was
too crowded; he therefore held back reinforcements and had them fire
long-range volleys at the Boers on Green Hill. Coke, having heard that
Crofton was severely wounded (he had been hit but was, apparently, still
exercising command), assumed that he was taking over command from
the next senior officer, Lieutenant Colonel Augustus Hill of the Middlesex Regiment. Hill, too, had heard that Crofton was badly wounded and
thought himself in command until he encountered Coke. Thus for a time
three or four officers—Thorneycroft, Hill, Coke, and perhaps Crofton—
each thought himself in charge of all the troops on Spion Kop.

About four o'clock in the afternoon Churchill and Captain Ronald
Brooke, 7th Hussars, started the climb up Spion Kop, and Churchill
recorded what he saw:

> Streams of wounded men met us and obstructed the path. Men were stagger-
> ing along, or supported by comrades, or crawling on hands and knees, or carried
> by stretchers. Corpses lay here and there. Many of the wounds were of a horrible
> nature. The splinters and fragments of the shell had torn and mutilated in the
> most ghastly manner. I passed about two hundred while I was climbing up. There
> was, moreover, a small but steady leakage of unwounded men of all corps. Some
> of these cursed and swore. Others were utterly exhausted and fell on the hillside
> in stupor. Scores were sleeping heavily.[9]

Churchill later wrote Pamela Plowden: "The scenes on Spion Kop were
among the strangest and most terrible I have ever witnessed."

On the summit the battle, which had swayed backward and forward
on different parts of the field, became stationary by the end of the day
as both sides, suffering from heat and exhaustion, lay where they were,
incapable of launching new assaults. But the musketry continued and the
Boers' guns went on firing.

The British now had some 2,000 men alive and on the summit, but
the trenches were clogged with 400, perhaps 500, dead and wounded.
The Boers probably had about 800 men on the hill, though Botha later
claimed that there were never more than 350 burghers there. For no
other battle of the war does there exist such a wide discrepancy in the
facts and figures provided by commanders, participants, and historians.

Coke finally found Hill and received from him a report on the situation as far as Hill understood it. To neither did it occur to consult with
Thorneycroft, who, as far as Coke was concerned, was simply "a junior

brevet lieutenant-colonel in command of a small unit . . . assisting Colonel Crofton in a position on the front line." At six o'clock Coke sent a
report to Warren which hinted that the battle might end in defeat: "The
situation is extremely critical. . . . Please give orders and should you wish
me to withdraw, cover retirement. . . ."

A half hour later Thorneycroft also sent Warren a report: "I request
instructions as to what course I am to adopt. . . . It is all I can do to hold
my own. If casualties go on occurring at present rate I shall barely hold
out the night. A large number of stretcher-bearers should be sent up and
also all water possible. The situation is critical."

On the British right Lyttelton had made a demonstration early in the
morning, but Buller had ordered it stopped. In the afternoon, however,
Lyttelton launched an attack on Twin Peaks with a battalion of the Kings
Royal Rifle Corps. He did not consult Buller, who he knew would disap-
prove.

The battalion crossed the Tugela at 1:00 P.M. and then divided:
Lieutenant Colonel Robert Buchanan-Riddell led half his battalion
towards the eastern peak and Major Robert Calverley Arlington Bewicke-
Copley took the other half towards the western peak. An hour later they
were at the foot of the hills and began the steep climb. The naval guns
covered Twin Peaks with their heavy shells. Schalk Burger, the Boer
general commanding on Twin Peaks, sent urgent messages begging for
reinforcements, and Botha was alarmed, as well he might be, for if the
British gained these heights and held them they could make Spion Kop
untenable for his burghers. Although short of men, he rushed reinforcements to counter this new threat, but the Rifles spread out, made use of
all available cover, and climbed steadily.

Botha's greatest support came not from his burghers but from Buller,
who, when he saw the attack developing, sent a furious message to Lyttelton demanding that he recall his men. Lyttelton, watching through his
glasses the battalion struggle up the steep slopes in the face of the Boer
rifle fire, was himself beginning to have doubts about the attack. Then an
unnerving message arrived from a staff officer he had sent with the Rifles
declaring that he did not think they would be able to take the peaks.
There seemed nothing else to do but heliograph the battalion to withdraw. The message was twice repeated within the next hour, but both
Buchanan-Riddell and Bewicke-Copley chose to ignore it.

Not able to stop the attack, the Boers withdrew their guns from Twin
Peaks and the burghers began to flee. At 5:00 P.M. Buchanan-Riddell sent
Lyttelton a message that if possible he would "recall the advanced sections." He then ordered his men to fix bayonets and they cleared the
enemy off the peak. Fifteen minutes later the other peak was captured and
the British were in full possession, although a few Boers still remained
hidden behind rocks on the slopes. Buchanan-Riddell, standing upon the
summit to look at the valley below, was shot through the head by one of
them.

Buller, meanwhile, was growing ever more angry that his orders were not being obeyed. He sent message after message to Lyttelton, who forwarded them to Twin Peaks. Bewicke-Copley, who had assumed command of the battalion, had already brought up ammunition, water, entrenching tools, and food, but he could not disobey the repeated direct orders. Reluctantly he withdrew. The Rifles lost 20 officers and men killed and 69 wounded in this ably conducted, gallant exploit now rendered purposeless. Officers and men alike in the Rifles were bitter, and one soldier wrote home: "We were wild at getting the order to retire after getting right up to the top." For Buller to order the withdrawal of the Rifles when success seemed improbable was an act of prudence; to continue to insist on the withdrawal when the improbable had been achieved and such an important tactical victory had been won was the purest folly.

Thorneycroft in his advanced and isolated position knew nothing of the activities of the Rifles. Coke saw that Twin Peaks had been captured, but it never occurred to him that he should now make a determined effort to clear the Boers from Aloe Knoll and link up with the Rifles. Instead he sent another discouraging dispatch to Warren:

The situation is as follows—
The original troops are still in position, have suffered severely, and the dead and wounded are still in the trenches. The shell fire is, and has been, very severe.
If I hold on to the position all night, is there any guarantee that our artillery can silence the enemy guns? Otherwise to-day's experience will be repeated, and the men will not stand another day's shelling. . . .
The situation is extremely critical. . . .
Please give orders, and should you wish me to retire cover retirement from Connaught's Hill.[10]

Just ten minutes later, at 6:00 P.M., Thorneycroft sent a similar report to Warren:

The troops which marched up here last night are quite done up. They have had no water, and ammunition is running short. I consider that even with the reinforcements which have arrived it is impossible to permanently hold this place so long as the enemy's guns can play on the hill. . . . It is all I can do to hold my own. If casualties go on at the present rate I shall barely hold out the night. . . . The situation is critical.[11]

Although Warren's headquarters on Three Tree Hill was not well sited to observe the battle, most of the staff officers could see some of the to and fro movements of the Boers and soldiers on Spion Kop. Warren, nearsighted, could see nothing; he was serenely unworried. All day he busied himself with minor details, which he handled splendidly; Warren liked to gnaw on small bones. It was not until late in the afternoon that he thought of the balloon and sent for it; although it was too late in the day to use it, it would be useful tomorrow, he thought. Not until even later did it occur to him that sandbags and entrenching tools ought to be sent up to Spion Kop. The signalling arrangements were deplorable, but he made no effort to better them; neither did he worry about pushing guns up onto the hill. Early in the day the mountain battery had been sent for and it arrived at Trichardt's Drift at 4:00 P.M., but Buller, instead of hurrying it on with all speed, sent a message to Warren saying, "They will have a devil of a march. You must give them a rest before they go up." So men and mules rested and the battery did not reach the foot of Spion Kop until three and a half hours later.

It was eight o'clock and growing dark by the time Coke's discouraging message reached Warren; this was followed shortly after by a staff officer sent down by Coke to report personally on the appalling conditions on the summit and to explain how critical the situation had become. Warren was inclined to dismiss the staff officer as an alarmist. But then came Churchill, who gave him a vivid word picture of the demoralised troops, the casualties, and the ineffectiveness of Coke.

Finally alarmed, Warren began thinking of useful things to do: he ordered the naval guns sent up, he sent off 200 men of the Somerset Light Infantry with entrenching tools and sandbags, and he sent Churchill back with a message to Thorneycroft. The only other thing he could think of was to order Coke to climb down and report to him in person.

No one, it seems, gave any thought to the possible effect of the battle on the Boers. Although Botha had been forced to weaken other parts of his line to send men up Spion Kop—and Warren or Buller might have reasonably assumed as much—no attempt was made by the British to take advantage of their tremendous numerical superiority by launching a full-scale attack all along the line, or even on Tabanyama, to relieve the pressure on Spion Kop. It appeared to the Boers on Spion Kop that the British were hanging on with that bulldog determination for which they were famous, and it was obvious that they were sending increasing numbers of men to hold it. The reports of burghers who had fled down the hill were alarming and grew more so as they were repeated in the laagers and trenches. All along the Boer line discouraged burghers prepared for flight. Towards evening, from a height at Ladysmith, H. H. S. Pearse could see the activity on the Boer side: "The Boers came hurrying down in groups from Spion Kop's crest, their waggons were trekking from laagers across the plain towards Van Reenan's, and men could be seen rounding up cattle as if for a general rearward movement. To us watching it seemed as if the Boers were beaten and knew it."[12]

Deneys Reitz described what it was like for the Boers on the summit at the end of the day:

Darkness fell swiftly; the firing died away, and there was silence, save for a rare shot and the moans of the wounded. For a long time I remained at my post, staring into the night to where the enemy lay, so close that I could hear the cries of their wounded and the murmur of voices from behind their breastwork.

Afterwards my nerves began to go and I thought I saw figures with bayonets stealing forward. When I tried to find the men who earlier in the evening had been beside me, they were gone. Almost in a panic I left my place and hastened along the fringe of rocks in search of company, and to my immense relief heard a gruff "werda." It was Commandant Opperman still in his place with about two dozen men. He told me to stay beside him, and we remained here until after ten o'clock, listening to the enemy who were talking and stumbling about in the darkness beyond.[13]

At last even Red Daniel Opperman came to believe that the situation was hopeless, and he led his tired men down the hill, stumbling in the dark over rocks, their boots sometimes striking with sickening thuds against the scattered bodies of the fallen. At the foot of the hill they found that most of the horses were gone, taken by those who had deserted the fight; only their own horses and those of the dead and wounded abandoned on the hill remained where they had been left standing without food or water all day. Close by was an old man who by the dim light of a lantern was tending to some of the seriously wounded burghers who had been carried down. Opperman and his men were hungry and, above all, thirsty. They got water for themselves and their horses from a nearby spring and ransacked saddlebags for food. Then they wearily mounted and rode slowly back until they came to the laager of the Carolina Commando.

STORMING THE BOER TRENCHES AT THE BATTLE OF SPION KOP.

They found it in chaos. The Carolina men had fought bravely and well, but now, feeling that all was lost, they were loading wagons and packing saddlebags in a panic. The first wagons were leaving when out of the night galloped Louis Botha, shouting at them to turn back. There were similar scenes elsewhere as throughout the night Botha rode from laager to laager trying to put heart into the dispirited commandos: "If only we stand firm our Lord will give us victory." In most places he was successful, but not in all. Schalk Burger and his men, having been driven off Twin Peaks, considered the battle lost and had already fled north.

All day long Thorneycroft had fought with great gallantry and grim determination. He had behaved splendidly as a soldier, but he had played a colonel's role, not a general's. He had stayed too far forward on just one segment of the line, and he knew nothing of what had happened elsewhere. He had received no messages from Warren since the one making him a general, there was no food or water that he knew of (although sandbags, water cans, and other necessities were piled only 300 yards down the slope behind him), Warren had not silenced the Boer artillery, his ammunition was low, guns had not arrived, his groaning wounded were all about him, his exhausted men were one by one leaving the firing line; worst of all, tomorrow would be a repetition of this dreadful day as far as he could see. Looking at the dead and wounded around him he murmured, "My poor boys. . . . my poor boys." He decided to call it all off.

Thorneycroft moved back from the front line a bit and summoned Crofton and Lieutenant Colonel Ernest Cooke, commanding the Cameronians. Coke with his bad leg was by this time making his way down the slope to report to Warren. Thorneycroft gave the two colonels his reasons for withdrawing—"Better six battalions safely off the hill than a mop up in the morning," he said—and they raised no objections. The order was given and the Cameronians were instructed to form the rear guard and to bring off as many wounded men as they could. Many of the troops were confused, and Captain Hubert Gough overheard a Cameronian ask: "What the hell are we leaving the bloody hill for?"

An hour later Thorneycroft on his way down encountered Churchill, who gave him Warren's message, told him of the guns and supplies that had been ordered up for him, and tried to dissuade him from continuing the flight, but Thorneycroft was not to be deflected and was as stubborn in his refusal to give up his retreat as he had been all through the day in not retreating. He stomped down the hill with Churchill in his wake. They were three-quarters of the way down when they met Captain Walter Braithwaite leading the Somerset Light Infantry with sandbags and entrenching tools. Braithwaite had a written message from Warren. Thorneycroft took it, but he was shaking from exhaustion and tension, Warren's handwriting was small, and he was unable to make it out. Churchill read it for him. The Somersets were to dig trenches for him, Warren wrote, and he should hang on. But Thorneycroft said, "I have done all I can, and I am not going back."

Thorneycroft ordered the Somersets to turn back. The mountain battery and a company of engineers they met were also told to turn around. Meanwhile, Captain Henry Phillips, whom Coke had left in charge of the signal station well below the summit, awoke from a short nap about eleven thirty; half of the troops had already moved past him

down the hill, but he at once tried to stop the retreat, insisting it was
contrary to Coke's orders. He managed to halt Cooke and Major Ernest
Twyford of the Cameronians. They agreed to delay a bit until Warren
could be contacted. Then Phillips discovered that the signal lamps were
out of oil.

Shortly after midnight a naval lieutenant with the unusual British
name of Schwikkard reached the summit of Spion Kop by a route which
avoided the retreating troops. He had been sent to select sites for the
naval guns. To his astonishment he found the battlefield deserted: on the
summit of Spion Kop, on Aloe Knoll and Twin Peaks, there were only
the dead and the wounded, whose groans were now the only sounds to
be heard. In the moonlight Schwikkard wandered over the hill and into
what had been the Boer lines. The Boers later claimed that a small group
of Prinsloo's men, led by Jan Kemp, had spent the night on the slopes,
but Prinsloo himself was certainly not there, for he had left the hill earlier,
carrying off the dead body of his brother Willie. On the summit itself
Schwikkard found only an ambulance man tending some wounded. Boer
and Briton, having fought each other to a standstill, had all given up in
despair and fled. Each side was prepared to grant the other victory, but
neither knew it.

It was not until two o'clock in the morning that Coke finally found
Warren. The headquarters on Three Tree Hill had received some unwel-
come attention from the Boer guns during the day, so Warren had shifted
his headquarters a short distance away; he had not thought to tell poor
Coke, who, ever stumbling about in the dark with his bad leg, again got
lost and went limping about for two hours after he reached the site of
Warren's original headquarters. At almost the same time that Coke found
Warren, Thorneycroft's message, sent eight hours earlier, also reached
Warren, who perhaps had not told his signallers of his change of headquarters either. In a few minutes Thorneycroft himself appeared. It was
only then that Coke and Thorneycroft discovered to their amazement
that each had thought himself in sole command on Spion Kop. It was at
this time, too, that Captain Phillips finally found some oil and sent off a
signal to Warren saying that an unauthorized withdrawal had taken place
but that some troops still held the lower slopes.

The time had now arrived for Sir Charles Warren to display what, if
anything, lay behind his monocle; what, if anything he possessed of military ability, moral courage, and resolution; and what, if anything, supported the jaunty self-confidence he had always displayed. There were
still some 1,600 troops, delayed by Phillips, on the slopes below the
summit; the mountain battery and the naval guns were at the foot of
Spion Kop, ready and willing to climb and fight; he had machine guns,
supplies, and a dozen fresh battalions in hand. As for his theories: in the
past twenty-four hours soldier and burgher had been truly and intimately
"introduced" to each other. He had only to act with energy and resolution, to throw his men and guns back onto that hilltop, to rally his officers

and men and infuse in them a sense of urgency, and the hill would have been his. More. The demoralised Boers would have fled from all their positions on the Tugela in confusion before his pounding guns and advancing bayonets, and Ladysmith would have been speedily relieved. But Warren looked into the glum face of Coke and the bloodshot eyes of Thorneycroft and resigned himself to defeat. He sent a pleading message to Buller: "Can you come at once and decide what to do?"

Blame for the British defeat must rest with the generals, but the inadequacies of the suffering soldiers was also pointed to, and Bron Herbert, writing in *The Times History,* passed a harsh and not entirely justified judgement on them: "Neither in skill with the rifle, nor in individual intelligence and moral endurance, was the British soldier equal to the terribly exacting demands of modern warfare. . . . Spion Kop might have been held by 500 men, but not by 500 ordinary British soldiers, nor by 5,000."[14]

In the first light of dawn some burghers at the northern foot of Spion Kop looked up and saw Boers on the summit waving their hats. The men on the crest were said to be some of Jan Kemp's Krugersdorpers or perhaps some burghers who had climbed back up to look for fallen comrades. In any case, those below grasped their message and dashed up to claim the battlefield. The British were gone. The Boers had, after all, won the battle. After such a victory who could blame them for believing that God had given them another miracle?

21

AFTER SPION KOP: VAAL KRANTZ

"Very bad news from Buller, my dear child," Wolseley wrote to his wife. "I am in despair at all our misfortunes. God seems to be with the Boers and against us." Queen Victoria wrote to Lansdowne: "I am horrified at the terrible list of casualties, twenty-two officers killed and twenty-one wounded. . . . Would it be possible to warn young officers not to expose themselves more than is absolutely necessary?" Doubtless she would have been more horrified had she known the true casualty figures. Even today no one knows the exact numbers and there appears to have been an understandable tendency on both sides to minimize their losses; even *The Times History* gives two sets of figures for the British, neither of which corresponds with the official casualty figures. Botha ordered Commandant William Prinsloo of Heidelberg to count the British corpses on the summit, but Prinsloo does not appear to have made an exact count: he reported 600 dead and 350 seriously wounded. However, those numbers which appear most plausible give the total as 1,740 British casualties, of which 383 were killed, 1,054 wounded, and 303 prisoners or missing (including the wounded left on the hill, many of whom were severely wounded and beyond recovery). This butcher's bill seems trifling when compared to the casualty figures in the European wars that followed in the next half century, but it seemed frightful at the time, and, considering the number engaged, it was indeed dreadful, being about half of the force involved.

The Boers gave their casualties as 58 dead and 140 wounded, but there were certainly more. A monument on Spion Kop today gives the names of 106 burghers who died there. At least 60 bodies were carried down and buried elsewhere.

Botha inspected the shambles of the battlefield and was appalled by the "gruesome, sickening, hideous picture." After speaking briefly with a British chaplain and arguing with Major Robert Wright, RAMC, about his right to remove the wounded (which Botha claimed were his prisoners), he climbed down to send off a report to Kruger:

Battle over and by the grace of God a magnificent victory for us. The enemy driven out of their positions and their losses are great. . . . The battlefield therefore is ours. . . . It breaks my heart to say that so many of our gallant heroes have also been killed or wounded. It is incredible that such a small handful of men, with the help of the Most High, could fight and withstand the mighty Britain.[1]

All who viewed the battlefield were awed by the sight. Hendrik Prinsloo said, "It seems a pity that we, belonging to two God fearing nations, should kill one another like that."[2] One old burgher, murmuring, "Poor lads, poor lads," shed tears as he walked among the piles of dead. Pieter Viljoen found the body of his son Henning when he came up with Botha, and he buried him where he and his comrades had fought and fallen. The correspondent for the *Standard and Diggers News* of Johannesburg wrote: "The field of battle was horrible. Men were literally blown to pieces by shells. I counted thirteen heads blown from bodies, some wholly, others from the ears upwards, and so on. It was a sight never to be forgotten. . . . I also saw a red hawk, so swift of wing, lying dead beside a dead soldier."[3]

Some souvenir hunters cut off the buttons and insignia of British officers. Rifles and equipment of the soldiers were gathered up, and it was in the course of doing this that Spion Kop saw its final casualty. Stiffened in death, one British soldier lay with his finger still curled around the trigger of his rifle. It took only the tug given by a young Boer collecting weapons to discharge it. He died of the stomach wound it inflicted.

The British were much blamed for not properly burying their dead.

A. D. W. Wolmarans, a member of the Transvaal Executive Council, visited Spion Kop five days after the battle and telegraphed a report to Kruger: "Parts of the bodies of the enemy dead, interred on the summit, still stick out of the ground. Three are quite unburied. It is high time that the famous cultured English nation were told that their way of burying the dead is worse than that of barbaric savages."[4]

It would appear, however, that blame lay not with the British but the Boers. In a dispatch to Kruger Botha said: "The enemy has asked me to remove their wounded and bury their dead, to which I have agreed."[5] Although disciplined soldiers can be made to bury putrid corpses, Botha's officers had difficulty convincing their burghers that they should, and those who did made a bad job of it. The stench was so bad that burghers even refused to stay on the hill to defend it. Thus the British soldiers achieved with their dead and decomposing bodies what they were unable to do when quick with life with weapons in their hands: they drove the Boers from the hill. And Spion Kop, which had seemed so important on that hot January day, was abandoned almost as soon as the fight for it ended, deserted by all except the vultures and the bodies of those who had died to possess it.

On the day after the battle there came to the top of Spion Kop long lines of Indians with stretchers, members of the South African Indian Ambulance Corps, which had been organized in Natal by a thirty-year-old Indian lawyer, Mohandas Karamchand Gandhi, later called the Mahatma. There were more Indians than Europeans in Natal, and although forbidden by the white-man's-war concept from taking up arms, they were eager to prove their loyalty to the Empire. In addition to Gandhi's unit there was also an ambulance corps formed by the Natal Public Works Department from indentured Indian coolies. Gandhi and his 1,100 Indian volunteers spent six weeks with the army on the Tugela, carrying off the mangled soldiers from Buller's battlefields. It was this corps which carried young Lieutenant Roberts from the field at Colenso and, as Gandhi later wrote, "Amongst the wounded we had the honour of carrying soldiers like General Woodgate." Woodgate, carried from the field pleading, "Let me alone. Let me alone," lived on in great agony before death mercifully came to him. He was the third major general killed by the Boers.

F. Treves, a distinguished surgeon, told one of the most poignant stories of the battle's aftermath:

One poor fellow had been shot in the face by a piece of shell, which had carried away his left eye, the upper jaw with the corresponding part of the cheek, and had left a hideous cavity at the bottom of which his tongue was exposed. He had been lying hours on the hill. He was unable to speak, and as soon as he was landed at the hospital he made signs that he wanted to write. Pencil and paper were given him, and it was supposed he wished to ask for something, but he merely wrote, "Did we win?" No one had the heart to tell him the truth.[6]

Some of the wounded who survived exposure on Spion Kop, the jolting journey down on a stretcher, the ride in the springless ambulances, and their treatment in the field hospitals were sent by train to Durban and taken on board a hospital ship called *Maine.* The government had chartered two ships from the Union Castle Line and had fitted them out in spartan fashion as hospital ships, but the *Maine,* lavishly equipped, was a private American charitable venture.

The idea of Americans providing a hospital ship had been conceived by the American wife of a South African mining executive who interested Lady Randolph Churchill in the project; Bernard N. Baker, founder of the Atlantic Transport Company of Baltimore, donated on behalf of his company an old cattle boat of 3,000 tons and agreed to maintain it at his company's expense. Lady Randolph Churchill formed a committee of American women in London and rallied her friends among the great and near-great to raise funds for refurbishing and equipping the vessel. In two months she and her committee raised £41,000. Lady Randolph explained the purpose of the enterprise:

> The *Maine* is to be essentially an American ship. We are not only to aid the wounded, but we are to show the world that American women can do the work better than anyone else can do it. . . . It is especially the province of American women to promote this cause, but it is a woman's function to foster and nourish the suffering. American women are more adept at it, we believe, than any others.[7]

The *Maine* was anchored in the Thames, refurbished, and fitted out with the latest that medical science could offer. According to *The Nursing Record and Hospital World,* it was "the most complete and comfortable hospital ship that has ever been constructed."[8] It provided accommodation for 218 patients in four large wards and one small isolation ward; it contained X-ray equipment and an operating room that boasted an enamelled iron operating table with a plate glass top.

The ship flew both the Union Jack and the Stars and Stripes—it was believed to be the first ship to sail under these two flags—and it also flew the flag of the Red Cross. When the *Maine* arrived in Durban one of the first patients to be taken on board was Lady Randolph Churchill's nineteen-year-old son Jack, a lieutenant in the South African Light Horse, who had received a leg wound in his first skirmish.

After Spion Kop Buller withdrew all of Warren's force behind the Tugela again. Henry Wilson wrote in his diary: "We stand where we did 10 days ago, with a licking thrown in." Hart in a private letter wrote: "The net result is that we have once more to chronicle a complete defeat." Behind his back Sir Redvers was called "Sir Reverse," and Lyttelton wrote home: "I have lost all confidence in Buller as a general and am sure he has himself." From Ladysmith Ian Hamilton smuggled out a letter to Spencer Wilkinson: *"Buller is no use. . . .* It is a question of life or death of ourselves here as well as the empire in general, and I write to beg you to use all your influence to get the man recalled before he does more mischief."[9]

But the rank and file retained their confidence in him. They had a simple, touching, pathetic faith in their blundering, incompetent commander who led them time after time to death and defeat. Throughout the war they remained loyal and grateful to the general who cared for them, who thought of them as human beings and knew their wants and needs. No matter that he led them from one tactical absurdity to another and that they suffered needless casualties, Buller thought about them, gave them hot meals, fresh bread, tents, and they, sensing instinctively his innate humaneness, loved him as they did no other general.

Even among those maimed as a result of his blunders, Buller was admired. In England a newspaper correspondent who went daily to the hospital reported that he had not encountered a single man who did not speak "in very warm tones indeed" of General Buller. Captain Blake Knox, a doctor in Buller's army, wrote:

> They had followed their leader, General Buller, never questioning, never doubting, even through the dark, dark days of Colenso and Spion Kop, and they were prepared to follow him anywhere and at any time. Never was a general more confidently looked up to through adversity than was our Natal chief.[10]

When the *Majestic* arrived in Southampton with 350 wounded, among them five amputees and one or two blind, a reporter noted: "The men . . . say they would have gone anywhere and done anything for Buller." Private H. Easterbrook of the 2nd Devons was indignant that anyone should criticize Buller, and he wrote home: "There is not a man here who would not follow Sir Redvers."

Although there was criticism of Buller in military and political circles at the highest levels and some in the press, the general public, like the soldiers, maintained their confidence in him, even in South Africa. At an entertainment in Cape Town where motion pictures taken by the cinematograph were shown, the audience cheered the various British leaders as they appeared, but, said one observer, "When the picture of General Buller appeared on the screen the audience went frantic." It was undoubtedly this popularity, which Buller neither sought nor encouraged, that prevented the politicians and Lord Roberts from removing him from his command.

After Spion Kop there were, of course, the usual military dispatches. The first news of the debacle that reached Roberts was a brief telegram from Buller saying that "Warren's garrison" had abandoned Spion Kop and adding some critical comments on Warren's abilities. Several days later Buller wrote three dispatches in which he maintained that he himself had not actually been present but said he thought "Colonel Thorneycroft exercised a wise decision." While he confessed that he ought to have assumed command himself, he threw all the blame for the disaster on Warren: "We had really lost our chance by Sir C. Warren's slowness. He seems to me a man who can do well what he can do himself, but he cannot command, as he can neither use his Staff nor subordinates. I can never employ him again on an independent command."[11]

Warren in his dispatch threw the blame on Thorneycroft. Roberts wrote a dispatch critical of all three—Buller, Warren, and Thorneycroft—and he bluntly told Buller: "Though portions of the force were engaged in different localities under subordinate commanders, you were present during the operations and in Chief command." In his confidential dispatch to Lansdowne he said:

But whatever faults Sir Charles Warren may have committed, the failure must also be ascribed to the disinclination of the officer in supreme command to assert his authority, and to see that what he thought best was done, and also to the unwarrantable and needless assumption of responsibility by a subordinate officer.[12]

He praised Thorneycroft's gallantry but added: "Colonel Thorneycroft issued an order, without reference to superior authority, which upset the whole plan of operations, and rendered unavailing the sacrifices which had already been made to carry it into effect."[13]

Lansdowne, to the surprise and indignation of both Salisbury and the Queen, published all the dispatches. Parliament and some of the newspapers were also indignant, for it was felt that this evidence of disagreement among the generals would shake the public's confidence in the army and its leaders. But the war was still young, most people were enthusiastic about it, and confidence in the army was not easily shaken. Perhaps many agreed with Churchill, who wrote at this time:

But when all that will be written about this has been written, and all the bitter words have been said by the people who will never do anything themselves, the wise and just citizen will remember that these same generals are, after all, brave, capable, noble English gentlemen, trying their best to carry through a task which may prove impossible.[14]

After Spion Kop Botha decided that he needed a rest; besides, he had some family affairs to attend to, so he went home for a while. Schalk Burger, A. P. Cronjé, and Joubert were unwell, and they, too, left the front. Many of the burghers drifted back to their farms. Between Buller's army and Ladysmith there were now probably not more than 4,000 Boers.

Although Roberts telegraphed to Buller advising him that unless he felt "fairly confident" of success he should not make another attempt to break through at this time, Buller on 28 January announced to his troops that he had at last found "the key to Ladysmith." Critics later remarked that while he may have found the key he appeared to have lost the lock. Buller did indeed have a plan, and a good one—at this stage almost any reasonable plan, swiftly and resolutely carried forward, had a good chance of succeeding. He sent a message to White telling him that he was going to have another "fair square try" to break through, although he added that he feared he was not strong enough.

To the right of the British lines, about 5 miles east of Spion Kop, north and east of the sinuous Tugela, was a hill called Vaal Krantz. Northwest of this was a kopje called Brakfontein, while to the northeast rose a larger height called Doornkop, all held by the Boers. Control of Vaal Krantz and Doornkop would enable Buller to break through to the Ladysmith plain to the north. On the morning of 5 February 1900 Buller made a feint towards Brakfontein with artillery and a brigade of infantry. The troops moved about smartly as though they were taking part in a field day at Aldershot, but they did not come within 2,000 yards of the Boers. *The Times History* neatly summarized this action: "It provided a magnificent spectacle to the rest of the army, and reflected credit on the previous company and battery drill of the troops engaged in it. As a military operation it was ludicrous."[15] Nevertheless, real bullets and shells were fired, and one soldier was killed and thirty-four were wounded in this demonstration.

The British next began to shell Vaal Krantz and a pontoon bridge was thrown over the Tugela. Buller's plan called for Lyttelton's brigade to seize Vaal Krantz, but, just as he was about ready to attack, Buller began, as Lyttelton put it, to "shilly-shally." It had taken too long to switch from the feint to the real attack, and Buller feared the kopje could not be taken before dark. Lyttelton finally persuaded him to change his mind, and the Durham Light Infantry swarmed across the bridge and stormed the hill. By four o'clock the British were in possession.

The capture of Vaal Krantz by the British was a discouraging blow to the Boers. General Tobias Smuts, commanding the Boer forces here, telegraphed to Lucas Meyer:

> The round kopje in the Standerton sector captured by the enemy. Reinforcements arrived too late. Do not know if I can regain it. General Burger's cannon do nothing as far as I can discover. The entire might of the enemy is falling on me and I get no help. I shall do my duty brother but God help me. If I have losses it is not my fault. Think upon what I have said.[16]

Lyttelton, having put most of his brigade on Vaal Krantz, now looked around for the reinforcements which were supposed to follow him. He looked in vain. Instead of reinforcements he received an order from Buller to withdraw. He ignored the order, hoping that his success would encourage his chief to proceed with the plan. Buller did not insist, but he took no further offensive action. He left the brigade sitting on Vaal Krantz all the next day while the Boers shot at it. The rest of the army sat idly by while he debated what he should do.

Unable to decide, he tried to get Roberts to make up his mind for him. In a long telegram he outlined the progress he had made but warned that to continue would cost 2,000 or 3,000 casualties and he was not sure of success. "Do you think the chance of the relief of Ladysmith worth the risk?"[17]

Roberts replied:

Ladysmith must be relieved, even at the cost you anticipate. I would certainly persevere, and my hope is that the enemy will be so severely punished as to enable White's garrison to be withdrawn without great difficulty. Let your troops know that the honour of the Empire is in their hands, and that I have no possible doubt of their being successful.[18]

Still Buller could not bring himself to assume responsibility for all those casualties. He called a council of war that included Warren, Clery, Lyttelton, and Hart. He did not read them Roberts's telegram with its stirring call to defend the honour of the Empire, although he did tell them that Roberts was in favour of continuing the offensive. He asked his generals for their opinions; only the impetuous Hart was in favour of pressing the attack. Warren suggested that they withdraw from Vaal Krantz and attack elsewhere. Where? Hlangwane, said Warren. Although a miserable general, Warren did have a surveyor's eye for topography. Buller agreed, and the meeting ended. Buller then telegraphed the decision to Roberts, stating that the Boer positions to the front and sides of Vaal Krantz were too strong, that he was "outclassed" by the Boer guns, and that it would be a useless waste of lives to go on. He would, he said, make another "desperate effort" elsewhere.

Lyttelton's brigade, after suffering the loss of 34 officers and men killed and 335 wounded, was withdrawn. Thus ended Buller's third attempt to pierce the Boer line on the Tugela; it was, said *The Times History,* "one of the feeblest performances in the history of war." The withdrawal was carried out at night in good order, and Buller remarked that he thought it was done "uncommonly well."

"Yes, sir," said a staff officer. "We've practiced it twice."

22

THE GREAT FLANK MARCH

On the evening of 6 February 1900 Roberts and Kitchener secretly left Cape Town on the northbound mail train for Methuen's camp on the Modder River. As Roberts needed to conceal his plans from the enemy for as long as possible, Colonel George Henderson, his chief intelligence officer, told newspaper correspondents in strict confidence that Roberts intended to concentrate his forces in the Colesburg area and then attack the Orange Free State from the south. When this was duly reported in the London papers the War Office telegraphed Roberts that there had been "a serious indiscretion on the part of someone on his staff"; later, when the true line of advance was revealed, the correspondents charged Roberts with "unfair and dishonest treatment."

Undeterred by the news of Buller's difficulties on the Tugela, unruffled by a spate of unrealistic suggestions from the War Office, and unyielding to the persistent demands of Milner that huge garrisons be maintained in Cape Colony, Roberts had vigorously carried forward the preparations for his own campaign. Over Milner's anguished protests, spoken and written, he had ruthlessly stripped central and eastern Cape Colony of troops. Even French's cavalry, which had been conducting a number of small but successful operations in the Colesburg area, was skilfully disengaged and sent to the Modder. The men, horses, mules, guns, stores, and supplies pouring off the ships at Cape ports were hustled forward to Methuen's camp. Every obtainable ox and every wagon was sent north. There were now some 180,000 troops in South Africa—more than double the entire population of the Orange Free State—but Roberts wanted every man and animal that could be spared, for he planned to strike the western flank of the Free State.

After two hot, dusty days on the train Roberts and Kitchener reached Methuen's camp, now a huge tent city set on the hot sands beside the Modder. The entire area was jammed with men, guns, wagons; all around were mountains of supplies. It was Roberts's intention to take the bulk of this army on a wide swing around the eastern end of the Boer positions at Magersfontein, boldly cutting himself off from the railway and launching his army onto the dry, barren veld. His objective was Bloemfontein, capital of the Orange Free State; Kimberley would be relieved on the way. He had to move quickly, and to do so he needed horsemen. He had already ordered as many infantrymen as possible to be mounted, and this was done by a process Kipling described in his poem "M.I.":

> . . . we are the beggars that got
> Three days "to learn equitation" an' six months o' bloomin' well
>   trot![1]

By scraping together all his cavalry, forming two brigades of mounted infantry, and adding seven batteries of horse artillery he hurriedly formed a cavalry division of three brigades which was placed under French's command. On the evening of 10 February Roberts assembled his senior cavalry officers and told them that they were about to have "the greatest chance cavalry has ever had. . . . You will remember what you are going to do all your lives, and when you have grown to be old men you will tell the story of the relief of Kimberley."

A few hours later the cavalrymen stood to their horses in the bright moonlight. At three o'clock in the morning of 11 February they rode out. The Great Flank March had begun. Methuen with only 5,000 men was left sitting on the Modder fronting the Boers at Magersfontein while Roberts took 18,000 infantry, 7,795 cavalry and mounted infantry, plus several thousand noncombatants,* and began his invasion of the Orange Free State.

Cronjé, thinking that Methuen was simply trying to create a diversion, sent out only a few small forces, including one under Christiaan de Wet, to counter Roberts's army, and there were several skirmishes. De Wet soon discovered the size and direction of Roberts's force and dispatched one of his bright young men, Gideon Scheepers, to Cronjé to sound the alarm.

The British march was an ordeal for men and animals. Many of the horses were newly arrived and had neither recovered from their long ocean voyage nor become acclimated. Within forty-eight hours some 500 horses were dead or too exhausted to move. Those in the artillery and in the ammunition columns, pulling their heavy loads, suffered worst of all; those that stood up best were horses which had come from the great London omnibus companies.

There were long delays getting men and wagons across the Riet River, but in spite of dust, heat, thunderstorms, and the shortage of water, Roberts's entire army was on the move. And it kept moving. French's cavalry was in the lead, pushing aside such groups of the enemy as it found. The first serious opposition was encountered on the morning of 15 February when the cavalry, having crossed the Modder at Klip Drift, found the Boers positioned in a broken semicircle of kopjes directly in front of them. Here John French made a momentous decision. It was an impetuous one, such as he was prone to make, and it might have led to disaster, but in the event it proved to be brilliant and it made his name. Putting his lancers in front and his horse artillery in the rear, he took them at a great thundering gallop right between the kopjes in the middle of the Boer line: "The whole division was set in motion. For nearly five miles in perfect order they galloped on until the head of the plain was reached. It was a thrilling time, never to be forgotten," said Captain Cecil Boyle. It was called a charge, but it was not; French's aim was not to attack the Boers, but to escape from them by breaking through their lines. The 5,000 horses and their riders in long lines sweeping across the veld raised

*These are the figures obtained by Captain S. L'H. Slocum, 8th United States Cavalry, who was the American military attaché with Roberts's force, but a wide variety of other figures exist. Wild as the Boer numbers generally were, those of the British often showed wide discrepancies too. *The Times History* gave Roberts's strength as "roughly 37,000 men," of whom 30,000 were combatants; Rayne Kruger, a modern writer, and A. Conan Doyle gave about 33,000 (over 25,000 infantry and nearly 8,000 mounted troops); American historian A. T. Mahan gave the total as 35,000 (24,000 infantry and 11,000 cavalry and mounted infantry), which is also the figure used by Brian Gardner. The number of guns is also in dispute: Kruger said "over 100," Mahan and Conan Doyle said 98, while Slocum gave 92.

such a huge cloud of dust that the Boer riflemen could not clearly see their targets. The entire cavalry division cleared the Boer line with the loss of only one officer killed and twenty of all ranks wounded.

French was now only 4 or 5 miles away from Cronjé's main laager, a plum he could have taken had he known of it, but unaware of his chance and obedient to his orders he pressed on towards Kimberley. By two thirty in the afternoon he was within sight of the waste tips of the diamond mines, and he paused to heliograph the news of his arrival to the besieged garrison. The heliograph winked away and those in Kimberley read the message—and refused to believe it. It took French an hour to convince the garrison that his message was not a Boer ruse, and it was not until 6:30 P.M. that he and his staff entered the town.

While French had been making his "charge" at Klip Drift an infantry brigade had been attacking Jacobsdal and had occupied it by 3 P.M., but Roberts's main concern this day was centred on the events taking place back at Waterval Drift on the Riet.

The oxen of the supply park had been overworked for the past two days and needed time to recuperate. They and the great convoy of wagons they pulled had been left behind when the last infantry brigade crossed the drift and marched away. Only about 500 men were detailed to guard them. On the morning of 15 February De Wet came upon them and opened a long-range fire from guns positioned on a kopje east of the drift. The British at once prepared to defend themselves and the convoy: most of the oxen were driven into the shelter of the riverbank, and sacks of oats and boxes of biscuits were hurriedly unloaded to make breastworks.

As soon as Roberts learned of the attack he ordered back two battalions of infantry and a battery; De Wet was also reinforced and now had about 1,000 men. The British, although immobilized, were able to hold their own without difficulty. They made one attempt to get the convoy away, but as soon as the oxen were brought out from cover, the Boers opened such a hot fire that the beasts stampeded—and made straight for the Boer position. More than half of the teams—1,600 oxen—thus deserted to the enemy and bullets took their toll of others.

Roberts grew increasingly worried by the messages he received from Waterval Drift throughout the day. Lieutenant General Charles Tucker was sent back with another battery and more infantry to take charge of the situation. He arrived at dusk and soon after reported to Roberts that he could drive off the Boers but would need another battery and two more battalions of infantry. Roberts now had to decide whether the oxen and supplies were worth the loss of time and men the struggle to extricate them would exact. Time was important, and he was reluctant to send more of his battalions back to Waterval Drift. Even if the enemy were driven off, the convoy, with half of its oxen gone, would be immobile and a strong force would have to be left to protect it.

He called in his supply chief, Colonel Wodehouse D. Richardson, and

asked him for an assessment of the damage that would be done if the
convoy was abandoned. Richardson told him that the troops had two
days' supplies with them, that there was a good supply of slaughter cattle,
and that there were other supply wagons on the way, although it would
take some time for them to catch up. Roberts asked if he had enough to
ration men and animals until they reached Bloemfontein. Richardson
said this was impossible.

"Can you give them three-quarter rations?"

"No, sir."

Roberts paused and then asked, "You can give them half rations
certainly?"

"Yes, sir, perhaps more."

The trim, dapper little general with the neat grey hair and mahogany
face paced up and down in the dust beside the covered wagon that served
as his headquarters in the field. At last he said, "I'll do it. I think the men
will do it for me."

Roberts had arrived at a bold decision. His physical courage was
proven—he wore the Victoria Cross on his chest—but it had taken courage of a different order to leave the railway behind and to cast his army
onto the veld. It took even more to abandon the convoy. But that is what
he did. Just before midnight he sent a messenger galloping off to recall
Tucker.

Abandoned to the Boers were 170 wagons containing 30,000 forage
rations and 150,000 men's rations plus 500 slaughter cattle—four days'
supply for Roberts's force—plus the heavy loss of his precious oxen. The
next morning to his "great surprise" De Wet found the British gone and
he hastened to take possession:

> Our booty was enormous. . . . On some of the waggons we found klinkers
> [biscuits], jam, milk, sardines, salmon, cases of corned beef, and other such
> provisions in great variety. Other waggons were loaded with rum; and still others
> contained oats and horse provender pressed into bales. In addition to these
> stores, we took one field-piece, which the English had left behind. It was, indeed,
> a gigantic capture; the only question was what to do with it.[2]

Hauling away all this loot consumed much time which De Wet might
better have spent elsewhere. It would have been wiser for him to have
destroyed it, but the urge to possess all these good things proved irresistible.

While De Wet was carrying off his plunder the fate of Piet Cronjé and
the main Boer army in the Free State was being determined. The news
that reached Cronjé's laager that day was mostly bad—very bad: French
and his host of troopers had dashed through the Boer lines into Kimberley, Jacobsdal had been captured, and in the afternoon Methuen's guns
opened a general bombardment of the Boer positions at Magersfontein.
The Free Staters were becoming demoralised. The mobility of Roberts's
army and the extent of his operations took them completely by surprise.

Cronjé had learned of the buildup of the British army on the Modder, of course, but he had assumed that the British would again launch a frontal attack, an attack for which he was well prepared. He had built an elaborate system of trenches and other field fortifications protected by barbed wire at Magersfontein. These all faced south. Cronjé could hardly bring himself to believe that the British had cut themselves off from their railway and that all of his careful preparations were useless. The stocky, bearded man sat inert in his tent, his wife gently patting his head, while all day long burghers came in and out, bringing him news and rumours and offering him advice. The advice was uniformly the same: escape while there was still time.

It was nearly sundown when he at last decided to act. S. P. Du Toit, in charge of the Transvaalers besieging Kimberley, was ordered to retire to Fourteen Streams; J. S. Ferreira, commander-in-chief of the Free State Forces, was asked to join him further up the Modder, where he planned to move in the hope of taking up new positions to protect Bloemfontein; his own men, some 5,000 burghers, were ordered to assemble at once in the main laager.

During the long stay at Magersfontein the Boers had grown increasingly domestic, and now the laager was crowded with women and children. Many of the burghers had lost their horses—there had been too many horses for the limited grazing—and now nearly a third of Cronjé's army were on foot (such men were called *voetgangers*). The laager broke up, oxen were inspanned, and in the bright moonlight they moved out —horsemen, voetgangers, women, and children, and more than 400 ox wagons—in no order, just a straggling mob of people. They travelled east, directly across the front of the British forces concentrated at Klip Drift, and although they passed only 3 miles from the British lines, not a soldier saw them. Methuen did not discover that he was no longer facing an enemy at Magersfontein until noon the next day.

Cronjé had selected the most direct route for placing himself between the British and Bloemfontein, but by doing so he had lessened his chances of escape. He probably thought that the British objective was simply to relieve Kimberley and that if he removed his force from Roberts's line of march he would not be molested. He could not know that for Roberts the relief of Kimberley was only incidental to his advance on the capital of the Orange Free State.

At 4:30 A.M. the next day, 16 February, Colonel Ormelie Hannay started out with 2,000 mounted infantry towards Kimberley. An hour and a half later Captain Chester Master, who was with the advance screen of Rimington's Guides, saw a great grey cloud of dust rising from behind some kopjes on his right front. A stray wagon directly before him was captured; it proved to be a straggler from Cronjé's convoy. Hannay, after some hesitation, made for the convoy, but his mounted infantry was driven back in great disorder by the Boer rear guard and Cronjé escaped —temporarily.

23

THE SIEGE OF KIMBERLEY

On 14 October 1899, two days after the declaration of war, Lieutenant Colonel Robert Kekewich in Kimberley was talking on the telephone with army headquarters in Cape Town when suddenly the line went dead. At the Kimberley telegraph office the keys, "which had been clicking away merrily like a lot of noisy crickets, one by one, in rapid succession, ceased their clattering and within a few seconds a dead silence reigned in the room." The Boers had cut the lines.

Kimberley, the "Diamond City," was the second-largest town in Cape Colony with a population of about 50,000 people, of whom more than half were Bantu and about 15 percent were Coloureds and Asiatics. It was the most unruly town in South Africa. Eleven years earlier the Diamond Laws Commission had reported that among its then 30,000 inhabitants there had been 11,000 criminal convictions. It had long been a hard-living, hard-drinking town with one saloon for every sixteen inhabitants, women and children included. John Merriman once described it as "a seething mass of opulent iniquity." Although in recent years a number of respectable and sober people, tradesmen and artisans, had come to Kimberley and a few substantial buildings had been built, there was still much of the boom town atmosphere.

It was an isolated place midway between the Vaal and the Modder rivers, each about 30 miles away, and nearly 500 miles from the next town of any size; the Kalahari Desert was nearby to the west, and in summer its hot winds stirred the dust that lay deep in the unpaved streets and on the corrugated iron roofs.

In anticipation of a Boer invasion of this part of Cape Colony a number of British troops had been stationed in Kimberley: the Northumberland Fusiliers, half of the North Lancashires, a few mounted infantry and Royal Engineers, and, arriving just before the siege began, the Munster Fusiliers and the 9th Lancers. In addition there were about 1,100 men in local volunteer forces—the Kimberley Regiment, the police, and the Diamond Field Horse. There were also a few old muzzle-loading cannons. A Town Guard was called into being, its members patriotically agreeing to serve as long as they were not asked to go more than 8 miles from the market square.

In charge of this force and of the defence of the town was balding, bullet-headed Lieutenant Colonel Robert Kekewich (1854–1914), commanding officer of the 1st North Lancashires. He was a Devonshire man who had joined the army in 1874 and had seen active service on the Perak Expedition in Malaya and on the Gordon Relief Expedition in the Sudan. He was a bachelor, as so many figures on the British side were—Cecil Rhodes, Lord Kitchener, Alfred Milner, Douglas Haig, Hector Macdonald, Robert Baden-Powell, Cornelius Clery, Thomas Kelly-Kenny. (All of the Boer leaders were married.) Kekewich appears to have been a good if undistinguished Victorian soldier, possessing only the ordinary man's fund of tact. It was his misfortune that tact was needed more than military skill in the defence of Kimberley, for on 10 October, just before the siege began, Cecil Rhodes arrived in town.

Rhodes's reasons for coming to Kimberley at this time are obscure. He must have known that his very presence there would be an added attraction for the Boers, that they bore him no love for his part in the Jameson Raid, that as former prime minister of Cape Colony, member of the Privy Council, and the richest Briton alive, he would make a fine catch for them. Rumour said that the Boers were already gloating over the prospect of capturing this proudest lion in Africa and parading him through the streets of Pretoria in a cage. Still, Kimberley was *his* town. It was here that he had amassed his first huge fortune, and he owned many of the enterprises, large and small, to be found there. Most important, he controlled the great De Beers Company which dominated the town. Perhaps, as was said, he thought his presence in the town would ensure its speedy relief. He certainly behaved as if this was his mission, but it is difficult to believe that Rhodes would deliberately allow himself to be among the besieged, or if he did that he understood what he was getting into, for, as Conan Doyle said, "Among other characteristics, Rhodes bears any form of restraint badly. . . ."

By proclaiming martial law Kekewich superseded the authority of the mayor and placed himself in charge of the town, at least in theory, but Rhodes, accustomed to having his own way in everything, always, had in the past run the town as he saw fit and he intended to go on doing so, martial law or not. The mayor had always obeyed him, and he undoubtedly expected Kekewich to be equally compliant. Rhodes had a low opinion of military men, but in the beginning he chose to be cooperative and Kekewich was appreciative. When it was decided to raise another mounted force, the Kimberley Light Horse, Rhodes provided the equipment from the resources of De Beers and Kekewich made him the regiment's honorary colonel. The first sign of a rift appeared when Kekewich discovered that, contrary to his order that all messages sent out of Kimberley be censored, Rhodes had instituted his own messenger service—a system he maintained throughout the siege in spite of Kekewich's objections—and it proved to be a more efficient system than any the army could devise. Kekewich sometimes found it difficult to get messages out; Rhodes never did.

He maintained unbroken his correspondence with political figures and friends; he even managed to carry on his usual business correspondence: one of his early messages was to his farm manager in Rhodesia about fences on his farms; in December he sent out detailed instructions concerning the payment of De Beers debentures and letters about a railway project; he sent word to Lady Cecil Bentinck asking her to take care of his home in Cape Town, and such messages as, "Hear Lady Chesham in coming. Tell her she may stay at my house."

The first ten days of the siege were quiet, marked only by the preparations being made on both sides; the first shots were not exchanged until 24 October and the Boers did not actually close in on the town until early November. Nevertheless, Rhodes was impatient from the beginning, and he wasted no time in demanding that the British army relieve Kimberley. He wrote to friends, officials, politicians, and men of influence in Cape Town and London. Three weeks after his arrival he was sending a flood of excited, almost hysterical messages demanding instant relief to save the city from "hordes of the enemy" and to avert a "terrible disaster." Prompted by Rhodes, the mayor, judges, and other prominent citizens echoed his demands. Lord Rothschild was asked to press the cabinet to make the military come at once to the rescue. "It is perfectly possible," Rhodes insisted, "but military authorities will do nothing."

He wrote Milner that "if Kimberley falls everything goes." There were plenty of soldiers available, he added; "I cannot understand delay." Milner complained to Lord Selborne, undersecretary of state for the colonies, that Rhodes kept sending him "panicky telegrams about immediate relief, which is impossible."

Ignorant of all this activity, Kekewich was astonished to receive a message from Buller saying, "Civilians in Kimberley representing situation there as serious. Have heard nothing from you. Send appreciation of the situation." Kekewich replied: "Situation in Kimberley not critical."

From a military viewpoint Kimberley was not important. Had Kekewich and his men abandoned it and fled south they probably would have been more useful, and had they destroyed the mining equipment before they left, the town would have been of little value to the Boers. But this was unthinkable; private property was sacred; the great Cecil Rhodes was in the town, and there was a mystique about Kimberley and its diamond mines. So it was that Buller, reluctantly, against his better judgement, sent Methuen on what proved to be his vain mission to relieve it.

In the first month of the siege Kekewich had an opportunity to evacuate the women and children in the town and to rid himself of the necessity of feeding some militarily useless mouths. Early in November General C. J. Wessels sent in a demand for unconditional surrender, adding that if this was not accepted he would still be willing "to receive all Afrikaner families who wish to leave Kimberley, and also to offer liberty to depart to all women and children of other nations desirous of leaving." This was a generous offer, and from both a military and a humanitarian viewpoint Kekewich should have accepted it. He drafted a proclamation which included Wessels's offer, but Rhodes disapproved and suggested that the offer be limited to Afrikaners. Redrafted, the proclamation was approved by Rhodes and published in the *Diamond Fields Advertiser* (owned by Rhodes). Only one family left.

At seven o'clock on Monday morning, 6 November 1899, the Boers fired two shells, the first of many, in the direction of Kimberley, and the hooters of the De Beers mine sounded the alarm. Dr. E. Oliver Ashe, a Kimberley physician, wrote: "It was a weird, ghastly sounding alarm and scared nervous people out of their senses. . . . the three blasts frequently repeated during this part of the siege fairly gave one the horrors, especially at night."[1]

In Kimberley, as in other besieged towns, shell fragments held a fascination for the civilians and unexploded shells were thought great prizes. Small boys, ever the first to dare, took to running out to snatch up pieces as soon as a shell had burst. Sold as souvenirs, they brought good prices, large fragments fetching as much as £2, while an unexploded shell brought £5.

Shelling was seldom heavy, and it was not very effective. No supply depots were destroyed, none of the defenders' guns were disabled, the mines were undamaged, and in the four months of the siege less than two dozen citizens were killed by shell fire. On 14 November, when the town received some sixty hits, total casualties were two cats and a cab horse killed outside the Queen's Hotel. There was usually a bombardment every morning, except on Sundays—and when it rained—"the morning hate," it was called. One of the first of the civilian casualties was a Bantu woman, killed in the street in front of the Kimberley Club. A barman, leaning out a window to watch an approaching shell, was decapitated. Near the railway station a shell hit a house, mortally wounding a woman and killing the baby in her arms. Winifred Heberden, wife of Dr. G. A. Heberden, who had fled with his family to Kimberley from Barclay West, wrote in her diary for 11 November:

Bombardment began at sunrise from three guns at Schmidt's Drift Road. . . . When they stopped we had breakfast and sallied forth to inspect the damage done, and to see if we could get any pieces.

The worst casualty had occurred in front of the Catholic Church, where a poor old native woman had been killed. I was looking at the spot where she had died, when a man near me kicked something soft and dusty, and remarked: "That's a piece of her brain, Missis—"; so, feeling rather queer, we went away.[2]

On 25 January a shell exploded in the dining room of A. T. Webster, blacksmith and wagon maker. Most of the family were in the room; five-year-old Andrew was mortally wounded, two other children were injured, and Webster's wife was so badly wounded in the leg that it was later amputated.

Such tragedies as these were rare, and, as sieges go, this one was not particularly ferocious. The Boers made no effort to storm the town, contenting themselves with camping around it and leisurely bombarding it. The British made some sorties, suffered a few casualties, and took a few prisoners, but, as seems to happen in all sieges, the aggressive spirit of the besieged diminished as time went on and there were fewer and fewer sorties. The Boers, too, grew indolent, and their laagers took on a domestic air; women joined their men, bringing their children, and to some it seemed like an extended picnic.

The combatants were courteous. When a doctor with the Boers came in under a white flag to ask for chloroform and brandy, they were readily given him, and Kekewich kept the Boers informed of the condition of the wounded prisoners, even offering to take in and nurse any seriously wounded men in the laagers. Kimberley had good hospital services and even an X-ray unit.

As the town settled in to siege life no one was more helpful, no one busier, than Rhodes. He established a soup kitchen and supplied fruit to the troops and milk for the sick and wounded in the hospitals. He employed nearly 10,000 Bantu on public works, including scavenging, tree planting, and the building of roads and bomb shelters. He formed a committee to help the families of those killed and wounded, he cared for Boer prisoners, and at Christmas he distributed plum puddings. In addition to his role in raising the Kimberley Light Horse, he put De Beers employees to work building a fort on the outskirts of town, and he allowed the De Beers workshops to be used for the fabrication of items needed by the military. Above all, he permitted the De Beers chief mechanical engineer, George Labram, to devote his considerable talents to problems created by the siege.

Labram was a remarkable man. A thirty-year-old American engineer, he had come to South Africa three years before and had quickly established a reputation as an ingenious inventor. He now turned his thoughts to the needs of Kimberley. There were too many cattle for the limited grazing available within the perimeter, but they could not be slaughtered without waste because there was no refrigeration, so Labram designed and built a refrigerator with a capacity of 14,000 cubic feet. He constructed a watchtower 155 feet high with a telephone exchange which linked it with all of the principal points of defence. He built powerful searchlights which covered the main approaches to the town and one large one (called "Rhodes's Eye") which was used for signalling to Methuen when he drew close. He invented a combination of dynamite and powder and manufactured shells for the British guns.

The Boers had modern Krupp guns, but the largest guns the Kimberley garrison possessed were old 7-pounders. Rhodes asked Labram one day if he had ever built a cannon. Only as a boy to shoot firecrackers on the 4th of July "to celebrate the time we licked the British," Labram said. "Well," said Rhodes, "build one now to celebrate the time you are to save the British." With no previous experience with ordnance, Labram designed a breech-loading, rifled gun with a 4.1-inch bore capable of firing

28-pound shells. Using such machines as were found in the De Beers workshops, he built it in just twenty-four days. As *The Times History* said, "The production of this gun must be considered one of the most remarkable events in the history of beleaguered garrisons." It was indeed. The gun, named "Long Cecil" in honour of Rhodes and mounted on an iron carriage, was fired for the first time with some ceremony on 20 January 1900, Mrs. Pickering, wife of the De Beers secretary, pulling the lanyard. Each shell was stamped: "With C.J.R.'s Comps."

Everyone liked George Labram. Many people saw as one of his most extraordinary feats the simultaneous friendship he was able to maintain with Rhodes and Kekewich. No one else in Kimberley achieved this.

When "Long Cecil" opened fire the Boers were shaken, for Labram's gun was more powerful than anything they had on hand. They hastily sent for one of their own "Long Toms"—a 6-inch Creusot which could fire a 96-pound projectile more than 10,000 yards. By 7 February the gun was in place and at 10:00 A.M. opened fire.

At the end of each day Labram was in the habit of taking a cup of chocolate with Dr. and Mrs. Heberden. They were all staying at the Grand Hotel. On 9 February Labram had to forgo this pleasure, for he was to dine with Rhodes and he was late. He was hurriedly dressing when a shell from the Boers' Creusot, the last of the day, crashed through the ceiling and exploded in his room. His body was partially dismembered and so unrecognizable that it was thought at first he had escaped.

Kekewich's relations with Rhodes rapidly deteriorated after Labram's death, and consequently his power and influence in Kimberley crumbled. Kekewich did his best to humour the great man, but Rhodes was so full of suggestions and advice, so bristling with ideas—some good and some very bad indeed—that he had of necessity to oppose him at times, and this enraged Rhodes. When Methuen started his march from the Orange River and relief seemed imminent, Rhodes advised Kekewich to send off a force of mounted men to relieve Mafeking. This was not one of his better ideas, and Kekewich wisely rejected it. Maddened, Rhodes accused him of being afraid of a handful of farmers: "You call yourselves soldiers of an Empire-making nation. I do believe you will next take fright at a pair of broomsticks dressed up in trousers. Give it up! Give it up!"

When Methuen drew closer, Rhodes sent a message outlining for him the strategy he ought to adopt. It was very good strategy, but Methuen was incensed that a civilian should presume to give him advice, and the unfortunate Kekewich was blamed for not controlling the uncontrollable Rhodes. Methuen told Kekewich flatly: "I am arranging military defence with you, and Rhodes must understand that he has no voice in the matter." Rhodes, of course, was incapable of understanding any such thing, and Kekewich, who was as inarticulate as were most regimental officers, found himself unable to explain why.

While the battle of Magersfontein was being fought, Kekewich watched the smoke and dust from the watchtower Labram had built for him without even attempting a sortie on the Boers around him. Together with everyone else in town, he expected to see advanced elements of Methuen's army enter Kimberley within the next twenty-four hours. But the Boers flashed them the bad news, "We have smashed up your fine column," and that night the searchlight south of Magersfontein blinked out a brief message from Methuen: "I am checked."

The disappointment in Kimberley was intense. The town's citizens angrily demanded to know what had happened, and when Kekewich, as disappointed and as uninformed as they, could tell them nothing, he was accused of deliberately withholding information.

It is not certain what Methuen would have done had he reached Kimberley. From evidence he gave to a royal commission after the war it would appear that he was not very clear himself:

Methuen: I had to relieve Kimberley, throw in a large supply of provisions, clear out the non-combatants, and return to the Orange river. These were, in short, the orders I got from him [Buller].
Question: The intention of your advance was simply to reinforce the garrison of Kimberley, and move the non-combatants, and come away again?
Methuen: No, I could not say my object was to reinforce Kimberley, but it was to clear out, I think, something like 11,000 useless mouths, who were black men, and so on. I was to send up the trains holding provisions sufficient for Kimberley to go on with for some time, and clear out all these black men and send them down country or where I could; at any rate get them out of Kimberley.[3]

If this was really what Methuen intended to do, it certainly would not have been satisfactory to Rhodes or other citizens of Kimberley. Kekewich actually did receive orders to prepare for the evacuation of all civilians when Methuen arrived, and he unwisely passed this information on to Rhodes—in confidence. Rhodes told the Town Council and then published the news in his newspaper. There was an uproar. Troubles rained down on the hapless Kekewich. The townspeople read the news in a rage. Unforgivably slow in coming to their relief, the military were now laying plans to dispossess them of their homes and to bankrupt the merchants. Dr. Ashe thought there might even be "a civil war in the town," and Winifred Heberden recorded: "People who have been quite cheerful and happy throughout the siege say that this is the first time they have felt the least depression, and in many cases there is great alarm."

There were, of course, thousands of Bantu, Coloureds, and Asiatics who under the whites's self-imposed rules could not take an active part in the defence except to dig trenches and build fortifications, but who nevertheless had to be fed. Early in the siege Rhodes tried to get rid of them by sending them en masse out of town during the night, but the Boers forced them to turn around and go back. As Rhodes had said nothing to Kekewich about this scheme, the British shelled them as they streamed back before it was realized who they were.

There was still enough food, at least for the white population, if one included horse meat. On 6 January 1900 Winifred Heberden wrote in her diary: "Today we had horseflesh for the first time, and very excellent it was, though many people foolishly refused to taste it." Before the end of the siege 164,183 pounds were consumed. The Bantu, caught in the middle of the warring whites, suffered most: some 900 developed scurvy. Kekewich estimated that he had enough food to last until 28 February. De Beers had large stocks of food which Kekewich, with Rhodes's permission, commandeered and rationed out—but only after the top De Beers officials had laid in their own private stocks. Prices soared: eggs, when they could be obtained, sold for £1 per dozen; among the Coloured servants kittens sold for 5s 6d and plump cats for 12s 6d.

On 29 January Kekewich was asked by Methuen if he could hold out for another six weeks and he replied that he could. The grumbling townspeople began to mutter that perhaps it would be better to surrender, and the mayor told Kekewich that Rhodes planned to call a mass meeting. When Kekewich, horrified at what might happen should the townspeople demand that he surrender, told the mayor that such a meeting must be prevented at all costs, he found an angry Rhodes on his stoep threatening to hold the meeting anyway unless he was given a detailed account of what the British army was doing towards relieving the town. Kekewich quickly sent off a message to Methuen intimating that he feared the inhabitants, led by Rhodes, would force him to surrender. Rhodes, he said, was "quite unreasonable." Roberts had now arrived at the Modder River, and he read Kekewich's message with concern.

The next day, 10 February, the *Diamond Fields Advertiser,* in an article entitled "Why Kimberley Cannot Wait," lauded "the heroic exertions of her citizens" and made plain the editor's opinion of the military: "Is it unreasonable, when our women and children are being slaughtered, and our buildings fired, to expect something better than that a large British Army should remain inactive in the presence of eight or ten thousand peasant soldiers?"

Kekewich closed down the paper and ordered the editor arrested, but Rhodes, anticipating this, had hidden him in a mine.

Soon after, Rhodes appeared at Kekewich's headquarters with the mayor in tow. He had met, he said, with "the twelve leading citizens in Kimberley" and they had drafted a message to Roberts which was to be sent off at once by heliograph. Kekewich read it. After painting a pitiable picture of conditions in the town, it demanded that Roberts inform them if he had any intention of making "an immediate effort for our relief. . . . It is absolutely essential that immediate relief should be afforded to this place."[4] Kekewich did not refuse to transmit the message; he only refused to send it off immediately, as his signallers were busy. Rhodes exploded and shouted: "You low damned cur!" To the startled mayor it appeared that Rhodes was about to hit the colonel, and he stepped between them. The two angry men glared at each other and then Rhodes turned his back and stomped out.

When Roberts received the message he replied at once to Kekewich, reminding him that he was in charge and telling him that if anyone, however grand, interfered with his conduct of the defence he should be arrested. He added that Kimberley would be relieved in a few days and that he should represent to Rhodes and the mayor the "disastrous and humiliating effect of surrendering." Kekewich marked a copy "Secret" and sent it to Rhodes, who at once read the part about imminent relief to a group at the Sanatorium Hotel and then to his friends at the Kimberley Club; then he wrote a message for Kekewich to relay to Roberts: "There is no fear of our surrendering, but we are getting anxious about the state of the British Army. It is high time you did something."[5]

Kekewich refused to send such a message to his commander in chief, and Rhodes was obliged to rewrite it in a less offensive style. Kekewich sent with it a message of his own. He found it necessary to explain—or to try to explain—the peculiar position he was in. Rhodes had done "excellent work," he admitted, but he "desires to control the military situation" and he had been "grossly insulting." He summed up his position: "The key to the military situation here in one sense is Rhodes, for a large majority of the Town Guardsmen, Kimberley Light Horse and Volunteers are De Beers employees. I fully realize the powers conferred on me by the existence of Martial Law, but I have not sufficient force to compel obedience."

With relief on the way at last, Rhodes felt sure that the Boers would intensify their bombardments of the town. On 11 February, without bothering to tell Kekewich, he had the town plastered with notices:

Sunday I recommend women and children who desire complete shelter to proceed to Kimberley and De Beers shafts. They will be lowered at once in the mines from 8 o'clock throughout the night. Lamps and guides will be provided.

C. J. Rhodes[6]

The town panicked. People arrived at the shafts early, and from 5:30 P.M. until 4:00 A.M. the mine lifts worked continually, carrying down women, children, and those men not directly involved with the defence, black and white. There were not enough latrines and the air was soon foul, but there were electric lights, it was cool, and plenty of food and tea was provided by the De Beers Company, an indication that not all the company's food supplies had been turned over to the army for equitable distribution.

On 15 February, the day of deliverance, Kekewich made an effort to capture "Long Tom," but its crew had fled, taking their gun with them. He then went wandering over the veld looking for French, while French and his staff rode into Kimberley and were welcomed by the mayor and Rhodes. Douglas Haig, French's chief of staff, looked around and thought the inhabitants appeared "fat and well."

That evening when Kekewich rode back into town he heard sounds of revelry coming from the Sanatorium Hotel (owned by Rhodes). Inside he found tables laid with luxury foods and champagne flowing freely. Like an awkward schoolboy he stood at the door until Rhodes saw him and pushed his way through his guests toward him. "You shall not see French," he growled. "This is my house, get out of it." But Kekewich had also been seen by one of French's staff officers, who came up and arranged for him to meet the general in a private room. Here French, having already heard Rhodes's views, did not conceal his own opinion that Kekewich had made a bad job of it.

Rhodes and his people had also got to the newspaper correspondents first, and every story sent out credited Rhodes and the De Beers Company with saving Kimberley.

So ended the four months' siege of Kimberley. As the *Daily Mail* put it: "Kimberley is won, Cecil Rhodes is free, the De Beers shareholders are full of themselves, and the beginning of the war is at an end."[7] There had been only 134 casualties among the armed defenders, only 21 citizens had been killed by the 8,500 shells the Boers had thrown into the town, but some 1,500 people, mostly Bantu and Coloureds, died of diseases. It proved a bad time and place to be born: infant mortality was 67.1 percent among whites and 91.2 percent among nonwhites.

24

PAARDEBERG

On 16 February, the day after French rode into Kimberley and drank Rhodes's champagne, the cavalry division went looking for the enemy. They rode over the positions the besiegers had occupied, but the Boers had gone and had taken their guns with them. A few commandos fighting rear-guard actions engaged them in some inconclusive skirmishes in which they suffered 28 casualties. Not much was accomplished. The most significant result of all this pounding across the veld and among the kopjes around Kimberley was the utter exhaustion of the horses.

French too was tired when at seven o'clock in the evening he returned to Kimberley, but he was to get little rest. Three hours later he received a message from Kitchener ordering him to move out and head off Cronjé, now trekking east along the Modder. He climbed back into his saddle and with less than 1,200 men—all that still had horses capable of moving or could be mounted on horses borrowed from the Diamond Fields Horse and the De Beers Company—set off that night on a 30-mile ride.

By eleven o'clock the next morning Cronjé had reached the Modder

River at Paardeberg Drift. He and his burghers felt reasonably safe here, believing that the main British force could not catch them before they crossed the river and took up suitable defensive positions blocking Roberts's path to Bloemfontein. Some of the wagons had already started to cross; others were outspanned and the oxen turned loose to graze. Some of the burghers and the women had built fires and were preparing to cook their midday meal; others had stretched out in the shade of their wagons to get some rest. Without warning, from only 1,200 yards away, guns boomed, and seconds later shells were bursting among them. Most of the Boers panicked, and it was lucky for French that they did, for it is unlikely that his exhausted men could have withstood a determined attack or that they could have escaped on their spent horses. Cronjé's force outnumbered French's by four to one.

All afternoon French held his own and prevented the Boers from moving while Kitchener energetically hustled forward more troops. The mounted infantry under Hannay came up before dark and occupied the high ground to the south and southeast. The 13th Brigade got lost in the dark, but the Highland Brigade marched 31 miles in twenty-four hours and reached Paardeberg just before midnight. The 19th Brigade marched all night and came up at 4:30 A.M. By the end of the second day the Boers were surrounded, the British perimeter stretching for 24 miles.

The senior commander on the spot was now Lieutenant General Sir Thomas Kelly-Kenny, commander of the 6th Division, but the energetic Kitchener quickly arrived, and although he held no command of his own, he was soon throwing orders in all directions. There arose the question of who was in charge.

Kelly-Kenny, the older man, had been nearly three years senior to Kitchener when the two men had been colonels, but Kitchener had been promoted to the rank of major general six months earlier than he. However, in South Africa Kelly-Kenny, like French and Colvile who were also on the scene, had been given the local rank of lieutenant general, while Kitchener held only his substantive rank as major general. Also, Kitchener, as chief of staff, could give orders only in Roberts's name, although quite obviously the orders he was giving at Paardeberg were his own, for Roberts had come down with a severe chill and was in bed at Jacobsdal, where he had established his headquarters. Sick or not, only Roberts could make the delicate and important decision as to who was to command at Paardeberg. A soldier was sent galloping off with the question. Roberts's reply was a courteous letter to Kelly-Kenny asking him to consider Kitchener's orders as being his own. Kelly-Kenny, piqued, huffily replied, "This is not the time to enter into personal matters. Till this phase of the operation is completed, I will submit to even humiliation rather than raise any matter connected with my command."

Kitchener proceeded to throw himself into this battle with all the energy for which he was justly famous and with a ferocity and ruthlessness which were to make him more famous still. Just before dawn on 18

February he rode forward to inspect the Boer positions.

It is probable that had Cronjé moved out on the night of 17 February he could have made his escape with at least most of his force. Such a course was urged on him by most of his commandants; some of his burghers on their own initiative did get away, but Cronjé, perhaps with thoughts of how the voortrekkers in their wagon laager with their backs to the Blood River had beaten back Dingaan's Zulu hordes, was determined to stay where he was. The coffee-coloured Modder provided water, and its steep banks lined with trees and bushes offered some protection for the cattle and horses and were themselves natural defensive works. He ordered the wagons parked together near the drift and started his men digging trenches and developing positions along the river's banks. The Boer position was now in the shape of a huge snail, its length the 2 miles of the brushwood-fringed riverbanks running east and west and its shell the bulge which formed the laager of animals and wagons on the north bank. North and south the Boers had clear fields of fire.

Kitchener viewed Cronjé's positions with satisfaction. Kelly-Kenny, who was with him, explained the plans he had made for mounting guns on the surrounding kopjes and distributing the infantry in defensive positions to prevent the enemy's escape. Kitchener thought the scheme was imbecilic. His tired troops had already been paraded and were on the move. He was going to throw them at the Boers. "To annihilate Cronjé's force, and then, with the terror of his dripping sword preceding him, to march straight on to Bloemfontein, was to Kitchener's mind, the only policy worthy of a soldier."[1] Impatiently he cut short Kelly-Kenny's exposition and ordered an immediate attack. Looking at his watch, he said confidently to the knot of staff officers around him: "It is now seven o'clock. We shall be in the laager by half-past ten. I'll then load up French, and send him on to Bloemfontein at once."

It was not to be so simple.

The soldiers were thrown recklessly at the Boer positions. Kitchener appears to have had quite clearly in mind what he wanted to do, but he had not troubled to explain himself to his subordinate commanders. Major General Horace Smith-Dorrien, commanding the 19th Brigade in Colvile's division, was told by one of Kitchener's staff officers to take his brigade and a battery across the river and "establish yourself on the other side." Smith-Dorrien asked where he was supposed to cross and was airily told: "The river is in flood and as far as I have heard Paardeberg Drift, the only one available, is unfordable; but Lord Kitchener, knowing your resourcefulness, is sure you will get across somehow." Smith-Dorrien cursed, but he did manage to get his brigade across. Once established on the other side he had no idea of what he was supposed to do next, and later said that he was "in a complete fog, and knew nothing of the situation either of our own troops, or of the Boers, beyond what I could see, or infer, myself."[2]

The Highland Brigade made a gallant charge across a bare, open stretch of veld in the face of a hail of bullets, but about 500 to 800 yards from the Boer positions the Highlanders were brought to a standstill and again found themselves, as at Magersfontein, lying on their stomachs on the veld in front of Boer positions.

THE YORKSHIRE REGIMENT CHARGED WITH BAYONETS INTO THE BOERS NEAR SLINGERSFONTEIN.

By two o'clock in the afternoon British attacks from east, west, and south had all been checked, but Kitchener, still determined to get into the laager with his bayonets, insisted that the Boer positions be taken "at all costs." In a frenzy he galloped about, tossing orders in all directions. Kelly-Kenny, ordered to rouse his troops and renew the attack, thought Kitchener was mad, but he obeyed. Smith-Dorrien was amazed to see his entire line, even the transport guard, suddenly rise up and charge. Kitchener was giving orders directly to subordinate commanders. Smith-Dorrien later complained that "the only man who was not told what 19 Brigade was to do was its commander." The brigade lost 22 percent of its strength.

Hannay's mounted infantry, its horses left behind, had pushed up to within 700 yards of the Boers' main position in front of their laager, but the fire was so fierce that it could make no further progress. Hannay sent Kitchener a message saying that it was futile to attempt to go further, but Kitchener fired back: "The time has now come for a final effort. All troops have been warned that the laager must be rushed at all costs. Try and carry Stephanson's brigade with you. But if they cannot go, the M.I. should do it. Gallop up if necessary and fire into the laager."[3]

Hannay appears to have been in a state of nervous exhaustion. The strain of the past few days had been great, and Kitchener had added to it by goading him unmercifully; with this last infeasible order Hannay reached his breaking point. He sent his staff away, hastily gathered up 50 mounted men, and led them in a wild charge straight at the Boer lines. Those who followed him were shot from their saddles; Hannay kept his until he fell riddled with bullets just inside the Boer position.

Hannay's dramatic, desperate act of self-immolation had a profound affect upon the officers and men, all of whom recognized it as a protest against Kitchener's ruthless indifference to the lives of his soldiers. Kitchener himself, completely unmoved, continued to throw his regiments at the enemy positions: three companies of the Duke of Cornwall's Light Infantry made a gallant charge, their colonel cheering his men on as he fell mortally wounded; the Canadians, too, attempted a charge. By the end of the day the exhausted troops could do no more. Many had had nothing to eat since the night before, and their water bottles had long been empty. An Oxfordshire soldier wrote: "I dreamed of a battle the night before, but I never thought it could be as terrible as this. We were mad with thirst and our officers flopped down like ninepins."[4] When the sun set on the bloody battlefield, even Kitchener was forced to give it up.

The Boers too were exhausted. Caught like animals in a trap, all were anxious, many were frightened. The laager was a scene of destruction and confusion. Wagons had been blown up or set on fire by the British guns. The ground was covered with debris; bits and pieces of boxes, bundles, casks, and broken wagons were everywhere. Hundreds of dead oxen and horses lay about. There were no doctors; the women, with faces pale and drawn, were doing what they could for the wounded amid the smoke and fire and din of exploding shells, while terrified children crouched whimpering in holes in the earth.

At the end of the first day Kitchener sent off a message to Roberts reporting that the laager was not yet taken and that casualties had been great, but he hoped to "do something more definite" the next day. Kitchener's furious assaults of 18 February had indeed produced high casualties for the British: 1,262 in all, including 20 officers and 300 men killed or mortally wounded.

When Roberts read Kitchener's report he decided that he must take over the conduct of the battle himself, and at once. Rising from his sick bed, he left Jacobsdal at four o'clock in the morning and reached Paardeberg six hours later. He found Kitchener, in spite of the objections of all his subordinate commanders, planning to renew the infantry assaults. Roberts, appalled by the losses on the previous day, wished to avoid "a further loss of life which did not appear . . . to be warranted by the exigencies of the situation." He was sure that Cronjé could be pounded into submission by his artillery without risking additional casualties in bloody bayonet charges. Kitchener was sent away—Roberts ordered him to expedite the repair of the railway and its bridges.

Cronjé asked for an armistice to bring in the wounded and bury the dead, but Roberts rejected this and sent him a demand for unconditional surrender. Cronjé's reply in Dutch was translated as: "Since you are so unmerciful as not to accord the time asked for, nothing remains for me but to do as you wish."[5] Roberts understandably assumed that this meant Cronjé had surrendered, and he sent troops marching towards the river to collect the prisoners. They were quickly driven back by a sharp fire from the Boers. Far from being a surrender, Cronjé's message had been one of defiance and correctly translated read: ". . . nothing remains for me to do. You do as you wish." He made himself clearer in a further exchange: "During my lifetime I will never surrender. If you wish to bombard, fire away. *Dixi.*"

Fire away is what the British did, shelling the Boer positions with every gun they possessed. At first Roberts did not realise that the laager contained women and children, but as soon as he learned of their presence he offered them a safe conduct out. Cronjé for unknown reasons refused this and so these innocents too were exposed to the full fury of the British artillery.

Nearly fifty British guns of all sizes were trained on Cronjé's laager and his positions along the river, while he had only four guns and a pompom with which to reply. All day long, every day, the lyddite shells rained on the immobile Boers. The gunners could hardly miss this easily defined target. Wagon after wagon was set afire and burned down to a pile of blackened scrap iron and smouldering wood ashes. The losses among the cattle and horses were enormous. It was impossible to bury them all; many were thrown into the river, but the current was not strong enough to carry them away. A Boer diarist recorded the conditions:

Bombardment heavier than usual. The burghers are recalcitrant and in consequence the General's authority wanes rapidly. There is hardly any food. . . . The stench of the decomposed oxen and horses is awful. The water of the river is putrid with carrion. . . . The sufferings of the wounded are heartrendering. Little children huddled together in bomb-proof excavations are restless, hungry and crying. The women are adding their sobs to the plaintive exhortations of the wounded. All the time the shelling never abates. . . . Nearly every man, woman and child is lyddite-stained. . . . It is too much for flesh and blood.[6]

News of Cronjé's plight spread rapidly. Throughout the republics there was anxiety. Kruger conducted a night-long vigil in the Dopper church in Pretoria, and similar services were held throughout the Transvaal. Out on the veld around the British encirclement hovered Boer commandos. In most of these there was much hand-wringing, but the leaders were uncertain and afraid. French in his dash from Kimberley had, unknown to him, frightened off J.S. Ferreira and his Free Staters who had intended to link up with Cronjé. The Transvaalers in the area hung back and sent a wire to Joubert in Natal asking what they should do. Joubert sent them a blistering reply:

How is this possible? Are there not instructions enough from the banks of the Modder, whence for so many days already General Cronje has been calling in his agony "Come relieve me"? What other instructions can now be given or demanded than, with one voice and one mouth, "Burghers of South Africa, go and help deliver your general from the might of the tyrant"? . . . Relieve Cronje, cost what it will. . . . trust firmly in God and He will give you strength. Relieve Cronje.[7]

Only Christiaan de Wet acted promptly with courage and resolution. On the south bank of the river was a hill which the British had christened Kitchener's kopje. The detachment of Kitchener's Horse stationed there were not actively engaged in the fighting, and on the afternoon of the 19th they rode to a nearby farm for water. Without warning De Wet pounced. With 500 burghers he captured the detachment and then occupied the hill. A quick-witted British staff officer gathered up some mounted infantry and three companies of the Gloucestershire Regiment and interposed them between Kitchener's kopje and the Yorkshires who were facing Cronjé's laager. Dusk found the British fighting back to back on this portion of the battlefield.

De Wet wrote a message to Cronjé urging him to abandon his laager and everything in it and fight his way out at night. If he would only move, De Wet stood ready to help in the breakout and to cover his retreat. The bearer of the message was Danie Theron, who was to become the most famous of the Boer scouts and a popular hero whose exploits are still remembered. (There is a Regiment Danie Theron in the South African army today.)

Carrying De Wet's message, Theron successfully inched his way through the British lines to Cronjé's laager and then made his way back again. Of this feat De Wet said: "He had performed an exploit unequalled in the war. Both in going and returning he had crawled past the British sentries, tearing his trousers to rags during the process. The blood was running from his knees, where the skin had been scrapped off."[8]

The mission was unsuccessful. Neither De Wet's message nor Theron's pleading could persuade the stubborn Cronjé to break out. A few burghers managed to slip away and join De Wet, including Commandant (later General) C. C. Froneman and that curious Boer prophet, Niklaas van Rensburg. De Wet fought to hold his position as long as possible, but he could not long remain without becoming surrounded himself. He got away just in time. The British could not then have known it, but the capture of De Wet would have been a more significant blow to the Boer cause than the defeat of Cronjé.

Conditions in the British camps did not compare with the frightful conditions in the Boer laager, but they were not pleasant. The polluted Modder was the only source of water, and it would appear that care was not taken to see that all water was drawn upstream. The soldiers called the water "dead horse soup." On 24 February Captain Slocum in his dispatch to the United States War Department reported: "But strange to say . . . there have been only 126 cases of enteric or typhoid fever, and those of a mild type." This favourable situation was not to last long.

Most of the sick and wounded had to lie on the ground exposed to sun and rain, for most of the tents had been left behind to reduce the baggage. Mr. Wilson Cheyne, a surgeon, had difficulty getting sterilized water and was short of dressings, but he made light of the sufferings of his patients, later testifying, "I think the hardships of the sick and wounded at Paardeberg was of very little consequence. . . . I do not think that the fact of the patients being in the open affected them a bit."[9]

On 26 February, after nine days of bombardment, Cronjé sent word to Roberts that he was ready to surrender. Conditions in the laager had become unendurable. Roberts's guns had done their work. Early on the morning of 27 February, the nineteenth anniversary of the battle of Majuba, Cronjé, accompanied by his wife and his secretary, rode out of the laager. General Sir George Pretyman and a small escort came to meet them and conduct them to Roberts's camp.

A crowd of officers and newspaper correspondents came to watch but stood respectfully back as Cronjé, alone on a bony grey pony, rode forward. One observer described him as "a great heavy bundle of a man. . . . Great square shoulders, from which the heavy beard was thrust forward so that he seemed humped; a heavy face, shapeless with unkempt, grey-tinged, black hair; lowering under heavy brows, from under which small, cunning, foxy eyes peered shiftily."[10] Another remarked that he was "rather fat, red-faced above his beard, a hard looking man."[11] Battersby told readers of the *Morning Post* that he "looked like nothing as much as a Welsh farmer going round his stock." Although observers disagreed as to whether his tattered coat was yellow, green, or brown and whether his blue trousers were serge or frieze, all agree that he wore a wide-brimmed, grey slouch hat and carried a sjambok.

In striking contrast to the shabby, hulking Cronjé was the dapper little field marshal who stepped out to greet him as he dismounted from his pony. Roberts, simply and neatly dressed in khaki, without any badge of rank but carrying the splendid presentation sword given him for his famous Kabul-to-Kandahar march, walked up and extended his hand.

"I am glad to see you," he said. "You have made a gallant defence, sir."

Roberts led Cronjé to his tent and offered him breakfast, but he refused. Later he took lunch and was given champagne; a staff officer sent him a cigar. The British stared at these unhappy people—Cronjé, his wife, and his secretary—with unabashed curiosity. The presence of Mrs. Cronjé in their camp seemed especially strange. Colonel N. J. C. Rutherford described her as "a small, dark, dried-up looking woman," and a newsman saw "a thin, decrepit woman," who "in her rough straw hat and dirty old black dress, without cloak or shawl of any sort, presented a hopelessly miserable, draggled and woebegone appearance." Still another found her "a motherly little old woman" with a toothless grin.

The arrangements for the surrender were soon made. The sixty-five-year-old Cronjé, who spoke little English, said almost nothing but sat sunk in a chair, his hands buried in his overcoat pockets, while his secretary (who was also his nephew) spoke for him. Defeat was bitter indeed for the "Lion of Potchefstroom." "His set, hardened face only suggested that the bitterest hour of his life was being barely endured," reported *The Times* correspondent.

All accounts of the surrender mention that Cronjé requested that his wife and secretary be permitted to accompany him into captivity. That a man of Cronjé's character, his mind numbed by horror and humiliation, would have made so personal a request seems unlikely. It is more probable that the request was prompted by his wife and made by his nephew without his knowledge. It may well have been a surprise to him to find his wife and nephew beside him when he set off in a closed carriage under guard for Cape Town.

The British watched with amazed curiosity as the rank-and-file Boers, escorted by a battalion of the Buffs, shambled out of their trenches and away from their foul and smoking laager, a nondescript crowd of about 4,000 burghers, many with weeping wives and children, their belongings done up in coloured handkerchiefs or striped blankets; many clutched their Bibles. A girl carried her arm in a stained sling, her pale face disfigured by a red scar almost hidden by her sunbonnet. "Clad in ill-fitting garments of extraordinary incongruity, laden with parasols, bundles, teapots, and bottles; many with umbrellas and many with galoshes . . . in appearance a mob of frowsy vagrants."[12] One observer thought them "the most singular lot of people to be seen at that moment upon earth."[13] "They are the worst-looking men I have ever seen," wrote Julian Ralph. "They are wild-eyed, savage, dull-witted, misshapen. Those who show symptoms of a brain appear to be unbalanced." Such were the impressions made by Cronjé's folk on the civilians present.

The soldiers who had fought these brave, resolute people reacted differently. "It was a great sight and they were a fine-looking lot of men," said Seymour Vandeleur. A tall Australian soldier ran up and kissed all the babies. "He did it," said Prevost Battersby, "with the indulgence of a man long deprived of such a pleasure, and the women seemed quite to understand."[14] Captain Slocum, the American military observer, wrote:

I do not know what history will say of these people, but personally, words fail to express adequately my admiration for their tenacious and brave defense under the conditions in which they were placed.

The women were at once given safe-conduct by Lord Roberts to go anywhere they wished, the wounded immediately cared for by the British doctors, and rations distributed to all.[15]

About two-thirds of the prisoners were from the western Transvaal; the rest were Free Staters. It would appear that they were fairly representative of the general Boer population: out of 1,000 prisoners, one in seven had one of the nine most common Afrikaner names. There were 21 named Pretorius, 23 named Van Vuren, and 19 Van der Merwe; there were 17 Van Zyls, 14 Bothas, and 13 Jouberts.

The British entering the Boer laager were horrified. Battersby found the smell overwhelming:

> Camping on the battlefield one became acclimated to the scent of death. But no human soul could have grown used to the reek of that slaughter-house. It was appalling. Shrapnel had scattered the bodies of beasts; lyddite had turned them inside out. Cattle, twisted out of the likeness of kine, stripped to a red and skinless horror, rent into mounds of broken pieces, lay on every hand and had lain there for weeks, under a sun that turns meat sour almost between the plate and the mouth.[16]

A subaltern wrote to his wife:

> Three horses lay piled one upon another. . . . Terrible was the agony expressed in the contortion of the topmost horse. His glossy bay neck, down which a thin crimson stain was oozing, curved back in a splendid arch, propped against the wither of the horse below. The lips were drawn back from the gums, and the glistening teeth clenched convulsively in the black mane of his prostrate comrade.[17]

James Barnes went among the prisoners and talked with them. A pretty girl in a sunbonnet with a tear-streaked face came up to him: "What are you going to do with us?"

Barnes, an American, answered, "Why, send you back to your homes safe and sound. What do you think the British are?"

One man asked Barnes if he thought he would be able to keep his cart and horse, as he had his old mother with him and she was unable to walk far. Barnes was astonished: "His old mother, forsooth! I thought to myself that a laager was a nice place to bring one's old mother, but I did not say so."[18]

The able-bodied men were sent off to Cape Town, the first stage of their long journey to the prisoner-of-war camp the British had established on the island of St. Helena. Some of the women were allowed to accompany their men as far as Cape Town. The wounded were sent to the Boer hospital in British-occupied Jacobsdal. Dr. H. Küttner, a German doctor with the Boers, described their condition:

> The wounded at Cronjé's laager . . . were almost all infected to some extent. So, whereas we should have had little operating to do, we now operate daily on many of the wounded, amputating, which would not have been necessary but for the sepsis from which many would have died, as some have, from tetnus.[19]

The surrender of Cronjé spread consternation among the Boers. De Wet spoke of the "indescribable panic throughout . . . all the laagers on the veld. . . . If the famous Cronjé were captured, how could any ordinary burgher be expected to continue his resistance!" It was the Boers' first major defeat, and it marked a turning point in the war. News of the disaster spread through the Orange Free State and the Transvaal. At Vereeniging, a small town on the Vaal River 35 miles south of Johannesburg, Dr. T. N. Leslie wrote in his journal:

On the 29th [February] we heard of a big battle in which Cronje had been made prisoner and his entire army either killed or made prisoners. All the Boers from this district were in this commando and a week later when the news began to filter among the farms, it was pitiable to see the women and children; and the scenes at the post office were indescribably pathetic. . . . all the women from that part, were crying and fainting.[20]

Gideon Scheepers had been with Cronjé but narrowly escaped capture, as he told his mother in a letter:

Dearest Mother,
I am still quite well through the blessings of the Lord. I was nearly also on my way to the Cape today, as just half an hour before the British surrounded the laager, I was called away to lay a cable, and thus escaped.
Old Cronjé has behaved very badly, and has now been taken captive with nearly 6,000 Boers. It is a hard blow for the Afrikaners, but they deserved it, otherwise it would not have happened. The Lord has helped us for so long, and in the end it was not fighting any more but the looting of cattle, one from the other—truly a disgrace the way they acted. No blessing could be expected here. So much injustice too was done here to the burghers. The poor always had to lie in the trenches, while the rich lay with old Cronjé in the tents. And now they are all going along to the Cape![21]

Already a feeling was developing that Cronjé had dishonoured and disgraced the Afrikaner cause. Although he survived his captivity and lived for nearly a decade after the war, he was never forgiven for his surrender at Paardeberg, and he never regained the respect or trust of his countrymen.

Adding to the ignominy of surrender, making it more bitter still, was the fact that Cronjé had surrendered on, of all days, the anniversary of the battle of Majuba. Kruger wailed, "The English have taken our Majuba Day away from us." De la Rey expressed the sentiments of all Boers: "But what shall I say about General Cronje! His stubbornness has cost us dear. . . . And why not have surrendered a day earlier, or a day later. Why, oh why, on 27 February! That was the greatest humiliation of all for the Afrikaner people, as henceforth any arrogant Englishman could say, 'Majuba is avenged!' "[22]

The significance of the day was not lost on the British. Roberts in his telegram to Lord Lansdowne said: "General Cronje and all his forces capitulated unconditionally at daylight this morning, and is now a prisoner in my camp. . . . I hope Her Majesty's Government will consider this event a satisfactory one, occurring as it does on the anniversary of Majuba."[23]

Her Majesty's government was pleased, and so was Her Majesty, who received the news at breakfast and wrote in her journal: "We are all greatly rejoiced, for it is indeed grand news." Her Majesty's loyal subjects were equally pleased. When the news reached the London Stock Exchange there were "rousing cheers" and everyone took off his hat and sang "God Save the Queen." Madame Tussaud's wax museum was not slow in offering a tableau depicting the meeting of Cronjé and Roberts. And in far-off Calcutta a statue of Roberts was decorated with flowers, one floral tribute bearing the legend: "Majuba Avenged."

There has been much after-the-fact debate as to whether Kitchener's attack plan or Roberts's siege plan was the best solution to the military problem presented at Paardeberg. The debate began almost immediately, but curiously it was a debate in which neither Roberts nor Kitchener participated. Although they obviously held opposing views and there were rumours both in South Africa and in England of a rift between them, neither man was ever heard afterwards to criticise the other.

The *Official History* and Conan Doyle came down firmly on the side of Roberts. "There was only one thing which apparently should not have been done," said Conan Doyle, "and that was attack him [Cronjé]." Both *The Times History* and the officers of the German Great General Staff disagreed. *The Times History* pointed out the "moral results": "Paardeberg . . . did not teach them to fear the British soldier. Only some direct act like the storming of the laager would have inspired that fear. . . . a thousand casualties would have produced an ineffaceable impression on them."[24]

The patient tactics of Roberts undoubtedly saved many of his soldiers from death by Boer bullets. Yet, had Kitchener been permitted to pursue his bloody assaults on the 19th and had he been successful, even at the cost of double the number of casualties, fewer men would have died. It is ironic and tragic that the protracted stay at Paardeberg, where the men daily drank the increasingly more polluted water of the Modder, caused more casualties than all the Mauser bullets the Boers had fired.

25

THE SIEGE OF LADYSMITH

Kimberley had been relieved, but on the eastern end of the theatre of war, on the Natal front, White was still bottled up in Ladysmith. "We are a victorious army besieged by an inferior enemy." So said Colonel Frank Rhodes after the British victories at Talana and Elandslaagte when White drew his entire army into Ladysmith and allowed himself to be besieged. True, White had tried to drive the Boers away, but only once, and he had been unsuccessful. He commanded more than an ordinary garrison; it was, at least in the beginning, a strong field army, complete with cavalry and field artillery, and yet, except for two small sorties, he did nothing further with it except to fend off the feeble attempts by the Boers to subdue him. He was much criticised later for not sending away his cavalry, which could have escaped and which, although of little use to the besieged town, would have been most useful to Roberts.

There were conflicting opinions as to whether Ladysmith was or was not an easily defended location. *The Times History* said: "The environs of Ladysmith lend themselves to a policy of pure defence far more readily than is generally supposed."[1] This had not been General Butler's opinion. On the selection of Ladysmith as the British garrison town in northern Natal he said, "Perhaps, in the whole history of modern strategic selection, no more unfortunate choice had been made than . . . Ladysmith."[2] This was also the opinion of Richard Harding Davis: "To anyone who has seen Ladysmith, the wonder grows not only that it was ever relieved, but that it was ever defended. . . . For a garrison at Ladysmith is in a strategic position not unlike that of a bear in a bear-pit at which the boys around the top of the pit are throwing shells instead of buns."[3]

Sir George White (1835–1912), the commander of the Ladysmith garrison, had had an extraordinary military career. After passing out of Sandhurst at the age of eighteen he had been sent to India, arriving just before the Indian Mutiny. His early career was undistinguished, promotion was slow, and after twenty-seven years' service he was still only a major in the Gordon Highlanders. Then came the Second Afghan War of 1879–1880, in which he so distinguished himself that he won the Victoria Cross, was made a Companion of the Bath, and was promoted to the rank of brevet lieutenant colonel. From this point on his career was spectacular: ten years later he was a major general and KCB; in 1893 he was given the supreme command in India over the heads of a number of his seniors. Just prior to his appointment in South Africa he had been quartermaster general at the War Office.

Sir George Younghusband called White "one of the bravest men, and an Irish gentleman to boot." Valorous on the battlefield he certainly was, but to live with defeat without being disheartened calls for a temperament and a courage he did not possess. After the battle of Ladysmith on 30 October 1899 he wrote to his wife: "I think that after this venture the men will lose confidence in me, and that I ought to be superseded." He appears to have been completely cowed by his defeat; the disaster near Nicholson's Nek particularly distressed him. It took much urging by his subordinates to get him to agree in December to two minor sorties to destroy Boer guns, and in spite of their success they were not repeated. Colonel Rawlinson complained: "If Sir George would go out a bit more and talk to the officers and men, he could do a lot to keep their spirits up." But apathetic and dispirited, White kept to his quarters.

Although Buller did not, as he could have, order White to attack or attempt to break out, he testified after the war that White had a better force theoretically, a more experienced force, and a larger available force to help himself than I had to help him. The onus of his relief was thrust on me . . . to bring the whole force of the Empire to get him out. I am satisfied in my own mind that if I had been in Ladysmith with that force I could have come out any morning or evening that I wished. . . .[4]

White was inactive, but so was Joubert. His burghers grew bored, and many were worried by reports that their homes were being looted. Botha telegraphed to the landdrost at Vryheid demanding that the properties of his soldiers back home be protected; and Assistant General E. Erasmus complained by telegraph to the landdrost in Pretoria over a report that the wife of one of his burghers was suffering from want.

Disquieting reports have been received by me . . . that properties are not suitably protected in your area. Since you are expected to protect everything there without exception, I am most annoyed to hear of this and also that, although evil-doers already accused of plundering have been sent to you for lawful punishment, not only has such not been done but, on the contrary, you have armed them. They don't come here I notice! Various houses of burghers at the front have been looted. . . .[5]

Commandant Ben Viljoen complained to Field Cornet De Vries in Fordsburg of the quality of recruits being sent him:

What the hell do you think I have here, a hospital, a reformatory, or a war on my hands . . . ? Among others who have arrived here with chronic and grave diseases are J. Elliot who is blind, G. van der Walt who has a large rupture and J. F. van der Merwe with a gastric ulcer, whereas G. Roestof throws an epileptic fit every day. . . . Why do you not commandeer plump over-nourished persons like the officials? . . .[6]

Unlike Kekewich in Kimberley, Sir George White had no trouble with the civil population of his besieged town, for he did not have a Cecil Rhodes to stir them up. He did, however, have the almost equally famous (or infamous) Dr. Jameson, Rhodes's friend and employee, leader of the Jameson Raid, and the future prime minister of Cape Colony.

Why Jameson was in Ladysmith and what he did during the siege are equal mysteries. Unlike Rhodes, he made no attempt to interfere with the military operations; neither was he helpful. By all accounts a good doctor and an able administrator, he was asked to serve in neither capacity, and as far as is known he did not volunteer. Lady Edward Cecil mentioned that he came down with enteric while at Ladysmith, but Dr. James Alexander Kay wrote in his journal: "I saw a lot of Jameson. He used to come to the hospital to have a yarn every morning." There is no evidence that he ever attended the sick and wounded. He stayed at first in the Royal Hotel with Colonel Rhodes, and although he was seldom to be found there during the bombardments, it seemed that the Boers made special efforts to hit this building. The *Ladysmith Bombshell,* a siege newspaper, ridiculed him for keeping so carefully to the safety of his bomb shelter.

The town was full of newspaper correspondents. No previous war had ever been so extensively covered by the press. There were "special correspondents" everywhere in South Africa. They were in the besieged towns and with the relieving columns, reporting gossip, describing what they saw or what others told them they had seen, writing conflicting accounts, giving military opinions, passing judgement upon the commanders. It was all read avidly, and in England people began sprinkling their speech with Afrikaans words; kopjes, dorps, the veld, neks, treks, and drifts—all became for the duration of the war part of the English language. The common Afrikaans suffix "fontein" on place names was somehow amusing, particularly "Stinkfontein," and would-be wits in London spoke of trekking to Kensingtonfontein.

The war was also covered by swarms of photographers, professional and amateur; no previous war had ever been so extensively photographed. In London several illustrated papers existed almost entirely on photographs, supplemented by a few drawings. *Black and White Budget* boasted of fifteen correspondents, photographers, and artists in South Africa; its circulation rose to more than half a million. *The Illustrated London News* sent out its best-known artist, Melton Prior (1845–1910), who was with the besieged in Ladysmith.

When it became obvious that Ladysmith was to be beleaguered the newsmen were forced to decide whether they would stay or leave. All but one stayed. "How could we ever think of quitting those famous British and Irish regiments gathered there at the centre of peril?" Harry Nevinson of the *Chronicle* wrote.[4] The one who did leave, Bennett Burleigh, famous correspondent of the *Daily Telegraph*, took the last train out on 2 November 1899, lying under his seat like the other passengers until out of range of the Boers' Mausers.

The newsmen did their bit to relieve the tedium of siege life by publishing two humorous newspapers, the *Ladysmith Lyre* (four numbers printed) and the *Ladysmith Bombshell*. Two samples from the *Bombshell:* "For Sale—One hundred Sworn Affidavits by Transvaal Burghers regarding the inhuman treatment they received at the hands of the 'Verdomde Engelsch' by being compelled to wash." "Wanted—a few Dutchmen to enter the Town of Ladysmith. A warm reception guaranteed."

It seemed witty at the time. Isabella Craw, a thirty-two-year-old spinster and a volunteer nurse, wrote in her journal: "It is very funny, most amusing."

The only real journalistic enterprise was shown by George Lynch, accredited by the *Morning Herald, Echo,* and *Illustrated London News,* who once went over to the Boer lines with some copies of the *Ladysmith Lyre* which he offered to exchange for copies of the *Standard and Diggers News,* the pro-Boer English-language newspaper from Johannesburg. The bored burghers, grateful for the diversion he created, made him welcome and invited him to spend the night. He was even allowed to send off a telegram to the *Morning Herald* before he left.

Not all the burghers were willing to accept Lynch at face value; one suspicious commandant wired the state secretary that he was "a highly dangerous person." Many Boers were convinced that their laagers had been infiltrated by British spies. The British too had spy fever; Dr. Kay thought he saw one:

> Ladysmith is full of spies. I saw one today, a man who had fought against us in the Boer War of 1880 and I knew him to be bitter towards us. I sent a friend with a message to the Intelligence Department that he had better be arrested; but the reply was, "Ladysmith is so full of spies that one more or less makes no difference."[8]

If there were indeed spies, they were inept, for neither side seemed to know very much about what the other was doing.

A steady stream of rumours kept people interested and amused until they grew cynical and refused to believe anything. Dr. Kay said, "Lying is becoming quite a fine art now; there are wonderful facilities for practice and it is evident that practice is making many perfect."[9]

Facts were scarce. Everyone, of course, was eager for information about the relief force and, to a lesser extent, for news of the outside world. When the sun shone, the heliographs set up by Captain John Cayzer with Buller's force winked and blinked continuously. (The large ones, with 14.137-inch mirrors, could be seen 90 miles away on a clear day, and even the smaller ones, with 7.087-inch mirrors, had a range of 48 miles.) Cayzer had had some difficulty at first establishing contact with Ladysmith; after several contacts with Boer helio stations he grew wary, and when at last he actually reached Ladysmith demanded proof, signalling: "Find Captain Brooks of the Gordons and ask him the name of Captain Cayzer's country place in Scotland." Captain Brooks, when found, remarked, "Well, I always thought Cayzer was an ass, but I didn't think he'd forget the name of his own home." Once, after two days of cloudy skies and rain, shortly before Buller attacked Vaal Krantz, when everyone in town was hungry for news of Buller's operations, the skies cleared and the sun shone through and Cayzer's heliograph resumed operations, blinking to the people of Ladysmith the tidings that "Sir Stafford Northcote, governor of Bombay, has been made a peer."

After the initial excitement Ladysmith settled down to the siege and the boredom of siege life. George W. Steevens, whom Churchill described as "the most brilliant man in journalism I ever met," and H. L. Mencken thought "the greatest newspaper reporter who ever lived," was in Ladysmith and wrote on 26 November:

> We know nothing of the outside; and of the inside there is nothing to know.
> Weary, stale, flat, unprofitable, the whole thing. At first, to be besieged and bombarded was a thrill; then it was a joke; now it is nothing but weary, weary, weary bore. We do nothing but eat and drink and sleep—just exist dismally. We have forgotten when the siege began, and now we are begining not to care when it ends.
> For my part, I feel it will never end.[10]

For Steevens the siege never did end. Within two months he was dead of enteric fever.

The people of Ladysmith accepted their fate more calmly than the citizens of Kimberley, although they grumbled about the food, the inconveniences of siege life, and the imposition of martial law. An order that everyone over the age of twelve had to carry a pass caused some bristling: "We felt rather indignant at the idea of having to have passes like kaffirs," wrote Isabella Craw in her diary. Citizens were also indignant about the soldiers who bathed naked in the river on Sundays, shocking the sensibilities of ladies passing by. A formal complaint was lodged with Colonel Edward Ward, who sensibly suggested that the ladies not look.

With little excitement and little to do, bored soldiers and civilians spent much time talking about food. It was not until the first days of February that horseflesh began to be eaten, and even then it was usually issued not as a meat but as an extract which was dubbed "chevril" (Bovril was a popular beef extract). H. H. S. Pearse of the London *Daily News* said, "I have tasted the soup and found it excellent, prejudice notwithstanding." And Dr. Kay waxed enthusiastic about it and complained, "You can never get enough of it."[11]

The rations, while not plentiful, were not such as people starve on. By 9 February the daily ration per adult had been reduced to one pound of meat (horse or ox) plus some sausage, four ounces of flour, four ounces of bread, and one-sixth of an ounce of tea. There was a great shortage of vegetables until it was discovered that a kind of wild spinach that grew everywhere was delicious. Food could also be purchased at auctions held at night, but prices rose steadily. Wits claimed that hens refused to lay eggs as soon as they learned they were worth 6s each, but in fact eggs never became more expensive than £1 17s per dozen.

George W. Willis wrote to his brother in New Zealand at the end of the siege: "The Military demanded delivery of all eggs and fowls. Over this question and the seizure of our cows and milk I got to loggerheads with them, and though threatened with arrest and imprisonment I compelled them to conditions by which we kept something for our families."[12]

To pass the time, soldiers and civilians arranged amusements for themselves. Since the Boers did not fight on Sundays, polo, cricket, football, and tennis could then be played in safety. Lotteries were held and bets taken on the date Ladysmith would be relieved. Concerts were arranged, and Isabella Craw described one:

Last night we went to the concert and simply enjoyed it immensely. . . . Men from the Naval Brigade (H.M.S. Powerful) contributed largely to the enjoyment of the evening, with comic songs etc. . . . . The songs were many and varied by a recitation and a mouth organ solo, which was the item of the evening, by one of the H.M.S. Powerful gunners.[13]

The garrison had a balloon and, at least in the beginning of the siege, its ascension was an event. Isabella Craw decided that she would not like to trust herself to such an "airy arrangement" and that it did not appear "by any means comfortable or pleasant." Count Gleichen, who made an ascent, complained that "there was remarkably little to see"—perhaps because he was made ill by the movement. Colonel Rawlinson said:

I went up in the balloon to 1,600 feet, and got a splendid view of the surrounding country in still, clear weather. I did not feel a bit sick, but was inclined to hold very tight. The Boers seem to be scattered all over the country around us, and not in any great numbers anywhere. Joubert's camp is visible about half a mile behind Pepworth Hill. I found it difficult to spot the guns, as the balloon rocks about and keeps revolving so much that one cannot keep one's glasses steady.[14]

The first shells landed in Ladysmith at 5:00 A.M. on 30 October 1899. Wakened from their sleep, the townspeople dressed hurriedly, excited but for the most part calm. People remembered afterwards one woman who, still in her night clothes, tied on her bonnet, snatched up her canaries and fled; most simply took to the streets, eager to see the action. Many, including one crippled gentleman who was wheeled out in a Bath chair, congregated on a slope just outside the town to watch. Isabella Craw described what it was like:

We got dressed, then strolled up the street. At every gate groups of men, women and children were standing talking over the latest rumours. We gathered at the corner by the Church. . . . While we were talking and the boom of cannon going every few seconds, another shell from "Big Tom" as we call it, burst not far away. . . . We all went in and had a cup of tea with the Barkers. After breakfast the shells were coming fast and thick. . . . At about half past nine . . . we walked up to the hill behind the Convent to see what we could of the battle. . . . We remained as long as we could or thought it safe.[15]

Under the hard reality of daily shelling, attitudes changed and most began seeking shelters. The high banks of the Klip River which looped around the town provided good protection; many dugout shelters were made and people spent their days there. Everyone slept in his own bed, for there was no shelling at night, and the evenings were often pleasantly spent in the company of friends, sometimes enjoying those immersions in sentimentality Victorians loved: singing "Swanee River," "Home, Sweet Home," and "Mother Come Back from the Echoless Shore."

As in the other besieged towns, people collected shell fragments and duds. One young man, trying to open an unexploded shell, was blinded when the powder exploded in his face.

Amid the shelling life continued to spring anew. Although no records were kept of births among the Bantu and Indian population, among the whites the first siege baby born was Tinta Siege Redvers Moore "at a farm on a hill in the centre of the defensive works," according to H. H. S. Pearse. Eight days after a son (still living) was born to the Willis family, shells from the Bulwana gun burst so close to the house that mother and child were placed on a stretcher and carried under fire to a shelter on the riverbank. Willis wrote to his brother:

When it became advisable to have the boy baptised we christened him Harry Buller Siege, being then daily in "suspectation" that General Buller's forces would relieve the town. . . . He is a fine child, and has been almost entirely reared on Mellins' food. . . . He was for a long time affected with convulsive symptoms owing to strain on the nerves due to the shell explosions, but is now seemingly getting over the affliction. His mother bore up most bravely and never evinced any nervousness under the peculiarly trying time and ordeal she underwent, and the other children showed no fear at any time, and generally looked on the whole business, notwithstanding many ghastly and harrowing sights and experiences, as a time of more or less fun and excitement.[16]

Of the babies born during the siege it would appear that few, if any, other than Buller Willis, survived infancy. Isabella Craw, writing of the death of one, said: "It was born in a cellar the first week the town was shelled so it had a short, sad, little existence."

The Boers had a naïve confidence in the effectiveness of their fine new cannons in the early months of the war, but they did little damage. Pearse wrote on 17 December: "Though more than 5,000 shells have been thrown into our defensive lines, and a vast number of these into the town itself, only one woman has been wounded so far, and not a single child hit."

That the bombardments were relatively harmless can be accounted for by the ease with which shelters could be made in the riverbanks and the leisurely, God-fearing working hours of the Boer gunners. Not only was there no shelling on Sunday or after dark, but the gunners regularly stopped to take their meals and the British could always count on a good undisturbed half hour for their tea while the Boers took their coffee. There were, however, occasional exceptions. When shells fell on the Naval Brigade one Sunday an exasperated captain declared, "That gunner is a German. Nobody but a German atheist would have fired on us at breakfast, lunch and dinner the same Sunday."[17]

Many developed a contempt for the guns and their shells. Pearse saw a woman knitting on the stoep of her cottage "and her busy needles only stopped for a moment when a shell burst in the roadway beyond, and then went on again as nimbly as ever."[18] The telegraph and postal clerks, having nothing to do, played cricket on the race ground within sight of the guns on Bulwana ridge, and Colonel Rawlinson wrote:

I spent a few idle moments watching the Imperial Light Horse play cricket. They kept a man to watch Bulwana Tom, and when he saw the flash he shouted "Here she comes!" The batsman pretended to play the shell, when, to his astonishment, it landed on the pitch about three feet from him. The concussion knocked him down, but he was not a bit hurt.[19]

The Boer guns mounted on Pepworth, Bulwana, and other hills around the town became familiar objects, and the soldiers gave them names: Puffing Billy, Fiddling Jimmy, the Meddler, Bulwana Tom, and

Silent Susan or the Bulwana Sneak (so called because the shell from this gun, a 6-inch Creusot, arrived before the report); three 9-pounders were dubbed Faith, Hope, and Charity; and it was said that soldiers of the Devonshire Regiment gave a Boer pompom "a coarse name." The British also christened some of their own guns: Lady Ann and Bloody Mary were the names given two 4.7-inch guns, and a pair of howitzers on Wagon Hill were called the Great Twin Brethren.

On the Prince of Wales's birthday, 9 November 1899, the British fired a twenty-one-gun salute with shotted guns and cheers ran through the regiments. The perplexed Boers manned their defences, expecting an attack. On the same day White released one of his 160 carrier pigeons (trained by the Durban and Coast Poultry Club) with a congratulatory message to the Prince.

Perhaps because there were so few casualties from the shelling, each death seemed more poignant. On 17 December a single shell blew six Natal Carbineers to bits and wounded three others; five severed legs were seen on the ground. When the young Earl of Ava was killed a sergeant paid him tribute: "You'd never take him for a lord, he seemed quite a nice gentleman."[20] Richard Harding Davis wrote: "He was a particularly gay, lovable, manly nature and he was brave to the edge of recklessness. . . . His father gave the city of Ava and all of Upper Burmah to the British Empire; his son gave his life. And in return the Empire gives him six feet of earth by the muddy waters of the Klip River."[21]

Of the nearly 600 deaths during the siege, only 59 were the results of enemy shelling, while 393 were from enteric fever. Dysentery was rife both in Ladysmith and in the Boer laagers. When the Boers ran out of chlorodyne (a popular anodyne composed of chloroform, morphia, prussic acid, tincture of Indian hemp, and other substances) they begged some from the British, who provided not only the medicine but some brandy as well. The Boers repaid courtesy with courtesy, and when Major Doveton of the South African Light Horse, a former mine manager on the Rand, was wounded in the shoulder they escorted his wife through the lines so that she could be with him.

Joubert generously offered to allow the British to establish a neutral camp for the sick, wounded, and noncombatants outside Ladysmith at a place called Intombi Spruit. A public meeting was held by the townspeople on 4 November to debate this. Charles Jones, who had been a transport rider in the First Anglo-Boer War, spoke up and said that it seemed to him they should not accept favours from their foes.

"But your wife and children are not here now," a man called out.

"No," said Jones, "but I can still say that if my wife and children were here, I would rather that they should trust to protection under the Union Jack with British soldiers than under the white flag at Joubert's mercy."

Rhetoric carried the day. It was decided that Joubert's offer should be rejected, and the meeting ended with three lusty cheers and a singing of "God Save the Queen." Neither the meeting nor the resolution had any effect upon General White, who sensibly accepted the opportunity to put his sick, wounded, and noncombatants out of harm's way. The Boers even allowed a train to travel between the camp and Ladysmith daily without interference. In addition to the sick, wounded, women, children, old men, and medical attendants, a number of able-bodied men also decided to wait out the siege in the safety of the Intombi Spruit camp, and it was sneeringly referred to in the town as Fort Funk or Funkersdorp. It was a matter of indifference to White, who made little use of the civilian manpower available; even the 273-man Town Guard was disbanded.

As the siege dragged on, the sickness rate rose alarmingly. On 10 February, the 101st day of the siege, Pearse noted that the "death rate at Intombi Hospital Camp has gone up to fifteen in a single day. Since the date of investment four hundred and eighty patients have died there from all causes."[22] The week of Spion Kop there were 842 cases of enteric and 472 cases of dysentery. During the course of the siege, out of a garrison of 13,497 there were 10,673 hospital admissions. Of the forty-eight doctors of the RAMC and the Indian Medical Service, five were killed or died of disease.

In the atmosphere of danger and tedium thievery flourished. Dr. Kay was most indignant:

> I lost a hat, a pair of boots, a white sunshade, a cigar box containing surgical instruments, a gold collar-stud, and a pair of Ross field glasses lent to a so-called friend who through deliberate carelessness had them stolen and also several boxes of tea tabloids. The disease develops so rapidly and becomes so acute that one suspects one's dearest friend, and in self defence one almost becomes a thief oneself.[23]

The good doctor who kept surgical instruments in a cigar box did indeed become a thief himself, for when he suspected a friend of stealing nine matches from him, he stole from him a can of candle drippings.

The siege was the greatest event in the life of Miss Isabella Craw. Nothing before had ever been so exciting; nothing after would be—and she knew it. She collected on a tablecloth the signatures of all the important people in town and embroidered them. (This is now in the Castle Museum in Cape Town.) And she did something quite extraordinary which she described in her diary on 18 January 1900:

> I did an awful thing today which I am afraid I will many a time regret, and that is to have on my arm tatooed:

1899
Ladysmith

Pro Patria
1900

No one knows it yet. I hardly know how to break it to Momma and the boys for I know they will say I am very foolish, as a good many have already told me. . . . However, it can't be helped now it is done.

The Christmas of 1899, the first Christmas of the war, seemed somehow special, not only in Ladysmith but throughout South Africa and in England as well. The Boers fired six shells into Ladysmith stuffed with Christmas pudding instead of powder, and each was engraved in bold capital letters: WITH THE COMPLIMENTS OF THE SEASON. One contained a note which said, "Come on out and fight you cowardly English," which rather spoiled the effect. For the shell collectors these were prize curios, and the finders were offered £5 each for them.

Major Karri Davies and Colonel Frank Rhodes organized a Christmas party for the 250 children in town. The officers bought up all the toys in the shops and provided four Christmas trees, which the women of the town decorated. Each tree was given a name—"Great Britain," "South Africa," "Australia," and "Canada"—and above them were the folds of the Union Jack. A hall was gaily decorated, and a trooper of the Imperial Light Horse played Father Christmas. General White attended and was amazed that so many children remained in Ladysmith. After the presents had been distributed and the children's party ended, the trees were removed and the young officers danced with the women of the town until midnight. But the day was a sad one for many, as it often is for those who must spend it far from their own firesides; perhaps this was particularly so for the men in the ranks. Sergeant W. E. Danton of the 2nd Rifle Brigade wrote to "My dearest wife and all at home":

I thought of you all on Christmas Day. Tell Mother and Dad I drank their health with water you would not wash clothes in. Our food was beef and water, bread for pudding. . . . I can't tell when this will reach you, but I trust in God that I shall be spared to write again and, in a few months, take you and the boy in my arms and never separate no more.[24]

There was no firing on Christmas Day except for the pudding-filled shells. Looking through the naval telescopes, those in Ladysmith could see the Boers celebrating too, and a number of women—some fashionably dressed, it was noted—were seen walking over the Boer positions. Women who stayed home sent gifts to their men at the front: silk handkerchiefs, spurs, food. The wife of State Secretary Reitz organized a group of women to bake cakes and pastry for the fighting burghers.

England remembered her soldiers in South Africa, and commercial firms as well as individuals sent gifts: Messrs. Willis & Co. sent 250,000 cigarettes and Messrs. Lyons sent 10,000 Christmas puddings. Some senders, full of good will but ignorant of geography, sent unseasonable gifts: a Lancashire firm sent 2,000 woolen comforters, and many sweltering soldiers received lovingly knitted balaclavas. One present was valued by everyone: a gift from Queen Victoria herself of a tin box of chocolate to each of her "dear brave soldiers." The box, designed by J. S. Fry & Sons of Bristol, carried the Queen's portrait and was bound with red, white, and blue ribbon. Every soldier in South Africa and on the high seas was to receive one, and the men had to sign receipts for them. An officer on board the hospital transport *Nubia* said: "The presentation of the Queen's chocolate to the poor wounded chaps was a very pleasant but pathetic function. I wish Her Majesty could have seen the gleam of joy it brought to many a despondent sufferer."[25]

The boxes were indeed valued highly. Some men refused £5 for theirs; two boxes auctioned at Christie's in London were knocked down at £5 5s and £4 10s. Many sent the boxes home to wives, mothers, and sweethearts. A widow in Cheshire received her son's chocolate together with a letter telling of his death and burial. Some of the empty tins are still to be found among the treasured heirlooms of the soldiers' descendants.

Private James Humphrey of the 2nd Royal Lancaster Regiment credited the Queen's chocolate tin with saving his life and asked that it be sent to the Queen. This was done, a doctor testifying that "had the bullet not been stopped by the chocolate, it would undoubtedly have passed through this structure into the abdomen, and have caused a fatal wound." Sir Arthur Bigge, the principal medical officer, sent the tin of chocolate with the bullet still in it to the Queen with a note saying, "Your Majesty would doubtless wish another box to be sent to Private Humphrey."

Boxing Day was not on the Boer calendar of holidays, and so the day after Christmas they resumed the war; the shells sent into Ladysmith were again filled with powder.

In early January 1900 the Boers made their only serious effort to crack the British defences when they launched an assault on a two-and-a-half-mile-long ridge known as the Platrand, located across the Klip River just south of the town. A hill stood at either end of the ridge: the larger, on the east, was named by the British Caesar's Camp, and the other, on the west, Wagon Hill. Ian Hamilton, in charge of the defences on the Platrand, had only a thousand men, and these he concentrated in several small forts with gun pits and minor works between them.

At three o'clock on the morning of 6 January the Boers attacked the western extremity of Wagon Hill and the eastern end of Caesar's Camp. The assault on Wagon Hill was led by Field Cornet Ignatias Vermaak of Utrecht, "a splendid old patriot of sixty-two years of age, who with flowing white locks and accompanied by four sons was the first to charge and the last to evacuate." Commandant C. J. deVilliers, a Majuba veteran, led another attack up the nek between the two hills. There was a great deal of confused fighting in the dark before dawn revealed to both sides their positions. The Boers had made some headway, but the British had put up a stubborn resistance. Throughout the morning a fierce fight moved backwards and forwards over the slopes; here one side gained an advantage, here another.

Second Lieutenant W. E. Davies of the Rifle Brigade led a small charge. He was glad, he said later, that the Boers retreated. "I found I had only brought my walking stick."

At 12:30 P.M. Hamilton was on Wagon Hill with Major Claude Miller-Wallnutt of the Gordon Highlanders and Lieutenant Robert Digby Jones of the Royal Engineers when, amid a furious burst of musketry, De Villiers and his men made a rush and pushed back the defenders just in front of them. Hamilton drew his pistol and, with Miller-Wallnutt, Jones, and a handful of men, dashed forward in a counterattack. The two opposing commanders found themselves face to face by a gun pit. There was a deadly shoot-out. De Villiers shot Miller-Wallnutt in the head, killing him. Digby Jones killed De Villiers. A few minutes later Jones was shot dead.

The fighting raged all afternoon. The British rushed up reserves from Ladysmith, the Devons made a gallant charge—losing all their company officers and a third of their men—and eventually the Boers were forced off the ridge. Philip Pienaar saw some of the burghers returning: "Down the hill our wounded dribbled, thirsty men, pale men, men covered with blood and weeping with rage. . . . One man is brought down lying across a horse. His face hangs in strips, shattered by a dum-dum bullet. Thank goodness, some of ours are using buckshot today."[26]

Conan Doyle was later to write: "There has been no better fighting in our time than upon Waggon Hill on that January morning."[27] Certainly it was a bloody day long remembered by the surviving participants, though perhaps not many thought of it as good fighting. It was remembered too by Prime Minister Winston Churchill, who, on hearing of the British victory at Bardia in Libya on 6 January 1941, wrote a note to Ian Hamilton, then eighty-eight years old: "I am thinking of you and Wagon Hill when another January 6th brings news of a fine feat of arms."[28]

The Transvaalers blamed their failure on the lack of support from the Free Staters, leaderless that day, because General Prinsloo and a number of his principal officers had left to attend a cattle sale in Harrismith.

The British suffered 417 casualties, including 168 killed—higher casualties than Buller had suffered at Colenso. The Boers reported 183 casualties, including 64 killed, but this was undoubtedly an understatement. When John Gough (Hubert's younger brother) of the Rifle Brigade ordered his meticulous sergeant major to collect the Boer dead, 99 bodies were found, a disappointment to the sergeant major, who had hoped for a tidy 100; he was troubled too by a kind of problem peculiar to sergeant majors: he had lined up the corpses by their heads, but if this was incorrect, he told Gough, he could easily line them up by their feet. Gough assured him that his arrangement was satisfactory: "This seemed to lift a considerable weight off the sergeant-major's mind."[29]

Three field cornets were killed; one was old Vermaak, who left seven grown sons to continue the fight. White, in a letter to his wife, wrote: "When we handed over the dead next morning, as each succeeding hero was brought down—for they were heroes—the Boers wrung their hands, and owned we had killed their best."[30]

The British were impressed with the ferocity of the Boer attack; the Boers, depressed by their failure, lacked the heart to launch any more, and the British were glad this was so. Neither side ever again embarked on serious offensive operations.

While Roberts was bombarding Cronjé's laager, Buller began his last attempt to relieve Ladysmith. He had with undue deliberation moved his force back to the Colenso area, where the incompetent Lukas Meyer had temporarily replaced Botha as commander of the Boer forces on the Tugela. After waiting several days because he thought the weather was too hot for fighting, he made a few abortive minor attacks. Finally, due to the initiative shown by Dundonald and Lyttelton, some important kopjes were taken and the Boers drew back. Hlangwane fell without a fight, thanks to the carelessness of the Boers; the Krugersdorp Commando occupying it had walked off the hill when the Heidelberg Commando, due to relieve it, was late in arriving.

By 18 February news of Roberts's successes had put the Boers on the Natal front in a turmoil, and under the pressure of Buller's army they gave way; many discouraged burghers simply gave up the fight and went home. Some of the commandants urged Joubert to raise the siege of Ladysmith and to take up new positions on the Biggarsberg, but he refused. Buller, who felt no compulsion to crush the Boer army but only to reach Ladysmith, gained the impression that the Boers were retreating, and so, instead of pushing forward vigorously, he decided to wait a few days for them to clear out of his way. This respite enabled the Boer leaders to rally their men; Botha returned to take command; President Kruger sent a long telegram replete with Biblical references and quotations exhorting the burghers to hold firm, to "stand fast in faith to fight." Inspired with fresh if still unsteady courage, the Boers prepared new defences.

On 21 February Buller sent a message to White: "I hope to be with you tomorrow night. I think there is only a rear guard in front of me." Thus, believing he would encounter only slight resistance, Buller gave his army its marching orders: troops, guns, and transport were to cross the pontoon bridge being thrown over the Tugela west of Hlangwane. By two o'clock in the afternoon the bridge was ready and Coke's brigade, led by the Somerset Light Infantry, crossed and debouched onto the small open plain beyond, the arena of an amphitheatre surrounded by hills from whose heights the Boer riflemen looked down. The infantry pushed forward bravely at first, but were soon brought to a halt by the Boer musketry and lay prone on the ground for the rest of the afternoon under a galling fire. The Somersets alone sustained 90 casualties, and there were another 20 in the rest of the brigade as a result of this encounter with the "rear guard."

It was the kind of tactical situation the Boers liked best: they could crouch behind comfortable defensive positions with a clear field of fire while the enemy ran at them with bayonets. Their spirits rose. At the end of the day Botha sent a jubilant telegram to Kruger:

> Thanks to our Father the burghers already showed to-day that they had taken heart again, when they had such splendid shooting at the enemy with their Mausers at 300 yards range. . . . With the help of the Lord, I expect that if only the spirit of the burghers keeps up as it did to-day, the enemy will suffer a great reverse.[31]

Not even the bloody result of this day's fighting shook Buller's unreasonable conviction that he was facing only a rear guard, and all night long he sent infantry, artillery, and supply wagons across the bridge until at dawn the next morning he had eleven battalions of infantry and forty guns packed into the amphitheatre behind the Colenso kopjes; during the course of the morning he added four more battalions and pushed in still more baggage. There was heavy fighting all this day and all the next as the troops struggled to dislodge the Boers from their hills flanking the road to Ladysmith. The British suffered 500 casualties in these two days, yet Buller still refused to believe that he was fighting the Boer main force on the Tugela, and the orders he issued were mere marching orders, the only reference to the enemy being to "snipers" in the hills.

Buller's state of mind can only be imagined. He had to get through to Ladysmith somehow. He knew that. Yet he could not bear the thought that he was sending his precious soldiers to face the full fury of the Boers' musketry. Only by deceiving himself, by pretending that he was not fighting a full-scale protracted battle, could he bear to continue the offensive. If he was faced by only a stubborn rear guard he could push on, soon the nightmare would be over, and the Boers would go away. It was only a rear guard. Only that.

The troops behaved gallantly, and in spite of their heavy losses— Hart lost 30 percent of the troops engaged in an attack on one hill— they did push on, and for once Buller shut his eyes and let them. But the resistance was stubborn indeed, and by the evening of the 24th the army had come to a complete standstill. Faced with the loss of 1,200 men in four days of fighting, even Buller had to accept reality, but he had no plan for remedying the perilous position in which he had placed his army:

> It was now strung out along the river in a chain of insecure positions, liable to be cut off from each other, difficult to reinforce, and still more difficult to escape in case of a reverse. . . . all the units had become hopelessly mixed up, while most of the artillery and mounted troops were in positions where they could be least effective.[32]

On 25 February Buller asked for an armistice to allow him to bring in the wounded and bury the dead; many of the wounded had been lying in agony for days in the hot sun without food or water. Botha and Lukas Meyer agreed, and stretcher parties moved onto the now silent battlefields. Soldiers and burghers also ventured forth to meet and talk, exchanging tobacco and views on the war.

General Lyttelton joined in the fraternization and told one Boer: "A rough time? Yes, I suppose so. But for us, of course, it is nothing. We are used to it and are paid for it. This is what we are paid for. This is the life we lead always—you understand?"

"Great God!" exclaimed the burgher.

Buller used the time of the armistice to sort out his troops and guns. He could see that at this point it was more dangerous to retreat than to try to go forward. He had to go on. After considering several plans he decided on a frontal attack along a 3-mile front using three brigades. For once he would make use of his overwhelming superiority in numbers of men and guns.

Another pontoon bridge was thrown across the Tugela further upstream and the Royal Engineers painted a signpost for it: TO LADYSMITH. Seventy-six guns were positioned to support the attack. As the infantry moved forward on the 27th the soldiers were heartened by the news of Cronjé's surrender to Roberts at Paardeberg. It took six hours of heavy fighting and cost another 500 men, but the British at last cleared the kopjes and opened the way to Ladysmith. "The British infantry has once more saved their generals," said Rawlinson.

The Boers had fought long and hard, but this sustained fighting was difficult for them. In a one-day battle they could be counted on, but fighting every day and being slowly driven back from position to position was beyond their capabilities; besides, the news of Cronjé's surrender had spread despair among them. Kruger appealed for a last-ditch stand, but Joubert simply ordered a general retreat and himself fled to Elandslaagte, leaving Botha to organize a rear guard as best he could. At 12:30 P.M. the Long Tom on Pepworth Hill fired its last shot, the shell exploding in Dunton's store in the middle of Ladysmith.

Botha had difficulty holding together enough burghers to form even a weak rear guard, and it was only after the greatest exertions on the part of his officers that the guns were brought away. One Long Tom was saved by an American, "Colonel" John Y. Fillimore Blake, a West Point graduate who commanded a group of Irish-American volunteers. He and his men, assisted by some American scouts, hitched oxen to the gun and during the night crawled with it past Ladysmith almost within earshot of the British outposts.

It was a mystery to most why the Boers were allowed to leave in peace. Richard Harding Davis wrote to his mother: "I watched the Boers for four hours the other day escaping from the battle of Pieters and I asked ... 'Why don't you send out your cavalry and light artillery and take those wagons?' The staff officer giggled and said, 'They might kill us.' I don't know what he meant; neither did he."[33]

It was raining, and through the mud the Boer ox wagons streamed away north in a disorganized mob—away from the Tugela heights and away from Ladysmith. "In all directions the plain was covered with a multitude of men, wagons, and guns ploughing across the sodden veld in the greatest disorder," wrote Deneys Reitz. "Had the British fired a single gun at this surging mob everything on wheels would have fallen into their hands."[34] But not a gun was fired. Buller did not, would not, pursue.

"Never, perhaps, has a general enjoyed such an opportunity for destroying a beaten and demoralised adversary," wrote Bron Herbert in *The Times History.* Urged by his senior commanders and staff officers to fall upon the fleeing Boers with the full weight of his army, Buller refused to sacrifice the life of a single additional soldier, although by doing so he would have shortened the war and saved the lives of many. White sent out a "flying column," but the men and horses were too weak to fight; Buller sternly rebuked him and ordered the pursuit halted. "Few commanders have so wantonly thrown away so great an opportunity," fumed Lyttelton. Even years later Colonel à Court said, "I cannot think of that day even now without rage."

The fleeing, panic-stricken burghers could hardly believe that they were not being pursued:

> The main column followed the railroad to Washbank, while part of the forces under Lukas Meyer, went towards Wessels Nek, where a scene of the wildest confusion reigned. Hundreds of canvas topped wagons converging to the narrow road, formed on the side of the hill a great solid triangle, two miles at the base and visible for miles. The recent rain had made the pass most difficult, every wagon having to be assisted over the steep incline with double teams. The clamor was fearful, each tried to be first, forcing their own vehicles into every crevice, in the hope of passing others, only to cause a more hopeless lock. The mounted men had carelessly gone before, seeking rest, regardless of this mass of wagons and field guns constituting the entire transport of the west wing, an inviting spoil for capture. Fortunately . . . by the heroic labor of the teamsters, the tangle was worked clear in twenty-four hours. The last wagon made the passage safely the following night, without any threatening demonstration from the British.
>
> The danger was passed, the entire army of the Tugela had made the perilous circuit of forty miles, without the loss of a gun or wagon not abandoned, and proceeding by slow stages, they commenced to recover their spirits.[35]

Just before sunset on 28 February Major Hubert Gough of the 16th Lancers splashed across a drift of the Klip River at the head of his squadron and rode into Ladysmith. Colonel Frank Rhodes described his reception:

> It is impossible to depict the enthusiasm of the beleaguered garrison. Cheer upon cheer ran from post to post, and staff officers, civilians, and soldiers flocked to greet them. At the ford of the Klip River, women, with children in their arms,

tearfully pressed forward to grasp the hands of the gallant band. Sisters and brothers, friends and relatives met again. The contrast between the robust troopers of a dozen battles and the pale, emaciated defenders of Ladysmith was great.[36]

It was, said Gough, "the most moving moment of my life." Although he later claimed that he had maintained "a dignified calm," Colonel Beachamp Duff saw him "sitting in his saddle with the tears in his eyes, unable to say more than, 'Thank God' over and over again." White was waiting for him in the main street and greeted him calmly: "Hello, Hubert, how are you?"

Thus ended the 118-day siege of Ladysmith.

Dundonald with the rest of the cavalry, some mounted infantry, and Winston Churchill soon followed Gough. That night Churchill dined with White, Ian Hamilton, Hunter, Dundonald, and Gough: "Never before," he said, "had I sat in such brave company nor stood so close to a great event."[37] He presented Hamilton with a copy of his recently published novel, Savrola. Miss Pamela Plowden's brother-in-law, Major Edgar Lafone of the 4th Hussars, had been among the besieged, and she had sent out a box of food for Churchill to give him. Finding Lafone too ill to appreciate the delicacies, Churchill ate them himself.

Lieutenant Claude Lafone of the 2nd Devonshire Regiment, Major Lafone's nephew, was also with the relieving force, and on 2 March he wrote to his mother: "Ladysmith at last. Thank goodness! God bless the Queen. . . . I don't think the Ladysmith troops can have been more glad to see us than we were to see them, as I think the relief of Ladysmith had begun to be looked on by most of us as rather mythical."[38]

Midshipman Wybrow Hallwright thought "the people in Ladysmith looked very ill and feeble, and the smells in the place were frightful, but as far as I could see there was not much damage by shell fire."[39]

News of the relief of Ladysmith raced around the world. Durban "went mad," and in London crowds in the street cheered Buller and White and sang "Soldiers of the Queen." H. S. Gaskell disembarked at Cape Town with the 10th Imperial Yeomanry on the day the news reached there:

The scene and sounds that followed baffle description. Every steamer in the harbour (and there were hundreds) gave vent to furious blasts on its fog-horn, flags were up every rigging in a trice, and the gunboats lying outside the harbour sent off rockets or let off guns for about twenty minutes; in fact, it all went on for about this time, and the din was something deafening. I bet that the Boer prisoners on board the gunboat, and old Cronje, who had been also brought down with a lot of his staff, felt pretty bad. . . .[40]

On 3 March 1900 Buller's army made its formal entrance into Ladysmith, and an exuberant Churchill was on hand to describe it:

The scene was solemn and stirring. The streets were lined with the brave defenders, looking very smart and clean in their best clothes, but pale, thin, and wasp-waisted—their belts several holes tighter than was satisfactory. . . . All through the morning and on into the afternoon the long stream of men and guns flowed through the streets of Ladysmith, and all marvelled to see what manner of men these were—dirty, war-worn, travel-stained, tanned, their uniforms in tatters, their boots falling to pieces, their helmets dinted and broken, but nevertheless magnificent soldiers, striding along, deep-chested and broad-shouldered, with the light of triumph in their eyes and the blood of fighting ancestors in their veins. It was a procession of lions. . . . I waved my feathered hat, and cheered and cheered until I could cheer no longer for joy that I had lived to see the day.[41]

The following day was a Sunday, and there was a thanksgiving service at the church in Ladysmith. "It was very impressive," said Isabella Craw, "and the way the congregation sang 'God Save the Queen' alone was worth going for."[42]

On the evening of his arrival Buller sat down and wrote to his wife:

Here I am at last. I thought I was never going to get here. . . .

Now it is all over and well over thank God. . . . It has all seemed to me like a dream. Every day there were complications to meet and every day the same roar of gun and rattle of musketry, with alas, every day the long list of killed and wounded, which is what I cannot bear. . . .

As for me I am filled with admiration for the British soldier; really the manner in which the men have worked, fought and endured during the last fortnight has been something more than human. . . .

There was a moment when I thought it was touch and go, but it was only a moment.[43]

It had seemed like a bad dream to the victorious soldiers and the fleeing burghers too. The war had now been in progress for only four and a half months, but for many of the participants its glory was fast fading.

Ladysmith, having had its brief moment in history, sank back again into a sleepy provincial town. The war moved on. A week after the lifting of the siege Isabella Craw wrote in her diary: "Nothing to write tonight. It seems an awful thing to say, but I quite miss 'Long Tom'; every day seems alike now, no excitement of any kind."

26

BLOEMFONTEIN

When Roberts sent Kitchener from Paardeberg to look after the railway line, he had more in mind than simply removing Kitchener from the scene, for the railway line was, and was long to remain, a worry. Among other calculated risks he had taken was his decision to leave this lifeline inadequately protected. It was a dangerous proceeding, for the Boers had some 8,000 men on the Orange River, while opposed to them along a 35-mile front in the Colesburg area after the withdrawal of French and his cavalry there were only half as many British soldiers. In command of this sector and charged with the delicate task of concealing its weakness from the enemy and protecting the railway junctions was Major General Ralph Clements, an able and experienced soldier with more than twenty-five years' service.

On 6–7–8 February 1900 Koos de la Rey, commanding the left wing of the Boer line, skirmished with the British and took a few prisoners; on 12 February he launched an attack on some of the main British positions and achieved considerable success. Had he pressed forward there is little doubt that he could have overwhelmed Clements's forces, captured the vital railway junctions of De Aar and Naauwpoort, and left Roberts's army stranded on the veld without supplies or reinforcements. But Roberts's great flank march had produced the desired effect of drawing off the Boer forces engaged in offensive operations on the borders. When news of Cronjé's entrapment at Paardeberg reached the Boers on the Orange, nearly half of the commandos there scurried back to defend Bloemfontein; a few days later De la Rey himself with most of his force also withdrew towards Bloemfontein. Clements, with the help of some reinforcements, was able to advance and reoccupy Colesburg.

The tide of war had now turned against the Boers; their days of victories were over. Everywhere the republican forces were in retreat. Only little Mafeking was still surrounded, but it showed no signs of capitulating and it was militarily unimportant. Buller's army, joined now by White's force, was larger than the combined armies of the Boers, and Roberts with another army threatened Bloemfontein. But the burghers, although badly shaken, were not palsied. Between Roberts and the capital of the Orange Free State was Christiaan de Wet with 6,000 men; he had been reinforced by A. P. Cronjé's force from Natal, and others were hurrying to join him. They were busily entrenching on kopjes around a place called Poplar Grove (also called Modderrivierpoort) 10 miles east of Paardeberg, and both Kruger and Steyn were on their way to inspire their men.

Roberts moved his army a short distance away from contaminated Paardeberg to a place called Stinkfontein. From here on 21 February he issued orders with explicit instructions governing the construction and use of latrines, the disposal of dead horses, collection of rubbish, and similar matters. Such orders ought to have been given and enforced much earlier. It was too late now.

For the moment all seemed well and Roberts was free to fix his attention on his next move. He whistled up reinforcements and worked out a plan of attack on De Wet at Poplar Grove. His scheme called for an enveloping movement with two infantry divisions moving in from the

south and southwest while the cavalry made a 17-mile swing south of the
Boer positions to cut off their line of retreat. It was a good plan. Had it
succeeded he would have dealt the Boers a resounding defeat which
might just possibly have ended the war. But all depended upon French
and his cavalry—and French, whom Conan Doyle called "the stormy
petrel of the war," was erratic. In fact, the temperamental French was
sulking and had already gone broody. The cause was horse fodder.

The long-suffering, overworked horses might have had an opportunity to recover somewhat at Paardeberg had there been enough fodder
for them, but this was in short supply, and many of the horses, unaccustomed to grazing, were unable to forage for themselves on the herbage
of the veld. When one battery turned its horses out to graze the puzzled
beasts simply wandered about until they heard the familiar bugle call that
announced feeding time, then rushed back to their lines and waited
expectantly for their nosebags.

Roberts had issued strict orders that horse rations were to be limited
to three pounds of fodder per horse. When, therefore, Colonel Richardson, his chief supply officer, reported to him that the horse rations drawn
far exceeded this limit, he summoned the brigade and division commanders and dressed them down. French, of course, had to bear the brunt of
this reprimand. Richardson's calculations were actually faulty; he had
divided the issue of horse rations by the number of fit horses, forgetting
that there were great numbers of unfit horses who also had to be fed. But
this was discovered only later, and it was no help at the moment to
French, who rode out in the darkness of the early morning of 7 March
to the battle of Poplar Grove burning with a sense of injustice.

To succeed in getting across the Boers' line of retreat it was necessary
that French move rapidly, but he had been an hour late starting, then just
two hours later he halted for forty-five minutes to wait for daylight.
Moving on, he came upon a large dam, and as this seemed to be a good
place to water his horses—since Roberts was so damned concerned about
them—he decided to make another halt and another hour was lost.

About eight o'clock in the morning Kruger arrived in De Wet's camp
escorted by some of the Pretoria mounted police. He had prepared a
speech, but there was no time to give it, for scarcely had he stepped down
from his wagon than word arrived that the British were coming. Roberts's
infantry was moving to the attack. De Wet hustled the old president back
onto his wagon and away, then quickly mounted and rode out to do
battle. But there was not to be a battle—or not much of one. At the first
sign of the enemy the burghers fled. De Wet wrote later:

Again I was confronted by the baleful influence of Cronje's surrender. A
panic had seized my men. Before the English had even got near enough to shell
our positions to any purpose, the wild flight began. Soon every position was
evacuated. There was not even an attempt to hold them, though some of them
would have been impregnable. It was a flight such as I had never seen before, and
shall never see again.

I did all that I could, but neither I nor my officers were able to prevent the burghers from following whither the waggons and guns had preceded them. . . . It was fortunate for us that the advance of the English was not very rapid. Had it been so, everything must have fallen into their hands.[1]

Probably the instincts of the burghers were sounder than De Wet's reasonings. Instant flight undoubtedly saved them from annihilation or from another, greater Paardeberg. They fled along the route Roberts had thought they would take, but the dilatory French arrived at his appointed place only in time to skirmish with the rear guard De Wet had skilfully managed to organise. Even then he dithered, withdrawing from one kopje and then ordering it to be retaken while the major portion of the Boer force streamed away to the east. By the time he was ready to launch a formal attack, the Boer rear guard had mounted their ponies and cantered off, leaving French and his cavalry sitting on their exhausted horses with nothing to attack.

The Boers had been successfully turned out of their positions, and this was satisfying, but they had not been defeated in the field in what could have been a major British victory. The British official history excused French on the grounds that his horses were in poor condition, which they were, but the fact is that the horses actually covered more ground this day and were worked harder than they would have been had French carried out the operation with the speed required. An apologist for French has said that he was "off his game"; the anonymous writer of this portion of *The Times History* said that French "never really seems to have had his heart in the business." Indeed he had not. Ian Hamilton, more than thirty years later, spoke of "the strange reaction of French," who at Klip Drift had gone "slap-bang like the Valkyrie Ritt" while at Poplar Grove "the pursuit was like 'Peace, Perfect Peace' played on a bad organ whilst the whole Boer army was allowed to escape to the sounds of the *Te Deum* being sung by the British mounted troops."[2]

Outwardly at least Roberts took French's ruination of his plan calmly and only remarked, "In war you can't expect everything to come out right." But in his report he wrote: "Had the Cavalry, Horse Artillery, and Mounted Infantry been able to move rapidly, they would undoubtedly have intercepted the enemy's line of retreat, and I should have had the satisfaction of capturing their guns, waggons, and supplies, as well as a large number of prisoners." He might also have captured Kruger.

Casualties on both sides were light. Still, every casualty is its own tragedy. A subaltern with Rimington's Guides wrote to his wife:

We saw many awful sights. . . . Sitting propped up against an ant-heap was a thing; it was no longer a man. Silent it sat, and immovable, with glassy eyes fixed staring into vacancy. The mouth was torn to twice its natural size by a Martini bullet; blood froze the chin to the tunic; the cheeks were purple and swollen. In the back of the neck a great wound showed where the bullet had entered. The poor creature was not dead, but he could make no sign. We could do nothing for him, and we left him sitting staring across the sunny plain.[3]

Eighteen miles away from Poplar Grove on the road to Bloemfontein, at a place called Abraham's Kraal, Kruger halted his wagon and attempted to stay the flight of De Wet's men streaming past him. Standing by the side of the road he pleaded with them to save Bloemfontein; he tried appealing to their patriotism; he called them cowards. They simply shook their heads and rode on. The old man lifted his stick and rushed at them. In his rage he ordered the mounted police to shoot every man that passed. They ignored him. But eventually a few stopped; then some more; and finally enough were assembled to make another stand. On 10 March, at a place near Abraham's Kraal called Driefontein, there was another battle. De la Rey with only 1,500 men successfully held off 10,000 British soldiers for a day—a remarkable feat of arms—but in the end he had to give way.

The fighting ranged over a wide area and lasted until after sunset. The British lost 82 killed and 342 wounded; they buried 102 Boer dead and took 22 prisoners.

There were also some innocent casualties in this fight: a herd of some 200 springbok found themselves in no-man's-land and "within the area of a square mile they galloped, and jumped, and stood to gaze." When the shooting started they circled frantically, seeking escape. An officer with Rimington's Guides was a witness: "Pitiable was their terror as shells hurtled over them, and bullets sang about their ears. Two, if not more, received the missiles meant for the lords of creation, for I saw their mangled bodies slung on two troopers' saddles. One poor wounded beast . . . came limping up alone to within a hundred yards of where I lay."[4]

The British were now but a few miles from Bloemfontein, and the disheartened Boers were ready to make peace. In fact, Presidents Steyn and Kruger had already sent off futile pleas to the governments of France, Germany, Russia, and the United States asking for their help in ending the war. They also dispatched a letter to Lord Salisbury, an offer to make peace if the British would only allow the republics to keep their independence and promise not to punish the rebel Afrikaners from the Cape who had joined them.

But the war was not to be stopped. As Richard Cobden once said, "You might as well reason with mad dogs as with men when they have begun to spill each other's blood." Not even half the blood and tears that would be shed had soaked the South African veld. The presidents were appalled by the misery and destruction thus far, but they had not seen a fraction of the total. The worst was yet to come.

The timing of this first peace offer was certainly unfortunate. After all their humiliating defeats in the first four months of the war the British were now tasting the sweets of victory; the tide had turned in their favour, and they were exaltingly running with it. They had tasted Boer blood and wanted more. To them it seemed that the war was almost won. They saw no need to grant any concessions at all. Six days after the peace offer— after Poplar Grove and Driefontein, after Gatacre had occupied Burgersdorp, Clements had pushed up to Norval's Pont, General E. Y. Brabant had occupied Jamestown, and Brigadier H. C. O. Plumer had captured a Boer laager in the north near Gopani—Salisbury gave the Boer presidents his answer in a long letter in which he reminded them that it was they who had started the hostilities by invading Her Majesty's colonies. "This great calamity has been the penalty which Great Britain has suffered for having in recent years acquiesced in the existence of the two republics." Salisbury unequivocally told the presidents that "Her Majesty's Government . . . are not prepared to assent to the independence either of the South African Republic or of the Orange Free State."[5]

The Boer leaders called a krygsraad and decided to make a last-ditch stand at Bloemfontein—to the horror of the townspeople, who had visions of their houses and other property destroyed. De Wet was certainly willing to fight: "For myself, I believed that the 13th of March should see a fight to the finish, cost what it might! for if Bloemfontein was to be taken, it would only be over our dead bodies." But the burghers were not so resolute. They had lost heart and would not stand. They continued their retreat northward. There was nothing to be done. President Steyn and his cabinet and such state papers as could be carried took a train for Kroonstad, 100 miles northeast of Bloemfontein. Roberts threw French forward as fast as he could go, and one of his cavalry officers, Major E. H. H. Allenby, who was to win fame in World War I in the Middle East, seized a key ridge outside Bloemfontein just at dusk on 12 March. The next day the town was captured by three newspaper correspondents.

Roberts had sent a captured burgher into the town to deliver a proclamation promising protection to all the inhabitants if his entry was unopposed while warning that any resistance would result in loss of life and destruction of property. On the morning of 13 March three enterprising newspaper correspondents entered the town and found the mayor and a group of prominent citizens assembled at the Bloemfontein Club debating what they should do. Appealed to for their opinion, the correspondents advised them to surrender. They did.

That afternoon Roberts formally entered the capital of the Orange Free State. There were citizens on hand to cheer and even a few Union Jacks displayed, for among the inhabitants who stayed were a number of Boer moderates who had opposed the war and also a number of British subjects. It was with considerable satisfaction that "Little Bobs" rode down the streets of Bloemfontein, for it was less than nine months since he had stepped off the ship at Cape Town and only a month after the beginning of his campaign.

On the flagstaff outside the Presidency the Union Jack was run up: it was a silk flag made by Lady Roberts herself, and she had worked a small shamrock into one corner. Then Roberts sent off a telegram to the Queen, telling her that "the British flag now flies over the Presidency vacated last evening by Mr. Steyn, late President of the Orange Free State."[6]

No one imagined that Roberts would remain long in Bloemfontein; all expected a rapid, victorious march to Pretoria and a speedy end to the war. H. S. Gaskell of the 10th Imperial Yeomanry expressed the expectations of most when he wrote: "I think the back of the war is broken and I give it another month at most."[7] Many Boers also thought the war was almost over. President Steyn later wrote in his memoirs:

No one who had not personally witnessed the despondency that existed after the taking of Bloemfontein can realise how great and deep it was. There was no courage and no wish to carry on the fight by the burghers. The Transvaalers left in great numbers, and the Free Staters had turned their faces to their homes. . . . The road to Pretoria was practically open for Lord Roberts.[8]

But the war was not about to end, and although Roberts certainly did not want to dally at Bloemfontein, logistics and infection caught up with him and his stay was longer than he or anyone else anticipated.

Stores, supplies, remounts, and men were pouring into South African ports at a prodigious rate. The Royal Navy had organised the movement of men and supplies in an exemplary manner, proving to the world Britain's ability to project its power 7,000 miles from its homeland. Reinforcements were arriving in South Africa at the rate of 30,000 per month, and there was no lack of food or fodder. But it was not easy to move men, animals, gear, and supplies into the interior where they were needed. East London, the nearest port, was 400 miles from Bloemfontein; Port Elizabeth was 450 miles away; and Cape Town, the main base, was now 750 miles from Roberts and his army. The railways were straining, but the last 90 miles, from Springfontein to Bloemfontein, were served by only a single track. Two trains of twenty-four trucks each were required daily simply to keep Roberts's army supplied with food—and in addition he badly needed horses, fodder, and equipment of all sorts. By the time he reached Bloemfontein he had only five days' supply of breadstuff for his 34,000 men; for his 11,500 horses there was practically no fodder at all. Colonel Richardson managed to secure twenty-seven days' additional rations and some fodder in the town, but the situation was critical. Through traffic on the railway was not open until 29 March, and from then until 7 April Roberts was able to obtain only 286 truckloads, scarcely more than half the number he needed.

Although the British had made some use of steam road transport, it was the horse, the mule, the ox, and the locomotive that were the decisive factors in the war. The shortage of horses was serious, for the value of mounted troops against a mounted enemy was becoming increasingly apparent. British purchasing agents had been sent to the United States, Argentina, Spain, Italy, and Hungary to buy horses and mules, but they could never get enough. The loss of horseflesh in the war was appalling. By the time French reached Bloemfontein he had killed two-thirds of the horses in his command. During the course of the war the British purchased 520,000 horses and 150,000 mules; of these, two-thirds of the horses and a third of the mules perished. The British, a horse-loving people, were horrified by these losses, and there were anguished cries in Parliament and in the press, but the mismanaged Remount Department, filled with officers who were overage or who had failed in the field or who were simply officers for whom no other place could be found, was not entirely to blame. There were never enough animals, and the urgent calls from the front for more and more, and quickly, required them to send forward horses and mules unaccustomed to the climate and the herbage; often animals were sent even before they had recovered from their long sea voyage, and the hard usage to which they were subjected on the veld killed them off rapidly. Cavalry horses also bore unnecessary burdens:

The amount of impedimenta strapped on and hung round each saddle was enormous. The saddles themselves . . . were of the heaviest cavalry pattern, the framework being made of iron. . . .

Saddle, and all upon it, swayed and rattled at every motion of the horse; and the noise made by a squadron at the gallop was like an iron-monger's shop let loose.[9]

The Boers, too, found that their horses and ponies did not always adapt to the changes in climate and herbage required of their far-ranging commandos. And their horses as well were subjected to hard usage. Roland Schikkerling wrote in his diary: "Will God forgive us for so torturing our willing horses? Their being so obedient and responsive makes our usage of them the more agonizing to us."[10]

A dead horse is difficult to bury or otherwise dispose of. Dead oxen and mules equally so. Already the veld was strewn with thousands of dead and putrefying animals in the wake of the contending warriors, and, plentiful as vultures were, there were not enough to consume all the carcasses. Many animals had died in or were thrown into rivers and spruits. And one dead mule could contaminate a stream for many miles and for many days. The germs of enteric (typhoid and paratyphoid) acquired in the field, particularly at Paardeberg, now flourished in the bodies of Roberts's soldiers. As reinforcements followed the path of the main army and drank the same water, disease also followed. It had not yet been learned that an unsanitary camp could be more dangerous than the most determined foe, more fatal to strategy than a major defeat on a field of battle.

There was no known cure for enteric fever; the treatment was merely symptomatic. The British army in South Africa suffered more casualties from this disease than had any other army before (as far as is known) or since. Of the 13,250 deaths from disease, most were from enteric; 31,000 men had to be invalided home because of it. Among the 30,000 troops Roberts had at Bloemfontein, Dr. Conan Doyle estimated that there were between 8,000 and 9,000 cases of the disease.

Water was a major problem for the British throughout the campaign. In his second dispatch, written in Jacobsdal on 16 February, Roberts had complained that there were not nearly enough water carts and that the ones he had were inadequate: "Moreover, these carts cannot follow the troops over strong or unbroken ground, and I have, therefore, asked for 2,000 bheesties, with a due proportion of mussacks and pokholes to be sent here from India."*[11] Colonel W. D. Richardson later testified: "Probably nothing harbours germs and disease more than our present type of wooden barrel water cart." Even if the water was drawn from a pure source and reached the soldier uncontaminated by the water cart, he still had little chance of tasting pure water, for his water bottle was also a source of contamination. As Richardson said: "After a few months' use the interior of the service water bottle is often covered with mould, which smells offensively and is very probably a fertile source of disease."

There were standing orders that water must be boiled, but fuel was usually insufficient and the orders were generally ignored. Besides, as Sir William Wilson, the principal medical officer in South Africa, said: the troops "have a great objection to the boiled water as they say it is insipid and they do not like it."[12] Conan Doyle wrote: "It is heartrending for the medical man who has emerged from a hospital full of water-borne pestilence to see a regimental water-cart being filled, without protest, at some polluted wayside pool."[13]

Inoculation against enteric was known, but it was a new thing—it was first used by Sir Almroth Wright in 1896. It was offered to most of the troops sent to South Africa while they were on shipboard, but it was not compulsory and only about 20,000 men (less than 5 percent of the force sent out) received the injection. As the inoculation was given in one huge dose, all who received it became violently ill, though none seems to have died from it. John Atkins described its effects: "Each of us was stabbed in the side with the hypodermic syringe dipped in the typhoid serum. . . . My own symptoms after receiving the minute wound were the symptoms of others—first an Elysian lassitude, and then headache and fever for perhaps twenty-four hours."[14] Inadequate records were kept, and at the end of the war the value of the inoculation was deemed "doubtful."

Buller, ever solicitous for the welfare of his soldiers, carried tents— and was much criticised for so pampering his men. Churchill wrote:

I have never before seen even officers accommodated with tents on service. . . . But here today, within striking distance of a mobile enemy, every private soldier has canvas shelter, and other arrangements are on an equally elaborate scale. The consequence is that roads are crowded, drifts are blocked, marching troops are delayed, and all rapidity of movement is out of the question. . . . It is a poor economy to let a soldier live well for three days at the price of killing him on the fourth.[15]

Roberts's men had no such luxury and camped in the open, rain or shine. The blankets issued, however, had eyelet holes along the sides so that

---

*A *bheestie* is an Indian water carrier; a *mussack* is the goatskin bag he carries. A *pokhole* (usually spelled *puckauly*) is a large waterskin made from an entire ox hide and holding about 20 gallons.

they could be laced together to form some shelter; the bottom edges could be pinned down and rifles used as uprights. No other shelter was provided for officers or men.

When Roberts's army entered Bloemfontein he had with him ten small hospital units and ten bearer companies carrying 200 sick and wounded. Three days later there were 327 men in hospital; in ten days there were 1,000; by 1 June there were 3,965 patients. Even this number does not accurately reflect the size of the epidemic that struck the army, for two hospital trains worked continuously carrying out the sick, and regular trains too carried out all who could be safely moved. The sick lay, many on the bare ground, in tents, and on the floors of makeshift hospitals in "Bloeming-typhoidtein," as Kipling once called it.[16]

The medical facilities accompanying the army, designed to accommodate not more than 4 percent of the force in hospital at one time, were engulfed; the medical staff, helpless, was unable to cope with the flood of sick. Every public building in Bloemfontein was converted into a hospital, including the Raadzaal itself, where beds were placed on the floor of the legislative chambers; schools and convents were pressed into service, although not the hotels where the staff officers stayed.

By the end of March fifty-six nursing sisters had arrived and by mid-April sixty-four more had come, but there were Victorian difficulties connected with employing female nurses. Sir William Wilson explained:

We can get any amount of good trained nurses. . . . the great difficulty is to get accommodation for them. A woman or a lady will always require a certain amount of accommodation; she must have all the bedroom equipment and everything else, and she must have servants. It was absolutely impossible to get female servants in South Africa as they are not to be had.[17]

The Army Nursing Service had been part of the regular establishment of the British army since the Crimean War, but its female complement at the beginning of the Anglo-Boer War was only one "lady superintendent" and fifty-six nursing sisters. The reasons given for this paucity of trained women nurses were numerous: it was cheaper to use untrained male orderlies, it was unsuitable to send women to the savage lands where most Victorian wars were fought, and, finally, it was unthinkable to ask females to care for soldiers with venereal diseases, and these made up a large portion of the hospital cases in peace time. Army doctors were still almost as prejudiced against women nurses as they had been when Florence Nightingale had gone out to Turkey nearly fifty years earlier. Miss Nightingale was still alive, age eighty, and much interested in sanitation problems, but she was not consulted about South Africa, although she was interested and made a financial contribution to one of the nine privately endowed hospitals that were sent out. With these were a number of women, venturesome and generous, though often ill-trained, who served as nurses. When criticism of the medical services erupted in England, two highly respected medical authorities maintained that the standard of service given the soldiers was excellent in spite of "a plague of flies and a plague of women."

By the middle of April there were two general hospitals—No. 8 and No. 9—and three private hospital units in Bloemfontein—Langman, Portland, and Irish. For three months (2 April to 5 July) Dr. Conan Doyle, already famous as the creator of Sherlock Holmes, practised at Langman Hospital, which set up shop in the Bloemfontein Club. The hospital was equipped to handle 100 patients but took in 150. "We had neither beds nor utensils enough to treat such a number properly," said Conan Doyle.[18]

In March 1900 there were 207,000 troops in South Africa but only 800 doctors and an equal number of nurses. General hospitals were equipped with 520 beds, but No. 8 General Hospital once had as many as 1,398 patients and No. 9 at one time had 1,644. There were never enough nurses, and convalescents were pressed into service as orderlies. While conscientious orderlies were overworked, others were simply inattentive, some were rough, some stole comforts and stimulants and were often drunk, and a few were actually brutal. In No. 8 General Hospital in the month of May more than 10 percent of the patients died.

Sir William MacCormac, five times president of the Royal College of Surgeons, and Frederick Treves, an appendectomy pioneer who two years later won fame and a baronetcy for successfully removing the appendix of King Edward VII just before his coronation, had been out to South Africa to inspect the medical arrangements, and Treves had actually worked there. Back in London they were given a dinner at the Reform Club, where Sir William said that "it would not be possible to have anything more complete or better arranged than the medical service in the war." Although at the time Treves did not dissent, he later told a royal commission that the supplies furnished the Medical Department "were certainly antiquated, and we were carrying about with us instruments which I should have thought would only be found in museums." There were also medicines which had been in their bottles "for 20 years possibly."[19] MacCormac and Treves had left South Africa just before the enteric epidemic. MacCormac's glowing description of the medical service was soon contradicted by a stream of letters home from the soldiers. Private T. G. P. Humphreys of the 14th Middlesex wrote: "All the stuff that has been written about the military hospitals and the care taken of the sick and wounded, is lies. It may be all right—in fact it no doubt is —for the officers; but as for Tommy Atkins, no one cares a straw whether he lives or dies."[20] Private Humphreys died of enteric.

The regular establishment of the Royal Army Medical Corps was of course insufficient for the needs of the great army Britain had hastily assembled for the war, and a number of civilian doctors had been taken in or contracted for. There was often conflict between these civilians in khaki and the regular RAMC officers. Surgeon Captain Morison from West Hartlepool wrote home:

Believe everything you hear as to mismanagement and even incapacity and wilful neglect. . . . Certainly if I were ill or had been wounded, I would not care to be left to the tender mercies of the majority of the men I have come across. . . . You would be surprised how the "Tommies" cringe from me because they see the R.A.M.C. badges on my shoulder, until they know that I am what is called an irresponsible civilian, or, as I have been called by senior officers in the R.A.M.C., a "broken down practitioner."[21]

Alfred Downing Fripp, a distinguished surgeon, took out a hospital that included a dentist (the only dentist for the entire army), a masseur, and a steam disinfector—all novelties. The regular RAMC officers scoffed, but Fripp was appalled to find that no systematic disinfectant procedures had been established. "I was roared at," he said, for bringing out the disinfector, "but very soon they sent them out to as many hospitals as they could get them to."[22]

Because of the many conflicting accounts, *The Times* sent out as a special correspondent W. L. A. B. Burdett-Coutts, a member of Parliament, to find out what the medical situation really was and to report on what he found. His first articles were temperate; then, after three weeks in Bloemfontein, he sent back a report which shocked the country:

Men were dying like flies for want of adequate attention. . . . On that night (Saturday, the 28th of April) hundreds of men to my knowledge were lying in the worst stages of typhoid, with only a blanket and a thin waterproof sheet (not even the latter for many of them) between their aching bodies and the hard ground, with no milk and hardly any medicines, without beds, stretchers, or mattresses, without pillows, without linen of any kind, without a single nurse amongst them, with only a few ordinary private soldiers to act as "orderlies", rough and utterly untrained to nursing, and with only three doctors to attend on 350 patients. . . . The tents were bell tents . . . affording accommodation for from six to eight men when working and in sound health. In many of these tents there were ten typhoid cases lying closely packed together, the dying against the convalescent, the man in his "crisis" pressed against the man hastening to it. There was not room to step between them. . . . The ground is hard as stone, and at night the temperature falls to freezing point. . . . The heat of these tents in the midday sun was overpowering, their odours sickening. Men lay with their faces covered with flies in black clusters, too weak to raise a hand to brush them off, trying in vain to dislodge them by painful twitching of the features. There was no one to do it for them.[23]

The Times also published an anonymous article which first appeared in the *Cape Times* headed "Seamy Side of War." It was written by W. A. Saunders, a former newsman from New Zealand, who had been in No. 9 General Hospital. He had seen money and valuables stolen by orderlies who threatened any man who complained. Although Saunders had enteric, he was placed in a ward for venereal cases:

The medicine glass was a broken measure glass, and I am sure it had not been washed for weeks, for all round the outside edge there was a thick rim of dried saliva and the discharge from sore lips, etc., making it a disgusting thing to take in one's hands, let alone one's lips. All sorts of medicines were administered out of the same glass, and even the thought of it made me sick.[24]

There was an outcry in England, and angry questions were asked in Parliament. Lord Roberts was asked to explain, and he replied:

It is obvious that a certain amount of suffering is inseparable from the rapid advance of a large army in the enemy's country, when railway communication has been destroyed. . . . I can quite understand that people who have no practical experience in such matters are much concerned to hear [of] the hardships which sick and wounded soldiers have to undergo in time of war.[25]

But the storm was not to be stilled, and eventually a royal commission was appointed to look into the matter. By the time the commission arrived in South Africa (August 1900) the worst of the epidemic was over; medical supplies had been rushed forward and improvements made in the medical arrangements. Still, the commission collected evidence from doctors, nurses, patients, and others who had seen the conditions at Bloemfontein in the terrible months of May and June when the epidemic was at its height.

In general, the regular doctors and nurses of the Royal Army Medical Corps, with eyes on their future prospects in the service, were reluctant to admit that anything was or had been wrong, or that anyone had erred. The long-service nursing sisters all spoke ambiguously of how wonderfully uncomplaining the men were. But the civilians in khaki—doctors and patients, officers and men—did not hesitate to speak up.

The medical, surgical, and administrative practices were probably no worse than they had always been in the British army, but not since the Crimean War more than fifty years earlier had they been exposed to public view. All soldiers able to do so were expected to stand at attention when officers entered their wards, thermometers passed from mouth to mouth without even being wiped; Dr. John Temple Leon (a civil surgeon) reported that the principal medical officer of his hospital did not visit his marquees for six weeks; Dr. Frank Fitchett said he never saw the PMO inspecting the medical tents, and he complained of the "apathy or indifference displayed by the senior officers." James Dunlop, professor of surgery at Anderson's Medical School, criticised the RAMC officers for being "not up to date": some of the heads of the Medical Department were unfamiliar with the advances of modern surgery, and were not "gifted with the experience and forethought and judgment necessary for men occupying such important positions."[26] Professor Dunlop once found that the bedpans had been removed from a ward because the men had been found using them as spitoons.

The major complaint heard by the commission was of the shortage of medical supplies and hospital equipment. Sir William Wilson said that although plenty of supplies were stocked on the coast he had difficulty getting them transported into the interior. This was undoubtedly true. The chief lack was of bedpans and chamberpots. Dr. Richard Whittington testified that at one time in No. 8 General Hospital there was only one night commode for forty bell tents. Dr. Fitchett said, "The night-stools were very small and soon filled, and on going round at night I frequently would hear piteous cries for the orderly, and found a man unable to relieve himself because the vessel was filled."[27] Dr. Albert A. B. Kirkman, also of No. 8 General Hospital, said he had had no bedpans and "the patients with enteric were walking down between the marquees evacuating down there. . . . all the patients had to get out of bed—men who were dying, as a matter of fact." Mr. Anthony Bowlby, the senior surgeon at Portland Hospital, said "there was an immense number of men suffering from diarrhoea. . . . The whole hillside for the circuit of a mile round Bloemfontein was contaminated." Dr. Little at No. 9 General Hospital testified that "we considered many patients lost their lives from the want of bed pans."

There were also insufficient beds, blankets, mattresses, cooking utensils, fuel, urinals, feeding cups, hospital clothing, and fresh milk. A private in the 3rd Grenadier Guards, who asked not to be identified when he appeared before the royal commission, testified that he had been put in a bell tent where for ten days he lay without a waterproof sheet. When he was finally moved to a marquee and given a bed and sheets, the mattress was infested with lice. He saw one orderly "take a delirious patient by the throat and throw him back upon the bed." Like many others, he complained of the food: "I had no fresh milk whatever in the hospital. The condensed milk was mixed with cold and dirty water. The beef-tea was cold and nasty, so that I could not drink it."

Kipling testified that on two occasions he had been told by RAMC officers that nothing was needed, but when he asked the nurses they begged for pyjamas, warning him to deliver them not to the Stores Issue Department but to the back entrance of the hospital. On one occasion he delivered medicines as well.

In striking contrast to the evidence of the civil surgeons and patients was the testimony of the senior RAMC officers. Lieutenant Colonel F. Edward Barrow, principal medical officer at No. 9 General Hospital, a hospital described by Burdett-Coutts as "a tented city of pestilence," admitted that he needed 60,000 gallons of water a day and could only get 6,000, but he admitted little else. "We were told to boil that water from the wells, but as we had no firewood or coals, we could not boil it." He does not appear to have regarded this as a serious matter, but he was concerned about the milk. He spoke of "the dirty habits of the Kaffir boys" and said he had deliberately stopped the supply of fresh milk because he thought it might be contaminated "with Kaffir boys doing all the work." He said his hospital had so much food that he had to bury fresh mutton and beef. He denied that his hospital had ever been overcrowded and said, "Lots of patients arrived with absolutely nothing the matter with them." When asked, "Did you fall short of necessities?" he apparently forgot his statements about the shortage of water and fuel or he did not regard these as necessities, for he replied: "I had more than enough of everything. . . . I never ran short of anything." Asked for figures, he said flatly that he never bothered with statistics and that he did not require his medical officers to give him reports: "There was no necessity to report to me. I knew everything what was going on." Given some statements made by wounded men regarding their handling, he shrugged and replied that "the wounded can be eccentric."

Colonel Barrow had some peculiar notions about the causes of illness. Although at one point he declared that he had never seen water in the hospital tents during heavy rains, he credited much sickness to rainstorms: "Men were washed out of their tents and were puddling about in mud four inches thick, the alluvial mud. By that means all those poisons were let loose." Another factor, he said, was that after the troops reached Bloemfontein they did not have enough work to do; idleness, he maintained, even more than rainstorms, was responsible for the epidemic. "If there had been war in the locality, and they had been at it again, there would not have been so much sickness."

Lieutenant Colonel R. T. Beamish, principal medical officer at No. 8 General Hospital, also affirmed that all had been well in his hospital. "It was never overcrowded," he said. Never at any time was the hospital undermanned; he had all the nurses and orderlies he needed. "The patients never suffered." In spite of all the evidence to the contrary, he swore that there were never more than five men housed in a bell tent. As to the great bedpan shortage, Beamish said: "I think there was no actual dearth of bed pans," and again, "I never knew there was any dearth of bed pans. On the contrary, I believe there was not." Except perhaps a shortage of feeding cups, Beamish thought there had been an ample supply of everything. As for the complaining civil surgeons, several were "very rowdy and not quite teetotal—they were more or less intemperate and very rowdy."

Sir Robert Romer, president of the royal commission, said he was very impressed with Colonel Beamish's testimony, as indeed he was with that of the other senior RAMC officers. When the commissioners' report was finally issued the following January it blandly stated:

We desire to say that in our judgement, reviewing the campaign as a whole, it has not been one where it can properly be said that the medical and hospital arrangements have broken down. . . . no general or wide-spread neglect of patients, or indifference to their suffering. And all witnesses of experience in other wars are practically unanimous in the view that, taking it all in all, in no campaign have the sick and wounded been so well looked after as they have been in this.

The war attracted an extraordinary number of visitors, people who just came out to see what it was like. While the war was still being fought Cooks organised tours of the battlefields. Admiral F. I. Maxse travelled to Bloemfontein to visit his son. Sir Claude and Lady de Crespigny went out to see their three sons and to take a look around. Lady de Crespigny did a bit of nursing in Bloemfontein, where their eldest son was in hospital, and Sir Claude, who wanted to see some action, attached himself to a colonial unit for a few weeks. A number of officers whose regiments were still in England obtained leave and went out to volunteer their services.

With all those fine young men in South Africa the seat of war became an attraction for a considerable number of women who (as Milner put it) "seem to have no particular call of duty or business." On 3 April 1900 Chamberlain wrote to Milner: "The Queen regrets to observe the large number of ladies now visiting and remaining in South Africa," and she deplored "the hysterical spirit which seems to have influenced some of them to go where they are not wanted." This observation was, of course, passed on to Lord Roberts, whose wife and daughter were then on their way to join him at Bloemfontein. He decided he had better write to the Queen and tell her this, which he did, adding: "I understand that Your Majesty does not approve of ladies coming out to South Africa from mere curiosity. I am forbidding any to enter the Orange Free State, except those who have a son or husband in hospital, or whose husband is likely to be quartered in Bloemfontein for some time."[28]

Soon after, John Maxwell wrote to his wife: "Lady Roberts has arrived here and, as Kitchener says, she has represented nearly 500 tons of supplies, for her ladyship came up in a special train and upset all arrangements. However, the old Chief must be looked after, and I'm sure we grudge him nothing."[29] As for his own wife, Maxwell told her not to come out, not even if she stayed in Cape Town, where, he said, "every hole and corner is crammed with ladies who alternate squabbling among themselves with the washing of officers' faces."

Young Lady Edward Cecil, herself in Cape Town, remarked that "there was a good bit of cackle" about the ban on women. In her memoirs she wrote: "Nobody in those free and spacious days objected to women who came out to see their husbands or brothers, but there were plenty of others, some of whom were even mischievous." Being the prime minister's daughter-in-law, she did not feel constrained to abide by the ban and, with Lady Charles Bentinck, went up to Bloemfontein. As she told her mother, they enjoyed themselves hugely:

Every man you ever heard of is in Bloemfontein and they nearly all came to see us that afternoon [the day of their arrival]. . . . We saw the Grenadiers on parade and as we rode—at some distance away—across their front, the eyes of every man in that Battalion followed us from right to left and until we had ridden away. It was an extraordinary feeling, being so looked at.[30]

Among the early visitors to conquered Bloemfontein was Rudyard Kipling, who, like many others, wanted to do his bit and see some action. Before the war Bloemfontein had produced an English-language newspaper called *The Friend of the Sovereignty and Bloemfontein Gazette.* Lord Stanley, the chief press censor, asked a group of newspaper correspondents to take it over and edit it as an official organ of the army for the amusement and instruction of both the troops and the inhabitants. And thus was founded the first army newspaper. The first addition of the new *Friend,* published on 16 March 1900, proclaimed: "The simple policy adhered to in these columns will be the maintenance of British supremacy in South Africa, equal rights for all white men, without respect for race or creed, which principles in our opinion embody the establishment of sound government, the prosperity of the country and the happiness of the people."

A number of the most distinguished correspondents in South Africa contributed to the paper during its thirty-day existence: Lionel James, Bennett Burleigh, A. B. "Banjo" Patterson (who wrote "Waltzing Matilda"), and, only a few days after its first appearance, Kipling, who contributed verses, epigrams, and articles, including "Kopje-book Maxims" such as:

> Two horses will shift a camp if they be dead enough.
> Abandoned women and abandoned kopjes are best left alone.
> Half a loaf is better than no bread, but a pound and a half of trek ox is an insult.

It was in *The Friend* that Kipling first published his remarkable poem on Joubert, after his death on 27 March 1900. Joubert, the moderate, the chivalrous, had always been admired by the British. When news of his death reached Roberts, he sent a note of condolence to President Kruger. Joubert had been in ill health for some time, and his condition was not improved by a fall from his horse. After the retreat from Ladysmith he had called together his commandants and sorrowfully told them that he was too ill to continue as their leader; he asked them to accept Louis Botha as his replacement. Although Botha had shown himself to be an able general and he was known to be a favourite of Joubert's, the request came as a surprise, for the Boers had a great respect for age and Botha at thirty-seven was considered very young for the chief command. It was also contrary to Boer custom for a commandant-general, or any general at this stage of the war, to be appointed rather than elected. Had an election been held, it is probable that De la Rey rather than Botha would have been the burghers' choice; however, in deference to Joubert's wishes, Botha was accepted and his appointment was eventually confirmed by the last session of the volksraad. Joubert retired to his farm, where he died, his faithful Hendrina by his side.

With the capture of Cronjé, the death of Joubert, and the passing of the military leadership of the Boer forces into the younger, more vigorous, and more able hands of Botha, De la Rey, and De Wet, the nature of the war began to change.

27

DECISIONS AT KROONSTAD

Bloemfontein was one of the enemies' capitals, but it did not impress the British. "Dust and flies and sunsets are the three outstanding things I remember about Bloemfontein," wrote General J. F. C. Fuller of his days as a subaltern. Lieutenant David Miller told his mother in a letter home: "Bloemfontein is very disappointing—just a little English townlet of some 6,000 inhabitants. Our camps are all around it. The hospitals are full, and a scarcity of nurses. Eighty soldiers were buried the day I arrived, nearly all enteric fever."[1]

There were few problems with the inhabitants, a number were helpful, and some of the women nursed the sick and wounded; it is said that one of President Steyn's brothers signed a contract to supply wood for fuel to the British army. People were not turned out of their homes, and the soldiers were given strict orders to be on their best behaviour. In the words of Corporal Murray Cosby of the 7th Mounted Infantry, Roberts warned them that "if any of us blackards were caught looting so much as a hen's egg from any private person, Dutch, English or Kaffir, we would be tried by drumhead court-martial and instantly shot."[2]

The staunchest republicans among the Boers, men and women, had fled Bloemfontein. Tibbie Steyn, the president's wife, although ill, had gathered up her son and two of her daughters and preceded her husband to Kroonstad. The flight of the refugees and wounded across the Orange Free State and the Transvaal before the advancing British increased the despair of the Boers; wild rumours spread; no one knew what to do or what to expect next. The world as they had known it was crumbling about them. Men and women scattered on farms across the veld travelled miles to the nearest railway station to glean news from refugees, wounded, and deserters.

Christian de Wet, seeing that it was a hopeless task to try holding his men together, gave them all leave to return to their homes and stay until he sent for them:

How can I describe my feelings when I saw Bloemfontein in the hands of the English? It was enough to break the heart of the bravest man amongst us. Even worse than the fall of our capital was the fact that, as was only to be expected, the burghers had become entirely disheartened; and it seemed as if they were incapable of offering any further resistance. The commandos were completely demoralized.[3]

President M. T. Steyn proclaimed Kroonstad to be the new capital of the Orange Free State. A three-man delegation had just been dispatched to Europe to plead for intervention on the part of the great powers. In the meantime it was necessary to fight on as best they could. On 17 March 1900 Steyn called all the principal Boer leaders to a krygsraad:

Notwithstanding the despondency of the burghers at the capture of Bloemfontein, there were no serious words spoken of making peace at the largest war council, over which I presided, at Kroonstad. . . . The matter of the most efficient manner of carrying on the war was discussed and in the Volksraad it was *unanimously* decided to carry on the war.[4]

Steyn the moderate, the man who more than any other on either side had sought to prevent the war, was now to emerge as the living, breathing spirit of the Boers' resistance. This man of peace was to be the only politician of iron and blood, the man with the firmest determination, the strongest will. It is curious that his name was, and is, so little known outside South Africa, for although Kruger had played his part in starting the war, Steyn was the major political figure to fight it. Kruger remained the living symbol of Afrikanerdom for the British, even long after he had faded from the scene, and they underestimated the vital role played by this stocky, long-bearded Free State president.

Some important decisions were made at the Kroonstad krygsraad. The need for greater discipline in the Boer forces was evident, and it was resolved that efforts would be made to make the independent-minded burghers conform to military necessities. Sick leaves were to be strictly regulated, and men who left their commandos without authorisation were to be punished. As Cronjé had demonstrated, the practice of carrying along wagons loaded with women and children and moveables could be disasterous; the krygsraad decreed that in future the numbers of wagons would be strictly controlled.

It was also decided to give more recognition to the foreign volunteers, of whom there were perhaps as many as 2,000, and to form them into a separate corps. They had been given a less than generous welcome in the early days of the war; Kruger had bluntly told one group: "Thank you for coming. Don't imagine that we have need of you. Transvaal wants no foreign help. But as you wish to fight for us, you are welcome. I take your coming as a gratifying sign that Europe is gradually beginning to recognize the right of the Afrikaner nation."[5]

European officers with impressive military credentials who had volunteered their services were told that if they could ride and shoot they could join a commando; their advice was not needed. Only the ambulance units sent by the French, Germans, Russians, and Dutch had called forth any expressions of gratitude. Since then the foreigners had proved themselves, for the most part, both useful and brave; besides, the republics now very much wanted help. Captain Carl Reichmann, the American military observer with the Boers, made some interesting observations on the foreign volunteers in his report to the United States War Department:

Volunteers, generally, have played a considerable part in this war; they were mostly foreigners, adventurers, amateurs, active, retired and ex-officers of foreign armies. Generally they behaved with much gallantry, and for that very reason failed to gain success. The Boers are hunters rather than soldiers, they are not much given to holding a position to the last unless their instincts tell them that the position is a safe one to hold. The foreigners, on the contrary, once posted would hold their ground. . . . Owing to lack of proper general staff service, the foreigners were frequently not informed when the burghers withdrew, remained in the position and lost heavily or were cut off. Owing to their offensive spirit, which is totally lacking in the burgher, the foreigners were particularly well suited for reconnaisance service. Whenever offensive operations were undertaken, the foreigners had to bear the brunt of the fighting.[6]

Comte Georges Henri Anne Marie Victor Villebois de Mareuil (1847–1900), sometimes called "the Lafayette of South Africa," was raised to the rank of vechtgeneraal and given command of the new corps. With his waxed moustaches and monocle he was the best known of the foreigners, though his name was usually misspelled. Certainly he was the most vocal and the most critical of the Boers' lack of discipline and of their dilatory strategies. He had moved about among the laagers from Ladysmith to Kimberley, criticising and offering his advice (largely unheeded) to Cronjé, Joubert, and Botha. Basil Williams in *The Times History* referred to his "quixotic nature"; Dr. James Kay called him "that notorious mercenary and swashbuckler." He was, however, the only foreigner among the Boers who had any real military reputation. He had had a distinguished career in the French army and had once commanded the 1st Regiment of the French Foreign Legion.

More than a dozen nationalities were represented among the foreigners. Cor van Gogh, brother of the painter, was one. (Captured, he committed suicide.) A few were noblemen, such as Count Pecci, a nephew of Pope Leo XIII; Prince Louis d'Orléans et Braganza, cousin of the French pretender; Baron von Goldek from Hungary; Count von Zeppelin, a relative of the inventor. Many had served in other armies in other places: the French Foreign Legion, the Dutch army in the East Indies, in South American revolutions, with the Americans in Cuba or against them in the Philippines. Some had come to South Africa specifically to fight and some had been there when the war began, uitlanders who, although not burghers, chose to fight for the Boers. Some were toughs looking for adventure and loot. Young Freda Schlosberg at Bronkhorstspruit recorded:

Members of the *Uitlander Korps* have been arriving all day. . . . The detachment consists of two or three hundred mercenaries—Hollanders, Germans, Frenchmen, Americans, Italians, Hungarians, Portuguese—all rough-looking, common men, evidently from the lowest classes. They are armed not only with the usual rifles and revolvers, but also with swords, daggers, etc., the Italians specially with home-made stilettos. . . .

The first thing they did after settling down was to steal some of our fowls, geese and ducks; then they took most of the wood lying in our yard without even asking permission. They are undisciplined and unprincipled, and under no control whatever by their officers. . . .

Their presence so near our house is terrifying. . . .[7]

There were also a few Britons to be found with the Boers, some of them deserters from the British army. Lieutenant David Miller in a letter home spoke of several fights in which he had taken part: "The leader in one case was a Glasgow man—and many of those who attacked our regimental outposts were Scotch and English."

Queen Victoria was particularly incensed when told that fifty German officers and noncommissioned officers had landed at Delagoa Bay and were on their way to the Transvaal. She instructed Lord Salisbury "to remonstrate at the presence of so many German officers and men with the Boers. It is monstrous." She herself wrote to the Kaiser, and in reply he assured her that no regular serving officers were in South Africa, which was not true.

Most of the foreigners were scattered throughout the Boer forces, but there were a number who from the first formed nationality units of their own. The German and Dutch contingents had been the largest, numbering perhaps 200 men each, but they had suffered severely at Elandslaagte. The Scandinavian unit had fought bravely but recklessly at Magersfontein and had been practically exterminated there. One of the best of the foreign units was the Italian contingent (which also included a few Frenchmen), led by an adventurer named Cumillo Richiardi. He had recently fought against the Americans in the Philippines, and he favoured a policy of taking no prisoners. In the later part of the war he specialised in blowing up bridges.

Most of the Americans with the Boers either had been born in Ireland or were of Irish extraction. Roland Schikkerling noted that whereas the Germans and Hollanders were closer in blood to the Boers they looked "out of place," but that "you could not pick Patrick out of a herd of the wildest Boers. There were field cornets bearing the names Kelly and O'Brien. This little band of men could curse like heretics, and their profanity was at times quite picturesque."[8] When one group of Irish Americans from Chicago, members of a Red Cross unit, reached the Transvaal, 46 out of 53 doffed their Red Cross brassards and picked up rifles, thus creating a scandal of international proportions. Most of them joined a unit led by John Y. Fillimore Blake, a huge American who habitually dressed in cowboy costume. Born in Missouri, he had graduated from West Point in 1880 and served with the 6th United States Cavalry in the Far West. He called himself "colonel," although he had never risen above the rank of first lieutenant in the American army. Unlike most foreign volunteers, who went home after a few months, Blake stayed on and fought to the end.

Blake's second-in-command was John MacBride, whom Deneys Reitz described as "a brave but ugly, red-headed little man." After the war he married Maud Gonne, the Irish revolutionary, took part in the Easter Rebellion in Dublin in 1916, and was executed by the British. Among other Americans were J. H. King, known as "Dynamite Dick," and James Foster, the "Arizona Kid," described as "a typical cowboy . . . frolicsome, lithe and reckless, always ready for any excitement, to take part in any sort of enterprise no matter what desperate chances were involved."[9]

The Arizona Kid, like many American volunteers on both sides, had come to South Africa with a shipment of mules. British purchasing agents buying horses and mules in the American Far West regularly advertised for men to tend the animals on the long voyage to South Africa, offering to pay a round-trip passage, New Orleans–Cape Town, and $15. Many men made it a one-way trip. An entire squadron of the South African Light Horse was composed of Texas cowboys and muleteers. One man who had served with Roosevelt's Rough Riders in Cuba wrote to his former commanding officer from South Africa: "Dear Teddy—I came over here meaning to join the Boers, who I was told were Republicans fighting Monarchists, but when I got here I found the Boers talked Dutch, while the Britishers talked English, so I joined the latter."[9]

Hassell's American Scouts, formed by J. A. Hassell, an American who had been given full citizenship by the Transvaal volksraad in recognition of his services during the Jameson Raid, saw action in a number of small battles and skirmishes. On 14 June 1900 they successfully attacked a party of British engineers working on a bridge across the Zand River. Among those killed by Hassell's Americans in this engagement was Louis Irving Seymour, thirty-nine, who, as his tombstone still proclaims, was a "Citizen USA, Major in Her Britannic Majesty's Railway Pioneer Regiment." Lieutenant Joseph Clement, another American, was killed in the same engagement.

At the Kroonstad krygsraad Villebois de Mareuil was given permission to try blowing up the bridge over the Modder River at Boshof. With about 100 foreigners, mostly Frenchmen, and Germans (Captain Reichmann was amused to see them sitting together one evening alternately singing the "Marseillaise" and the "Wacht am Rhein"), and 25 Boers, he set off for Boshof under the impression that it was lightly defended. So it had been, but on the very day he and his men arrived in the area Methuen had concentrated six and a half battalions of infantry, a thousand mounted men, and twenty-two guns there. Methuen was alerted and dispatched 750 troopers and a battery to take him. The Boers bolted before they were surrounded; the foreigners stayed and fought until Villebois de Mareuil fell mortally wounded by a shell fragment. Methuen buried him with full military honours.

The affair at Boshof was only one of a series of small engagements that would continue to be fought over a vast area. The battleground widened, and the days of the big set-piece battles were almost over.

28

THE BOER REVIVAL

To the British, both in South Africa and in Britain, the end of the war appeared near at hand, the final outcome certain; nothing more was required other than a bit of final mopping up in the conquered areas. While waiting for his stocks of supplies to build up at Bloemfontein, Roberts sent Kitchener off to put down an incipient rebellion in the western Cape, and he dispatched small columns into the southern part of the Orange Free State. On 15 March he issued a proclamation to the burghers of the Free State offering to allow all those willing to give up their arms and take an oath of neutrality to return to their homes unmolested. Many did, although the British noted how few Mausers and how many venerable hunting pieces and antiques from the Kaffir wars they collected. At the end of the month Roberts made a preliminary movement north along the railway, and on 29 March his troops fought a small battle at Karee Siding that was witnessed by Kipling.

Although he had written much about soldiers, this was the first battle Kipling had ever seen. He was astonished to see how the "enormous pale landscape swallowed up seven thousand men without a sign," and it was strange "seeing nothing in the emptiness and hearing only a faint murmur as of wind along gas-jets, running in and out of the unconcerned hills."[1]

Karee Siding was not a very well managed battle: the attack of the infantry was not well prepared and the flanking movements of the cavalry were too slow. Still, at a cost of 189 casualties to the Boers' 34 the British dislodged their enemy from positions astride the railway. The first stage of the route north to Pretoria was now secure. But new and unexpected problems developed.

The war might indeed have been brought to a close as quickly as Roberts anticipated had it not been for one of the most remarkable men to emerge from the Boer ranks, a leader who did truly become a legendary figure in his own time: Christiaan de Wet. Born of voortrekker parents on a farm near Dewetsdorp, a Free State village named after his father, he had as a young man taken part in one of the wars against the Basuto, and in the First Anglo-Boer War he had joined the Transvaal forces and had been with the party that captured Majuba. Most of his life had been spent as a farmer—and he looked like one. Now forty-six years old, of medium height, with sloping shoulders, straight brown hair, and a small moustache and beard, he spoke with a slight lisp. "I can't help laughing at the idea of his being a general," said Count Sternberg, a foreign volunteer. He was married and the father of sixteen children. Three of his sons—Kootie, Isaac, and Christiaan—accompanied him when, as a simple burgher in the Heilbron Commando, he set out again to fight the British. He served first on the Natal front, where, after his commandant took sick, he was elected to succeed him. He led the attack near Nicholson's Nek and shortly after was made a vechtgeneraal. After Piet Cronjé's capture at Paardeberg, he was made commander-in-chief of the Free State forces.

Just at dusk on the evening of 28 March De Wet led a column of 1,600 men with five guns, a Maxim machine gun, and a pompom out of Brandfort. He had recalled his men from their furloughs, and many had rejoined him, rested and ready again for battle. The commandos with him were under good leaders; A. P. Cronjé, J. B. Wessels, C. C. Froneman, and his brother, Piet de Wet. Beginning a practise he was to continue for the rest of the war, he told no one his plans. Leaving Brandfort in a northeasterly direction, he turned abruptly south during the night. He rested most of his force the following day and that evening moved out to a position 17 miles north of the waterworks pumping station on the Modder River that supplied Bloemfontein with its water.

Here he had an altercation with one of his commandants, Frans Vilonel. De Wet was determined to enforce the decision reached at the Kroonstad krygsraad to limit the number of wagons. "I made up my mind," he said, "to hold the reins of discipline with a firmer hand." When Vilonel refused to obey his order to abandon his wagon, De Wet took the unprecedented step of relieving him of his command and reducing him to the ranks, appointing a field cornet to replace him as commandant.

This internal problem solved, he turned to the project at hand. It was his intention to capture the waterworks, which he knew to be guarded by only 200 men. He discovered, however, that Brigadier General R. G. Broadwood, an experienced and able cavalry commander, had just arrived on the scene with 1,800 cavalry and mounted infantry on his way to Bloemfontein from Thaba 'Nchu. As Broadwood was ignorant of his presence, De Wet changed his objective from the mere capture of the waterworks to something grander, and he decided upon a bold and clever course of action.

The battlefield can be imagined as being roughly in the shape of the letter **A**, pointing north, the east side being formed by the Modder River, on the west bank of which stood the waterworks, and the other by the Koornspruit, which flows into the Modder several miles north. Between them, forming the crossbar of the **A**, ran a road which crossed the Koornspruit at a drift, and, roughly parallel to the road, ran a partly constructed railway line. The distance between the Modder and the Koornspruit at this point is about two and a half miles. About three-quarters of a mile from the Koornspruit on the unfinished railway line were three buildings that formed what was called Sanna's Post.

De Wet positioned his brother Piet with most of his men and all his guns in kopjes on the east bank of the Modder opposite the waterworks. He himself with only 350 men lay concealed along the steep banks of the Koornspruit near the drift. He planned a partridge shoot. His brother Piet and his men would drive the British towards the blind, but instead of shooting his game, he planned a wholesale capture. The men with him were given strict orders not to fire until he gave the command.

The British sent out no patrols until morning and relied simply on a few sentries close to their bivouac. About six o'clock on the morning of 31 March, just as the troops were breaking camp, a lieutenant who had led a patrol across the Modder reported that he had been fired upon. Not much importance was attached to this, but twenty minutes later a Boer gun banged out a shell; it was followed by others, which fell among Broadwood's transport.

Although Broadwood's patrols had failed to uncover the trap laid by De Wet, there was one man who had: behind the Boer lines Major Frederick Russell Burnham, an American who had come all the way from Alaska to be Roberts's chief of scouts, was hurriedly scrambling up a kopje. He had discovered De Wet's trap too late to slip through the Boer lines and warn Broadwood, but he had hopes of giving an alarm. Mounting a rock in full view of both forces he stood waving a red handkerchief he habitually used as a signal. If anyone in the cavalry brigade had noticed the figure frantically waving on the hillside the brigade might have been saved, but no one did. None of the British, that is. The Boers saw him and captured him.

When the first shells from Piet de Wet's guns fell among Broadwood's wagons the transport drivers quickly inspanned and in some confusion fled west, away from the guns, towards the Koornspruit drift and into the waiting arms of Christiaan de Wet. The drive had begun.

De Wet himself stood at the top of the drift with two of his commandants as over the brow of the rise of land came the first wagons and carts. The drivers were met by a quiet "Hands up!" and an order to keep silent and not to give any alarm. Wagon after wagon rode into the trap. Dozens of them. Then came soldiers, and some 200 were disarmed before they knew what was happening. "The discipline among the burghers was fairly satisfactory until the disarming work began," said De Wet:

If my men had only been able to think for themselves, they would have thrown the rifles on the bank as they came into their hands, and so would have disarmed far more of the English than they succeeded in doing. But as it was, the burghers kept asking:

"Where shall I put this rifle, General? What have I to do with this horse?"

That the work should be delayed by this sort of thing sorely tried my hasty temper.[2]

Broadwood knew that a Boer force of 5,000 men under Cornelius Hermanus Olivier was in the vicinity, and he assumed that it was this force, vastly larger than his own, which was now attacking him. His guns tried to reply to the Boer artillery across the river, but the enemy was beyond the range of his 12-pounders, and he ordered the battery commanders to limber up and follow the wagons. "U" and "Q" batteries, Royal Horse Artillery, were ordered to cross the Koornspruit and take up a position on a kopje beyond to cover his retreat. They trotted off, "U" Battery in the lead, towards the drift where De Wet and his men were busily and quietly capturing wagons and men.

When Major Philip Taylor with "U" Battery clattering behind him rode up to the drift, De Wet himself met him with the curt order: "Dismount. You are prisoners. Go to the wagons." In the moments of confusion which followed, Taylor slipped back to "Q" Battery and warned Major Edmund Phipps-Hornby, its battery commander. At the same time, Colonel H. L. Dawson, commanding Roberts's Horse, coming up on the left of the batteries, saw what was happening. He reined up sharply, shouting "Files about! Gallop!" Phipps-Hornby also wheeled his guns and teams about and galloped back. De Wet, seeing that his prey was startled and fleeing, called out to his men to open fire.

A scene of the utmost confusion ensued around the drift. Excited and frightened men and horses and oxen milled about. A gun and two ammunition wagons overturned, and their horses were killed in the flight of "Q" Battery for the shelter of the buildings at Sanna's Post. The soldiers of "U" Battery had dismounted and were prisoners, but their untended horses panicked when the Boers opened fire so close to them, and they galloped off in all directions, dragging their guns and limbers behind them. The Boers shot down most of them, but one gun team, on its own and without drivers, ran after "Q" Battery and escaped.

Phipps-Hornby halted his battery at Sanna's Post, unlimbered his guns in front of the buildings, put his horses and limbers behind, and opened fire. It was a brave show, but the field guns with their flat trajectories had little effect on the Boers in the shelter of the Koornspruit's high banks, while the gunners, without the protection of shields on their guns, were completely exposed to the Boers' musketry.

Broadwood himself arrived on the scene and for the first time realized what was happening. He called off "Q" Battery's gallant, futile engagement and ordered the guns withdrawn. But by this time only Phipps-Hornby, Captain Gardiner Humphreys, and ten gunners were still left on their feet. They managed to get two guns away by themselves. Then Phipps-Hornby called out for volunteers from the mounted infantry, now dismounted and lying prone along the railway embankment behind Sanna's Post. As these men left their cover and ran forward they were met by such a sleet of bullets that they involuntarily pressed their helmets down on their heads and bent forward as if running against a strong wind. They tried bringing out the teams, but men and horses were bowled over.

A "Q" Battery gunner lying wounded in the hip was a witness: "O! it was an awful sight—dead and wounded all around and the poor horses smothered in blood and struggling about."[3] Driver Horace Glasock had six horses shot from under him.

Through it all Humphreys and Phipps-Hornby behaved like model Victorian officers, incredibly cool and brave. When a Boer bullet knocked Humphreys's stick from his hand, he calmly stopped to pick it up and then strolled on. When one of Broadwood's aides suggested to Phipps-Hornby that he take cover, he replied, "Perhaps it would be as well, but I have been here for some hours now," and he continued to walk about, apparently in the possession of a charmed life.

One gun and its limber had to be left in the open for lack of horses, but five guns, including the one brought back by the riderless team of "U" Battery, were brought away. As the mutilated remains of the horse artillery galloped back through the lines of the mounted infantry, the soldiers, careless of the bullets flying about them, rose up and cheered. Phipps-Hornby and three of his men received the Victoria Cross.

Broadwood sent cavalry around to try to outflank De Wet, but they failed. About noon he managed to extricate nearly all of his remaining men by retiring south and west, crossing the Koornspruit further upstream, but the Boers left their positions to press hard on his rear guard. Broadwood lost 159 officers and men killed or wounded and 421 captured. Boer losses according to De Wet were 3 killed and 5 wounded. In addition to the guns, the Boers captured 83 wagons loaded with stores.

In the middle of the battle of Sanna's Post, at about eight o'clock in the morning, Colonel Cyril Martyr with a weak brigade of mounted infantry arrived at Boesman's Kop, about 5 miles west of the Koornspruit. He had been sent out by Lord Roberts to reinforce Broadwood should he be attacked by Olivier. From the top of the hill Martyr could plainly see the battlefield through his glasses, and although his brigade was weak (about 600 men), he could have moved smartly forward and taken De Wet in the rear. Instead, he divided his force into small units and sent them flying in different directions on futile errands. At 11:15 A.M., as Broadwood was getting his troops away to the southwest, General Sir Henry Colvile, following Martyr, reached Boesman's Kop with an entire infantry division. He too could have saved the day by pouncing on De Wet, now struggling to get away with his prisoners and wagons. But Colvile, instead of pressing forward, sat on Boesman's Kop and sent a staff officer to summon Broadwood to come to him and explain the situation while his troops were given an hour's rest. Broadwood wisely decided that his place was with his men and that a 10-mile ride to and from Boesman's Kop to chat with Colvile was nonsense. He sent back a message urging Colvile to make a direct and immediate advance on the Boers. Colvile ignored it. Instead, after his men were rested he marched most of them northeast to Waterval Drift, about 5 miles north of Sanna's Post where the Koornspruit meets the Modder.

Colvile finally did send a small force under Colonel T. C. Porter east across the Koornspruit, and the next day he sent Smith-Dorrien's brigade to join him and to recapture the waterworks. He then changed his mind and ordered Smith-Dorrien to withdraw. Meanwhile, Smith-Dorrien, having learned that the Boers had left 87 of Broadwood's wounded in the buildings at Sanna's Post, sent back staff officers to bring up ambulances and carts, but Colvile refused to permit this. It was up to the mounted units to take care of their own wounded, he said; it was not the responsibility of the infantry. Smith-Dorrien later wrote: "I shall never forget the indignation of Porter and his men when they heard of this inhuman order."[4] Smith-Dorrien withdrew as ordered, but reluctantly and slowly, and not before his troops had brought the wounded men back.

Colvile's behaviour at Sanna's Post is difficult to understand, and he appears to have had some difficulty in trying to explain it to Lord Roberts later. The only plausible explanation appears to be that Colvile, a proud as well as stupid man, was unduly piqued that Broadwood, his junior, failed to obey his order to report to him and in retaliation deliberately ignored Broadwood's request for assistance, refusing to support or help him in any way.

Even though De Wet was reinforced by Olivier, Colvile and Broadwood had sufficient force to drive off the Boers, but they chose to withdraw, leaving the waterworks in Boer hands. Bloemfontein's main water supply was thus cut off.

So impressed were the British officers by the brilliant battle plan of De Wet that they could not at first bring themselves to believe that an "ignorant Boer" had conceived it. A curious rumour spread that the Boers had been led by Captain Carl Reichmann, the American military attaché, who had indeed been present, but only as an observer. During the battle Reichmann appears to have been primarily concerned with attending to Lieutenant Nix, the Dutch attaché, who was severely wounded by British shrapnel.

Immediately after his victory De Wet left his men with his brother and A. P. Cronjé and rode off with three aides in the direction of Dewetsdorp. There he found such a tempting target for another strike that he sent orders for 1,500 burghers and three guns to join him with all speed. While he waited, he collected an additional 110 men locally, men who had given up the struggle after the fall of Bloemfontein but who now readily took up their arms again at his call.

Roberts had instructed Gatacre to occupy Dewetsdorp if he had enough troops at his disposal. These instructions were vague (Who knows how many are enough?), and Gatacre sent only 500 infantry under the command of Captain William M'Whinnie. It was not until 1 April that Roberts discovered how small the force was. Then, knowing the nearness of De Wet and Olivier, he ordered it withdrawn. Gatacre passed on the order to M'Whinnie but neglected to alert him to his danger. M'Whinnie marched his men towards Reddersburg, unaware of his peril; two days later, 3 April, while still 4 miles northeast of the town, he became aware that he was being pursued. He then quickly made for a horseshoe-shaped ridge known as Mostert's Hoek and there threw up some stone sangars and sent off a messenger asking for help.

De Wet had hurried his men on by forced marches. Those who could not keep up the pace or whose horses foundered were left behind. Finding the British brought to bay, he at once sent in a demand for their surrender, to which M'Whinnie replied, "I'm damned if I surrender!" De Wet immediately opened fire with his three Krupp guns while his men, sheltered behind rocks and folds in the ground, crept up on the British position, but it was late in the day and night fell without any decisive action.

It was seven o'clock that evening when Gatacre and Roberts learned of M'Whinnie's difficulties. Roberts at once ordered Gatacre to go to his relief. By ten o'clock the following morning Gatacre was on a ridge overlooking Reddersburg and could hear the sounds of the battle at Mostert's Hoek about 5 miles away, but in and about the town of Reddersburg were Boers covering De Wet's main force. Gatacre, after some indecision, decided not to press forward but to fall back on the railway at Bethany. After moving back about 4 miles he received orders from Roberts to seize Reddersburg. He then countermarched and occupied the town, encountering little resistance, but he was too late to help M'Whinnie and his men at Mostert's Hoek.

De Wet had opened fire with his Krupps at 5:30 A.M. About noon M'Whinnie surrendered. His casualties amounted to only 10 killed and 37 wounded, and he was later blamed for not holding out longer, but he was unable to reply to De Wet's guns and, in view of Gatacre's timidity, it is difficult to see how further resistance would have saved them. De Wet claimed 470 prisoners.

Roberts by now had had enough of Gatacre. He relieved him of his command. Gatacre, bitter and resentful, returned to England—to be greeted by cheers from the people and to receive a medal from the Queen. But he never again held a command.

The week which extended from 29 March to 5 April 1900 had been a bustling one. The score seemed almost even—the British had defeated the foreign volunteers at Boshof and driven off the Boers at Karee Siding; De Wet had scored two striking victories at Sanna's Post and Mostert's Hoek—but Boshof had been little more than a skirmish and Karee Siding had been an expensive victory in terms of casualties suffered for results obtained, while De Wet's two brilliant successes in less than a week, resulting in the capture of a thousand prisoners, seven guns, and a convoy of stores had an electrifying effect on Boer morale. It stiffened the resolve of those in arms, rallied the waverers, and inspired many burghers who had gone home to pick up their Mausers and resume the fight.

Roberts was now anxious, and rightly so, about his lines of communication. De Wet was in a position to sweep south along the railway line, stranding Roberts and rousing thousands of Cape Afrikaners to the republican cause. This certainly would have been his wisest course. But he became diverted, allowing passion to replace logic—a bad exchange for generals as for others.

At Wepener, on the Basutoland border, about 1,800 colonials and a few regulars, a part of the Colonial Division, were stationed under the command of Colonel E. H. Dalgety; against these De Wet assembled an army of 6,000 burghers, and on 9 April he attacked. Most of the men in the Colonial Division were South Africans from Cape Colony, and the Boers had a special hatred for these men. De Wet told why:

> To tell the truth, there was not a man amongst us who would have asked better than to make prisoners of the Cape Mounted Rifles and of Brabant's Horse. They were Afrikaners, although neither Free Staters nor Transvaalers, they ought, in our opinion, to have been ashamed to fight against us.
>
> The English, we admitted, had a perfect right to hire such sweepings, and to use them against us, but we utterly dispised them for allowing themselves to be hired. . . .[5]

The colonials took up excellent defensive positions on some kopjes 3 to 5 miles northeast of the town on the east bank of the Caledon River. De Wet surrounded them, but after wasting seventeen days he gave up the fight and withdrew, just managing to slip past forces sent to their aid.

The diversion had cost him dear, giving the British time to protect their vital line of communication. He had lost his chance. His decision to attack the colonials instead of the railway was the worst De Wet ever made.

29

ON THE MARCH TO PRETORIA

While sitting in Bloemfontein waiting until he was able to resume his march northward, Roberts had much to occupy his mind: the shortage of men and supplies, the enteric which was carrying off the men he had, the dangers to his long line of communications, his planning for the advance to Johannesburg and Pretoria, the worrying activities of De Wet—and there was Buller.

After the relief of Ladysmith, Buller's army in Natal numbered 55,000 men—more than the total number of Boers in the field—but he was doing absolutely nothing with this large force. Roberts wanted to make a two-pronged invasion of the Transvaal—Buller operating on the eastern flank while his own forces pressed up from the south. Between early March and May 1900 more than forty telegrams were exchanged between Roberts and Buller in which Roberts tried everything—except a direct order—to get Buller to move, to do *something* (even some slight pressure from Buller on the eastern front would have been helpful), and Buller found reasons why he could not budge.

Buller could not decide what he should do or determine what he could do—whether he should make a western advance over the Drakensberg into the Orange Free State, or advance northward through Natal towards the Transvaal, or do both simultaneously. On 2 March he proposed to attack in both directions; on 5 March he thought he would attack only by the northern route; two days later he proposed the western route. His mood vacillated between extravagant optimism and profound pessimism. Roberts, exasperated, was prepared to agree to anything that would move him out of Ladysmith. Still Buller delayed. His excuses were endless: the Boers were too strong, the Ladysmith garrison was still recovering from the effects of the siege, he did not have enough cavalry or engineers, his men needed boots and other clothing, he needed more remounts. At one point he even suggested that Roberts send his cavalry 200 miles across the Free State to clear the Drakensberg passes for him so that he could safely move his army through. Roberts, ever decisive himself, did not know what to make of him. To Lansdowne he wrote: "He certainly is an extraordinary man. His first intentions are generally correct, but his second thoughts invariably lead him astray. . . . I can never feel sure that he will carry out anything that has been decided upon, even though the idea may have originated with himself."[1]

Buller, like most timorous commanders, greatly overestimated the difficulties before him. He guessed that 25,000 Boers would block his advance when, in actual fact, there were only about 8,000 on the Biggarsberg under the command of Lucas Meyer, the Boers' most incompetent general. Botha, with a sizable number of his men, had moved from the Natal front into the Free State to oppose Roberts's further advance. Buller, with a fighting strength of 45,000 men and 119 guns, ought to have moved inexorably forward, but he remained glued to Natal. Military observers were puzzled. "The slowness of General Buller's advance in Natal since the relief of Ladysmith over two and one-half months previous is inexplicable," wrote Captain Slocum in his report to the United States War Department.[2]

At last Roberts concluded that it was useless to expect anything from Buller. When he had first suggested that Buller might spare him a division, Buller had protested so vigorously that Roberts had not pressed the point, but finally he ordered one division and the Imperial Light Horse to be sent to him. He also pulled out a few good officers, such as Ian Hamilton and Archibald Hunter, and relieved Warren of his command.

Warren, instead of being shipped home as he deserved, was sent to take charge of small operations in northwestern Cape Colony where some Cape rebels were creating disturbances.

Why Lord Roberts did not relieve Buller of his command or at least give him direct orders to follow is difficult to understand. The two men were not friends. Far from it. Buller was the protégé of Wolseley, Roberts's chief rival in the army, and there had never been any love lost between them. Yet, though Roberts made his dissatisfaction with Buller quite clear to his political superiors at home, and the Cabinet had questioned whether it was wise to retain him in his command, Roberts did not replace him. Six years later Roberts said in a letter to William Blackwood: "I doubt if any one has realized how impossible it was to supersede him."[3]

The Times History guessed that Roberts, who had not personally visited the Natal front, thought that Buller, as the man on the spot, was best able to judge of the military situation there, and also that Roberts had "a chivalrous disinclination to treat a general who had once been commander-in-chief in South Africa in the same way as he treated his other subordinates."[4] There were perhaps other considerations as well. One was Buller's immense popularity, not only among his own troops but with the general public at home. In spite of his blunders (not all of which were generally known) they loved him still. Then too there appeared to be no one to replace him; Warren was incompetent, and Sir George White had been invalided home. Finally, there was perhaps a personal consideration: it was Buller who had been responsible for the death of Roberts's son; he would not want to appear to be taking personal revenge. Still, when all has been considered, it is impossible to justify the retention of Buller in his high command.

With or without Buller's cooperation, Roberts was determined to invade the Transvaal. On 3 May 1900 he left Bloemfontein behind, left too all those sick and wounded, and with bands playing began his march north to Pretoria with 38,000 men and more than 100 guns. He marched on a broad front, his troops moving in three columns. He himself commanded the centre column based on the railway while French and his cavalry marched parallel to him on his left and Ian Hamilton (now a general) with a column consisting mostly of mounted infantry was on his right. Brandfort was captured without difficulty, and in ten days Roberts was in Kroonstad, from which Steyn and the Free State government had just fled.

The Boers wanted desperately to stop Roberts's steamroller advance, but they lacked any sound plan for doing so and relied only on what *The Times History* called "an almost unreasoning and obstinate patriotism." In Pretoria on 7 May the last session of the Transvaal volksraad opened. Although the bayonets and sabres of the invaders glistened on the frontiers, this last session was begun with all the usual ceremony. Foreign consuls and attachés were there in uniforms or formal dress, and Kruger wore his white gloves and sash of office. Over the chair of the captured Cronjé the Vierkleur was draped, and over the chairs of Joubert, Kock, and other dead volksraad members hung strips of black crepe and wreaths of immortelles. The volksraad sat for three days without accomplishing much of importance except the confirmation of Botha as commandant-general.

If the Boers could not stop Roberts, they could and did harass him and slow him down. He had to halt for ten days at Kroonstad to attend to his supply situation, for he had always to be looking over his shoulder at his long, tenuous, vulnerable line of communication to Cape Town. On just the 128 miles of railway between Bloemfontein and Kroonstad the Boers had cut the line in seventeen places, blowing up bridges and culverts or tearing up track in 1,000-yard stretches.

While waiting at Kroonstad, Roberts sent Ian Hamilton to take Lindley. After a short skirmish Hamilton entered the town, but he did not stay long and the Boers at once reoccupied it. Lindley, named after an American preacher who had ministered to the spiritual wants of the voortrekkers, was a storm centre of Boer resistance in the Free State, and it was to change hands more than half a dozen times in the next few weeks.

On 22 May Roberts resumed his march northward. Two days later part of French's cavalry crossed the Vaal into the Transvaal, and on this day, the Queen's birthday, Roberts issued a proclamation annexing the Orange Free State and changing its name to Orange River Colony. Roberts now girded his loins for an attack on Johannesburg, where he expected to encounter stiff resistance. French was sent off to the west to find the Boer right flank, and Hamilton followed behind with his infantry. On 28 May French found the flank near Doornkop, within sight of the Rand's gold mines, and started to move around it. This drew off some of the Boers, and Hamilton launched his Gordon Highlanders in a gallant charge across open country at the Boer positions. At a cost of 9 officers and 84 men killed and wounded they carried the position and routed the enemy. A jubilant Hamilton congratulated them on the battlefield and assured them that within hours all Scotland would be cheering their exploit. The next day the ubiquitous Winston Churchill, who had transferred himself here from the inactive Natal front, rode over the battlefield:

> Near a clump of rocks eighteen Gordon Highlanders lay dead in a row. Their faces were covered with blankets, but their grey stockinged feet—for the boots had been removed—looked very pitiful. There they lay stiff and cold on the surface of the great Banket Reef. I knew how much more precious their lives had been to their countrymen than all the gold mines the lying foreigners say this war was fought to win. And yet, in view of the dead and the ground they lay on, neither I nor the officer who rode with me could control an emotion of illogical anger, and we scowled at the tall chimneys of the Rand.[5]

Johannesburg, the city of gold, was now at Roberts's feet. Although it was half deserted after the flight of the uitlanders, many of the foreigners had sought and received permission to stay, but *The Times History* said that "a large proportion of the normal inhabitants still left in Johannesburg were either very poor or very rascally." The only real excitement in the city since the beginning of the war had been on 24 April when Begbie's Foundary and Engineering Works, which had been making munitions for the Transvaal forces, blew up. The Boers thought this was a deliberate effort on the part of the British, but more probably it was simply the result of the workmen's carelessness.

For most of those remaining in "Joburg" it was business as usual. The *Standard and Diggers News* was still publishing, and its pages were filled with the usual advertisements: the Continental Restaurant offered lunch for three shillings and dinner for four shillings; W. Reuter, an attorney, was looking for a cook-housekeeper; R. H. Akers was seeking his lost greyhound, offering a reward for its return while adding a threat to anyone found keeping it. There were advertisements for "Mr. W. Goldstuck's valuable remedy for dysentery," "Victoria's brand bacon and hams," and a timely one from W. S. Duke & Co.:

THE GOLDEN THREAD CIGARETE [sic]
Draws wisdom from the lips of the philosopher and shuts up the mouth of the foolish. This is the kind of cigarette appreciated in such critical times.

The British were only a few miles away, but on 18 May the Alberti brothers' "Italian String Quartette's Best Band" gave a concert with mandolin, violin, flute, and harp; H. Simpson was still selling wedding rings; J. Gau was peddling insurance for the Manchester Assurance Company and the Mutual Life Insurance Company of New York; Doctors S. C. Smith and L. S. Rubinsohn were still operating the City Dental Institute ("Painless Extraction of Teeth a Specialty. Artificial Teeth Made while you wait. Teeth filled with Gold and other Material on the latest American systems"); and Miss A. Lindblom ("Specialist in all kinds of Massage and Midwifery") continued to ply her trade.

Knowing of the existence of the Johannesburg forts, which the Boers had constructed at great expense, Roberts had ordered huge siege guns brought out from England, and these, with their "armour-piercing, deferred-explosion" shells, had been carried over seas and land for 7,000 miles and were now at hand. They were not needed. The Johannesburg forts were not manned and the Boers had long since removed all their guns; the burghers preferred to trust to their mobility, and they had no intention of allowing themselves to be caught cooped up in forts. When Roberts had the town almost surrounded, he sent in a demand for its surrender. Dr. Fritz Krause, governor of the town, rode out with a member of the volksraad to talk with him about the situation. There were still some die-hard burghers in town, and Krause was afraid that if the British occupied it they would resist; there might be women and children killed —and even property destroyed. Roberts, worried about the safety of the as yet undamaged gold mines, made an extraordinary deal: Krause promised to hurry the commandos out of town and to protect the mines, while

Roberts agreed to delay his entry to allow the fighting burghers to escape.

On 31 May 1900 Roberts formally marched into a quiet Johannesburg where "the motley crowd of white foreigners and blacks gave little
appearance of animation."[6] But in the middle of a road off the main street
four old burghers knelt in prayer, asking God to forgive the sins of their
people and to restore their country to them. One patriarch with a white
beard, leaning on the shoulder of a friend, sobbed as if his heart had
broken.

Roberts felt that the taking of Johannesburg, the place where all the
uproar over the franchise and the rights of the uitlanders had originated,
was a milestone in the war, and he celebrated with a repetition of the
ceremony at Bloemfontein. The troops paraded, Lady Roberts's silk
Union Jack was raised over the courthouse, and there were the usual three
cheers for the Queen. The ceremony was witnessed by the troops and an
interested crowd of Bantu and European civilians, but Prevost Battersby
reported that "the entry of the troops into Johannesburg was no account
as a spectacle."[7] There was a brief scuffle when a uitlander, outraged by
a burgher who refused to take off his hat when the Union Jack was run
up, tried to snatch it off his head. One of the soldiers put a quick end to
it. "Leave him alone," he said. "He fought for his flag. You fight for
none."

England received the news of the capture of Johannesburg calmly
with none of the enthusiastic celebrations which had marked earlier victories. Many were more interested in the results of the Epsom races. Roberts's triumphal march towards Pretoria had been anticipated, his successes expected. It seemed clear to all that the war in South Africa was
nearly ended and that there was no longer any danger of a major setback.
There was much anxiety over the fate of the little garrison at Mafeking,
but for the rest the suspense was over, the drama gone; the remaining
steps to victory seemed well defined and public interest turned to other
wars in other places. The third war against the Ashantis was being fought
on the Gold Coast, and in China the Boxer Rebellion had broken out and
the fate of those in the European legations at Peking was more engrossing
than the bloodless capture of Johannesburg. But the Boers were still
capable of delivering surprises and shocks, and one jolt was delivered on
the very day Roberts marched into Johannesburg.

Following behind Roberts's main advance and sweeping the country
in wide swathes were other bodies of troops. One of these was Colvile's
division, which had been marching behind Ian Hamilton to support him
if need be. On 17 May Colvile was ordered to extend his lines across the
eastern Free State. On 22 May he marched out of Winburg towards
Ventersburg, where he was ordered to concentrate his forces and where
Kitchener told him he would be reinforced by the 13th Battalion of
Imperial Yeomanry. His orders also stated that he was to reach Lindley
on the 26th and Heilbron on the 29th. When the yeomanry failed to show
up on the 24th, he marched out of Ventersburg without them. He fought

a short battle near Lindley on the 26th and the next day continued his march north. Early on the morning of the 28th he received a message from the missing yeomanry:

Found no one in Lindley but Boers—have 500 men but only one day's food, have stopped three miles back on the Kroonstad road. I want help to get out without great loss.

—B. Spragge, Lieutenant-Colonel
27.5.1900

Colvile's first reaction was to lift his nose and ask, "And who is Colonel Spragge?" Even when told that he was the colonel of the yeomanry who were supposed to be under his command, he declined to turn back and rescue him; it was more important, he felt, to keep to his timetable. The 13th Yeomanry, surrounded by 2,000 burghers under Piet de Wet, surrendered after suffering 80 casualties.

The Times History said "this incident acquired a somewhat undue importance at the time." Yes indeed. There was an uproar in Britain, particularly when it was learned that one company of the 13th Yeomanry consisted of "men of gentle birth and wealth" who had bought their own equipment, paid their own way to South Africa, and donated their pay to the Widows and Orphans Fund. The man blamed for the disaster was Lieutenant General Sir Henry Colvile, and Roberts "awarded him a bowler"—he was relieved of his command and sent home.

Four days after the capture of the 13th Yeomanry Christiaan de Wet succeeded in sweeping up a small convoy of 56 wagons and 160 men carrying supplies to Colvile's column. These activities of the De Wet brothers were more than annoying to Roberts, particularly as they were taking place in his rear, but they did not slow his advance to Pretoria. He did not foresee—nor did anyone else at the time—that these isolated attacks by mobile commandos adumbrated the new style in which the war was to be carried on.

30

MAFEKING

Exactly two weeks before Roberts marched into Johannesburg and the 13th Imperial Yeomanry surrendered to Piet de Wet, an important event took place in the small town of Mafeking 160 miles due west of Pretoria.

It was not important strategically or because what took place there had any effect on the course of the war, but because Britons everywhere thought it was important. Roberts's march to Pretoria may have lacked suspense, but there was drama enough in the events surrounding the siege of Mafeking, or so it seemed, and the garrison commander, Colonel Robert Stephenson Smyth Baden-Powell, displayed exactly those qualities Britons of all classes delighted in. Brian Gardner called it "the most . . . jauntily withstood siege in modern history,"[1] and Baden-Powell set the tone with his first message to the outside world: "All well. Four hours bombardment. One dog killed." Britons everywhere had a good laugh; they were captivated. But as the siege dragged on to become the longest of the war, anxiety grew in spite of the plucky resolve expressed by Baden-Powell. When, then, word reached London that the tiny garrison, after withstanding a siege of 217 days, had at last been relieved, England went wild with joy. Londoners staged the greatest, most hysterical, spontaneous celebration ever seen in Britain. For years afterwards, "to Maffick" meant to celebrate uproariously.

Mafeking Night began in London when at 9:17 P.M. on 18 May the Reuters News Agency received a message from its correspondent in Pretoria saying that it had been officially announced by the Transvaal government that the Boers had abandoned the siege. Eighteen minutes later a footman at Mansion House ran out to post a placard: MAFEKING RELIEVED. As the news was shouted through the streets the excitement spread over the city. Squares and thoroughfares were rapidly filled with hysterically cheering, shouting, singing men, women, and children. The Lord Mayor appeared on the balcony to say: "I wish the music of your cheers could reach Mafeking. British pluck and valour, when used in the right cause, must triumph." But the crowds did not want speeches; they were in a mood for singing and exultation. Policemen rushed from their stations to control the crowds, but there was no controlling the mobs of deliriously joyous people. There was much hugging and indiscriminate kissing, and one constable said later: "I wouldn't go through that kissing again for something. Right in the public street it was."

At the Royalty Theatre Mrs. Patrick Campbell, whose husband had been killed six weeks earlier at Boshof, announced the news from the stage and led the audience in singing "Rule Britannia" and "God Save the Queen." At Covent Garden, where the Prince and Princess of Wales were watching a performance of *Lohengrin,* someone shouted, "Mafeking is relieved!" The audience got to its feet, cheered, and lustily sang "God Save the Queen" while the Prince beat time on the ledge of his box. It was, said *Punch,* "Best operatic chorus ever heard!"

Although people talked for years of Mafeking Night as if the celebrations stopped at daybreak, they actually went on sporadically for five days. One reporter called it the "most wonderful and harmless saturnalia of the century."[2] Generally good-humoured, in a few places the crowds turned rowdy, attacking the homes and shops of people thought to be pro-Boer.

The name that the crowds shouted in the street was not Mahon or
Plumer, the rescuers of Mafeking, but Baden-Powell, the town's plucky
defender. Mafeking's hero inspired a rash of musical compositions.
There was "Our Hero B-P," "The Baden-Powell Schottische," and
"Major-General British Pluck." Pictures of Baden-Powell, usually showing him wearing the felt campaign hat later to become familiar to millions
of Boy Scouts, appeared everywhere. He was an instant hero.

Scenes similar to those in London on Friday night took place in every
town in Britain. At Newcastle-Upon-Tyne the *Chronicle* sent up rockets;
at Bedford the factory sirens were sounded; in Glasgow all the church
bells were rung. Everywhere there were cheering, singing, flag-waving
crowds. The St. Pancras Orphan School at King's Langley in Hertford-
shire, in an astonishing burst of generosity, gave each of its 150 orphan
boys twopence to spend as he pleased. Seven-year-old William Wright
bought a farthing's worth of matches and firecrackers and joined the
celebrations. One of his firecrackers, thrown into a shop door on the high
street, set the store alight. Identified by one of the villagers as the culprit,
William celebrated the next day on the raised platform of the orphan
school, where he was given "six of the best" on his bare buttocks.

As the news reached Canada, Australia, New Zealand, and other parts
of the Empire there were scenes similar to those in Britain. In Montreal
and Melbourne salutes were fired and church bells rung; in Brisbane and
in New Zealand public holidays were announced; in the hills around
Wellington huge bonfires were lit; and in Singapore all business came to
a halt.

Four minutes after the news reached the London office of Reuters the
Associated Press in New York received the same message. Crowds hungry
for more details formed around newspaper offices, but Americans received the news more calmly. That very day President McKinley had met
with his cabinet in Washington to discuss the possibility of the United
States offering its good offices to the combatants, but the decision taken
had been "to hold absolutely aloof." Americans remained divided in their
sentiments.

Naturally the news was received somewhat differently in the Transvaal. The *Standard and Diggers News* reported the event in a matter-of-fact
way but devoted more space to the trial in New York of Olga Nethersole,
who had appeared in a play called *Sapho* which the police considered
indecent. It is pleasant to report that Miss Nethersole, who appeared in
court "attired in a robe of heliotrope silk, trimmed with mink fur and
lined with white silk satin," was acquitted.

The prologue to the drama at Mafeking and the wild celebration of
Mafeking Night may be said to have begun some three months before the
war started when the War Office decided to send a handful of "special
service officers" to South Africa to raise local regiments among the colonists. Colonel Baden-Powell (he pronounced his name to rhyme with

"maiden noël," but most people called him simply B-P) was taking lunch at the Naval and Military Club in London on Monday, 3 July 1899, when he was summoned by Lord Wolseley.

"I want you to go to South Africa," said Wolseley.

"Yes, sir."

"Well, can you arrange to go Saturday next?"

"No, sir."

"Why not?"

"There's no ship on Saturday, but I can go on Friday."

This account of the interview was told by B-P—many times—and it is typical of his theatrical sense.

He was born in 1857, the son of an Oxford geometry professor who sired fourteen children. Robert was the eighth child by his third wife, a woman who claimed to be a descendant of that Captain John Smith whom the beautiful Pocahontas saved from being clubbed to death by her friends and relations. Robert was educated at Charterhouse, where, although he did not do well in either studies or games, he distinguished himself in the school plays. Two of his brothers had done brilliantly at Oxford, but Robert, in spite of two attempts and the distinguished reputation of his father, failed to gain admission. He had not thought much about the army, but the tests were easier, he passed, and without any military education whatsoever he was gazetted straight to the 13th Hussars in India.

Baden-Powell had some military assets (he could ride and shoot), and he was able to enliven the dullness of garrison life with his sketches and caricatures (he was ambidextrous) and by his talent in amateur theatricals. He could play the piano, whistle, and sing, including comic songs sung in an hilarious falsetto. He was "as good a skirt dancer as ever 'brought down the house,' "[3] and he was said to be "the most inveterate practical joker in the British army."[4] He loved to dress up in costumes and disguises: George Younghusband encountered him at Simla disguised as an Italian count. *Punch* once referred to him as "Barnum Powell." *Black and White Budget* summed up his personality: "He is a delightfully breezy beggar is B-P."[5]

From India he sent home sketches which were published in *Graphic*, and he tried to make a name for himself by writing military manuals. When he sent home the manuscript for *Reconnaissance and Scouting* he wrote his brother: "Even if it did not sell twenty copies it would be a grand advertisement for me—because I could send copies to all the brass quartermaster-generals, Wolseleys, etc.,"[6] and he dedicated his *Manual of Cavalry* to the Duke of Connaught. It took him twenty years to reach the rank of major, but thereafter his rise was rapid. He saw service in Zululand, in the Ashanti campaign of 1895, and in the Matebele campaign of the following year. In 1897 he was promoted colonel and given command of the 5th Dragoon Guards.

His assignment in South Africa was to raise two regiments of mounted infantry in Bechuanaland and Rhodesia for the purpose of defending those colonies' frontiers. He took with him Major Lord Edward Cecil of the Grenadier Guards, the son of Lord Salisbury, and Lieutenant the Honourable Algernon Hanbury-Tracy of the Royal Horse Guards, a son of Lord Sudeley. Lady Edward Cecil accompanied her husband as far as Cape Town, leaving behind their four-year-old son George. In Cape Town, before making his way to Bulawayo, B-P found time to contribute to a charity bazaar a parody of Longfellow's poem "Psalm of Life," signing it "Wrongfellow."

Baden-Powell experienced some difficulty raising his two regiments, but he did manage it, for as Sir William Butler had said: "There is always in South Africa a floating population of loafers, mostly men who have made Europe too hot for them, who are ready to join any corps raised for them." Not all of the recruits were British and not all could ride—or at least many were unable to ride the half-broken horses provided them. It was while he was at Bulawayo that Baden-Powell acquired the services as his aide-de-camp of Captain Gordon Wilson, whose wife, Lady Sarah, née Churchill, was Winston's aunt. Lady Sarah was with her husband at Bulawayo, spending her time practicing first aid "on the lanky arms and legs of a little black boy."

It was not in the minds of anyone in London or Cape Town that Baden-Powell should make any preparations to defend Mafeking, which was not in either Bechuanaland or Rhodesia but over the border in Cape Colony and only 8 miles from the Transvaal frontier, but he began to use it as a base. The firm of Julius Weil & Company had ample storage space there, and Major Lord Edward Cecil, as Baden-Powell's chief of staff, opened negotiations with Mr. Benjamin Weil for enormous quantities of supplies. Anticipating war and difficulty in obtaining supplies after it had started, Cecil asked the government for £500,000. The request was refused. Cecil then turned to the Weil Company, offering his personal guarantee of payment, frankly telling Benjamin Weil: "I place this order with you without the authority of my superiors. I may have to pay for it myself, but I will take the responsibility on my own shoulders." And so he did, giving Messrs. Weil his personal note of hand for £500,000. As his wife later said: "It was very sporting and very shrewd of the Weils to take this risk; they must have known that he himself had not a tenth of this money. But they banked on Lord Edward's personality and his father's position, and the deal saved Mafeking."[7]

It was indeed a deal which saved Mafeking, and in doing so it made Baden-Powell a hero. One might imagine that B-P would have been grateful, but at the end of the siege, in a private letter accompanying his dispatch, he wrote: "Cecil did his best but was not much use."

As trains loaded with supplies poured into Mafeking and the Weil storehouses began to bulge, Baden-Powell asked for permission to put an armed guard there to protect his supplies. The size of the guard was not specified, so when permission was granted he put an entire regiment there, half of his total force, and moved to Mafeking himself, setting up headquarters quite comfortably in Dixon's Hotel and making preparations for the town's defence. He also took time to correct the proofs for his seventh book, *Aids to Scouting,* the first chapter of which was concerned with "pluck." This was a word much loved by the Victorians, and "plucky" was an adjective often applied to B-P. It seemed to strike the right note of casual bravery, to describe what all late Victorians most admired in men and what all the world imagined Baden-Powell to be.

Mafeking (the name is a Bantu word meaning "place of stones") was the most northerly town in Cape Colony. It was not much of a town really. Baden-Powell described it as "a very ordinary-looking place. . . . Just a small tin-roofed town of small houses plumped down upon the open veldt." The European section had been laid out by Sir Charles Warren in 1885 and by 1899 occupied roughly 1,000 square yards with two open spaces named Government Square and Market Square. The only two-storied building was the Sisters of Mercy Convent, inhabited by a Mother Superior and eight nuns. The European population consisted of 1,074 men, 229 women, and 405 children; about 200 of these people were Boers. There were some 7,500 Bantu, partly from the local Barolong boo Ratshidi tribe and partly families who had left the Rand area when the uitlanders fled and the mines closed, depriving them of employment.

There was never any doubt in anyone's mind that when hostilities began Mafeking would be attacked. It was isolated; although small, it was the second-largest town, after Kimberley, in northern Cape Colony; it was close to the Transvaal border; and it sat on the railway line that joined Rhodesia with Cape Colony. Aside from Baden-Powell and the handful of officers with him, there were no regular troops in the area. The total force for the defence of the town consisted of the newly raised Protectorate Regiment (469 men), the Bechuanaland Rifles (82 men), the Town Guard (302 men), some police, a railway detachment, and a "Cape Boy Contingent"—in all, about 1,200 men. Less than half were armed with magazine-load rifles; the rest were equipped with Martini-Henry single-loaders. In addition, Baden-Powell armed about 300 Bantu with obsolete firearms to act as cattle guards. At the start of the siege the only British artillery consisted of four muzzle-loading 7-pounders, a 1-pounder Hotchkiss, and a 2-inch Nordenfeldt; there were also seven Maxim machine guns and two armoured locomotives. With this meagre force B-P began planning to defend the town for what was expected to be a siege of at most six weeks.

A number of proclamations were issued. One suggested that since the town would almost certainly be shelled, women and children should leave while the railway was still in operation. Another gave notice that mines were being laid, adding that small red flags would mark their locations "in order to avoid accidents." Most curious of all was one that read:

Notice
SPIES

There are in town to-day nine known spies. They are hereby warned to leave before 12 noon to-morrow or they will be apprehended.

By order
E. H. Cecil, Major
C.S.O.

Mafeking
7th October 1899

On 13 October the Boers tore up the railway track and cut the telegraph lines. Mafeking was isolated, although not surrounded, and the siege of the town began. Estimates of the size of the Boer forces around Mafeking varied widely, but at the most it was probably not more than six or seven thousand, and most of the time considerably less. Brian Gardner did an amusing comparison of the various figures Baden-Powell himself gave for the number of enemies he faced.[8] For example, October 1899: 5–6,000; May, 1900: 8,000; 1907: up to 9,000; 1933: 10,000; 1937: 12,000.

On 14 October the British attacked a Boer contravallation and lost 2 killed and 16 wounded—B-P called it a "smartly fought little engagement," claiming in his official report 55 Boers killed and more than that number wounded. The Boers reported 3 casualties. British stretcher-bearers were fired on as they worked after the battle, and the next day Baden-Powell sent a letter of complaint to Piet Cronjé; Cronjé dispatched a Boer doctor to deliver a personal apology: young men who did not understand the significance of the red cross flag had fired the shots and had been reprimanded. The doctor was given lunch and sent back with a bottle of whiskey for Cronjé.

The following day the Boers bombarded the town, but no one was hurt. Many of the European inhabitants had already prepared dugouts. After the bombardment Cronjé sent in a demand for an unconditional surrender. It was carried by an Englishman named Everitt who was fighting on the Boer side; he, like the doctor, was treated with elaborate courtesy, given lunch at Dixon's Hotel, a few drinks, and a polite refusal to take back with him.

Mafeking was never completely invested. Hardly a week went by without a Bantu messenger passing through the lines carrying a "Kaffir-gram," as the messages were called. The system of runners and dispatch riders was organized by the enterprising Benjamin Weil. It was Weil too who provided interpreters, artillery spotters, and frequent and generous gifts from his stocks. The siege, though long, was not ferocious and there was seldom much action. B-P never pretended otherwise in the frequent messages he sent out. It was the British public who filled in a background of hardships and danger, choosing to see heroism in B-P's cheery jauntiness.

On the night of 27 October 53 men of the Protectorate Regiment, led by Captain Charles Fitzclarence, made a successful bayonet raid on a Boer trench. Baden-Powell reported Boer losses as one hundred; *The Times History* said three. British losses were six killed, nine wounded, and two missing. Fitzclarence, on Baden-Powell's recommendation, was given the Victoria Cross for his night's work. It was unfortunate that the trench so ferociously attacked had been mostly held by young boys. J. Emerson Neilly of the *Pall Mall Gazette,* one of a number of correspondents in Mafeking, wrote: "It is not too much to the taste of your soldier to bayonet a lad of thirteen or fourteen; but if any shame attaches to the killing of the youngsters, it must rest on the shoulders of those fathers who brought them there."[9]

On 31 October the Boers launched a small-scale attack on one point of the perimeter. Losses were light on both sides. That the Boers never made an all-out attack on the town can be explained not only by their temperamental reluctance to undertake offensive operations but also by the orders from Kruger, who had rightly seen that Mafeking was of no military importance—the primary Boer objective on the western front was Kimberley—and had told Cronjé that if it would cost more than fifty casualties to take the town the attempt should not be made.

After another night raid by the British on 7 November there were, except for some shelling, seven weeks of quiet. The Boers, ignorant of the vast quantities of stores and supplies Cecil and Weil had piled up, expected the British to run out of food and capitulate; the British thought the Boers' patience would run out and they would leave. In lieu of bullets, the antagonists exchanged messages.

A recurring complaint of Baden-Powell's was that the Boers shelled the convent, which had been converted into a hospital. Cronjé countercharged that the British stationed artillery near the convent. Although an article in the Mafeking *Mail* (9 November 1899) denied this, the unpublished diary of Mother Mary Stanislaus confirms that there were indeed guns near the convent, and Lady Sarah saw a Maxim there. Officers who knew about the guns later claimed implausibly that they had been put there to protect the convent.

At Mafeking, as elsewhere, the Boers did not, unless forced to, fight on Sundays. Guy Fawkes' Day fell on a Sunday in 1899, and B-P, who planned to celebrate it with the traditional fireworks, sent an explanation of this peculiar holiday to Cronjé, telling him "not to be alarmed."

For the British Sundays at Mafeking, as at Kimberley and Ladysmith, were a time for sports, entertainments, washing clothes, paying visits—almost every activity, in fact, except fighting and attending church. Solomon Tshekisho Plaatje* (1877–1932), the only black African to leave a

---

*A remarkable young man who, as he spoke Afrikaans and English as well as several Bantu languages, served as an interpreter in Mafeking. He also knew how to type. After the war he became a Lutheran lay preacher, editor of an English-Setswana weekly newspaper, and in 1912 the first general corresponding secretary of the South African Native National

diary of his experiences during the war, noted that the "gymkhana meetings and merryments" on Sundays were "strong counter-attractions to Divine Services": "These surely must be one of the causes of the deadliness of the Dutch weapons now. I had entered my pony for a run in next Sunday's races . . . but I had decided to withdraw him today lest I be guilty of blatant sacrilege and thereby further imperil my already dangerous condition."[10]

The British, not sharing Plaatje's sense of sin, looked forward eagerly to their Sundays. J. Angus Hamilton, correspondent for *The Times* and *Black and White Budget,* wrote: "We drink, we accept one another's invitations to meals of surpassing heaviness; we even invite ourselves to one another's houses. We eat, we drink, we flirt, we live in every second of the hours which constitute Sunday."[11] Sometimes on Sundays Boers and Britons met to chat and the Boers would exchange newspapers for whiskey.

No one enjoyed Sundays more than the garrison's commander. B-P energetically organized sports events and a wide variety of entertainments. On Sunday mornings the band played, and on Sunday evenings there were concerts, plays, and sketches in which B-P took a prominent part: he recited, played the mouth organ and the piano (once imitating Paderewski by putting a mop on his head), sang songs (some of his own composition), and acted parts. He also arranged for agricultural, art, and horticultural exhibitions and organized teas, dances, and a baby show. There were complaints of the tedium of the siege, of course, but in general the people in Mafeking complained less about their boredom than did the inhabitants of Ladysmith and Kimberley. There is, perhaps, much to be said for having as commander of a besieged town an energetic buffoon.

After sitting around Mafeking for five weeks Cronjé moved off with most of his commandos, leaving only about 2,000 men (B-P said 4,000) under Assistant Commandant-General J. P. Snyman to continue the siege. The Boers engaged in no further offensive operations. Most of the burghers were from the western Transvaal, their farms were not far away, so their wives and children visited them; to many it seemed "little else than a pleasant picnic." No attempt was made to encircle the town completely, and the British messenger service improved. Private citizens posted personal letters, and even small packages were received from the outside world. Sometimes the Boers themselves passed on messages, as when in November through their courtesy Lord Edward Cecil was told of the death of his mother.

The adventures of Winston Churchill's Aunt Sarah enlivened the scene. She had gone with her husband to Mafeking when Baden-Powell

Congress. His novel, *Mhudi,* written in English, was the first by a South African Bantu; he also made many translations from English into Setswana. His diary of the siege was not discovered until 1969.

ENGLISH ARTILLERYMEN BRINGING UP A GUN NEAR COLENSO WERE
SCATTERED BY A BOER SHELL.

moved there, staying at Benjamin Weil's house by the railway station and
taking her meals at Dixon's Hotel, where, she said, "the food was weird."
Just before the siege began she left the town and established herself in
a tiny settlement 75 miles away on the edge of the Kalahari Desert. This
proved much too dull, and she began to roam the countryside. Although
by this time the area was controlled by the Boers, she encountered little
difficulty. Stopped once by a Boer patrol and asked for her pass, she
flourished her British passport and was waved on. All might have gone
well for her if a Reuters correspondent she met in her wanderings had
not presented her with a pigeon. It was the pigeon, that "idiotic bird,"
that undid her.

The Reuters man assured her that the bird would carry a message to
Mafeking, and Lady Sarah, delighted, dashed off a note to B-P offering
to collect intelligence for him. The note was attached and the bird
released. It circled uncertainly a few times and then headed straight for
Snyman's headquarters, a farmhouse about 40 miles away. It was sighted
there perched on the roof and shot; the message was read and Lady Sarah
was taken into custody. She was indignant. No one had any right to hold
her, she told Snyman, and she insisted that she be permitted to go to
Mafeking. Snyman said he would consider the matter.

Spies, of course, could be shot, but Lady Sarah could not be so simply
dealt with. Snyman offered to exchange her for Petrus Viljoen, a Boer
then in the Mafeking jail serving a sentence for horse stealing. Baden-

Powell refused. Her captors politely suggested that she would find "pleasant ladies' society" in Pretoria and offered to send her there, but Lady Sarah bristled: "I remarked that I had no intention of visiting their capital . . . I would not for an instant admit they had any right to detain me or to send me to any place against my will." "I could see," she said later, "they were taking a cowardly advantage of me because I was a woman."[12]

For several days Snyman and B-P negotiated without getting anywhere. On 4 December Snyman telegraphed to Kruger, explaining the situation and asking plaintively, "What shall I now do with Lady Sarah Wilson? Please answer speedily."[13] Meanwhile, Lady Sarah was making herself disagreeable, as she herself admitted: "In fact, I was on every occasion so importunate that I am quite sure the General's Staff only prayed for the moment that I should depart." Alternating demands that she be released with complaints about her accommodations, she raised a storm in the laager. She was quartered in the hospital, and she objected to the couch she slept on and the people she was forced to associate with; in particular she objected to a woman doctor, the first she had ever seen. A female physician, and a badly dressed one at that, was a phenomenon Lady Sarah did not approve of, and to hear her addressed as "doctor" was insupportable. She hammered incessantly on poor Snyman, showering him with letters when she could not see him to speak her mind, and by 6 December she had reduced him to begging the state secretary: "Please, please send me at once your decision concerning Lady Sarah Wilson. She is unwilling to stay here any longer."[14]

The negotiations dragged on and B-P fidgeted. He had Cecil at his side pressing him to make the exchange and warning how bad it would look to permit an Englishwoman to remain a Boer prisoner, especially an Englishwoman of Lady Sarah's rank, but on the other hand he was afraid of trouble from the authorities if he released a convicted horse thief. He tried offering another burgher, but Snyman, as much as he wanted to rid himself of Lady Sarah, would have Viljoen or no one.

So things might have remained, and Lady Sarah might have spent a few weeks longer sleeping on her detested couch, had not Cecil put an end to the impasse by offering to shoulder the entire responsibility for the exchange himself. Greatly relieved, B-P declared a truce, and on 7 December, a mile outside of town, the horse thief was traded for the lady. B-P and Cecil were on hand to welcome Lady Sarah. Her husband seems to have been elsewhere.

Cecil's own wife, the beautiful Lady Violet, twenty-eight years old, was meanwhile keeping busy in Cape Town, where she was living at Rhodes's house and seeing a great deal of Milner, her future second husband. "I do not know how I have got through this time. I should not have but for Milner, I think," she told her mother. When news of the relief of Mafeking reached her, she went to bed with a sick headache.

Safe in Mafeking, Lady Sarah was not idle; she ordered the construction of a bomb-proof shelter, the finest in town. There were, in fact, few rooms even above ground in dusty little Mafeking that could compare with it, for it measured a generous 18 by 15 by 8 feet and boasted white painted panelling among other amenities. Lady Sarah celebrated its completion with a dinner party for the senior officers of the garrison. She became correspondent for the *Daily Mail,* and she helped with the nursing of the convalescents in the convent. A few weeks after her arrival she was wounded—well, bruised—by an exploding Boer shell.

As at Ladysmith and Kimberley, guns were given names. One Boer Creusot was known as "Creaky," or sometimes "Big Ben"; another was named "Gentle Annie." The British had a 6-inch gun they had made themselves which they called "the Wolf"; it could fire an 18-pound shell about 4,000 yards. And another local gun, "Lord Nelson" or "Skipping Sally," was a real curiosity: it was a smooth-bore, muzzle-loading naval gun that fired round balls. It had been constructed in 1770 and at some time in the nineteenth century had been presented to Montsioa, chief of the Barolongs. For the past twenty years it had been buried in the ground, but now the Barolongs dug it up and gave it back to the British. The initials of its manufacturer were stamped on it, and they seemed most apposite: "B.P. and Co." Powder bags for this antique were stitched together by a group of women, including the Sisters of Mercy nuns.

In Mafeking as in the other besieged towns the British were struck by the curious regularity of the Boer shelling, and Emerson Neilly, of the *Pall Mall Gazette,* went so far as to report that some people "timed their watches by the fire."[15]

At first the Boers experienced some difficulty with their shells; not all of them exploded. But at Mafeking there was at least one deliberate dud. Opened, it was found to contain a note:

Mr. Baden-Powell—Please excuse me for sending this iron message i have no other to send at present. He is rather exentric but forgive him if he does not behave well. I wish to ask you not to let your men drink all the whisky as i wish to have a drink when we all come to see you. Cindly tell Mrs Dunkley that her mother and vamily are all quite well. I remain, Yours trewly, A Republican.[16]

The next morning B-P dispatched a bottle of whiskey in care of Snyman for the thirsty republican. Snyman investigated and discovered that the note sender was a burgher named C. H. Perrin. He reported the incident to Kruger by telegraph, adding: "What must I do? I had him court-martialed. He said he meant no harm."[17]

Thanks to their dugouts, there were few casualties among the Europeans from the Boer shells—only four white civilians were killed during the entire siege, not counting E. G. Parslow, correspondent for the *Daily Chronicle,* who was murdered by an officer of the garrison. Among the civilians wounded was the town's special constable; a shell "fractured his private parts in a most pitiful manner."[18] The Bantu, however, did not make shelters for themselves and none were made for them; 329 were killed. They also suffered from the neglect, or at least the indifference, of the white men. Vere Stent, the Reuters correspondent, claimed that at least one doctor did not use anesthetics when he operated on Bantu patients.

The Barolong tribe, which was native to the area, had cattle and gardens of their own, but the Bantu who had come from the Rand had no food and no money to buy any. They killed and ate dogs, and when they could and when they dared they stole. The penalty for theft was death, and five Bantu were executed during the siege, one for stealing a goat.

Such stern measures might have been excusable had there been a shortage of food, but although stocks of certain items ran out, there was plenty of food in town. Even after one hundred days of siege Weil still had 2,450 pounds of sardines, 10,488 pounds of boiled mutton, and vast quantities of corned beef and other tinned foods. Beef was issued to Europeans throughout the siege; rations of horse meat were supplied only during the last two months, and then only three days a week. There was a large quantity of rice, which might have been used to feed the Bantu but was not. Eventually "a foul-smelling horse-meat factory" was established southwest of town and a soup kitchen was organised to supply them with horse meat stew mixed with oat husks, but there was a charge of threepence and most could not pay. For the Europeans rationing did not begin until the sixth week of the siege, and even then the allowance was liberal: one pound per day each of meat, bread, and vegetables, plus milk, eggs, and poultry; a wide variety of luxury foods was available at Weil's store.

At Christmas the Boers also wanted to celebrate in peace, and so a truce was arranged. There were, though, eight shots fired accidentally by a British soldier showing a young woman a machine gun. The British formally apologised. The Christmas menu offered by Mr. G. Riesle, proprietor of the Mafeking Hotel, included anchovy croûtons, olives, oyster patties, tongue, ham, veal, beef, lamb, suckling pig, mutton, bacon, potatoes, peas, mince pies, puddings, and jellies. B-P and his staff were given a turkey dinner in Lady Sarah's dugout.

C. G. H. Bell complained that he was bothered all Christmas Day by Bantu who leaned against his garden wall hitting their bellies and complaining of their hunger. "These people will soon be a source of anxiety to us," he wrote that night.

Conditions among the Bantu worsened as the siege dragged on. Emerson Neilly wrote a pathetic account of their plight: "I saw them fall down on the veldt and lie where they had fallen, too weak to go on their way. The sufferers were mostly little boys—mere infants ranging in age from four or five upwards."[19]

Plaatje, whose job as an interpreter provided him with money to buy food, wrote in his diary: "It is really pitiful to see. . . . Last month one died in the Civil Commissioner's yard. It was a miserable scene to be surrounded by about 50 hungry beings, agitating the engagement of your pity and see one of them succumb to his agonies and fall backwards with a dead thud."[20]

Although Plaatje accepted the sufferings of his countrymen as a siege necessity, some of the newsmen were roused to indignation. Angus Hamilton wrote: "There can be no doubt that the drastic principles of economy which Colonel Baden-Powell has been practicing in these later days are opposed to and altogether at variance with the dignity and liberalism which we profess."[21]

The Bantu, it was reasoned, were free to leave the town whenever they chose, so it was wasteful to give them food. Unfortunately, there was no place for them to go, except to the Boers, who did not want them either.

The problem was partially solved when Lieutenant Colonel Herbert Plumer established a depot some 60 miles from the town for their reception. Plumer, in command of the second regiment Baden-Powell had raised, had been skillfully doing the work on the frontier that B-P had been sent to South Africa to do and with his small force had been successfully operating along the Transvaal-Rhodesian border. Eventually about 1,200 Bantu were persuaded to leave Mafeking and make their way to him.

The Bantu were encouraged to steal from the Boers, and a number of those armed as "cattle guards" went out on armed expeditions to raid the Boer cattle herds. They frequently exchanged shots with the owners, and a Barolong named Mathakgong was said to have killed many Boers, including women and children, on farms he raided. Most of the cattle taken were used to feed the Europeans, and on 16 February the Mafeking *Mail* gave thanks to Mathakgong for the "succulent, juicy undercut" that appeared on "certain breakfast tables." In arming the Bantu Baden-Powell aroused the intense indignation of the Boers; Snyman frequently protested, and John E. Dyer, an American doctor with the Boers, wrote to B-P:

> You have committed an enormous act, the wickedness of which is certain, and the end of which no man can foresee. . . . It has hitherto been a cardinal in South African ethics, both English and Dutch, to view with horror the idea of arming black against white, and I would ask you . . . to disarm your blacks and thereby act the part of a white man in a white man's war.[22]

Curiously, Baden-Powell was not criticised by his compatriots, either in South Africa or in Britain.

The day after Christmas B-P launched an attack with 260 men on a Boer position called Game Tree Fort. It was a badly managed affair. Baden-Powell, the advocate of scouting, had failed to have the Boer position properly scouted, and the British suffered 50 casualties, of whom 24 were killed or mortally wounded. After the battle the Boers, who had lost 3 men, fell to and helped the British carry off the dead and wounded, Angus Hamilton was struck by the sudden change: "People who had been pitted against each other in mortal combat the moment before were now fraternizing with every outward sign of decency and amity." Baden-Powell wrote Snyman: "This kind action is much appreciated by the comrades of the fallen men."[23]

This was not the only time Boer and Briton came together in amity. Later in the siege, when in places the lines were quite close, James Barnes reported this exchange:

"Hey! I say, one of you Boers stand up and I'll take a photograph of you."

"Have you got a camera?"

"Yes."

"On your honour?"

"Yes."

"You won't shoot me if I stand up, upon your word?"

"No, we won't shoot."

"Pass it down the line."

The word was passed, and a young Boer, about twenty-three, stood up, buttoning his jacket. He was well over 6 feet tall.

"How will you have it?"

"Turn it a little more sideways. There."

The camera clicked.

"Thanks."

"Send me a picture."[24]

For a few moments afterwards all was quiet. Then an English soldier lifted his hat on a stick and a bullet went through it. "War is a strange thing to understand at times," said Barnes.

There were a few desertions from the British forces. One, Trooper E. J. Hays, was believed to be directing the Boer artillery. "I shouldn't care to be Hays after the war," wrote F. D. Baillie for the *Morning Post*, "as there is £50 on his head, and the Boers are hard up." In general, however, the morale of the besieged held up remarkably well, and on the 200th day B-P reported to Roberts:

I desire to bring to your Lordship's notice the exceptionally good spirit of loyalty that pervades all classes of the garrison. The patience of everybody in Mafeking in making the best of things under the long strain of anxiety, hardships, and privation, is beyond all praise, and is a revelation to me. The men . . . have adapted themselves to their duties with the greatest zeal, readiness, and pluck, and the devotion of the women is remarkable.[25]

When currency ran short B-P personally designed some notes to "be exchanged for coin at the Mafeking Branch of the Standard Bank on the resumption of Civil Law." Postage stamps, too, were scarce, and special ones were made. On the three-penny stamps the head of the Queen was replaced by that of Baden-Powell. Later criticised for this, he claimed that the stamps had been printed without his knowledge, that he did not know of their existence until they were printed. But in a letter to his mother he spoke with delight of the new stamps with his head on them. The one-penny stamps carried a picture of a boy "cadet," representative of a group of boys who had been dressed in khaki and trained to act as orderlies and carry messages. Although B-P took the credit for forming the "Cadet Corps," which became the inspiration for the Boy Scouts, it was Lord Edward Cecil who conceived the idea, and it was he who drilled them, trained them, and organized games for them.

On 23 April 1900, when the siege had been in progress for more than six months, a board of officers took stock of the food still available and found that there remained meat for ninety days and breadstuffs (oat and meal) for fifty-two days, and that there was still a good supply of whiskey, brandy, and wine. The amount laid in had been so ample that Baden-Powell (who neither drank nor smoked) once closed down all the bars in town for a week because there was so much drunkenness.

Roberts had been determined that his main thrust through the Orange Free State and the Transvaal would not be diverted or his main force reduced by sending off columns to conduct sideshows. But Mafeking was very much in the public eye, and there were political pressures for its relief. At last Roberts, perhaps with a weary sigh, arranged for a force to go relieve the place. A battery of Canadian artillery which had landed at Cape Town on 26 March was reembarked less than three weeks later and sent up to Beira in Mozambique, where 100 men of the Queensland Mounted Infantry joined them. From there by rail, mule, and horse this little force made its way to Plumer in western Rhodesia, reaching him on 14 May.

Meanwhile a flying column was being assembled under Colonel Bryan Mahon at Barclay West, some 20 miles northwest of Kimberley. Roberts carefully arranged that when this force was joined by Plumer's it would include troops from all corners of the Empire: Australia, Canada, New Zealand, Natal, and Cape Colony were represented, as well as 25 selected men each from English, Irish, Scottish, and Welsh regiments. On the morning of 4 May Mahon's force, 1,149 strong, rode out of Barclay West and the Empire was off to the rescue of Mafeking.

It had been a long but reasonably quiet siege, and B-P, aware that the eyes of the world were upon him, had gone whistling about his duties. He loved to whistle. "He warbled operatic airs and music hall ditties from morning to night," said Neilly. The besieged in Mafeking had faith in their plucky, dapper, ever-whistling, fun-loving commander. But, as Neilly said later: "Frankly our defender's pluck did not save Mafeking, great and heroic though that pluck was. The cowardice of the enemy saved us." It was less cowardice than lassitude that affected the Boers, but this attitude was shaken by the arrival of Commandant Sarel Johannes Eloff, an impetuous twenty-eight-year-old grandson of Kruger. Eloff wanted to take Mafeking before the relief force arrived.

As soon as the moon came up on the night of 11 May Eloff led 300 men, many of them foreign volunteers, quietly down the bed of the Molopo River. They slipped past two British outposts and emerged in the Bantu section of town. There they set fire to several huts as a signal to Snyman that the defences had been pierced and that they were inside the town. Of course, this signal also told the British garrison the same thing. Eloff siezed a barracks and captured Colonel C. O. Hore, commanding officer of the Protectorate Regiment, three other officers, and eighteen men. Angus Hamilton wandered over to see what was happening and was also captured. The prisoners were locked in a storage room, where they opened some cases of whiskey and wine and sat down philosophically to wait things out.

According to the Boer plan, Snyman was to follow up Eloff's success with a major attack. Eloff now waited for it to begin. While waiting, his men replied to the British musketry and found ways to amuse themselves in the barracks they held: ex-trooper Hays, the traitor, buckled on his former commanding officer's sword; Comte de Frémont, a foreign volunteer, played French songs on a piano in the officers' mess; another Frenchman took a bottle of wine onto the roof and, while shouting taunts at the British, unwisely stood up and was shot in the abdomen.

The major attack failed; Snyman's men made no more than a few half-hearted attempts to get through. Many of Eloff's men, with the Boer instinct for self-preservation when threatened with entrapment, made their way out of the British lines and back to their laagers. One by one the groups of Boers and foreigners who remained inside the perimeter were rounded up and forced to surrender. Finally only Eloff and 73 men were left in the surrounded barracks. At six o'clock in the evening Eloff gave up. The burghers and foreign volunteers were marched to the jail; Eloff was taken to Baden-Powell, who shook his hand and said breezily: "Good evening, Commandant, won't you come in and have some dinner?"

The next day Baden-Powell sent Snyman a letter giving him the results of the fight, concluding with: "I should like to record my admiration for the gallant way in which your burghers fought yesterday." Kruger was properly indignant when he heard of Snyman's failure to support Eloff and asked if Snyman had been drunk. F. D. Baillie in his account of the attack for the *Morning Post* said, "It gave a pleasant finish to the siege. It wanted just a finishing touch to make it satisfactory."

The Boers were watching the progress of Mahon's column, and on 12 May, not far north of Vryburg, they attacked it. Mahon drove them off, and three days later he joined Plumer with his 800 men 18 miles west of Mafeking. There was no further opposition, the besiegers withdrew, and finally, at seven o'clock on the evening of 16 May 1900, Major Karri Davies with a patrol of ten men of the Imperial Light Horse rode into Mafeking carrying a box of the Queen's chocolate for Baden-Powell. Davies was astonished by the lack of enthusiasm on the part of the first people he encountered. One man to whom he identified himself said, "Oh, yes, I heard you were knocking about."

The next day, when the main body of the relief force marched in and paraded with the garrison, an appropriate amount of enthusiasm was displayed. Neilly was perhaps somewhat carried away when he wrote: "I did not think it was possible for human joy to reach such a white-hot pitch."[26] The relief force was surprised to see how healthy and hearty were the besieged, at least the Europeans; only the Bantu looked emaciated. Many of those in the flying column, certainly those who had been pounding along the border with Plumer, had experienced a more exhausting seven months than had the garrison of Mafeking. The besieged town was able to supply Plumer and his men with luxuries they had not seen in months.

The defenders of Mafeking soon learned what heroes they were to the Empire. Thousands of letters and telegrams poured into the town. The Queen herself sent a message of congratulations, and Baden-Powell was rewarded by being made a major general; at forty-three he was the youngest general officer in the British army. Lady Sarah Wilson was awarded the Royal Red Cross.

The sieges of Kimberley, Ladysmith, and Mafeking, avidly followed while they were in progress, widely celebrated when they were raised, have been given their place in history. Rarely mentioned, however, is the siege of Schweizer Reneke, a small town in the western Transvaal which was invested on 19 August 1900 and was not relieved until 9 January 1901. No one remembers the name of George Chamier, the garrison's commander. The gallant defenders of Schweizer Reneke had the misfortune to be besieged at a time when the people at home were bored with sieges; they had had enough; besides, there were no newspaper correspondents there. And the British public, which exhausted itself cheering for plucky B-P and the relief of Mafeking, raised not a single cheer for the relief of Schweizer Reneke.

31

PRETORIA

The sideshow of Mafeking over, attention again focussed on the two principal arenas of the war: the central Transvaal where Roberts was poised for his assault on Pretoria, and the area around Ladysmith where

Buller, finally, at long last, began to move. Although one of his excuses for remaining inactive had been that he did not have enough mounted men, he left two regiments of cavalry sitting in Ladysmith. On 14 May, thanks to the energy of Dundonald and the poor generalship of Lucas Meyer, the Biggarsberg was forced. Two days later Dundee and Glencoe were occupied and on the 18th, Newcastle. Buller then advanced cautiously on the Drakensberg. He did not move far, but at least he was in motion. Roberts, never one to dally, moved quickly out of Johannesburg; leaving a garrison of 3,000 men there, he marched out with the bulk of his force on Sunday, 3 June 1900, to cover the remaining 40 miles to Pretoria.

On that same warm and bright winter Sunday James F. J. Archibald attended church in Pretoria:

In many a pew there was no father or brother, but only a sad-faced woman in sombre black. . . . There was not one in the whole church who was not weeping. Near me sat a young girl of twenty, who sobbed aloud during the entire service, as if her heart was broken beyond all comfort; and I afterwards learned that her father and four brothers were all dead, and that her one remaining brother was at St. Helena with Cronjé. In the pew in front of me sat an old grizzled burgher with a heavy gray beard; he needed no rifle to show that he had been for months on commando, for his face was burned by wind and sun. His arm was around his wife, whose head rested on his shoulder. She did not weep, but at frequent intervals she huddled closer to him and grasped his arm more firmly, as if afraid he would leave her. On his other side sat a little girl, who looked around with big, frightened eyes, wondering at the scene.[1]

That Sunday evening Deneys Reitz and his brother Hjalmar rode into the Pretoria suburb of Sunnyside and found their house there deserted. They knocked on the doors of several neighbors before a shrinking figure finally opened a door a crack and told them that their father, along with Kruger and the rest of the government, had fled. The door was then shut in their faces. The young men returned home, broke into their own house, built a fire, and for the first time in weeks slept in a real bed. "It was nevertheless a dismal homecoming," said Deneys.

It was a sad and bitter time for the Boers. Since their retreat from the Modder and the Tugela there had been few victories to raise the hearts of the burghers. Jan Smuts summed up the situation and the feelings of his countrymen:

It was everlasting retreat; retreat—wearying, dispiriting retreat. At every stage of the retreat the Boer cause became more hopeless, the Boer army smaller in numbers, and the Boer resources more exhausted. Pretoria—that holy of holies of the Republic of South Africa—was generally expected to mark a decisive stage of the war; to the British commanders the expected final stand at Pretoria and its capture seemed to be the *coup de grâce* to the Republics; to the Boer rank and file it appeared in advance as the great Armageddon where the Boer force, concentrated from all points of the compass in defence of their central stronghold, would deliver the final united blow from which perhaps the British forces might be sent reeling back to the coast. Perhaps and perhaps not; at any rate the action there would be decisive and thousands of burghers stuck to their commandos in the course of this disastrous retreat simply because they believed that the decisive battle would be fought at Pretoria, and at that battle they were determined to be present.[2]

But this was not to be. On 29 May the Transvaal Executive Committee had met and decided that their capital could not be saved and that the government should be moved to Middelburg. The gold and the state archives were loaded on a train that night. Archibald was a witness:

> Even cabs had been pressed into the service of transferring the treasure of the State from the mint to the train. Bars of the precious metal were thrown out of the cabs on wagons like so much rubbish.
>
> There was bustle and activity, but no noise and no excitement. . . .
>
> It was an extraordinary sight, under the glare of the electric lights, to see this train being loaded with all that was left of the capital of the Republic. It was done decently and rapidly.[3]

President Kruger, somewhat deaf and suffering from an eye disease, was now almost at the nadir of his career. When it was decided to abandon Pretoria to the British, he boarded a train and turned his back on his capital, his home, and his ailing wife. He was never to see any of them again. This was certainly the saddest day of his life, but before he left Pretoria, in the midst of all the turmoil, the packing, the sad farewells, the anxiety and the worry, the old man took a few minutes to see a young boy who had come a very long way.

In the drawing room of Kruger's Presidency was a large carved and painted eagle, a present from American admirers. In this room Kruger was introduced to James Francis Smith, a handsome fifteen-year-old messenger boy from New York. The American District Telegraph Company had sent him all the way to South Africa to deliver two packages to the president: one was a long scroll bound up in heavy silk containing a memorial signed by 15,000 schoolboys in New York, 10,000 in Philadelphia, and 4,000 in Boston; the second item was a specially made leather case containing cuttings from the Philadelphia *North American,* the newspaper which had promoted this scheme. Kruger, his mind on more important matters, was puzzled by these curious gifts, but he courteously thanked young Smith before hurrying off.

With the departure of the government Pretoria turned into a place of confusion and unrest. The Reverend Henry James Batts, the English Baptist minister who had been allowed to remain, said: "Such a medley and riot has never before been seen in the streets of Pretoria. . . . The confusion that prevailed was indescribable; nobody seemed to have power really to act."[4]

Deneys and Hjalmar Reitz, riding through the streets after their cheerless night at home, found them "swarming with leaderless men, knowing less of the situation than ourselves. . . . All was utter confusion

. . . and a great deal of criticism of our leaders."[5] The roads were filled with horses, oxen, carts, and wagons, with agitated and anxious men and women, European and Bantu. Rumours flew about. There was talk of defending the town and rifles were passed out. The government warehouses were broken open, and there was a mad scramble as people fought to get into them and then struggled to make off with their booty in carts, wheelbarrows, children's wagons, and even baby carriages. One large woman stood guard at a door and with her umbrella beat the heads of all Bantu who tried to enter. There were some who honestly believed that the government had given permission for the looting, but this was not so. Young Jan Smuts, the state attorney, had been left in charge, but his authority was challenged by other politicians, and he struggled unsuccessfully to maintain order. When through the town the weary dispirited burghers passed in retreat there was no one to cheer them. "They found scarcely anything to eat," said Smuts bitterly, "and thousands passed with sad hearts and empty stomachs through the ungrateful capital."[6] Captain Reichmann wrote in his report: "The Boers were demoralized and absolutely worn out. Patriotism was still alive there, but the enthusiasm had burnt out, and the Boers were not held together with the cement of discipline which makes a formidable unit of so many harmless individuals and which holds men to their work in adversity."[7]

In an attempt to shore up their crumbling spirits, Louis Botha rode into town and made a speech in front of the Raadzaal, reminding his listeners that the Americans had once surrendered their capital to the British but had still triumphed. Kruger sent a telegram, which was read aloud, adjuring them to fight on in the name of the Lord. Thus goaded, some made brave talk of making a stand, but when Lieutenant W. W. R. Watson rode into town under a white flag and demanded Pretoria's unconditional surrender, it was given up without a shot being fired. Botha sadly said good-bye to his wife Annie, heaved himself into the saddle, and rode off behind his retreating burghers. Pretoria, capital of the Transvaal, lay at Lord Roberts's feet.

Unlike Bloemfontein, Pretoria was a pretty little city with a population of 12,000; almost everyone who saw it was charmed by its appearance. Churchill described it as "a picturesque little town with red or blue roofs peeping out among masses of trees, and here and there an occasional spire or factory chimney."[8] Even Milner, seeing it a few weeks after its capture, had to admit that "Pretoria is a lovely little spot," but, he told Lady Edward Cecil, it was "ruined by the most *horrible* vulgarities of the 10th rate continental villadom—German architecture of the Bismarckian era at its worst."[9] Prevost Battersby's aesthetic sense was also affronted: "Alike in its squalor and its pretentiousness, the place is damned with the dregs of style. It is daubed with the decaying decoration of the Greek and the Goth, and plastered with every fatuity of a false Renaissance."[10]

Beautiful or ugly, Pretoria represented Afrikaner civilisation on the veld. The houses were widely separated and a number of them were quite large, some having been built by wealthy uitlanders. As in Johannesburg, it was business as usual in spite of the war. Tilanus and Van Griethuysen sold champagne, whiskeys, brandies, and imported wines; C. Christopulo ran the American Candy Factory; and at Keinton House Restaurant, which prided itself on its "French kitchen," one could sit down to dinner at the "best table in town" for five shillings. Hot and dusty farmers could come to the baths in Vermeulen Street and have a warm tub, a shower, or a swim in "as fine a bath as any in South Africa." Still, the wide streets were unpaved, dusty in dry weather and seas of mud when it rained.

In the centre of town was Church Square, dominated by the Raadzaal and the Dutch Reformed Church where Kruger had often preached. It was an imposing structure but in no way a handsome one. On Church Street, the principal thoroughfare, was the modest house of President Kruger. It was here on 29 May that Kruger had said good-bye to his dying wife, leaving her to the care of their daughter (Mrs. F. C. Eloff), who lived next door, and to the British. Further down Church Street, west, near the race course, was the house of Captain J. W. "Koos" Bosman of the staatsartillerie. He was still with the fighting burghers, but his beautiful Scots wife Eva, née Turnbull, and his three small daughters were still there. Unlike the loyal inhabitants of Bloemfontein, the citizens of Pretoria did not flee. Indeed, there now seemed no place for them to go. The wives of Botha, Lucas Meyer, Jan Smuts, and other Boer leaders remained in town.

Among the first soldiers to enter Pretoria were Winston Churchill and his cousin, the young Duke of Marlborough, who early in the morning on 5 June raced ahead of the troops to free the imprisoned officers. The Model School was no longer used as a prison. Richard Harding Davis, the American war correspondent, in an article for *Scribners* said it was because some of the officers had made rude remarks to women passing by, but more probably overcrowding and the need for tighter security prompted the move. Churchill and Marlborough were directed to a barbed wire enclosure on the edge of town. The prisoners called it "the bird cage."

Here more than 100 officers were housed in a long shed with a corrugated zinc roof, the interior decorated with pictures cut from illustrated British magazines of the Queen, Lord Roberts, and celebrated actresses. Living conditions were not as pleasant as they had been at the Model School, but books and magazines were allowed and the prisoners hectographed a little newspaper called the *Gram* which was edited by Lord Roslyn and "kopje-righted." British interests in the Transvaal had been looked after by Adalbert S. Hay, the American consul general, and John Coolidge, the vice-consul. Hay had taken an interest in the welfare of the prisoners, both officers and men, and he had represented their grievances to the Transvaal government.

When Churchill and Marlborough rounded a corner and saw the "bird cage," Churchill took off his hat and gave a cheer which was echoed by the prisoners who came tumbling out of their barracks into the enclosure. Marlborough found the commandant and demanded the surrender of the prison. The gate was opened, the guards were made prisoners, and Lieutenant Cecil Grimshaw of the Dublin Fusiliers produced a Union Jack he had made. It was hoisted in place of the Transvaal Vierkleur; the time, as Churchill carefully noted, was 8:47 A.M.

Early in the afternoon Roberts made a triumphal entry with his army: 25,531 officers and men, 6,971 horses, 116 guns, and 76 machine guns. Lord Roberts and his staff sat their horses in Church Square to review the troops. The released British officers lined the streets. As the troops came marching down Church Street the three little Bosman girls raced out to climb on their garden gate and watch them. Julie Hennie, the eldest (then about eight years old) remembered the awesome sight:

> The road leading from the west in the main street (Church Street) leading to the square was full from side to side, probably the other main streets were just as full because they numbered thousands. Silent, with music at intervals, one could almost not realize they were humans. I could hear my own young voice singing, "Jesus Loves Me" where I sat on the gate. . . .[11]

One of her sisters called out: "Where is our daddy?" A Highlander stopped before them, held out a penny to Julie Hennie, and patted the head of three-year-old Bessie, the youngest. "What a bonnie lassie," he said.

The troops were tired, grimy, and footsore, but they felt that at last they had reached their final destination, the end of a very long road. Johanna (called Hansie) van Warmelo, an attractive twenty-two-year-old Boer girl, watched them. She had two brothers on commando and a third was a prisoner of war. Defiantly she wore a Vierkleur ribbon around her hat. At one rest halt a weary soldier sank down and groaned, "Thank God the war is over." Hansie leaned over and hissed at him: "Tommy Atkins, the war has just begun!"

The soldier looked up at her, sighed, and closed his eyes.

"I do not like you," one girl said to a trooper while patting his horse. "You have come to take away my country."

"Bless you, miss," he said cheerfully, "we've come to give it yer."

In Church Square the Union Jack which had been made by Lady Roberts and flown over Bloemfontein and Johannesburg was raised by the Duke of Westminster, an officer on Roberts's staff. The Reverend Batts watched the ceremony with emotion: "I saw a big Australian mop his eyes at the moment and I felt a lump in my throat."[12] Roberts gave Westminster an envelope addressed "To the officer who hoists the Union Jack (when that happy event takes place), Pretoria, South Africa." Inside was a cigar and a note from a Mr. W. H. Knowles: "Thanks! Have a cigar!" Lady Roberts's flag, having been ceremoniously raised, was then taken down and replaced with another Union Jack, 12 feet long: this one had been made by three women living near Cape Town who had given it to Roberts with the request that it fly over the capital of the Transvaal.

The Reverend Batts noted the delight with which the Bantu greeted the conquering British and that they "for a few days showed a disposition to be troublesome . . . because they thought all the old laws as they affected them were suspended, and they could take liberties which were not allowed under Boer rule." They were soon disillusioned, and "it was rather a surprise to them to discover that there was no alteration whatever in their conditions."[13]

The day after his entry into Pretoria Roberts sent a brigade to free the rank-and-file prisoners. Originally the British other ranks had been held at the race course, where Jameson's men had also been confined, but after a few months they had been moved into an enclosure prepared for them about 12 miles outside of town. Sergeant W. J. Wade of the 2nd Devonshire Regiment, who had been captured during the fighting on the Tugela, wrote home from there:

> I daresay you know I have been taken prisoner, and am in Pretoria, where I am safe till the end of the war; so you need not be in any way about me, as I shall have no more fighting to do, and they are treating us very well indeed. We are not confined in Pretoria but in an enclosure fenced round with wire, with long rows of iron sheds. . . . How thankful I shall be to get home. . . . I have had only two letters since we left England.[14]

Later, when enteric broke out, one contemporary British historian, H. W. Wilson, had bitter words to say about conditions: "It was Andersonville, with all its nameless horrors, over again, and without the faintest shadow of excuse. Meanwhile the Boer prisoners in the hands of the British were living in plenty and comfort at St. Helena."[15] Wilson exaggerated. The St. Helena camps were not really that grand, nor was the Transvaal camp that bad.

With the approach of Roberts's army the Boers had made an effort to move their prisoners away, but they had managed to evacuate only about 1,000; there were still 3,000 left in the camp. To prevent the rescue of these De la Rey had taken up positions nearby with 2,000 men and four guns. As the British brigade moved out of Pretoria towards the prison camp, accompanied by a train to carry back the men they hoped to free, a squadron of the 2nd Dragoons (Scots Greys) trotted ahead, driving in a Boer outpost. When the dragoons came in sight of the prison enclosure an extraordinary event took place.

The prisoners knew that Roberts had taken Pretoria and they were in a state of high excitement as they waited impatiently to be delivered. Their guards, about 300 old men and young boys, were nervous, frightened, and uncertain. When prisoners posted on the roof of their barracks saw the dragoons trot into view they raised a cheer, and at once the men below turned into an excited mob. Snatching up their belongings, they pushed past their bewildered guards, climbed the fences, and surged across the veld. De la Rey saw them and fired a few warning shells, but he did not, as he easily could have done, advance and mow them down. Perhaps, as the British believed, De la Rey assumed there was a cloud of cavalry behind the dragoons; perhaps, as the Boers believed, he was too humane to butcher the unarmed jubilant men. In any event, the prisoners streamed away towards the waiting train with their bundles under their arms, and the British suffered only one casualty.

While Roberts was enjoying his triumph in Pretoria many of the disheartened Boer leaders, mostly Transvaalers, were meeting in a whiskey distillery only a few miles away. Neither Steyn nor De Wet was present. Botha had called them together to discuss their next step, and there were some who thought it might have to be surrender.

Even before Roberts crossed the Vaal and entered the Transvaal Kruger had begun to have doubts concerning the wisdom of continuing the war. He had discussed the situation with his close friend Samuel Marks (1850–1920), a Russian Jew who had come to South Africa as a young man and had amassed a fortune. Marks suggested that the Boers lay down their arms "under protest," avoiding the hated word "surrender." Kruger had laid this suggestion before Steyn, who indignantly rejected it, reminding Kruger of the rebels from Cape Colony whom they had urged to join them and who in the event of defeat faced the possibility of being shot as traitors. They had a responsibility to these men, Steyn insisted. When, two weeks later, with Roberts about to capture his capital, Kruger again sounded out Steyn about making peace, he received a blistering reply:

1st June 3 A.M. I have received your telegram with amazement. . . . Only a small part of the Transvaal is in the hands of the enemy; nearly all our land lies under his heel. Fourteen days ago I made plain my opinion to Your Honour, and now Your Honour comes with the same proposal again. My policy remains unchanged. We must fight to the bitter end.[16]

Still, the facts were plain: Buller had begun to stir in the east and Roberts was marching steadily north; there was no Boer army large enough to bar the way of either; further resistance could not bring victory. The war could not be won. This was evident to most of those who answered Botha's call and assembled at the whiskey distillery on Sammy Mark's model farm. Botha opened the meeting with a prayer, and then they all spoke their minds. Gloom hung over them. Smuts was later to recall their mood:

I shall never forget the bitter humiliation and despondency of that awful moment when the stoutest hearts and strongest wills in the Transvaal army were, albeit but for a moment, to sink beneath the tide of our misfortune. What we all felt so deeply was that the fight had gone out of the Boers, that the heroes who had stood like a stone wall on the Tugela and the Modder River, who had stormed Spion Kop and Ladysmith and many other forlorn hopes had lost heart and hope, had gone home and forsaken their officers. It was not Lord Roberts's army that they feared, it was the utter collapse of the Boer rank and file which staggered these great officers.[17]

There was talk of surrender even from Botha, and De la Rey, listening, grew so angry that, like the belligerent voortrekkers of old, he threatened to go off and found his own republic. In the end it was decided to postpone the inevitable a bit longer, to wait a few days. Perhaps a miracle would happen. Meanwhile, it would be best to find out what terms Roberts would give them.

It is not clear whether it was Marks's manager or Annie Botha who first made it known to Roberts that the Boer leaders wanted to discuss peace, but it was Annie Botha certainly who acted as intermediary. When she proposed a meeting Roberts quickly agreed and suggested that it be held the following morning. Mrs. Botha took the message to her husband, but the meeting did not take place, for just at this crucial juncture word was received of De Wet's successes at Sanna's Post and Mostert's Hoek. Though they were not major victories, they were good enough to send the hopes of the Boers soaring and they provided excuse enough to fight on. The conduct of the war was placed entirely in the hands of Louis Botha. There were to be no more krygsraads, and Botha determined to attack Roberts.

There were at this time probably not more than 20,000 Boers still in the field, and they were widely scattered. The largest concentration was a force of about 7,000 under Botha and De la Rey which had taken up strong positions 15 miles from Pretoria astride the railway that ran from Pretoria to Delagoa Bay.

Roberts's army was camped in and around Pretoria, which was to remain until the end of the war the headquarters for the army. Here, as at Bloemfontein, there was enteric, but medical arrangements were much improved; there were no further complaints of inadequate facilities or lack of medical personnel. Dr. James Kay visited three of the hospitals in the area and said: "No critic, however captious, could find fault with these three hospitals." The Welsh hospital even boasted a French chef from the Hotel Cecil.

Except for the soldiers, the town was largely inhabited by the wives and children of men who were British prisoners, fugitives, or on commando. And some women were widows now, and some children orphans. Gezina Kruger, the president's wife, was allowed to remain in the Presidency, a guard of honour posted at her door, until on 20 July she died of pneumonia. Boer women helped nurse the soldiers in the hospitals, and relations between Annie Botha and the British officers were cordial indeed: she even sang for them at a party, and once Roberts lent her a military band for a garden party she gave.

Still, there was no lack of martial spirit on the part of most women. It was forbidden to fly the Vierkleur or to display its colours, but many defiantly sported ribbons of red, white, blue, and green. Lord Roberts, out riding one day, spied Helen Botha, the commandant-general's young and pretty daughter, with a Vierkleur ribbon around her hat. He stopped and asked why she was wearing it. To honour her father and to show her admiration for his cause, she said. "Good show," said Roberts, and rode on.

James Archibald noted that "the women of Pretoria were intensely bitter against the British, and did not scruple to show it." Many of the men who broke their oath of neutrality and took up arms again did so to escape the taunts of their women. One woman had a half dozen tiny branding irons made in the shape of a cross; with these she wanted the foreheads of traitors branded. Major George Younghusband wrote: "The Boer women hated us with a pure and unalloyed, albeit carefully concealed hatred."

In May, just before Roberts's arrival in Pretoria, an attempt had been made by some of the younger women to form an Amazon Corps. Several of them wearing riding skirts had their photographs taken with rifles in their hands, but the scheme went no further. Still, if women could not ride and fight beside their men, there were other ways in which they could be useful. Dr. Kay wrote in his diary: "The Boer women are so bitter that they would be willing to run any risk to assist their people. . . . That Pretoria is full of active spies and zealous over-sympathisers with the enemy is beyond dispute and yet no steps are taken against them."[18]

There was indeed a good bit of amateur spying done by the women. J. J. Naude, a twenty-two-year-old Boer, made frequent visits to Johannesburg and Pretoria disguised as a British officer in order to bring out the information they had collected. Jan Smuts's wife Isie rolled up secret documents and stuffed them in hollow curtain rods. Both Hansie van Warmelo and her mother busily wrote messages with lemon juice and sent them out concealed in match boxes, behind picture frames, in tins of insect powder, and once even in dolls. They also sent letters to pro-Boer newspapers in England.

Young Hansie van Warmelo sometimes found her position difficult. Her brother, who had been a student in Holland before the war, had been captured by the British and was in a prisoner-of-war camp in Johannesburg. Hansie had no trouble obtaining passes to visit him from General John Maxwell, the military governor of Pretoria. Maxwell was uniformly courteous and kind and did many favours for the Van Warmelo women. Hansie once rebelled against her role and returned from British headquarters determined never to go again. "The English must not be so good to us!" she told her mother. "It is not right to accept favours at their hands, for it places us in a false position."[19]

When caught, women spies were treated leniently: Miss Maggie Joubert, an attractive Afrikaner girl in Cape Town, was sentenced to only six months in prison for sending secret messages to her cousin in Pretoria. Of course spying women were not confined to the cities; women on farms gave such help as they could to local commandos.

Roberts was well aware that the Boers were kept informed of his strength and his movements. While at Bloemfontein he had written to Landsdowne: "We are all working at great disadvantage owing to the enemy knowing exactly what we are doing from day to day, where our troops are, what their strength is, in fact, everything about us, while we are in great doubt, and at times in total ignorance of their plans and movements."[20]

At last Roberts decided that he could at least rid himself of one segment of his problem, and he wrote to Botha telling him that he intended to ship all the women whose husbands were still fighting into the Boer lines. In a letter dated 4 September 1900 Botha replied: "The pretext mentioned by you, viz., that by such action you wish to protect yourself against any information being brought over to us, is doubtless a delusion. . . . It is unnecessary to add that we have never received any information through women and children with regard to military operations."[21] That this was not true, everyone knew, but Botha wanted the women and children no more than did Roberts, for with them on his hands his mobility would be disastrously impaired. Roberts did indeed send thousands of women and children to the Boers, thus marking the beginning of that phase of the conflict in which the women and children were to be the war's chief losers.

Women do not seem to have taken any part in the terrorist plots that were hatched in Johannesburg and Pretoria. Indeed these were mostly the schemes of foreigners. The first plot was uncovered only two months after Roberts entered Pretoria. The plan was to set fire to several houses and in the confusion to kidnap Lord Roberts and kill several senior officers. Thanks to an American informer, fifteen men, all foreigners, were arrested. The ringleader (or at least the man against whom the evidence was strongest) was a twenty-three-year-old German, Hans Cordua. Tried and convicted by a court-martial, he was shot by a firing squad in the garden of the Pretoria gaol. The other plotters were deported. Cordua was the first man to be executed by either side, although as the war grew increasingly nasty executions became a regular feature.

In addition to the spying and the plots there was also sabotage, or so the British believed. In July Roberts expelled a number of pro-Boer foreigners, including most of the Hollanders who were key employees of the railway, for they refused to work for the British.

Roberts's problems were increased by the inadequacies of his staff. He was not alone in his failure to understand how to select, organise, and use a staff. There was perhaps no British general who did. When Buller arrived in South Africa his designated chief of staff was shut up in Ladysmith; he never bothered to replace him. In spite of the heavy price paid fifty years earlier during the Crimean War for having the most complex and unworkable arrangements imaginable for supplying an army with its needs, the British staff system was still primitive. At the highest level there was no general staff, and generals in the field had staffs no better than and little different from that employed by Wellington a hundred years before.

There were about seventy officers on Roberts's staff. Some were quite capable men whom he had known in India and Afghanistan, while others were "pleasant aristocrats" such as the dukes of Norfolk, Westminister, and Marlborough. Something might have been made of this collection of officers had there been a proper staff system, but there was almost none. Kitchener was technically chief of staff, but he never functioned as such, even when he was at Roberts's headquarters. Roberts habitually transmitted his orders through the person nearest to him at the time, a secretary, a deputy assistant adjutant general, or an aide-de-camp. It was only due to Roberts's good memory and his constant attention to detail, as well as the presence of a number of conscientious and able officers with some initiative, that the headquarters of the army in South Africa was able to function as well as it did, but there was considerable confusion.

At one time it was discovered that for nine days no one had been in charge of the vital railway line from Bloemfontein to the front. Roberts had ordered Colonel Rainford Hannay to be placed in command, reporting direct to army headquarters, but Hannay, unknown to Roberts or his staff, was in hospital.

Worst of all the staff operations was the handling of intelligence. The British army in general had a low opinion of intelligence activities. As Captain (later Field Marshal) E. R. Robertson said, "The intelligence branch was treated as a separate, not very important part of the War Office organization." Colonel Henderson, who had gone out with Roberts to be his intelligence officer, was taken ill at Bloemfontein and invalided home. His successor, Lieutenant Colonel C. V. Hume, had served in a similar capacity in Burma, but he did not know South Africa. Nevertheless Hume was conscientious and intelligent, and in July 1900 he made a number of wise recommendations for putting intelligence gathering on a sounder, more effective basis, urging that all columns, regardless of their size, should have an intelligence officer assigned to them, that intelligence gathering should be coordinated, and that the army should have a counterespionage unit. His ideas seemed too radical at the time, although eventually most of the proposals were adopted. Eighteen months later there were 132 intelligence officers; not many, but more than the British army had ever had in its long history. None, however, had received any training in his duties. Even when a rough intelligence department was organised and began to pass on useful information, it was largely ignored.

One newly arrived officer was told by his commander how simple staff work was: "The right pocket will be a receptacle for 'business' telegrams, the left one for 'bunkum.' " "It is superfluous," the officer recorded, "to mention that the whole of the messages sent by the local Intelligence Departments were dismissed as 'bunkum.' "

Lack of adequate knowledge of the dispositions and strength of the enemy was to plague the British to the end of the war, and their failure to organise a sophisticated intelligence system enabled the Boers to make frequent unexpected strikes on the long lines of communication. One such strike took place just two days after Roberts's occupation of Pretoria.

32

AFTER PRETORIA:
ROODEWAL AND BRANDWATER BASIN

On 6 June 1900 De Wet divided his force into three parts for a three-pronged attack on the railway line about 30 miles northeast of Kroonstad: at Vredefort, Rhenoster River, and Roodewal. The next day all three forces struck simultaneously. The northern column, 300 men and a Krupp gun under Commandant Lucas Steenekamp, overwhelmed the small garrison at Vredefort but then became engaged in a running fight with British reinforcements under Major Douglas Haig that came hurrying up by rail. The largest force, under the command of C. C. Froneman, launched an attack on positions held by seven companies of the 4th Derbyshires at Rhenoster River.

The 4th Battalion of the Derbyshire Regiment was a militia unit. The militia, unlike the yeomanry, was composed of men from the working classes who possessed few useful military assets and were ill-trained. In this war they were largely employed in guarding the lines of communication, and the 4th Derbyshires guarding the railway bridge on the Rhenoster River were destined to be the only militia unit of any size to be seriously engaged in the course of the war. Miners and farm labourers for the most part, they had been in South Africa only four months, and, as Conan Doyle said, they "had never seen more bloodshed than a cut finger in their lives." Then, without warning, at dawn on the winter morning of 7 July the shells of Froneman's four field guns fell upon them and a pompom scattered its 1-pound shells in their midst. Raw as they were, they put up a gallant fight, but by ten o'clock in the morning, having lost 36 killed and 104 wounded, they surrendered. Froneman then destroyed the bridge which the Royal Engineers had just finished repairing.

De Wet himself led the attack on Roodewal Station (today, Rooiwal) just 2 miles away. This was his main objective, for there the British had piled up immense quantities of stores. Informed that the force guarding these riches was a small one, he took with him only one Krupp gun and 80 burghers. The force at Roodewal Station was indeed weak—a company of the Railway Pioneer Regiment and one weak company of the 4th Derbyshires, altogether about 150 men—but it was not as small as he had expected. His message demanding surrender was returned with a cryptic "We refuse to surrender" scrawled on the back, and the fire of his one Krupp and his Mausers had little effect, for the soldiers had excellent cover along the railway embankment and behind hastily thrown-up barricades of the boxes and bales of the stores.

Not until he was reinforced by two of Froneman's guns, ordered up as soon as he heard the firing cease at Rhenoster River, did the British seek terms. They tried to negotiate, offering to surrender if they could retain their personal possessions and the mail bags, but although De Wet willingly agreed to the first, he insisted that the mail bags were his. These terms they were forced to accept.

Once the prisoners were collected and disarmed, the burghers were caught up in an orgy of looting. The captured stores, valued at £100,000 (some said £250,000), included vast quantities of ammunition of all calibres, boxes of boots, bales of blankets and winter clothing (including 12,000 "coats, British warm"), and a treasure trove of other items. "You could have found there practically anything from an anchor to a needle," said Commandant C. A. van Niekerk. The burghers fell upon the 1,500 mail bags, dumping out the contents, tearing open the packages of food, cigarettes, stockings, and underclothing. Letters and goods were soon scattered everywhere. The contagion spread; two of the prisoners asked if they too could open mail bags, and De Wet told them to go ahead. "It was a very amusing sight to see the soldiers thus robbing their own mail!" said De Wet. "They had such a large choice that they soon became too dainty to consider even a plum pudding worth looking at."[1]

De Wet was anxious to get away before the British could catch up with him, but first he wanted to preserve some of the captured ammunition by hiding it nearby. He had the greatest difficulty getting his men to help:

I did succeed, however, in dragging a few of the burghers away from the post-bags, but the spirit of loot was upon them, and I was almost powerless. Even when I induced a burgher to work, he was off to the post-bags again the instant my back was turned, and I had to go and hunt him up, or else find some other man to do the work.[2]

Some 600 cases were hidden, and with these he had to be content. At sundown he marched his men away. The burghers had so loaded their horses with loot that they had to walk beside them; the prisoners too trudged along with their arms filled with the booty from their own army. When they were clear of the station De Wet sent fifteen men back to set fire to all that was left. The conflagration lit up the sky, exploding shells providing De Wet with "the most beautiful display of fireworks that I have ever seen."

De Wet was, quite naturally, pleased with himself. At small cost—he claimed a loss of only one killed and four wounded—he had demolished a bridge and cut the railway in three places (completely rupturing Roberts's communications with Bloemfontein and all his other bases of supply); he had captured 800 prisoners and destroyed vast quantities of supplies and ammunition. "It was a wonderful day for us," he said. "A day not easily forgotten." It was certainly not forgotten by the lucky burghers who had taken part in the affair. Philip Pienaar saw De Wet shortly after: "It was interesting to see his entire band in complete khaki, with only the flapping, loose-hanging felt hats to show their nationality. Wristlets, watches, spy-glasses, chocolate, cigarettes, were now as common as in ordinary times they were rare."[3]

Mail has always been sacred to the British; the deliberate destruction of all those letters and packages seemed, as Conan Doyle said, "unsportsmanlike." Colonel W. H. Mackinnon of the CIV damned it as "a most uncivilized act." Prevost Battersby called it "a most stupid and uncivil action." To Churchill it seemed "a poor and spiteful thing to burn up soldiers' letters, nor can I see how this can benefit the cause of his campaign," but later he noted that the destruction of the mail "has caused, and is causing, intense annoyance and distress throughout the army, and perhaps some dissatisfaction at home."[4]

Letters from the looted mail sacks blew about the veld near Roodewal for weeks and, curiosity about other people's mail being universal, many were read. Unable to resist temptation, the British felt excuses were necessary: Battersby was careful to explain that he "read for information and not from curiosity," and Conan Doyle quoted from a letter he "could not help observing." De Wet had no such qualms and read the letters with obvious relish: "I never realized how many love-sick women there were in Britain," he said.

H. S. Gaskell arrived with his unit at Roodewal shortly after the raid and described the scene there:

It was indeed a sorry spectacle. . . . The station buildings were knocked down in all directions, the line torn up, and the whole veldt for literally acres was strewn ankle deep, with burnt clothing, destroyed ammunition, and parcels that might have been gladdening the hearts of poor Tommy further up the line. About a ton or more lay about the place wasted and destroyed out of pure cussedness by brother Boer.[5]

Gaskell and his friends began to poke about: "We didn't fare so badly. Several men in rummaging about managed to get hold of lumps of tobacco only a little burnt around the edges, and many more got illustrated papers, etc. I secured a Sketch, and a very respectable thick serge jacket, only a little burnt in places. . . ."[6]

De Wet later had some interesting reflections on the raid:

Undoubtedly Lord Roberts would be very angry with me; but I consoled myself with the thought that his anger would soon blow over. . . . He should have kept his supplies at Kroonstad, or better still, at Bloemfontein, until he had reconstructed all the railway bridges which we had blown up on the line to Pretoria. Lord Roberts had already begun to trust the Free Staters too much; and he had forgotten that . . . never for a single moment had we thought of surrendering our country.[7]

But perhaps De Wet himself placed too much confidence in his countrymen. Three days after the raid a field cornet and twenty men deserted. One of the prisoners, Captain Wyndham White of the 4th Derbyshires, gave them passes which allowed them to turn in their rifles and return to their farms. De Wet was enraged. It was, he said, "an event which filled me with disgust."

Even important officers were on the point of defecting, including De Wet's own brother, Piet. De Wet opened negotiations with the British, offering to surrender with the Bethlehem commando if he were allowed to return to his farm, an offer that was rejected at this time, for on 15 May Roberts had decreed that while he was quite willing to allow ordinary burghers to lay down their arms and go home, Boer leaders must be made prisoners of war. Buller meanwhile was negotiating with another Boer general, Christiaan Botha, brother of the Transvaal commandant-general, but nothing came of these negotiations either.

On 8 June Buller advanced and captured Botha's Pass; three days later he occupied Alleman's Nek. He was in the rear of the Boer positions at Laing's Nek, but failed to realise the strategic effect of his victories, to see that his advance made the Boer positions untenable. He thought he would have to attack and made plans to do so, but the Boers, quick to realise their plight, evacuated their positions. Buller, surprised, now marched with ease into the Transvaal.

Roberts, alarmed about his severed supply line and by the loss of such large quantities of stores and supplies, sent Kitchener, the trouble-shooter, south with Smith-Dorrien's brigade and ten guns to put things in order along the railway and to protect Kroonstad, which Christiaan de Wet now threatened. But De Wet, who had remained west of the railway for several days, doubled back and crossed it near the point where he had mopped up the Derbyshire militia. In the process he attacked a construction train which was trying to repair the damage he had done earlier. Froneman ordered his men to attack a second train brought to a halt by the fighting, but they balked and thus lost a great prize: Kitchener was aboard.

In addition to sending off troops to protect his exposed railway line, Roberts resorted to schemes which had been used by the Germans in their war with France thirty years earlier: he ordered that farms near any place where the railway was cut or from which attacks were made on British troops were to be burned and the owners taken into custody; hostages were also to be taken and forcibly carried on military trains, a practice which created such an uproar in Britain that it was hastily abandoned.

The wide-ranging commandos in his rear were disturbing, but Roberts's primary concern was the concentration of Boers under Botha now entrenched in strong positions on a long range of kopjes about 16 miles east of Pretoria. This force guarded the last remaining stretch of railway left to the Boers: the line that ran east to Middelburg, to Machadodorp —where the Transvaal government was attempting to carry on its business from offices in railway carriages—thence down off the high veld to Komatipoort on the Mozambique border, and on through Portuguese territory to Lourenço Marques on Delagoa Bay. It was the free Boers' only link to the outside world, the only way by which supplies from abroad could reach them, and the only route by which they could escape.

On 11 June Roberts marched out of Pretoria with 14,000 men, 70 guns, and some pompoms to engage a force of 6,000 men and 23 guns under Botha and De la Rey. They fought all that day and the next around and near Diamond Hill. By the night of the 12th the two armies appeared to be stalemated. The following day the British again attacked, but over empty ground; the Boers had packed up and stolen away. When the CIV advanced they found only a young boy of thirteen or fourteen, shot through the head but still alive; with him was his father, who had refused to leave his son.

Although Ian Hamilton maintained that the battle of Diamond Hill was "the true turning point of the South African campaign"[8] because it

A GALLANT TROOPER RESCUES A DISMOUNTED COMRADE JUST IN THE
NICK OF TIME.

proved that, "humanly speaking, Pretoria could not be retaken,"[9] not much was accomplished and it was not a ferocious battle. Boer morale was shaky, and the burghers, as always, were careful not to lose too many lives, while Roberts in his orders to subordinate commanders stressed that they were to take no action that would result in heavy losses. In terms of dead and wounded, this cautious two-day battle resulted in only 200 casualties for the British. The Boers said they lost only 4 killed and 20 wounded; whatever their true losses, they were not high. As usual, although driven from the field, they were not defeated.

It was in this action that the aristocratic and gallant Lord Airlie, commanding the 12th Lancers, was killed just after leading his men in a boot-to-boot charge. *The Times History* recorded that his last words were an order: "Troops, right about wheel!" Churchill reported the order as "Files about!" but according to Conan Doyle his last words were addressed to a cursing sergeant: "Pray moderate your language."

There was other fighting in other places, particularly around Lindley, and on 11 July there were three attacks by De la Rey's commandos on British forces, all within 35 miles of Pretoria, but the most significant action occurred in the eastern Free State in an area called the Brandwater Basin, a huge horseshoe-shaped arena formed by the Wittebergen and Roodebergen mountain ranges and described by Erskine Childers as "an immense amphitheatre of rich, undulating pasture land, with a white farmhouse here and there, half hidden in the trees. Beyond rose tier upon tier of hills, ending on the sky-line in snow-clad mountain peaks."[10] It was into this beautiful country on the Basutoland border that the bulk of the Free State fighting forces, about 9,000 men, were chivied by relentless columns of British troops under the command of General Archibald Hunter. De Wet was here, and so were President Steyn and his cabinet.

In the mountains surrounding the Brandwater Basin there are only four passes and a few smaller, difficult means of egress. The Boers had fled into this area as to a safe refuge, for they felt that they could defend the passes and keep the British at bay. Among the more credulous burghers it was believed that they had only to hold out until after the American elections, when they would be relieved by an American army, but many began to have doubts as to whether this sacrifice of their mobility for safety was really wise. Hunter was concentrating his forces around Bethlehem; if he blocked the passes they would be trapped. Steyn called a krygsraad to discuss the situation, and it was decided to break out of the basin and to do it by dividing the army into three parts which would leave separately.

On 5 July Hunter moved to close the passes. That same evening De Wet, carrying Steyn and his government officials with him, left the basin with 2,600 men, 5 guns, and 400 wagons. This column, 5,000 yards long on the march, passed undetected within a mile of a sleeping British camp and escaped.

Back in the Brandwater Basin De Wet had left General Paul Roux in

charge. He was to have led the bulk of the Free State army out on the
following day while the Wittebergen burghers under Marthinus Prinsloo
held the passes. No sooner had De Wet left, however, than quarrelling
broke out among the leaders. A number of commandants objected to
Roux being in command and demanded that an election be held.

Paul Hendrik Roux, thirty-eight years old and a minister of the Dutch
Reformed Church, was an educated man who had studied in Europe.
Personally brave and a reasonably good general, he is said never to have
fired a shot or even to have carried a weapon. Instead of facing down his
rebellious officers and ending their bickering, he unwisely consented to
the election they were clamouring for, and on 17 July Prinsloo by a bare
majority was elected their leader.

A prosperous farmer in the Winburg district and an elder of the
church, Prinsloo had earned his military reputation in the Basuto War of
1866. He had a dignified look and a long white beard, but he was well
past his prime as a military leader.

By 26 July—three weeks after De Wet and Steyn had left—all of the
major passes had been taken by the British and there was only one exit
left, and that a difficult one. Two British columns were already inside the
basin. Still the Free Staters quarrelled. Two commandos had been away
when the voting took place, and as they had favoured Roux they demanded that a new election be held.

Many of the burghers, convinced that it was useless to hold out any
longer, were ready to surrender; many were just as ready to fight on.
There were disputes about this while the wrangling over a choice of
commander continued. This preoccupation with their internal problems
in the face of the peril before them seems almost unbelievable. They even
asked the British to give them a four- to six-day armistice, a holiday from
fighting so that they could quarrel in peace, candidly admitting that they
wanted to consult with Steyn and De Wet to resolve who should be in
command and whether or not they should surrender.

The request for an armistice was, not surprisingly, refused, but still
the burghers argued. Wild rumours swept through the laagers, and even
wilder schemes were proposed. There was no one capable of giving
central direction, and neither Prinsloo nor Roux did anything construc-
tive. An air of defeat hung over most of the laagers. Panic seized some.
The British were all around them and they were trapped. Some still
hoped for deliverance, a miracle. All lamented their fate. Brave men shed
tears of rage.

Prinsloo, under the pressure of the arguments of demoralised commandants, at last concluded that he had no choice but to surrender, and
he set about seeing what terms he could get. As a further indication of
the fatuity into which the Boer leaders had tumbled, they chose as their
emissary to the British a man they had recently tried and condemned as
a traitor. Frans Vilonel, the ex-commandant whom De Wet had reduced
to the ranks for failing to obey his orders, had defected to the British and

then had been caught in the act of trying to induce others to do the same. Instead of being shot, as he would have been later in the war, he was sentenced to five years' imprisonment at hard labour; however, as there was no prison, he was simply carried about from laager to laager. This was the man selected to represent the Free Staters in their negotiations with the British.

Roberts, kept informed of developments by telegraph, dictated the terms of surrender: rifles, guns, horses, wagons, oxen, and mules were to be given up; the burghers could keep other personal possessions, but all were to be made prisoners of war.

On the evening of 29 July Roux informed Prinsloo that a new election had been held and that he, Roux, had been elected. It was too late. The deed had been done. Prinsloo simply handed him Hunter's acceptance of their surrender. Now came the final act in this extraordinary drama. Roux impulsively jumped on his horse and galloped off to the British lines to argue with General Hunter. Prinsloo was not really in command, he contended, and the surrender was unauthorized and illegal. Prinsloo had no right, no authority. It was all a mistake. As De Wet wrote later, "He acted like a child."

Word of the surrender spread among the scattered laagers. Most wearily resigned themselves to their fate, but several commandants, including such stalwarts as Olivier and Froneman, refused to accept defeat. Late that night they led their commandos out of the Brandwater Basin, taking them over seemingly impossible paths. They even carried out a pompom, two Maxims, and eight guns. When the paths became too narrow for the gun carriages, they jettisoned them, lashed the guns to logs, muscled them labouriously up slopes, and slid them down. About 1,500 burghers escaped.

On the morning of 30 July 1900 Hunter formally accepted the surrender of Prinsloo with the Ficksburg and Ladybrand commandos at a place aptly named Verliesfontein (*verlies:* loss or bereavement). Sadly the burghers came up and threw down their rifles and ammunition. Some were mere boys; some white-bearded patriarchs. For them the war was over. All dreaded being sent to St. Helena, but St. Helena was already too crowded and the British had opened up a new prisoner-of-war camp in the mountains of central Ceylon at a place called Diyatalowa ("Happy Valley"). From the fountain of bereavement to the happy valley.

Throughout the Brandwater Basin the surrender scene was repeated as the commandos turned in their arms to the nearest British unit. A British staff officer found Olivier 8 miles outside the basin and took his promise to stay where he was until he received instructions from Prinsloo, but Olivier had no intention of surrendering and he made off with all speed. Hunter thought this unfair: "I regard it as a dishonourable breach of faith upon the part of General Olivier, for which I hold him personally responsible. He admitted that he knew that General Prinsloo had included him in the unconditional surrender."[11]

A few burghers tried to conceal themselves in caves and other hiding places, but eventually most of these were flushed out. Strangely, even some who had made their escape—men of the Vrede and Harrisburg commandos—changed their minds and rode into Harrismith to surrender to General Hector Macdonald. By 9 August the British had captured 4,314 prisoners in and around the Brandwater Basin. They had also captured three guns (two of which were "U" Battery guns taken by De Wet at Sanna's Post) and nearly 2 million rounds of ammunition, most of which was destroyed. The spot where they exploded it is to this day still bare of vegetation and littered with cartridge cases. They also took possession of 2,800 head of cattle, 4,000 sheep, and nearly 6,000 good horses.

Among the Boers who surrendered was Pieter Schutte, twenty-two years old, whose sweetheart, Cecilia Senekal, wrote one of the war's most beautiful songs: "Zeit gy Ginds de Blaawe Bergen?" (Didst Thou See the Blue Mountains?). The first of its ten verses is:

> Didst thou see those Blue Mountains
> where our friends were sold?
> Taken prisoner by the enemy
> and sent so far away.*[12]

The belief that the burghers were sold out soon became general; De Wet certainly thought so: "The circumstances of this surrender are so suspicious that it is hard to acquit the man who was responsible for it of a definite act of treachery; and the case against him is all the more grave from the fact that Vilonel . . . had a share in the transaction."[13]

Prinsloo did not have an opportunity to defend himself, for he died shortly after. So too did Piet Schutte. His sweetheart married his brother, and the song she wrote is now almost forgotten.

33

ADVANCE TO KOMATIPOORT

It was now obvious: the Boers ought to give up. They could not possibly win. The capitals of the two countries, all of the towns of any importance, and most of the railway system were in British hands, as were about 15,000 prisoners of war. Most of the Free State army had surrendered.

---

*This translation is by J. H. Schoeman, whose father and two uncles rode with De Wet.

above   General Piet Joubert and staff at Newcastle, Natal, 17 October 1899.

left   Three generations in arms, 1900.

below   First meeting between the British commander and the Boer envoys at Middelburg, the Transvaal, 28 February 1901. Botha and Kitchener are seated in the center surrounded by their staffs.

General Cronjé after his surrender at Paardeberg sits disconsolately with a member of Lord Roberts' staff.

Lieutenant General Lord Methuen.

Lieutenant General Ian Hamilton.

Jacobus Wynand ("Koos") Bosman as a lieutenant in the Transvaal Staatsartillerie. (*Courtesy of Miss Maria Bosman*)

General Sir Redvers Buller, V.C.

top   Colonel Jan Smuts with his favorite horse, "Charlie."

above left   President Paul Kruger with his sash of office.

above right   General "Koos" de la Rey.

right   Major General R. S. S. Baden-Powell.

A 6-inch creuzot gun, called a Long Tom. Long Toms were used in the sieges of Ladysmith, Kimberley, and Mafeking.

Boer picket on Spion Kop.

British staff headquarters at Paardeberg Drift.

Boers manning the trenches outside Mafeking.

Bullock wagon crossing drift from Boer laager with loot (Paardeberg).

British field guns crossing the Modder at Paardeberg Drift to outflank General Cronjé.

Boers with a Krupp quick-firing cannon.

Six-inch naval gun on a railway truck being sent forward from the Modder River Station.

A section of Deadwood Camp, St. Helena.

"IK ZAL U NIET BEGEVEN" "IK ZAL U NIET · VERLATEN"

A scene inside British concentration camp as depicted by the famous South African sculptor, Anton van Wouw, at the base of the Women's National Memorial outside Bloemfontein. The text is from Joshua 1:5 and reads: "I will not fail thee nor forsake thee." *(George Aschman)*

A field hospital at Paardeberg Drift.

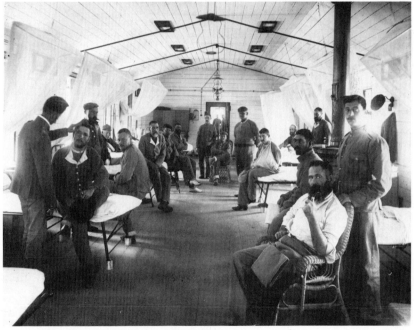

Wounded Boer prisoners at the Wynberg Hospital.

Signaling station on the top of a kopje. Instrument on right is a heliograph and center a field telephone.

left Attending the injured after the Battle of Driefontein.

Begbie lamp and heliograph station at Bloemfontein.

Cannon captured from the English on 30 October 1899 by Koos Bosman (in dark
trousers). *(Courtesy of Miss Maria Bosman)*

A. McCoelree, a Boer woman
dressed in her best and posed
beside an ox wagon.

Transvaal burghers with their families before leaving for the Natal front.

Newcastle — hospital prisoners before being sent to India, 1900.

Newcastle Station — Boer women and children in trucks, 1900.

The entry of Lord Roberts and Lord Kitchener into Pretoria.

Boer prisoners being transported to prisoner-of-war camps outside South Africa.

Cronjé's surrender.

Alfred Milner, British Administrator in
South Africa. *(The Bettmann Archive)*

Lieutenant General Sir George
White, V.C. *(Culver Pictures)*

President Marthinus Steyn, President of
Orange Free State and supporter of
President Kruger at declaration of Boer
War. *(Culver Pictures)*

Lord Roberts in his
traveling headquarters wagon
preparing for the Great Flank March.

Kimberley notables of 1894. Seated, from left to right, Sir Richard Solomon,
D. J. Haarhoff, Sir Starr Jameson, Cecil Rhodes, F. Newton, H. Robinow, and
C. E. Nind. Standing, from left to right, R. Harris, Mr. Craven, G. W. Compton,
Sir H. Goold Adams, Gardner Williams, Sir J. H. Lange, and Col. Sir David Harris.

British troops swarmed over the land. President Steyn no longer pretended to have a capital; his government was where he dismounted for the night as, a fugitive, he fled north into the Transvaal with De Wet. There were some important defections. Piet de Wet came to his brother to ask if there was any point in continuing the struggle. "Are you mad?" De Wet answered, and turned his back. Piet de Wet had fought bravely and well, but now he had had enough. He mounted his horse and rode off to turn in his rifle and surrender.

Still, many Boers, in spite of the hopelessness of their position, refused to give up and thought contemptible those who did. Christiaan de Wet never spoke to his brother again and even swore he would shoot him on sight. Over both countries there was sporadic fighting, and in the western Transvaal De la Rey had some striking successes. Kruger, interviewed in his railway carriage at Machadodorp, was asked if he did not feel that the war was over now that Roberts had captured his capital: "The capital! What is a capital?" he asked. "It does not consist of any particular collection of bricks and mortar. The capital of the republic, the seat of government, is here in this car. There is no magic about any special site."

Steyn, when asked why he continued such a hopeless struggle, would reply with another question: What hope had the two little republics at the beginning of the war of winning the fight against the might of England? If they had trusted in God at the beginning, why not continue to trust in Him?

Roberts sent out columns to try to deal with De la Rey while other columns tried to catch the slippery De Wet (this became known as the First De Wet Hunt), but he remained convinced that he had only to capture the last 250 miles of railway on which Botha and Kruger were perched to end the war. On 23 July he launched his army along the railway towards Komatipoort, determined to force the fighting burghers to surrender or flee the country. Four days later Middelburg was occupied and the Boers began to retreat to the east. Buller meanwhile was slowly moving along the railway that ran from Durban to Ladysmith and on into the Transvaal through Volksrust, Standerton, and Heidelburg, joining the main north-south line just south of Johannesburg. Roberts was naturally eager to have this second, shorter supply line open for his use, but for a time the hunt for De Wet occupied his attention.

Not for the first or the last time De Wet managed to outmarch and outwit the British columns sent to hem him in. Steyn wanted to meet with Kruger, so De Wet assigned the bulk of his force to accompany him on a wide swing north to reach Machadodorp while he with only 250 men doubled back towards the Free State. He counted on this movement to confuse the British and divert their attention from Steyn and the main force. He was right. He diverted so much attention to himself that at one point he was trapped, his little band pushed against the Magaliesberg, a 100-mile range of mountains about 40 miles west of Pretoria, with British columns moving in for the kill.

De Wet rode up to a Bantu hut and consulted its occupant about the feasibility of crossing the mountains before him. The Bantu assured him it was not possible.

"Do baboons go across?" asked De Wet.

"Yes. Baboons do, but not a man."

"Come on!" De Wet cried to his burghers. "This is our only way, and where a baboon can cross, we can cross."[1]

Young Adriaan Matthijsen looked at the mountains soaring 2,000 feet above him and sighed, "O Red Sea!"

Leading their horses, slipping and sliding, they forced their way up and then scrambled down the other side to safety, leaving the British columns holding an empty bag.

The First De Wet Hunt lasted a month. When it was over Roberts collected his scattered forces and turned to his primary objective: capturing the entire railway line to Komatipoort. Buller was asked to cooperate by leaving his Natal-Transvaal railway and marching north to form the right flank of Roberts's advancing army. Taking 9,000 men and 42 guns, Buller, with some trepidation, left the railway, source of all comforts, and moved to join forces with Roberts. For the first time he left tents behind, but he took with him half again as many wagons and carts in proportion to the number of troops as had Roberts on his march to Bloemfontein. Buller's men would not want.

Boer commandos under Christiaan Botha fell back fighting before Buller's advance, while the main force under Louis Botha was also forced to retreat back along the railway. Kruger and his government moved their railway carriages still further east to Waterval Onder.

Buller had orders from Roberts to place himself behind Dalmanutha, a village on the railway halfway between Pretoria and Komatipoort, and to attack the Boer flank. He had started to execute this when he received a report from the 19th Hussars that they had found the Boer flank at Bergandal, several miles west of Dalmanutha. This was surprising, but Buller changed directions to attack what was, in fact, the centre of the Boer line. Actually, the hussars had found a small gap in the Boer defences and assumed that it was the end of their line. For the British the mistake was a stroke of luck. Botha, knowing that Roberts always attacked the flank when he could, had left his centre weak in order to strengthen his flanks.

The exact point at which Buller launched his attack was a small salient in the Boer line held by only 74 men of the Johannesburg police, the Zarps whom the uitlanders had so hated, under the command of Commandant Philip Oosthuizen. They were supported by 1,000 burghers ranged on either side, but behind and not directly connected to them. The Zarp position then was well forward and isolated. Against these 74 men Buller could throw 8,000 troops and bring to bear 38 guns.

The battle began at eleven o'clock on the morning of 27 August with a three-hour bombardment of the Zarps' position by all 38 British guns. It was perhaps the heaviest bombardment of the war. "Smoke and sulphurous gases and rocks shooting up into the air made the place look like a Vesuvius in eruption."[2] Roland Schikkerling of the Johannesburg Commando was positioned on the right of the Zarps where he had a good view of the bombardment: "I thought everything human had perished, even to the lizards and insects in the rent and battered rocks, and felt sick at heart to think that, while we looked idly on, this infernal fury should fall on these few wretches alone."[3] The Zarps, well entrenched, lay low. They could do nothing else. As one said later, "We dared not leave the post. We dared not—it was certain death." When at last the bombardment ceased, two battalions of British infantry rose up and, bayonets bared, moved forward to the attack: 1,500 soldiers against what was left of the contingent of 74 policemen. Roberts himself had ridden up, and he and Buller watched the attack through their field glasses.

As the infantry advanced across nearly 1,500 yards of open ground, the Zarps left alive raised their heads and opened a steady, accurate fire. A liver and white springer spaniel trotted in front of the advancing men, tail in the air, nose to the ground, sniffing at the puffs of dust raised by the bullets striking around him, puzzled by what caused them. The men advanced in rushes, and each time they threw themselves on the ground, the dog trotted up and down the prone line, puzzled by this behaviour too. Then a bullet struck him just behind the left shoulder and he went down, but when the men rose to move on, he too struggled up and hobbled painfully after them.

Newspapers reported that as the Rifles rose for their final rush they gave a "ringing cheer," but Lieutenant E. T. Aspinall reported that it was an inhuman yell and that the men, their blood up, cursed savagely— "Corporal Porter, a good judge, said he had never heard worse." The Zarps maintained their cool, deadly musketry until the soldiers were almost upon them, then some turned and ran for their horses; others stayed on and fought to the end.

Conan Doyle said of the Zarps: "No finer defence was made in the war." They suffered 40 killed, wounded, or captured, including the severely wounded Commandant Oosthuizen; the British lost 12 killed and 85 wounded. When the heat of battle subsided a reaction set in among the soldiers, and a number busied themselves in binding up the wounds of the Boers: "One, a lad of about fourteen, with a severe wound in his shoulder, was the object of much pity among them and some were almost in tears about him, yet a few minutes before they would probably have put a bayonet in him."[4]

With the capture of the Zarp position the rest of the Boers lost heart and fled; the line crumbled. As was so frequently the case, the British failed to make a vigourous pursuit, and by nightfall most of the Boers had scrambled to safety.

Everywhere the beaten, dispirited men fell back. Kruger and Steyn retreated still further to Nelspruit; Louis Botha was ill with quinsy, and without his voice the Boer leadership dissolved in confusion. Even he was for a time discouraged and wrote to Kruger suggesting that as the two presidents were now together they should discuss peace terms, for he saw no way of continuing the war.

Roberts, anticipating an imminent end to hostilities, proclaimed the annexation of the Transvaal on 1 September 1900.

At this point it was decided that Kruger, suffering from his diseased eyes, should go to Europe. It would have been too demoralising to have him fall into British hands; he was too old and ill for campaign life, and perhaps in Europe he could enlist the help of some of the European powers. Ostensibly it was to be but a six months' absence, but on 11 September he crossed the border at Komatipoort and left the Transvaal, never to return. Schalk Burger was left as acting president, but the real leader of the Transvaal Boers was now Louis Botha.

Steyn had joined Kruger just two days before the battle of Bergandal and stayed with him during the retreat to Nelspruit, but he had no intention of leaving South Africa or of surrendering. This iron-willed leader moved among the dispirited burghers breathing fire and exhorting them to fight on: "What answer can you give to your children when they ask what you have done with the independence you inherited?"

The Boers continued to fight rear-guard actions, to snipe and to tear up the railway, but the British force pressing against them was overwhelming, and was made even greater by the release of the remaining 2,000 prisoners of war who had been held at Nooigedacht. Back along the railway line, east to the Mozambique border, the Boers were driven. Still, there were no mass surrenders. As long as they could retreat they would; they were discouraged but not completely demoralised, and they would not surrender if they could avoid it. It now appeared, at least to the British, that they would have to, that there was no choice left but surrender or flight across the frontier into Mozambique.

Faced with what appeared to be certain defeat, the Transvaalers in this crisis arrived after debate among the leaders at a remarkable decision: they would reorganise their army. It hardly seemed the time to do this, but extraordinarily enough, this decision did in fact save them from annihilation. The best men and the best horses and wagons were organised into commandos of about 300 men, each under a commandant appointed by Commandant-General Botha, not elected; a field cornet commanded each hundred and a corporal each ten. This left a surplus of officers, all of whom were reduced to the ranks. At this time too a pay scale was introduced, although no pay was ever given. It was also decided to divide the Transvaal into five areas of operation with the burghers fighting in their own districts as far as possible.

The Transvaalers with their streamlined fighting force now broke away from the heavy British columns to continue the war in other places and in other ways. Left behind at Komatipoort to face the British or flee over the border were some 3,000 men under two easily spared generals. Included in this force were the weak and the weary, the voetgangers and the sick, the faint of heart, the misfits, most of the foreign volunteers, the unnerved and unneeded of the government officials, and many Cape rebels.

Although smaller in numbers, the Transvaal forces were more wieldy and effective, composed as they were of the strongest and staunchest, the enthusiasts who were willing and able to fight. They kept one Long Tom and a few field guns, destroying the remainder of their artillery; they took the most useful of the stores and set fire to the rest. Then in numerous small bands and in two large parties, one under Botha and another under Ben Viljoen, they trekked north into the wild bush veld, the "thirstland" —what is today the famous Kruger National Park. They were anxious to escape from the low country with its fevers and tsetse flies before the onset of hot weather, but they had to stay off the high veld until they were far enough north to escape around the British left flank. Roberts was alerted to the movement, but his troops failed to move fast enough to prevent their escape.

Although unmolested by the British, some of the straggling groups of Boers lost their way and some were attacked by hostile tribesmen; animals died and men fell sick. Some lost all their horses and trudged along on foot. The sick and wounded, carried along on litters, were such a burden that their bearers, abhoring themselves for the thought, often wished them dead. It was a hard journey.

After going far enough north to be out of reach of the British columns, they turned west and back onto the high veld to Pietersburg, their assembly point.

Remote Pietersburg had never seen so many men, horses, oxen, and wagons as had now descended upon it, and the girls had never in their lives seen such a magnificent collection of young men, ragged but spirited. Every evening the town vibrated to singing, dancing, and games of "Kiss in the Ring." Schikkerling, handsome and ardent, wryly recorded that he "came away without any regrets to comfort me."[5]

When the reorganised Transvaal army rode north the burghers left behind at Komatipoort threw themselves into an orgy of destruction, blowing up or setting fire to supplies, guns, ammunition, locomotives. Only the railway bridge was spared, for the Portuguese had persuaded Kruger to forbid its destruction. The Portuguese, who had moved most of their 1,500 European troops to the frontier, offered good treatment to those who crossed the border and laid down their arms.

By 22 September some 2,500 Boers and foreign volunteers had crossed over into Portuguese territory. Four out of five were completely destitute. All ended up at Lourenço Marques, an embarrassment and a worry to the local authorities. The correspondent for the *Standard* reported on the foreign volunteers: "A worse collection of scoundrels could not be found in Paris, New York, or London."[6]

The foreign military observers who had been with the Boers, concluding that the war was now over, also left the Transvaal. Captain Reich-mann in his report to the American War Office tried to sum up:

What I saw of the struggle of these simple farmers against the trained troops of the British empire was pathetic to behold; it was the old story of enthusiasm and valor as against organization and discipline, and it had the same invariable result. Yet the farmers were undaunted. When I took leave of Mr. Reitz, the state secretary, he was on horseback carrying bandoliers and carbine and leading three spare horses; he smiled and said to me, "If your people could fight eight years for their independence, we can!"[7]

On 24 September advance elements of a British column under General R. Pole-Carew entered an almost deserted Komatipoort.

The British could now look about them and see no more armies to fight, no other major cities to conquer, no more railways or other installations to capture. The soldiers began to think of returning home.

34

THE END OF THE SECOND ACT

The war was over. Lord Roberts reported to the secretary of state for war that "with the occupation of Komati Poort, and the dispersal of Commandant-General Louis Botha's army, the organized resistance of the two Republics might be said to have ceased."[1] There did not appear to be much more for the army to do; the civil administration would soon be able to take over, and on 8 October Alfred Milner was appointed administrator for the new colonies. "There is nothing now left of the Boer army but a few marauding bands," said Roberts publicly. Although he was later condemned for his lack of foresight, he cannot, in fairness, be blamed for his assessment; no one else in the British Empire was any wiser at the time. All his officers thought the war was over and that only some police actions were required to bring the Pax Britannica to South Africa. The politicians in London thought it was over, and so did prominent South Africans such as Cecil Rhodes. Many, perhaps most, Boers thought so as well. A small dissenting voice in the victory chorus was a trooper in Paget's Horse who wrote home:

"The Transvaal is annexed," "the war is over," "sailing orders may be expected at any moment," and yet I am writing this with a loaded rifle by my side and with the sound of rifle fire in my ears; also with the happy consciousness that at any minute a "sniper" may honour me with his attentions, and yet "the war is over," for do not the month-old papers we receive from home persistently call our attention to this, to them, patent fact? It is not quite so obvious, however, out here.[2]

Conan Doyle thought the war was over, and he had a great thick history of the conflict all but finished. He dashed through the final bit— there was a penultimate chapter entitled "The End of the War"—and hastened into print with it. While admitting that there were "scattered bands of Boer warriors" still on the veld, he explained: "My time and my space forbid the inclusion of these last incidents, which could have no bearing on the ultimate result." This first history of the war was a popular book and went through many editions, but by the time the eighteenth version—called "The Final Edition"—was published two years later (when the war was indeed and at long last really ended) there were an additional nine chapters and the original "The End of the War" chapter was retitled.

The politicians, whose business it was ever to keep an ear cocked to the public voice, viewed the course of the war with one eye on its effect on their own careers. The Unionist government in England decided that there would be no better time to test its strength than in this hour when the British army stood on the threshold of victory. On 25 September, the same day British troops occupied Komatipoort, Parliament was dissolved. The general election that followed was called the "Khaki Election," for there was but one primary issue: the war. The election campaign was short and vicious. Since this was "Chamberlain's war," it was he, the colonial secretary, not the prime minister, who was the chief representative of the Unionist party. There was, said Winston Churchill later, more enthusiasm for Chamberlain at this time than there was after World War I for Lloyd George and Douglas Haig combined.

In one of his speeches Chamberlain repeated the words of the mayor of Mafeking: "A seat lost to the government is a seat gained by the Boers." This was picked up and much quoted. Unionist posters twisted it slightly to "A vote for a Liberal is a vote for the Boers." To many voters the issue did indeed seem black or white: one was pro-Empire or pro-Boer; one was loyal to the government or a traitor.

The government had much to live down. There had been the dismal defeats in the field at the beginning of the war; there was the scandal over the inadequate medical attention given to the troops; there was the vast (so it seemed) expenditure of funds and loss of life. But the war was almost won now, it was believed, and there was a fear that the Liberals if elected would repeat "the magnanimity of Majuba."

The government was not without its critics, and there was even some criticism of Milner and demands that he be removed from his South African post. Churchill, however, in one of his most extravagant statements, argued that to remove Milner at this time would be "a greater blow to Imperial interests than the defeats of Magersfontein, Stormberg, Colenso and Spion Kop put together."[3]

These attacks on Chamberlain and Milner were mere pin pricks. The Liberals were hopelessly divided on the war issue, and the antiwar groups had no prominent men of stature to support them. Even such unlikely people as Bernard Shaw and Swinburne supported the government, although Shaw confessed to being somewhat embarrassed at finding himself "on the side of the mob." Much has been written about the Khaki Election, but in spite of the excitement among the politically minded there was considerable apathy among the voters and 1,276,089 fewer votes were cast than there had been in 1895. The Unionists won, and although they increased their majority by only two, they obtained a significantly higher percentage of the popular vote. Among the new members taking their seats for the first time was Winston Churchill, who, believing that the war was almost over, had hurried home in July to capitalise on his family name and his newly won reputation in South Africa.

The people of Britain had demonstrated their overwhelming support of the government's policy in South Africa, but there was, and there remained for the duration of the war, a small but vocal band, damned as pro-Boers, who denounced the war. Most of these belonged to one of two groups: the South African Conciliation Committee, which in November 1900 had only 1,700 members, and the Stop-the-War Committee, the most extreme group, founded by that flamboyant journalist W. T. Stead. Besides Stead the only leaders of note were Leonard Courtney, M.P. for Liskeard, and David Lloyd George, who nearly lost his seat in Parliament, his law practice, and his life through his antiwar activities.

The thirty-seven-year-old Lloyd George was not, in fact, well known in the country as a whole before the war, but came into national prominence as a result of his antiwar speeches and his vigorous attacks on the popular Chamberlain. He told the House of Commons:

> The right honourable gentleman [Chamberlain] admitted that he had no right to meddle in the affairs of the Transvaal and that there was only one possible justification for it—that our motive was an unselfish one. We have thrown that justification away now. . . . You entered into these two republics for Philanthropic purposes and remained to commit burglary. . . . Our critics say you are not going to war for equal rights and to establish fair play, but to get hold of the goldfields.[4]

Lloyd George's was a voice in the wilderness. Chamberlain and his views were popular; Lloyd George and his views were not. Outside of the House of Commons he often had difficulty finding an audience. The *Cornish Times* reported at length on one attempt he made to speak in Liskeard under the auspices of the South African Conciliation Committee:

> It was anticipated from the first that the proceedings would not pass off without some demonstration of opposition to the views set forth by the commit-

tee. These expectations proved only too well justified. . . . the platform was stormed by a party of young fellows, many of whom wore miniature Union Jacks, and the meeting was broken up in confusion.[5]

When the chairman tried to speak he was interrupted by shouts and whistles; someone blew on a tin trumpet and the audience roared out "Soldiers of the Queen," "Rule Britannia," and other patriotic airs. These were followed by a rendering of the Cornish ballad "Trelawny," which while not very relevant was a tune everyone knew. "It was some time before the noise in any way abated; flags were waved, chairs knocked about, and as a khaki-clad soldier from the front tried to leave the building, he was lifted shoulder-high, and this led to an outburst of cheering for 'Tommy Atkins'."

Miss Emily Hobhouse, secretary of the Conciliation Committee, rose to speak and with more truth than wisdom reminded the audience that "manners maketh man." This was greeted with hoots of laughter followed by cheers for Buller and Baden-Powell and Chamberlain. When from the back of the hall someone started the singing of "Men of Harlech" to the accompaniment of stamping feet, Miss Hobhouse gave up and sat down.

Mr. Lloyd George stood smiling at the table, he did not attempt to utter a syllable. It was perfectly evident that the crowd would not hear the Welsh MP at any price. . . . Presently a further demonstration attracted attention to the floor from the hall. The khaki-clad soldier from Hassenford was hoisted onto the shoulders of half a dozen men, who carried him around the hall. . . . At this point the police made their appearance on the platform.

Aided by the police, the speakers left in safety while the crowd cheered for Lord Roberts and leading politicians.

This was a peaceful demonstration compared with one that took place five months later when Lloyd George attempted to speak at the Town Hall in Birmingham, Chamberlain's home town. Before the meeting began brass bands defiantly played patriotic songs in the snow outside the hall, and a street vendor did a brisk business selling half-bricks "three a penny, to throw at Lloyd George." It did not appear to be an auspicious occasion, and indeed it was not. But Lloyd George was a brave little man: he appeared on the platform. He was greeted by a roar of angry voices. Cries of "Traitor!" and "Pro-Boer!" and, more ominously, "Kill him!" filled the hall. Above the shouts could be heard the crash of breaking glass and the whistles of the police. As the Birmingham *Daily Mail* reported it, "the outcome . . . was that considerable damage was done to the Town Hall, and one young man was killed, and several members of the police force and the general public were more or less severely injured."[6]

Including the young man killed by an overzealous policeman wielding a baton, there were twenty-seven casualties. The problem of removing Lloyd George safely from the hall was solved by dressing him in a

policeman's uniform, although because of his size there was some difficulty in finding one small enough. In this disguise and with his police
helmet pulled well down over his face the future prime minister scurried
out a side exit into Paradise Street and made his escape.

Pro-Boers were unpopular everywhere. Zealous patriots broke the
windows of their homes or places of business, disrupted their meetings,
hurled insults at them, and such conduct was condoned by some newspapers. The *Yorkshire Post* said: "When pro-Boers . . . insult the living and
the dead by extolling the nation's enemies, they do what is not only
foolish but wicked, and openly invite the ill-usage they afterwards receive."[7]

Only a few newspapers were antiwar: the *Manchester Guardian,* the
Daily News, the *Star,* the *Westminister Gazette,* for which H. H. Munro (better
known as "Saki") wrote, two working-class newspapers, the *Morning
Leader* and *Reynolds News,* and W. T. Stead's *Review of Reviews.* No one was
more violently opposed to the war than Stead, whose newspaper was full
of antiwar articles. Among his contributions to the Khaki Election was
The Candidates of Cain, a 70,000-word book he wrote in just six days. He
also put out special antiwar pamphlets such as *Shall I Slay My Brother Boer?,*
billed as an "appeal to the conscience of Britain." This particular piece
provoked a counter pamphlet entitled *Shall I Kick My Brother Stead?*

Neither Stead nor anyone else was able to stem the tide of opinion
in favour of the war. The only community in the country which was
strongly pro-Boer was Battersea, which went so far as to name a street
after Commandant-General Joubert. (It still bears his name.)

Never before nor since has a war been so popular. Even antiwar
speakers had to be careful not to disparage "our brave soldiers." Tommy
Atkins had never been so esteemed; only the Irish Nationalists dared to
damn the British army and openly to cheer Boer victories. Lines were
sharply drawn, and there was no place for the man who loved his country
and was proud of the Empire but deplored the war.

It was widely held that the war was prolonged by the antiwar activities
in Britain, and it was true that those trying to stop the war did, in fact,
help to prolong it. Selected statements made by antiwar Britons, translated and read to the commandos, gave hope to many that Britain would
give up the struggle. This, together with the equally groundless hopes of
foreign intervention excited by the pro-Boer sentiments expressed in the
European and American press, helped to sustain Boer morale.

The antiwar movement in Britain has been much studied, not because it had any real influence on the government or public opinion, but
because it was a new thing in British history. None of the dozens of other
imperialistic wars had brought forth such a movement. Earlier in the
century Gladstone had denounced Britain's wars in Afghanistan and
Zululand, but he had merely used them as sticks with which to beat the
existing government; there were no pro-Afghan or pro-Zulu organiza-
tions. To see the antiwar movement in perspective one can look at its

strength in Parliament: of the 670 members elected to the House of Commons in the Khaki Election, only 52 were pro-Boer while 402 were Unionists.

Undoubtedly some of the steam was taken out of the movement at the time of the election by the general belief that the war was already over, or would be within a matter of weeks, and perhaps many among those who found it hard to justify were nevertheless unwilling that Britain should give up what had been so hardly won. There were few indeed who seriously considered the complete withdrawal of British troops and the return of the Orange Free State and the Transvaal to the republican Boers.

Roberts, having done all the conventional things expected of a general in the field and having, by any ordinary standards, won the war, now prepared to go home. His accomplishments were impressive. He had marched through the enemy's countries, seizing both capitals; he had captured Cronjé and his army, and in every engagement the enemy had been routed; the besieged towns of Kimberley, Ladysmith, and Mafeking had been relieved; what remained of the Boer forces had scattered before him, and their governments' leaders and officials had been driven into exile or made fugitives on the veld; he was in firm control of all the means of communication and supply and, agriculture excepted, of all the wealth-producing resources of the former republics. And he had done all this in less than a year.

True, President Steyn and Acting President Schalk Burger still attempted to head their governments on the open veld. True too that scattered over the vast countryside there were still a few thousand armed and mounted men determined to continue the fight—"bitter-enders" they came to be called—led by Botha, De la Rey, and De Wet. But these could not be expected to survive, and the mopping-up operations could safely be entrusted to the ruthless efficiency of Kitchener—or so it was believed. Who could blame Roberts for thinking he had won the war? That he could now return home to his triumph? And who would deny him the honours of a conqueror?

The lustre of his greatness dimmed somewhat as it slowly dawned on soldiers and civilians alike that the war was not, after all, ended, that the fighting had simply taken a new form. History has not always dealt kindly with Roberts, and he has been called the most overrated general in British history.[8] Perhaps a fresh judgement is not out of place. Naturally, Roberts did not deserve quite all of the encomiums heaped on him. Few heroes do. However, he ought not to be denied his rightful place in military history. It is true he was not a genius; he only appeared to be when contrasted with generals such as Buller, Methuen, Warren, and Gatacre.

His triumphal march through the Orange Free State and the Transvaal was exactly what the War Office had had in mind from the start, what

Buller had at first intended to do, and there was nothing particularly singular about his variations on the plan, for to outflank strong enemy positions rather than attack them frontally is only good sense. But plans remain valueless unless they can be implemented, and it is in the execution of strategy that most of the qualities desired in generals are put to the test. Roberts had confidence in his own abilities, he possessed physical and moral courage, and he had that most important quality of all: resolution, the determination to win through. Obstacles and reverses did not shake him; the suggestions and advice of politicians did not cause him to hesitate; he refused to be diverted from his major objectives by lesser crises. Genius was not required of him, only competence, and by Victorian standards Roberts was a very competent general.

Roberts's departure from South Africa was delayed by a series of misfortunes. One of his aides-de-camp, Major Prince Victor of Schleswig-Holstein, a grandson of Queen Victoria, came down with enteric and died after only a few days' illness. Two days later Roberts's eldest daughter, Aileen, caught the disease and was for two weeks on the danger list. Scarcely had she recovered than Roberts was thrown from his horse and broke his arm. It was not until 11 December that he and his family were able to set off for home, going to Cape Town by way of Durban so that he could visit his son's grave. At Colenso Roberts stared in silence over the battlefield where his son had been killed, finally murmuring to his companion, "It was murder."

At three o'clock on 2 January 1901 Roberts stepped onto Trinity Pier, East Cowes, and England gave him a hero's welcome. Crowds cheered, newsmen jostled to interview him, every ship at anchorage blew its whistle or rang its bell, guns banged out a nineteen-gun salute, and the mayor read a formal address. Roberts was taken to Osborne to see the Queen, the same sovereign who nearly forty-two years before had pinned on his chest the Victoria Cross. He had won many honours since, and now he was raised to the rank of earl with a special remainder to his daughters —there no longer being a son to inherit the title—and he was made a Knight of the Garter, the first and only victorious general in Queen Victoria's reign to be so honoured. It was almost the Queen's last official function, for she was seriously ill and died just twenty days later. From Osborne Roberts proceeded to London, where the Prince and Princess of Wales came to meet his special train at Paddington Station and 14,000 troops lined the way to Buckingham Palace to keep back the tens of thousands on hand to cheer him.

Roberts was now appointed commander-in-chief of the army, replacing Wolseley. It was a popular appointment, for, as usual, the War Office was blamed for all the disasters and the lack of preparedness and had to shoulder not only its own mistakes but those of the politicians as well. A cartoon advertising "Monkey Brand," a popular soap, aptly summed up public sentiment. Depicting an oversized monkey dressed in evening clothes in front of the War Office handing a box of soap to Lord Roberts, it was captioned, "Clean up that place, my lord."

Sir Redvers Buller also returned to England, arriving in Southampton on the *Dunvegan Castle* exactly thirteen months from the day he had left. He was loudly cheered by the public, but the official honours given so generously to Roberts were not accorded him. When a grateful Parliament awarded Roberts £100,000 and nothing at all to Buller, a large crowd gathered in Hyde Park to protest. It seemed that nothing could diminish his popularity. Even when his message to White suggesting surrender was revealed and newspapers made the most of the disclosure, he was still cheered when he appeared in public, and at Exeter an equestrian statue of him was erected, an honour unprecedented in England for a living general. But Buller's days as a soldier were soon ended. When he tried to explain away his surrender message to White in a public speech, the War Office retired him.

Along with the generals, most of the swarm of war correspondents also left South Africa, and thousands of troops were sent home in the belief that they would no longer be needed; local South African units were disbanded.

Almost equally disastrous for the future operations of the British in South Africa was the dismantling of its remount organization. The officers engaged in buying horses and mules in Europe, South America, and the United States were ordered back to England. The flow of remounts to South Africa dried up. Certainly no greater evidence of overconfidence could be offered than the assumption that no more horses would be needed to round up the elusive mounted burghers ranging the veld.

This illusory end of the war was a time for adding up the cost. In flesh and blood, 4,185 British officers and men had been killed in action or died of wounds, but the total death toll was 10,678, for 6,493 had died of disease (mostly enteric) or from accidents. In addition, 34,499 sick or seriously wounded men had been invalided home. Of these, 208 died and 1,030 had to be discharged as unfit. No one imagined that only half the blood price had been paid.

There was also a counting of deeds of valour, or rather the awards given for such deeds. Twenty-five Victoria Crosses had been awarded, thirteen to officers. Of the eleven given to the infantry, five went to men in one regiment: the Gordon Highlanders. In addition to the Victoria Crosses and a sprinkling of Distinguished Service Orders, there was another, a singular award never before or since given. Queen Victoria before her death crocheted five scarves of khaki-coloured Berlin wool with the initials VRI on one of the knots to be presented to a British, an Australian, a New Zealand, a South African, and a Canadian soldier voted by his comrades to be "the best all-round man taking part in the South African campaign." The South African scarf was presented to Trooper Chadwick of Roberts's Horse, an American who had served in the United States Navy during the Spanish-American War.

There were many who thought that Lord Roberts, although a fine general, had been too easy on the Boers, too humane and magnanimous. It had been a mistake, they felt, to allow so many to lay down their rifles, take an oath, and ride back to their farms, and the large number of burghers who broke their oaths and returned to their commandos enraged them. It was believed that Kitchener, who was left in South Africa to wind up the war, would adopt sterner policies. *Black and White Budget* said: "Now that Lord Roberts has left, it is to be hoped that these people will be dealt with in the proper and only way. For months they have treated the British nation as a people of 'Jugginses.' Now is the time to show the mercy exhibited at Culloden."[9]

Captain David Miller of the Gordon Highlanders reflected a popular view among the soldiers when he wrote to his mother: "The Government should declare the war over and shoot anyone found with arms—this is the way to treat them."[10] Even later, when the war was finally and truly over, another officer, George Younghusband, wrote: "There is only one thing the Dutchman understood in the war, and that was the fist, the almighty fist, and an exceedingly heavy fist."[11]

This feeling appears to have been even stronger among the civilians in Natal and Cape Colony. Roberts's fair-minded treatment of his enemies was much criticised; in Cape Town notices of a mock performance appeared that included "A Lecture on 'Magnanimity and How to Fight with Kid Gloves' by Field Marshal Lord Roberts (Bobs)."

But now Kitchener was in charge. He would take off the kid gloves. Kitchener had the "almighty fist" to pound the Boer into his place. Kitchener knew how to deal with these people.

ACT III

35

COMMANDOS IN CAPE COLONY

In only two actions, at Paardeberg and the Brandwater Basin, had the British done more than simply drive the Boers from their positions. Both of these defeats had been inflicted on the Free State's army, the smaller of the two, and even so De Wet was still at large. The Transvaalers had suffered no serious defeat involving mass surrenders. The Boers had little need for cities or towns; they could do without their railways. Their home was the veld, and the veld had not yet been conquered. Out on those vast open spaces, free and armed, roamed men determined to fight. And these were the very best fighters, serving under strong and able leaders. The old generals who had begun the war—Cronjé, Joubert, and Prinsloo—were gone now, dead or in captivity. In their places were Botha, De la Rey, De Wet, and new, as yet untried, younger men such as Jan Smuts, Barry Hertzog, Ben Viljoen, and Christoffel Kemp, who were to prove themselves equally capable—a new, tough, vigorous, stubborn, clever breed. Kruger was gone, but Steyn was still free on the veld, and his strong voice, his very presence, encouraged the burghers to fight on.

The British would not be cruel masters—at least not deliberately. Most Boers knew this. But the flame of independence burned within them as brightly as it had in their voortrekker forefathers. No people ever desired their independence more. No people in history, not faced with the alternative of death or cruel tyranny, ever fought so hard for so long with so little hope of ultimate success.

From the seizure of Komatipoort until the close of the year the British were so busy ending the war—sending generals and troops home, reorganising their reduced army, and dismantling their supply structure—that they were incapable of undertaking offensive operations and the Boers were given a much needed respite. They were able to pull themselves together, to rorganise and consider how they could best carry on

323

the war. They also demonstrated their ability to strike and to hurt.

During the month of October 1900 they launched attacks on a number of small towns. Near Vlakfontein they tore up railway track in several places and cut up the work parties dispatched to repair the breaks. There were numerous small engagements: Mahon was attacked at Geluk; Methuen fought three small, sharp battles; De Wet was active, although General C. E. Knox, soon to emerge as one of the better guerrilla hunters, was busy chasing him and came so close that he captured some of his guns and wagons. These engagements were not, as the British believed, the last struggles of a defeated and dying enemy. They marked the beginning of the kind of combat the Boers would engage in for the next year and a half. It was the start of a whole new war, a war in which the British would suffer more men killed in action than in all the previous battles. There would be no more set battle pieces; henceforth there would be dozens of small actions, the Boers striking unexpectedly at widely separate locations, snapping up a convoy here, attacking small garrisons there, destroying railway bridges, blowing up locomotives, sniping. It was guerrilla war, and the Boers were to prove themselves most adept at this kind of fighting.

They had no overall strategy, no master plan for winning the war. The activities of the various commandos were not coordinated, and there was not even a statement of policy regarding purposes or objectives. From first to last the Boers were always long on tactics and short on strategy. Each independent commander was left to harass the British as he thought best. The general effect of Boer operations was of a blind lashing out in all directions by stubborn men who found in guerrilla activities not a way to win the war but simply their only alternative to surrender.

Guerrillas by themselves cannot win wars, not in the military sense. They can keep their enemies from winning; they can hope that in time their strength will increase to the point where they can put orthodox armies in the field to confront and defeat their enemies in conventional battles; they can hope to so wear down, annoy, exasperate their foes that they will wring concessions from them; or they can hope for foreign intervention.

In the face of the massive British army arrayed against them, still many times larger than their own in spite of troop reductions, the Boers had little hope of again amassing an army sizable enough to face the British in open battle; remembering what Gladstone had done after the First Anglo-Boer War and listening to the antiwar voices in England gave hope to some that if they fought on long enough the British might quit and perhaps give them back their independence, but those in power in Britain gave no such encouragement. After scorning foreign aid at the beginning of the war, the Boers now made feeble efforts to enlist active foreign intervention—delegations were sent to Europe and the United States, and Dr. Willem J. Leyds, a Hollander who had been state secretary of the Transvaal before the war, put forth a stream of propaganda—but it was all amateurish, and only the most optimistic could bring themselves to believe that foreign armies would actually march to their defence; the United States even refused its good offices.

There was little hope to be found by a reasoning man in the Boers' plight. But it was not facts or logic that kept the burghers fighting; it was something more impellent than either. In spite of hardships, which steadily increased, the idea of surrender seemed to these strong, free-dom-loving men an impossible alternative as long as they had rifles in their hands, horses under them, and the vast open veld in which to roam.

Their struggle was indeed without hope of success, at least of the kind they could imagine. Their deliberate, hopeless prolongation of the war resulted in the deaths of additional thousands of brave men. It resulted in the destruction of their farms, which they and their fathers and grand-fathers had worked so hard to build, and in the slaughter of their herds of cattle and sheep on which their future existence and way of life de-pended. Worst of all, it resulted in the decimation of their women and children.

These proud, stubborn men had much to answer for.

Their struggle did not in any way produce tangible military results commensurate with the hardships, sufferings, and deaths they exacted, but it did engender in their adversaries a grudging but genuine admira-tion for their stubbornness and bravery, qualities which the British have always admired. More importantly, there emerged among the Boers a consciousness of their own vitality and identity, for in the fire of their desperate struggle was forged the Afrikaner character. As long as they were alive and active, it was the fighting burghers, not those reasonable men who saw the futility of the fight, who provided South Africa with its leadership. Their spirit and character live on to this day in the Afrikaner and his leaders—and their concepts and prejudices too, making them in some ways anachronisms in today's world. When sixty years after the war Harold Macmillan tried to tell them of the wind of change blowing through the world, it seemed to the Afrikaner but a far-away breeze compared with the hot blast from the fire generated by the guerrilla warriors which blows upon them still.

The military history of the last eighteen months of the war is the story of innumerable small engagements which took place in widely scattered parts of the Transvaal, the Orange Free State, and Cape Colony, even some in Natal. Few had by themselves any special significance. They were important because they indicated continuing vigour on the part of the Boers, and because their cumulative effect was to sustain the concept of legitimate belligerents fighting on behalf of republican governments which, in fact, no longer existed.

Statistics can sometimes be more eloquent than words. Perhaps the best index of Boer guerrilla activity in the twelve months after Komati-poort is a simple list of the number of times the railway line was cut:

October 1900	32
November	30
December	21
January 1901	16
February	30
March	18
April	18
May	12
June	8
July	4
August	4
September	2[1]

The Boers did not concentrate their efforts on destroying British communications, which in the early stages of the guerrilla war they might have
done. Even so, there were enough attacks on the railway to worry the
British. After July 1900 all night running stopped between Bloemfontein
and the Vaal, and three months later between Bloemfontein and the
Orange. For a time in January 1901 the British did not dare run a train
at night anywhere in the conquered territory.

Instead of trying to strangle the British army by a complete disrup-
tion of its supply lines, the Boers looked to Cape Colony with its large
Afrikaner population for support. From a strictly military point of view
this was a mistake, although had the Boers cut off Roberts's supplies and
kept the line broken they could only have prolonged the war; military
victory was from the beginning an impossibility. Victory was possible only
in political terms, and the well-developed Boer political instincts told
them that their best hope of success lay in rousing the Afrikaners in the
Cape to stage a massive demonstration of their support.

It had been a disappointment at the beginning of the war that the
Cape Afrikaners had not, as hoped, risen in rebellion. Here and there
small areas revolted, and when Free State commandos actually rode into
Cape Colony they were cheered and aided; this gave the fighting burghers some hope that they might yet strike the sparks that would ignite
their blood brothers to do more than give them bread and sympathy.

Cape Colony was the most populous British possession in South
Africa, and probably half or more of the white colonists were Afrikaners.
Had there been a mass uprising it would indeed have been a serious
matter for the British, a civil war on a large scale. Besides, the Cape was
the British invasion base, and all of the supplies for Roberts's army came
from or passed through the colony. The desire of the Boers to carry the
war into British territory was strong, and as the war progressed there was
the additional lure of plentiful supplies and fresh sources of manpower
to be found there. The British, well aware of Boer ambitions, made
strenuous efforts to keep commandos north of the Orange. They were so
vigilant that the Boers were never able to pass any large force over the
river.

An early invasion of Cape Colony in the Prieska area in February and

March 1900 had achieved some success initially, but it was easily thrown back, the invaders all retreating over the border except for one commando filled with rebels and led by twenty-four-year-old Chaim David Judelewitz, an uitlander. He and his commando, about 300 strong, were able to remain and operate in the Prieska area until 28 May 1900 when he was surprised in laager by a British column with four guns under Colonel John Adye. Most of his men fled when the first shells landed, and Jedelewitz was killed. There was no more trouble for the British in the Prieska area.

In mid-January 1901 De Wet marched south to try another invasion, but the British were vigilant, and two weeks later he was forced to abandon the attempt. Although De Wet failed, other Boer leaders did manage to make incursions into the Cape with smaller forces. Pieter Henrick Kritzinger (1870–1935) and James Barry Hertzog (1866–1942) led two of these. Kritzinger was a powerfully built man with a luxuriant moustache, small ears, and a massive chin. Although born in Cape Colony, he had been taken to the Free State by his parents when he was twelve and he grew up in the Rouxville district. When the war began he rode off with the Rouxville Commando under Commandant J. H. Olivier, and after Olivier's capture in August 1900 he was elected commandant.

Kritzinger made three excursions into Cape Colony. Then on 16 December 1901 his career as a guerrilla came to an end. Racing from pursuing troopers he ran into heavy fire while crossing the railway near Hanover. While attempting to rescue some of his wounded men, he was himself shot, a bullet tearing through the muscles of his left arm and passing through his lung, and he was captured.

Hertzog was a quite different type. He was a scholar, and with his wire-rimmed spectacles he looked more like a professor than a soldier. Deneys Reitz described him as "a thin high-cheeked man with angry eyes" who was "a fierce hater." He possessed a brilliant mind and had studied law at Amsterdam. At the age of twenty-nine he had been appointed a judge in the Orange Free State and he was always called Judge Hertzog—except by British soldiers, who called him Hedgehog. He was to prove himself one of the most audacious of the Boer guerrilla leaders, and he was never captured. After the war he became the champion of Afrikaner nationalism in the Union of South Africa, and he served for fifteen years as prime minister.

These and other commandos in Cape Colony were a source of great anxiety to the British authorities. Perhaps nothing did more to convince the British that the war was not yet won than these guerrilla bands roving about in their oldest and most heavily populated South African colony. To succeed guerrillas must have the support of the people, for, as Mao Tse-tung has so aptly put it, guerrillas are like fish swimming in the sea of the population. A sympathetic population is the guerrilla's natural element; he cannot exist without it. The republican Boers succeeded as well as they did because they had the sympathy of a substantial portion

MOUNTED TROOPS WERE ESSENTIAL FOR SCOUTING.

of the farmers and villagers in the Cape. The Cape Afrikaners would not rise in revolt, but they made no secret of their sentiments. At Graaf-Reinet in the eastern Cape there had even been a riot when the British tried to celebrate Roberts's victory at Paardeberg with a fireworks display.

On 17 January 1901 martial law, which had before been put into effect only in the most disaffected parts of Cape Colony, was extended to include the entire colony except the ports and the Bantu areas. The British had been reluctant to impose martial law in Cape Colony, and in the beginning its application was strictly limited and mild. It was intended merely to supplement the civil authority, and military courts tried only clear cases of treason, sabotage, or trafficking with the enemy. Although district commanders could make their own regulations for preserving order and protecting their troops, they were instructed "to interfere as little as possible with the civil rights of peaceful inhabitants and their freedom to pursue their ordinary occupations."

At first the British living in Cape Colony welcomed martial law, many feeling as did the "lady contributor" to *The Owl* (published in Cape Town) that this would put the Afrikaners in their places:

Martial law has driven home to the Dutch in a way that no other method could possibly have accomplished, the fact that Britain means to settle once and for all the question of superiority in the Colony. . . . I stood outside the Dutch Church and listened to their singing. The old defiant ring and sonorous gladness were no longer there, and every now and then a strong man's voice trembled.[2]

The Afrikaners, with their hatred for any restriction of their liberty, did indeed resent what they, finding the English words difficult to pronounce, called Martie Louw. Eventually, everyone came to resent the new order, for it applied to the just and the unjust, British and Afrikaners alike, and it grew more and more restrictive and onerous: passes were required to enter, leave, or move from a district; a curfew was imposed; sale of liquor was controlled; bicycles were registered; neutrality became unacceptable and farmers were ordered to give information and actively aid British columns; all horses not actually needed on farms had to be given up; the licences of travelling pedlars were suspended; hotels had to file daily reports on their guests; and there were harsh restrictions on a long list of "prohibited goods" that included food for men and animals (only a limited amount could be kept on hand), leather goods, blankets, tobacco, and horseshoes. H. W. Wilson complained:

Martial law in many of the districts was administered with a want of tact which added fuel to the secret fire of indignation. Business was impossible; chaos ruled in place of order; and the freaks of some of the military despots were such as to irritate almost beyond endurance those who were devoutly loyal to the flag.[3]

It was the military courts which brought the realities of war to the farmers and villagers of Cape Colony. After the annexation of the Orange Free State and the Transvaal all of the burghers in the field became technically rebels, but to avoid mass executions of men who were in fact prisoners of war the British did not attempt to apply this logic. They were adamant, however, in the case of Cape Colony Afrikaners who took up arms and joined the enemy; some 700 of these were tried and sentenced to death as traitors, although only 35 were actually executed.

The execution of Cape rebels did not begin until 1901. It was an expression of the new feeling of bitterness which marked the last year of the conflict when, as Conan Doyle observed, "The war had lost much of the good humour which marked its outset. A fiercer feeling had been engendered on both sides. . . ."[4] It is difficult to say whether the executions accomplished their purpose, whether they deterred Cape Afrikaners from joining commandos, but it is certain that they engendered in the Afrikaners a sense of outrage and a bitterness against the British which persists among many to this day.

To make their point, the British usually compelled leading citizens, and sometimes the entire population of a town, to witness the reading of the death sentence and, in a few instances, the actual execution.

The executions of Johannes Lötter and Gideon Scheepers attracted the most attention and are today best remembered. Lötter had been a successful guerrilla leader until he was captured on 5 September 1901. He had become a Free State burgher after the war started, but the British brushed this aside and claimed him as a traitorous subject. He was convicted on nine counts, two for murder and one for flogging a British subject. The British subject in question was J. van der Merwe, a Cape Afrikaner who had fought with a commando and then voluntarily surrendered. Given a light sentence, he offered to try persuading his brother in Lötter's commando to do the same. He was caught in the attempt, and on Lötter's orders he was whipped with wet stirrup straps and then released. Without considering what would be their treatment of a soldier who deserted and tried inducing others to desert, the British were incensed. Ivie Allen, a photographer at Graaf-Reinet, took a picture of Van der Merwe's lacerated back and it was widely reproduced in British journals.

On 11 October 1901 at Middelburg in Cape Colony all business was suspended and leading citizens were ordered to appear in the public square. In what one correspondent called "a most impressive ceremony," the death sentence was read to Lötter, who fainted and had to be carried back to the gaol. The next day he was taken to a kopje just west of the town, tied to a chair, and shot. The following day Piet Wolfaardt, another Cape rebel, was executed on the same spot.

The execution which most stirred the hearts of men and women around the world was that of young, handsome, dashing Gideon Scheepers on 18 January 1902. He was not, as the British claimed, a British subject, for he was born on a farm near Middelburg (formerly Nazareth) in the eastern Transvaal on 4 April 1878, the second of ten children. When he was sixteen he enrolled as an apprentice telegraphist in the

Transvaal staatsartillerie, and four years later he transferred to the Orange Free State staatsartillerie to organise their telegraphic and helio-graphic corps. During the early months of the war he served under Cronjé and took part in the battles against Methuen. Later he served under De Wet and established a reputation as a scout. When De Wet's attempt to invade Cape Colony failed, he sent Kritzinger and Scheepers with smaller forces there with orders to encourage Cape Afrikaners to join them, to wreck trains, and to burn the farms and homes of Afrikaners regarded as traitors to their people.

It was hard for a Cape Afrikaner to be law-abiding and at the same time safe, to obey his conscience and to obey the law. If he obeyed Martie Louw and helped the British soldiers he earned the enmity of his neigh-bours and his home or farm was likely to be burned to the ground by a visiting commando; if he helped the commandos he ran afoul of the British authorities and risked gaol.

Farm burning in the Cape was in part a retaliation for the policy of wholesale farm burning which had recently been adopted by the British in the conquered territories, but this did not prevent the British from finding it heinous. The two situations were not comparable, they said, and H. W. Wilson, using some peculiar logic, tried to explain. Speaking of the burning of public buildings and private homes by Scheepers at Murraysburg on 6 July 1901, he wrote: "The case was altogether different from the British burning of farms in the Boer territories, where there was a strategic purpose and an ulterior aim, which could only be secured by such acts. . . . This savage and senseless act of his caused fresh panic throughout the colony."[5]

For months Scheepers and his commando ranged over Cape Colony from Aliwal North to Wocester pursued by British columns, and Scheep-ers, only twenty-two years old,* made himself into a living legend. His commando was filled with boys and young men who had left off helping their fathers farm or had abandoned their schoolbooks to join his bold, far-ranging riders. More than half of his "men" were in their teens.

Petronella van Hearden was a little girl when Scheepers and his commando, dirty and unshaven, with tattered clothes, rode into her vil-lage. The villagers took them into their homes, and a few hours later Petronella saw them emerge, clean and shaven, their clothes mended and washed. When they rode out that night Petronella's older brother Alec went with them.

Not all the inhabitants of Cape Colony were happy to see the com-mandos. There were, after all, a great many people of British descent as well as some thoroughly loyal Afrikaners. Mrs. Sarah Glueck, a twenty-six-year-old widow with two children, was the postmistress in the town

---

*Scheepers was not the youngest Boer leader. Commandant Piet van der Merwe, leader of another commando operating in the Cape, was only nineteen when he was killed in action.

of Lady Grey. When a Boer commando rode in and demanded the keys to the post office she refused to part with them. When the Boers posted a proclamation on the post office notice board, she tore it down and put up one of Milner's, underlining the parts referring to the obligation of subjects to support the crown, and above it she wrote RULE BRITANNIA— "to add further zest to it," she said later. The story of her bold defiance, much embroidered, was told throughout the Empire, and Mrs. Glueck found herself a heroine. A truthful woman, she was not responsible for the additional colouration given her story. Popular versions made her into a British Barbara Fritchie who refused to haul down the Union Jack or who actually pulled down the Vierkleur and hoisted the Union Jack.*

Johannes Smith grew up to be an artist and a trustee of the National Gallery of South Africa, but when he was only a fourteen-year-old boy he and some companions slipped between the strands of barbed wire which surrounded the village of Aberdeen, cut across an ostrich farm, and sought out Scheepers's commando. The British army, in spite of constant searching, had not been able to find Scheepers, but this fourteen-year-old Afrikaner boy and his friends appear to have had little trouble. Young as they were, Scheepers allowed them to join him.

Typical of Scheepers's operations was his occupation of Uniondale. The town was unguarded and he rode in unopposed. He released all the Afrikaner prisoners in the gaol, locked up the local magistrate, burned all the records he found, hauled down the Union Jack, and hoisted the Vierkleur. Then in celebration he galloped down the main street of the town with the Union Jack tied to the tail of his horse.

To blow up a locomotive was fun, and to ride into a village where one was welcomed by admiring young girls who willingly darned worn stockings and sewed up patched shirts was romantic, but for the most part the life of the Boers on commando in the Cape was that of fugitives. They were hunted and harried relentlessly. Although it is doubtful there were ever more than 3,000 men on commando in Cape Colony at any one time, nearly 45,000 British troops were deployed to guard military assets and to track down and destroy them.

With little time for sleep, never free from tension and danger, men had to ride on in all weather, sick or well, wounded or not, if they wanted to escape capture. It was, then, a serious matter when Scheepers developed pains in his abdomen and right side. In his diary he wrote: "Have been ill from 28 Sept. [1901] and on 4 Oct. the pains increased to such an extent that I could not mount a horse."[6] In a few days he was too ill to travel at all, and on 10 October 1901, Kruger's birthday (as Scheepers noted), he had to be left behind at a farmhouse. He was quickly captured.

---

*An interesting aspect of the story, not revealed at the time, is that Mrs. Glueck was not British. Born Sarah Bella Abrahams in Lithuania of Jewish parents, she was educated in Europe and it was there she met and married Max Glueck. The couple emigrated to the United States, where their two children were born, and she had been in South Africa only seven years.

He was removed to a hospital, and his illness was variously diagnosed as gastric fever or acute appendicitis. While still weak and in much pain he was sent to Graaf-Reinet. He wrote in his diary: "The real reason why I was transferred from Beaufort West is a mystery to me. My only conclusion is that I am considered a very important criminal."

He was indeed. On his arrival he was taken to a gaol and searched: "After my name and everything had been written down, I was taken in another direction and put in a hospital room, a most pleasantly cool room, but oh, the bars, the bars!"[7] Here Scheepers learned that he was to be tried by a military court: "On 16 December the final evidence was read out. Thirty accusations were brought against me of 'murder,' seven of 'arson,' 'rough' handling of prisoners, 'barbaric' treatment of kaffirs, etc."[8]

In his defence Scheepers maintained that he had a right to flog or shoot spies and that in burning farms he had been following orders from his superiors. He denied ill-treating soldiers taken prisoner, and he denied some of the killings laid to him; they had been the work of other commandos. He freely admitted that he had flogged "kaffir spies" and he admitted too that he had executed Afrikaner "traitors."

Obviously some of the responsibilities which fell upon the head of the young commandant had been too heavy. Judgement, particularly moral judgement, is difficult to exercise, especially for a youth with life-or-death responsibilities, a god unto himself with his roving band of young men, and Scheepers's decisions sometimes made justice quixotic and cruel, however logical they seemed to him. When two Afrikaner spies (or so they were thought or judged to be) were once caught by his men, it seemed to him that with no courts or gaols available he either had to shoot them or free them. Arbitrarily he decided to release one to carry a letter back to the officer who had sent them and to shoot the other. They were made to draw lots. Perhaps Scheepers felt, as had Jozua Joubert at Colenso, that the choice of the lot was the will of God, but whatever the reasoning, one man drew the short straw and was shot; the other was freed.

Charges that he mistreated Bantu incensed Scheepers, not because the charges were untrue but because they seemed to him unjust; it seemed to him monstrous that Bantu were allowed to testify in court and, even worse, that they were allowed to be gaolers and order about white prisoners. In his diary he wrote: "We Afrikaners will never find justice under the English. Everything is for the kaffirs; their own soldiers go short and the barbarian, the kaffir, gets all the benefits."[9]

On 17 January 1902, a hot summer's day, Scheepers was taken to Church Square where soldiers were drawn up and the townspeople assembled. There Colonel Arthur Henniker-Major read the death sentence and announced that Kitchener had confirmed it. It was reported that Colonel Henniker-Major's whole body trembled as he read and that it almost seemed as if he rather than the condemned man would collapse. The Reverend A. C. Murray visited Scheepers in his cell when he was brought back to it: "I found him so excitable and indignant that it was not possible to have much discussion about his spiritual well-being, and I thought it advisable for us to kneel and lay his circumstances and condition in prayer before the Lord."[10]

The next day Scheepers was taken in an ambulance to his place of execution outside of town. Dismounting, he walked past the open grave waiting to receive him and raised his manacled hands in salute. One of the soldiers asked for the badge he wore on his hat which had the word "Liefde" (Love) on it. He refused, saying he wanted it buried with him. He sat on the chair and the soldiers prepared to tie him to it. He begged them not to, but they had orders to obey. Bound and blindfolded, he was shot by a squad of soldiers from the Coldstream Guards.

Scheepers's body was cut loose, put on a blanket, and carried to the grave. As they were about to lower it an officer called, "Let him drop." He was dropped.

"When the adjutant ordered us to drop him," said one of the soldiers later, "it made me feel sick."

The chair on which he had sat to be executed was broken up and thrown in the grave. His hat too. Then unslaked lime was thrown in and the soldiers shovelled the dirt over him and levelled the grave while the band of the Coldstream Guards played "More Work for the Undertaker."

Back in their quarters that night a comrade said to Private Wilfrid Harrison, who had been one of the firing squad, "Well, that's another of them dispatched." Harrison hit him.

Scheepers was dead and buried, and the British had done their best to make certain there would be neither relics nor shrine. But his ghost lived on, and in the hearts of Afrikaners he was enshrined as a martyr. Shortly after the war, Jacobus and Sophia Scheepers came to Graaf-Reinet to look for the grave of their son, but could find no trace of it. When, later, it was discovered, it was found to be empty; only some pieces of the chair and his hat remained. His final resting place has never been found.

Commandant Pieter Kritzinger almost suffered Scheepers's fate when he fell into British hands; after his wounds healed he was tried by a military court for a similar list of offences, but he was acquitted of them all. Perhaps he profited by the public clamour against the executions. British politicians, Winston Churchill among them, decried the folly of creating another martyr. The trials of Scheepers and Kritzinger brought forth howls of outrage in Holland, Germany, France, and the United States. Senator Henry Moore Teller of Colorado was among those who protested the sentence given Scheepers, and he moved in the United States Senate that President Theodore Roosevelt ask Britain "to set aside the sentence in the interest of humanity," but he was too late. Scheepers had already been shot.

To the Afrikaners rebellion did not seem as heinous a crime as it did to the British; after all, rebellion had always been a part of the Boer tradition. They were as horrified by the executions as their grandfathers had been by the hanging of the rebels at Slachter's Nek in 1816. Now a new generation of Afrikaners was hardened in the belief that the British were unjust, cruel, and bloodthirsty.

There were other Boer commanders who led commandos into Cape Colony and who committed all, or most, of the offences for which Scheepers and Lötter were executed, but they were fortunate enough not to be caught. Hertzog was one of these; another was a future field marshal of the British army who became a member of the Council for Imperial Defence in World War I, prime minister of South Africa in World War II, and one of the founders of the United Nations: Jan Smuts (1870–1950).

Smuts was technically a British subject, for he was born on a farm 3 miles from Riebeck West in Cape Colony. Like all Afrikaners, whatever their profession, he ever remained proud of being a farmer; at the age of seventy-seven, after a life largely devoted to politics in towns and cities, he still claimed, "I am just a son of the veld. . . . I am a farmer's son, and my people have been farmers through the centuries." His early boyhood was indeed spent on a farm, and of course he learned to ride and shoot. Until the age of twelve he received no schooling, but he possessed a remarkable intellect and he entered Victoria College at Stellenbosch at the age of sixteen. He went on to Cambridge, where he performed the astonishing, perhaps unique, feat of taking both parts of the Law Tripos at the same time; he also collected prizes for papers on constitutional law, Roman law, and jurisprudence. He entered the Middle Temple and at the age of twenty-five was a practicing barrister.

Friends and relations have taken pains to point out that Smuts was not really haughty, unfeeling, and unsociable, that he was actually a warm, sensitive human being. This needed pointing out because it was not evident. Most of his contemporaries saw him as a man of cold intellect. He was shrewd too, and many thought him "slim" (foxy, crafty). Even among those who respected his abilities he was often called Slim Jannie. Intensely loyal to those he served, he spent most of his career serving two men, neither of whom was in the least like him: Paul Kruger and Louis Botha. Both of these masters had remarkable qualities of personal leadership and liked close, personal, direct contact with people; both, too, appreciated and knew how to use the powerful intellect of Jan Smuts.

When Kruger had decided to appoint the brilliant young lawyer as state attorney there had been some grumbling and the Johannesburg *Star* said: "Though he may have all the precociousness of a Pitt, we still consider twenty-eight is rather too young an age for the State Attorney of the South African Republic."[11] But Kruger never heeded the advice of newspapers—he didn't even read them. The appointment was made and Smuts was serving in this office when war was declared. His relationship with Kruger was, he said later, as "between a father and his son." After the fall of Pretoria there was not much need for a state attorney, and Smuts joined De la Rey in the western Transvaal, where he quickly learned his new trade as a guerrilla leader.

Most of the invaders of the Cape had been neighbouring Free Staters, but at a conference of Transvaal leaders on 20 June 1901 it was decided that Jan Smuts should lead a commando into Cape Colony. With a hand-picked force of 362 men he started off on an arduous and dangerous 2,000-mile ride with Jacobus van Deventer and Ben Bouwer as his two chief lieutenants. Into his saddlebags went the essentials: confidential papers, a photograph of his wife Isie (née Sybella Krige), the New Testament in Greek, a Bible in English, the complete works of Schiller, and—appropriately, as it turned out—Xenophon's *Anabasis*.

The jumping-off place for the expedition was near Vereeniging, where ten months later it was all to end.

36

SMUTS'S INVASION OF THE CAPE

One of the men who followed Smuts into Cape Colony was Deneys Reitz, only eighteen years old but already a veteran. All five of State Secretary Francis Reitz's sons by his first marriage fought in the war, even the youngest, age twelve when the war began. Deneys had seen action in the early fighting around Ladysmith and at Spion Kop; he had taken part in the eastward retreat after the fall of Pretoria and had escaped into the bush veld to continue fighting. He had several times changed commandos before joining Smuts, and it was his fortune to see more action than most in the course of the war.*

Calamity marked the very beginning of Smuts's expedition; while still gathering up his command at Krugersdorp in the Transvaal, a tremendous thunder storm struck and six of his men were killed by a single bolt of lightning. It was not a good omen. Riding into the Free State, Smuts stumbled into a trap of Kitchener's making, a drive to round up all the commandos operating in the area. In addition to the men manning the garrisons and blockhouses along the railway, 15,000 troops organised into seventeen columns were engaged in sweeping the area he had en-

---

*He was later to see even more soldiering: he took part in suppressing the rebellion of 1914, and in World War I he rose to the command of a British battalion. Later still he became a cabinet minister in the government of a united South Africa.

tered. To lead his commando through the meshes of such a net took skill and luck, hard riding, much fighting, and artful dodging. By the time they reached the Cape Colony border thirty more men had been lost.

On 5 September they slipped across the Orange River by night and, entering Cape Colony, began a trial more arduous than any of them had ever imagined. Almost at once they lost three killed and several wounded in skirmishes with Basutos. Foul weather proved their greatest trial. Until then the nights had been cold but the days had been cloudless and the sun had given some warmth; now rain set in and they rode for days shivering under blankets thrown over their shoulders. Through the bitterly cold nights they lay dismally in the mud. "The nights were evil dreams," said Reitz. Three days after entering the colony they encountered the British for the first time at a pass (a narrow defile, actually) called Moordenaas Poort (Murderer's Pass); one man was killed and two severely wounded. Smuts himself had a narrow escape; he lost his horse and his saddlebags with his books, papers, and his wife's photograph. The following day there was another fight. The British began to hem them in. Three days later Smuts wrote in his diary: "Eleven forces move to surround me."

With no doctors and no bandages or medical supplies of any sort and no wagons, the wounded had to ride; when they could no longer mount they were left in farmhouses to be collected by the British. Deneys Reitz said:

Amid all the cruelty . . . there was one redeeming feature, in that the English soldiers, both officers and men, were unfailingly humane. This was so well known that there was never any hesitation in abandoning a wounded man to the mercy of the troops, in the sure knowledge that he would be taken away and carefully nursed, a certainty that went far to soften the asperities of the war.[1]

Smuts and his men were short of almost all necessities. Reitz did not have a shirt or even underclothes, only "a ragged coat and worn trousers full of holes. . . . On my naked feet were dilapidated rawhide sandals, patched and repaired during eight months of wear, and I had only one frayed blanket to sleep under at night."[2] Few of his companions were better off, and every day saw conditions worsened. Chivied mercilessly by a strong and numerous enemy, men and horses suffered from the cold, the damp, and the fatigue of long, hard rides. One by one the horses faltered and dropped.

Near sunset one evening they came within sight of Jamestown, but as there was a strong British column nearby, Smuts ordered his tired men to keep moving. The night was dark, a cold rain drove into their faces, and their local guide lost his bearings. The men walked, pulling their exhausted horses behind them. While crossing a spruit Reitz's feet stuck in the clay and his wretched sandals came apart when he tried to pull them out. He was now reduced to cutting corners from his thin blanket and tying the scraps around his naked feet. At last, after five hours of floundering about in the mud and cold, the entire commando stumbled to a halt. Men and horses, stiff and numb, dumbly huddled together, ankle deep in mud, an icy rain pouring down on them. When it grew light they counted thirty dead horses.

There was some comfort to be found at the occasional farmhouse they came upon where they were sometimes given bread and coffee. At one large farm they were even able to build fires and eat a hot meal, unimaginable luxuries both. Here the farmer's wife gave Reitz a pair of boots, and he made a coat for himself of a grain bag by the simple expedient of cutting holes for his head and arms. His companions laughed, but they soon followed his example.

Although unwilling to leave their farms and fight, many Cape farmers were willing to help the ragged, harried band with information or to act as guides. Near Dordecht a young farm boy led them expertly on a 30-mile march around the flank of a threatening British column. The tired men halted at a farm and slaughtered a few sheep, but before they had time to cook their mutton there was the familiar cry of "Opsaal!" (saddle up). A long column of British troops was coming towards them.

Detailing some of the men to fight a rear-guard action, Smuts led his depleted force towards a pass in the Stormberg range near Pen Hoek. The troopers swinging around to follow him were slowed down enough by the fire of the rear guard to give them time to make their way up the mountain and onto a large plateau. Looking down on the plain from the far rim of the plateau, scouts could see trains off-loading soldiers and horses; some units were already mounted and making their way towards them. Smuts tried desperately to find some way to escape. He led his men he knew not where, in circles, seeking now here, now there, for an opening in the ring of troops drawing ever tighter around them. A gale blew dust and grit into the faces of the cold, tired, desperate men as they searched unsuccessfully for a weak spot in the gathering noose.

All day long they fought skirmishes and beat hasty retreats. Dusk found them stranded at a small farmhouse. They had been forty hours without sleep; men and horses were famished and exhausted; their ammunition was almost gone; the expedition so far had achieved nothing. Short of a miracle the next day's sun would see their surrender. But the Boers believed in miracles, and what men believe in often happens. As Smuts stood in the farmyard with his lieutenants, Van Deventer and Bouwer, a hunchback on crutches came out of the house. He hardly looked like their deliverer as he hobbled up to Smuts, but he was. He knew a way out over a bog-like area that was unlikely to be guarded, and he offered to guide them. Once again the men heard the familiar cry of "Opsaal!" Six or seven burghers had been wounded in the day's skirmishing, yet all but two went on.

Mounted insecurely on a horse, their guide led them in the dark over a slippery, squelching, twisting path. At one point they slipped past a British unit, passing so close that they could hear the soldiers' voices and the champing of their horses. At the edge of the escarpment their guide slid from his horse, adjusted the crutches under his arms, and set off in the night to make his way home.

Smuts quietly gave the order, and in the dark the men led their horses over the rim, slithering and sliding down the steep, grassy slope. It was, said Reitz, "probably the nearest approach to the vertical attempted by any mounted force during the war. . . . At times whole batches of men and horses came glissading past, knocking against all in their course."[3] Even when they reached the plain below they had to press on. Their greatest need was for sleep, but sleep was impossible. Ahead of them were the tracks of the railway they had seen that morning, and several miles beyond was another set of tracks. Both would have to be crossed before daylight if they were to escape fresh swarms of troops which the trains could quickly bring to the scene. Only the cold, biting wind kept them awake. Not for another twenty-four hours would they rest.

It was about eleven o'clock that night when they reached the first set of tracks. A train was approaching, and some of the men were for derailing and attacking it, but Smuts refused: there might be civilians on board, he said. The lighted windows of the train rolled by as they sat their horses in the dark. Framed inside them were fresh, smartly dressed officers drinking wine, laughing and talking. It seemed an incredible world they gazed at. When the last carriage clattered past they were left in the silence to dismount and wearily lead their horses across the tracks. They had missed an opportunity to change history. General John French was on that train.

They rode all night. Held up briefly by a fence or a ditch, men would slip to the ground and, crouching at their horses' feet, fall so soundly asleep that they had to be shaken awake. The sun was rising as they crossed the second set of tracks at a siding about 5 miles from Sterkstroom. There were some deserted railway buildings there, and Van Deventer and a few men stayed behind to search for anything useful. While they were scrounging, a goods train came clanking up. Van Deventer stopped it by switching the points. It proved to be an empty coal train with only a driver, stoker, and brakeman aboard, but Van Deventer did find a mail bag which he extracted before allowing the train to go on its way. The idea of destroying the train to prevent its use by the British or to prevent its crew from reporting their presence seems not to have occurred to him.

Most of the mail proved to be personal letters of little interest, but there were newspapers and these were eagerly scanned for news of the war. They were delighted and amused to find an item about themselves: Smuts had invaded Cape Colony with "the riff-raff of the Boer armies." Also of interest was Kitchener's first and only attempt to end the war by threats: a proclamation announcing that all Boer officers who did not surrender by 15 September would be "banished forever from South Africa; and the cost of maintaining the families of such burghers shall be recoverable from, and become a charge on, their properties, whether land or movables in both colonies." De Wet later said of it: "It had no effect whatsoever. . . . I know of no single case where an officer in consequence of this proclamation surrendered; on the contrary . . . the burghers had more reason to trust their officers than before."[4] He was probably right. The Boers called it a *papierbomme* (paper bomb). Steyn, De Wet, and De la Rey all made defiant replies. On 15 September Steyn wrote Kitchener a long letter in which he said: "May I be permitted to say that your Excellency's jurisdiction is limited to the range of your Excellency's guns."[5] As for the threats to the Boer officers:

> Our country is ruined; our hearths and homes wrecked; our cattle are looted, or killed by the thousand; our women and children are made prisoners, insulted, and carried away by armed kaffirs; and many hundreds have already given their lives for the freedom of the fatherland. Can we now—when it is merely a question of banishment—shrink from our duty?[6]

Even in Britain Kitchener's proclamation did not sit well. Conan Doyle, the greatest apologist for Britain's war policy, wrote: "The imposition of personal penalties upon the officers of an opposing army is a step for which it is difficult to quote a precedent. . . . the whole proceeding must appear to be injudicious and high-handed."[7]

Although the proclamation had been issued on 7 August, it was 13 September when Smuts and his men saw it. They had two days left in which to surrender, but they had no intention of giving up the struggle as long as they were physically able to fight, although it was not at all certain how much longer this would be.

On the banks of the Klaas Smits River Smuts paused long enough for his men to prepare a hasty meal and for the long-suffering horses to pluck a few tufts of grass. There was time for no more. Another British column appeared on the horizon to hustle them. Retreating from kopje to kopje, Smuts kept off his pursuers until sunset, when they gave up the chase. He then led his men to a large farm where, after sixty hours of marching and fighting, they were at last able to sleep.

A night's rest was welcome indeed, but it was all they got. At nine o'clock the next morning another British column was seen bearing down on them. It was again "Opsaal!" and away. All that day and the next they fled from the doggedly pursuing British. More cold rain added to their misery. Then one night their guide lost his way and they floundered about, ankle deep in mud and water. About midnight the rain turned to sleet. The grain bags the men wore froze solid into stiff and cutting coats of mail. They had to keep moving to avoid freezing. Men who had endured all previous hardships without complaint now audibly groaned. "We had known two years of war," said Reitz, "but we came nearer to despair that night than I care to remember. . . . and for my part I passed through no greater test during the war."[8] It was worse than anything that had gone before, worse than any battle they had fought; fourteen men and dozens of horses were lost on this dreadful night. Xenophon and his Greeks in western Armenia did not suffer worse.

It was almost dawn before they came upon a deserted homestead. They stumbled inside the empty buildings and stood shivering in the dark, men and horses huddled together, waiting dumbly for daylight. With the dawn the rain stopped and fires were built; men and their clothes were dried. At midday Smuts ordered them to move on, and they headed for a large farm 8 or 9 miles away where a Bantu had told them they would find fodder for their famished horses. Although nearly every man had begun the expedition with two horses, there were now not enough to go around, and nearly a quarter of the force were without mounts; of the horses still alive, not one was fit.

At the farm they found a large supply of oat sheaves and even sheep for slaughter and wood to burn. That night they slept in relative comfort, but local Bantu told of British columns that were forming a cordon to the south, their direction of march. The next day, 17 September 1901, was to see the most dramatic and significant action of the campaign.

When scouts reported 200 British cavalry waiting for them at the end of a valley just ahead, Smuts decided to attack, for unless he could capture fresh horses and ammunition he was lost. Van Deventer and about 20 men, Reitz among them, were sent ahead while Smuts brought up the remainder of the commando. Van Deventer's men had just crossed a small stream and were passing through a fringe of thorn trees on the other side when they collided with a British patrol of about 15 or 20 troopers. Reitz and three or four of his companions were in the lead. Leaping from their horses, they opened fire, bringing down several troopers from a distance of only 10 yards. The patrol wheeled and bolted. Reitz, having fired his last two cartridges in this encounter, ran forward to grab the Lee-Metford and bandolier of a fallen soldier. Thus rearmed, he jumped on his horse and joined the others in the chase. The soldiers were delayed by a gate, and two or three more were shot from their saddles.

When the Boers reached the gate, Van Deventer and a half-dozen men veered off and made for a nearby kopje while the others continued their hot pursuit of the cavalry patrol. The troopers raced to an outcropping of rocks where a British picket had been posted. There they leaped from their horses, scrambled behind rocks, and opened a point-blank fire on their pursuers. A mountain gun and a machine gun also opened up. Three burghers were hit, but the rest rode straight for the rocks, jumped off, loosed their horses, and returned the fire, soldiers and burghers only a few feet from each other.

Looking around from the shelter of his rock, Reitz was surprised that the tents of the British camp were so near that he could see the soldiers running and clearly hear the shouts of their officers. Smuts and the remainder of the commando were coming up on the other side, and from where he lay Reitz could see a mountain gun with a four-man crew opening up on them, apparently unaware that any of the Boers were so close. He shot at the tallest of the four and saw him spin and fall back in a sitting position, his back against the wheel of the gun. The other three bolted, and he shot one more as he ran.

Some troopers from the camp came running towards them, and Reitz shot a big, heavily built sergeant in the abdomen; he folded up and rolled on the ground in agony until he died. Young Lieutenant Richard Brinsley Sheridan rose up from behind a rock and fired at Reitz but missed. When he tried again Reitz creased his temple with a bullet. Sheridan swayed unsteadily, blood running down his face, but raised his rifle; another burgher shot him through the brain.

The British, taken by surprise and caught in a fast and accurate fire from all sides, panicked. Only one group of soldiers held out, fighting valiantly from a stone kraal. It took fierce hand-to-hand fighting to subdue them and put the Boers in undisputed possession. They had lost only 1 killed and 6 wounded, while the British, out of 145 men, had suffered 26 killed and 39 wounded. Of the 6 officers, 4 were killed and 2 wounded.

Masters of the camp, the burghers began joyously to loot. Tents and wagons were ransacked; grain bag coats were thrown off and exchanged for warm British uniforms; fresh horses were acquired, along with saddlery, Lee-Metfords, and all the ammunition they could carry. Reitz rifled an officer's tent and emerged dressed in riding breeches, a cavalry officer's tunic, a sporting Lee-Metford, and full bandoliers of ammunition. He also selected a superb grey Arab pony which had belonged to Lieutenant Sheridan and a strong riding mule. Then, flushed with victory and resplendent in his finery, he strode about the camp and battlefield; not even the sight of the men he had killed could dampen his spirits: "I looked upon them with mixed feelings, for although I have never hated the English, a fight is a fight, and while I was sorry for the men, I was proud of my share in the day's work."[9]

Smuts gained much by this little victory. Not only was he able to reequip, reprovision, and rearm his commando, but he had broken through the circle of British troops surrounding him and out of the mountainous country into the open plain. He was now free to go marauding in the Cape Midlands, where he soon created an uproar. Equally important, the battle had renewed the confidence of his men in him as a leader. The weather improved and they rode gaily into the heart of Cape Colony, helping themselves from the larders of farms, to the fruits of orchards, and to sheep from the flocks.

The Boers were usually punctilious in the observance of the rules of war as they understood them, but both sides tended to let their principles slip in the last, more bitter months of the conflict. Smuts must have known very well that it was against the accepted rules of warfare to don the enemy's uniform and that men caught doing so could be, and often were, shot as spies if captured. Yet, understandably if not excusably, he permitted his ragged, shivering men to wear the uniforms of the 17th

Lancers. While there was some justification at the time for wearing the clothing, there was no excuse for not removing the badges and insignia, and there was no excuse for not discarding the uniforms altogether when the commando entered the Midlands and supplies of other clothing became available. For some of his men this wearing of the British khaki was fatal.

Most were ignorant of the enormity of their crime. They liked the warm clothes, and many also enjoyed presenting a military appearance. Reitz took pride in wearing all of the badges and insignia of an officer of the 17th Lancers. He and his companions were often mistaken for British troops, and when asked by civilians the name of their unit their stock witticism was to reply that they were "English-killing dragoons," and doubtless some mistook them for the 6th Inniskilling Dragoons. One day the commando stopped at a wayside inn, and, as most of the men had not tasted liquor for more than a year, some took the opportunity to make up for time lost. Piet de Ruyt, a Hollander, overindulged and was sleeping when Smuts cried "Opsaal!" and the commando moved on without him. He was still asleep in his lancer's uniform when the British arrived shortly after. They shot him.

Piet de Ruyt was the first but not the last of Smuts's men to face a firing squad. Although the Boers claimed that in the last days of the war they had no clothes other than the uniforms they stripped from prisoners —and this was certainly true in the Transvaal and the Orange Free State —the British were justly indignant at the use of their uniform to deceive them. Reitz admitted that at least twice he was saved from death or capture by posing as a British soldier. More serious was another incident involving Smuts's men.

Two young burghers were out scouting one day when they unexpectedly encountered a British patrol. One of the burghers, an English-speaking boy from Johannesburg, called out: "Don't fire, we are 17th Lancers!" Captain Watson, in charge of the patrol, hesitated for a fatal moment; both burghers fired, killing Watson and one of his men. Smuts, according to Reitz, "pulled a long face" when told of the incident but apparently made no attempt to discourage such deceptions. The death of Captain Watson was much publicized; Kitchener used it as a justification for shooting burghers caught in British uniforms.

Smuts worked his way south, successfully dodging the columns sent to catch him, until he was only 50 miles from Algoa Bay on the eastern Cape coast. The taciturn Smuts did not tell his men where he was leading them or why, and some speculated that he actually intended to attack Port Elizabeth, but then an unexpected misfortune overtook the commando. On 29 September, hard pressed by British columns, Smuts retreated into a nearby mountain range. He was probably not seriously concerned, for he could retreat further into the mountains and take his men where it was unlikely that British columns would follow, but in the populated plains food had been so plentiful that the men no longer carried supplies with

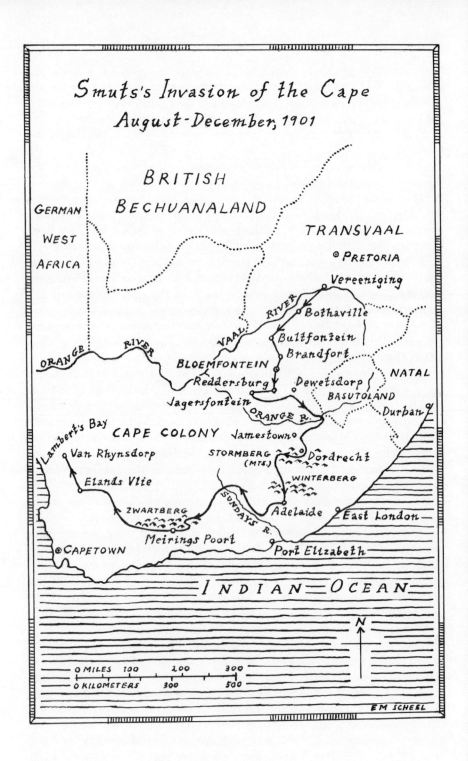

Smuts's Invasion of the Cape
August - December, 1901

GERMAN
WEST
AFRICA

BRITISH
BECHUANALAND

TRANSVAAL

⊙ PRETORIA

Vereeniging

VAAL RIVER

Bothaville

Bultfontein

Brandfort

ORANGE RIVER

BLOEMFONTEIN

Reddersburg

Jagersfontein

Dewetsdorp

NATAL

BASUTOLAND

ORANGE R.

Durban ⊙

CAPE COLONY

Lambert's Bay

Jamestown

Van Rhynsdorp

STORMBERG
(MTS.)

Dordrecht

Elands Vlie

WINTERBERG

ZWARTBERG

SUNDAYS R.

Adelaide

East London

Meirings Poort

⊙ CAPETOWN

Port Elizabeth

INDIAN OCEAN

N

0 MILES   100   200   300
0 KILOMETERS   300   500

EM SCHEEL

them; now they found themselves in an uninhabited mountain region and they were soon hungry.

Scattered about in this wild area was a plant bearing a fruit somewhat resembling a pineapple and locally known as "Hottentot's bread" *(Encephelartos Altensteinii)*. It does not grow on the high veld and was unknown to the burghers from the north. One man tasted it and found it good. Others followed his example. It seemed that God had provided them with manna in this wilderness—and so it might have proved at another time of year, for although wholesome and edible in its season the fruit is indigestible at other times, and this was such a time. Like Xenophon's Greeks who ate the honeycombs, men began to retch and roll on the ground, groaning in agony. More than half the commando was soon *hors de combat*—and sickest of all was Jan Smuts.

Just at this juncture British troops were seen moving to attack them. Smuts appeared to be in a coma; Van Deventer was too sick to move. Ben Bouwer, although ill himself, managed to assemble all those still able to function along the top of the ridge they were occupying. It was nearly sunset and the light was uncertain, but they shot well enough to discourage the assaulting troops, who retreated to the hillside opposite to wait for morning before resuming the attack. To the Boers it was obvious that they ought to retreat during the night, but it was equally obvious that half the commando, including their leader, was unable either to walk or to ride. The night was dark and a cold wind sprang up to add to their misery. The groans and retching continued; those who had not eaten the poisonous fruit sat shivering and hungry, wondering what was to become of them.

Towards morning most of the sick men began to recover, and one by one they stumbled to their feet. When the first light appeared in the eastern sky only about twenty remained prostrate. Smuts was still on his back, but he had recovered sufficiently to appreciate the danger of their position and he ordered the commando to move; all who were unable to saddle and mount by themselves were to be tied to their horses. Smuts himself had to be held on his horse. In the early dawn they started off, following a game track which led them deeper into the mountains. Making their way south, they reached a point from which they could see in the distance the Indian Ocean and at night the lights of Port Elizabeth. No other commando had ever or would ever penetrate so far south.

Scouts sent out under Jack Borrius to find a way still further south ran into a British patrol and were forced to turn back. There had been fighting, and Borrius returned in a pitiable condition: his left eye shot away, its socket filled with dried blood, and his right hand smashed to a bloody pulp.

Benjamin Coetzee led the next scouting party, but two of his men walked into a British ambush and were captured. As they were wearing British uniforms, they were shot out of hand and buried where they fell. Their graves are the most southerly of all the fighting burghers.

Smuts now abandoned his attempt to go further south and headed for the western Cape. He had been reinforced by small bands of Boers, some Cape rebels, and remnants of other commandos, including that of Gideon Scheepers. For more rapid movement, easier provisioning, and to confuse the British, he divided his force, Van Deventer taking charge of one half and leading them by a separate route to a rendezvous in the Calvina district, hundreds of miles to the west. When at last Smuts reached the western Cape he linked up with numerous small bands of Cape rebels and 600 well-armed men led by Salomon Gerhardus ("Manie") Maritz, described by Reitz as "a short, dark man, of enormous physical strength, cruel and ruthless in his methods, but a splendid guerilla leader, and according to his lights an ardent patriot."[10]

Smuts had failed to create a general uprising of the Cape Afrikaners, but his invasion, considered in any other terms, was a success, and it drew off large British forces which Kitchener would have liked to have used against the larger forces of De la Rey, De Wet, and Botha. Although Smuts was later to refer to this campaign, in spite of its horrors, as being the happiest period in his life, he was at least once close to despair. From Nieuwoudtville, near Calvina, he wrote a letter to his brother Koos (delivered by the British postal system) in which he said: "I have had numerous narrow escapes, for which I am grateful; but each person has his turn . . . I hold out little hope of seeing you all again: I know you will do your best to help Isie."[11]

It was in the western Cape that a colonial named Lambert Colyn (or Lemuel Colaine; accounts differ), who said he had escaped from a British prison, joined the commando. "He was a man of about forty-five," said Reitz, "in appearance a typical back-veld Boer, with flowing beard and corduroys." His story was believed, and he was given a rifle. A few days later he disappeared and when next seen was leading a British column in a dawn surprise attack on their laager that resulted in 17 casualties.

A short time after, when Smuts successfully attacked a British camp near Vanrhynsdorp, Colyn was captured and brought to him. "Take him out and shoot him," snapped Smuts.

Colyn fell to his knees, begging for mercy, but Smuts was adamant: "For you there can be no mercy. You have done the dirty work of the English."

Colyn, still pleading, was dragged away, stood in front of a firing squad, and shot.

Smuts was never allowed to forget this episode. Many years later, when he had become prime minister of the Union of South Africa and one of the British Empire's most loyal servants, he was making a speech at a political meeting at Beaufort West. Continually interrupted by an old man with a high voice, he was finally forced to stop and let him speak out:

"General, do you remember the day you shot Colyn?"

"Yes."

"Do you remember how Colyn implored you to spare his life?"

Smuts did not answer.

"General, do you remember what you said to him? You said, 'Colyn, you are one of those rotten Afrikaners who allow themselves to be used by the British to do their dirty work.' General, are you not perhaps one of those Afrikaners?"

There can be no doubt that Smuts felt justified in ordering the execution, politically difficult as it was to live with afterwards. His son remembered hearing his father tell the story "in such matter-of-fact terms that I was left without any doubt that he considered it a minor incident of the campaign."[12] Of course at the time it was impossible for Smuts to look ahead to the day when he would be a privy councilor to the King of England, would accept from his hands the Order of Merit and be made a Companion of Honour, but he may have thought back to Xenophon's story of Cyrus and the traitor Orontas in the *Anabasis*.

The incursions of other commandos into the Cape had been little more than raids, but in the western Cape Smuts became undisputed master of a sizable chunk of British territory stretching from the Oliphant to the Orange and only 150 miles due north of Cape Town. He made his headquarters on the Oliphant River only 25 miles inland from the Atlantic Ocean and distributed his men in small groups over his conquered territory. There was time now to make new plans, and even time for some relaxation. Gathering up all those who had never seen the sea, he led them, some 60 or 70 farm boys, most of whom had never seen any body of water larger than a pond, to a small deserted inlet called Fishwater. When they rode over the last sand dune and saw the great expanse of ocean shimmering before them they reined in their horses and stared with amazement and delight, calling out, as did Xenophon's soldiers on Mount Theches, "The sea! The sea!" Throwing off their clothes and the saddles of their horses, they rode naked and bareback into the surf, shouting and laughing. That night they camped on the beach, built fires of driftwood, and sitting around them talked quietly of the wonders they had seen, the hardships, the fighting, and all the tales they would have to tell when they got home—if they got home.

Six of Maritz's men also rode to the sea and made their way along the coast to Darling, where they saw a British warship lying at anchor near the shore in Lambert's Bay. It was an irresistible target, and they loosed a few rounds at its steel sides. When the ship's crew returned the fire, using their guns, they bolted, happy to be able to boast of having fought the only naval action of the war.

But this was not the first time the Royal Navy had had a chance to fire on the Boers from a man-of-war. Earlier, in January 1901, some of Hertzog's men had reached this same point in the hope of finding a ship from Europe bringing them supplies and foreign volunteers. It was a scheme that went awry: instead of the friendly ship they expected they found HMS *Sybille* anchored there. As Erskine Childers in *The Times History* said,

the ship "saluted the raiders with a volley of shell as a reminder that they
had reached the element where Britain, under Providence, was undisputed mistress."[13]

Smuts now felt himself strong enough to undertake offensive operations, and he moved against three fortified British posts some 150 miles
to the north: Springbok, Concordia, and O'okiep. The first two were
captured without difficulty, thanks to some homemade hand grenades
manufactured out of dynamite found in a nearby copper mine, but
O'okiep proved difficult and Smuts laid siege to it. It was while engaged
in this operation in April 1902 that he received under a flag of truce a
message from Kitchener saying that a meeting had been arranged between the Boer and the British leaders at Vereeniging to discuss peace.
He was invited to attend.

37

FIGHTING THE GUERRILLAS

The guerrilla phase of the war called for new strategy and new tactics on
the part of the British, and Kitchener was not slow to develop these once
he realised that the war had not ended and that more than just police
actions were required. He did not hesitate to employ most of the ruthless
methods necessary to fight guerrillas, but he was slow to see their political
and psychological implications, to understand that, however justifiable
militarily, many of his methods were politically unsound and that military
measures alone cannot conquer guerrillas.

The nature of guerrilla warfare has changed little since it was first
used in modern times by the Spanish and Portuguese in the Peninsular
War, for in spite of technology, it remains a primitive form of warfare and
its concepts, tactics, and strategy remain very much the same in all eras.
The methods by which guerrillas are overcome are, for humane men,
unpalatable because they involve making war upon entire populations,
upon those who in orthodox warfare are considered noncombatants. But
as guerrillas are dependent upon the noncombatant population for supplies, information, and other necessities, and the passive, if not active,
support of the people among whom they move is essential, these people
—housewives who count the men and guns in the passing column, small
boys who have seen the hiding soldiers in their ambush, old men who
know forgotten paths—become a danger to the counter-guerrilla forces

and minatory action is taken against them. So terrorism becomes a standard feature of guerrilla wars.

Terrorism is a tool for coercion. To achieve maximum effectiveness the usual devices of terrorism—executions, destruction of property, imprisonments, torture, et al.—must be employed brutally and indiscriminately without regard to fairness or justice. It requires the willing suspension of humane feelings and all sense of fair play. The British by temperament have usually been incapable of this.

"Humane" was never an adjective applied to Kitchener, but before describing the measures he actually employed it is only fair to say at the beginning that the British did not use one of the oldest, usually effective, but most repulsive techniques, one which in the past fifty years has been a common feature of guerrilla wars: the use of torture to obtain information. Although rarely acknowledged as an instrument of policy, torture is frequently countenanced by higher commanders or, even when it is not, is indulged in by at least some subordinate commanders. The temptation is often strong. It is a remarkable thing that in this war there is not a single recorded instance of this ever having taken place. As far as is known, no one even suggested it. Amid all the angry charges flung by each side against the other, neither Boer nor Briton ever claimed that physical torture was used.

Torture can be mental as well as physical, of course, but the only recorded incident of the deliberate infliction of mental anguish is the story told by Captain James Seeley (later Lord Mottistone), who apparently never felt that he had done anything reprehensible. He had ridden all night with 20 men to capture Boers who he had learned were at a farm owned by a man named Greyling in the Orange Free State. He surrounded the farm and three Boers rode out; all of them managed to escape. After a futile pursuit, he led his troopers back to the farm, now occupied only by a boy, Jappie, his mother, and two sisters. Singling out the boy to question, he demanded to know where his father had gone. All of his questions were met with silence; the boy refused to talk. Determined to break him, Seeley ordered up a firing squad, stood him in front of it, and threatened to order it to shoot; still the boy refused to betray his father. In the face of such resolution it was Seeley who broke, called off his bluff, and shook the boy's hand, telling the terrified mother that she had a son to be proud of, one it had been a privilege to meet. Then he mounted and rode off with his men. Telling the tale in later years, he wrote: "As long as I live, I shall never forget that wonderful moment when love of father, home and country triumphed over certain death. Never shall I forget the expression on the face of that Boer lad when, lifting his head, he said to me with glistening eyes: *I shall not tell!*"[1]

The Anglo-Boer War has been called the last gentlemen's war, but then, so has the Crimean War. It is debatable whether any war can be so described, but certainly few wars, and no guerrilla wars, have been fought with so many of the leaders on both sides personally displaying so much humanity, even when carrying out policies which were sometimes far from humane.

Both sides neglected one of the most valuable, perhaps *the* most valuable, guerrilla warfare weapon. As fifteen years later T. E. Lawrence discovered, "The printing press is the greatest weapon in the armoury of the modern commander." Kitchener had all the printing presses in his hands, but he failed to make full use of them.

Although Kitchener disdained to use torture and was ignorant of the power of propaganda, he made use of every other tool available to him for use against the Boer guerrillas: destruction of the enemy's sources of supply through farm burning and the slaughter of livestock; control of the population by a pass system and by herding noncombatants into concentration camps; protection of his own supply routes and restriction of the enemy's movements by lines of blockhouses; continual pressure on the enemy by mobile columns and drives; and demoralisation through the use of "traitors."

That the railways were vital to the British forces in South Africa had been obvious to all commanders from the beginning, and they obviously had to be protected. To this end a number of strong points were established along the way by constructing a series of blockhouses. The first line of blockhouses was built between Jacobsdal and Ladybrand, and it was found that not only did it protect the railway, but it served as a barrier of sorts which restricted the mobility of the Boer commandos. Kitchener saw that his task would be made easier if he could prevent the Boers from freely moving about, if he could prevent them from combining forces and hinder their communication with one other. By extensive use of the blockhouses along the railway he could divide the sea of the population in which the guerrillas swam (to use Mao Tse-tung's analogy) into polders which could be drained of supplies and population and in which the fighting burghers might more easily be caught. So the blockhouse system was extended until some 8,000 were built, stretching for 3,700 miles along the railways. By November 1901 some 14,700 square miles of the Transvaal and 17,000 square miles of the Orange Free State were enclosed. The construction, once started, was continued right up to the last day of the war. Although De Wet contemptuously referred to the policy of blockhouses as "the policy of the blockhead," it played an important part in reducing the mobility and thus the effectiveness of the commandos.

Some of the first blockhouses were of stone, but such substantial structures were expensive and time-consuming to build. It was not until the invention by a Royal Engineer officer of a cheap model capable of being easily and quickly constructed that the use of blockhouses on a large scale became practicable. Two cylinders of corrugated iron 6 feet high, one 2 feet smaller in diameter than the other, were used. The smaller, 12 feet in diameter, was placed inside the larger and the gap between them filled with earth or stones. A 4-foot-square door and a dozen loopholes were punched and an overhanging pitch roof added. Placed quite close together, seldom more than a mile apart and often separated by only a few hundred yards, they were surrounded by barbed wire and along both sides of the tracks wire festooned with tins containing pebbles was strung to give warning when anyone tried to cross. Sometimes there were also ditches and stone walls. Telephones and telegraphs were used to maintain communications, and armoured trains with guns and searchlights patrolled the tracks.

The idea of hampering the movement of guerrillas by using fortified lines was not new; the Spanish army in Cuba had tried a similar system, throwing *trochas* from coast to coast across the width of the island. It had not worked well for the Spanish, but if Kitchener knew of the experience he did not allow it to discourage him.

The principal objection to the blockhouse system was that it tied down to fixed defences an enormous number of men, so many in fact that Kitchener never had more than 50,000 troops actually available for offensive operations. In the beginning the employment of infantry on blockhouse duty was not a serious drain on effective manpower, for there was little other use to which infantry could be put; soldiers on foot tramping about the veld trying to catch nimble horsemen were ineffectual, although this was a use to which they were often put. As the lines of blockhouses were extended, however, more and more men were needed.

No special skills or powers of endurance (other than the ability to endure boredom) were needed for blockhouse duty; it was for the most part a tedious and lonely life. J. F. C. Fuller, who served as a subaltern, wrote:

The worst feature of blockhouse life was its demoralizing influence on the soldier. Apart from sentry duty and minor fatigue work, there was absolutely nothing to do except talk, smoke and gamble. Frequently no sign of civilization, or even of life, except for the two neighboring blockhouses, could be seen for miles around, and this utter blankness of life carried with it a bad moral influence. . . . Though they were in complete safety, men would become jumpy and bad-tempered.[2]

The temptation to use the great numbers of idle Bantu and Coloureds for this irksome task and thus free soldiers for other duties proved irresistible, and the British laid aside their scruples about not arming "natives," gave them guns, and employed them on blockhouse duty. Soldiers facetiously called these guards "the Black Watch." The experiment was not a success, for the undisciplined men were not always vigilant, and British officers testing the system once "captured" with ease several blockhouses whose Coloured guards were absorbed in playing cards.

The simple cylindrical blockhouses would not have been able to withstand artillery fire, but in the later stages of the war the Boers had few guns: most had been captured, destroyed, or buried when the ammunition ran out—and besides, they found that guns, like wagons, hampered mobility and were often more of an impediment than they were worth. Occasionally blockhouses were attacked with homemade grenades or dynamite charges, but usually they were left alone and the Boers attempted crossings at night by cutting the wires between them.

A commando crossing a railway was not a common occurrence. Many soldiers spent their entire tour of duty in South Africa without ever seeing a hostile burgher. This lack of activity made for a relaxation of vigilance that often enabled the Boers to slip through, although at times the guards became jumpy and nervous, firing at any noise they heard. Wild animals stumbling into the wire at night provoked outbursts of musketry, and, as firing from one blockhouse usually caused neighbouring blockhouses to open fire, a chain reaction was sometimes created which, once started, was difficult to stop. In one instance the firing spread along a hundred miles of track and thousands of bullets were sent off into the dark and empty veld. Fuller remembered lying in bed listening "to a battle on the railway line between Kaffir watchmen who were blazing away at each other."[3]

For offensive operations the traditional combat units—battalions, brigades, and divisions—were no longer practical and the fighting unit became the column. Although sometimes infantry was included, the most effective columns consisted of mounted infantry, sometimes cavalry and a few guns. Their size varied between 200 and 1,500, but typical was the description by Kipling in "Columns": "A section, a pompom, an' six 'undred men."[4]

Columns were used not only to hunt down Boer commandos but also to plough furrows of destruction through the former republics. The two functions did not complement each other: one being the swift pursuit of a mobile enemy and the other the slow process of systematic destruction. It was cruel logic that dictated the burning of farms and the slaughter of livestock, and it aroused deep and long-lasting resentment. At first farms were burned only when British troops had been fired on from them. Then Roberts ordered that farms lying nearest any spot where Boers had cut a railway or telegraph line were to be burned. These were punitive measures, of course, but Roberts was careful to issue orders (18 November 1900) that farm burning was to be strictly limited to the stated offence: "The mere fact of a burgher being on commando is on *no account* to be used as reason for burning the house."

Roberts knew all about farm burning, for it had been a common practice on India's Northwest Frontier where he had long served, but he did not like it; he knew, as he told the House of Lords, that it would result in "a rich harvest of hatred and revenge." Nineteen years after the war (27 January 1921) Field Marshal William Robertson wrote to T. W. Mackensie, editor of *The Friend* (Bloemfontein):

I had been greatly struck when serving on the staff of Lord Roberts in South Africa with the way in which he always kept in view that the two Republics might one day become members of the British Empire and throughout the operations insisted upon the people being treated with every possible consideration consistent with military requirements.[5]

Many soldiers thought Roberts was too soft. Lieutenant David Miller wrote to his mother:

The great mistake they are making here, as far as I can see, is that they leave all the farms and small tenure standing. The result of this is that the Boers have always means of getting fresh supplies. I would burn all the farms in the disaffected parts, and also all the towns which we are not occupying, sending the women and children out to the nearest commando.[6]

Lieutenant Miller got his wish when Kitchener took command. The new commander-in-chief undertook deliberate, thorough, wholesale destruction of farms: all buildings burned to the ground, all crops set alight, all animals slaughtered, hundreds of square miles turned into a wasteland. An estimated 30,000 farms were burned and 3,600,000 sheep slaughtered. "Our course through the country is marked as in prehistoric ages by pillars of smoke by day and fire by night," wrote one soldier with a British column. "We usually burn from six to twelve farms a day."[7] All who travelled through the Orange Free State and the Transvaal commented on the desolation they saw. Miller, who was now seeing the results of the policy he had advocated, wrote his mother: "The country is now almost entirely laid waste. You can go for miles and miles—in fact you might march for weeks and weeks and see no sign of a living thing or a cultivated patch of land—nothing but burnt farms and desolation."[8]

Miller was writing of conditions as he saw them in September 1901. One month later, young Freda Schlosberg, travelling with her parents from Rhenosterkop to Bronkhorstspruit, wrote in her diary, "On the road there are many burned houses or ruins of former dwellings which the British had burnt. There was not a sign of life for miles, nothing but black ruins and endless stretches of bare dry veld."[9] Smuts, making his perilous way south through the Free State to invade Cape Colony, wrote in his diary, "Dams everywhere filled with rotting animals. Water undrinkable. Veld covered with slaughtered herds of sheep and goats, cattle and horses. Hungry lambs run bleating around."[10]

There was an outcry in England—even Churchill condemned the policy as "a hateful folly"—and Campbell-Bannerman, leader of the opposition and future prime minister, created an uproar when at a dinner of the National Reform Union on 14 June 1901 he referred to Kitchener's activities as "methods of barbarism." The British, who for the past two hundred years at least had regarded themselves as the most civilised people on earth, were more horrified by Campbell-Bannerman's calling them barbarians than by Kitchener's methods. Explaining himself to the House of Commons, Campbell-Bannerman protested that he intended no calumny against the army, but he stuck to his conviction that Kitchener's policy was barbarous, and in a subsequent speech at Stirling he said:

The farms are burned, the country is wasted. The flocks and herds are either butchered or driven off; the mills are destroyed, furniture and instruments of agriculture smashed. These things are what I have termed methods of barbarism. . . . If those are not the methods of barbarism, what methods did barbarism employ?[11]

The Boers obtained copies of this speech and reproduced it for distribution to the commandos, proof that even the British themselves were sickened by Kitchener's policies.

Milner in a dispatch defended the policy and clearly stated the position of the British military:

The fight is now mainly over supplies. The Boers live entirely on the country through which they pass, not only taking all the food they can lay hands upon on the farms—grain, forage, horses, cattle, etc., but looting the small village stores for clothing, boots, coffee, sugar, etc., of all which they are in need. Our forces, on their side, are compelled to denude the country of everything moveable, in order to frustrate these tactics of the enemy. . . . Indeed, the loss of crops and stock is a far more serious matter than the destruction of farm buildings, of which so much has been heard.[12]

In South Africa there was (and still is) something almost sacred about a farm. A farm was more than the means for making a living, more than just a home. This feeling was well expressed by Victor Sampson, himself a loyal British Cape colonist: "Personally, the burning of a town house would lie no heavier on my conscience than shooting a cock pheasant, but to burn a farm or a haystack is, according to my ethics, utterly heartless and damnable."[13]

For precedent the British pointed to Sherman's farm- and- crop-burning operations in the Shenandoah Valley during the American Civil War and the destruction wrought by the Germans in France in 1870. But it was, as Conan Doyle said, a policy "which warfare may justify but which civilization must deplore."[14]

Burning farms, depriving the commandos of food and supplies, was only half of Kitchener's strategy; the other half was to catch the slippery burghers on the veld, and this he found an exasperating task. In his dispatch of 8 July 1901 he explained his problem:

Divided up into small parties of three to four hundred men, they are scattered all over the country without plans and without hope, and on the approach of our troops they disperse, to reassemble in the same neighborhood when our men pass on. In this way they continue an obstinate resistance without retaining anything, or defending the smallest portion of this vast country.[15]

In effect, the Boers fought where and when they wished, retaining the initiative. Although many uitlanders had returned to the Transvaal, the mines could be worked and fields ploughed only as long as there were British bayonets to protect the workers and farmers, mines and crops. The extent of British rule was still measured by the range of their guns.

There was a highly protected zone around Johannesburg, roughly a rectangle 120 miles long and 60 miles wide, within which the mines were working, producing by December 1901 some 53,000 ounces of gold per month. Even so, there were sometimes attacks on them, and these particularly incensed Milner, who saw "no reason or justification" for such raids. The destruction of mining equipment was, he said, "pure vandalism, and outside the scope of civilised warfare." It took a Milner to make the fine distinction between the destruction of farms and the destruction of mines.

It was impossible for Kitchener to be equally strong everywhere. There was too much land and too much property to be defended. To eliminate the menace of the maurading commandos he had to go into the countryside and first find and then kill or capture the burghers in arms. To this end his columns combed the veld.

The columns marching to and fro across the Transvaal and the Orange Free State seldom obtained results commensurate with the effort expended. Perhaps the column commanded by Lord Rawlinson was as successful as any. It was composed of two battalions of mounted infantry and, for part of the time, the Imperial Light Horse. It was therefore more mobile than those containing infantry. Between 1 April 1901 and 10 June 1902 it marched 5,211 miles and halted in 276 camps. The column killed 64 Boers, wounded 87, and took 1,376 prisoners; 3 guns, 1,082 rifles, and 68,600 rounds of ammunition were captured. The operation cost the lives of 12 British soldiers, and 42 others were wounded.

Rawlinson did not say how many of his prisoners were noncombatants, but as there were more Boer prisoners than rifles taken it is safe to assume that not all were fighting burghers. He also failed to record the numbers of livestock taken or destroyed, but Smith-Dorrien, leading a larger column, rounded up 5,000 head of cattle and tens of thousands of sheep while picking up only a few sick or wounded Boers. Driving the livestock was a problem, he found, so he decided one day to slaughter 15,000 sheep to get rid of them, but the following day he swept up 23,000 more and 4,000 head of cattle.

Major General E. Locke Elliot was in charge of a large drive in the Orange Free State in June–July 1901. A month's hard work costing 3 casualties netted 17 Boers killed or wounded and 61 prisoners. Although he also collected 7,000 horses, 7,000 cattle, 6,000 rounds of ammunition, and 300 vehicles, some wondered whether the game was worth the candle.

Sometimes individual enterprise accomplished more than the heavy columns. Three colonial troopers, hearing that a strong patrol was to be sent to Ladybrand, then in republican hands, obtained permission to go there too and buy saddle stuffing for their company. The patrol was cancelled—perhaps because it was feared that the town was too strongly held—but the troopers rode boldly in. Meeting no opposition, they went straight to the landdrost and demanded the surrender of the town. All of the official keys were yielded up to them; they tore down the Free State

Vierkleur and raised the Union Jack; they arrested the gaoler and made themselves comfortable in the government offices while they received the rifles they had demanded be turned in to them. A few townsmen became suspicious, and eight armed burghers came to seek an explanation. Their general with 1,000 men was near at hand, the troopers assured them, and General French with 16,000 was not far away. They had been sent ahead, they explained, to accept the town's surrender in the hope of avoiding bloodshed. Satisfied, the burghers turned in their arms.

The three spent the night in town, and the next morning, after a hearty breakfast, they commandeered some carts, loaded them with the surrendered weapons—as well as the saddle stuffing they had come for —and drove back to their unit. The following day, when a column rode into Ladybrand, the Union Jack was still flying.

The most successful of the independent columns, and the only one the Boers really feared, was that led by Lieutenant Colonel George Elliot Benson, an artillery officer who had been twenty years in the army, passed through the staff college, and seen much active service in the Sudan and on the Gold Coast. A square-faced man with a small nose, large eyes, and a bushy moustache, he had been in South Africa almost from the beginning of the war, and it was he who had guided Wauchope's Highland Brigade at Magersfontein.

Principally responsible for the success of Benson's column was its intelligence officer, a remarkable character, Aubrey Woolls-Sampson (1856–1924). Benson had the acumen to use him properly and the ability to make effective use of his advice.

It was Woolls-Sampson who had advocated the formation of a colonial unit before the war started, a suggestion which had recommended itself to Milner but was rejected with disdain by General Butler. He was born plain Aubrey Sampson in Cape Town, but later added his mother's family name of Woolls. According to his brother, Victor Sampson, "His whole life had been one long wooing of danger and adventure."[16] When he was twenty-three he fought in the Zulu War and shortly after in the campaign against the Bapedi. He and a companion had the misfortune to be captured in that campaign, and the Bapedi had turned them over to their women, who had used "sharp thorns and thin pointed sticks to have their way with them." He survived this treatment and recovered too from a severe wound he received in the First Anglo-Boer War. He had been an active plotter on the Johannesburg Reform Committee and after the failure of the Jameson Raid had been, along with the other members, arrested and imprisoned. Although Rhodes paid the fines and the others went free, he and Karri Davies stubbornly refused to petition for their release (part of the conditions imposed) and spent thirteen months in prison until the Queen's Diamond Jubilee gave the Boers an excuse to free them.

When the war started Woolls-Sampson helped to raise the Imperial Light Horse. He was given command of a squadron and fought at Elandslaagte, where he was severely wounded. As a commander he was too impetuous; he found his true métier when he was made an intelligence officer.

He had an implacable hatred of the Boers, and it exasperated him that most of the British officers fought them without rancour as honourable foes. "He is a fanatic, a fanatic," said Cecil Rhodes, adding, "but nothing is ever done in this world except by fanatics."

Officers who knew him admired his abilities, although they found him somewhat strange. Colonel Bruce Hamilton spoke of him as "a quick tempered man" and commented on his habit of not messing with the other officers but eating alone or with his scouts and spies. Captain Frederic Shaw said, "He never mixed with us in a social sense." To General Bindon Blood it was curious that "he never took any pay for himself and wanted to pay all his men himself." He clung superstitiously to a talisman, a stick he was never without. "Where ever he might go and whatever danger he might encounter," said his brother, "so long as he had the stick with him he felt safe." When he died more than twenty years after the war it was buried with him.

Major Woolls-Sampson's intelligence-gathering methods depended upon the use of Bantu scouts sent out to locate Boer laagers; then, as Bruce Hamilton described it:

He would spend hours talking to his boys on their return, encouraging them, cross-questioning them, and checking what they told him. It was dangerous work for the boys, as the Boers killed any they caught and we found their bodies left as warning on the veldt. . . . He had an extraordinary sense of what the Boers were likely to do, and over and over again, after marching all night, we would find them where he expected.[17]

Of 28 such attacks by Benson, 21 were successful. Lax about posting sentinels, the Boers were usually caught unawares. On one night attack Benson nearly captured Louis Botha himself, who was forced to flee so precipitously that he lost all his possessions. Kitchener courteously returned his Bible, hymn book, personal papers, and a hat thought to be (but was not) that of Botha's son.

Benson's was a hard-riding column that suffered more casualties by falls from horses than from Boer bullets. It was made up of 1,400 men, 4 guns, and 2 pompoms, the men being drawn from 14 combat units, and it included Australians and South Africans as well as British regulars— an indication of the way normal units were scrambled during the guerrilla phase of the war.

Benson's column became such a terror to the Boers in the central Transvaal that they were afraid to laager in the same place two nights in succession. Anxious to destroy this menace, they at last, on 30 October 1901, had their chance.

The events leading up to Benson's destruction began on 7 September when Louis Botha marched out of Blaawkop with 2,000 men to invade

Natal. Warned of his movements, Kitchener sent four columns in pursuit. Slowed down by the first spring rains, it was not until 17 September that a force of 285 cavalry and three guns under Lieutenant Colonel Hubert de la P. Gough made contact with Botha's main force. Gough, unfortunately, did not know it. Assuming he had discovered only an isolated commando, he decided, with that impetuosity which ever characterised British cavalry commanders (much lauded as "the cavalry spirit") to charge. The result was disastrous. In less than a quarter of an hour half of his officers and 38 of his men were killed or wounded; the rest surrendered.

Kitchener, ever prone to swatting flies with sledge hammers, reacted to this minor disaster by mobilising 16,000 men and 40 guns into seven columns and sending them after Botha. However, it was not Kitchener's heavy columns but the determined resistance of the men in two small British forts, Itala and Prospect, on the Transvaal-Zululand border which did more than anything else to discourage Botha's men.

The Boers seldom attacked fortified positions and rarely succeeded when they tried. Still, in this instance the forts were small, the Boers had overwhelming numerical superiority, and success seemed sure, but they had not counted on the stubborn spirit of such men as the Durham miner who, when Fort Prospect was called on to surrender, shouted out: "I'm a pitman at home, and I've been in deeper holes than this before."

On 25/26 September the Boers attacked Itala and Prospect and were thrown back at both places. Of the fight at Fort Itala, Conan Doyle claimed that "there have been battles with 10,000 British troops hotly engaged in which the Boer losses have not been so great as in this obscure conflict against an isolated post."[18] Discouraged by their failures and aware of the heavy columns bearing down on them, Botha and his men turned back. At the sacrifice of most of their wagons the main force eluded the columns and reached the safety of the high veld again.

Here Botha heard from Commandant H. S. Grobler, 70 miles away at Brakenlaagte (also called Noitgedact, about 40 miles from Middelburg) that his commando had made contact with Benson's column but that alone he was too weak to do much more than harass it. Hurriedly gathering up 500 men, mostly from the Ermelo and Carolina commandos, Botha set out by forced marches to join him.

Early on the morning of 30 October Benson started out in the rain with his column for a 35-mile trek back to the railway to replenish his supplies. In the previous week there had been a number of small engagements, short and indecisive; he knew that the Boers, although still too weak to launch an all-out attack on him, were gathering their strength. They had been exceptionally wary, and he had been unable to catch them off guard with his usual tactics. He had no more than started out that morning before Grobler's commando darted out to harass his rear and flanks. A difficult drift over a spruit delayed the column for several hours.

A cold rain driven by a southerly wind made the work of the rear guard under Major F. Gore Anley of the Essex Regiment increasingly difficult, but the rear guard was skilfully handled, the men dropping back in successive rushes covered by a pompom; there seemed nothing to worry about.

At midday the situation was altered radically when Louis Botha and his men arrived, tired but eager for battle. Botha had so screened his movements and had ridden so rapidly, taking the last 30 miles at a rush, that Woolls-Sampson and his scouts had had no time to learn of his approach. About one o'clock in the afternoon Major Anley, feeling an increasing pressure on his rear guard, dispatched a warning message to Benson. Fifteen minutes later he sent another, and Benson decided to go back himself, taking with him about 100 men of the Scottish Horse.

Until he actually arrived on the scene Benson probably did not realize the seriousness of the situation. To hustle and harass a rear guard was a common Boer tactic, but it rarely constituted a major threat. He had been busy getting his convoy of wagons over the drift and parked, and putting his infantry into camp at Noitgedact Farm so as to be free to manoeuvre with his mounted troops. Doubtless he was only annoyed by Anley's messages and thought his rear-guard commander was overreacting to the pressure on him. Only when he rode back to see for himself did he begin to realise his danger. For a number of reasons, a considerable part of his force was scattered over some 2 miles of country in weak detachments. The pompom had jammed and was on its way back to camp with a small escort. The situation was perilous.

Botha, who had been able to concentrate 800 men in a key position in Benson's rear, examined the field with satisfaction: the scattered detachments, some in the act of retiring, and the convoy of wagons 2,000 yards beyond offered an attractive opportunity. He ordered a charge.

Benson, meanwhile, had given orders for his men to retreat to better defensive positions. He personally led the Scottish Horse and 40 men of the Yorkshire Light Infantry in a rapid retirement to a low kopje (subsequently called Gun Hill) where two guns of the 84th Battery and 20 men of the King's Royal Rifle Corps were in position. Anley, with a company of the North Lancashire Regiment, made for a ridge about 1,000 yards east.

Benson and the Boers began a race for Gun Hill. The Boers were extended in a long line, making a front of nearly a mile and a half. Goading their tired horses to their best speed, they pounded across the sodden veld, yelling and firing from the saddle. A heavy mist made visibility difficult, but Anley, looking back over his shoulder, caught a glimpse through a rift of a cloud of horsemen streaming over the veld. An Irish trooper looked back too: "There's miles of 'em, begob!" he exclaimed.

A portion of the Boer force on the extreme right made for the ridge held by Anley, but the larger part raced for Gun Hill. A company of the

Buffs (East Kent Regiment) and, separate from them, a detachment of 30 more Buffs were all that stood in their way. These knots of soldiers proved trifling obstacles. The first was overwhelmed with scarcely a struggle, the young subaltern in charge being shot down at the onset; the second put up a fierce but brief resistance, 19 out of 30 quickly becoming casualties. The Boer horsemen swept on, engulfing a covering section of the Scottish Horse and pressing on the heels of Benson's men who, on reaching the hill, threw themselves on the ground in defensive positions around the guns. The Boers drew rein in a hollow at the foot of Gun Hill, dismounted, and began an attack at close quarters.

The two guns of the 84th Battery, posted 20 yards apart, fired only three rounds and then fell silent. Every gunner was shot down. Corporal Atkins, though wounded, tried to reach up and remove the breech block from his gun. As he raised his hands to the block a bullet passed through them. Sergeant Hays, badly wounded and the only survivor of his gun crew, managed to crawl forward and pull the lanyard for a round before he fainted. Lieutenant Colonel Eustace Guinness, the battery commander, fired the last round from the other gun himself and then called for the limbers and teams waiting on the reverse slope of the kopje. They came up at a gallop, but as soon as they appeared on the skyline they were mowed down "like corn under the scythe." Guinness, too, fell. Most of the officers were killed or wounded. Benson himself was hit in the knee, but he crawled about from point to point in the firing line, encouraging his men and directing their fire.

Lieutenant Thomas Henry Eyre Lloyd of the Coldstream Guards, Benson's assistant staff officer, was in camp when he heard the sounds of the fighting. He galloped to Gun Hill, drew up at the rear of the guns, and tossed his reins to a trooper. Trooper and horse were instantly shot dead. Upright and unarmed, he coolly walked towards Benson. A few paces from his chief he fell mortally wounded.

Quartermaster Sergeant Warnock of the Scottish Horse was an old soldier who had served twenty-one years in the Scottish Borderers. His place was with the convoy, but like the old fire-horse who hears the alarm he could not resist the sounds of battle so near. Loading himself and two others with boxes of ammunition, he made for Gun Hill. There they crawled forward until they could throw cartridges to the hard-pressed men on the firing line. One of his men was killed, but Warnock kept at the work until the boxes were all but empty, then he picked up a dead man's rifle and joined the fight, keeping up a cool fire until he collapsed, wounded in three places.

Although badly outnumbered, the British refused to give up. When a burgher called out to the Scottish Horse to surrender, the only reply he got was a laconic "We're Scots." Some Boers got to their feet as if to rush the position, but a ragged volley greeted them and they sank to earth again. Benson received a second wound, in the arm this time. Worried about his guns, he called for a volunteer to take a message to the camp:

an order not to send out ambulances, as the Boers might use the mules to carry away the guns. The trooper who rose to take the message was immediately shot in the foot; the same bullet hit Benson in the abdomen.

Suddenly the entire line of Boers rose up and directed a fierce, indiscriminate fire on everything that moved. Then they ran forward to claim the hill and the guns. "So ended," said *The Times History,* "a fight unique in the annals of war." But it was not quite ended. The British guns in the camp opened fire on the hill—on both the Boers and their own wounded. Conan Doyle said it was Benson who had signalled for this fire to be laid down on his own position, but this is doubtful. The Boers withdrew, but the British made no attempt to counterattack, and under cover of night the Boers carried off the two guns.

Only 6 of the Scottish Horse out of 79 on the hill came out unscathed; of the 32 gunners, only 3 escaped; of the 20 men of the Rifle Corps, but 3 were untouched; and among the Yorkshiremen, only 5 out of 40 were unhit. Every officer was killed or wounded. All in all, the column on this day lost nearly a third of its strength: 238 men killed or wounded; about 120 taken prisoner. The Boers lost about 100 of their best men, but they had destroyed Benson's column. Benson too. The gallant commander was brought into camp about 9 P.M. and died early the next morning. His last words were: "No more night marching."

This disaster to Benson's column reverberated through the army in South Africa, and shock waves were felt by those at home. Kitchener, as usual, reacted emotionally. In his dispatch to London he averred that if his best column could be scuppered in this fashion he did not know how he would be able to go on unless he received "a large addition to our forces to carry on the war." This unfortunate phrase caused head shaking in England. It had been difficult enough to understand why with so many soldiers in South Africa and so few Boers in the field the war had dragged on for so long, and now Kitchener wanted even more men. It had been nearly a year since Roberts, thinking the war ended, had turned over his command and gone home. Was Kitchener losing his grip? Ian Hamilton, who had gone home with Roberts, was sent back to be Kitchener's chief of staff and was asked privately to report when he got to South Africa on "Kitchener's health and general conditions."

Search-and-destroy columns such as Benson's, which operated independently, were rare. Most of the columns worked together on coordinated schemes devised by Kitchener. Sometimes these were hunts for a particular body of Boers, often futile pursuits of the wily De Wet, but Kitchener favoured drives, particularly after the Benson catastrophe. At first these were simply great sweeps of areas by troops acting as beaters to flush Boers. Then he developed what were called "new model drives," employing large bodies of troops sweeping through large areas and using blockhouse lines as walls against which the enemy were pushed. David Miller, now a staff officer with Colonel James Spens's column, described in a letter home how Kitchener's new model drives worked:

We are "driving" now, and it is curious work, and shows what an extraordinary stage the war is now in—if, indeed, you can call it war at all. We "drive" as follows. Two points are selected by the chief—one probably on a blockhouse, and another on the railway, thus—

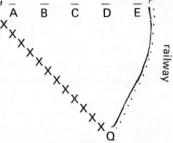

A, B, C, D, E are columns, and they drive down to the point Q, and the Boers cannot get out. The columns at starting point probably cover a front of about sixty miles which gradually lessens.

At night we form a chain of outposts at about 150 yards' interval, and a hasty wire entanglement is put up in front of each regiment. We march about twenty-five miles a day. Sometimes the Boers try to get out, generally by rushing the picquet line at night, but they frequently make no effort, running along in front like sheep until caught in the cover.[19]

The first of the new model drives, 5–8 February 1902, involved (in round numbers) 300 blockhouses, 7 armoured trains, and 17,000 men, and it ranged over the area between Liebenberg's Vlei and the railway in the Free State. De Wet was known to be in this area, and Kitchener was confident he would net him. But clever men can outwit the best of systems, and De Wet was clever. Ignoring the driving columns, he led his men to a point on the blockhouse line between Kroonstad and Lindley. On the night of 7 February, an exceptionally dark night, his men quietly cut the wires between two blockhouses and he passed his entire force through the gap without a shot being fired. Then he brought his herd of cattle through as well. Driven by four brothers named Potgieter, the herd came through with a rush; they were fired on, but there was little loss. De Wet then marched men and cattle 40 miles to Doornberg and halted. When the drive was over, he coolly returned to Elandskop in the middle of the area that had just been swept.

The net result of the drive was a total of 286 Boers killed, wounded, or captured. It seemed a small bag for such a mighty effort, but Kitchener at once decided on another, grander drive, and it began only five days later. Again De Wet gathered his force and punched a hole through the British cordon, but this time there was fighting in the dead of night and he suffered 14 killed and about 20 wounded before he managed to get away. Even though the grand prize had once again slipped through, the drive was counted a success, yielding 50 Boers killed and 778 captured; 25,000 head of cattle and 200 carts and wagons were taken.

Ahead of the driving columns men, women, and children fled like animals before a fire. Schikkerling wrote a description of the turmoil created by one of Kitchener's early drives, and the scene was doubtless often repeated:

Shall I ever forget the sight? The shouting and confusion of excited people, each with his wagon, mule or donkey, to which he selfishly clung, loading and preparing to get away or meditating to remain and surrender. Oxen and mules were being inspanned and outspanned by women, many of whom were once wealthy. . . . Wandering about with the commandos with which they remained for safety, they had slowly shed the bulk of their fortunes. These unfortunate people were now to lose the last of their possessions. Many women sat in their wagons weeping, and even some men sobbed unrestrainedly. One girl of about eighteen, barefoot, and with hardly a dress to her body, was all alone catching and harnessing donkeys. No one cared to help her, each being too engaged in his own affairs.[20]

Some managed to hide and thus escape; others tried ingenious methods without success. Three Boers buried themselves, leaving only a tube sticking up through which they could breathe, but soldiers found the new-turned earth and ran their bayonets into it until they heard muffled screams. Another burgher trying the same stratagem was stepped on by a horse.

By 27 February 1902, when the second new model drive ended, the troops were exhausted, but Kitchener gave them little rest; on 4 March a third drive was launched over the same area covered by the first. A massive effort, lasting a week, it netted only about 100 Boers and De Wet again escaped, but Kitchener's appetite for drives remained unabated. He made column commanders drag telegraph lines after them, and Ian Hamilton (in his old age, when Kitchener was long dead) described the commander-in-chief's delight in using them:

He was like one of those stage performers who plays six instruments at once. . . . K. worked over the wires direct with the four principal columns, and twice a day at least, and sometimes half a dozen times a day, gave them their orders. K. was perfectly enchanted with the game of making Generals dance at the end of wires like so many marionettes. . . . It was clear he regarded his column commanders as babes in the woods when deprived of his guiding telegrams.[21]

Once when the telegraph line to headquarters broke or was cut, Kitchener "rose from his chair, went straight to his room, and refused for the best part of two days and two nights to take a bite. Not one single crumb."[22]

No Boer leader of any importance was ever captured in Kitchener's drives. The cleverest and best always escaped. The one British tactic the Boers really feared was the night attack. De Wet said, "We soon discovered that these night attacks were the most difficult of the enemy's tactics with which we had to deal." He had too low an opinion of the British military mind to think that his enemy could have conceived of such tactics unaided: "They never would have thought of them at all if they had not been instructed in them by the National Scouts—our own flesh and blood."[23]

When in war one side is unable to sustain enthusiasm through either victories or propaganda, there will be defectors in appreciable numbers, and some will become actual traitors to their original cause. As the war in South Africa dragged on, more and more Boers turned to helping the British.

Some of these "renegade Boers"—or, as the British called them, "tame Boers"—were formed into "burgher corps" which were used as police or as cattle guards, wearing red neck bands to distinguish them. The motives of such men varied. Some fought for money, some to win favours from their conquerers, some because they thought British rule might after all not be bad, and many because they saw the futility of the struggle and wanted it ended before their entire homeland was turned into a desert.

As early as December 1900 a group of influential Boers formed themselves into a Burgher Peace Committee and met with Kitchener. On their advice Kitchener issued a proclamation promising that all who voluntarily surrendered would be allowed to live with their families in government camps until peace was signed and they could return to their farms. Members of the committee sought out the laagers of the commandos and acted as peace emissaries, or tried to. The effort was not a success. The would-be peace makers were roughly handled, the fighting burghers regarding them as traitors and spies. Several were flogged and a few were actually put to death.

In September 1901 a number of leading Boers, including former generals A. P. Cronjé and Piet de Wet, offered to form military units to fight their fellow countrymen. Kitchener gave his consent, and the National Scouts were raised in the Transvaal and, at a later date, the Orange River Colony Volunteers. At first they were paid only in loot and occasional gifts; later they were given regular pay and treated as colonials— well, almost. The British never quite trusted them, and they were a negligible military factor, their total number never exceeding 2,000, but the formation of the National Scouts had its effect on the fighting burghers. That men would surrender was at least understandable; that they would turn and fight against their own people seemed monstrous, and the republican Boers held a detestation for them far exceeding their hatred for the British. When National Scouts were caught they were executed, and no quarter was shown in fights with them.

In England the antiwar and pro-Boer factions raised an outcry against this system of turning brother against brother. The Irish radicals were particularly incensed. In the House of Commons an acrimonious exchange took place between Chamberlain and John Dillon when Chamberlain quoted Frans Vilonel, the former commandant who had deserted when De Wet reduced him to the ranks. Now an officer in the National Scouts, he had written a message to the burghers in the field from which

Chamberlain read a passage containing the phrase: "the enemies of the country are those who are continuing a hopeless struggle." At this Dillon leaped to his feet to protest that Vilonel was a traitor. Chamberlain replied to the effect that doubtless the honourable gentleman from Ireland was a good judge of traitors. The exchange ended with Dillon calling Chamberlain "a damned liar," an outburst which caused him to be suspended from the House.

Fireworks in Parliament did little to revive interest or enthusiasm for the war at home, and meant nothing at all to the soldiers "sloggin' over Africa."

38

SOLDIERING ON THE VELD

The inland plateau that forms the high veld impresses all who see it. Vast and bare, with its high-banked, unnavigable rivers that are raging torrents one day and muddy trickles the next, with its strange vegetation and exotic animals, with its peculiarly shaped hills, and above all, its great open skies that stretch away forever—this land, this veld, affected the men from the north who came to conquer it. Sitting in a lonely blockhouse day after day staring at a limitless horizon or marching on foot or horse for endless miles, many a British soldier hated it, longing for the green, well-manicured land of his birth. Yet there was something alluring about it. One young officer wrote: "The veldt is like the eye of the basilisk; it fascinates, no one knows why."[1] Herbert Lionel James described a feeling shared by many: "Immense,—a land without a horizon, a land every characteristic of which inspires a sense of independence and freedom. A sensation—an intoxication to be felt, not be described. Why should men fight in a land such as this? Surely there is room for all!"[2]

The soldiers' work on the veld was inglorious, even demeaning. The burning of farms, the wanton slaughter of farm animals, the rounding up of women and children—these things did not seem proper soldiers' work. Even the manhunting lacked glory. The prisoners they took, the men they killed, did not look like soldiers: bearded old farmers and ragged, hungry young men; they did not apear to be foes requiring the might of a huge army drawn from all parts of the Empire to subdue. Yet these slouching, undisciplined, dirty civilians, equipped only with rifles, bandoliers, and horses, were formidable fighting men. This was clear. It was equally clear that the Boers were a stubborn race. Roberts had been lenient; now Kitchener was being tough and ruthless; they responded neither to magnanimity nor to severity. But the British too were a stubborn breed. And so the soldiers marched on and fought on and did their duty as best they could.

Young Lieutenant Miller's reaction was shared by many officers who in the beginning had been in favour of Kitchener's ruthless policies but who were now forced to put them into practice. He told his mother: "I have seen many pitiful sights—such as make the heart bleed . . . and I have seen what may make a man think." There were indeed such sights, and many a British soldier found the work of burning farms and slaughtering livestock hateful; few became hardened to the sight of women and children sobbing before their flaming homes and bleeding animals.

Many of the Boer families stranded on the veld after their farms were burned led miserable lives. British columns began to see such sights as Miller described: "The other day we discovered several families living in a great hole in a rock by the banks of the Vaal River. They are living entirely on fresh meat and mealie meal. . . . [They] are, for the most part, in a frightful state of destitution—clothes made of blankets patched with bits of tablecloth or carpet."[3]

Ian Hamilton, when he had become a very old man, still remembered how he had been able to dry the tears of one little girl of about twelve at Oliphant's Nek in the Transvaal by saving her pet calf from the clutches of his own men. Hamilton even remembered his conversation with her. She told him nothing of the movements of De Wet, whom he was chasing, but she did tell him about her best friends, that she liked to dance, and that her favourite book was an English novel, *Cometh Up as a Flower,* by Rhoda Broughton.

While soldiers must obey, generals can sometimes take liberties with standing orders. Old Mrs. de Kok and her grandson stood at the gate of their farmhouse worrying about the safety of their little herd of cattle when "a respectable soldier" rode by. He stopped when Mrs. de Kok called out to him, and he listened attentively when the boy ran up to tell him their troubles. Sitting his horse, he scribbled a note and handed it down to the boy. It read: "Don't interfere with these cows—Hector Macdonald, General."

It was usually only women, children, and old men whom the soldiers found on the farms. Crops were sown and harvested by Bantu under the supervision of the women with such help as the children could give. It was difficult trying to keep up the house, rear children, and do the men's work on the farm, and heart-rending to see the fruits of their efforts wantonly destroyed. As De Wet said, "It was hard indeed for them to watch the soldiers fling the corn on the ground before their horses' hoofs. Still harder was it to see that which had cost them so much labour thrown into the flames."[4]

Most of the officers, at least, disliked the work, and, as Frederick Howland said, "It was certainly not an inspiring sight to see a Lieutenant-General of the British army [Methuen] sitting on the stoep of a dingy farmhouse saying he hoped the war would soon be over, to a group of women wringing their hands in his face."[5]

Captain L. March Phillips of Rimington's Scouts described one farm burning:

At another farm a small girl interrupted her preparations for departure to play indignantly their national anthem at us on an old piano. We were carting the people off. It was raining hard and blowing—a miserable hurried home-leaving; ransacked house, muddy soldiers, a distracted mother saving one or two trifles and pushing along her children to the ox wagon outside, and this poor little wretch in the midst of it all pulling herself together to strum a final defiance. One smiled but it was rather dramatic all the same, and exactly like a picture.[6]

Many went about their work of destruction without enthusiasm and without guilt or rancour, impersonally, with little feeling for or against the folk whose ruin they were accomplishing. Corporal Murray Cosby Jackson of the 7th M.I. described how his company carried out its task:

We wetted all the grain, burnt the forage, and killed the livestock, leaving merely enough for the family. The women couldn't quite make Tommy out, I think. A soldier, hot and grimy from burning their best haystack, and bloody with the blood of the old frou's pet Minorcas and Anconas, would go up to the back door without a trace of ill feeling and ask very civilly for a glass of milk, and then proceed to kill the pig.[7]

Such workaday attitudes did not always prevail. It is unhealthy for an army to be put to such work, for it tends to corrupt and to brutalize. Captain Phillips wrote:

Soldiers as a class (I take the town bred majority) are men who have discarded the civil standard of morality altogether, they simply ignore it. . . . Looting, again, is one of his perpetual joys. Not merely looting for profit . . . but looting for the sheer fun of the destruction; tearing down pictures to kick their boots through them; smashing furniture for the fun of smashing it, and maybe dressing up in women's clothes to finish with, and dancing among the ruins they have made. To pick up a good heavy stone and send it *wallop* right through the works of a piano is a great moment for Tommy.[8]

Although their mission was simply to destroy, the temptation to loot was sometimes irresistible: Why not take and use what otherwise would be burned? Some soldiers talked openly of this, and Private Stanley from New South Wales wrote a letter home that was published in the Sydney *Telegraph:*

When within 800 yards of the farm we halted, and the infantry blazed a volley into the house; we broke open the place and went in. It was beautifully furnished and the officers got several things they could make use of. There was a lovely library—books of all descriptions, printed in Dutch and English. I secured a Bible, also a rifle, quite new. After getting all we wanted out of the house, our men put a charge under and blew it up. It seemed such a pity, it was a lovely house.

Farmhouses were not the only buildings looted. The predikant at Schweizer-Reneke complained that a British officer had carried off the communion plate, and at Witpoort a Boer woman declared she had seen the soldiers carry away all of the church plate.*

Sarah Raal saw a spot where soldiers had chased a large flock of sheep into tall, dry grass, encircled the area, and then set fire to the grass:

It was dreadful to see the groups of animals. Those which had not been burned to death had twisted legs. They crept on their knees, and others had their eyes bursting out of their heads, and some had lips curled up above the teeth. I could never have believed that there are such cruel people if I had not witnessed it myself.[9]

Cavalry came to the homestead of Hans Botha, an old burgher who had fought and been wounded in the First Anglo-Boer War but was too old for this one. He was away when the cavalry came, and only his wife, seventy years old, and two small grandchildren were at home. They were given three pillows and three blankets and told to leave. The three went off a way and then stood, the old woman with her grandchildren beside her, looking back as the smoke curled up from the house in which she had lived most of her life and which contained all the possessions she cherished.

The 7th M.I. came to destroy one farm and found only a lone woman who did not realise what the soldiers were going to do when they put her in a wagon. As they were driving off she saw smoke coming from her house. What was happening? "Oh, that's your house going up," she was told. She screamed, leaped from the wagon, and ran back to rescue her husband hidden under the floor.

Lieutenant Cyril Rocke, occupying a group of kopjes one day while on outpost duty with a farm-burning column, sat helplessly on his horse and watched a farm being burned. "I could have sobbed," he said. "In fact I think I did."

A few months earlier he had lain in one of the bedrooms there recovering from a broken shoulder and from head injuries sustained when his horse had thrown him during a skirmish nearby. The two women who lived there alone, a grey-haired Boer matron and her young and attractive niece Anna, had cared for him tenderly. It had been Anna's fiancé, Piet, and his brother who had picked Rocke up unconscious from the veld and brought him there. "We couldn't leave you for the vultures," they said laughing.

In spite of their kindness, Rocke had no doubt he was a prisoner; the

*Such plunder is still to be found and sometimes in strange places. In 1972 an American from Fairfax, Virginia, returned to the South African Embassy a beautifully worked pulpit cloth looted by one of his forbears.

two young Boers were fighting burghers, probably part of the group he had been skirmishing with. When they returned one day, this time with a cart driven by a Zulu boy, and told him, "You're leaving here today," he was sure he would be taken to a Boer laager and that his days of real captivity had begun. The young men helped him dress and helped him into the cart. He said good-bye to his nurses, the elder woman refusing the watch he offered her, and the cart moved off.

After a jolting and, to Rocke, painful three-hour ride they stopped at a fork in the road. "Get down, please," Piet said. "This is where we part. Standerton is about ten miles in that direction. We are going the other way."

War tells strange stories, and one such unfolded for Lieutenant Rocke as he watched the burning farm. Snipers had been firing on the soldiers as they did their work of destruction; one had been captured and was brought to him. It was Piet. Rocke dismissed the soldiers who had brought him in, and the two men looked at each other. Rocke owed this young burgher much. He knew that, unlike most prisoners of war, Piet was in a perilous position: born and raised in Natal, he was a British subject, a rebel who could be shot. Still, he had been caught sniping at his own men. Rocke hesitated. Then, "Take my horse and go," he said.

The two met still another time eighteen months later when Rocke watched De la Rey lead his ragged, dirty, unbowed veterans into Balmoral to surrender. Standing among the "irreconcilables" (those who chose exile rather than signing an oath of allegiance to the King) was Piet. Rocke went up to him, eager for news. Rocke's horse had served him well, Piet said, until it died of horse sickness. His aunt had died in a concentration camp; he did not know what had become of his brother, but he thought he was dead. Was that all, Rocke asked. In a flat voice Piet said, "You killed my Anna."

Telling the story many years later, Cyril Rocke still remembered the shock: it was, he said, as if he had been lashed with a whip.

Captain Francis Fletcher Vane was with a column in the northern Free State trying to catch Hertzog when one day he surrounded a farmhouse and captured six Boers. One of them, Vane was astonished to discover, was a slender, blue-eyed, attractive girl dressed as a man and carrying a rifle and bandolier. She was Ella Jacobs, who had been with her mother in a concentration camp at Springfontein before she ran off with another girl to find her brothers, Hendrik and Gideon. For six months she had been fighting in Hertzog's commando.

"It had never fallen to my lot to have the honour to capture a fighting girl," said Vane. "It was not the sort of thing one expected . . . and it was embarrassing." He did not know what to do with her, for to send her to a prisoner-of-war camp was unthinkable. According to Vane, he sent her under escort to her farm; according to her son, S. Marais, now a farmer in Trompsburg, Orange Free State, she was returned to the concentration camp.

Not long after the war Vane looked up Ella Jacobs and arrived at her parents' farm on the day she was to be married. He stayed for her wedding dinner and gave her a miniature of his Queen's South African Medal; she gave him a photograph of herself. She had become one of the war's heroines, known as the "Boer Joan of Arc," and only she, it would seem, was unimpressed with her fame: in later years she always referred to her days as a fighting burgher as "the follies of my youth." She died in 1969 at the age of eighty-five. Ella Jacobs made a lasting impression on Vane, for she gave him "the first inkling of what women could do when they believe themselves oppressed."

Captain Herbert James had a less pleasant experience. He rode up to a Boer farm one day and, without dismounting, asked a young woman for a glass of milk. She brought the milk, but as James reached down for it, she dashed it in his face and doubled over with laughter as two men with rifles stepped out of the farmhouse doorway and shouted, "Hands up!" James dug his spurs into his horse and made a successful dash for safety.

Even in the final, bitter phase of the war, decency and humanity did not entirely disappear, and there were numerous occasions when it was exhibited. No man on either side showed finer qualities of civilised manhood than Koos de la Rey, the skilful and fierce fighter who looked like a patriarch and behaved like a gentleman in the very best sense of that term.

Major Tudor C. Trevor was leading a patrol of 60 men in the Klerksdorp district when he was attacked by 200 Boers under De la Rey who fell upon his patrol like a whirlwind. Within minutes twenty of his men were down. One, a young subaltern, was badly wounded, shot in the chest. There was little Trevor could do but put his hat over his face to ward off the sun. Then he had to make a dash for it; he had almost lingered too long; the Boers were upon him, sweeping over the position, and he had barely time to throw himself on his horse. He galloped away in a hail of bullets, and it later seemed to him strange that not a shot had been fired at him until he had reached his horse. Over a rise in the ground he met the main body of his column, which wheeled in the direction of the enemy, back to the site of the skirmish.

The Boers had disappeared like the wind; the wounded were still on the ground, including the young subaltern. Trevor bent over him and the young man said something inexplicable: "If you ever meet De la Rey again, give him the best hat money can buy for me."

The subaltern died in hospital, but from one of his nurses Trevor heard his story. When the Boers had overrun the position, they had immediately begun to strip the dead and wounded of their clothing and equipment. One had taken the young man's hat, and he cried out in protest. De la Rey, nearby, had ordered the hat restored and had seen that he was given water and made comfortable.

It was not until after the war when De la Rey passed through Cape

Town that Trevor was able to comply with his dead subaltern's request. He bought a splendid black silk top hat (it still exists) and presented it to him. He also used the occasion to ask why he had not shot him before he mounted his horse, as he easily could have done. De la Rey answered, "You don't shoot partridges on the ground, do you? Neither do I."

Lieutenant David Miller was with a column under Colonel James Spens when it descended on a farm named Buffleskloof. It was an ordinary Boer farm: house and outbuildings set down in a clearing on the open veld. The owners fled at the column's approach. Before setting fire to the buildings a search was made for anything living, and a soldier found a newborn puppy. He presented it to Miller, who put it in his tunic pocket, hardly thinking it would live. When the farm had been fired the column moved on. That evening he nursed the pup with milk from the fingers of a glove. Buffles, named after the farm, thrived and grew into a strongly built Labrador retriever that outlived its master.

Dogs are always acquired somewhere, somehow, in the course of every campaign. In South Africa the New South Wales Bushmen had a sheepdog and the 2nd Middlesex Regiment had a collie that followed them when they marched out of Estcourt (and so it was named Estcourt). Nell, the terrier of the 2nd Battalion of the Rifle Brigade, gave birth to twins during the battle for Caesar's Camp and Wagon Hill; the pups were named Shot and Shell.

There were other pets as well: the Scots Guards had a goat, always called "Billy Muffit's Goat," which was found in the Boer trenches at Magersfontein; the 2nd West Yorkshires had a baboon; several units had monkeys, usually named Jock; the 2nd Shropshire Light Infantry was given an ostrich by a friendly farmer (or so they said); one battalion of the CIV had a white kitten named Emergency Ration. The ammunition column of the Third Cavalry Brigade had a pet hen which had been found in Cronjé's laager at Paardeberg; it travelled in a box on a limber and gained such fame that it was suggested "the Zoological Society should find it a home." Pets did not escape the dangers of war: Estcourt was with his regiment on Spion Kop; a monkey belonging to an Imperial Yeomanry battalion saw action at Nooitgedacht and survived being hit three times by bullets.

The fighting burghers had fewer pets, but Schikkerling tells of a baboon belonging to a gun section of the Transvaal staatsartillerie which always rode the gun on the march until the gun was buried when its ammunition was exhausted.

Kitchener's policy of deliberate wholesale destruction was intended to deprive the guerrillas of supplies, and in this he was successful. Even De Wet, ever scornful of British tactics, admitted that "had not the English burnt the corn by the thousand sacks, the war could have been continued." Although the generals on both sides understood the underlying reason for the farm burning, it was widely believed among the

Boers, and among many Britons as well, that the policy was intended to intimidate the Boers; in fact it only provoked anger and bitterness; it did not lessen their will to resist, only their means for doing so.

Roland Schikkerling with the Johannesburg Commando recorded his reaction. He was on his way to attack a train near Bothasberg in the Transvaal when he came across a woman and her buxom, rosy, eighteen-year-old daughter living among the blackened ruins of their home. He listened with rising indignation to their story: how the British had visited their farm and applied "the Torch of Civilization." Schikkerling promised the woman that if his commando was successful in its attack on the train (it was not) he would "spare no pains and shun no danger" to get them some sugar and coffee; a promise he later regretted, reflecting wryly: "What a pity that heroism must always be accompanied by risk, charity by expense, and politeness by discomfort."

For the British, life on the veld became a dull routine and even the fighting was seldom exciting. David Miller tried to answer his mother's questions about what his life was like:

There is so little to describe. The infantry soldier sees nothing except the men on either side of him and the enemy in front. He hears the crackle of the enemy's fire somewhere—he does not know where—and he hears the whit! whit! of the bullets, and every now and then he knows vaguely some one near him is hit—he feels the smell of the powder (cordite) and the hot oily smell of his rifle. He fires at the range given, and at the given direction, and every now and then he hears "Advance!" and he gets up and goes on and wonders why he is not hit as he stands up. That is all. Then the bullets cease to come and the action is over . . . he marches to the chosen camping ground and perhaps goes on picket—very tired and dirty—and he does it all again next day. That is the infantry soldier's battle—very nasty—very tiring—very greasy—very hungry—very thirsty—everything very beastly. No glitter—no excitement—no nothing. Just bullets and dirt.[10]

"Eternal damnation on Steyn and De Wet for keeping us out!" exclaimed Major George Younghusband. There seemed no end to the hard marching and little fights:

"Where are you and what have you been doing?" was the burden of our letters from home. And echo answered "where" and "what" indeed? Perhaps Kitchener knew, though I doubt it. . . . to the rank-and-file the past was merely an endless vista of double treks. Reveille at 3:30 A.M., trek from dawn till noon; grazing the horses in the blazing sun or driving rain till 2 P.M.; up saddle and then trek on till dark. Now and again a "scrap" with brother Boer, and now and again a small town passed. But on the whole a weary dreary nightmare, and not worth writing about.[11]

Younghusband was a professional soldier, an officer; the volunteers and the common soldiers were even less keen. Back in Britain enthusiasm for the war waned as dispatches from the front increasingly recorded captures of sheep and cattle rather than of armed Boers. There was a noticeable drop in the quality of the men who enlisted and a drop in the number who reenlisted. All the defeats of the first three months of the war had not dampened British ardor, all of Buller's blunders had failed to quench the fighting spirit of the troops, but the guerrilla war did. Soldiers complained that they were "fed up," and it was said that never before had homesickness been so manifest in a British army.

There were less generous feelings towards "brother Boer." Atrocity stories began to appear. Edgar Wallace, not yet famous for his novels, first began trying his hand at fiction in his news dispatches. The *Daily Mail* carried one of his stories, accompanied by a lurid sketch of Boers bayoneting British wounded:

Abandoning the old methods of dropping the butt end of a rifle on the wounded soldier's face when there was none to see the villainy, the Boer has done his bloody work in the light of day, within sight of a dozen eye-witnesses, and the stories we have hardly dared to hint, lest you thought we had grown hysterical, we can now tell without fear of ridicule. The Boers murder wounded men.[12]

His story created a sensation in Britain. Kitchener, asked to investigate, reported that it was without any foundation in fact.

Black and White Budget published a letter purporting to be from "an officer writing from camp near Pretoria": "One of our native scouts was caught by the Boers the other day. They cut the lad open alive and took his insides out. A Boer woman put a little black boy's head in a carpenter's vice and twisted it round until his neck was broken. They really are for the most part savages."[13]

The Boers too at this stage of the war had their atrocity stories, the brutal treatment of Boer women by British soldiers being a favourite theme. In Cape Colony the editor of *Ons Land* was fined £100 for publishing "a seditious libel attributing atrocities to British troops."

Boers were increasingly accused of using explosive or expansive bullets, firing from behind women, wearing British uniforms to deceive, using the red cross or white flag as a ruse, whipping prisoners, robbing or killing wounded, and violating their oaths of allegiance.

The charge of using improper bullets was one left over from the early days of the war when both sides were guilty of the practice; they were seldom used during the last two-thirds of the war. That the Boers ill-used prisoners or wounded was largely untrue, but of course there were exceptions, and De la Rey once had some of his men flogged for ill-treating prisoners. There is no evidence of burghers deliberately hiding behind women to shoot, but there were "women's laagers" on the veld and occasionally women with commandos; sometimes they did get in the way of the fighting males. It was certainly true that thousands of Boers who had given up the fight and had taken the oath of neutrality or oath of allegiance to the crown later took up arms again and joined commandos, a practise which undoubtedly incensed the British.

The wearing of British uniforms was indeed common, and not infrequently Boer commandos pretended to be British, riding like British soldiers in formation. Most burghers, if reduced to wearing captured British uniforms, kept their own easily identifiable wide-brimmed slouch hats, but it became difficult indeed to tell friend from foe when many British units adopted the practical and comfortable Boer hat. Some Highland units, which kept their kilts but exchanged their helmets for slouch hats, were described as being "Boer above and bare below."

Misunderstandings and mistakes about the use of the white flag did not diminish, and the belief was widespread among the soldiers that the Boers deliberately and regularly lured soldiers to their deaths with white flags. An Australian trooper wrote home:

> There was a most impressive scene at the burial of Lieutenant White, near Lichtenburg. He was treacherously shot at Manana, four miles east of Lichtenburg, while going to answer the white flag displayed by the Boers. . . . At the funeral his comrades replaced their hats on their heads, and joined hands together and swore most solemnly never to recognize the white flag.[14]

Ceremonies of this sort were repeated elsewhere, and the war became crueler. There is evidence that soldiers did sometimes ignore the white flag, and the Boers collected sworn statements from witnesses.

Colonials, towards whom Englishmen have usually exhibited a supercilious disdain, had never stood so high in the public estimation in Britain; it was expected that South Africans would fight, but the way in which the Australians, New Zealanders, Tasmanians, and Canadians volunteered to aid the cause of Empire inspired new feelings of brotherhood,* a sentiment not widely shared by the British regulars, who resented the higher pay the colonials were given. For their part, the colonials, an independent lot, chafed under British army discipline and red tape, and they resented having British regular officers placed over them.

On the night of 12 June 1901 some 120 Boers completely routed 350 Australians (Victorian Mounted Rifles) at Wilmansrust, between Middelburg and Ermelo, looting their camp and carrying off a pompom. The Victorians had been easy prey that night because they had neglected properly to post sentinels and pickets. Lieutenant Colonel Stuart Beatson, in charge of the column to which they were attached, was enraged; he assembled the remains of the unit and not only told them that they were "a lot of wasters and white-livered curs" but added some unpleasant opinions about Australians in general. The Victorians mutinied. They had always disliked Beatson and had resented his attempts to infuse some discipline into them; now they swore they would never serve under him again. Three of the leaders were court-martialled and condemned to death; Kitchener commuted the sentences to three years' imprisonment, but the Victorian government protested even this sentence and the three were pardoned.

---

*One out of every fifty men of fighting age in the Australian colonies volunteered for service in South Africa.

Volunteers from Britain also complained of their treatment at the hands of regular officers. In general, both the British and the colonial volunteers, once trained, made better soldiers than the regular rank and file who were recruited from the poorest, least intelligent, and least skilled, but regular officers, unaccustomed to dealing with higher-calibre men, did not always know how to handle them.

Tommy Atkins had never enjoyed such esteem in Britain, but the correspondents and officers who saw the regular in South Africa were aware of his deficiencies. Praise for him was sometimes backhanded. Herbert Lionel James wrote: "Know, therefore, that there is no keener judge of human character and human mind than the cherub of the gutter. It is from these gutter-snipes, grown into men, that the fighting ranks of the great British army are filled."[15]

Captain Slocum made a comparison of the British regular with his American counterpart. "The British soldiers have not the individuality or resources of our men, but for indomitable courage, uncomplaining fortitude and implicit obedience, they are beyond criticism."[16]

John Atkins would have agreed, but he thought that the sturdy discipline of the British regulars was "matched with an equally sturdy want of natural resource, intelligence, or eye for the country." And Churchill, now a young and reckless politician, dared to say that "the individual Boer, mounted in suitable country, is worth three to five regular soldiers." After the war most of the officers who testified before the Commission on the War in South Africa admitted that the average British regular was inferior in intelligence and ability to the colonials and to the Boers. *The Times History* passed a harsh but true judgement: "They were indifferent shots, careless of cover, slow to comprehend what was taking place or to grasp the whereabouts of the enemy, always getting surprised or lost, helpless without their officers. In a word, the British soldier was well disciplined but ill-trained—one might almost say untrained."[17]

The ability to endure was the regular's most signal feature. General Hector Macdonald, a Scotsman who had himself served for nine years in the ranks, appreciated this: "Poor fellows, the work is hard, hard indeed; but not a growl among them all. They march, march, hour after hour, day after day, sometimes without boots or shoes, and often in rags, but they are always cheery and never complain." In all of the previous wars of the Victorian era the stolid qualities of the British regular had made up for his inadequate training and lack of skills. It was only in this war, for the first time, that bulldog tenacity, blind obedience, and brave endurance did not suffice.

Not much is known of what these simple, illiterate men thought or felt. They did not write books or articles, and few writers of books and articles considered their thoughts or feelings worth recording. Most of what we know about life in the ranks comes from literate volunteers.

James Barnes saw the body of a soldier being brought in after a skirmish. Walking beside the stretcher was a tall comrade, his bronzed face drawn with grief, who kept a hand on the stretcher to steady it, as if he felt the dead man could be hurt by the jolting. A trooper came up to commiserate. "Was he your pal?" he asked.

"Aye!" he said brokenly. "And man! You should 'ave 'eard 'im play the penny whistle!"

It is only in such casually observed or overheard bits that we catch a glimpse of the regular army soldier. Neither officers nor newspaper correspondents made any real attempt to understand him. His bravery and endurance were praised, his military deficiencies were deplored, but there was no attempt to discover what he felt. For this we must turn, curiously, to fiction and to poetry—the work of a man who never spent a day in the army. That the work of Rudyard Kipling hit the proper note for the rank and file is attested by the thousands of crudely spelled letters he received from men in the ranks and by their lusty cheers whenever he appeared among them. In fact, Major General George Younghusband maintained that Kipling created the British soldier:

> I myself had served for many years with soldiers, but had never once heard the words or expressions that Rudyard Kipling's soldiers used. Many a time did I ask my brother officers whether they had ever heard them. No, never. But sure enough, a few years after the soldiers thought, and talked, and expressed themselves exactly like Rudyard Kipling had taught them in his stories! He would get a stray word here, or a stray expression there, and weave them into general soldier talk, in his priceless stories. Rudyard Kipling made the modern soldier. . . .
>
> My early recollections of the British soldier are of a bluff, rather surly person, never the least jocose or light-hearted, except perhaps when he had too much beer. He was brave always, but with a sullen, stubborn bravery.[18]

More than anything, perhaps, this passage illustrates how little officers associated with or even spoke to their men. A wide, insurmountable social and cultural gulf divided officers and other ranks. They shared the dangers of campaigns, but little else; they lived in different worlds. Kipling did not so much create the British soldier as open his officers' eyes to him.

It is extraordinary that Kipling, who was certainly not of a class from which private soldiers were recruited, who had never been in the army himself, and whose contacts with soldiers were not really extensive, could so vividly and accurately portray their feelings and attitudes in such a variety of situations. He made three trips to South Africa during the war, staying each time for several months, but only once—and that only for about ten days—did he ever leave Cape Colony and see the fighting soldiers at work. Only a genius with an exceptional ear for language and an extraordinary empathy could have written of the soldier's life in South Africa as he did.

He wrote only three full-length stories about the war but more than two dozen poems. The most famous at the time was "The Absent-Minded Beggar," but perhaps the best known today is "Boots." "The Islanders," a passionate plea for conscription, is remembered now for the phrase that caused an uproar among his sports-loving countrymen: "the flannelled fools at the wicket or the muddied oafs at the goals." Poems such as this and "A Song of the White Men" were political; more interesting today are those which describe the lives and feelings of ordinary soldiers, poems such as "M.I.," "Columns," "Half-Ballad of Waterval," and "Two Kopjes." These poems are written without any concessions to the uninitiated reader, to those unfamiliar with the war as seen by the soldiers. They bristle with jargon and slang and Afrikaans words, and today need either footnotes or an understanding of the war in South Africa to be entirely comprehensible.

Kipling was passionately patriotic and convinced that the British cause was a just one, but he was incapable of a blind hatred for the enemy. He wrote a poetic tribute to Joubert when he died, and in "Piet" (as, earlier, in "Fuzzy-Wuzzy") he reflected the soldier's respect for his foe:

Ah there, Piet!—Picked up be'ind the drive!
The wonder wasn't 'ow 'e fought, but 'ow 'e kep' alive,
With nothin' in 'is belly, on 'is back, or to 'is feet—
I've known a lot o' men behave a dam' sight worse than Piet.[19]

This was an attitude more prevalent in the first half of the war than the last half, and it is significant that Kipling took pains to explain that the speaker is not a colonial or a volunteer but a "Regular of the Line."

In the beginning there had been a number of gentlemen rankers, but in the guerrilla phase of the war these had largely disappeared, gone home when their time was served. The social level of the volunteers declined, and there were no longer architects, barristers, or even bank clerks in the ranks. Recruits came from the working class. Perhaps the best explanation of why they enlisted after the glamour of the war had worn thin can be seen in an anonymous article published in a working-class magazine:

Here I was cooped up in a city warehouse a strong active fellow full of high spirits and a desire to see the world. What more to the taste could there be than a few months in a different land. . . . to see life and to escape the continual sameness inseparable from trade in the city. . . . it was to escape for a time the monotony of existence, and if other volunteers were to speak the truth they would tell you the same thing.[20]

Although the quality of the British soldiers decreased and their enthusiasm waned, the situation among the Boers was the reverse. Their numbers in the field grew ever fewer, but those remaining were the best fighters; they were those most enthusiastic for their cause, those most skilled in the arts of survival—the hardest to catch and kill.

39

GUERRILLA LIFE

Britons and Boers both inhabited the veld, playing the same deadly game; the same sun and the same rain fell on both, but life was not the same for the hunted as for the hunters. The British had bases to draw upon, inexhaustible supplies, overwhelming force; the Boers' sources of men and supplies steadily dwindled. In one sense time was on the side of the British, for the Boers could not continue indefinitely. Yet, in another sense, time was on the side of the Boers, for the nature of guerrilla warfare makes the objectives of the war different for the two contestants. In order to win, the British had either to kill or to capture all their foes or force them to capitulate; the Boers on the other hand needed only to exist, they needed only to stay alive on the veld to deny the British their victory. They could not win, but they could keep the British from winning. The guerrilla phase was a war of wills, an endurance contest. Each week that the Boers prolonged the struggle added to Britain's embarrassment, for while each minor victory of the Boers was a humiliation for their enemy, British victories, using crushing force on small bands of exhausted burghers, were without glory and added no credit to the army or the Empire.

The average British soldier could not understand why the Boers kept on fighting when they were certain to lose. A prisoner once asked young Reitz why they persisted: "Oh, well, you see," said Reitz, "we're like Mr. Micawber. We are waiting for something to turn up."

Back-veld Boers, like British Tommys, did not keep diaries or write many letters; most of what we know of the guerrilla life led by the fighting burghers comes from the pens of town Boers, the best accounts being those of Deneys Reitz from Pretoria and Roland Schikkerling from Johannesburg. But educated young townsmen and wild, bearded Boers from the Zoutpansberg, diverse as they might be, lived and fought under the same conditions, nor was the life of a commandant or general much different from theirs; guerrilla life rubbed men down to essentials.

With Kitchener's columns sweeping the country clean of livestock and burning the crops, food grew ever more scarce and the fighting burghers were forced to live frugally indeed. Daniel Morgan, guerrilla leader in the American Revolution, put his finger on the fundamental requisite of a guerrilla: he had in his unit a number of "Pennsylvania Dutch," a stock not unlike the Afrikaners. "As for fighting," he said, "the men of all races are pretty much alike. . . . But sir, for the grand, essential composition of a good soldier, give me a 'Dutchman'—he starves well."

There was a wide variety of game on the veld, and the British could not denude the country of all animal life. If the burghers were left in peace long enough and could spare the ammunition, they hunted antelope and other game, jerked it, and made biltong. The great staple was mealies (maize), which grew in such profusion that they were seldom without it. It was eaten boiled, roasted, and green, made into porridge and ground up for flour. It was even toasted and used to make an ersatz coffee. Schikkerling was probably not exaggerating when he said of mealies: "Take it away and we could not remain in the field ten days longer. Without it we would have had to abandon the war more than a year ago. A mealie cob should be on our coat of arms."[1]

There was also food to be had from the British, sometimes in quantity when they successfully attacked and captured a goods train or supply convoy, but with no safe place to establish depots they were able to use only what they could carry with them or eat on the spot. Some of it was too strange for the unsophisticated back-veld Boers. One old burgher, having pried open a tin of oysters, asked plaintively, "Who will give me some jam for this little tin of bird's bellies?"

THE WOUNDED WERE TENDED ON THE BATTLEFIELD AT A COLLECTING STATION BEFORE BEING TAKEN TO A FIELD HOSPITAL.

Hunger sometimes drove the Boers to raid Bantu kraals, and this led to retaliatory attacks. The Bantu were not slow to see who was winning the war; their fears of the Boers decreased and they became bolder. Their increasingly hostile attitude made the Boers feel freer to make raids on them for food. This bad feeling between Boer and Bantu, particularly in the Transvaal, increased the dangers the burghers faced.

As the war dragged on, clothing became increasingly scarce. Cloth had never been manufactured in the republics, and after the capture of Komatipoort by the British the Boers received no more imports. Commandos operating in the Cape suffered less than did those in the north, and some even developed a kind of uniform with their own distinctive hat bands: Scheepers's men wore white bands, Willem Fouché's men yellow, and Wynand Malan's men blue with white polka dots.

Deneys Reitz was not the only one to discover that grain bags could be made to serve as clothing. Schikkerling, writing in August 1901 from the Transvaal, said: "The local farmers have better clothes than we of the Johannesburg Commando. The material is from a better class of grain-bag, more closely knit, and without names and advertisements on. They, however, betray their bad taste and vanity by the goat-skin, and clashing colours of their patches."[2]

Describing a meeting of General Ben Viljoen with a group of his officers, he wrote:

The astonishing assemblage looked very much like a cannibal fancy dress meeting. One officer wore a jacket of monkey skin, hair to the outside; another officer a jacket of leopard skin. One looked a cross between Attila the Hun and Sancho Panza. Others wore odd garments of sheep, goat, and deer skin, and of green baize and gaudily coloured kaffir blankets. Quite evidently the apparel does not here proclaim the man.[3]

To the British it seemed humiliating that these bands of ragamuffins could prove such formidable foes. Herbert Lionel James looked at a batch of prisoners and found cause for reflection:

The majority had neither coats nor boots; and their remaining costume was in the last stages of decay. . . . They were emaciated and drawn with hunger and hardship. . . . But what is more humiliating than anything else, is the realization that these miserable creatures are an enemy able to keep the flower of England's army in check, to levy a tax of six millions a month upon this country, and render abortive a military reputation built upon unparallelled traditions. This is indeed a bitter reflection . . .[4]

James was writing in February 1901. The war was to go on for more than a year longer, and the Boers learned to look to the British army as unwilling supplies of clothing. When prisoners were taken, the Boers, having no prisons, simply stripped them of their clothing and accoutrements and freed them to "walk man-naked in the 'eat" (as Kipling put it) back to their units.

Clothing was not the only item in short supply. Kitchener's scorched-earth policy made everything scarce. Tobacco adicts suffered, and desperate men smoked horse dung, calling it Wayside Mixture. The Boers became skilled at making do with what they could find on the veld. From British telegraph wire they made nails for their horses' shoes; when there were no more matches they made tinder boxes, using flints they found and, for tinder, the fluffy substance found inside the pods of a common shrub.

Ammunition for their Mausers became very scarce indeed, and when it was nearly exhausted the Boers took every opportunity to exchange their Mausers for Lee-Metfords; eventually almost the entire Boer force in the field was armed with British rifles shooting British ammunition. "It is an extraordinary thing when we think of it," wrote David Miller in a letter home, "that the Boers depend almost entirely for their ammunition on captures they make from us."[5] But the Boers did not have to rely entirely on captures. British soldiers carried their cartridges loose in ammunition pouches, an unsatisfactory arrangement, for a loose strap made it easy for them to spill out. The burghers often followed behind a British column gleaning cartridges; camp sites always yielded a supply, for the British usually broke camp before daylight and did not police their areas before leaving. The Canadians had a superior cartridge belt invented by a retired American general, Anson Mills, and toward the end of the war the British also acquired some, but there were always enough captures, enough of the old ammunition pouches, and enough careless soldiers to keep the Boers supplied and fighting.

Someone once suggested to Kitchener that he ask the ordnance department in England to produce cartridges that resembled the ordinary issue but which would explode when fired and that these be scattered about for the Boers to pick up. Kitchener considered this idea, but Ian Hamilton talked him out of it. "To my mind," said Hamilton, "this stood on a level with the poisoning of wells, and heaven be praised, K. never touched it."[6]

The Boers had begun the war with hymns and sermons, had ridden off to join their commandos with their Bibles stuffed in their saddlebags; many commandos had been accompanied by predikants of the church, some of whom had become officers. "The men who led the Boers in prayers also led them in battle," Captain Carl Reichmann observed. "In camp or at a halt on the march he read his Bible or hymn book, and at night after dark, groups of men would sing psalms and hymns, whose weird solemnity subdued the frivolity of any would-be scoffer."[7]

The altered character of the war did little to change this picture. There were church services, prayer meetings, thanksgiving services after victories or narrow escapes, and confirmation classes for the young men. At least one commando even formed a religious debating society—and this during the guerrilla war.

Absent from the hymn singing and other pious observances were the foreign volunteers, whose free-ranging ways were not to be checked. It was a rare burgher who drank to drunkenness; many foreign volunteers did so as often as they had the opportunity. They were also more profane, and many had a wild exuberance of language that bewildered the more literal-minded Boer. One old burgher sat amazed, a plug of tobacco halfway to his mouth, while an Irish-American with whom he had refused to share it ranted at him, "You are lower than a snake's arse, and I wouldn't spit on you if your guts were on fire."

Most of the men with the guerrilla commandos were no more disciplined at the end of the war than they had been at the beginning, although much depended upon their leaders. De Wet was probably the most successful, but even in his forces the state of discipline never reached what would be considered an acceptable standard in any other army; orders deemed unacceptable were still disregarded. Schikkerling in his diary for 22 February 1901 recorded one such time: "In the afternoon the General [Ben Viljoen] sent to arrest a young fellow who, without leave, had left some distant commando to visit someone in our laager. About seventy of us congregate and refuse to allow violence to our visitor, and there the matter drops."[8]

Leaders found it difficult to restrain their burghers from pillaging and even from stealing from each other. Although the foreigners were credited with being the worst thieves, the Boers were not far behind. Schikkerling was the proud possessor of a spoon, a rare article, but he was forced to carry it in his pocket at all times to prevent its being stolen by his comrades, and in his diary he once wrote: "It is today two years since I fled out of Johannesburg. On this historic day a depraved person steals the twelve bars of soap I made."[9]

Commandant Botha (a relative of the commandant-general) one night listened patiently to the fulminations of a burgher who had come to him with the news that they were losing the war because God was punishing them for their sins, especially for the sin of thieving, and in particular for the heinous crime of stealing from comrades. The harangue was brought to an end only by the exhausted Botha rolling himself in his blankets and falling asleep. He awoke cold and shivering, his blankets gone. So, too, were his coat and saddle. So too was the burgher.

Schikkerling's diary reveals repeatedly the depredations of his own commando:

During our wanderings last night [16 May 1901] we stopped at a farmhouse to make some enquiry, but received scant courtesy from the woman in command. She approached, followed by a long diminishing file of children, the whole looking like a monstrous sea serpent, herself in the van forming the formidable head. With tearful fury she denounced us as thieves, drunkards, and cowards who, having left our manhood behind us in the big cities and other idolatrous centres, had come here to rob and ruin helpless Christian women and children, and to be instrumental in causing their homes to be burnt down, by drawing, through our uninvited presence, the enemy to their houses with fire and sword and, when he came, by fleeing and leaving the distracted household to face him. The painful part of the reproach was the coarse grains of truth therein embedded. We admitted defeat and moved on.[10]

The Boer officers generally did their best to discourage indiscriminate looting from their own people, but, without power to punish, their words often fell on deaf ears. At one farm the housewife welcomed the men of the Johannesburg Commando warmly, but they stole her pigs and turkeys anyway, causing her to break into tears: "If only she had cursed us," said Schikkerling, "we could have stood it; but she merely wept; and this drew from me all that I had to leave her—a tear of pity."[11]

Some commandos were worse than others, carrying reputations that made their visits dreaded. Jack Pienaar's field coronetcy, consisting mostly of foreign volunteers, earned a name for poultry thieving, and the approach of the Machadodorp Commando, noted for plundering, was cause for alarm to any farm, although when they came to her parents' farm Freda Schlosberg recorded that they were "so utterly discouraged that they did not have enough pluck to loot us, though they stole as much as they could. . . . So the much dreaded commando passed harmlessly."[12] But there were others, and, as Freda wrote in her diary, "some of them were exceedingly troublesome." One carried off the little pony on which she and her sister used to ride. When a commando came to a neighbouring farm the woman there snatched up a revolver and ran to the stable. The two horses inside were all she had left after the depredations of another commando only a week before, and she vowed she would shoot any man who touched them. They simply took the revolver out of her hand and led the horses away.

The Schlosbergs finally abandoned their farm, and Freda recorded its fate in her diary:

> As soon as we left Rhenosterkop the Boers took away the doors and windows of our house, all the furniture and everything else useful, broke into our warehouses and took all the forage and mealies that we left.
> Then Colonel Plumer arrived with his regiment and burnt our home and warehouses to the ground.[13]

Schlosberg, born in Russia, was not a burgher, and he had tried to be neutral, but any farmer found that impossible; whatever he did he seemed certain to be accused of partisanship and to lose all he possessed. On 6 October 1900 Botha issued the following order to his subordinate commanders: "Do everything in your power to prevent the burghers laying down their arms. I will be compelled, if they do not listen to this, to confiscate everything movable and also to burn their farms."[14]

So the Boers did their share of farm burning too, and they were not always judicious. Marthinus Becker was with his commando when a group of Boers came to the thatched cottage where he had left his wife and children. They accused Becker of having gone over to the British and refused to believe his wife's protestations that he had not. They burned the house and all its contents.

The Boer leaders did their best to see that their commandos did not take on the appearance of mere bands of banditti, and they struggled to maintain a semblance of formal government. In spite of Lord Roberts's annexation proclamation, Steyn still claimed to be president of the Orange Free State, and although Kruger was gone, Schalk Burger remained as acting president of the Transvaal; cabinet officers were appointed and they did as much government business as they could, although it was not much. Their capitals were wherever the heads of state laagered for the night. Schikkerling lightheartedly made fun of the Transvaal government:

The Government is. . . . a portable and peripatetic body, the head and executive mounted on horses and mules, on which are packed the State Documents and worthless paper money; of coin currency they have none. This fugitive assemblage wanders about, making the Capital and seat of Government any humble hill, valley or grotto, that gives shelter and sanctuary. When it stands for any length of time on one spot, it acquires impedimenta and poultry and gets into easy habits, the Ministry often eating real bread and sometimes putting sugar in their mealie coffee.[15]

Effective national leadership in the Transvaal was really given by Louis Botha rather than the weak Schalk Burger, but in the Orange Free State the fiery Marthinus Theunis Steyn was a flaming torch of patriotism, giving to the cause of independence every ounce of his energy. Although De Wet and faithful burghers tried to protect him, Steyn led a precarious life. Several times he came close to being captured, and once he came very close indeed.

On 6 July 1901 a British column passing through the village of Reitz in the northern Free State discovered that the Boers were in the habit of vacating the town as soon as a column approached and returning as soon as it passed on. Three days later Brigadier General R. G. Broadwood was ordered to double back by forced marches and take the town by surprise.

The Boers, who kept track of British columns, knew (or thought they did) that the nearest column was 20 miles away when, on the night of 9 July, Steyn and his government were camped at Reitz. As a precaution, however, some men were posted between the town and the column. But Broadwood, taking 400 well-mounted men and a pompom, moved fast. When the Boer picket dashed into town shouting "The English are on us!" the British were pounding at their heels.

Steyn shared a tent with his brother-in-law and aide, Gordon Fraser, but this night Fraser had sat up until one o'clock playing cards at a home in town and, not wanting to disturb the President, had decided to sleep there. He had slept only a few hours when shouts woke him. He tumbled out of bed and grabbed up his clothes, but at the door of the house he was met by soldiers and the order, "Hands up!"

About two o'clock in the morning Steyn had awakened, as he frequently did, to get up, look around, and see that all was well. Everything was quiet, and he went back to sleep. Just before dawn his Coloured servant, Ruiter, got up to make the morning coffee and heard, faintly at first, a sound he took to be made by cattle. Then he saw, looming up in the darkness, Broadwood's hard-riding dragoons, and he rushed into Steyn's tent shouting, "Oubaas! Here are the English!" Steyn leaped up and ran outside. Only about 400 yards away were the British, riding with loose reins as fast as they could straight towards him. He and Ruiter made a dash for it, Steyn wisely following Ruiter, who knew where the horses were, and they managed to round a corner and race to the barn where the horses were stalled without being seen. Another servant, who had dashed back into the tent to fetch Steyn's saddle, was met by the troopers as he ran outside with it. Steyn had thrown a rope over his horse's neck and was about to mount bareback when a young burgher named Curlewis, a former schoolmaster, thrust his saddle at him. He was a small man and the stirrups were too short, but there was no time for niceties.

Mounted and outside the barn, Steyn and Ruiter could see that the town swarmed with soldiers, and Steyn instinctively turned that way, but Ruiter managed to dissuade him and they galloped for a nearby kopje. A dragoon sent a shot after them, and Steyn, looking over his shoulder, saw Ruiter tumble from his saddle.

Dawn found the President of the Orange Free State hatless, coatless, and alone, a fugitive on the veld. Behind him in the hands of the enemy were all his official and personal papers; his staff and most of his cabinet were prisoners.

Early in the morning he came upon some Boer scouts, one of whom gave him a handkerchief (a rare article among the guerrillas) to cover his balding head. Another scout he encountered gave him a hat, and at the farm of a recently married man the bride gave him the only man's jacket in the house—her absent husband's wedding coat.

Although the British had failed to capture Steyn, they had done well. Among the prisoners were one of the president's brothers, Pieter Gysburt Steyn; Gordon Fraser, the president's brother-in-law; Rocco de Villiers, secretary of the Executive; Alec McHardy, secretary of the War Committee; and two Boer generals: A. P. Cronjé and J. B. Wessels. Broadwood also had the satisfaction of recapturing the remaining guns De Wet had taken from him at Sanna's Post. It was quite a haul.

All accounts except the most reliable—that of Steyn himself—say that the president fled Reitz in his nightshirt. But Steyn, like his burghers, slept in his clothes. He had been wearing a nightcap, but this he had thrown aside while running with Ruiter for the horses. Later, Major Hamilton Goold-Adams, then military governor of Bloemfontein, stopped the carriage of Steyn's wife and asked, "Mrs. Steyn, can it be true that President Steyn barely escaped in his nightshirt?"

"I would like to think that it *is* true," she replied. "If the President can still sleep in a nightshirt then I know he still has clothes enough.

. . . But he certainly got away, your excellency, and that is the most
important thing to us."

The deprivations and dangers of living on the open veld fighting for
a lost cause required men who were exceptionally brave, hardy, determined, and skilful. Not all men by any means could measure up to the
demands made upon them. They were cut off from their families and, for
most of the time, cut off from any news at all. Their leaders, particularly
Steyn, gave inspiring speeches when they could; occasionally the burghers would see a newspaper, but this would be British; and from time to
time news and propaganda would be sent to them. Kruger in Europe sent
messages—"flinch not and fall not into disbelief" was the usual theme—
and sometimes they gathered around their commandant or general to
hear news of minor victories, words of encouragement from Boer sympa-
thizers, or selected quotations from articles and speeches written by
antiwar enthusiasts in England. Sometimes too the British sent out news
that circulated among the commandos. Schikkerling wrote:

> The enemy has sent to inform us that Commandant Trichardt had a hundred
> and sixty-two of his men captured, that Commandant Scheepers in the Cape
> Colony has been put to death, and that Kritzinger is awaiting trial. An enemy
> seems to have no regard for one's feelings. Who wanted this news? This is the
> sort of thing that makes enemies bad friends.[16]

From first to last Schikkerling retained his sense of humour. He had
need of it. But even he was sometimes homesick, and on 28 November
1901, his twenty-second birthday, he wrote: "I am so tired, and do so long
to be home."[17] And he was sometimes discouraged:

> The enemy is wearing us down and huddling us together, and we seem
> unable to offer resistance. We are far out of courage, and our days are becoming
> one continuous extremity. We are at a loss to know what Saint to humour. The
> roomy days of our talkative forefathers, who never had such protracted cam-
> paigns, are gone and past, and the fates seem weary of doing Majuba miracles.
> There used to be a time when we were entitled to look forward to a miracle as
> naturally as to a shock of corn in its season.[18]

"One does not fight because there is hope of winning," said Cyrano
de Bergerac. "It is much finer to fight when it is no use." Such appeared to be the attitude of the burghers on the veld during the final
year of the war, and Schikkerling seemed to echo Cyrano's sentiments:
"Any fool can glory in victory, but only the brave can endure defeat
upon defeat. A victory is glory to the meanest, but the test of courage
is reverse. . . . There is more in the strength to endure than in the
power to inflict. . . ."[19]

Even in the worst of times there came for most commandos brief
respites, occasional lulls, when men could rest and play. Charles B.
Holme, an Australian, was one of five men from the Queensland Mounted
Infantry captured by the Johannesburg Commando and kept for a time
unconfined in their laager. He was surprised to see the young Boers

playing such childish games as leapfrog and "egg in the hat,"* and a game called "mill," a variant of the morris game. Group singing was popular, and although the Doppers sang only hymns and psalms, those belonging to the less strict sects of the Dutch Reformed Church sang secular songs. Some men managed to carry fiddles or concertinas strapped to their saddles, and there were frequent concerts. In September 1901 a group of burghers wrote and produced a play at Pilgrim's Rest in the northern Transvaal; women in the town took part, and even General Ben Viljoen played a role. The plot has not survived, but the final scene, played to great effect, featured the execution of a traitor to the accompaniment of a song.

The most charming, certainly the most pleasant picture of guerrilla life is that of a group of young Boers who on New Year's Day 1901, after bathing in a stream, decorated their horses and themselves with ferns and wild flowers and rode gaily back to their laager.

The British did not, could not, occupy all of the two former republics. Although they held the railways, the cities, the mines, and the most populous areas, there were still places where Kitchener's columns never ventured. De la Rey, "the Lion of the West," successfully held back the British in the western Transvaal, and the British gave up as an impossible task the occupation of the sparcely settled north, the wild Zoutpansberg district. The one railway running north from Pretoria went only as far as Pietersburg, which the British first occupied when a column under Plumer rode into town on the night of 8 April 1901. Pietersburg's only defender was the village schoolmaster, who hid in the tall grass just outside the town and shot two Tasmanian officers and a trooper before he was run to earth. Plumer's column did not remain long, but he destroyed four steam mills, a repair shop, and the plant of the two newspapers.

From the Zoutpansberg came some of the most rugged and intractable burghers. Conan Doyle described them as "tough frontiersmen living in a land where a dinner was shot, not bought. Shaggy, hairy, half-savage men, handling a rifle as a mediaeval Englishman handled a bow, and skilled in every wile of veldt craft, they were as formidable opponents as the world could show."[20]

These were takhaaren, people who seemed strange and wild even to the other Boers. Many of the town Boers had never before encountered them. Schikkerling on seeing them for the first time wrote:

These people are wretched indeed. Some, I am told, hardly till the soil, subsisting mainly on stamvruchten and other wild fruits, and even eating mon-

---

*In this game each participant puts his hat on the ground. One takes a stone or ball and tries to throw it in a hat. When he succeeds, the owner of the hat must run and get it and throw the ball at someone else. The person hit then has to throw the ball in a hat. I am indebted to Advocate Gladys Steyn for this explanation of a game now seldom played.

Holme, incidentally, returned to South Africa after the war and worked at the Aukland Park race course in Johannesburg, making friends of some of his former captors.

keys. One of them had sold his daughter for two oxen to a man who did not seem quite white. (I saw her, and I certainly think she was worth three.) They are ignorant and unschooled in civilized ways, having been reared in the wilderness in a chronic state of withering poverty.[21]

Boer tactics remained basically unchanged, but occasionally ingenious leaders could startle the British with something new, as Brigadier General H. G. Dixon discovered three days after setting out from Naauwpoort on 26 May 1901 with 430 mounted men and 800 infantry, seven guns, and a pompom. Most of his mounted men were newly arrived yeomanry who had seen no serious fighting, but the infantry and gunners were veterans. He discovered a cache of ammunition buried on a farm called Elandsfontein and, although it was only one thirty in the afternoon, decided it was too late in the day to start the removal, so he withdrew the bulk of his force to Vlakfontein farm about 2 miles away, leaving as a guard at Elandsfontein a company of Derbys, the yeomanry, and two guns, all under the command of Major Henry Chance, an artillery officer.

Chance and his guard were attacked suddenly and with exceptional ferocity by one of the most daring of the young Boer generals: twenty-nine-year-old Christoffel Greyling Kemp. The Boers set fire to the veld, taking advantage of a westerly wind that blew the smoke and flames towards Chance's position. Behind the flames and obscured by the smoke, Kemp boldly advanced with 500 burghers, secure from the fire of the British guns. Chance withdrew 1,200 yards towards Dixon's camp at Vlakfontein and sent for reinforcements; the fire was gaining on him. Suddenly, through the smoke and flames, looking like blackened, smoking fiends, rode the Boers, firing from the saddle as they bore down on Chance and his men. Nine out of 16 yeomanry officers fell, dead or wounded. The yeomanry recruits fled in terror and were shot down by the dozens as they did so. The gunners, embued with the traditions of their regiment, stuck to their guns; 17 out of 19 fell.

Kemp turned the captured guns on the British, but Dixon, coming up rapidly to the rescue, led the Derbys and the King's Own Scottish Borderers in a counterattack with the bayonet that drove the Boers from the field.

After the battle there were many and persistent reports that Kemp's men had killed British wounded. Conan Doyle said, "There is no question at all about the fact, which is attested by many independent witnesses. . . . the incident is too well authenticated to be left unrecorded."[22] But Conan Doyle did not document the charge or even cite the witnesses. When all the evidence was sifted it came down to one burgher, a man named Van Zyl, wounded himself and out of his head, who crawled about and shot three wounded soldiers before he could be stopped.

The most spectacular Boer victory of the guerrilla war was, like Vlakfontein, against newly arrived, unblooded troops, and it took place on 7 March 1902, almost at the end of the war. It was spectacular not in the number of killed and wounded (impressive though this number was in relation to the forces involved) or in the tactics displayed (brilliant though the Boer tactics were) but because it resulted in the capture of Lieutenant General Lord Methuen.

In his attempt to march to the relief of Kimberley in December 1899 Methuen had behaved arrogantly and stupidly, and his campaign had ended in disaster at Magersfontein. He had been humbled and he knew it; he had been taught a lesson and he was not such a fool as to ignore it. Since then he had worked hard to redeem his tarnished reputation. When Buller and all the other senior officers who had come out with him returned home, Methuen remained, accepting any job given him and doing it willingly, conscientiously, and usually doing it well. He was the senior officer in the country, senior even to Kitchener, but he served without complaint under younger and junior generals. There were few senior officers in the British army who would have suffered this indignity. At one time his command was reduced to a single column such as would normally have been commanded by a colonel, but he manfully soldiered on—and he fought.

On 2 March 1902 Methuen, now in charge of the western Transvaal theatre of operations, left Vryburg with four guns and 1,300 men. Only a week earlier disaster had struck one of his principal columns under Colonel Pelham von Donop. De la Rey had scuppered it and in the process had acquired guns, mules, horses, and a half-million rounds of ammunition.

The column Methuen personally led out of Vryburg consisted mostly of ill-trained and inexperienced troops. Culled from fourteen different units, they were a mixture of yeomanry, mounted police, regulars, and colonials. Only the gunners, 200 Northumberland Fusiliers, and 100 Loyal North Lancashires were seasoned veterans, but Methuen intended to link up with another column of 1,500 men under Colonel Grenfell. The country over which he marched was arid, water supply was uncertain, and his oxen were in poor condition, so his rate of march was slow. On 6 March a small Boer commando followed the column and skirmished with the rear guard, made up of the 86th Yeomanry and some colonials. At one point, when the Boers pressed forward with some vigour, the colonial officers lost their heads and the men panicked. A few shells dispersed the Boers, but Methuen had personally to restore order among his shaky men. It was an ominous sign.

When Methuen camped for the night at a place called Tweebosch his intelligence officer reported that the small commando with which they had skirmished that day had linked up with a large force under De la Rey, but he could not say where it was, nor had he discovered the location of Grenfell's column. De la Rey, on the other hand, knew exactly where Methuen was, and undoubtedly he knew the composition and quality of his column; taking 1,100 picked men, he set out to get him. Methuen the hunter was now the hunted.

Early on the morning of the next day Methuen's column lumbered off northward. It did not get far. At five o'clock, just after daybreak, in the angle formed by the Little Hart's and Great rivers, De la Rey's skirmishers began to harass Methuen's rear guard. An hour later De la Rey's horsemen were also on the column's right flank. Next De la Rey threw out three successive lines of skirmishers on the left rear of the column; then he brought up a fourth line of horsemen who passed through their own skirmishers at a gallop and, firing from the saddle, charged home. The yeomanry and colonials panicked and fled. A section (two guns) of the 38th Battery remained, but there was not a rifle to protect them. They fought to the end. Lieutenant Cuthbert Nesham, in charge of the section, was the last survivor. He refused to surrender and was shot down. Methuen and the regular officers tried in vain to halt the flight of the colonials and yeomanry, but it was a "battle of the spurs" and many did not stop until their horses were blown. Methuen gathered together his infantry regulars and the remaining two guns for a hopeless last stand.

A lance corporal of the Northumberland Fusiliers described the scene where Methuen stood:

It was a dreadful sight around the guns, just like a slaughter-house. I have never seen men work so hard in my life. They kept on firing the guns under the heaviest fire that I have ever been under, never seeming to heed their dead comrades or horses, because a similar fate awaited them. The last gunner, finding himself alone, was just leaving when he was shot through the head. Lord Methuen did not quit the guns until then. He came over to us and stood about fifteen yards from where I was. Five minutes later he got his first wound—in his right side— and then tried to mount his horse. I do not know what he was going to do, but his horse was shot in the leg, and he had to get off. A few moments later he got his second wound—in the thigh—and lay down as if nothing had happened. His horse was shot dead immediately afterwards, falling on him and breaking his leg. The doctor went to him to dress his wounds, but, before he had half finished he was shot, too, and our General had to lie there till he surrendered.[23]

It was quickly over. The British lost 4 officers and 64 men killed, 10 officers and 111 men wounded, and about 600 were captured. De la Rey acquired another four guns.

No one could know that this was to be the Boers' last victory. At British army headquarters it was thought that it might be the first of many, marking a turning point in the war. Ian Hamilton wrote: "I can't tell exactly how folk felt about all this in England. At Pretoria I do know that it really almost seemed as if everything might crash back into chaos. In fact, the whole issue of the war seemed now to hinge on the Western Transvaal."[24] When Kitchener heard the news he took to his bed for thirty-six hours; his nerves, he confided to his aide-de-camp, Captain Francis Maxwell, had "gone to pieces."

Methuen was the highest-ranking officer the Boers ever captured: a lieutuenant general and a real lord besides; he was indeed a prize. His cattle killing and farm burning had made him a much hated man, although the policy which dictated his actions was not of his making. He had even burned down De la Rey's own farm. And it was in a fight with Methuen that De la Rey's son had been mortally wounded. The British had shot Gideon Scheepers and other Boer officers—why should they not shoot Methuen? Such was the temper of De la Rey's men. At the thanksgiving service held after the battle the predikant took as his text that "it would be displeasing to the Lord did we allow such a man who had dealt so cruelly with women and children to go untried." But De la Rey had his own ideas of what would be displeasing to the Lord, and he did not think that God was as bloody-minded as his predikant. He determined to send Methuen to the nearest British hospital. His men almost mutinied when they heard this decision, but De la Rey was adamant: Methuen was sent with a British doctor under a flag of truce into Klerksdorp along with a personal message of sympathy from De la Rey to be forwarded to Lady Methuen.

Almost from the moment that Roberts began his invasion of the Orange Free State there were women who fled from their homes, preferring a life on the veld to living under the rule of the British. They wandered about from place to place with their ox wagons, some chickens perhaps, a few cows, living as best they could, often with their daughters and small sons. Sometimes they attached themselves to commandos, but they were not really welcome; they were an encumbrance to the fighting burghers.

There were many of these wandering groups, and scattered over the veld there eventually came to be women's laagers. It was a hard life indeed for most of the women. For them, as for the men, clothing was scarce, and they made frocks out of captured British blankets when they could get them. De la Rey's wife, who spent eighteen months on the veld with six of her children and three Bantu servants, made dresses for her daughters from captured Union Jacks. Steyn received a report on conditions in some of the women's laagers: "The women and children, suffering almost every one from malaria, fever and other diseases in consequence of privations and bad food, without physicians, without medicines, without any consolation in this world, almost without any clothes, and after hostile raids, without any food at all."[25]

With the beginning of the wholesale farm burning such women's laagers became more and more numerous until the British decided to sweep up the women and their children and put them in concentration camps.

40

THE CONCENTRATION CAMPS
AND EMILY HOBHOUSE

War is many things. Above all else it is a tragedy. How does one measure the depth of a tragedy such as war? How, in human terms, does one count the cost? One way is to count the killed; another is to assess the consequences of the calamity for future generations. By any such measurements the saddest statistic of the war in South Africa is not the number of homesteads burned or even the number of burghers and soldiers killed in the fighting, but the death toll of the women and children.

More Boer boys and girls under the age of sixteen died in British concentration camps than all the fighting men killed by bullets and shells on both sides in the course of the entire war.

The exact number of Boer children who died in the camps is unknown; the most conservative estimate puts the figure at 16,000, but the actual number was probably closer to 20,000—and most of these died within one twelve-month period. This does not include the unknown and unestimated number of Bantu and Coloured children who also died in great numbers.

On a month-by-month basis, the death rate among the Boer women, children, and men in the camps ranged from a low of 20 per thousand to a high in October 1901 of 344 per thousand. As a basis of comparison, the average death rate in England at this time was 19 per thousand and today is less than 11 per thousand. The average death rate of the children in the camps was about 300 per thousand.

How could such a disaster occur?

Soldiers and fighting burghers alike would have had to agree that in their efforts to kill each other the women, the children, the old men, and the helpless got in their way. The fighting burghers were unable both to fight and to care for their families; the British, by their farm burning, livestock slaughtering, and destruction of crops, made it increasingly difficult for the families to care for themselves. There were, too, the burghers who had laid down their arms and who wanted only to live in peace but were made homeless by their fellow countrymen whose threats and depredations drove them to seek British protection.

The first indication that the British would have to do something for these people was found in a dispatch by Roberts dated 3 September 1900 in which he mentioned that ten men with women, children, cattle, and wagons had come into the British camp at Eerst Fabricken seeking protection. On 22 September Major General J. G. Maxwell, military governor of the Transvaal, announced that "camps for burghers who voluntarily surrender are being formed in Pretoria and Bloemfontein." Thus these first "burgher camps" or "refugee camps" were indeed simply that: places where the peaceful burghers and their families could come in and be guarded by British bayonets.

The next step came when Kitchener sent out a memorandum to all general officers (21 December 1900) pointing out the advantages of bringing into the camps "all men, women and children and natives from the Districts which the enemy's bands persistently occupy." This, he said, would be "the most effective method of limiting the endurance of the Guerillas. . . . Moreover, seeing the unprotected state of women now living in the Districts, this course is desirable to ensure their not being insulted or molested by natives." This same order pointed out that there would be two classes of inmates in the camps: the first, who would be entitled to preference in accommodation and food, were the families of "neutrals, non-combatants, and surrendered burghers"; the second would be "those whose husbands, fathers and sons are on commando." Thus the nature of the camps changed; henceforth they were to hold the willing and the unwilling, the pro-British, the neutrals, and the defiant. The Boers too saw themselves as a people divided into the "joiners" or "hands-uppers" (hensoppers) and the bitter-enders (bittereinders). There was to be much friction in the camps between these two elements. So much animosity was shown towards the families of National Scouts that special camps had to be established for them.

The idea of sweeping up the inhabitants of entire districts and herding them into guarded camps was not new. Like the blockhouse system, the Spaniards had tried it in Cuba. In 1896 Don Valeriana Weyler y Nicolau, captain general of Cuba, had forced the inhabitants of the four westernmost provinces of the island into fortified areas where they died in great numbers of neglect, starvation, and disease. It is not known if Kitchener was aware of the Spanish reconcentrado system and its effects, but if he was it did not discourage him. Conan Doyle knew of it, but he protested that there was an "essential difference" in that "the guests of the British Government were all well fed and well treated during their detention." There was to be considerable debate about this.

Although a number of Boer families were brought into the concentration camps from certain districts soon after Kitchener's memorandum was issued, the wholesale rounding up of women and children did not begin until after the meeting between Kitchener and Botha at Middelburg on 28 February 1901. This meeting was the first attempt on the part of the combatants to sit down together and seriously discuss peace terms, the first attempt by either side to find out what sort of terms each was prepared to accept.

Botha later described his preparations for the meeting and his reception:

> We selected the best horses in our camp and applied a piece of soap to my own white stallion—a wasteful, profligate sort of thing to do, as soap is a rare luxury with us. But we wanted to look our best. Three miles outside the village we were met by a large military escort, and greeted with military honours. . . . Arrived at the British headquarters, Lord Kitchener came out to meet us, and offering me his arm, led me into a room.[1]

Kitchener and Botha discussed a wide range of subjects and lodged protests with each other. Milner, who had been raised to the peerage, had recently been appointed administrator of the two new colonies; Botha protested the appointment and condemned the employment by the British of armed Bantu and Coloureds. Kitchener objected to the treatment given the Boer peace envoys he had sent and to the wearing of British uniforms by the fighting burghers. As to the peace terms, Botha asked that the legal debts of the republics, including IOUs issued by commandants of commandos, be honoured, that Dutch as well as English be taught in schools, that amnesty be granted for all bona fide acts of war and to the Cape rebels, that British financial assistance be given to rebuild and restock the farms, that prisoners of war be returned as soon as possible, and he asked for assurance that there would be no franchise for the Bantu. Most of all, Botha said, the Boers wanted their independence or, at least, early self-government.

The meeting was friendly. The generals had a photograph taken together, Botha looking spruce in a tunic, riding breeches, boots, and a hat turned up on one side, Kitchener in khaki with a black arm band (Queen Victoria had died in January). Kitchener even taught Botha a new card game that was sweeping Britain: it was called bridge. Not even a translator (which he used) could dampen Botha's charm, and Kitchener felt it and responded to it. In his report on the meeting he made a shrewd prophecy: "He will be, I should think, of valuable assistance to the future good of the country in an official capacity." Afterwards, in a letter to Roberts he wrote:

> If the Government wish to end the war, I do not see any difficulty in doing so, but I think it will go on for some time if the points raised by Botha cannot be answered. I do not think Botha is likely to be unreasonable; there is a good deal of sentiment about it—particularly as regards giving up their independence, which they feel very much.[2]

Kitchener, ever practical, thought that suitable peace terms could be worked out. But when the enemy begins to talk of peace the brutality of the soldier is replaced by the ruthlessness of the politician. Soldiers develop respect for a gallant foe; diplomats and politicians feel none of this; they want more than the defeat of the enemy's armies; they want their enemies grovelling before them, stripped, humble, and helpless. The original aims of the war are forgotten in the determination (harboured by the most democratic of politicians) to crush completely and then dictate to a beaten foe. The words "unconditional surrender" spring more readily to the lips of the politician than to those of the soldier. As soon as Milner arrived on the scene the possibilities for peace vanished.

Milner examined the list of Boer aspirations and agreed with none of them. He was as unwilling to compromise then as he had been at the Bloemfontein conference eighteen months earlier. And it was Milner's uncompromising views that were accepted by Chamberlain and Salisbury. To take but one issue, the treatment of the Cape rebels, Milner was vindictive and insisted that they be treated as traitors; the Boers could not in honour turn their backs on these men who had helped them. Kitchener thought Milner's intransigence was absurd, and in a letter to Broderick he said:

I did all in my power to urge Milner to change his views, which seemed to me very narrow on the subject. . . . Milner's views may be strictly just, but to my mind they are vindictive, and I do not know of a case in history where, under similar circumstances, an amnesty has not been granted.

We are now carrying on the war to be able to put 2–3000 Dutchmen in prison at the end of it. It seems to me absurd, and I wonder the Chancellor of the Exchequer did not have a fit.[3]

When word of the disagreement between Kitchener and the politicians leaked out, Lloyd George blamed Chamberlain: "There was a soldier, who knew what war meant; he strove to make peace. There was another man, who strolled among his orchids, 6000 miles from the deadly bark of the Mauser rifle. He stopped Kitchener's peace!"[4]

There was general disappointment in Britain that the Middelburg meeting failed to bring peace. Still, it is doubtful if Botha would have been able to persuade the other Boer leaders to accept terms even if he and Kitchener had been able to agree. Steyn was furious that Botha had even met with Kitchener. Independence was the basic issue for the Boers, and this the British would not agree to give. When Kitchener telegraphed the report of his meeting to London, Chamberlain was quick to reply that the British government "cannot take into consideration any proposals which have as basis the sanction of the independence of the former republics, which are now formally annexed to the British crown."

On one major issue, however, Kitchener was able to reassure Botha. The British had always advanced the protection they stood ready to extend to the rights of the Bantu and Coloureds as one reason their rule was preferable to that of the Boers. The Boers almost believed them and feared that Britain would go so far as to give them the vote, but Kitchener assured Botha that "it is not the intention of His Majesty's Government to give such franchise before representative government is granted to these colonies, and if then given it will be so limited as to secure the just predominance of the white race."[5] So much for the rights of the blacks.

There was another agreement of sorts reached at Middelburg. In essence this was that the women and children at the seat of war were not to be allowed to interfere with the fighting. This came about, it would appear, when Kitchener protested against the Boer practice of putting pressure on burghers who had surrendered and taken the oath of neutrality to rejoin commandos. Botha replied: "I am entitled by law to force every man to join, and if they do not do so, to confiscate their property and leave their families on the veld."

Kitchener tried to make a deal with Botha: he would spare the farms and families of burghers on commando if Botha would agree to leave in peace those who had surrendered or who wanted to remain neutral. Botha would not agree. The fate of tens of thousands of women and children was thus sealed.

There was some correspondence on the subject after the conference, but the doom of thousands of innocents was pronounced when on 16 April 1901 Kitchener wrote Botha:

As I informed your Honour at Middelburg, Owing to the irregular manner in which you have conducted and continue to conduct hostilities, by forcing unwilling and peaceful inhabitants to join your Commandos, a proceeding totally unauthorized by the recognized customs of war, I have no other course open to me, and am forced to take the very unpleasant and repugnant steps of bringing in the women and children.[6]

Neither Kitchener nor Botha foresaw all the consequences of their decisions. Neither could see that between them they had contrived the war's greatest tragedy. "From the one side or the other it was clear that the Boer women with their little ones must suffer," wrote Emily Hobhouse. "They were between the devil and the deep sea."[7]

They were indeed.

Only a few Britons but all Afrikaners now have an historical remembrance of the concentration camps. The British view at the time was well expressed by W. Basil Worsfold: "Judged by the laws of war, they [the Boers] had been saved from the alternatives of physical annihilation or abject submission by the almost quixotic generosity of the enemy who fed and housed their non-combatant population."[8] Far from considering the British quixotically generous, the Boers saw the internment of the women and children as vindictive, a punishment meted out to the innocent because their men were fighting. State Secretary F. W. Reitz wrote a poem expressing the Afrikaner view—then and now:

> Lord Roberts burns our houses down;
>   The women out he drives;
> He cannot overcome the men
>   So he persecutes the wives.[9]

And De Wet wrote:

> Any one knows that in war, cruelties more horrible than murder can take place, but that such direct and indirect murder should have been committed against defenceless women and children is a thing which I should have staked my head could never have happened in a war by the civilized English nation. And yet it happened.[10]

Between December 1900 and February 1902 about 120,000 Boers, mostly women and children, were inmates of some fifty camps which ranged in size from 7,400 people in the Potchefstroom camp to the small Waterval North camp which contained two men, three women, and three children. There were also camps established for Bantu and Coloureds. The standards, discipline, and quality of life varied considerably from camp to camp depending upon a number of factors such as the capabilities of the camp superintendent, the location of the camp—its proximity to wood and water, its distance from a base or source of supplies—the date the camp was opened (later camps were usually better than earlier ones), and the functioning of the railway system, which the guerrillas constantly disrupted. There were well-run camps in good locations at Kimberley, Norval's Pont, Johannesburg, and Krugersdorp; there were badly run and poorly situated camps at Aliwal North, Mafeking, Kroonstad, and Standerton. It is generally agreed that the worst camp was at Merebank. The death rates also varied considerably from camp to camp. In January 1902 the Potchefstroom camp had 7,126 inmates, of whom 35 died in that month; in the same month the camp at Bethulie, with only 4,088 inmates, had 139 deaths.

The reaction to the camps by the inmates depended not only upon actual camp conditions but to a marked degree upon the status and quality of the people before they entered them. For some who had been *bywoners* (squatters or poor tenant farmers) or back-veld Boers, living conditions in the camps were sometimes better than anything they had previously known; for the families of prosperous farmers and town Boers the conditions seemed intolerable. Inmates' attitudes also depended, of course, on the reasons for their being there. It made a difference whether they had actually sought British protection from their own countrymen, whether they had been forced by the farm burning to seek shelter and food at the camps, or whether they had been rounded up on the veld and put into the camps against their will.

Men were paid for any work they did, usually from 3s to 8s per day, but at the Kimberley camp the men refused work offered by De Beers and would not even work around the camp or grow vegetables. The same was true at the Krugersdorp camp, where the superintendent tried to encourage men to work by offering "first-class rations" to those who did and "second-class rations" to those who did not: this was not a success, for on 31 July 1901 he reported that his daily issue was only 246 first-class rations and 2,692 second-class rations. At Potchefstroom, however, there were more men willing to work than there were jobs available.

Paying Boers to work in the camps aroused some resentment. Corporal Murray Jackson wrote:

> They lived in a way that used to make the brutal soldier's mouth water when he came into town after trekking. Our food in the Mounted Infantry was generally good enough, but we never had shelter. . . . These persecuted people, however, were living in roomy, cool marquees and were paid for doing things for themselves. Thus, if they wanted an oven to bake their bread in, the men made one and got paid for it. This I know for a fact in some camps.[11]

The inmates of the camps were not totally confined and were generally free to leave for short periods, although rules varied in different locations. At Heidelberg people could go out only once a week, while at Pietermaritzburg they could leave camp every day from eight in the morning until six in the evening. Still, most found the confinement a hardship. Dr. T. N. Leslie at Vereeniging wrote in his diary: "The confinement to a camp of a people whose whole lives are spent isolated from the rest of the community. . . . who feel themselves crowded if another family should live within a mile of them . . . is in itself the greatest hardship that they endure."[12]

In establishing the concentration camps the British authorities gave little thought to what they were doing or how they ought to go about doing it. They began by providing hospitable refuges and ended by herding people into semiprisons. They had no idea of the numbers of people they would have to provide for; they had only vague ideas concerning the equipment and services they would have to provide; and they seriously underestimated the problems involved. There was little advance planning; difficulties were solved only after they became apparent or pressing or could no longer be overlooked. Sites selected by the army with military security in mind were not always the most healthy locations for permanent camps.

The British military mind also failed to take into account the emotions and states of mind of the women and children they uprooted. The officers responsible were, in fact, remarkably obtuse. To a soldier's mind life in a settled camp did not appear to be a bad thing. The life of Boer women on the veld, alone on a farm with only her children and Bantu servants, miles from neighbours or towns, struggling to keep going while their men were gone, did not smack of the good life to the average Englishman, but it was the only existence most of the women had ever known; it was the life their mothers and grandmothers had led. They missed their men, but they could cope. The concerns, cares, and comforts of children, farm animals, crops, Bantu servants; the acquistion of possessions; the simple pleasures of farm life—all this provided an active, full life. It made a world where happiness could be found. For a woman to be possessed of all this one day and the next to see her treasured animals killed, her precious crops destroyed, and her house containing all she owned go up in flames, to be herded with others like cattle and carried off to the alien environment of a crowded camp with strangers pressing around her, to be guarded by and dependent upon the enemy who had destroyed the work of her and her husband's lifetime, foreigners who did not even speak her language—all this was traumatic in the extreme.

Camp life has its own rules that must be followed if those who live in camps are to remain healthy or reasonably comfortable, rules of which the Boer women were ignorant. It is no wonder that the bewildered, saddened, frightened women did not immediately adjust to this new life into which they were suddenly thrust, did not change at once their habits of a lifetime. But the authorities complained that the women did little to help themselves, that they did not at once cosily settle down to make themselves comfortable. It was a sad, depressing, unworthy insensitivity.

The authorities could not plead ignorance of the conditions in the camps, for they were set forth in two Command Papers (No. 819, November 1901, and No. 853, December 1901). As first established, ten of them had no stores and the Command Papers reported that "these people are bare-footed and in rags." At the Bloemfontein camp, "The children are mostly not well or warmly clad. There was a shortage of boys' clothing and materials for shirts. Boots are very badly wanted." At Potchefstroom, the largest camp, there were no tents and the "refugees" had to be housed in crude reed huts. In Johannesburg families were put in stables and had to hang up blankets for privacy. At Irene water was drawn from an open ditch in which cattle and sheep often strayed. At Middelburg some families had only one blanket each and hundreds of children were without shoes. Here too a measles epidemic was followed by an influenza epidemic and there were no isolation wards; a shortage of coffins necessitated burying children in packing cases. In November 1901 there were no qualified nurses at the Orange River Station. Some of the doctors in the camps were foreigners who could speak little English and no Dutch or Afrikaans.

Although there were a few camps in Natal and Cape Colony, most were in the Orange Free State and the Transvaal. In retrospect it seems extraordinary that all the camps were not established outside the theatre of war at locations where they could more easily be maintained and supplied. The reason given for keeping them in the war zone was that the inmates wanted to remain in their own districts. This was probably true, but it added to the difficulties of the British and to the hardships of the inmates. New camps were opened only when their need became obvious, and the absence of forethought continued as long as the camps remained under military control. Kitchener had suggested that all of the inmates be transported and settled somewhere outside South Africa—then "there will be room for the British to colonize"—but this idea did not find favour with the politicians.

The camps originally established by the army remained under Kitchener's control until 1 March 1901 when those in the Orange Free State and the Transvaal passed over to civil control under Milner. On 1 November 1901 all were turned over to the civil government. The army treated the inmates as though they were so many soldiers. The rations issued were those served out to regular soldiers in garrison, but what the uncomplaining Tommy meekly accepted the Boer civilians complained of bitterly—and with reason. After the war Kitchener said, "I consider that the soldier was better fed than in any previous campaign,"[13] but civilian politicians had not realized how bad the food was they served to their soldiers. For the first time it occurred to those in authority that the rations of the British army were execrable.

People in institutions, particularly when they have little to do, always complain of the food, even when it is good. In the concentration camps the food was neither good nor plentiful, and certainly it did not make for a balanced diet. Still, no one died of starvation. The amount of food issued varied somewhat from camp to camp: in the Transvaal and in Natal the meat ration was usually four pounds per adult each week; in the Orange Free State it was three and a half pounds. When Milner took charge of the camps he increased the ration and took pains to see that the diet was more varied.

Discrimination in the issue of food—first-class rations for the families of hands-uppers or men who worked and second-class rations for the families of fighting burghers or men who refused to work—created cries of protest even from supporters of the government in Britain, and there were questions in the House of Commons. It did not seem right that women and children should be given less or inferior food because their men were fighting. The practice was discontinued in the Transvaal on 27 February 1901 and in the Orange Free State nine days later.

Bad though the food was, particularly in the first months, it was not as bad as many Boers claimed. Nor were the rumours that flew from camp to camp true: it was said that ground glass was put in the food, there were "blue things," poison, in the sugar, and fish hooks in the bully beef (most of which was processed in the United States). Many were afraid to eat the food they were issued. The only basis for any of these charges was that there were indeed sometimes "blue things" in the sugar, a harmless colouring agent used in processing sugar to make it white.

Miserable as they were, the women of the fighting burghers remained defiant. On President Steyn's birthday a large number of women and children marched about one camp waving Transvaal and Free State flags and singing the volkslieds. Sometimes they saved up their rations and tried to smuggle food out to commandos on the veld. Kitchener, who regarded the back-veld Boers as "uncivilized Afrikaner savages with a thin white veneer," wrote to St. John Broderick: "The Boer woman in the refugee camps who slaps her great protruding belly at you and shouts, 'When all our men are gone these little khakis will fight you,' is a type of the savage produced by generations of wild lonely life."

Kitchener wrote as though reporting an incident he had witnessed, but it must have been reported to him, for he never visited a concentration camp. Although the deaths of the women and children were the most poignant, the most tragic consequence of the war, Kitchener took no interest in the camps at all until he was forced to. And he *was* forced to take note of their conditions by a remarkable English spinster, Emily Hobhouse, who came to be called by Kitchener simply "that bloody woman."

Emily Hobhouse (1860–1936) was born in the rectory of St. Ives, a village near Liskeard in eastern Cornwall, and spent the first thirty-five years of her life there. Her mother died when she was nineteen, and her father, the Reverend Reginald Hobhouse, became a chronic invalid. Emily spent her youth nursing her domineering father and busying herself obediently with parish affairs. When she fell in love with a farmer's son her father thought the match unsuitable; the lovers parted and the young man went to America. When she was thirty-five her father died, and without hesitation Emily left the village in which she had lived all her life. She never returned.

With the intention of doing missionary work, she went, strangely enough, to Virginia, Minnesota, a rough, raw mining town in the Masabi iron range. If she was shocked by her new surroundings, it was not for long; she took the people as she found them: "Four houses of ill-fame are looked on as a necessity which alone makes it possible for respectable women to walk abroad." Although she accepted the miners' sexual customs, their drinking habits were something else and she launched a temperance campaign. Could an archdeacon's daughter in her late thirties find happiness in a Minnesota mining town? She tried. For two years she was engaged to J. C. Jackson, the lean and handsome mayor of the town who also ran a general store.

In 1897 Jackson fell into financial difficulties and left town in some haste for Mexico, where Emily joined him. There she lost what money she had in a speculative venture probably suggested by Jackson. When her money vanished so did Jackson. She returned to England. Exit all notions of romantic love.

For a while Emily worked for the Women's Industrial Council. Then came the Boer War. In it Emily Hobhouse found a mission that was to make her a heroine in the eyes of Afrikaners for all time. Her first involvement was with the South African Women and Children's Distress Fund, for which she was the chief fund-raiser; soon after she began to work with the South African Conciliation Committee. Then she decided to go to South Africa and see conditions for herself. On 7 December 1900 she sailed, second class, for Cape Town. There she heard for the first time of the existence of the concentration camps and contrived to obtain an interview with Milner, who finally consented, reluctantly, to allow her to visit the camps and to distribute food and clothing paid for from the monies she had raised for the Distress Fund. On the afternoon of 24 January 1901 she arrived on a military train at Bloemfontein with a letter

of introduction to General George Pretyman, military governor of the
Orange River Colony, who greeted her cordially, gave her a permanent
pass to visit the camp at Bloemfontein, introduced her to the camp
superintendent, and politely told her that he would be interested in any
comments she might have after her visit. He could hardly have realized
the consequences.

Emily did not merely tour the camp, she examined it minutely, asked
questions, talked with the women, listened with a ready sympathy that
drew from them their stories. While no one can be sure which histories
she first heard, those now known are doubtless similar enough to give an
idea of the sufferings revealed to her.

Mrs. Lillian du Preez, née Pienaar, was a little girl of six when the
British came to her parents' farm. Her father, Johannes, and her two
eldest brothers were on commando. Her mother, Christina, was on the
farm alone with five of her children. The soldiers allowed them to take
some clothes, bedding, and small articles and then they were loaded onto
a horse-drawn trolley and taken away. They travelled all afternoon across
the veld, being joined by wagon loads of other women and children
guarded by soldiers. That night the wagons were drawn into a circle and
they watched the soldiers kill their poultry and cook the fowls over fires.
No one offered them anything. The next day they were given their only
food, a loaf of bread, and eventually they reached the Standerton concentration camp. While sitting with her confused and frightened children,
waiting for a bell tent to be erected, Christina asked another woman if
it was possible to get anything to eat. "Our tears are our sustenance," was
the reply.[14]

There were touching stories of children being parted from their pets,
taken or slaughtered by the soldiers. At one farm where the women and
children fled at the approach of the troops, a child pinned a note to the
door: "Please feed my chickens and turkeys." Little Lillian Pienaar had
rescued and kept with her a lame chicken, a pet she nursed and cared for.
Not long after her arrival at Standerton, a woman came to her mother
begging for her grandfather who was ill and hungry; could she have the
chicken? Christina Pienaar persuaded her little girl to "give it to the sick
old man, as it would die in any case." Lillian handed over her pet; nearly
seventy-five years later she remembered: "My first sacrifice, but it broke
my heart to part from that lame chicken."[15]

When the soldiers came for Alida Badenhorst they gave her fifteen
minutes to collect what she could, but "I was so crushed," she said, "I
did not know what I was doing, and they kept saying, 'quick, quick,' so
I gathered a few necessities together, and thus was driven forth from my
home."[16]

Catherine Labuschagne had buried her baby only a week before the
British came to her farm. Suspecting a buried arms cache, the soldiers
dug open the grave.

On 11 May 1901 Dr. T. N. Leslie wrote in his diary:

A large column under Major Weston crossed the river [Vaal] with guns, prisoners and women and children. . . . the poor women and children were ragged and unkempt, and looked half-starved. . . . They wore a haunted look and their fragile bodies, worn down with the long privations and hardships they had shared with the men, were in striking contrast to the old-time buxom Boer vrow whose size and capacity was so long a byword throughout South Africa.[17]

The war had become a bitter experience indeed for some. One woman said to Leslie: "What is the independence of the country to me when my man is dead?"

Emily Hobhouse was a woman of strong passions, a sharp sense of righteous indignation with a compulsion to help underdogs, the disadvantaged, and the unpopular. All of the accumulated force of the suppressed rebellion of her first thirty-five years under her stern-willed father seems to have erupted when she saw other women and their children paying a male-exacted price for the determination of their men to fight. One wonders how her father managed to keep her bridled, for from this time on no other man ever succeeded in suppressing her except by brute force. She was intelligent, persuasive, energetic, determined, and resourceful; no hardship, no indignity, no sense of propriety, no criticism prevented her from carrying out what she set her mind to do. British officialdom, military and civil, had unwittingly allowed a most formidable enemy to penetrate its lines and view its most disgraceful example of ineptness. A male relative, a member of Parliament, was asked later if he was related to *"the* Miss Hobhouse"; when he told Emily she said, "I thought I was really *that* Miss Hobhouse."

The conditions of the women and children might well have remained largely unknown and the disaster might have been of greater magnitude had it not been for the light of publicity thrown on the camps. This light was flicked on in a dramatic fashion by Miss Hobhouse.

Only two days after she had visited the Bloemfontein camp she wrote to the Distress Committee at home:

I call this camp system wholesale cruelty. It can never be wiped out from the memories of the people. It presses hardest on the children. They droop in the terrible heat. . . . If only the English people would try to exercise a little imagination and picture the whole miserable scene. Entire villages and districts rooted up and dumped in a strange bare place. To keep these camps going is murder for the children. Of course by judicious management they could be improved; but do what you will, you can't undo the thing itself.[18]

She had found conditions worse than she had imagined. Both soap and water were scarce; many were sleeping on the bare ground, and swarms of flies buzzing through the heat and filth added to the misery. In one tent she entered, a puff adder, common in South Africa, crawled out of hiding. The Boer women sensibly fled; Emily, typically, stayed and flailed away at it with her parasol.

In her recommendations to General Pretyman she included a want list: a boiler large enough to boil all the drinking water, a wash house with soap and running water, better medical equipment, more nurses, and more clothing, particularly for the children. In a letter home she wrote: "The authorities are at their wits end, and have no more idea how to cope with the one difficulty of providing clothes for the people than the man in the moon. Crass male ignorance, stupidity, helplessness and muddling. I rub as much salt into the sore places of their minds as I possibly can because it is good for them."[19] General Pretyman must at this point have had at least an inkling of the character of the extraordinary woman who had suddenly appeared on his horizon.

Emily was impressed by the Boer women she met: "simple . . . calm and composed in manner, but always brimming over with hospitable impulses. They possess shrewdness and mother-wit in abundance, and they are wrapped in suspicion like a coat of mail." The Bloemfontein camp was but one of many; Emily wanted to see others, was determined to do so, and did. But a lone Englishwoman travelling about the war-torn country was regarded by the military authorities as an eccentric, and she found that being a woman was a handicap: "I should get on better," she told those at home, "if I were shaped like a truck and ran on wheels."

At Springfontein she sat on the stoep of a farmhouse with three boxes of clothes. The women were brought to her, and she heard their stories and dispensed what she had; even the boxes themselves were coveted, for wood was scarce. To the Distress Committee she wrote:

> But it is interesting to note the various ways in which the great common trouble is met by divers characters. Some are scared, some paralysed and unable to realize their loss, some are dissolved in tears; some, mute and dry-eyed, seem only able to think of the bleak, penniless future; and some are glowing with pride at being prisoners for their country's sake.
>
> A few bare women had made petticoats out of the brown rough blankets. . . .
>
> I have been giving some material for women to make their own boys' clothing, but we are stopped by the utter famine of cotton or thread. Scissors are handed round from tent to tent; thimbles are very few. Everything here is so scarce. . . .
>
> The crying need in this camp is fuel. Wood there is none. . . .
>
> I just want to say, while it's on my mind, that the blouses sent from England, and supposed to be full grown, are only useful here for girls of twelve to fourteen or so—much too small for the well developed Boer maiden, who is really a fine creature.[20]

From camp to camp she went, discovering their inadequacies and complaining of them in her letters home and to the authorities in South Africa. At Norval's Pont, however, she found a well-run camp; the tents were neatly arranged, there was some furniture in them—even some beds and mattresses—a tennis court had been laid out and a school started. Emily suggested that Mr. Cole Brown, the camp superintendent, be sent to other camps to show how things ought to be done.

In many of the camps the inadequacies were beyond the powers of the superintendents to remedy. When Emily first visited Springfontein in February the camp held 500; by April the superintendent was trying to cope with 3,000. It became a frequent occurrence for a camp superintendent, warned by a telegram to expect several hundred people by a certain date in the near future, to find that no provision had been made to supply him with additional tents, food, and medical supplies.

Emily was horrified by the number of sick she found and by the mortality rates. In her letters home she described in vivid detail the sights she had seen:

Next, a girl of twenty-four lay dying on a stretcher. Her father, a big gentle Boer, kneeling beside her, while in the next tent his wife was watching a child of six also dying, and one of about five also drooping. Already this couple had lost three children in the hospital, and so would not let those go, though I begged hard to take them out of the hot tent. "We must watch these ourselves," they said.[21]

Although she compared the sickness and mortality rates with the "Black Death and the Great Plague," they were not nearly as bad as they were to become. She had returned to England before these rates reached their height. No one wanted thousands of children to die in the white tents of the concentration camps. But die they did—of measles, typhoid, dysentery, pneumonia, scarlet fever, influenza, bronchitis, whooping cough, diphtheria, and malaria.

At the time there was much finger pointing, and there has been much since, by those who would fasten on one side or the other the entire guilt for this slaughter of innocents. The burghers who refused to recognise the right of their fellow countrymen to be neutral, who left their families in the hands of the enemy, acquiesced in the formation of the camps, and then attacked convoys and trains and destroyed railway tracks, cutting off supplies, even occasionally cutting off the water; those Boer women who through ignorance or fear or superstition unwittingly allowed many to die; the British authorities who formed the camps, forced the people into them, and then failed to provide proper facilities and necessities—all must bear their share of the blame. That the British authorities must bear the ultimate responsibility seems irrefutable, but that among these guilty parties the blame is not evenly distributed gives none cause for self-righteousness.

A close examination of the causes of the high mortality rates among the children in the camps can only lead one to echo Schiller: "Against stupidity the very gods themselves struggle in vain."

"All superintendents agree that most of the mortality is amongst the new arrivals," said W. K. Tucker, general superintendent of all the Transvaal camps, in October 1901 when the death rate was the highest.[22] This was probably true and led many Englishmen to maintain that the women and children would have died anyway if they had not been brought in. Dr. Alexander Kay wrote in his diary: "It is my firm belief that if the camps had not been established, sickness and mortality would have been far greater on the farms and villages, and even in the towns."[23] Perhaps so, but the crowded and often unsanitary conditions of the camps, the failure of the authorities immediately to isolate new arrivals carrying infectious diseases, and the transportation of persons suffering from those diseases from one camp to another, spreading the infection, must also be taken into account.

The women who with their children had struggled to live alone on the veld or in women's laagers or had tried to follow commandos certainly endured great hardships and suffered much. So did their children. One woman had lost twelve of her eighteen children from malaria before being brought into a camp; another had lost nine out of ten from dysentery. An inquiry into the history of twenty families at the Irene camp revealed that the parents, who among them had had 168 children, had lost 71 before they arrived in camp. The British used such facts and figures to demonstrate that mortality was high outside the camps too. It was a poor argument. That women and children on the open veld after they had been dispossessed by Kitchener's farm-burning tactics suffered as badly as or worse than they did in the camps was hardly an adequate excuse.

The people brought into the camps were indeed often in dreadful condition. Dr. Pratt Yule, British medical officer in the Orange Free State, reported:

> Those who followed the commandos were in miserable condition. They were worn out, half clad, riddled with disease. At Kroonstad one batch brought in eight moribund and three dead. Many had lost from one to four children on commando. The Heidelberg refugees came into Kroonstad in terrible condition. They started the terrible measles in July, August, September.[24]

One detects in all such statements the desire to believe that the sufferings of the women and children were somehow their own fault. Although the authorities were soon aware of the condition of the people on the veld, the columns sent to bring them in were not equipped in any way to alleviate their misery, and when those rounded up arrived at the camps they were seldom given prompt and proper care. There appears to have been, at least in the beginning, no processing and no medical inspections; those newly arrived were often put into areas already crowded, and naturally diseases rapidly spread. Medical facilities in the early months were often inadequate, and there were not enough doctors and nurses. Even where facilities and medical personnel were on hand the system, at least initially, was to make the medical aid available; the sick were not forced to go into hospital.

John Maxwell (who was to receive a CMG for services rendered as military governor of Pretoria "and in connection with the Concentration Camps") wrote to his wife:

You can tell anyone who asks that they [the camps] are going well, the inmates are well cared for, and though the death rate amongst the children is excessive, it is in most cases the fault of the mothers themselves. There has been a severe epidemic of measles and as you know this only requires care. They won't have anything to do with doctors or nurses and prefer their own squalid methods and truly wonderful nostrums.[25]

Many were indeed suspicious, fearful even, of the camp doctors and nurses. They were in most cases foreigners, the mortality rate among their patients did not inspire trust, and yielding up children to them was to put them into alien hands and to subject them to unfamiliar medical practices; small wonder then that so many preferred their own home remedies, some of which were undeniably horrifying:

Tar on the feet was a common remedy for reducing fever.
Dog's blood was in demand as a medicine.
Cow dung was smeared on the chest for bronchitis and applied to limbs affected by rheumatism.
Horse dung, boiled and strained, was given to those convalescing from enteric.
A black chicken was cut open and applied bleeding to the chest for inflammation of the lungs.

Dr. Kendal Franks, writing from Bloemfontein in January 1902, said:

Mr. Randle [the camp superintendent] one day visited Abram Strauss, a man who had been selected as one of the head men of the camp and in virtue of his office was housed in a marquee. Mr. Randle was surprised to see a cat running about the tent with all its fur clipped off. He inquired the cause and was told that the fur had been cut off and roasted and then applied to his child's chest as a remedy for bronchitis.[26]

Medical science in this era knew no cure for most of the diseases rampant in the camps; early and careful nursing offered the best chance of recovery. Doctors confronted with the sick brought to them only as a last resort had little chance of saving them. One exasperated doctor at Standerton shouted at a distraught mother: "Why have you brought me a dying child?" Most doctors did the best they could; often their advice was ignored. At Krugersdorp Dr. Franks reported that milk had been prescribed for a four-month-old infant with bronchitis, but the mother fed it sardines and it died within two days.

In general the doctors were supported by the administrators of the camps. In August 1901 W. K. Tucker issued the following instructions to the superintendents of the Transvaal camps:

There must be no stint in the distribution of medical comforts to the sick and convalescent, old and infirm people and young children. When necessary, stimulants may be freely given under doctors' orders. There must be an adequate supply of milk, which should be liberally supplied to children and deserving people, as well as the sick and convalescent.[27]

Similar orders appear to have been issued in the Orange Free State, for in October 1901 the following stimulants were issued at the Bloemfontein camp:

Champagne	32 bottles
Brandy	171½ bottles
Port wine	73½ bottles
Claret	29 bottles
Stout	19 bottles
Whiskey	19 bottles

And 5,004 tins of milk.

Milner—who, it must be said, was not responsible for the formation of the camps and, in fact, disapproved of the whole scheme—did everything in his power to improve conditions as soon as they came under his control. On 20 November 1901 he wrote to the military governor at Pretoria and to the deputy administrator at Bloemfontein:

It is clearly the desire of His Majesty's Government that expense should not be allowed to stand in the way when it is a question of providing anything necessary to improve the health of the camps. . . . And it would be better to err, in the present emergency, on the side of liberality than to leave anything unprovided which would promote the health of the inmates of the camps for fear of adding a few thousands to an expenditure which must in any case be heavy.[28]

Milner's generosity with government funds was, of course, wise from every point of view, even if it did come a bit late, for considerable publicity had by this time been given to conditions in the camps, and in spite of all the champagne, brandy, whiskey, and tinned milk, the children continued to die. Typhoid killed one in five inmates who came down with it; pneumonia one in three. Between 1 September 1901 and the end of the year, one person out of every ten died. We do not know the exact number of children in the camps, only that most of the deaths were of boys and girls under the age of sixteen. Perhaps as many as one in six children died in just this four-month period. The following are the statistics for one year. The sources cited are British government Blue Books:

		Camp Population	Deaths	Blue Book
1901	June	85,410	777	Cd 608
	July	93,940	1,412	Cd 694
	Aug.	105,347	1,878	Cd 789
	Sept.	109,418	2,411	Cd 793
	Oct.	113,506	3,156	Cd 853
	Nov.	117,974	2,807	Cd 934
	Dec.	117,017	2,380	Cd 902
1902	Jan.	114,376	1,805	Cd 934
	Feb.	114,311	628	Cd 939
	March	111,508	402	Cd 939
	April	112,733	298	Cd 942
	May	116,572	196	Cd 1161

Much of the death-dealing sickness was the result of unsanitary camps and unhygienic habits. The authorities, reluctant in the face of the mounting death toll to admit even to themselves that the ultimate responsibility for conditions was theirs, preferred to blame the unhygienic habits of the women, although they did little to enforce or even to lay down regulations which would have modified such habits. The chief fault of the British was not that they ruled and regulated the lives of the inhabitants of the camps, but that they did not exert enough authority; given the premise that the people were forced to live in the camps, they were given too much freedom. Unless rules regarding washing, airing, eating, sleeping, and toilet arrangements are rigidly enforced, any camp, regardless of its inhabitants, will quickly become fouled. Trekboer women, for example, accustomed all their lives to defecating on the open veld and moving on, ought to have been instructed in the use of latrines and made to use them. Instead, they simply used the space around their tents. The toilet facilities provided by the British were not always such as to encourage their use. At the Standerton camp, and probably at other camps as well in the beginning, the latrine was simply a long narrow trench with a pole across it lengthwise on which people were expected to perch. The area was surrounded by a fence of sacking and there was but one entrance. Privacy there was none.

Boiled water ought to have been provided and the necessity for using it ought to have been explained instead of expecting the women to boil their own. Even soldiers could not be made to boil their water when fuel was scarce, as it usually was. Although water for washing was generally available, soap was often in short supply. The authorities appear to have had little understanding of their responsibilities for hygiene and contented themselves with being disgusted by the filth they observed. Dr. G. B. Woodroffe, camp medical officer at the Irene camp, reported:

> The habits of the people in general are such as would be a disgrace to any European nation. . . . Napkins for babies are seldom used. They are allowed to mess their beds, which lie for days without being washed or aired, and the tents absolutely stink of decomposing urine, etc.
>
> A mother had two children with diarrhoea. They all slept in one bed, and she never attended to them from the time they went to bed until breakfast time the next morning.[29]

In her travels about South Africa Emily Hobhouse won friends and made enemies. Her friends were the Boer women in the concentration camps; her enemies were more influential. Among the latter was Miss Dora Fairbridge, one of the founders of the Guild of Loyal Women of South Africa, an organisation which proclaimed itself to be nonpolitical —except, of course, for its "determination to uphold the Imperial Supremacy in South Africa." Miss Fairbridge wrote to Sir Walter Hely-Hutchinson, now governor of Cape Colony, that Emily had "sown discontent and dissatisfaction among the women she is supposed to benefit.

They were all satisfied and grateful to the English Government until she came amongst them to invent grievances where none existed." Hely-Hutchinson passed on to Chamberlain the Guild's opinion that "Miss Hobhouse exercises a bad influence on the Boer women in the Refugee Camps." Milner received more than sixty complaints about her. News of her activities began to precede her, and Major Hamilton Goold-Adams refused to permit her to visit the camp at Kroonstad because, as he told her, he had heard that she showed "personal sympathy" for the Boers. Emily did not deny it. "I replied with astonishment that that was just what I had come to do—to give personal sympathy and help in personal troubles." Goold-Adams remained adamant. He had also heard that one of her letters from South Africa had been read at a pro-Boer political meeting in London. Though she denied this, it was true.

Miss Hobhouse's letters home and her speeches after her return to England created a furore. Questions were asked in the House of Commons, but the members were told that Kitchener believed the people in the camps had "a sufficient allowance and were all comfortable and happy." When her report on conditions in the camps was published, many were appalled, but soon there came a flood of counter statements and arguments from British South Africans. R. B. Douglas, a Presbyterian minister in Johannesburg, wrote: "I have walked through every department of the camp at Johannesburg and have seen nothing to suggest hardship and privation. . . . Everywhere there is evidence of cheerfulness and contentment."[30]

Mrs. K. H. R. Stuart, delegate for the Guild of Loyal Women of South Africa, who was in Britain to raise funds for the erection of gravestones for soldiers killed in the war, wrote this of Miss Hobhouse's report:

> [It] is apt to give wrong impressions to those who are unacquainted with the habits of life and conditions of things in South Africa, where intense heat, crowded tents, flies, scarcity of milk, snakes, etc. are every-day occurences. We South Africans wonder to hear so much made of things which we have always had to put up with. . . . On the whole, Miss Hobhouse's report is unintentionally a marvellous testimony to the exceeding care our military have expended upon the women and children of the very men who are shooting our brave soldiers down.[31]

Dr. Kay wrote of "some agitation about concentration camps raised by a few unsexed hysterical women who are prepared to sacrifice everything for notoriety." He admitted there was sickness in the camps but said that improvements were taking place and that these "would have taken place whether or not there was this agitation by sexless busybodies with nothing better to do than decry everything and everybody."

Kitchener continued to send back reassuring messages. On 3 August 1901 he telegraphed:

> Goold-Adams has made a tour of inspection refugee camps Orange River Colony and reports people well looked after and completely satisfied with all we are doing for them. . . . Male refugees at Kroonstad presenting most loyal address and peace movement is spreading fast in all camps.[32]

There was a good bit of understandable confusion in the minds of many honest people as to exactly what conditions really were in the camps. In spite of Kitchener's assurances, a great many were left uneasy. Something had to be done, the politicians realised. What they did was most uncharacteristic and unusual for a British government, or any other government, at this period in history: six women were appointed to a Ladies Committee to go to South Africa, to investigate and to report.

41

THE CONCENTRATION CAMPS:
THE LADIES COMMITTEE

The government obviously wanted the concentration camp issue white-washed, but, unintentionally perhaps, it selected conscientious, intelligent, honest, and energetic women for the Ladies Committee. It was headed by Mrs. Millicent Garett Fawcett, widow of Professor Henry Fawcett, the extraordinary man who though blind became postmaster general of England. Mrs. Fawcett was a remarkable woman: she was a feminist, an able public speaker, and the author of a book on political economy, but perhaps her chief recommendation to those who appointed her was an article she had recently published in the *Westminster Gazette* criticising Miss Hobhouse.

Dr. Jane Waterson, a beautiful and intelligent sixty-one-year-old spinster, daughter of Lieutenant General Lord Abinger, was also on the committee. She had earned medical degrees in both London and Brussels, and she had been the first woman doctor in South Africa. She too had expressed in print her displeasure with the "hysterical whining going on in England" while "we feed and pamper people who had not even the grace to say thank you for the care bestowed on them." Other members of the committee were Miss Katherine Bereton, a former nursing sister at Guy's Hospital in London, who had served in an army hospital in South Africa; Dr. the Honourable Ella Campbell Scarlett; Lady Anne Knox, wife of General Sir William Knox, who had done some nursing of soldiers at Ladysmith; and Miss Lucy Deane, government inspector of factories in Britain, who had some experience in infant welfare work.

Emily Hobhouse had asked to be included but was blandly told that the government wanted an impartial committee and she was obviously biased. Undismayed, she decided to go to South Africa again anyway. On the afternoon of 27 October 1901 the *Avondale Castle*, carrying Emily and a companion, dropped anchor in Table Bay off Cape Town. Before they could disembark an officer came aboard and, taking Emily aside, informed her that she was not to be allowed to land and must remain on board, communicating with no one ashore, and that within three days she would be transferred to another vessel and shipped back to Britain. She tried to argue: the officer had no warrant for her detention, and she had committed no crime; not being able to send a message to anyone ashore deprived her of any appeal. The most the officer would agree to do for her was to take a letter to his superior.

Emily wrote hastily, first to the commandant in Cape Town, pointing out that "the summary arrest of an Englishwoman bound on works of charity, without warrant of any kind or stated offense, is a proceeding which requires explanation." With this she enclosed letters to be forwarded to Milner, to Kitchener, and to Hely-Hutchinson. It was, however, as she doubtless suspected, Kitchener himself who had taken this high-handed action. Nevertheless, she was determined to fight her deportation and to make matters as unpleasant and as awkward as possible for the authorities. She demanded a guard so as to make it clear that she was being held prisoner; she refused to give her parole; she demanded that she be told in writing the conditions of her imprisonment; she claimed to be ill and in need of rest on shore; she asked to be transferred to a prison on land; she refused to pack her bags or to leave the *Avondale Castle* for another ship. In the end soldiers had to be brought on board; she was wrapped in a shawl and bodily carried off to a troopship bound for England.

In July the women from England appointed to the Ladies Committee went to Cape Town and were joined by the other committeewomen already in South Africa. Kitchener did not like the idea of their coming, but as he told Lord Roberts, "I hope it will calm the agitators in England. I doubt there being much for them to do as the camps are very well run." Kitchener was wrong. The members of the Ladies Committee found a great deal to do. For more than three months they travelled about, visiting twenty-one camps. They examined water supplies, refuse disposal, trenching, hospitals, latrines, fuel, abatoirs, schools, clothing, camp regulations, food—everything pertaining to the camps. They maintained a proper scepticism and paid surprise visits: "In no case . . . did we announce beforehand our proposed visit to the superintendent."

They were not always welcomed; both inmates and administrators often resented their presence. At the Bloemfontein camp they were treated to a noisy demonstration:

> Women threw large portions, which had been newly served out, of good though thin meat, into the wide roadway of the camp. It would have made very good broth or stew. We supposed that this wicked waste was a sort of bravado for the purpose of showing us how discontented they were; but we took it as proof that, at any rate, the people in the camp were not short of food.[1]

When they had finished their work the women of the Ladies Committee wrote a report in clear, objective prose that indicated how thoroughly they had grasped the problems. They did not consider the morality of, or the advisability of, establishing or maintaining the camps—this was outside the scope of their mission; they devoted themselves to the problems which their existence presented. As to the causes of the high mortality rate, they properly discussed these under three headings: those under the control of the inmates, those under the control of the administrators, and those caused by the nature of the war itself.

Although generally praising the work of the medical staffs, the women did not hesitate to point out exceptions and to detail slack and negligent practises that had caused deaths: scarlet fever and diphtheria cases in the same hospital tent with other patients, for example, and children with measles sent to camps which had previously been free of the disease. Most administrators too were praised for doing their best under difficult conditions, but not all, and they recommended the removal of several superintendents. Men possessing all the qualifications needed were, as the committee recognised, difficult to find:

The Superintendent required rare mental and moral gifts. He had to control thousands of people unaccustomed to discipline. He had to be just, strict, kind, inexhaustibly patient. He required a knowledge of sanitation, enough of the engineer to use the water supply to best advantage, he had to be interested in education, able to enlist the cooperation of doctors, nurses, everybody. He required business training and some of the aptitudes of a grocer and corn factor. If he could add to these a practical knowledge of gardening and half-a-dozen industries, such as brickmaking, tanning, carpentering, he would be ideal.[2]

The committee did not hesitate to give its recommendations for improvements in camp administration. It was all very well for the army to put sixteen men in a bell tent, for soldiers were always moving on, but in a semipermanent camp more than five in a tent was overcrowding. They criticised the location of some camp sites, the bad water, the laziness and inefficiencies of some of the administrators, the lack of supplies, et al.

At the Howich camp they found that although there were twenty-six cases of scarlet fever, no attempt had been made to isolate them. At Potchefstroom the committee found much to criticise during their four-day stay. For the 4,900 inmates of the camp there were only 65 latrine pails for women and 23 for men, and the "accommodation is inconveniently high for little children"; also, "screens in front of the latrines do not sufficiently protect all the occupants."[3] The mortuary was used as "a receptacle for soiled linen, which lay upon the floor." Half of the inmates had no bedsteads of any kind. The sheets of typhoid patients were "neither boiled nor disinfected"; they were not even washed in hot water. Worst of all: "The drinking water for patients is neither boiled nor filtered." Nearly a third of all the patients who entered the hospital died there.

At Merebank camp they found that the camp contained 5,154 people (534 men, 2,145 women, and 2,475 children) but only one bath house with ten baths for women, two for men, and two for boys. The camp was badly situated: "It is a swamp, and unless it can be drained, it will continue to be hopelessly water-logged. We earnestly deprecate the continual sending of large drafts of people to Merebank in its present condition."[4] There was much overcrowding: "Such crowding would only occur in the poorest slums in England," the ladies reported. In the three months preceding the committee's visit, 112 persons had died, all but seven under twenty years of age. The camp had a bad rationing system, there was a lack of beds or kartels, and there were not enough doctors, nurses, or administrative personnel. "The Merebank camp is in a peculiar position," said the ladies in their report, "from the fact that, morally, undesirable people have been sent there from a number of Transvaal camps."[5] They were much occupied with morals.

When military camps were located next to concentration camps they were made mutually out of bounds, but iron bars and bolts will scarcely maintain a separation of the sexes when they are in proximity. The ladies learned that at Harrismith three women had "absented themselves all night, it is feared for immoral purposes." At Vereeniging the superintendent told them that three times he had found soldiers in his camp and that a few women "who were more than suspects" would be sent to Natal, where "the authorities would be warned of their characters." At Heidelberg the superintendent said he had had some difficulties with soldiers "knocking about" but that he had put a stop to it.

Recalcitrant women were disciplined by having their rations docked, by being put in wired-in enclosures, or by being sent away. All camps had special enclosures for unruly and obstreperous people—"If women cannot govern their tongues they are put there." Those regarded as "incorrigibly filthy" were also put in these enclosures sometimes, or in special "dirty lines" that were known as "Hogs' Paradise." David Murray, superintendent of the camp at Belfast, was in the habit of placarding the camp with the names of women he considered "incorrigibly dirty," and this, he said, "has had a very good effect." Withholding of passes or of sugar, coffee, or meat was a common punishment—"You can reach these people through their stomachs," said R. L. Cowat, superintendent of the Mafeking camp.

High on the list of procedures to be investigated the Ladies Committee had placed provision for the care of orphans, and in every camp they visited they inquired about this. Camp after camp reported that there were no provisions and none were needed; here at least no problem existed. "Orphan children were almost invariably taken by their relatives. . . . Boers are very good about this." In only one camp, Middelburg, was there a need for an orphanage, and even here only 22 out of 186 orphans in the camp had no one to care for them.

The Ladies Committee made a number of sound recommendations.

They praised the efforts to start schools in some camps, but noted that more and better teachers were required. They advised that "more hospital accommodation, improved equipment and increased staff are needed." They recommended an increase in the weekly meat allowance to five pounds for each adult and three pounds for each child. They also recommended the fencing of all camps and more controls: "restrictions of free ingress and egress are desired from the point of view of health and morals."

The Ladies Committee did not confine itself to generalisations but made specific recommendations for each camp they visited. When the Standerton camp was visited on 23 November it contained 620 men, 1162 women, and 1,251 children. There were no bathrooms and no receptacles for rubbish. "The camp is soaked with enteric and the water is bad." The boilers for boiling water were inadequate. About the only good thing they had to say about this camp was that coffins and shrouds were provided free. They recommended that the hospital be doubled in size and that the superintendent, a Mr. Wingfield, be sacked, as "he has no grasp of the importance of sanitation."

At the Aliwal North camp, which also contained a number of "loyal" burgher families, conditions were so bad that the ladies' recommendation was simply: "Remove the Superintendent, and thoroughly reorganize the camp." There was only one latrine to every 177 women and children and "the smell was abominable." There was a shortage of most necessities: tents, blankets, mattresses, slop buckets, medicines. "It was the worst [ration] system, or rather want of system, we have seen in any camp." Worst of all was the hospital accommodation: in August 1901 there were 710 cases of measles and nearly a quarter of those afflicted died.

The ladies' criticisms were not confined to the camp administrators; the inmates themselves came in for their share. The committee concluded that "a large number of deaths in the concentration camps have been directly and obviously caused by the noxious compounds given by Boer women to their children."

As the notion prevailed that it was wrong for people to be given anything for nothing, the Ladies Committee noted with approval that in most camps an account was kept against every family for all rations, clothing, and supplies issued "with a view to recovering the value when the war is over," and they were quite incensed that men in the camps did not always perform satisfactorily the work they were paid to do: "It is in itself a demoralising influence to receive all the necessaries and some of the luxuries of life from the Government as a free gift, and this demoralising influence will be intensified if men are allowed to receive wages and neglect the work they are supposed to do in exchange for them."[6]

Though the ladies' views were not those embraced today by welfare states, they were acceptable at the time, and on the whole their report was a fair one, accurate and honest. Certainly it was not the whitewash many had assumed it would be, and it brought about many improvements, but it did not still the outraged voices of the antiwar faction in Britain or the European and American critics of the war. In the House of Commons Campbell-Bannerman described the camps as "an offense against civilization, as a military mistake, and as a political disaster." Lloyd George used even more violent language, comparing the British government to Herod, for the British, he said, were trying "to crush a little race by killing its young sons and daughters." He looked to the future, and in passionate language he spoke of the bitterness and hatred which the death of so many children would create: "At this rate within a few years there will not be a child alive on the veld. . . . A barrier of dead children's bodies will rise up between the British and the Boer races in South Africa!"[7]

The French, Austrian, Dutch, and Scandinavian press accused Britain of waging a war of extermination. In the Transvaal itself the representatives of a number of countries, even Turkey (recently involved in massacring Armenians), protested the continuance of the camps. In the United States there was such a groundswell of indignation that the camps became an embarrassment to the American government, officially friendly to Britain, but John Hay in a letter to H. C. Lodge wrote: "The Boer women and children are in the Concentration Camps simply because their husbands and brothers want them there, and as to the war with all its hideous incidents and barbarities, it will stop the instant Botha and De Wet wish it to stop."[8]

It was true that the burghers preferred to have the British take care of their families rather than be burdened with them and with the now impossible task of providing for them as long as the fighting continued. Most of the camps were practically undefended, and it would have been a simple matter for the fighting burghers to rescue their women and children had they chosen to do so. There were, in fact, several attacks made on camps, but in no instance were any of the women and children taken away.

Young Commandant Willem Fouché, operating in Cape Colony, heard that the administrators of the camp at Aliwal North were traitors from the Orange Free State. On 17 July 1901 he led an attack on the camp, killed two Bantu, and carried off four of the alleged traitors; he also tried while there to drum up some recruits, but out of 689 men in the camp only 5 elected to join him. On 15 September 1901 the Belfast camp was raided, apparently only to get supplies, but the attack was repulsed; one woman and two children were wounded. In December about 800 Boers captured the Pietersburg camp, and J. E. Tucker, the superintendent, and his staff were made prisoners. After a gay, all-night party with wives, sweethearts, friends, and relations the burghers released their prisoners unharmed and rode off into the sunrise.

There was one—perhaps only one—beneficial result of the concentration camp system, a result which was to have an enormous effect on the future of South Africa. In January 1901 Milner appointed E. B. Sargant as educational adviser. Taking several boxes of books, he went to the Norval's Pont camp, collected such teachers as he could, acted as headmaster himself, and began lessons in English for all children whose parents would consent to it. The experiment was a success, and other schools were soon begun.

By May 1901 there were 1,800 children attending such schools in the Transvaal and 2,000 in the Orange Free State; by the end of the year there were 32,500—far more Boer children than had ever before been in school. Sargant was appointed commissioner of education for both new colonies, and he sent out an appeal for good teachers. From more than 2,000 applicants, 200 of the best qualified were selected from Britain and another hundred from Canada, New Zealand, and Australia.

It was dark when Margaret Hulburd with several other young English and Scottish women, all tired and hungry, descended from the train at the Irene camp. They were a contingent of Sargant's "lady teachers" sent out (accompanied by a chaperone) to teach school in the concentration camps. It had been a long, hot, dusty journey from Cape Town, and Miss Hulburd had not been impressed by what she had seen from her carriage window as the train crawled up country in the heat of a South African summer: the veld was brown, dry, and monotonous, there were the innumerable blockhouses beside the tracks, and everywhere the carcasses of animals in varying stages of decay.

The tents to which the young women were assigned seemed "terribly unsafe places to sleep in. Only a canvas flap and a thin cord between us and a possibly attacking enemy!" Nevertheless Miss Hulburd brushed a frog from her pillow and slept soundly. Once adjusted to her new life she found the camp and its surroundings beautiful. Nearby was a stream bordered by mimosa in full bloom, giant willows with drooping branches, and eucalyptus trees; she was pleased that destiny had placed her "in such a pleasant spot." The Irene camp, located between Pretoria and Johannesburg, was the largest in the Transvaal with some 7,000 inmates. By the time Miss Hulburd and the other teachers arrived the greatest evils had been corrected; it was no longer the place that Emily Hobhouse and the Ladies Committee had seen. It was by this time laid out in neat blocks of about twenty-five bell tents each; wide roads marked with whitewashed stones divided each block. At least two brick ovens for baking bread were provided for every line of tents. Margaret found that "the rules for cleanliness are most stringent" and the whole arrangement "so cleverly organized. The system is perfect in every way." A large church had been built, and here, as by this time in every other camp, there was a Dutch Reformed Church predikant.

Some camps had brick or stone schoolhouses by the end of the war, but at Irene the classrooms were large store tents arranged to form three sides of a square, the centre being used as a playground. Here at eight thirty daily came 4,200 boys and girls from five to twenty years of age who formed up in lines according to their class, the boys in their patched but clean clothes, the girls in their frocks and stiffly starched sunbonnets. When a bell rang they stood, arms folded and eyes closed, for a short church service. This was followed by a song in English—"We Are But Little Children Weak" or "All Things Bright and Beautiful"—and a few prayers in Dutch; then, led by their teachers, they marched off to their classes.

In addition to academic work there were courses in needlework and knitting for the girls and manual training for the boys. Margaret Hulburd found the children "decidedly docile and amenable to discipline." When a concert, to be concluded by the schoolchildren singing "God Save the King," was planned for the camp, the headmaster carefully explained that in England it was customary for all entertainments to close with the national anthem, but he went even further and asked that all the children obtain their parents' permission: 94 percent gave their consent. This was not the case at all camps. Earlier, at Bloemfontein, a Boer teacher refused to conduct a singing competition held on the King's birthday.

At Irene there were also classes in English for adults, and Margaret Hulburd wrote home: "It is odd to see quite old men with grey beards and stout, elderly matrons sitting patiently and seriously spelling out the easiest words and learning the alphabet like little children."[9]

For the children who survived the diseases that swept the camps this chance to acquire some education was an excellent thing. Young Boers on scattered farms rarely had an opportunity to study. There was, of course, opposition on the part of some of the inmates to classes in English; they accused the British of trying to anglicize them—which indeed they were—but most Boers, as is common among pioneering folk, had a great respect for education, and an education in English was better than no education at all. For the students, most of whom would spend the rest of their lives under the Union Jack, it was an invaluable acquirement. But learning English did not always succeed in changing the political views of the children. Isie Malan, in school at the Belfast camp, wrote as her first school paper: "I will try to learn English that I can say to the Kakky, hands up. I am twelve years old. This is my first English writing."[10]

It was not easy for Boers and Britons to overcome their feelings of distrust, suspicion, and dislike for each other while the war was still in progress, yet in at least one instance love bloomed: Wim Hopford, an inmate of the Volksrust camp, and one of the English teachers fell in love and were married, but life was not easy for the couple and Hopford wrote:

> Strange to say, this conquest in love cost me nearly all my friends. The refugees could not understand my falling in love with an English girl, and the girl's English friends could not appreciate her attachment to a fellow who might be nice enough in some ways, but who was, after all, a nondescript Boer refugee.[11]

Little information was collected about the camps for the Bantu and Coloureds or for those established for the British refugees who had fled from the Orange Free State and the Transvaal just before the war began. In the early days of the war there had been considerable sympathy for the plight of the British refugees and a Mansion House fund provided aid, but as the war went on, interest in their fate waned and outside funds, when exhausted, were not replenished. Many of those waiting out the war in Natal and Cape Colony became embittered by the preoccupation of the public and government with the conditions in the Boer concentration camps; it was easy for them to believe that they, loyal subjects, were not only neglected but deprived of essentials which were given instead to the families of their enemies.

To this day Doris Heberdon remembers a story often told by her mother—how she once, in search of much-needed cotton cloth, went to a store in Pietermaritzburg and was told that none was available. Standing before her she could see great stacks of cloth as well as tinned meats and jams and other goods in short supply. When she pointed these out she was told that all were destined for the concentration camps.[12]

Of the separate camps established for the Bantu and Coloureds little is known and reliable statistics are scarce. They were not visited by Emily Hobhouse or the Ladies Committee. The inmates were for the most part servants and farm labourers swept up as part of Kitchener's policy of "clearing the country." An estimated 80,000 persons were in these camps, and mortality rates were said to be high, but no one knows exactly how high. Some idea may be obtained from such statistics as exist: in July 1901 there were 23,000 inmates of camps in the Orange Free State, and in this month 256 died (169 of these were children); of the 39,000 Coloureds in Transvaal camps in December 1901, 956 died—one out of 40 in just one month. The Aborigines Protection Society of London suggested that in view of the high mortality rates in the camps a "committee of South African ladies" be appointed to investigate, but the government refused its sanction. A number of Bantu and Coloureds also lived in the concentration camps for the Boers; some were servants and others were employed by the administration for the more disagreeable camp chores, such as emptying latrine buckets.

At first the "native refugee camps" were organised in the same manner as those for the Boers, but as "it was thought undesirable that so large a native population should be fed in idleness"[13] the camps were broken up and the former inmates were distributed along the railway lines and given plots of ground on which to raise their own food or put to industrial work.

The concentration camps (which continued in existence for nearly a year after the end of the war), although never intended to inflict punishment or injury or to impose deliberate hardship, nevertheless found themselves the instruments of all three in great measure. Emily Hobhouse saw clearly when she wrote: "Whatever the authorities do—and they are, I believe, doing their best with very limited means—it all is only a miserable patch on a great ill."[14]

Milner wrote on 7 December 1901 a remarkably candid appraisal of the camp system:

It was not until six weeks or two months ago that it dawned on me personally (I cannot speak for others), that the enormous mortality was not incidental to the first formation of the camps and the sudden inrush of thousands of people already starving, but was going to continue. The fact that it continues is no doubt a condemnation of the camp system. The whole thing, I think now has been a mistake.[15]

Yes. It was a mistake. A terrible, a tragic mistake.

42

PRISONERS OF WAR

In striking contrast to the fate of the women and children in the concentration camps was that of the captured burghers sent to prisoner-of-war camps. At first they had been kept on board transports converted into prison ships and anchored in Simon's Bay, where their health suffered from the close confinement. But the British soon abandoned the prison ships, concluding that the practise was an "expensive, unsatisfactory and troublesome experiment."[1] Conditions were much improved when the prisoners were moved ashore to the sports grounds at Green Point (now a suburb of Cape Town) or to the camp established at Simonstown— although an outbreak of enteric fever there took a number of inmates' lives and also killed the charming and attractive Mary Kingsley, traveller and ethnologist, who had gone to South Africa to nurse Boer prisoners. In general, however, the captured burgher had a far better chance of surviving the war than did his mother, wife, and children, for the prisoner-of-war camps were in healthy locations and the treatment of the prisoners was wise and humane.

Of the 4,619 prisoners sent to Bermuda, only 35 died, all but one of natural causes. (Prisoner No. 16870, "a persistent escapist," was shot and killed while making his last attempt.) Seventeen-year-old B. J. du Toit said the "provision supplied was splendid." Commandant Pieter Ferreira, interviewed in New York after his release at the end of the war, told a reporter: "Really, I do not think we have much to complain about in regard to our treatment. It is certain the British cared for us much better than we could possibly have cared for them had we been in their place."[2]

The first overseas prisoner-of-war camp was established on the island of St. Helena when 514 Boers arrived on the *Milwaukee* on 16 April 1900. Eleven days before its arrival the governor, Robert A. Sterndale, issued a public notice:

His Excellency the Governor expresses the hope that the Inhabitants will treat the Prisoners with that courtesy and consideration which should be extended to all men who have fought bravely in what they considered the cause of their Country and will help in repressing any unseemly demonstration which individuals might exhibit.[3]

The first prisoners were sent to Deadwood Camp, about 6 miles by road from Jamestown toward the eastern end of the island. An exception was made for Cronjé and his wife (she was the only woman with the prisoners of war), who were allowed to live under guard at Kent Cottage, 3 or 4 miles southwest of Jamestown, and later at Longwood, which had been Napoleon's home. A second camp was established on the island when quarrels broke out among the prisoners between the irreconcilables and those who were willing to take the oath of allegiance and forget the war. This second camp for the "tame Boers" was known as Deadwood No. 2, or the "Peace Camp." Then there were further quarrels between Free Staters and Transvaalers and they had to be separated. So a third camp, Broadbottom, was established about 5 miles away.

St. Helena eventually held both the first and the last of the important Boer generals captured by the British, for besides Cronjé it also held General Ben Viljoen, who was ambushed and captured near the end of the war. On 25 February 1902 Viljoen arrived at St. Helena on board the *Britannic* and recorded his first sight of the island:

"The Rock" rose out of the ocean, bare and rugged, the imprisonment upon it offered a gloomy prospect. No animal was visible, and foliage was wanting. I never saw a less attractive place than Jamestown, the port at which we landed. . . . I must confess that the feeling grew upon us that we were to be treated as ordinary criminals, since only murderers and dangerous people are banished to such places to be forgotten by mankind.[4]

In this mood Viljoen was hardly off the ship when he began a quarrel with Colonel H. S. Price, the commanding officer at Deadwood, a man he called "arrogant, cruel and generally unbearable." Colonel Price's offence would seem to have been his refusal immediately to accept Viljoen's parole or to issue him a pass to leave the prison camp—at least this is the only grievance Viljoen recorded, and he refrained from mentioning that Price had a reason, and a good one, for refusing to allow prisoners to wander about soon after their arrival: all new men were wisely put in quarantine to prevent the spread of infectious diseases. Later the truculant Viljoen was allowed to live in a small house outside the camp, and for the remainder of his brief stay he found it difficult to find fault with his gaolers.

As the number of prisoners increased, other camps were opened in Ceylon, India, and Bermuda, in that order. The Bermuda camps were established on five small islands ranging in size from 7 to 15 acres. There were eventually six camps in Ceylon, the first and largest being at Diyatalawa, about 140 miles from Colombo, where a Wesleyan mission had for years operated a reformatory. F. G. M. Carver, a prisoner, de-

COLONEL PILCHER'S EXPEDITIONARY FORCE TO DOUGLAS DISTINGUISHED
ITSELF BY CAPTURING FORTY BOER PRISONERS.

scribed the camp in a letter to an uncle in California: "Our camp is
. . . at an altitude of between four and five thousand feet. It is situated
upon the lower hills, within a circle of high and beautiful mountains. The
climate is fresh and mild, not unlike that of Johannesburg during the
December rains. . . . We are well housed and amply fed."[5]

Ceylon's second camp was a convalescent centre opened at Mount
Lavinia, a pleasant place by the sea. Ragama was set up as a special camp
for troublemakers. "Parole camps" were later established at Urugasman-
handiya and Hambantota.

There were thirteen camps established in India (including what is
today Pakistan), and all appear to have been well situated in healthy
locations. A camp at Ahmednagar, a delightful hill station 2,000 feet
above sea level with a dry, healthy climate, recorded one five-month
period in which there was not a single death from disease among its 500
prisoners.

To be sent to a prison camp so far from their homeland was a fate
much dreaded by the captured. Families, formerly so closely knit, were
torn apart and flung over the world. Deneys Reitz had one brother,
Hjalmar, in a prison camp in India and another, Joubert, in Bermuda.
Even the distance between Simonstown and the Transvaal seemed far to
Frikkie Badenhorst when he was a prisoner. He wrote to his wife: "We
are separated from the outer world—it is more than a year since I last saw

a woman or heard the voice of a child. How often I long to talk to a child. We do not even see much of animals. We smoke—and are more or less getting used to it all."[6]

There were heart-rending scenes as prisoners, collected in temporary camps, were moved by trains to Cape Town or Durban, the embarkation points. Mrs. Mostyn Cleaver described the scene at noon on a cold, gusty day in Bloemfontein when prisoners were marched to the railway station and she went to have a last look at her son:

Out of the cottages as we passed, sprang forlorn women and children, weeping and shouting farewells. . . . Just outside the grounds of the railway a weird throng of dishevelled women stood. All of the poorest class, some without any head covering and with dishevelled looks, they stood lamenting and crying out frantic farewells.[7]

Harry Fraser obtained permission to visit his brother Gordon (captured in the raid on Reitz, where Steyn had had such a narrow escape) when he was temporarily imprisoned in Pretoria. In a letter to his sister, President Steyn's wife, he wrote:

His appearance was undoubtedly ragged, but I am glad to say he looked very well and healthy. I gave him a good outfit. Three suits of clothes, pair of boots, couple of hats and a fair supply of underclothing, so that he is fitted out at any rate for some little time. . . . They have been treated very well and had every consideration shown them. Gordon says he will long remember the kindness of the Seventh Dragoon Guards who captured them.[8]

Prisoners had few complaints about their treatment while in British hands. Cronjé was always shown great respect while a prisoner. Instructions were issued that he was to be styled "general" and to receive the same courtesies as "a British general not in employ." En route to St. Helena on HMS *Doris* Admiral Robert Harris gave up his cabin to Cronjé and his wife. Field Cornet F. G. M. Cleaver wrote to his mother from the *Mohawk,* which was carrying him to Ceylon: "We are travelling in great comfort. The burghers are forward with the soldiers, and the Krijgsofficieren enjoy the accommodations and privileges of first class passengers, along with the British officers."[9] It was the same when they reached Ceylon, and Cleaver wrote from Diyatalawa camp: "We travelled in nice, roomy carriages to this place."

Still, it was a sad thing to be sent from one's homeland, and on board the *Montrose* bound for Bermuda G. J. van Riet wrote in his diary on leaving Cape Town: "In evening on losing sight of Table Mountain the National Anthems were sung by all the burghers. It was really quite impressive." Christmas was a sad day, and he wrote:

The sea rough and unpleasant . . . not even a photo or letter to remind me of my dear ones. I have just finished my daily search and found 2 lice. The misery of this day I shall never forget. I cannot get a quiet corner to hunt up some consoling words, of which I feel oh, so much in need. . . . To our surprise we actually got a piece of pudding each for our Xmas dinner.[10]

Gerhardus Botha, sixteen years old, was sent to Green Point after his capture at Reitz. There he and others attempted to escape by digging a tunnel but were caught in the act and hurriedly put aboard the *Catalonia* bound for Ceylon. At Diyatalawa Botha fell seriously ill. Tended by a Sinhalese doctor, to whom he felt he owed his life, he recovered and was sent into the hills to recuperate. "I enjoyed my stay immensely," he said. "On my return the officer in charge, Col. Vincent [Lieutenant Colonel A. C. F. Vincent] of Diyatalawa camp insisted on me continuing with my studies. This was an excellent thing for me."[11]

Included among the prisoners of war were several old men (one prisoner in Bermuda was seventy-nine years old) and a considerable number of young boys, some mere children. No one knows how many there were, but in one camp in Bermuda, on Darrell's Island, there were 113 prisoners under sixteen years of age. Two prisoners, Pieter Cronjé and Johannes van der Veldt, were not yet eight years old when they were captured, and Jan Viljoen was only ten. These youngsters were treated no differently from the men until they reached the camps, where, in at least several places, they were separated and put in schools.

In Bermuda the boys were collected and sent to a special camp on Hinson's Island, where they were put in what they called the "Khaki School." Some boys rebelled. One, A. J. Vercuel, recalled sixty years later: "About twenty of us refused to go. After three days, food and water were cut off, well then we had to go. . . . We found all the other children at Hinson's and were informed that we were there for schooling and trades."[12] Some of the boys continued to rebel: soldiers one night had to rescue an unfortunate schoolmaster who was dumped in the sea, bed and all.

Older boys were given the opportunity to work and earn a little money. B. J. du Toit was seventeen when on 1 August 1901 he arrived in Bermuda and was put in school: "On and off," he said, "we were allowed to cut coral bricks at one shilling per day allowing me to buy an english [sic] dictionary for one shilling and six pence."

Cricket matches were arranged between the boys on Hinson's Island and the boys of Saltus Grammar School in Hamilton. A number of British residents in Bermuda interested themselves in the young prisoners. Vercuel remembered some of them bringing over a vat of ice cream. "It was amusing to see some of the boys from the back veld eating it, never having seen it before," he said. Lord Geary, governor of Bermuda, and his wife had lost a son in the war, but they made friends with young Vercuel and corresponded with him for twelve years after the war.

General Anson Mills, the retired American soldier who made his fortune manufacturing cartridge belts, wrote to the American consul in Bermuda in March 1902 and asked him to try to arrange for Jan Viljoen and Pieter Cronjé, then ages eleven and nine respectively, to be sent to him in the United States. General Mills offered to pay their passage and to educate them at his own expense until such time as they could return home.

Some of the adult prisoners organised classes among themselves. In Bermuda Jacob de Villiers, onetime state attorney of the Orange Free State, gave lectures in law. Gordon Fraser studied French and learned shorthand. And, of course, there were religious study groups. Gerhardus Botha, many years later, told of his religious instruction in Ceylon: "During the time I was in camp I was confirmed by the Rev. Papenfus. I found my little Bible, which my mother had given to me when I left for the war, most useful. I still have my confirmation certificate and at the bottom of it is printed 'Diyatalawa, Ceylon. 11 September 1901.' "[13]

In some camps religious services were held twice daily. "I tell you they can pray," said one of the British soldiers on guard duty in Bermuda. "They pray . . . until we outside get tired of it and call out 'Oh, gag yourselves!' "[14]

Commercial enterprise was not discouraged; there were camp canteens run by prisoners; St. Helena boasted a coffee house; M. J. Slabbert opened the President Café; Carl le Roux operated a brewery; and Henry Cox set himself up as an auctioneer and pawnbroker. In Bermuda R. J. Schutte became a photographer when he was sent an early Ilford camera as a present; on Darrell's Island a tailor made trousers for one shilling and shirts for one shilling, sixpence. The British made some work available and paid two shillings a day for skilled labour and one shilling a day for unskilled work, but most of the burghers refused to work for the British.

The major prison camp industry on Bermuda was carving. The making of curios became an organised affair when the prisoners on Burt's Island formed an Industrial Association, and soon every curio shop and tourist spot on the islands sold their souvenirs.

There were recreations too. On St. Helena there was a drama society, and a Hollander named Houtzaager wrote plays that were produced in the camp, J. H. L. Schumann wrote songs and had them published in England, and St. Helena camps could boast of a string quartet, a piano trio, a brass band, a male choir, and a minstrel group as well as a debating society, a German club, an anti-smoking society, and many sports teams. Sometimes there were parties (each man brought his own liquor) where the invariable toasts were to Kruger, Steyn, and "our fighting burghers in the field." Pranksters abounded. The prisoners on Darrell's Island in Bermuda made up a life-sized dummy, labelled it "Joe Chamberlain," and floated it out to sea one night. Searchlights picked it up and a guard ship full of soldiers captured it.

Some camps produced newspapers. On St. Helena there was *De Krijgsgevangene* (The War Prisoner) and in Ceylon the *Diyatalawa Dum-Dum,* printed "by means of a gelatine copying apparatus." The prisoners on Burt's Island in Bermuda published *Die Burt's Trompet.*

European and American sympathisers sometimes sent gifts. Americans took a special interest in the prisoners on nearby Bermuda, particularly after Joubert Reitz smuggled out a letter that was published in the Boston *Globe* asking for food and clothing. A number of pro-Boer organisations in the United States, notably the Lend a Hand Society of Boston, the Boer Relief Fund of New York, and the American Transvaal League of Paterson, New Jersey, sent packages. So many rumours and horror stories about the treatment of prisoners and the conditions of the camps circulated in the United States that several Americans went to Bermuda to see for themselves. The Reverend W. S. Key of the Lend a Hand Society was appalled by the food (the standard field ration of the British army), but Frank Vizetelly, author and traveller, wrote: "So far as general care is concerned . . . there must be many people in our own cities who would gladly exchange their present surroundings . . . to share the life of the burghers."[15] Dr. J. B. Mattison of Brooklyn, probably a reliable source, wrote a letter (dated 17 February 1902) which was published in the New York *Tribune:* "I talked with many, noted their food, their clothing, their sanitary and hospital conditions, and must say that stories started by sensation mongers about poor food, bad clothes, much sickness and great mortality among the Boers in Bermuda are not true."

In Bermuda an energetic Englishwoman, Miss Katherine Elwes, formed an Association for Boer Recreation that provided books, magazines, fishing tackle, and playing cards. Another local group, headed by Miss Anna Maria Outerbridge, was called the Boer Relief Committee and was said to have German connections. Its members harboured pro-Boer sentiments and even aided prisoners who tried to escape.

Politics, their own local politics, absorbed the men in the camps as it had at home. They held elections for landdrosts, judges, public prosecutors, and other officials, establishing little republics in each camp. The most contentious issue, of course, was whether they should accept the inevitable and take the British oath of allegiance. The irreconcilables exhibited a rancour towards those who took the oath such as they never showed the British.

So serious was the division that in Bermuda as elsewhere those who took the oath had to be separated from the rest. On the other hand, prison forged closer bonds between the Boers and the foreign volunteers. On St. Helena, when the British tried to separate the foreigners from the others, the prisoners protested and the camp newspaper declared: "Fellow warriors who have fought with us and shared our trenches in the veld are just as much Boers as we are."

Only Cape rebels were handled differently from all others. Tried by military courts and sentenced to from three years' hard labour to life imprisonment, they were kept apart, wore the broad arrow on the backs of their jackets, and were treated not as prisoners of war but as common criminals.

Well cared for though they were, to be a prisoner was a hard, sad lot for most; men suffered keenly the loss of freedom and their exile from country and family; news that came in eagerly awaited letters was frequently tragic. Frikkie Badenhorst, writing to his wife in the Klerksdorp concentration camp, eloquently expressed the longing most felt:

You wrote of the weeping in the night. We hear no one cry, notwithstanding that many tears arise. . . . Many men have had letters to tell them that their wives are dead and also their children, so by this you know that here also is sorrow. But in the night all is silent save the night watch, who calls from time to time: "All's well." It will be wonderful for us when once again we hear women and children weep![16]

At Simonstown those who received letters mounted a stone and read them out; they were sure to contain news of other families and of friends, so men crowded around to hear. The prisoners themselves tended to write more and more often: on St. Helena outgoing letters and cards increased from 14,000 a month between January and September 1901 to nearly 16,000 during the same months in the following year. The men were given envelopes and paper and there were no restrictions on the number they could send, but they had to buy their own stamps and all letters were censored. When it was discovered that some prisoners wrote secret messages under the stamps, letters had to be turned in unsealed with the stamp placed loose inside. Cleaver, in Ceylon, once added a postcript to a letter: "Five pounds reward for the man in de Wet's commando who captures this letter out of the post before it reaches Johannesburg."[17] But the letter was delivered.

There were a number of escapes. Most of the successful ones were made at Green Point and Simonstown before the prisoners were shipped out of South Africa. At the Simonstown camp the prisoners were frequently taken to the beach to wash and swim in the sea, and on one of these occasions Hjalmar Pettersen-Janek, one of the Scandinavians captured at Magersfontein, had himself buried in the sand with a reed to breathe through. This ruse worked, and he made his way from Cape Town to Lourenço Marques and back into the Transvaal, where he joined the Lichtenburg Commando.

There were several escapes in India, but all of the escapees were recaptured. No one escaped from St. Helena, although Sarel Eloff and some friends stole a boat and made an attempt. One man tried to escape from Bermuda by putting a box over his head and paddling off in broad daylight. An alert guard took an interest in the box that was making such steady headway against wind and tide, and a party of soldiers was waiting for it when it reached the shore.

Escape from Bermuda was made feasible by the SS *Trinidad,* which plied regularly between Hamilton and New York. If a prisoner could reach this ship and hide on board he could find freedom in the United States. The first successful escape was by this method: on 5 July 1901

David du Plooy stowed away on the *Trinidad* and was not discovered until the ship reached New York. A few days later four prisoners from Darrell's Island tried to duplicate his feat but were caught.

In September 1901 three men swam from Darrell's Island to the Warwick shore and walked around to Hamilton. One went to seek the help of Miss Outerbridge and was captured at her garden gate. The other two, explaining their moist and bedraggled appearance by saying they were sailors whose boat had been swamped by a sudden gust of wind, boldly hired a horse and carriage to take them to the *Trinidad;* they too were caught. It was soon after this that the Bermuda government belatedly passed a law against harbouring escapees and offered a £3 reward for information leading to the capture of an escaped prisoner.

The war was over and peace was signed when on the night of 25 June 1902 F. J. du Quesne and a man named Du Toit swam off their island and made their way to Miss Outerbridge. For some unexplained reason she agreed to help one if the other would surrender. This was agreed to, and Du Toit voluntarily gave himself up while Du Quesne, with the help of Miss Outerbridge, escaped and lived to become a secret agent for German naval intelligence during World War I. Adolphus de Wet, a nephew of the Free State general, also escaped from Bermuda and eventually made his way to Peru, where he went to work for a mining company.

A German named Albrecht was actually assisted by the British in making his escape. He made a long swim, stopping to rest on various islands, and he was picked up, wet and exhausted, by a British search party. They readily believed his inspired story that he was a stoker off the *Trinidad;* they were looking for two other escapees. He was delivered to the ship and reached New York with ease.

As far as is known, only five prisoners of war ever escaped after being sent out of South Africa and succeeded in returning to their homeland to fight again.

On 10 January 1901 the *Catalonia* entered the harbour of Colombo, Ceylon, with a load of prisoners of war, among them five young men bent on escape: Willie Steyn, Pieter Botha, Ernest Hausner (a German), and two brothers, George and Lourens Steytler. When a Russian troop ship, the *Kherson,* commanded by Captain Vladimir Petroff Kissimoff, also entered the harbour the five young men slipped over the side of the *Catalonia* in the dark and swam to it through the shark-infested water. The Russians took them up, gave them dry clothes and hot tea, and Captain Kissimoff at once weighed anchor and steamed away. At Aden, where the *Kherson* had to stop for coal, the British tried to search the ship, but Kissimoff hid the Boers in one of the ship's funnels.

They had intended to disembark at Port Said and make their way somehow from there to Lourenço Marques, but Kissimoff learned that the British were anticipating this move and he persuaded them to stay on board until he reached a Russian port.

From the moment the *Kherson* docked at Feodosiya in the Crimea on

2 February the young Boers were treated as heroes. They travelled by troop train to St. Petersburg, pampered all the way by the Russian officers; crowds waited at each station to catch a glimpse of them. They were lionized in St. Petersburg, presented with money and clothing, and whirled through a round of entertainments before setting off for Berlin and then on to Utrecht, where President Kruger greeted them jovially with: "Are you the five swimmers?"

Kruger arranged for them to be provided with money and passports, and after purchasing Mausers, ammunition, and other supplies, they took a German ship to what was then German West Africa. With some difficulty they made their way overland to South Africa and again became fighting burghers. Their odyssey had lasted nearly a year and they had travelled some 20,000 miles.

43

VEREENIGING: THE BITTER END

It could not go on. The British had an almost inexhaustible supply of men; every day saw the numbers of the Boers diminish. The war slithered to a stop. A meeting between Kitchener and the Transvaal leaders on 12 April 1902 in Kitchener's quarters in Pretoria* marked the beginning of the end.

The British had not exactly asked for the meeting, but Kitchener found a way to let the Boer leaders know that he thought it would be a good idea. On the day of Methuen's defeat at Tweebosch (7 March 1902) but probably before he had heard of it, he sent Botha and Schalk Berger copies of correspondence between the governments of Britain and the Netherlands concerning the Dutch government's proposal that it lend its good offices to arrange a peace. Britain had refused the offer, and Lord Lansdowne had told the Dutch: "The quickest and most satisfactory means of arranging a settlement would be by direct communication between the leaders of the Boer Forces in South Africa and the Commander-in-Chief of His Majesty's Forces." Although Kitchener sent these papers without any covering letter or comment, the Boers got the point: it was an unspoken invitation to come in and talk.

The meeting opened with Schalk Burger solemnly reading, article by article, a long proposal drawn up by the Boer leaders. Kitchener listened

*Melrose House on Jacob Maré Street, now a national monument.

in amazement, for it seemed as if time had stopped two and a half years ago; Burger was covering all the issues which had been discussed at the Bloemfontein conference, issues which the British had long since forgotten or in which they were no longer interested. Now it appeared that the Boers were willing to agree to nearly all that the British had then asked for—a franchise for the uitlanders; customs, postal, and railway unions; English as well as Dutch to be used in the schools; disputes to be settled by arbitration; and, in what *The Times History* sneeringly called the "sublimest touch of all," they agreed to demolish the forts at Johannesburg, Pretoria, and Bloemfontein.

Considering their plight at this moment, it certainly was ingenuous and, from the British view, impertinent for the Boers seriously to bring forth such proposals. Kitchener interrupted Schalk Burger's reading: "Must I understand from what you say that you wish to retain your independence?"

"Yes," said Steyn. "The people must not lose their self-respect."

A futile discussion followed. At the insistence of the Boers, the proposal—"in all its naked absurdity," as *The Times History* put it—was telegraphed to London. The reply, of course, was that His Majesty's Government could not "entertain any proposals based on the continued independence of the former Republics which have been formally annexed to the British Crown." On 14 April they met again, this time and henceforth with Milner in attendence.

It would appear that neither side realised that the Boers had just won their first concession. The presence of Milner at the negotiating table meant that the conference was not to be the meeting of opposing military commanders on the battlefield that Lansdowne and the government in London had envisaged, not simply a meeting to arrange an Appomattox-type surrender, but a meeting of the representatives of Great Britain with the representatives of two other nations, neither of whose existence Britain recognized.

The Boer leaders did not think of themselves as professional soldiers; they were, and had always been, politicians: almost all had at some time been elected to public offices; they easily switched from their temporary role as warriors to their political roles, and it was as representatives of their people, not as military commanders, that they wanted to meet with the British. Kitchener, a professional soldier who had never held a public office, had little interest in the political issues; he was interested only in a satisfactory conclusion of the hostilities. Instead of insisting that the discussions be kept on the military level, the British sent Milner to discuss the very issues which most interested their opponents. Milner tried to sidestep these and to keep the discussions on a military level, for he was not enthusiastic about meeting with the Boers for any purpose other than to arrange for their unconditional surrender.* He felt that "every conces-

---

*The term "unconditional surrender" was still fairly new, having been first used during the American Civil War.

sion we make now means more trouble hereafter." In his terms, he was right. Steyn, Burger, and the rest were technically rebels and outlaws; the people they claimed to represent were British colonials. But even Milner seems to have realised that the British could not be too stiff about this.

During these first talks it became evident to the Boers that Milner and Kitchener did not share the same views, Kitchener being more willing to compromise, not so prone to stand on technicalities, and quite willing to forget the earlier proclamations banishing the Boer leaders. For their part, the British could see a schism between the Free Staters and the Transvaalers, Botha and Burger being more interested in making peace than were Steyn and De Wet.

At the 19 April meeting the Boers asked for an armistice so that they could consult with all the scattered guerrilla leaders. They did not receive an immediate answer, but at a subsequent meeting Kitchener, while refusing to grant an armistice, agreed to arrange for the Boer leaders to meet at Vereeniging, a sleepy little town with a population of about 2,000 whites and 3,000 nonwhites on the Free State–Transvaal border, and he promised immunity from capture to the leaders chosen to attend as from 11 May. It was to be an extraordinary convention. Nothing quite like it had ever taken place before, and it remains a unique historical event. To the Boers it seemed a natural thing to do, conforming to all their political instincts, but already the peace talks were becoming more political than the British had ever envisioned.

It was certainly a bizarre proceeding to be taking place inside a British colony: Kitchener provided all facilities for his rebel enemies to hold a closed, secret meeting; furthermore, he granted immunity to all their leaders, military and political, the very men he had been trying to catch and imprison. Not only was the meeting an acceptance by the British of the Boers' contention that the republics still existed, but it was an acceptance of the fact—made a fact by the character of the meeting itself—that it was the fighting burghers in the field, and they alone, who spoke for the Afrikaner people. There was not even a suggestion that the prisoners of war or the men in the concentration camps or the hands-uppers or the National Scouts or anyone else should have any say in the matter. The "representatives of the people" were to be the leaders, for the most part generals and commandants, selected by the fighting burghers, together with their acknowledged political leaders.

Kitchener did not care about diplomatic forms; the Boers could be as politically peculiar as they liked as long as he achieved his own ends, and he felt quite sure the meeting of the delegates at Vereeniging would result in an end to the war. His optimism was reflected in a letter he wrote on 20 April to Lady Cranborne: "It is quite exciting to think that by the 20th of next month we may have peace. It would be such a good thing for all if it came before the Coronation. How I would like to see Botha, De Wet and De la Rey in the procession; it is quite in the cards, and it would do them a world of good to see the crowds."[1]

The Boer leaders had no thoughts of marching behind Kitchener's chariot in a triumph when they made their way to this remarkable meeting on the banks of the Vaal. From all over the Transvaal, the Orange Free State, and Cape Colony the delegates came, many riding without charge on British ships and trains, to meet at Vereeniging and there decide on peace or the continuation of the war. And if for peace, on what terms. The destiny of their people was in their hands.

It was said that many a British officer thought he had made an important capture before his prisoner produced his pass. One young subaltern, the story goes, fancied for a few heady moments that he had captured the much-hunted De Wet.

Smuts, like the other Boer leaders, was told he could bring to the meeting an aide and an orderly. He chose Deneys Reitz as one of these, asking him in which capacity he preferred to go. Young Reitz, not knowing the difference, chose to be the orderly and found himself riding in an open truck with the baggage while a laughing companion designated as the aide rode in a first-class carriage with Smuts.

Steyn was seriously ill, but he went to Vereeniging, travelling with Cornelis ("Corneels") du Preez as his aide and Ruiter, his Coloured servant, as his orderly. Ruiter had not been killed, as Steyn had feared, when he tumbled from his horse at Reitz. He had simply thought it prudent to stop when shot at. When the train drew up at Vereeniging station Steyn looked out the window and saw the tents of the concentration camp there. "Corneels," he called. "Look at that!"

Du Preez, busily collecting the baggage, glanced out the window and said, "Forget it, President. We have arrived."

But Steyn sat in his seat as though stunned. "Now I have seen one —a concentration camp. It is . . . *terrible!*"

By train and on horseback they arrived at Vereeniging: sixty delegates, thirty each from the Orange Free State and the Transvaal, and, in addition, the political leaders (neither Steyn nor Schalk Burger was an official delegate). They had had little contact with one another—more than a thousand miles had separated the burghers and rebels fighting in Cape Colony from the commandos in the northern Transvaal—and the contrasts in their appearance and physical condition indicated the varying fortunes of their cause in the different sectors of the theatre of war. Those from the well-fed forces in the Cape were shocked by the appearance of the men from the eastern Transvaal—"these starving, ragged men, clad in skins and sacking, their bodies covered with sores from lack of salt and food."[2]

The British had erected two camps, one for each set of representatives, and between them a large marquee to be used as a meeting hall. There on the cold, crisp autumn morning of 15 May 1902, after two years and seven months of war, the Boer delegates met. C. F. Beyers from Waterberg was elected chairman, and the great debate began.

From the beginning the difference in the composition of the delegates from the two republics was apparent: all the Free Staters were generals or commandants; the Transvaal delegation, while including all the principal commanders, also had six field cornets, four rank-and-file burghers, and even two noncombatants (the landdrosts of Wakkerstroom and Zoutpansberg). Most important of all, the Free Staters, at the instigation of Steyn and De Wet, had pledged before they left their commandos not to vote for any peace terms that involved the surrender of their independence; Botha and other leaders anxious for peace saw at once that the pledges of the Free Staters made the meeting pointless, for they had already faced the fact that they would have to give up their cherished independence, that their real purpose was simply to wring from the British all the concessions they could. The situation was saved by J. B. M. Hertzog, the judge turned general, who addressed the meeting and assured the Free Staters that it was a principle of law that a delegate could not be a mere mouthpiece but had to vote as he thought best. Smuts rose and reaffirmed this. The Boers, always respectful of legal learning, accepted these assurances from the two intellectual giants among them and the point was never seriously raised again, although many Free Staters remained uneasy about their pledges. Peace was now possible, but it was still far away.

The rest of this first day was taken up with reports of conditions in the various sectors. In some areas supplies could still be found; others were simply blackened wildernesses. Some of the speakers talked bravely of continuing the war; others spoke of the hopelessness of trying to carry on. All larded their talks with quotations from the Bible. For three days the Boers wrestled with their dilemma. Reason and sentiment contended in an atmosphere charged with emotion. Deneys Reitz wrote: "Even in adversity the Boer instinct for speeches and wordy wrangling asserted itself, and the time was passed in oratory."[3]

Kemp, still the fiery young general, gave a bellicose speech ending with, "As far as I am concerned, unless relief comes, I will fight on till I die." J. G. Celliers, who commanded the best-equipped commando in the field, also spoke in favour of continuing the war. But the commandants from the eastern Transvaal pointed out the futility of it all, saying that if the meeting did not result in peace many of the burghers would surrender anyway. C. Birkenstock, a burgher from Vryheid, told how "the presence of women and children causes great difficulty" and spoke of the shortage of food and of the increasing hostility of the Bantu tribesmen: "That peace must be made at all costs is the opinion of all the families in my district, and I feel it my duty to bring this opinion before you."[4]

There was not much in the way of positive proposals, although Francis Reitz, Deneys's father, suggested that they offer to give up the gold fields, which, he said, had caused the war in the first place. Their enemy was already in possession of the gold fields, of course, but some burghers snatched at this straw, hoping the British might be satisfied if all the gold was voluntarily yielded to them. A commission was elected to meet with

Schalk Burger and Steyn and draw up a proposal to be presented to the delegates. The debate went on.

The men whose words carried the most weight at Vereeniging were the three great military leaders: Botha, De la Rey, and De Wet. The delegates would follow these men through the moral thicket in which they found themselves, but the three were themselves divided: Botha was for peace, De Wet was for war, and De la Rey wavered uncertainly between the two.

Botha spoke at length, stressing the hopelessness of their position: the destruction of crops and the slaughter of animals had cut off all supplies of food in some districts; the "Kaffir question," he said, grew more serious every day and attacks on burghers by Bantu were increasing; the condition of the women was pitiable; the number of men on commando grew fewer and fewer; and their horses were giving out. "We must face the fact that things are not at a standstill; we are slipping back every moment."

Then De la Rey, who remained silent until the second day, rose to speak. Some had spoken of foreign intervention, he said, but he himself had never believed in this possibility; he felt that this was the time to negotiate with the British. On the main issue his message was contradictory, reflecting his own indecision. In his own area he could and would continue to fight: "So far as I myself am concerned, I cannot think of laying down my arms." Now, however, he had heard of the piteous conditions elsewhere and he was not certain the war could be continued: "There has been talk of fighting to the bitter end. But has the bitter end already come? Each man must answer that question for himself. You must remember that everything has been sacrificed—cattle, goods, money, wife and child. Our men are going about naked and our women have nothing but clothes made of skins to wear. Is not this the bitter end?"

De Wet followed De la Rey. There were no doubts in his mind: he was for war. His theme was: "Persevere. We have everything to lose, but we have not yet lost it." He would not agree to giving up any part of their territory, not even the gold fields. He called on the delegates to keep their faith in God, for the conflict, he said, was really a war of religion. "At all costs let us continue the fighting."

On Saturday the draft of the proposed terms drawn up by the commission was read and it was agreed to accept a position as a protectorate, to let Britain handle all foreign relations, and "to conclude a defensive alliance with Great Britain in regard to South Africa," but not to sacrifice complete independence. Then a committee was appointed to treat with Milner and Kitchener. This group, consisting of Botha, De la Rey, De Wet, Hertzog, and Smuts, went to Pretoria and on 19 May began talks with the British.

The meeting did not begin well. The Boers laid before Milner and Kitchener the list of those things they were willing to give up if they could still retain their right to govern themselves. Milner rejected their proposal out of hand. He would not even consider it as a basis for negotiations. He took the position that the Middelburg proposal contained "the utmost concessions that the British Government is able to grant." Milner entertained peculiar notions regarding the nature of the negotiating process: as usual, he wanted to begin with his final offer and not budge from it.

From 19 May until 28 May the Boer leaders argued and pleaded. At last, in spite of Milner's arrogance and intransigence, a draft document was drawn up stating that the burghers would lay down their arms and acknowledge King Edward VII as their lawful sovereign. In return the British agreed that none of the burghers would lose his freedom or his property, that Dutch as well as English would be taught in the schools, that "as soon as circumstances permit it a representative system tending towards autonomy would be introduced," that no special taxes would be levied to pay for the war, that the British would contribute £3,000,000 towards rehabilitating the country, and that all prisoners of war who took the oath of allegiance would be speedily returned. It was also agreed that there would be no vote for the Bantu or Coloureds until there was representative government—in effect, never—a concession Milner later characterised as the greatest mistake of his life.

It was a curious surrender document. There was, of course, the agreement on the part of the Boers to lay down their arms, but the bulk of the document consisted of political agreements applicable to the postwar period. It was unique in that it was an agreement between a *people*, not a nation, and a conqueror who claimed these people as his subjects. No thought was given as to how in future the Boers were to be represented; no guarantees other than the document itself were given by the conquerors that they would abide by the agreement; no system was envisaged for the arbitration of misunderstandings or disputes regarding the terms. There was a considerable amount of trust on both sides; trust that was not misplaced. The importance of the document lay not in the concessions themselves, which were slight, but by all that was implied in the British acceptance of any concessions. There was, for example, the implied threat that if the British did not abide by the agreement the Boers would and could again take the field; and this, in turn, implied acceptance on the part of the British of the fact that the Boers had not been completely subjugated, that their morale, their martial spirit, their will to resist, had not been completely crushed; although the Boers had been forced to agree to things they did not want to agree to, the British had been manoeuvred into making promises they would rather not have made. It was also implied that the Boers, as represented by the fighting burghers, were still, and would remain, a political force to be reckoned with in the future; and this was the most important implication of all.

The Natal and Cape rebels were dealt with in a separate document. They were to be disenfranchised for life (although this was later reduced to five years and eventually to less than four); rebel officers and officials were to stand trial for high treason, but it was promised that none would be executed.

That the British agreed to anything, to make even minor concessions, was due to Kitchener. "He does not care what he gives away," wailed Milner. It was also in large measure through Kitchener's efforts that the Boer stance was softened. Perhaps his most important contribution to the conference was a stroll he took with Smuts. In the course of one meeting, when Smuts was trying unsuccessfully to reason with Milner, Kitchener touched his arm and said, "Come out, come out for a little," and he led Smuts out of the room. They walked up and down in silence for a minute and then Kitchener said, "Look here, Smuts, there is something on my mind that I want to tell you. I can only give it to you as my opinion, but I believe that in two years' time a Liberal government will be in power. And if a Liberal government comes into power it will grant you a constitution for South Africa."

"This is a very important pronouncement," said Smuts. "If one could be sure of this it would make a great difference."

"As I say, it is only my opinion. But I honestly *do* believe that will happen."[5]

Smuts, of course, passed on this opinion to his colleagues, as Kitchener intended he should, and it had a decided influence on them. It was the first, the only, hope the Boers were given that they might have some form of independence in the near future.

Milner, who had fought every concession, now demanded that the Boer leaders return to Vereeniging, present the proposal to the delegates, and bring back a yes or no answer. The delegates would have to take the terms or leave them as a whole. They were nonnegotiable. Milner further demanded that they give their answer within two days, by the evening of 31 May.

At seven o'clock on the evening of 28 May the Boer negotiators sadly boarded the special train for Vereeniging, and the following day they laid the terms, the best they had been able to obtain, before the delegates. The burghers were now faced with three choices: they could refuse to sign the peace terms and simply surrender unconditionally (this was discussed but never seriously considered); they could continue to fight; or they could accept the British terms. There was much heated debate, much soul searching, much emotional oratory. There were also many small meetings outside the convention marquee; both Botha and De la Rey argued and pleaded with De Wet to accept the terms. On the afternoon of 31 May 1902 they proceeded to the voting. The vote was 54 in favour of accepting the terms and 6 against. All the important leaders, even the fiery De Wet, who until the last moment had argued for the continuation of the war, voted to accept the unpalatable terms.

Now it was over. The bitter end had come at last. Schalk Burger rose and said, "We are standing here at the grave of the two republics." Gloom hung thick in the marquee where they had sat for so long with their aching consciences and heavy hearts. They were visionaries, these men, and they had dreamed a great dream, had striven mightily for it, and failed. They were strong, proud men, and they were tasting now the bitterness of defeat, the wrenching agony of failure. Withal, they were practical men, farmers most of them, who knew that dream's end left practical problems, and so Commandant F. P. Jacobsz of Harrismith was able to rouse them from their sad, bitter mood by a practical proposal. He suggested that a committee be appointed to provide for "the suffering women and children, widows and orphans, and other destitute persons" and that De Wet, Botha, and De la Rey go abroad to raise funds for this purpose. After this was agreed to, the last meeting of the two republics closed with a prayer.

The painful deliberations of the delegates were secret—neither officers nor government officials attempted to spy on them—but all the world awaited the decision. An enterprising reporter named Edgar Wallace, later to win fame as a novelist, arranged to be the first with the news by bribing one of the guards stationed at the big marquee and supplying him with three handkerchiefs, each of a different colour, with which to signal the progress of the meeting: blue if the talks were going satisfactorily, red if some difficulty had occurred, and white if peace had definitely been accepted. Wallace sat in a carriage some distance away, smoking and reading and watching. When the guard produced the white handkerchief, he raced to Johannesburg, and that evening he cabled the news to the *Daily Mail,* which had it nearly twenty-four hours before the official announcement was made. Wallace had made the scoop of the decade—or so it ought to have been. It was unfortunate for him and his paper, however, that 31 May 1902 was a Saturday, Wallace's message arrived that night, and the *Daily Mail* had no Sunday edition.

Late that Saturday afternoon those deputed to sign the peace terms (it had no formal title) left by special train for Pretoria, and the actual signing took place in the dining room of Melrose House shortly after eleven o'clock that night, less than an hour before Milner's deadline. The document itself was typed on parchment, and there were four copies. The Reverend J. D. Kestell, who was present, wrote: "The document has been signed. Everything has fallen silent in this room where so much was said. They remain motionless for yet another moment. A shattering feeling of loss overwhelms our men. The members of the Government rise, as if bewildered, to leave the hall. Speak they cannot."[6]

Kitchener tried to break the mood of depression, to cut through the gloom; he went from one to the other, shaking the hand of each and saying, "We are good friends now." He spoke as a soldier to brave and honourable foes who had earned his respect and admiration. The Boers tried to accept his words in this spirit, but they were brokenhearted men.

"I have just come from signing the terms of surrender—surely one of the strangest documents in history," Milner wrote to a friend. "If anything could make me relent towards Boers, it was the faces of the men who sat around the table tonight. . . ."

It was De la Rey who broke the funereal atmosphere. Looking around at the long faces of his colleagues and, speaking slowly in broken, accented English, he said, "We are a bloody cheerful-looking lot of British subjects!"

Back in Vereeniging a group of delegates gathered in a tent where a small grave had been dug. Solemnly they folded and buried a Transvaal Vierkleur, and Francis Reitz, his voice quivering with emotion, recited a poem he had written for the occasion.

On 2 June Kitchener went to Vereeniging and addressed the delegates. He congratulated them upon the gallant fight they had made; he told them they should be proud of their record and that it was no disgrace to be defeated by such overwhelming numbers; he said that he wanted them to be his friends and he asked for their cooperation.

When the first rumours of peace reached the women's laager with De la Rey's forces, it was thought that the republics had retained their independence; there were joyous shouts and children danced on the veld waving a Vierkleur. Nonnie de la Rey quickly loaded her wagon, gathered up her children, and started for Lichtenburg, where she hoped to meet up with her husband and her son Koos. On the road she learned the real terms of the peace agreement. The children wept and Nonnie de la Rey exclaimed bitterly, "Why was all the bloodshed, the suffering? What was the purpose of it all?"

Marthinus Theunis Steyn, who had proved one of the most fervid bitter-enders, had been able to exert little influence over the convention, for he was a very sick man. He had insisted on going to Vereeniging, even though his doctor had advised against it, but the exertions of the journey left him too weak to leave his tent, and only occasionally was he able to talk with De Wet and the other Free State generals or with the Transvaal leaders. He had worn himself out in the cause and had contracted a baffling disease.* Among other symptoms, he suffered from double vision and his legs pained him so severely that walking was impossible. Many years later his son Colin said in a radio interview: "Had he remained well, I doubt if the peace terms of Vereeniging would have been accepted." This might well have been the case.

Steyn's physical condition worsened at Vereeniging, and he was not made any better by the reports he received of the deliberations. Lying helpless in his tent he must have sensed the slackening resolve of the delegates pledged to continue the war and the slipping away of his country's independence. It was finally decided that he must be moved to Krugersdorp where he could be properly cared for; De Wet was appointed acting president. After an emotional farewell to his officers, Steyn was taken to the station and carried on board a train, his health broken, his cause lost, his career ended.

---

*The nature of Steyn's illness is still being debated. Dr. T. Fichardt, Steyn's grandson, summed up the varying diagnoses in the *South African Medical Journal* (24 November 1973) and concluded that it could have been either myasthenia gravis or botulism, but probably the latter, the result of eating spoiled sausage.

In Cape Colony the war wound down while the peace conference was in progress, and near Springbok some of the Boers under Manie Maritz played football with a British unit under Major Clement Edwards. But this slackening of military operations was not typical, and elsewhere the fighting continued unabated. Ian Hamilton was engaged in a final drive in the western Transvaal and fought the last major engagement of the war at Roodewal. He thought it a marvellous battle with which to end the war:

And what a sequel to shake hands upon! There's been no better in the birth of nations bar perhaps the battle of Hastings. . . . F. J. Potgieter, foremost of the brave. . . . Potgieter in his blue shirt leading the line of 1200 Boers—the pick of the back-veld—at a steady canter, over ground that could not give cover to a mouse; straight—a mile and a half in bright sunlight—at a massed column of 1500 British bayonets and another similar column standing by in support. Every rifle, pom-pom and field gun that can be brought to bear is firing for dear life. The charge of the Light Brigade at Balaclava was child's play to this. Miraculously—incredibly—on and on they came until Potgieter falls with a bullet through his brain only seventy yards from the centre of the Scottish Horse.

When we buried these heroes we did so reverently as if they had been our comrades.[7]

On 29 May, only two days before the peace treaty was signed, some Boers made a cattle raid near Frederikstad in the southwestern Transvaal; a handful of mounted infantry gave chase and were ambushed. Most of the troopers managed to escape, but Second Lieutenant Sutherland, a boy still in his teens, fresh out of Eton into the Seaforth Highlanders, lost his horse. He scrambled to his feet and, firing as he ran, tried to break his way free. It was impossible; he was outnumbered and surrounded, but he refused to surrender. Finally the circling Boers shot him down. Conan Doyle thought this a glorious death: "It is indeed sad that at this last instant a young life should be thrown away, but Sutherland died in a noble fashion for a noble cause, and many inglorious years would be a poor substitute for the example and traditions which such a death will leave behind."[8]

Reactions to the peace varied. Not all the soldiers in South Africa were glad to see the war end. Lieutenant J. F. C. Fuller, twenty-three years old, was on blockhouse duty. He was riding to Kroomdraai to get the mail on 1 June when he encountered another officer who rode up and said, "Have you heard? Peace was proclaimed last night!"

"Well, I am sorry," Fuller replied, and, telling of this later, he added, "And so I was."

Murray Cosby Jackson, now a sergeant, was given news of the peace at church parade on the same day: "We gave the regulation cheer. I don't know that I was much elated though, on the whole. We had had a pretty good time all round and will probably never get the same experiences again."[9]

One Englishman who was glad to see the war ended and who lost no time in hurrying home was Lord Kitchener. On 20 June he turned over his command of the forces in South Africa to General Neville Lyttelton and three days later sailed for England. He took with him four bronze statues of Boers, the creation of sculptor Anton van Wouw, and President Kruger's stinkwood ox wagon. He gave two of the statues to the Royal Engineers and kept the other two for himself; Kruger's wagon he presented to the City of London. Eventually, after Kitchener's death, his heirs, the Royal Engineers, and the City of London were persuaded to return this booty. The ox wagon is now in the Kruger museum, and the bronze figures stand where they were intended to be placed around the statue of Kruger in Church Square, Pretoria.

In Britain there was general rejoicing at the news of the peace, except among the pro-Boers. When Kipling's Aunt Georgie (Lady Burne-Jones, née Georgiana Macdonald), who did not share her nephew's jingoistic attitudes, heard of the surrender she hung a black cloth from the window of her cottage at Rottingdean and put up a large notice that read: WE HAVE KILLED AND ALSO TAKEN POSSESSION. Kipling had to rescue her from a band of angry young patriots.

It had been hard indeed for the delegates to the peace conference at Vereeniging to bring themselves to agree to the British terms; now they had the unpleasant task of returning to their commandos to explain to their burghers what they had done and why. Equally unpleasant was the task of arranging for their men to surrender their arms and take the oath of allegiance. Major General E. Locke Elliot described the procedure:

> On receipt of a signal that the commando had assembled I proceeded with my personal staff to the meeting. On arrival, General De Wet introduced the generals and commandants, the latter their field cornets. . . . The men were then fallen in, counted, and had their arms collected in convenient places. Passes were given to each burgher to the effect that they had surrendered.[10]

De Wet also wrote a description:

> I left Pretoria on the 3rd of June with General Elliott [sic] who had to accompany me to the various centres to receive the burghers' arms.
> On the 5th June the first commando laid down their weapons near Vredefort. To every man there, as to myself, this surrender was no more and no less than the sacrifice of our independence. I have often been present at the death-bed and at the burial of those who have been nearest to my heart—father, mother, brother and friend—but the grief which I felt on those occasions was not to be compared with what I now underwent at the burial of my Nation![11]

In all, 21,256 burghers and rebels surrendered: 11,166 in the Transvaal, 6,455 in the Free State, and 3,635 in Cape Colony. Their reactions to the surrender varied, but for none was there joy. Some cried, a few fainted. Some were relieved, many were bitter. When Smuts spoke to his men, one burgher cried out, "Jan Smuts, you have betrayed us!"

As the shaggy, unkempt burghers came off the veld and into the towns, soldiers, women and children, black and white, stood along the sides of the roads to stare at them; some produced cameras and took their pictures. They rode to surrender locations, these proud, hardy veterans, led by their leaders. They rode with the easy slouch of men long accustomed to living in the saddle; most were dirty, their clothing a stained assortment of rags, skins, grain bags, and captured British uniforms. They had fought long and hard and well, holding at bay an army more than ten times their number. The world had watched and wondered at such warriors. They had been defeated, but their spirit remained unbroken, their pride unbent.

Many burghers fired off their ammunition and smashed their rifles on rocks before turning them in. Some irreconcilables refused to sign the oath of allegiance, preferring exile.

Of the 30,000 prisoners of war held by the British at the war's end, some 24,000 were in camps outside South Africa. Many of these refused to believe that peace had been signed, suspecting that the news was simply a British trick. When peace was definitely confirmed and the news could not be denied, many still refused to sign the oath of allegiance, even though refusal meant they would not be repatriated. The form each man was asked to sign read:

I . . . [name and home address] adhere to the terms of the agreement signed at Pretoria on 31 May 1902, between my late Government and the representatives of His Majesty's Government. I acknowledge myself to be a subject of King Edward VII and I promise to own allegiance to him, his heirs, and successors according to law.

There were so many prisoners in India and Ceylon who refused to sign that finally, at the end of 1903, the British had to ask De la Rey to go there and personally persuade some 500 of them that the war was really over and that they ought to take the oath and go home. In November 1902, six months after the end of the war, there were still 376 irreconcilables in Bermuda. In December the British asked the leading Boer generals to send them letters advising them to sign the oath. This was done, but in August 1903, more than a year after Vereeniging, there were still 63 stubborn men who refused.

The British were in a quandary. The prisoners refused to work, refused to take the oath, and even refused the offer of free passage to any country they chose. Finally seven of the most recalcitrant were simply dumped on the wharf in Hamilton. They immediately established a "laager" in the sheds on the waterfront and, ever faithful to the democratic process, proceeded to elect a leader. The city fathers of Hamilton then debated the wisdom and legality of lodging a charge of vagrancy against them. A month later the police evicted them from the sheds and left them sitting on their boxes and bundles in the street with orders to be off by nightfall. They drifted off; no one seemed to know or care where.

This procedure having worked, the military authorities then unloaded the remainder of their prisoners onto the city of Hamilton. This time, when they were put on the wharf, the police were ready and promptly arrested them for loitering. Sent to gaol, they refused to work and were put on bread and water. Still they held out. When after ten days they were released, they simply sat in the street outside the gaol until they were rearrested.

Eventually some took the oath and some drifted away from Bermuda, but there were a few who never signed and never left. They found work and became part of the population; two married local girls. It is not known when the last one died, but twenty-five years after the war there was at least one irreconcilable left there, still proclaiming himself a citizen of a republic which no longer existed.

While most of the prisoners of war eventually returned to South Africa, those who had fought to the end but still refused to sign the oath were deported, and for a time there were Boers scattered all over the world. Deneys Reitz went to Madagascar; Francis Reitz, Ben Viljoen, and many others went to the United States, where some of them accepted the offer of free land made by a number of western states; others were scattered about Europe; some went to South America, and in remote Patagonia there is to this day a Dutch Reformed Church and a group of Spanish-speaking Argentines called Juan or Pedro with Afrikaner surnames.

Wherever they went the Boers were welcomed, for men admire bravery and endurance and the Boers had earned the admiration of the Western world. Theirs seemed such an incredible military achievement that even they themselves were a bit awed by it. De Wet saw the hand of God behind it all:

> England's great power pitted against two republics, which, in comparison with European countries were nearly uninhabited! This mighty Empire employed against us, besides their own English, Scotch, and Irish soldiers, volunteers from the Australian, New Zealand, Canadian and South African Colonies, hired against us both black and white nations, and, what is worst of all, the National Scouts from our own nation. Think, further, that all harbours were closed to us, and that there were therefore no imports. Can you not see that the whole course of events was a miracle from beginning to end? A miracle of God in the eyes of every one who looks at it with an unbiased mind, but even more apparent to those who had personal experience of it.[12]

The British did not believe in miracles, but they recognised courage, stamina, and stubborn persistence when they encountered it, and they joined the world in admiration of their former enemies. L. S. Amery best expressed their attitude at this time:

> The decision of the Boer leaders to prolong the war was an assertion of individual and national character over mere calculating reason. In the long, heroic struggle that followed that character was strengthened, purified and chastened. . . . The Boers, surrendering when they did and as they did, were a greater asset to the British Empire than they would have been if they had surrendered two years earlier.[13]

And so it all ended. But in history there can be no end, and what we call endings are also beginnings, for life goes on, leading to new endings and new beginnings for ever and ever.

44

EPILOGUE: THE DUST SETTLES

If a chief villain is to be selected, a man most responsible for the tragedy of the war in South Africa, all fingers must point to Milner. The Boers had hated Rhodes (who died just before the war ended), and they detested Jameson, Kitchener, and Chamberlain, but above all they entertained an implacable hatred for Milner. To them it seemed particularly humiliating, the grossest insult, that he should have been selected to be Britain's proconsul, the man who would now rule over them. Churchill too thought the appointment unwise: "After the Peace of Vereeniging no more unsuitable agent could have been chosen to discharge the functions of High Commissioner."

Certainly there could have been no greater contrast in temperament than that of Milner and the people he was to govern. The Boers were an unpretentious people; Milner was proud and clothed in an impervious arrogance. The Boers had a passion for politics and debate; Milner distrusted democratic processes, and since it was nearly impossible for him to understand how anyone could disagree with him, he regarded debate as an empty form, a sheer waste of time. The Boers' dislike of Milner was reciprocated; he disliked and distrusted them. Yet, having said this, it must also be said that Churchill was wrong and the Boers were shortsighted. In those first postwar years South Africa in general and the Boers in particular were fortunate indeed to have had the services of Lord Milner.

"The unsettling of a nation is easy work; the settling is not"—so Vincent Gookin had said 250 years before. He was speaking of Ireland, but his words were no less true when applied to the former Boer republics. All of the institutions of Boer society were in disarray if not completely shattered. The economy of the Orange Free State and the Transvaal had rested upon agriculture and mining. This economy was now in ruins. The people, both black and white, who had supplied the labour for the farms and mines had been uprooted and were now scattered about the world or huddled in concentration camps. To restore the economy, to repatriate the people, and to re-create their institutions in a new society—these were the urgent tasks that faced the new rulers. To accomplish this—and quickly—the British resorted to that least desirable but most efficient form of government: a dictatorship, and a dictatorship of the most difficult kind: a temporary one, intended to lead to eventual self-government. The man chosen to head such a government had to possess an extraordinary combination of talents and abilities: Milner was such a man and Britain was fortunate in having him at hand, for he was also a man she could trust, just as forty-three years later the United States was fortunate to have a remarkably similar autocrat in Douglas MacArthur to rule Japan. Both were born dictators completely dedicated to the service of democratic governments.

Milner was not in the least daunted by the immensity of the tasks before him; he rubbed his hands with delight at the prospect of reassembling the pieces of the two republics in a new way; he was at last in his element. He set about his great work of "restarting the new colonies on a higher plane of civilization" with energy, enthusiasm, and determination, and to assist him he assembled a personal staff of young men who were copies of himself—clever, energetic, cocksure. Most were but a few years out of the university; most came from Oxford, and many, like Milner, from Balliol. And all, like Milner, were bachelors. They came to be known collectively as "Milner's kindergarten."

In spite of opposition from man and nature, Milner accomplished much in a relatively short time. Nothing escaped his zeal: he completely reorganised the police and prison administrations, developed a government hospital in Pretoria, established asylums for the insane, founded leper colonies, reformed the labour laws and the whole machinery for the administration of justice, formed a public health department, built the finest zoo in Africa, enlarged and improved the railway system and the telephone and telegraph service, constructed public buildings, and, using the schools started in the concentration camps as his foundation, established farm schools wherever a group of children could be collected (more than two hundred of these schools were started in 1903 alone). Milner's approach to problems was not only intelligent but often imaginative, as when he sent groups of former prisoners of war on tours of Canada, Australia, and New Zealand to study new crops and new methods of cattle raising.

The greatest of his labours was the resettlement of the land and the reestablishment of the agricultural base of the economy, to put the people back on the farms. The problems involved in repatriation, of resettling men, women, and children, black and white, on a devastated land, were tremendous. There were, in round numbers, 200,000 whites and 100,000 Bantu to be put back on the land and given the means for survival. This included not only 30,000 prisoners of war and 110,000 people in concentration camps, but also the 4,500 South Africans who were discharged from the British army and some 30,000 others, remnants of the Boer nations, still at large, homeless on the veld.

Nature itself seemed to conspire against Milner in his great repopulation effort. The winter that immediately followed the peace at Vereeniging was the most severe in South Africa's recorded history, bitterly cold and punctuated by violent storms. Then came drought, epidemics of cattle diseases, and a plague of locusts.

Milner attacked his major problem by establishing a Repatriation Department, using the concentration camps as bases from which families were dispatched to what was left of their farms. Thus, the concentration camps remained in existence for nearly nine months after the end of the war. The Repatriation Department worked hard, but there were innumerable difficulties with which it could not cope, and problems seemingly without end.

The shortage of farm animals was crucial. Milner arranged to import long-horned steers and two-year-old heifers from the United States and, after weeks of haggling, managed to purchase from the army 80,000 oxen, mules, and donkeys. Seeds, building materials, ploughs, horses, sheep, harnesses, and wagons were offered to the Boers by the Repatriation Department at cost without charge for administration or delivery. But many of the animals obtained from the army were in wretched condition; when glanders broke out among the mules, the results were disastrous. The most urgent need was for ploughing cattle, and even though teams of government animals were sent round to plough a certain number of acres on farms that lacked draft animals, there were never enough.

In spite of the severe winter and the hardships, the people were anxious to go back to the land, and day after day clouds of dust blew over the veld, stirred up by wagon trains pulled by mules or oxen moving away from the concentration camps and repatriation centres, carrying families, their possessions, one month's rations, and materials for a new start in life. Packed in somehow were the broken bits of furniture and personal possessions that had been saved from their former lives, the curios bought or made by the men while in prison camps, and the toys and new schoolbooks of the children.

Milner had hoped to have the farms reestablished and the people settled within a year, but this proved impossible. When the wagons arrived at the blackened ruins of the old homestead the goods were off-loaded and the wagons of the Repatriation Department lumbered off to move another family. Left to themselves on their land, despondency must have overwhelmed many as they looked about them. Strong hands and hearts were needed if families were to survive. Most Boer families possessed both, but in spite of this, and in spite of the energetic efforts of the government, it became obvious, even before the first winter was over, that more British aid would be needed, and for a longer period, if the landscape was not to be strewn with starving families. Milner recognized this: despite the grumblings of those inside and outside the government at home, he pushed ahead with his resettlement program. He spent lavishly; far more than the £3,000,000 promised in the peace agreement was expended on reconstruction and repatriation, and millions more were made available for loans.

It is impossible to see how Milner could have done more than he did, given the existing political atmosphere, the prevailing Victorian attitudes towards charity, the lack of understanding in England of conditions on the veld, and the resentment of the British taxpayers towards the use of their money to help their former enemies. It must be remembered that this was the first time in history that a conqueror had ever attempted such a mass repatriation and rehabilitation of a conquered people. It was altogether a new thing.

The attitude of the Boers to their new rulers varied: some could never suppress their hatred for the British and did not want to; others wanted to forget the war and get on with the business of rebuilding their farms and their lives. Stompie van Rensburg, surrendering at the end of the war, carried his rifle in his left hand as he walked up to a soldier and, holding out his right, said, "Englishman, here is my rifle and here is my hand."

Although he and others were willing to come to terms with the British, few indeed were willing to forgive those of their own countrymen who had sided with the enemy. One who did was Jozua Joubert, the commandant who had drawn the lot which placed him on Hlangwane at the battle of Colenso. Joubert had come home from the war without his right arm to find his farmhouse burned and all that he possessed destroyed. Yet he was able to confront his neighbour, a hands-upper responsible for the destruction, by holding out his remaining hand and saying: "Revenge belongs to God, not to man, so we must shake hands and be friends."

Jozua Joubert was a remarkable man, by no means typical. Stompie van Rensburg lived for more than forty years after the war without speaking to a former friend on an adjoining farm who had been a hands-upper and, he claimed, had tried to betray him.

Although the hands-uppers and National Scouts had chosen the winning side in the war, their place in postwar society was unenviable. Their fellow countrymen regarded them as traitors, and the feeling against them was intense. They were socially ostracised, insulted, boycotted, and even banned from churches unless they publicly admitted their guilt and repented. In some areas it was a disgrace to have an unburned farmhouse. (Even today, farmhouses built before 1902 are pointed out as belonging to the families of hands-uppers.) The political influence to which such men as Piet de Wet and A. P. J. Cronjé might have aspired was denied them by the fact that the peace treaty, made with the fighting burghers without reference to them, gave unstated but effective recognition to the bitter-end guerrilla leaders, not the hands-uppers, as the true representatives of the Afrikaner people in the new colonies.

After the war the army regarded those Boers who had fought on their side simply as irregulars to be paid off and forgotten; the civil administration saw them only as more Boers to be resettled. Thanks to the efforts of a staff officer who recognised their peculiar status, Kitchener was persuaded to pay them an extra month's salary and to give each of them a pony, saddle, and bridle; further, wagons, rations, and tents were offered at moderate prices and a fund was established for their benefit.

Many of the National Scouts and ORC Volunteers had come from the lower strata of Boer society. A large proportion had been *bywoners,* squatters without land of their own, who now that the war was over had no place to go, for few of the farmers would allow them back on their land. A group of former leaders of the National Scouts formed a Farmers Association and rented land near Standerton where some might settle. The venture seemed so promising that other associations and settlements were formed, but unfortunately this well-intentioned scheme came to grief.

The bywoners were not made of the sternest stuff—which is perhaps why they went over to the British in the first place. Many were shiftless and most were too easily discouraged. The associations themselves, private ventures, suffered from mismanagement and actual dishonesty. In the Orange River Colony little effort was made to settle the bywoners on the land; instead, a system of public works projects was initiated and they were employed as manual labourers.

Boers who owned their own lands, however, were determined to remain on the veld, to rebuild their farms, and, in spite of all difficulties, they persevered. But not until the closing weeks of 1903 was there a good rainfall, and not until 1904 did a degree of normalcy return to the veld. By 1905, however, only three years after Vereeniging, there were few reminders that this was a land recently aflame with war—only a few blockhouses to be seen; some fences along the railways festooned with rusting tins, the pebbles inside causing them to tinkle when the wind blew; and, of course, the scattered graves on the veld.

To make the new colonies bright jewels in the crown of Empire was Milner's great ambition, and he was not to be distracted from his single-minded devotion to his task. When in 1903 Chamberlain resigned from the Cabinet on the issue of Imperial preference and the post of colonial secretary was offered to Milner, he refused—perhaps wisely, for he was not a politician; still, there were few other men who would have given up an opportunity to be a key Cabinet minister in order to be proconsul for a pair of devastated colonies inhabited by truculent and ungrateful subjects for whom they had no affection.

In spite of a chronic shortage of labour, the mines increased their production, but they were unable to reach their prewar level. This vast land, never overpopulous and now depopulated by war, needed hands and brains if it was to grow and develop. Even before the end of the war Milner had pleaded for government encouragement of emigration to the new colonies. In a dispatch written 25 January 1902 he wrote:

If we do nothing, we shall be confronted, sooner or later, with an industrial urban population, rapidly increasing, and almost wholly British in sentiment, and, on the other hand, a rural population, wholly Dutch, agriculturally unprogressive. It is not possible to contemplate such a state of affairs without grave misgivings.[1]

It had been Milner's fond hope that swarms of British emigrants would come to settle in the new colonies. Conan Doyle even suggested that the Boers be put on reservations to make room for them: "Let them live there as Basutos live in Basutoland, or Indians in Indian territory, or the inhabitants of a protected state in India."[2]

Some Britons did come, but not nearly enough to fulfill Milner's dream of making the Boers a minority. Many of the new colonists, not having the knack of raising crops and livestock on the veld, soon became discouraged and left.

What Milner feared is exactly what happened. Even today, the urban white population, controlling commerce and industry, is predominately Anglo-Saxon; the rural white population, controlling agriculture and the government, is predominately Afrikaner. Milner's failure to change the composition of the white population to assure a predominance of Anglo-Saxons was a bitter disappointment to him, for in his mind this was the prime purpose of all his schemes, the justification of the war itself.

There were few problems in repopulating the towns with whites. Most of the uitlanders had returned to the Rand before the end of the war, and Johannesburg, the largest town in the new colonies, quickly returned to its prewar white population level. Milner even had some success in redressing the imbalance of sexes: he persuaded the British Emigration Association in Britain to form a South African Expansion Committee, and through their efforts some 4,000 women were sent out between 1902 and 1908. He established a Women's Immigration Department in the Transvaal which contributed to the women's transportation costs, received the immigrants at government hostels when they arrived, and undertook to find employment for them until they found husbands.

The hand of Milner was everywhere, and certainly he deserved much credit for his part in revitalising the colonies. But this credit was denied him. To say that he and his good works were unappreciated is to understate the case. Smuts called his administration "the darkest period in the history of the Transvaal"; "Milnerism" became a pejorative term. Since Plato, intellectuals have been puzzled by men's rejection of intellectuals as rulers. Milner provided honest, intelligent, and efficient government, failing to realise that in spite of the lip service paid to these virtues they are really low on any candid list of political desiderata. What people most want is a "voice"; they would rather have the opportunity of expressing their views on all manner of political problems, to make their own decisions, to decide their own fate, than to be given the best solutions, the best government, by the wisest of autocratic rulers. And of all peoples, this was most true of the Boers, now denied all voice in their political affairs.

There was an appointed legislative council in the Transvaal, and in January 1903 Milner invited Botha, De la Rey, and Smuts to serve on it. They refused. The British were still regarded as the enemy, and they would not collaborate with them. Smuts, whose views probably influenced the others, answered for the three of them, telling Milner that they would serve on a legislative body only if it was elected by the people. Botha continued to sit on his stoep and listen sympathetically to the discontented, talk of what he would do, make friends, and solidify his political foundations. Smuts, the intellectual, became Milner's gadfly—a very noisy, persistent, stinging gadfly.

The Boers were not alone in their feelings about Milner. Even the uitlanders turned against him. They had greeted him as their champion, one who would give them the preferential treatment they felt they deserved and exact from the Boers all the penalties of defeat. They were disappointed. Milner was fair, just, and placed administrative efficiency above political expediency. He disliked the Boers, but he saw no purpose in persecuting them; on the contrary, he saw how necessary it was to the well-being of the country that they be helped. The uitlanders, taxed to support their recent enemies (Milner slapped a 10 percent tax on gold mining profits—double that which the republic had imposed) and as completely shut out of the business of running the country as were the Boers, were soon loud in their complaints against Milner and his "imported bureaucracy." They formed the Transvaal Political Association, the avowed purpose of which was to support the government by criticising it. It was not, Milner felt, the kind of support he needed.

Others were also under the impression that with British victory the millennium had arrived. They were quickly and rudely disillusioned. Asiatics, mostly Indians, had been pro-British and supportive during the war; many speeches had been made, some by responsible members of government in London, that led the Indians to believe they would no longer be considered second-class subjects; in particular they anticipated that they would no longer be forced to live in segregated areas and would be allowed freedom to trade wherever they chose. Nothing of the sort happened, and Indian discontent grew.

The Bantu had also helped the British; they had heard the British talk of improving the lot of the natives, and many had believed it. They too had lived in expectation of a better life after the war, but their condition was, in fact, little altered. *The Times History* put the matter succinctly:

The natives had in many instances become insolent, owing to unduly high wages and to the familiarity with which the soldiers had treated them. They expected the Boers to be treated as a conquered race, to whom they would no longer stand in a dependent relation. But they soon discovered that the British conquest, though it might give the black man greater security against oppression and more clearly defined rights, involved no essential alteration in the superior status of the white man, be he Briton or Boer.[3]

The British continued the system of registration, and each Bantu was required to have a pass. They were herded into compounds, put to breaking stones, and doled out to various companies and work projects. At the beginning of the war the Boers had reduced wages to £1 per month; the Bantu expected the British to raise this to at least prewar levels, but in this they were disappointed. Many simply refused to work.

Not even all the Britons whom Milner tried so hard to lure to the new colonies were happy with him, nor was he particularly happy with all of them: one was Emily Hobhouse, who in May 1903 came there to live and to help the Boer people in the difficult work of reconstruction. She founded a school which taught home industries for women and girls at Philippolis, and she travelled through the devastated countryside, writing letters and reports on the sufferings of the Boer families she found on the veld, making herself a constant irritant.

Many South Africans in Natal and Cape Colony, as well as patriots in England, grumbled at the expense of Milner's programs and what they regarded as the coddling of the Boers. The final verse of Kipling's "Piet" spoke for them:

> No more I'll 'ear 'is rifle crack
>   Along the block'ouse fence—
> The beggar's on the peaceful tack,
>   Regardless of expense;
> For countin' what 'e eats an' draws,
>   An' gifts and loans as well,
> 'E's gettin' 'alf the Earth, because
>   'E didn't give us 'Ell!
>   Ah there, Piet! with your brand-new English plough!
>   Your gratis tents an' cattle, an' your most ungrateful frow,
>   You've made the British taxpayer rebuild your country-seat—
>   I've known some pet battalions charge a dam' sight less than Piet.[4]

So in the end Milner satisfied no one. For his part in instigating a destructive, expensive, profitless war he had won acclaim and had been raised to the peerage; for all his splendid efforts under difficult circumstances to put the country right again afterwards he was denounced and vilified.

It was the Chinese, in the end, who brought about Milner's downfall.

In spite of every effort—short of raising wages and improving working conditions—the mines were unable to attract a sufficient number of Bantu labourers. At the very end of the war Milner had appointed Dr. C. L. Sansom to investigate the treatment of native labourers, and the result was a horrifying report of men crowded into compounds with filthy quarters, supplied with food unfit for human consumption, of lamentably inadequate medical treatment and poor hospitals. The mortality rates were enormous. When Milner put pressure on the Randlords to improve conditions—further exasperating them—the mine owners countered by demanding that the government find cheap labour for them. Finally, after much debate, it was decided to make an agreement with the Chinese government for the importation of coolies to work in the mines. The scheme was imaginative, it relieved the labour shortage and the output of the mines more than doubled in two years, but it was unsound for a number of reasons.

With the fantastic mixture of races already in South Africa and the tensions which invariably developed among them, the last thing this corner of the world needed was the introduction of another race. The importation of Chinese coolies, which began in June 1904, was the most bizarre episode in the history of the reconstruction era.

By March 1905 there were 34,355 Chinese in the Transvaal, and by January 1907 their numbers had increased to 53,856. Naturally among so many, a number of outrages occurred, murders and robberies, which somehow seemed more terrifying than the same crimes committed by whites or blacks, especially when made sensational by the press. Those not afraid of the Chinese were afraid for them. Milner unwisely sanctioned flogging as a punishment at the mines, and the cry went up in England that Britain had instituted slavery in South Africa. In Britain, South Africa, and indeed throughout the Empire, the Chinese question created an uproar. Even the Australians indignantly protested, seeing the importation of Chinese into a "white colony" as a dangerous precedent.

The government at home, which had supported Milner, was staggering towards its fall, reeling under the attacks of the Liberals, who were busily fanning the flame of public indignation over the Chinese coolie policy. Milner was obviously a political liability. Abruptly he resigned, and on 2 April 1905 he left Johannesburg for England, not to return until nearly twenty years later when he came back for a visit and contracted the sleeping sickness that killed him. He had failed in his chief aim: British paramountcy was not established, Afrikaner culture and the Afrikaans language were not swamped by a tide of British culture, and Britons had not emigrated to South Africa in sufficient numbers to provide an Anglo-Saxon majority; in fact, the Afrikaners' pride in themselves as a separate people was intensified. Afrikaner culture flourished as never before: in 1902 the first Afrikaans dictionary was published and Afrikaans literature began to replace Dutch.

In January 1906 the general elections in Britain swept Campbell-Bannerman's Liberal Party into power with a record majority, one of the main issues being the Chinese in South Africa. Throughout the country during the electioneering, hoardings featured lurid pictures of Chinese being tortured, and political meetings were often enlivened by men parading through the streets dressed as Chinese coolies in chains. The following March there was a motion in the House of Commons for a vote of censure on Milner. It was during the debate on this issue that the young under-secretary at the Colonial Office, Winston Churchill, used the expression for which he was much ridiculed for many years: to describe the conditions under which the Chinese in South Africa laboured as slavery, he said, was a "terminological inexactitude." In the end, although the treatment of the Chinese was condemned, Milner was not censured by name; still, he had suffered a slap in the face.

Paul Kruger died in Clarens, Switzerland, on 14 July 1904; his body was returned to the Transvaal, and his funeral on 16 December (Dingaan's Day) was a large public affair. The funeral and the political orations in connection with it raised the Boers' nationalistic feelings to a high pitch. The following month a Boer political party, Het Volk, was formed. In January 1906 the Liberals came to power in England, as Kitchener had predicted they would, and less than one year later, on 6 December 1906, to the intense indignation of all Unionists, a Transvaal Constitution was promulgated by Letters Patent; a general election was held the following February. Balfour denounced this granting of self-government to the Transvaal as "the most reckless experiment ever tried in the development of a great colonial policy." Contrary to all expectations and hopes in London—Churchill had assured the King that "a clear racial Boer majority is outside the bounds of possibility"—Het Volk obtained a majority of five in a legislative assembly of sixty-nine, and Louis Botha became prime minister. Behind him in serried ranks stood the old Boer generals and commandants to take up the ministerial posts. Less than five years after the war the Boers, although now part of the British Empire, were again self-governing, and they have remained so. Britain, after winning a long and costly war in which 21,942 of her soldiers gave their lives to establish British paramountcy in South Africa, had now simply abandoned the whole idea.

Botha wasted no time in taking up the reins of power and in replacing British officials with Afrikaners. In 1907 he started to repatriate the Chinese, and the last to go left in 1910, taking their dead with them, the ashes neatly packaged in little tea boxes.

One residue of the war left by the British still flourishes. With the fodder they imported from South America during the war came a pungent-smelling, noxious weed with a small flower (*Althermarathera achyrantha*) which South Africans call "khaki weed." In spite of strenuous efforts to eradicate it, the weed still crops up in the Afrikaners' mealie fields.

In 1907 the Orange River Colony was also given a constitution and self-government. Abraham Fischer became prime minister, with De Wet and Hertzog in his cabinet. Steyn's health never recovered from his exertions during the war. He spent two and a half years in Europe under a doctor's care, returning to South Africa in 1905 and retiring to his farm. Although he retained his interest in politics—he neither forgot nor forgave—he was never again able to assume active leadership. He died in 1916, still irreconcilable. His wife, Tibbie, had donned a black dress after Vereeniging and for forty years continued to wear only black.

On 12 October 1908—the ninth anniversary of the start of the war —political leaders from all four colonies met in Durban to consider a merger. After a series of such meetings an agreement was reached, and on 31 May 1910—exactly eight years after the signing of the peace of Vereeniging—the Union of South Africa came into being. Louis Botha was the first premier, and in his cabinet sat Smuts, Hertzog, and other Boer heroes; F. W. Reitz was elected president of the Senate. The Boers now controlled not only the Transvaal and Orange River Colony but Natal and Cape Colony as well. There were squabbles, for, as De la Rey said, "Now that we no longer have to fight Kaffirs or English, we are bound to quarrel among ourselves—it is the way of the Boer." In 1914, when Botha carried South Africa into the war on the side of Britain, quarrels flared into an open revolt led by De Wet, Kemp, and Manie Maritz.

De la Rey too might have been planning to join the rebels, but no one knows, for he was killed in Johannesburg on the eve of the rebellion in a bizarre accident. Riding with Christiaan Beyers, then commandant-general, on the night of 15 September 1914, their Daimler was driven through a police roadblock set up to intercept a band of desperados; the police fired, and De la Rey slumped over dead in his seat. Had he lived and lent his enormous prestige to the rebel cause there might have been a civil war on a grand scale. It was bad enough as it was. Boers again seized their rifles, mounted their horses, and formed commandos, about 13,000 on the rebel side against 30,000 government troops, two-thirds of whom were Afrikaners; Boer against Boer.

When some government scouts rode into a village and an old woman called out in Afrikaans, "Where are the *verdoem* English?" a young Boer called out, "We *are* the *verdoem* English, old vrow!"

In less than three months it was over. Maritz and Kemp took their forces over the border to join the Germans in Southwest Africa, and De Wet and his commando were brought to earth by Coen Brits, who pursued them with a fleet of motor cars. It marked the end to the picturesque horse commando system. Government forces suffered 374 casualties, the rebels 540. De Wet was tried and sentenced to serve six years in prison and pay a fine of £2,000. Kemp too finally surrendered and was sentenced to seven years' imprisonment. None served his full sentence. De Wet stayed in gaol only one year; two years after the rebellion all were freed. Lesser participants were merely banned from holding public offices for ten years. Only one man, Joseph Johannes ("Jappie") Fourie, was shot for treason, and this execution shocked many people, for Jappie Fourie had been a minor hero of the Anglo-Boer War.

The 1914 Rebellion was the last attempt of the Afrikaners to win complete independence by violence rather than negotiation, by their commandos rather than their cunning; never again would they take up their rifles in revolt. As the wiser among them had already discovered, they did not need to. Not only were they already self-governing; their leaders were becoming world figures. Jan Smuts was soon sitting on Lloyd George's War Cabinet, and Louis Botha was to sit side by side with

Milner (who became secretary for war) at the peace conference at Versailles.

Although in World War II there was a sizable pro-German faction in the Union of South Africa, Smuts kept the country within the Empire for one more war. Then, in October 1960, with Britain's acquiescence, a referendum was held to decide whether or not South Africa should become a republic. The vote was close, but the republicans won (850,458 versus 775,878, a difference of only 74,580), and on 31 May 1961—exactly fifty-nine years after Vereeniging—the Republic of South Africa was founded with C. R. Swart as its first president. In October of that same year South Africa withdrew its application for membership in the British Commonwealth and the last ties with Britain were finally and completely severed.

The wildest, most improbable political dreams of Kruger's and Steyn's Boers—to be free of British interference and to make all South Africa a Boer republic—became reality for their children and grandchildren.

GLOSSARY

bergen—mountain
donga—ravine
dorp—hamlet, small town
drift—ford
fontein—spring
hoek—corner or secluded valley
impi—a Zulu "regiment"
kappie—sunbonnet
kloof—mountain pass or gully
kop—isolated hill
kopje—small hill
krysraad—council of war
laager—*(n.)* camp, often one formed for defence; *(v.)* to form a camp, to make camp
laagte—valley, dale
landdrost—magistrate
mealie(s)—maize
nek—neck, applied to depression between two hills
predikant—preacher
raadzaal—legislative building
rand—highland or ridge
spruit—creek
uitlander—foreigner
veld or veldt—grassland
vierkleur—"four colour": used for the flag of the Orange Free State and the South African Republic (Transvaal)
vlei—swamp
voetgangers—men on foot
volksraad—parliament of a Boer republic
voortrekker—pioneer
vrow—woman
Zarps—Transvaal police, from Z.A.R.P. *(Zuid-Afrikaansche Repupliek Politie)*

NOTES

Only the shortened form of the reference is given here; a complete description of the works cited is given in the bibliography.

Chapter 1. The Birth of a People

1. Quoted in Rosenthal, *Stars and Stripes in Africa*, p. 86.
2. Reitz, *No Outspan*, p. 21.

Chapter 2. Voortrekkers and Their Republics

1. Haggard, *The Last Boer War*, p. 49.

Chapter 3. The First Anglo-Boer War

1. Quoted in Carter, *A Narrative of the Boer War*, p. 127.
2. Quoted in Fitzpatrick, *The Transvaal from Within*, p. 44n. This book, written by an uitlander, has been called the *Uncle Tom's Cabin* of the First Anglo-Boer War.
3. Doyle, *The Great Boer War*, 3rd impression, pp. 20, 22.
4. Carter, *A Narrative of the Boer War*, pp. 492f.
5. *Ibid.*, p. 501.

Chapter 4. The Jameson Raid

1. Warner, *The Geography of British South Africa*, pp. 177f.
2. Quoted in Nutting, *Scramble for Africa*, p. 340.
3. Quoted in Meintjes, *President Steyn*, p. 61.

Chapter 5. Moving Towards War

1. Words spoken to Graham Bower, imperial secretary at the Cape. Quoted in Nutting, *Scramble for Africa*, p. 299.
2. Quoted in Symons, *Buller's Campaigns*, p. 55.
3. *The Times History*, V. 1, p. 183.

Chapter 6. Eve of War

1. All of the quotations here are taken from the British Government Blue Book, Cd 1792.
2. *The Times History*, V. 1, p. 13.
3. Blue Book, Cd 1792, p. 44.
4. Mahan, *The Story of the War in South Africa*, pp. 203f.
5. Belmont, *Adventures and Letters of Richard Harding Davis*, p. 289.

6. Steevens, *From Cape Town to Ladysmith*, p. 21.
7. Quoted in Nutting, *Scramble for Africa*, p. 414.
8. *Ibid.*, p. 423.

Chapter 7. War Begins

1. Quoted in May, *The Music of the Guns*, pp. 6f.
2. *Ibid.*, p. 17.
3. Quoted in Jones, *Lloyd George*, p. 26.
4. Blunt, *My Diaries.*
5. Sinclair-Stevenson, *The Gordon Highlanders*, p. 74.
6. Quoted in Cornwallis-West, *Edwardian Hey-Days.*
7. Mackinnon, *The Journal of the C.I.V. in South Africa*, pp. 3f.
8. "Pearson's Illustrated War News," 25 November 1899.
9. *Morning Post*, 27 November 1899.
10. Souza, *No Charge for Delivery*, p. 160.
11. Reitz, *Commando*, p. 24.
12. *Ibid.*, p. 26.
13. Schikkerling, *Commando Courageous*, p. 10.

Chapter 8. Talana: The First Battle

1. Quoted in *The Times History*, V. 2, pp. 164f.
2. *Ibid.*, pp. 168f.

Chapter 9. Elandslaagte

1. Sampson and Hamilton, *Anti-Commando*, p. 117.
2. Quoted in *The Times History*, V. 2, p. 193*n.*
3. Quoted in Beck, *History of South Africa and the Boer-British War*, pp. 403f.
4. Reitz, *Commando*, p. 34.
5. Steevens, *From Capetown to Ladysmith*, p. 61.
6. Souza, *No Charge for Delivery*, p. 116.
7. Hobson, *The War in South Africa*, p. 222.
8. Pearse, *Four Months Besieged*, p. 75.

Chapter 10. The Battle of Ladysmith

1. Sampson and Hamilton, *Anti-Commando*, p. 157.
2. Reitz, *Commando*, pp. 32f.
3. De Wet, *Three Years War*, p. 25.
4. Steevens, *From Capetown to Ladysmith*, pp. 75f.
5. *Ibid.*, p. 80.

Chapter 11. Buller

1. Jerrold, *Sir Redvers Buller, V.C.*, p. 234.
2. Churchill, *A Roving Commission*, p. 234.
3. Quoted in Pemberton, *Battles of the Boer War*, p. 124.
4. Atkins, *The Relief of Ladysmith*, pp. 30f.
5. *The Times History*, V. 2, p. 285.
6. *The Letters of Queen Victoria*, 3rd series, V. 3, p. 416.

Chapter 12. Methuen

1. Quoted in Meintjes, *Sword in the Sand*, p. 39.
2. Quoted in *The Times History*, V. 2, p. 336.
3. Jeans, *Naval Brigades in the South African War*, p. 22.
4. Quoted in Milne, *The Epistles of Atkins*, p. 73.
5. Quoted in Wilson, *With the Flag to Pretoria*, V. 1, p. 164.
6. Souza, *No Charge for Delivery*, p. 187.
7. *Black and White Budget*, 14 April 1900.
8. Wilson, *With the Flag to Pretoria*, V. 1, p. 166.

Chapter 13. Magersfontein

1. Quoted in Sutherland, *The Argyll and Sutherland Highlanders*, p. 61.
2. Quoted in Sinclair-Stevenson, *The Gordon Highlanders*, p. 76.
3. Wilson, *With the Flag to Pretoria*, V. 1, p. 193.
4. Barnes, *The Great War Trek*, pp. 41f.
5. Doyle, *The Great Boer War*, 3rd impression, p. 161.
6. Badenhorst, *Tant' Alie of Transvaal*, p. 95.

Chapter 14. Stormberg Junction

1. Gatacre, *General Gatacre*, p. 56.
2. Steevens, *From Capetown to Ladysmith*, p. 10.
3. Quoted in Meintjes, *Stormberg*, p. 107.
4. *The Official History* gives the final figure as 135 killed and wounded and 571 missing.
5. Quoted in Gatacre, *General Gatacre*, pp. 235f.

Chapter 15. Before Colenso

1. Atkins, *The Relief of Ladysmith*, p. 118.
2. Butler, *Sir Redvers Buller*, p. 81.
3. Quoted in Pemberton, *Battles of the Boer War*, p. 162.
4. Atkins, *The Relief of Ladysmith*, p. 128.
5. Quoted in Meintjes, *General Louis Botha*, p. 44.
6. Quoted in Barnard, "General Botha at the Battle of Colenso," *Military History Journal*, V. 2, No. 1, June 1971.

Chapter 16. Colenso

1. Blue Book, Cd 1793, p. 341.
2. Gough, *Soldiering On*, p. 70.
3. Wilson, *With the Flag to Pretoria*, V. 1, p. 97.
4. Quoted in Symons, *Buller's Campaigns*, p. 165.
5. Quoted in Bryant, *Jackets of Green*, p. 185n.
6. Quoted in Atkins, *The Relief of Ladysmith*, p. 174.
7. Quoted in Hamilton, *Listening to the Drums*, p. 32.
8. Blue Book, Cd 1792, pp. 341f.
9. Dickson, *The Biograph in Battle*, p. 83.
10. *Black and White Budget*, 10 March 1900, 21 April 1900.
11. Quoted in Butler, *Sir Redvers Buller*, p. 71.
12. Quoted in *The Times History*, V. 2, p. 461.

13. Quoted in Pemberton, *Battles of the Boer War*, pp. 147f.

14. *Ibid.*, p. 134*n*.

Chapter 17. Black Week

1. Wilson, *With the Flag to Pretoria*, V. 1, pp. 105f.

2. Maurice, *The Life of General Lord Rawlinson of Trent*, p. 51.

3. Doyle, *The Great Boer War*, 3rd impression, p. 197.

4. *The Times History*, V. 3, p. 3.

5. Rice, *Letters and Friendships of Sir Cecil Spring Rice*, V. 1, pp. 303f.

6. New York *Journal*, 7 January 1900.

7. *Black and White Budget*, 30 December 1899.

8. Quoted in Trevelyan, *Grey of Fallodon*, p. 77. Letter is dated 17 October 1899.

9. Blunt, *My Diaries*, V. 1, p. 341.

10. Webb, *Our Partnership*, ed. B. Drake and M. I. Cole (New York, 1948).

11. Churchill, *Winston S. Churchill*, V. 2, p. 7.

12. Rice, *Letters and Friendships of Sir Cecil Spring Rice*, pp. 303f. Letter is dated 20 December 1899.

13. Quoted in Hamilton, *The Happy Warrior*, p. 145.

14. Quoted in James, *Lord Roberts*, pp. 262f.

15. Letter from Lord Lansdowne to Lady Aileen Roberts, 11 May 1921. Quoted in James, *Lord Roberts*, p. 266.

Chapter 18. Lord Roberts and Lord Kitchener

1. The Amery quotation is from James, *Lord Roberts*, p. v; the Herbert quotation is from *The Times History*, V. 3, p. 332.

2. Quoted in *The Letters of Queen Victoria*, 3rd series, V. 3, p. 441*n*.

3. Younghusband, *A Soldier's Memories*, pp. 228f.

Chapter 19. Tabanyama: Prelude to Spion Kop

1. Churchill, *Winston S. Churchill*, V. 1, Pt. 2, p. 1059.

2. *The Times History*, V. 3, p. 221.

3. Quoted in Wilson, *With the Flag to Pretoria*, V. 1, p. 248.

4. Quoted in Symons, *Buller's Campaigns*, p. 184.

5. Quoted in Williams, *The Life of General Sir Charles Warren*, p. 251.

6. Burne, *With the Naval Brigade in Natal*, p. 3.

7. Quoted in Dundonald, *My Army Life*, p. 125*n*.

8. *Report of the Royal Commission on the War in South Africa*. Buller's remarks quoted in Symons, *Buller's Campaigns*, p. 202.

9. Barnard, *Military History Journal*, V. 2, No. 1, June 1971.

10. Churchill, written 23 January 1900 and published in *Morning Post*, 17 February 1900.

11. Quoted in Symons, *Buller's Campaigns*, p. 207.

Chapter 20. Spion Kop

1. *The Times History*, V. 3, p. 239.

2. Quoted in Symons, *Buller's Campaigns*, p. 211.

3. Hiley and Hassell, *The Mobile Boer*, p. 120.

4. Reitz, *Commando*, pp. 73f.

5. Quoted in Wilson, *With the Flag to Pretoria*, V. 1. p. 296.

6. Churchill, written 23 January 1900 and published in *Morning Post*, 17 February 1900.

7. Letter from Benjamin Walker to his father, J. B. M. Walker. Unpublished.

8. Reitz, *Commando*, pp. 76f.

9. Quoted in Symons, *Buller's Campaigns*, p. 226.

10. *The Times History*, V. 3, pp. 278f.

11. *Ibid.*, p. 282.

12. Pearse, *Four Months Besieged*, p. 215.

13. Reitz, *Commando*, p. 77.

14. *The Times History*, V. 3, p. 298.

Chapter 21. After Spion Kop: Vaal Krantz

1. Bernard, *Military History Journal*, V. 2, No. 1, June 1971.

2. Quoted in Ramsford, *The Battle of Spion Kop*, p. 8.

3. *Standard and Diggers News*, 29 January 1900.

4. Souza, *No Charge for Delivery*, p. 174.

5. Quoted in Bernard, *Military History Journal*, V. 2, No. 1, June 1971, p. 6.

6. Quoted in Wilson, *With the Flag to Pretoria*, V. 1, p. 304.

7. *New York Times*, 9 November 1899.

8. *The Nursing Record and Hospital World*, 18 November 1899.

9. Quoted in Symons, *Buller's Campaigns*, p. 276.

10. Quoted in Butler, *Sir Redvers Buller*, pp. 77f.

11. Quoted in *The Times History*, V. 3, p. 305n. and Blue Book, Cd 968, p. 17. This is from Buller's covering note on Warren's dispatch.

12. Quoted in *Letters of Queen Victoria*, 3rd series, V. 3, p. 533n.

13. Quoted in Mahan, *The Story of the War in South Africa 1899–1900*, p. 260.

14. Churchill, *Frontiers and Wars*, p. 437.

15. *The Times History*, V. 3, p. 317.

16. Quoted in Souza, *No Charge for Delivery*, p. 6.

17. *The Times History*, V. 3, p. 323.

18. *Ibid.*, pp. 323f.

Chapter 22. The Great Flank March

1. "M.I.," *Rudyard Kipling's Verse*, p. 538.

2. De Wet, *Three Years War*, p. 48.

Chapter 23. The Siege of Kimberley

1. Ashe, *Besieged by the Boers*, p. 34.

2. Unpublished diary of Winifred Heberdon.

3. Blue Book, Cd 1790, V. 2, p. 119.

4. Quoted in O'Meara, *Kekewich in Kimberley*, p. 115.

5. *Ibid.*, p. 112.

6. Reproduced in Wilson, *With the Flag to Pretoria*, V. 2, p. 388.

7. *Daily Mail*, 17 February 1900.

Chapter 24. Paardeberg

1. *The Times History*, V. 3, p. 424.
2. Quoted in Magnus, *Kitchener*, p. 167.
3. *The Times History*, V. 3, p. 438.
4. Quoted in Wilson, *With the Flag to Pretoria*, V. 2, p. 411.
5. *The Times History*, V. 3, p. 454.
6. Quoted in Meintjes, *De la Rey*, pp. 156f.
7. Quoted in Kruger, *Good-bye Dolly Gray*, pp. 241f.
8. De Wet, *Three Years War*, p. 63.
9. Blue Book, Cd 453, p. 23.
10. Reported by a Mr. Hands in Wilson, *With the Flag to Pretoria*, V. 2, p. 430.
11. Maxse, *Seymour Vandeleur*, p. 264.
12. Wilson, *With the Flag to Pretoria*, V. 2, p. 433.
13. O'Meara, *Kekewich in Kimberley*, p. 345.
14. Battersby, *In the Web of War*, p. 73.
15. U.S. War Department, *Reports on Military Operations in South Africa and China*, p. 37.
16. Battersby, *In the Web of War*, p. 65.
17. Anonymous, *A Subaltern's Letters to His Wife*, p. 50.
18. Barnes, *The Great War Trek*, pp. 164f.
19. *South African Medical Journal*, V. 5, No. 39, October 1971.
20. Quoted in Leigh, *Vereeniging*, p. 43.
21. Quoted in Meintjes, *Sword in the Sand*, pp. 72f. Letter dated 2 March 1900.
22. Quoted in Meintjes, *De la Rey*, p. 157.
23. Quoted in James, *Lord Roberts*, p. 295.
24. *The Times History*, V. 3, p. 457.

Chapter 25. The Siege of Ladysmith

1. *The Times History*, V. 3, p. 150.
2. Quoted in Butler, *Sir William Butler*, p. 416.
3. Davis, *With Both Armies in South Africa*, p. 26.
4. Quoted in Symons, *Buller's Campaigns*, p. 169.
5. Souza, *No Charge for Delivery*, pp. 74f.
6. *Ibid.*, p. 184.
7. Quoted in Furneaux, *News of War*, p. 193.
8. Quoted in May, *Music of the Guns*, p. 23.
9. *Ibid.*, p. 58.
10. Steevens, *From Capetown to Ladysmith*, pp. 122f., 125.
11. Quoted in May, *Music of the Guns*, p. 60.
12. Unpublished letter in possession of Buller Willis.
13. Diary of Isabella Craw.
14. Quoted in Maurice, *The Life of General Lord Rawlinson*, pp. 47f.
15. Diary of Isabella Craw.
16. Unpublished letter in possession of Buller Willis.
17. Steevens, *From Capetown to Ladysmith*, p. 135.
18. Pearse, *Four Months Besieged*, p. 46.
19. Maurice, *The Life of General Lord Rawlinson*, p. 48.
20. Quoted in Furneaux, *News of War*, p. 201.

21. Davis, *With Both Armies in South Africa,* p. 37.
22. Pearse, *Four Months Besieged,* p. 226.
23. Quoted in May, *Music of the Guns,* pp. 56f.
24. Quoted in *Rifle Brigade Chronical,* 1958, pp. 63–65.
25. *Black and White Budget,* 14 April 1900.
26. Pienaar, *With Steyn and De Wet,* p. 28.
27. Doyle, *The Great Boer War,* 3rd impression, p. 230.
28. Hamilton, *Listening for the Drums,* p. 238.
29. Gough, *Soldiering On,* p. 72.
30. Quoted in Hamilton, *The Happy Warrior,* pp. 177f.
31. *The Times History,* V. 3, p. 515.
32. *Ibid.,* p. 529.
33. Quoted in Davis, *Adventures and Letters of Richard Harding Davis,* p. 273.
34. Reitz, *Commando,* p. 90.
35. Hiley and Hassell, *The Mobile Boer,* p. 147.
36. Quoted in Beck, *History of South Africa and the Boer-British War,* p. 504.
37. Quoted in Churchill, *Winston S. Churchill,* V. 1, Pt. 2, p. 1153.
38. Printed sheet in Jackdaw, No. 68.
39. *Black and White Budget,* 9 June 1900.
40. Gaskell, *With Lord Methuen in South Africa,* pp. 23f.
41. Churchill, *Frontiers and Wars,* pp. 492f.
42. Diary of Isabella Craw.
43. Letter reproduced in facsimile in Butler, *Sir Redvers Buller,* opposite p. 84.

Chapter 26. Bloemfontein

1. De Wet, *Three Years War,* p. 69.
2. Sampson and Hamilton, *Anti-Commando,* p. 158.
3. Anonymous, *A Subaltern's Letters to His Wife,* p. 226.
4. *Ibid.,* p. 7.
5. Quoted in Doyle, *The Great Boer War,* 3rd impression, pp. 366f.
6. Quoted in *The Letters of Queen Victoria,* 3rd series, V. 3, pp. 511f.
7. Gaskell, *With Lord Methuen in South Africa,* p. 54.
8. Trans. by Adv. G. E. Steyn in letter to the author.
9. Gaskell, *With Lord Methuen in South Africa,* pp. 31f, 33.
10. Schikkerling, *Commando Courageous,* p. 178.
11. Blue Book, Cd 457, V. 1.
12. Blue Book, Cd 1790, V. 1.
13. Doyle, *The Great Boer War,* 3rd impression, p. 375.
14. Atkins, *The Relief of Ladysmith,* p. 32.
15. Churchill, *Frontiers and Wars,* p. 418.
16. "The Parting of the Columns," *Rudyard Kipling's Verse.*
17. Blue Book, Cd 1790, V. 1.
18. Blue Book, Cd 454.
19. Blue Book, Cd 1789.
20. *Black and White Budget,* 18 August 1900.
21. *Ibid.,* 15 September 1900.
22. Quoted in Martin, *The Concentration Camps,* p. 27.
23. Written 29 May and published in *The Times* on 29 June 1900.
24. *Cape Times,* 23 June 1900, and *The Times,* 20 July 1900.

25. Quoted in Wilson, *With the Flag to Pretoria*, V. 2, p. 657.

26. Blue Book, Cd 455.

27. This and subsequent quotations, except where noted, are from Blue Book, Cd 454.

28. Quoted in *The Letters of Queen Victoria*, 3rd series, V. 3, p. 529.

29. Quoted in Arthur, *General Sir John Maxwell*, p. 87.

30. Milner, *My Picture Gallery*, p. 180.

Chapter 27. Decisions at Kroonstad.

1. Miller, *A Captain of the Gordons*, p. 38.

2. Jackson, *A Soldier's Diary.*

3. De Wet, *Three Years War,* p. 78.

4. Steyn's memoirs, trans. for the author by Adv. G. E. Steyn.

5. Seiner, Franks, *Esinnerungen einer Burenkampfers.* Quoted in *The Times History*, V. 3, p. 73*n.*

6. Included in *Reports on Military Operations in South Africa and China* (U.S. War Department), p. 123.

7. Quoted in May, *Music of the Guns*, pp. 30f. and 48.

8. Schikkerling, *Commando Courageous,* p. 27.

9. Hiley and Hassell, *The Mobile Boer*, p. 159.

10. Lyttelton, *Eighty Years*, p. 206.

Chapter 28. The Boer Revival

1. Quoted in Carrington, *Rudyard Kipling*, p. 309.

2. De Wet, *Three Years War*, pp. 89f.

3. *Black and White Budget*, 26 May 1900.

4. Quoted in Smithers, *The Man Who Disobeyed*, p. 69.

5. De Wet, *Three Years War*, pp. 104f.

Chapter 29. On the March to Pretoria

1. Quoted in James, *Lord Roberts*, p. 316.

2. Included in *Reports on Military Operations in South Africa and China* (U.S. War Department), p. 70.

3. Quoted in James, *Lord Roberts*, p. 317*n.*

4. *The Times History*, V. 4, p. 85.

5. Churchill, *Frontiers and Wars*, p. 544.

6. *The Times History*, V. 4, p. 152.

7. Battersby, *In the Web of War*, p. 211.

Chapter 30. Mafeking

1. Gardner, *Mafeking*, p. 54.

2. "The Seer," in *Club Life*, 23 May 1900.

3. *Black and White Budget*, 23 June 1900.

4. Beck, *History of South Africa and the Boer-British War*, p. 433.

5. *Black and White Budget*, 23 June 1900.

6. Quoted in Hillcourt and Lady Baden-Powell, *Baden-Powell*, p. 59.

7. Milner, *My Picture Gallery*, pp. 125f.

8. Gardner, *Mafeking*, p. 230.

9. Neilly, *Besieged with B-P*, p. 91.

10. Plaatje, *The Diary of Sol T. Plaatje*, pp. 35f. Entry for 8 December 1899.

11. *Black and White Budget*, 21 April 1900.

12. Lady Sarah Wilson, *South African Memories*, p. 151. Subsequent quotations of Lady Sarah in this chapter are from this book.

13. Souza, *No Charge for Delivery*, pp. 164f.

14. *Ibid.*, p. 165.

15. Quoted in Wilson, *With the Flag to Pretoria*, V. 2, p. 602.

16. Quoted in Gardner, *Mafeking*, p. 109.

17. Souza, *No Charge for Delivery*, p. 72.

18. Plaatje, *The Diary of Sol T. Plaatje*, p. 77. Entry for 20 January 1900.

19. Neilly, *Besieged with B-P*, pp. 227–330.

20. Plaatje, *The Diary of Sol T. Plaatje*, p. 122. Entry for 12 March 1900.

21. Quoted in Neilly, *Besieged with B-P.*

22. *Ibid.*, p. 98.

23. Souza, *No Charge for Delivery*, p. 26.

24. Barnes, *The Great War Trek*, pp. 350f.

25. Quoted in Wilson, *With the Flag to Pretoria*, V. 2, pp. 619f.

26. *Ibid.*, p. 626.

Chapter 31. Pretoria

1. Archibald, *Blue Shirt and Khaki.*

2. Quoted in Smuts, *Jan Christian Smuts*, pp. 54f.

3. Archibald, *Blue Shirt and Khaki.*

4. Batts, *Pretoria from Within During the War*, p. 164.

5. Reitz, *Commando*, p. 109.

6. Quoted in Smuts, *Jan Christian Smuts*, p. 56.

7. Included in *Reports on Military Operations in South Africa and China* (U.S. War Department), p. 220.

8. Churchill, *Frontiers and Wars*, p. 555.

9. Quoted in Meintjes, *General Louis Botha*, p. 69.

10. Battersby, *In the Web of War*, p. 222.

11. Private correspondence. Maria Bosman to author, 30 November 1971.

12. Batts, *Pretoria from Within During the War*, p. 177.

13. *Ibid.*, p. 192.

14. Sergeant Wade's letter was dated 18 December 1899 and was printed in *Black and White Budget*, 2 June 1900.

15. Wilson, *With the Flag to Pretoria*, V. 2, p. 655.

16. Souza, *No Charge for Delivery*, pp. 42f.

17. Quoted in Smuts, *Jan Christian Smuts*, pp. 57f.

18. Quoted in May, *Music of the Guns*, p. 90.

19. Brandt, *The Petticoat Commando*, p. 97.

20. Quoted in James, *Lord Roberts*, p. 314.

21. Quoted in Meintjes, *General Louis Botha*, p. 75.

Chapter 32. After Pretoria: Roodewal and Brandwater Basin

1. De Wet, *Three Years War*, p. 135.

2. *Ibid.*

3. Pienaar, *With Steyn and De Wet*, p. 107.

4. *Morning Post*, 25 July 1900.

5. Gaskell, *With Lord Methuen in South Africa*, p. 115.

6. *Ibid.*, p. 116.

7. De Wet, *Three Years War*, pp. 137f.

8. Hamilton, *Listening for the Drums*, p. 240.

9. *Ibid.*, p. 249.

10. Wilson, *After Pretoria*, V. 1., pp. 23f.

11. Quoted in Doyle, *The Great Boer War*, 3rd impression, p. 480.

12. Unpublished.

13. De Wet, *Three Years War*, p. 165.

Chapter 33. Advance to Komatipoort

1. De Wet, *Three Years War*, p. 187.

2. *The Times History*, V. 4, p. 452.

3. Schikkerling, *Commando Courageous*, p. 51.

4. Quoted in Bryant, *Jackets of Green*, p. 198.

5. Schikkerling, *Commando Courageous*, p. 88.

6. Quoted in Wilson, *After Pretoria*, V. 1, p. 140.

7. Included in *Reports on Military Operations in South Africa and China* (U.S. War Department), p. 259.

Chapter 34. The End of the Second Act

1. Quoted in Worsfold, *Lord Milner's Work in South Africa*, p. 322.

2. *Black and White Budget*, 26 September 1900.

3. Churchill, *Winston S. Churchill*, p. 1210n.

4. *Hansard*, 25 July 1900. Parliamentary Debates, 4th series, LXXXVI.

5. *Cornish Times*, 7 July 1900. Subsequent quotations describing this meeting are from the same source.

6. Birmingham *Daily Mail*, 19 December 1901.

7. *Yorkshire Post*, 9 March 1900.

8. See Kruger, *Good-bye Dolly Gray*, pp. 374f.

9. *Black and White Budget*, 8 December 1900.

10. Miller, *A Captain in the Gordons*, p. 115.

11. Younghusband, *A Soldier's Memories*, p. 184.

Chapter 35. Commandos in Cape Colony

1. Quoted in Worsfold, *Lord Milner's Work in South Africa*, p. 459.

2. Reprinted in *Morning Leader*, 17 September 1901.

3. Wilson, *After Pretoria*, V. 1, p. 494.

4. Doyle, *The Great Boer War*, final edition, pp. 467f.

5. Wilson, *After Pretoria*, p. 704.

6. Quoted in Meintjes, *Sword in the Sand*, p. 157.

7. *Ibid.*, p. 165.

8. *Ibid.*, p. 171.

9. *Ibid.*, pp. 177f.

10. *Ibid.*, p. 187.

11. Johannesburg *Star*, 2 June 1898.

Chapter 36. Smuts's Invasion of the Cape

1. Reitz, *Commando,* p. 169.
2. *Ibid.,* p. 209.
3. *Ibid.,* p. 219.
4. De Wet, *Three Years War,* p. 309.
5. Quoted in *ibid.,* p. 315.
6. *Ibid.,* p. 316
7. Doyle, *The Great Boer War,* final edition, pp. 661f.
8. Reitz, *Commando,* pp. 223f.
9. *Ibid.,* p. 231.
10. *Ibid.,* p. 278.
11. Quoted in Smuts, *Jan Christian Smuts,* p. 78.
12. *Ibid.,* p. 79.
13. *The Times History,* V. 5, p. 131.

Chapter 37. Fighting the Guerrillas

1. Quoted in Anderson, *Heroes of South Africa.*
2. Fuller, *The Last Gentlemen's War,* pp. 111f.
3. *Ibid.,* p. 114.
4. *Rudyard Kipling's Verse,* p. 530.
5. Quoted in private correspondence from George Aschman.
6. Miller, *A Captain in the Gordons,* p. 57.
7. Quoted in Popham, *The Somerset Light Infantry,* p. 94.
8. Miller, *A Captain in the Gordons,* p. 107. Letter is dated 13 September 1901.
9. May. *Music of the Guns,* p. 158.
10. Quoted in Smuts. *Jan Christian Smuts,* p. 68.
11. Quoted in Worsfold, *Lord Milner's Work in South Africa,* pp. 467f.
12. *Ibid.,* pp. 437f.
13. Sampson and Hamilton, *Anti-Commando,* p. 27.
14. Doyle, *The Great Boer War,* final edition, p. 525.
15. Quoted in Worsfold, *Lord Milner's Work in South Africa,* p. 454.
16. Sampson and Hamilton, *Anti-Commando,* p. 36.
17. Quoted in Parritt, *The Intelligencers,* p. 197.
18. Doyle, *The Great Boer War,* final edition, p. 667.
19. Miller, *A Captain in the Gordons,* pp. 130f. Letter of 25 April 1902.
20. Schikkerling, *Commando Courageous,* p. 179.
21. Sampson and Hamilton, *Anti-Commando,* pp. 163, 116.
22. *Ibid.,* pp. 166f.
23. De Wet, *Three Years War,* p. 342.

Chapter 38. Soldiering on the Veld

1. Butler, *Sir William Butler,* p. 22.
2. [James, H.L.] "The Intelligence Officer," *On the Heels of De Wet,* p. 46.
3. Miller, *A Captain in the Gordons,* p. 102. Letter of 5 August 1901.
4. De Wet, *Three Years War,* p. 112n.
5. Quoted in Howland, *The Chase of De Wet,* p. 110.
6. Quoted in Meintjes, *De la Rey,* pp. 179f.

7. Jackson, *A Soldier's Diary.*
8. Phillips, *With Rimington.*
9. Sarah Raal, *Met die Boere in die Veld.* Quotation trans. by Maria Bosman.
10. Miller, *A Captain of the Gordons,* pp. 103f. Letter of 5 August 1901.
11. Younghusband, *A Soldier's Memories,* pp. 181, 184.
12. Quoted in Meintjes, *De la Rey,* p. 233.
13. *Black and White Budget,* 16 March 1901.
14. Quoted in Wilson, *After Pretoria,* V. 2, p. 190.
15. [James, H.L.] "The Intelligence Officer," *On the Heels of De Wet.*
16. Quoted in Pemberton, *Battles of the Boer War,* p. 170.
17. *The Times History,* V. 2, p. 34.
18. Younghusband, *A Soldier's Memories,* pp. 187f.
19. *Rudyard Kipling's Verse,* p. 548.
20. Anonymous, "A South African Trip," *Club Life,* 4 May 1901. Quoted in Price, *An Imperial War and the British Working Class,* pp. 229f.

Chapter 39. Guerrilla Life

1. Schikkerling, *Commando Courageous,* p. 326.
2. *Ibid.,* p. 285.
3. *Ibid.,* p. 250.
4. [James, H.L.] "The Intelligence Officer," *On the Heels of De Wet,* pp. 265f.
5. Miller, *A Captain in the Gordons,* p. 114.
6. Sampson and Hamilton, *Anti-Commando,* pp. 161f.
7. U.S. War Department, *Reports on Military Operations in South Africa and China,* pp. 240f.
8. Schikkerling, *Commando Courageous,* p. 158.
9. *Ibid.,* p. 388.
10. *Ibid.,* p. 198.
11. *Ibid.,* p. 217.
12. Quoted in May, *Music of the Guns,* p. 146.
13. *Ibid.,* p. 165.
14. Blue Book, Cd 902.
15. Schikkerling, *Commando Courageous,* p. 138.
16. *Ibid.,* p. 362.
17. *Ibid.,* p. 333.
18. *Ibid.,* p. 277.
19. *Ibid.,* p. 300.
20. Doyle, *The Great Boer War,* final edition, p. 418.
21. Schikkerling, *Commando Courageous,* p. 350.
22. Doyle, *The Great Boer War,* final edition, pp. 265f.
23. Quoted in Wilson, *After Pretoria,* p. 954.
24. Sampson and Hamilton, *Anti-Commando,* pp. 160f.
25. Quoted in Martin, *The Concentration Camps 1900–1902,* p. 14.

Chapter 40. The Concentration Camps and Emily Hobhouse

1. Quoted in Wilson, *After Pretoria,* V. 2, p. 413.
2. Quoted in Meintjes, *General Louis Botha,* p. 81.
3. Quoted in Magnus, *Kitchener,* p. 184. Kitchener's letter dated 22 March 1901.

4. Quoted in Kruger, *Good-bye Dolly Gray*, p. 413.
5. Quoted in Worsfold, *Lord Milner's Work in South Africa*, p. 569.
6. *Ibid.*, p. 464.
7. Hobhouse, *The Brunt of the War and Where It Fell*, p. 102.
8. Worsfold, *Lord Milner's Work in South Africa*, p. 579.
9. Quoted in Meintjes, *Stormberg*, p. 154.
10. De Wet, *Three Years War*, pp. 242f.
11. Jackson, *A Soldier's Diary.*
12. Quoted in Leigh, *Vereeniging*, p. 50.
13. Blue Book, Cd 1791, V. 1, p. 9.
14. Personal correspondence from Mrs. Lillian du Preez.
15. *Ibid.*
16. Badenhorst, *Tant' Alie of Transvaal*, p. 210.
17. Quoted in Leigh, *Vereeniging*, pp. 49f.
18. Quoted in Fisher, *That Miss Hobhouse*, p. 129.
19. Quoted in Napier Davitt, "The Concentrations Camps in South Africa" (pamphlet), p. 40.
20. Quoted in Fisher, *That Miss Hobhouse*, pp. 133f.
21. *Ibid.*, pp. 130.
22. Blue Book, Cd 853.
23. Quoted in May, *Music of the Guns*, p. 163.
24. Blue Book, Cd 835.
25. Quoted in Arthur, *General Sir John Maxwell*, p. 96.
26. Quoted in Fisher, *That Miss Hobhouse*, p. 190.
27. Blue Book, Cd 819.
28. Quoted in *Archives of South African History* (1968). Report dated 23 November 1901.
29. Blue Book, Cd 819.
30. Quoted in Fisher, *That Miss Hobhouse*, p. 155.
31. *Ibid.*, p. 157.
32. *Ibid.*, pp. 161f.

Chapter 41. The Concentration Camps: The Ladies Committee

1. Blue Book, Cd 893, p. 43.
2. *Ibid.*, p. 14.
3. *Ibid.*, p. 129.
4. *Ibid.*, p. 12.
5. *Ibid.* See pp. 33–38 for report on this camp.
6. *Ibid.*, p. 156.
7. Quoted in Fisher, *The Afrikaners*, p. 161.
8. Quoted in Ferguson, *American Diplomacy and the Boer War*, p. 174.
9. Unpublished letter of Margaret Hulburd in possession of Mr. S. Beadle.
10. Quoted in Fisher, *That Miss Hobhouse*, p. 184.
11. Hopford, *Twice Interned.*
12. Letter to author from Mrs. Doris Heberden.
13. *The Times History*, V. 6, p. 25.
14. Quoted in Methuen, *Peace or War in South Africa*, p. 262.
15. Quoted in Martin, *The Concentration Camps*, p. 22.

Chapter 42. Prisoners of War

1. *The Times History,* V. 6, p. 292.
2. Benbow, "Boer Prisoners of War in Bermuda."
3. *Black and White Budget,* 16 June 1900.
4. Viljoen, *An Exiled General,* p. 281.
5. Quoted in Cleaver, *A Young South African,* p. 127.
6. Quoted in Badenhorst, *Tant' Alie of the Transvaal,* p. 217.
7. Cleaver, *A Young South African,* p. 111.
8. Unpublished letter, dated 24 July 1901, in possession of Adv. G. E. Steyn.
9. Quoted in Cleaver, *A Young South African,* p. 116. The letter is dated 20 July 1900.
10. Quoted in Benbow, "Boer Prisoners of War in Bermuda."
11. Unpublished memoir of Senator G. M. Botha.
12. Quoted in Benbow, "Boer Prisoners of War in Bermuda."
13. Unpublished memoir of Senator G. M. Botha.
14. Quoted in Hassel, "The Boer Concentration Camps of Bermuda," p. 10.
15. Quoted in Benbow, "Boer Prisoners of War in Bermuda."
16. Quoted in Badenhorst, *Tant' Alie of the Transvaal,* p. 248.
17. Quoted in Cleaver, *A Young South African,* p. 173.

Chapter 43. Vereeniging: The Bitter End

1. Quoted in Meintjes, *De la Rey,* p. 250.
2. Reitz, *Commando,* p. 320.
3. *Ibid.,* p. 321.
4. Quoted in De Wet, *Three Years War,* p. 412.
5. Quoted in Crafford, *Jan Smuts,* p. 53.
6. Quoted in "Melrose House" (booklet).
7. Sampson and Hamilton, *Anti-Commando,* pp. 179f.
8. Doyle, *The Great Boer War,* final edition, p. 735.
9. Jackson, *A Soldier's Diary.*
10. Quoted in Wilson, *After Pretoria,* V. 2, p. 988.
11. De Wet, *Three Years War,* p. 391.
12. *Ibid.,* pp. 275f.
13. *The Times History,* V. 5, p. viii.

Chapter 44. Epilogue: The Dust Settles

1. Worsfold, *Lord Milner's Work in South Africa,* p. 538.
2. Doyle, *The War in South Africa,* final edition, p. 153.
3. *The Times History,* V. 6, p. 52.
4. *Rudyard Kipling's Verse,* p. 548.

SELECT BIBLIOGRAPHY

A virtually complete list of all books on the war published before 1909 is included in Volume 7 of *The Times History of the War in South Africa*. I have not duplicated this bibliography here, but I have included some of those works which I have found helpful as well as most of the more modern published sources in English. I have not included all of the South African, British, and American periodicals consulted, but where they are quoted in the text I have given the complete reference in the notes.

Books

Amery, L. S., general ed. *The Times History of the War in South Africa*. 7 vols. Sampson, Low, Marston, London, 1900–1909.
Anderson, Ken. *Heroes of South Africa*. Purnell & Sons, Cape Town, n.d.
Anonymous. *A Handbook of the Boer War*. Gale and Polden, Aldershot, 1910.
Anonymous. *A Subaltern's Letters to His Wife*. Longmans, Green, London, 1901.
Anonymous. *The Transvaal War*. The Illustrated London News, London, n.d.
Archibald, James F. T. *Blue Shirt and Khaki*. Silver, Burdett & Co., New York, 1901.
Arthur, Sir George. *General Sir John Maxwell*. John Murray, London, 1932.
Ashe, E. O. *Besieged by the Boers*. Hutchinson, London, 1900.
Atkins, John Black. *The Relief of Ladysmith*. Methuen, London, 1900.
Bacon, A. O. *Resolution of Sympathy for the South African Republics*. Senate of the United States, May 29, 1900, Washington, D.C., 1900.
Badenhorst, Alida. *Tant' Alie of the Transvaal, Her Diary 1880–1902*. Trans. by Emily Hobhouse. George Allen and Unwin, London, 1923.
Barnes, James. *The Great War Trek*. D. Appleton, New York, 1901.
Barnett, Corelli. *Britain and Her Army*. Allen Lane, London, 1970.
Battersby, H. F. Prevost. *In the Web of War*. Methuen, London, 1900.
Batts, H. J. *Pretoria from Within During the War*. John F. Shaw, London, n.d.
Baynes, Arthur Hamilton. *My Diocese During the War*. George Bell & Sons, London, 1900.
Beak, G. B. *The Aftermath of War*. Arnold, London, 1906.
Beck, Henry Houghton. *History of South Africa and the Boer-British War*. Globe Bible Publishing Co., Philadelphia, 1900.
Benians, E. A., Butler, Sir James, and Carrington, C. E., eds. *The Cambridge History of the British Empire*. Vol. 3. Cambridge University Press, Cambridge, 1967.
Biggar, E. B. *The Boer War*. Biggar Samuel & Co., Toronto, 1900.
Blake, J. Y. F. *A West Pointer with the Boers*. Angel Guardian Press, Boston, 1903.
Blood, Bindon. *Four Score Years and Ten*. G. Bell & Sons, London, 1933.
Blunt, Wilfred Scawen. *My Diaries*. 2 vols. Alfred A. Knopf, New York, 1922.
Brandt, Johanna. *The Petticoat Commando*. Mills & Boon, London, 1913.

Brent, Peter. *The Edwardians.* British Broadcasting Co., London, 1972.

Brett-Smith, Richard. *The 11th Hussars.* Leo Cooper, London, 1969.

Bryant, Arthur. *Jackets of Green.* Collins, London, 1972.

Buckle, George Earle, ed. *The Letters of Queen Victoria.* Third series, 3 vols. John Murray, London, 1932.

Bull, Rev. P. B. *God and Our Soldiers.* Methuen, London, 1904.

Burdett-Coutts, W. L. *The Sick and Wounded in South Africa.* Cassell, London, 1902.

Burne, Lieutenant C. R. N. *With the Naval Brigade in Natal.* Edward Arnold, London, 1902.

Burnham, Frederick Russell. *Scouting on Two Continents.* William Heineman, London, 1927.

Butler, Lewis. *Sir Redvers Buller.* Smith, Elder & Co., London, 1909.

Butler, W. F. *Sir William Butler: An Autobiography.* Constable & Co., London, 1911.

Caldwell, Theodore C., ed. *The Anglo-Boer War.* D. C. Heath & Co., Boston, 1965.

Carrington, Charles. *Rudyard Kipling, His Life and Work.* Macmillan, London, 1955.

Carter, Thomas Fortescue. *A Narrative of the Boer War.* John Macqueen, London, 1900.

Cartwright, A. P. *South Africa's Hall of Fame.* Central News Agency, South Africa, n.d.

Chilvers, Hedley A. *Out of the Crucible.* Cassell, London, 1930.

Churchill, Randolph S. *Winston S. Churchill.* 2 vols. Heinemann, London, 1966, 1967.

_____. *Winston S. Churchill,* Companion vol. 1, part 2, 1896–1900. Houghton Mifflin, Boston, 1967.

Churchill, Winston S. *Frontiers and Wars.* Eyre & Spottiswoode, London, 1962.

_____. *A Roving Commission.* Charles Scribner's Sons, New York, 1930.

Clammer, David. *The Zulu War.* St. Martin's Press, New York, 1973.

Cleaver, Mrs. M. M. *A Young South African.* W. E. Hortor, Johannesburg, 1913.

Cloete, Stuart. *African Portraits.* Collins, London, 1946.

Cook, E. T. *Rights and Wrongs of the Transvaal War.* Edward Arnold, London, 1902.

Cornwallis-West, George. *Edwardian Hey-Days.* Putnam, New York, 1930.

Crafford, F. S. *Jan Smuts.* Greenwood Press, New York, 1968.

Crane, Stephen. *The War Dispatches of Stephen Crane,* ed. by A. W. Stallman and E. R. Hagemann. New York University Press, New York, 1964.

Crankshaw, Edward. *The Forsaken Idea: A Study of Viscount Milner.* Longmans, Green, London, 1952.

Creswicke, Louis. *South Africa and the Transvaal War.* 7 vols. Caxton, London, 1900–1902.

Cross, Colin. *The Fall of the British Empire.* Hodder & Stoughton, London, 1968.

Davis, Charles Belmont. *Adventures and Letters of Richard Harding Davis.* Charles Scribner's Sons, New York, 1913.

Davis, Colonel John. *The History of the Second, Queen's Royal Regiment, Now the Queen's (Royal West Surrey) Regiment.* Vol. 5. Eyre & Spottiswoode, London, 1906.

Davis, Richard Harding. *With Both Armies in South Africa.* Charles Scribner's Sons, New York, 1900.

Davis, Webster. *John Bull's Crime or Assaults on Republics.* The Abbey Press, New York, 1901.

Davitt, Napier. *Memories of a Magistrate.* H. F. & G. Witterby, London, 1934.

De Crespigny, Sir Claude Champion. *Forty Years of a Sportsman's Life.* Mills & Boon, London, 1925.

De Kiewiet, C. W. *A History of South Africa, Social and Economic.* Clarendon Press, Oxford, 1941.

De Villebois-Mareuil, Colonel. *War Notes.* Trans. by Frederic Lees. Adam and Charles Black, London, 1901.

De Wet, Christiaan Rudolf. *Three Years War.* Archibald Constable, London, 1902.

Dickson, W. K.-L. *The Biograph in Battle.* T. Fisher Unwin, London, 1901.

Downey, Fairfax. *Richard Harding Davis.* Charles Scribner's Sons, New York, 1933.

Doyle, A. Conan. *The Great Boer War.* Smith Elder, London, 1900 (3rd impression) and 1902 (18th impression).

———. *The War in South Africa, Its Cause and Conduct.* Smith, Elder & Co., London, 1902.

Dundonald, The Earl of. *My Army Life.* Edward Arnold, London, 1926.

Ensor, Sir Robert. *England 1870–1914.* Oxford History of England, Vol. XIV. The Clarendon Press, Oxford, 1936.

Ferguson, John H. *American Diplomacy and the Boer War.* University of Pennsylvania Press, Philadelphia, 1939.

Fisher, John. *The Afrikaners.* Cassell, London, 1969.

———. *That Miss Hobhouse.* Secker & Warburg, London, 1971.

Fitzpatrick, J. P. *The Transvaal from Within.* Heinemann, London, 1899.

Fortescue, J. W. *Military History.* Cambridge University Press, Cambridge, 1923.

[French, John] Ypre, The Earl of. *Some War Diaries, Addresses and Correspondence.* Herbert Jenkins, London, 1937.

Fry, A. Ruth. *Emily Hobhouse.* Jonathan Cape, London, 1929.

Fuller, J. F. C. *The Last of the Gentlemen's Wars.* Faber & Faber, London, 1937.

Furneaux, Rupert. *News of War.* Max Parrish, London, 1964.

Gandhi, Mohandas K. *An Autobiography.* Trans. from the Gujarati by Mahalev Desai. Beacon Press, Boston, 1957.

Gardner, Brian. *Mafeking: A Victorian Legend.* Cassell, London, 1966.

Garvin, J. L. *The Life of Joseph Chamberlain.* 3 vols. (a fourth by Julian Amery). Macmillan, London, 1934.

Gaskell, H. S. *With Lord Methuen in South Africa.* Henry J. Drane, London, 1906.

Gatacre, Beatrix. *General Gatacre.* John Murray, London, 1910.

Gibbs, Peter. *The Death of the Last Republic.* Frederick Muller, London, 1957.

Gilbert, Martin, ed. *Lloyd George.* Prentice-Hall, Englewood Cliffs, N.J., 1968.

Goldman, Charles Sydney. *With General French and the Cavalry in South Africa.* Macmillan, London, 1902.

Goodinge, Anthony. *The Scots Guards.* Leo Cooper, London, 1969.

Gough, Sir Hubert. *Soldiering On.* Arthur Barker, London, 1954.

Haggard, H. Rider. *The Last Boer War.* Kegan Paul, Trench, Trübner & Co., London, 1899.

Hamilton, Ian. *Listening for the Drums.* Faber & Faber, London, 1944.

———. *The Happy Warrior: A Life of General Sir Ian Hamilton.* Cassell, London, 1966.

Hammond, John Hays. *The Autobiography of John Hays Hammond.* Holt, New York, 1935.

Headlam, Cecil, ed. *The Milner Papers—South Africa, 1899–1905.* Cassell, London, 1933.

Hiley, Alan, and Hassell, John A. *The Mobile Boer.* Grafton Press, New York, 1902.

Hillcourt, W., with Olave, Lady Baden-Powell. *Baden-Powell: The Two Lives of a Hero.* Heinemann, London, 1964.

Hobhouse, Emily, *The Brunt of the War and Where It Fell.* Methuen, London, 1902.

Hobson, J. A. *The Psychology of Jingoism.* G. Richards, London, 1901.
──────. *The War in South Africa, Its Causes and Effects.* Howard Fertey, New York, 1969. (First published in 1900.)
Hogg, Ivan V. *The Guns of 1914–18.* Ballantine, New York, 1971.
Holt, Edgar. *The Boer War.* Putnam, London, 1958.
Hoppford, Wim. *Thrice Interned.* John Murray, London, 1919.
Howard, Philip. *The Black Watch.* Hamish Hamilton, London, 1968.
Howland, Frederick Hoppin. *The Chase of De Wet.* Preston and Rounds, Providence, 1901.
Israel, Milton, ed. *Pax Britannica.* Oliver & Boyd, London, 1968.
Jackson, Murray Cosby. *A Soldier's Diary.* Max Goschen, London, 1913.
James, David. *Lord Roberts.* Hollis & Carter, London, 1954.
[James, Herbert Lional] "The Intelligence Officer." *On the Heels of De Wet.* William Blackwood & Sons, Edinburgh, 1902.
Jeans, T. T., ed. *Naval Brigades in the South African War.* Sampson Low, London, 1901.
Jenkins, Roy. *Asquith, Portrait of a Man and an Era.* Chilmark Press, New York, 1964.
Jerrold, Walter. *Sir Redvers Buller, V.C.* S. W. Partridge, London, 1900.
Johnson, Harry H. *The Story of My Life.* Bobbs-Merrill, Indianapolis, 1923.
Jones, Thomas. *Lloyd George.* Harvard University Press, Cambridge, Mass., 1951.
Keppel-Jones, Arthur. *South Africa: A Short History.* 3rd revised ed. Hutchinson, London, 1961.
Kipling, Rudyard. *Rudyard Kipling's Verse.* Inclusive edition. Doubleday, Page & Co., Garden City, N.Y., 1925.
Koss, Steven, ed. *The Pro-Boers, The Anatomy of an Anti-War Movement.* University of Chicago Press, Chicago, 1973.
Krige, Uys, ed. *Olive Schreiner: A Selection.* Oxford University Press, Cape Town, 1968.
Kruger, D. W. *The Making of a Nation.* Macmillan, Johannesburg, 1969.
Kruger, Rayne. *Good-bye Dolly Gray.* Cassell, London, 1959.
Lehmann, Joseph. *The First Boer War.* Jonathan Cape, London, 1972.
Leigh, Ramon Lewis. *Vereeniging.* Courier-Gazette Publishers, Johannesburg, 1968.
Leslie, Anita. *Lady Randolf Churchill.* Scribner's, New York, 1970.
Lines, G. W. *The Ladysmith Siege.* No publisher, n.d.
Lockhart, J. G., and Woodhouse, C. M. *Rhodes.* Hodder and Stoughton, London, 1963.
Longford, Elizabeth. *Victoria R.I.* Weidenfeld and Nicholson, London, 1964.
Lyttelton, Neville. *Eighty Years.* Hodder and Stoughton, London, n.d.
McCourt, Edward. *Remember Butler.* Routledge and Kegan Paul, London, 1967.
Mackinnon, Major-General W. H. *The Journal of the C.I.V. in South Africa.* John Murray, London, 1901.
Magnus, Philip. *Gladstone.* John Murray, London, 1963.
──────. *Kitchener: Portrait of an Imperialist.* John Murray, London, 1958.
Mahan, Captain A. T. *The Story of the War in South Africa, 1899–1900.* Sampson, Low, Marston & Co., London, 1900.
Marais, J. S. *The Fall of Kruger's Republic.* Clarendon Press, Oxford, 1961.
Marquard, Margaret. *Letters from a Boer Parsonage.* Ed. by Leo Marquard. Purnell, Capetown, 1967.
Marson, T. B. *Scarlet and Khaki.* Jonathan Cape, London, 1930.

Martin, A. C. *The Concentration Camps, 1900–1902.* Howard Timmins, Cape Town, 1957.

Martin, Ralph G. *Jennie: The Life of Lady Randolf Churchill.* Vol. 2. Prentice-Hall, Englewood Cliffs, N.J., 1971.

Maurice, F. M., and Grant, M. H. *History of the War in South Africa, 1899–1902.* Compiled by Direction of His Majesty's Government. 8 vols. HMSO, London, 1906–1910.

Maurice, Frederick, ed. *The Life of General Lord Rawlinson of Trent.* Cassell, London, 1928.

Maxse, F. I. *Seymour Vandeleur: The Story of a British Officer.* The National Review, London, 1905.

May, John Henry, ed. *Music of the Guns.* Hutchinson of South Africa, Johannesburg, 1970.

Meintjes, Johannes. *The Commandant-General.* Tafelberg-Uitgewers, Cape Town, 1971.

———. *De la Rey, Lion of the West.* Hugh Keartland, Johannesburg, 1966.

———. *General Louis Botha.* Cassell, London, 1970.

———. *President Steyn.* Nasionale Boekhandel, Cape Town, 1969.

———. *Stormberg, A Lost Opportunity.* Nasionale Boekhandel, Cape Town, 1969.

———. *Sword in the Sand.* Tafelberg-Uitgewers, Cape Town, 1969.

Methuen, A. M. S. *Peace or War in South Africa.* Methuen, London, 1901.

Miller, David S. *A Captain in the Gordons.* Ed. by Mrs. Margaret Miller and Helen Russell Miller. Sampson, Low, Marston & Co., London, n.d.

Milne, James. *The Epistles of Atkins.* T. Fisher Unwin, London, 1902.

Milner, The Viscountess. *My Picture Gallery, 1886–1901.* John Murray, London, 1951.

Mockler-Ferryman, A. F., ed. *The Oxfordshire Light Infantry in South Africa.* Eyre & Spottiswoode, London, 1901.

Morley, Viscount John. *Recollections.* 2 vols. Macmillan, New York, 1917.

Nathan, Manfred. *Paul Kruger.* Knox Publishing Co., Durban, South Africa, n.d.

Neilly, J. E. *Besieged with B-P.* Pearson, London, 1900.

Newton, A. P., and Benicans, E. A., general eds. *The Cambridge History of the British Empire.* Vol. VII. Cambridge University Press, Cambridge, 1936.

Nutting, Anthony. *Scramble for Africa: The Great Trek to the Boer War.* E. P. Dutton, New York, 1971.

O'Meara, W. A. J. *Kekewich in Kimberley.* Medici Society, London, 1926.

Pearse, H. H. S. *Four Months Besieged: The Story of Ladysmith.* Macmillan, London, 1900.

Pemberton, W. Baring. *Battles of the Boer War.* Batsford, London, 1964.

Phillips, L. March. *With Rimington.* Arnold, London, 1901.

Pienaar, Philip. *With Steyn and De Wet.* Methuen, London, 1902.

Plaatje, Sol T. *The Diary of Sol Plaatje.* Ed. by John L. Comaroff, Macmillan, Johannesburg, 1973.

Pohl, Victor. *Adventures of a Boer Family.* Faber and Faber, London, 1944.

Popham, Hugh. *The Somerset Light Infantry.* Hamish Hamilton, London, 1968.

Price, Richard. *An Imperial War and the British Working Class.* Routledge and Kegan Paul, London, 1972.

Ralph, Julian. *An American with Lord Roberts.* Frederick A. Stokes, New York, 1901.

Ransford, Oliver. *The Battle of Spion Kop.* John Murray, London, 1969.

Reckitt, B. N. *The Lindley Affair.* A. Brown & Sons, Hull, 1972.

Reitz, Deneys. *Commando.* Faber and Faber, London, 1929.

———. *No Outspan.* Faber and Faber, London, 1943.

———. *Trekking On.* Faber and Faber, London, 1933.

Rice, Sir Cecil Spring. *The Letters and Friendships of Sir Cecil Spring Rice.* 2 vols. Ed. by Stephen Gwynn. Houghton Mifflin, Boston, 1929.

Robinson, Ronald, and Gallager, John. *Africa and the Victorians.* Macmillan, London, 1961.

Rosenthal, Eric. *Encyclopaedia of Southern Africa.* Frederick Warne, London, 1961.

———. *South African Surnames.* Howard Timmins, Cape Town, 1965.

———. *Stars and Stripes in Africa.* Nasionale Boekhandel, Cape Town, 1968.

Rutherford, Col. N. J. C. *Soldiering with a Stethescope.* Stanley Paul, London, 1937.

Sampson, P. J. *The Capture of De Wet.* Edward Arnold, London, 1915.

Sampson, Victor, and Hamilton, Ian. *Anti-Commando.* Faber and Faber, London, 1931.

Saron, Gustav, and Hotz, Louis, ed. *The Jews in South Africa.* Oxford University Press, Cape Town, 1955.

Schikkerling, Roland William. *Commando Courageous.* Hugh Keartland, Johannesburg, 1964.

Sinclair-Stevenson, Christopher. *The Gordon Highlanders.* Hamish Hamilton, London, 1968.

Smail, T. L. *Monuments and Battlefields of the Transvaal War 1881 and the South African War 1899.* Howard Timmins, Cape Town, 1966.

Small, J. L. *Those Restless Years.* Howard Timmins, Cape Town, 1971.

Smithers, A. J. *The Man Who Disobeyed.* Leo Cooper, London, 1970.

Smuts, J. C. *Jan Christian Smuts.* Cassell, London, 1952.

"S.N.D.," collated, trans., and arranged by. *The Boers and the War.* Simpkin, Marshal, Hamilton, Kent and Co., London, 1902.

Souza, C. W. L. de, ed. *No Charge for Delivery.* Books of Africa, Cape Town, 1969.

Steevens, G. W. *From Capetown to Ladysmith.* William Blackwood, Edinburgh, 1900.

Sternberg, Count (Adalbert). *My Experiences of the Boer War.* Longmans, Green, London, 1901.

Storrs, Sir Ronald. *The Memoirs of Sir Ronald Storrs.* G. P. Putnam's Sons, New York, 1937.

Strachey, John. *The End of Empire.* Victor Gollancz, London, 1959.

Sutherland, Douglas. *The Argyll and Sutherland Highlanders.* Leo Cooper, London, 1969.

Symons, Julian. *Buller's Campaigns.* Cresset Press, London, 1963.

Taylor, Don. *The British in Africa.* Robert Hale, London, 1962.

Terraine, John. *Douglas Haig, the Educated Soldier.* Hutchinson, London, 1963.

Thomson, S. J. *The Transvaal Burgher Camps, South Africa.* Pioneer Press, Allahabad, 1904.

Trevelyan, George Macaulay. *Grey of Fallodon.* Longmans, Green, London, 1937.

Viljoen, Ben J. *An Exiled General.* A. Noble Printing Co., St. Louis, 1906.

———. *Under the Vierkleur.* Small, Maynard, Boston, 1904.

Vroom, Eugen. *The Hapless Boers.* Flanders Hall, Scotch Plains, N.J., n.d.

Wade, Major A. G. *Counterspy.* Stanley Paul, London, 1938.

Warner, George Townsend. *The Geography of British South Africa.* Blackie & Son, London, 1905.

Waters, W. H. H., trans. *The War in South Africa.* John Murray, London, 1904.

Whyte, Frederic. *The Life of W. T. Stead.* 2 vols. Houghton Mifflin, Boston, n.d.

Williams, W. W. *The Life of General Sir Charles Warren.* Blackwell, Oxford, 1941.

Wilson, H. W. *After Pretoria: The Guerilla War.* 2 vols. Amalgamated Press, London, 1902.

———. *With the Flag to Pretoria.* 2 vols. Harmsworth Brothers, London, 1900.

Wilson, Monica, and Thompson, Leonard, eds. *The Oxford History of South Africa.* 2 vols. Oxford University Press, New York, 1969.

Wilson, Lady Sarah. *South African Memories.* Edward Arnold, London, 1909.

Wood, Herbert Fairlie. *The King's Royal Rifle Corps.* Hamish Hamilton, London, 1967.

Woods, Frederick, ed. *Young Winston's Wars.* Leo Cooper, London, 1972.

Worsfold, W. Basil. *Lord Milner's Work in South Africa.* E. P. Dutton, New York, 1906.

Younghusband, Sir George. *A Soldier's Memories.* Herbert Jenkins, London, 1917.

Articles

Anonymous. "A South African Trip." *Club Life,* 4 May 1901.

Barnard, C. J. "General Botha at the Battle of Colenso." *Military History Journal* (South Africa), V. 1, No. 7, December 1970.

———. "General Botha in the Spioenkop Campaign." *Military History Journal* (South Africa), V. 2, No. 1, June 1971.

Bond, Brian. "The Disaster at Majuba Hill, 1881." *History Today,* XV, No. 7, July 1965.

Boyle, Captain Cecil. "The Cavalry Rush to Kimberley." *The Nineteenth Century,* June 1900.

Brett-James, Anthony. "War and Logistics, 1861–1918." *History Today,* XIV, No. 9, September 1964.

Bryce, James. "The Historical Causes of the Present War in South Africa." *Contemporary Review,* October 1899.

Crane, Stephen. "The Great Boer Trek." *Cosmopolitan,* June 1900.

Drus, Ethel. "The Question of Imperial Complicity in the Jameson Raid." *English Historical Review,* LXVIII (1953).

Gomm, Neville. "Commandant P. H. Kritzinger in the Cape." *Military History Journal* (South Africa), V. 1, No. 7, December 1970.

James, Theodore. "Gunshot Wounds of the South African War." *South African Medical Journal,* V. 5, No. 39, October 1971.

Oxford, J. G. "The Verdict of History." *Military History Journal* (South Africa), V. 2, No. 2, December 1971.

Rabinowitz, L. I. "The Jewish Ambulance Unit." *Jewish Affairs,* April 1959.

———. "Joel Charles Duveen." *Jewish Guild Annual,* September 1952.

———. "President Kruger's Jood." *Jewish Affairs,* October 1948.

Rathbone, J. H. "Prisoner-of-War Camps in St. Helena, 1900–02." *The South African Philatelist,* August–September 1958.

Reichmann, Carl. "Personal Reminiscences from the Campaign in the Orange Free State in March 1900." *Journal of the Military Service Institution of the United States,* XXIX, July–November 1901.

Saron, Gus. "The Jews in Kruger's Republic." *Jewish Affairs,* May 1971.

Stokes, Eric. "Great Britain and Africa: The Myth of Imperialism." *History Today,* X, June 1960.

———. "Milnerism." *The Historical Journal,* V (1962).

Symons, Julian. "Buller in South Africa." *History Today,* XI, No. 11, November 1961.

Walker, E. A. "Lord Milner and South Africa." *Proceedings of the British Academy*, XXVIII (1942).
Woodhouse, C. M. "The Missing Telegrams and the Jameson Raid." *History Today*, XII, June–July 1962.

Government Publications

Blue Books, HMSO: Cd 453, Cd 454, Cd 457, Cd 819, Cd 853, Cd 893, Cd 902, Cd 934, Cd 1789, Cd 1790, Cd 1791, Cd 1792.
Kaplan, Irving, and others. *Area Handbook for the Republic of South Africa.* GPO, Washington, 1970.
Reports on Militray Operations in South Africa and China. U.S. War Department, Adjutant General's Office, DPO, Washington, July 1901.
Selected Translations Pertaining to the Boer War. U. S. War Department, Office of the Chief of Staff, GPO, Washington, 1 April 1905.

Other Sources

Benbow, Colin. "Boer Prisoners of War in Bermuda." Pamphlet of Bermuda Historical Society. Occasional Publications, No. 3, Hamilton, Bermuda, 1962.
_____ and Snowden, Neil. "The Handling, Censoring and Distribution of Boer Prisoners' Mail: 1901–02." *Bermuda Historical Quarterly*, XXIX, No. 4, Winter 1972.
"The Boer War: Official Dispatches from Generals De la Rey, Smuts and Others." Pamphlet published by George H. Buchanan, Philadelphia, n.d.
Botha, G.M., Senator. Memoir. Unpublished manuscript.
Craw, Isabella. Diary. Mimeographed by the Ladysmith Historical Society.
Davitt, Napier. "The Concentration Camps in South Africa." Pamphlet. Schuter and Shooter, Pietermaritzburg, 1941.
Fichardt, Etrechia. Account of the escape of Laurens Steytler, written by his daughter. Unpublished manuscript.
Hattingh, J. L. *Archives Yearbook of South African History* (1968). Published for University of Pretoria.
Heberden, Winifred. Diary. Unpublished manuscript.
Hulburd, Margaret. Memoir. Unpublished manuscript.
Parritt, B. A. H. *The Intelligencers.* Mimeographed.
Publications of the Anglo-Boer War Philatelic Society: No. 1, "Prisoners of War Camps in South Africa and the Burgher Camps," No. 2; "Prisoner of War Camps Overseas." Mimeographed, n.d.
Rabinowitz, L. I. "Herman Judelewitz, 'Russian Rebel' of the Boer War." Lecture delivered before the South African Jewish Sociological and Historical Society, 17 June 1948.
_____. "Transvaal Jewry in the Boer War." Unpublished.
Schroeder, Stephan. "Britain and the Boers." Pamphlet. Berlin, 1940.
Tatham, G. F., Major, of the Natal Carbineers. Diary. Mimeographed by the Ladysmith Historical Society.
Willis, George W. Letter from Ladysmith to his brother, Archdeacon William Willis, in Cambridge, New Zealand. 29 March 1900. Unpublished.

INDEX

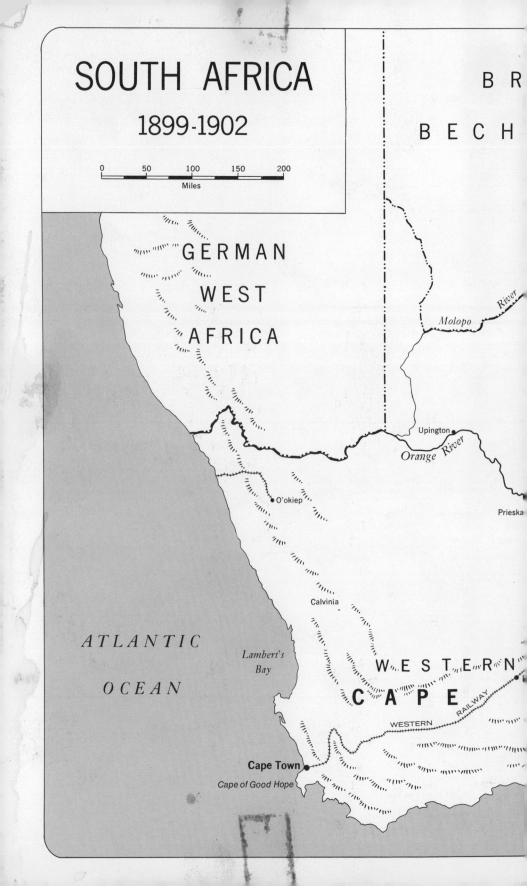

SOUTH AFRICA
1899-1902

0   50   100   150   200
Miles

B R

B E C H

GERMAN

WEST

AFRICA

Molopo *River*

Upington

Orange River

O'okiep

Prieska

Calvinia

ATLANTIC

Lambert's
Bay

OCEAN

W E S T E R N

C A P E

WESTERN   RAILWAY

Cape Town

Cape of Good Hope